*Menahem
Pressler*

Menahem Pressler

ARTISTRY IN PIANO TEACHING

William Brown

Indiana University Press

BLOOMINGTON AND INDIANAPOLIS

This book is a publication of

Indiana University Press
601 North Morton Street
Bloomington, IN 47404-3797 USA

http://iupress.indiana.edu

Telephone orders   800-842-6796
Fax orders   812-855-7931
Orders by e-mail   iuporder@indiana.edu

MANUFACTURED IN THE UNITED STATES OF AMERICA

Library of Congress Cataloging-in-Publication Data

Brown, William Paul, date–
  Menahem Pressler : artistry in piano teaching / William Brown.
    p. cm.
  Includes bibliographical references and index.
  ISBN 978-0-253-35241-5 (cloth : alk. paper)   1. Pressler,
Menahem.   2. Pianists.   3. Piano teachers   4. Piano—Perfor-
mance.   5. Piano music—Interpretation (Phrasing, dynamics, etc.)
I. Title.
  ML417.P75B76 2009
  786.2092—dc22
  [B]
                                                        2008022724

1   2   3   4   5   14   13   12   11   10

To Menahem Pressler,
mentor and friend, whose teaching and performing have
enriched and transformed generations of musicians.

CONTENTS

PREFACE: A FEW WORDS BEFORE

We were returning from a Beaux Arts Trio concert in Bloomington, Indiana, when my wife, Kathy, remarked, "Someone must write a book
about Mr. Pressler." My thoughts returned to her comment again and
again over the next few days, and I realized the significance of her statement. I phoned Menahem Pressler the following week. He shared with
me that a biography by Cynthia Wilson was indeed already being prepared for publication and added, "There have been so many things—
articles, documentaries, and the Nicholas Delbanco book about the
Beaux Arts Trio." But nothing like the present book: no comprehensive
study of Pressler's teaching legacy had been attempted. I told him I had
accumulated many pages of notes transcribed from my lessons with him
from 1969 through 1977, as well as hundreds of pages of scores with his
markings, images, fingerings, and phrasings; and I realized that there
were many others who also cherish their remembrances of studying with
Menahem Pressler. What a treasure it would be to have access to all those
comments and markings that this world-renowned performer/teacher/
mentor/friend has made over the fifty-plus years of his career!

As I suspected, the resources were abundant. It was only necessary to
collect these materials and organize them for use by future pianists and
teachers. Indiana University's Jacobs School of Music generously provided names and addresses of Pressler's students from 1955 through
2007. I sent each of these persons a survey and a request for any tapes
they might have of their lessons with Pressler and copies of musical
scores he had marked for them. Additionally, participants from the Adamant Music School in Vermont contributed their remembrances, musical scores, and tapes and Mr. Pressler directed me to several former students for personal interviews that provided tremendous help in enlarging
my perspective of Pressler's impact on the world of pianism.

These participants represent more than five decades of Pressler's
teaching, the impact of which is international in scope and includes es-
teemed concert artists; college, university, and conservatory professors;
teachers with private studios; and gifted amateur musicians. Pressler's
influence on the lives of these people is apparent by what they have told

me: "His influence has become part of everything I do." "I think about him every day." "I keep his picture on my door so that I see it every day." "I think about what I've accomplished, and I think, 'He would be pleased.'"

Part 1 of this book is based on interviews with Pressler and comments from musical scores, lessons, and master classes. Included for the first time in published form are Pressler's technical exercises as well as a compendium of technical and expressive details for interpreting many piano masterpieces. Part 2 offers twenty-three measure-by-measure lessons. These are composites of Pressler's markings made in students' musical scores as well as transcripts of lessons and master classes. Measures for all pieces are numbered in the conventional manner, beginning with the first complete measure and skipping first endings unless otherwise indicated.

For this volume, Mr. Pressler allowed the inclusion of his lecture-recital on Beethoven's Sonata in A-flat Major, Op. 110, which he presented at the Metropolitan Museum of Art in New York City in February 2004, as well as the transcript of a lecture he presented at the TCU/Cliburn Piano Institute in Fort Worth, Texas, in 2005. These presentations show aspects of his influence apart from his teaching.

A chart of Pressler's musical ancestry is included as Appendix A and is expanded in Appendix B, tracing his teachers through many of the great pianists and musicians of history, including Franz Liszt, Frédéric Chopin, Ludwig van Beethoven, and even J. S. Bach. Appendix C comprises tributes from students, and Pressler's student rosters, 1955–2008, are included as appendix D.

When asked what he would like the book to accomplish, Mr. Pressler replied, "What a book like this can do is share with teachers what in my life has been my primary activity. If someone reads it and sees how one teacher went about doing it and how in some ways he succeeded, that is what the book can show."

Menahem Pressler has given the world a tremendous legacy of artistic piano performance and teaching, and it is essential that we preserve and maintain this legacy. As we gain an appreciation for both the technical and expressive facets of Pressler's teaching, we will discover that our eyes are opened to a deeper understanding of the composers' intentions, and our ears are better attuned to a limitless palette of musical colors and possibilities. And by applying his principles in a broader manner, we can learn about setting goals, appreciating beauty, and striving for excellence in every area of our lives.

ACKNOWLEDGMENTS

Those who contributed anecdotes, tributes, comments from Pressler during lessons and master classes, and other remembrances are myriad and include Pressler's friends, colleagues, students, former students, and acquaintances. I am especially grateful to my family members for their support, to Tim McCarty who helped in taping my interviews with Mr. Pressler, to Susan Guymon and Eric Schramm for their editing work, to Melinda Baird who made available numerous resources, to Indiana University Archives for their assistance, to Sara Pressler for her thoughtful insights, to Edna Pressler for her encouragement, and most of all to Menahem Pressler himself for his willingness to devote the time, energy, and insight needed to bring this project to completion.

Contributors from Pressler's former Indiana University students include Jane Abbott-Kirk, John Adams, David Alpher, Fernando Araujo, Konstantine Athanasakos, Mi Jai Auh, Melinda Baird, Margaret Barela, Paul Barnes, Jonathan Bass, Alasdair Beatson, Gayle (Cameron) Blankenburg, Jimmy Briere, Madeline Bruser, John Burnett, Diana (Haddad) Cangemi, Mark Cappelli, Ted Carnes, Susan Chan, Angela Cheng, Mikyung (Carrie) Choi (Koh), Winston Choi, Alan Chow, Alvin Chow, Jeanne-Minette Cilliers, Lynda Cochrane, Jack Cohan, Jeffrey Cohen, Paula da Matta, Andrew DeGrado (deceased), Henry Doskey, Jerry Emmanuel, Paula Ennis, Zoe Erisman, George Fee, John Ferguson, Anne-France Fosseur, William Goldenberg, Frances Gray, Pamela Griffel-King, Charlene Harb, Christopher Harding, Robert Hatten, Wen-Ting Huang, Mia (Kim) Hynes, Sherri Jones, Manami (Naoe) Kawamura, Pieter Kuijken, Julia Lam, Marilyn (White) Lowe, David Lyons, Gordon Macpherson, Stephen Mann, Pauline Martin, Robert Mayerovitch, Roger McVey, Fred Moyer, Kevin Murphy, Megumi Nagai, Saori Ohno, Tongsook Han Park, Rebecca Penneys, Mary Rucker, Ann Saslov, Scott Schillin, Jacqueline Schmitt, Joshua Seedman, Kevin Sharpe, Karen Shaw, George Shirley, Jill (Trudgeon) Sprenger, Mark Sullivan, Rámon Tamaran, William Tucker, Daria van den Bercken, Charles Webb, Sandra Webster, Mei-Huei Wei, and Mary Wong.

Many participants from Pressler's master classes and those who took private lessons (apart from Indiana University) from Pressler were graciously willing to share their remembrances. These include Jan Deats, Patricia Drew, Elaine Felder, Kevin Fitz-Gerald, Mary Lou Francis, Lily Friedman, Celeste O'Brien Haugen, Janet Hickey, Daniel Paul Horn, Roger Keyes, Barbara Kurdirka, Yvonne Lang, Linda Lienhard, Dina Namer, Jeannete Nettleton, Elaine Newman, Janice Nimetz, Del Parkinson, Dmitry Rachmanov, Lynn Raley, Mark Reiss, Tiffany Seybert, Richard Sogg, Joyce Ucci, Ludolph van der Hoeven, and Vicki von Arx.

Research for the book required interviewing many people, including Melinda Baird, Margaret Barela, Jonathan Bass, Angela Cheng, Alan Chow, Alvin Chow, Jeffrey Cohen, Paula Ennis, Robert Hatten, Mia (Kim) Hynes, Stephen Mann, Pauline Martin, Robert Mayerovitch, Sara Pressler, Edna Pressler, Ann (Heiligman) Saslav, Joshua Seedman, Karen Shaw, and Jill (Trudgeon) Sprenger.

Musical scores were contributed by John Adams, Melinda Baird, Jonathan Bass, Diana (Haddad) Cangemi, Mark Cappelli, Angela Cheng, Alvin Chow, Jeffrey Cohen, Paula Ennis, Anne-Francis Fosseur, Robert Hatten, Wen-Ting Huang, Mia (Kim) Hynes, Minami (Naoe) Kawamura, Pieter Kuijken, Stephen Mann, Megumi Nagai, Tongsook Han Park, Mary Rucker, Joshua Seedman, Kevin Sharpe, Jill (Trudgeon) Sprenger, Mark Sullivan, Joyce Ucci, Daria van der Berchen, and Ludolph van der Hoeven.

Recordings and transcripts of lessons with Pressler were provided by Melinda Baird, William Brown, Andrew DeGrado, Anne-Francis Fosseur, Frances Gray, Wen-Ting Huang, Mia (Kim) Hynes, Linda Lienhard, Stephen Mann, and Joshua Seedman.

Recordings and transcripts of master classes with Pressler were also provided by Adamant Music School (Vermont), Indiana University, Northwestern University, Shelburne Farms (Vermont), Steinway Hall (New York City), Mark Sullivan Studio Classes (California), University of Missouri–Columbia, Vanderbilt University, and Wayne State University.

And finally, I would like to thank Jane Behnken, Katherine Baber, and Brian Herrmann at Indiana University Press for their encouragement and expertise in completing this manuscript.

Menahem
Pressler

Part One

A LIFE IN TEACHING

ONE

A Brief Biography

Menahem Pressler was born on December 16, 1923, in Magdeburg, Germany. In 1939 he and his family fled to Palestine as the Nazi regime made life increasingly difficult for Jews in Europe. Pressler, who had begun playing the piano at age six, continued his musical studies during these years of turmoil. In 1946, while still a student, he flew to San Francisco where he won first prize at the First International Debussy Competition. Soon after, he began his solo career, which included an unprecedented four-year contract as soloist with the Philadelphia Orchestra under the direction of Eugene Ormandy.

While continuing his successful career as a soloist in recital and with orchestras, Pressler co-founded the Beaux Arts Trio, which today is considered the world's foremost piano trio, regularly appearing in major international music centers and festivals. Since its debut concert on July 13, 1955, the Trio has performed throughout North America, Europe, Japan, South America, and the Middle East, as well as at the Olympics in South Korea and Australia. Annual concert appearances include series at the Metropolitan Museum of Art, the Celebrity Series of Boston, and the Library of Congress. The Trio has recorded fifty albums, including almost the entire chamber literature with piano on the Philips label, and has been awarded numerous honors, including England's Record of the Year Award, four Grammy nominations, Musical America's Ensemble of the Year, the Toscanini Award, the German Recording Award, the Prix Mondial du Disque, three Grand Prix du Disques, the Union de la Presse Musicale Belge Award, and Record of the Year awards from both *Gramophone* and *Stereo Review*. On July 14, 2005, the Trio celebrated its fiftieth anniversary with a performance at the Tanglewood Festival.

In the same year that he co-founded the Beaux Arts Trio, Pressler joined the faculty of the Indiana University Jacobs School of Music. He was named to the Dean Charles H. Webb Chair of Music in 1998 and currently holds the title of Distinguished Professor. In addition to presenting master classes worldwide, Pressler also has served as a juror for the Van Cliburn, Queen Elisabeth of Belgium, Arthur Rubinstein, and Paloma O'Shea piano competitions and the International Piano-e-Competition.

In 1994 Pressler was honored with Chamber Music America's Distinguished Service Award, and in 1995 he won the German Critics' Ehrenurkunde award for having set the standard for chamber music over the previous forty years. In 1998, he received one of only five Lifetime Achievement Awards granted in the last fifty years by *Gramophone* magazine, placing him in the distinguished company of Dame Joan Sutherland, Sir Georg Solti, Dietrich Fischer-Dieskau, and Sir Yehudi Menuhin. In 2002 Pressler was awarded the Gold Medal of Merit from the National Society of Arts and Letters, which recognized him for "a long and distinguished career not only as an internationally recognized concert artist but also a teacher and mentor of young artists." In 1986 he was invited to dinner at the White House. In 2005, he was named a commander in France's Order of Arts and Letters, France's highest cultural honor, and soon after received the German President's *Deutsche Bundesverdienstkreuz* (Cross of Merit), Germany's highest cultural honor. In 2006 he was awarded the Concertgebouw Prize, and in 2007 he was named an Honorary Fellow of the Jerusalem Academy of Music and Dance. In addition, Pressler has been elected to the American Academy of Arts and Sciences and received honorary doctorates from the University of Nebraska-Lincoln, the North Carolina School of the Arts, and the San Francisco Conservatory of Music.

Pressler has continued to perform as a soloist, having made his Carnegie Hall recital debut in 1996 in the Great Performers Series. He has also recorded thirty solo albums. He lives in Bloomington, Indiana, with his wife, Sara. Their son, Ami, is a hospital laboratory technician in Bloomington and their daughter, Edna, is a clinical psychologist and director of the University of Massachusetts-Boston Counseling Center.

The *New York Times* has called Pressler "a prodigious talent" with "exceptional gifts." The *Washington Evening Star* praised him as "a poet of the piano." And *Le Figaro* in Paris has hailed him as "one of the greatest living pianists."

T W O

THE STUDIO

On many days Menahem Pressler can be found in his piano studio, Room 105, in the Jacobs School of Music at Indiana University. His daily schedule is to practice from 8:00 AM until lunch at noon and then to teach from 1:30 until 5:00 PM. Late afternoons are frequently spent in recital hearings for the school's hundreds of piano students. Evenings often include attendance at some of the school's more than 1,100 annual recitals, many of which are presented by Pressler's own students. Some evenings Pressler goes to bed at 10:00 PM and then gets up at 1:30 or 2:00 AM to practice for another hour or two. His health, eyesight, and level of energy surpass people many years his junior. His work ethic is extraordinary in that he has never cancelled a concert or a lesson.

For more than fifty years, since 1955, Pressler has maintained a full class of fifteen to thirty students. This would be remarkable in itself even without the twenty-four weeks of the year that he is on tour, presenting more than 120 concerts with the famed Beaux Arts Trio or performing solo piano recitals. His former students are now faculty members of conservatories and music schools around the world, and the influence of his performance and teaching has shaped the way many people perform and listen to music, especially in the realm of chamber music.

Pressler presents students with a technical regime that ensures their ability to play without physical tension, an approach that frees the student from injury or abuse from strain, despite hours of daily practice. Pressler's method produces finger dexterity, sonorous sound, a command of touches, and a myriad of tonal colors.

Perhaps the most remarkable aspect students gain from working with Pressler is to begin to share his ability to hear the limitless possibilities of color that are available in piano playing. His keen ear, musical sensitivity, and tremendous insights are easily recognized by the perceptive listener and can be systematically transmitted from teacher to student so as to affect the shaping of melodies, balance of musical lines, and rhythmic flow.

People often ask Pressler how he maintains his boundless enthusiasm, to which he offers this standard reply: "When you wake up and you see a very beautiful new day is coming, that is the way you keep your enthusiasm up. You take a piece of music and you feel renewed. You feel, 'That's what I wanted to do all my life, and now that I have the opportunity and the privilege of being able to do it, should I not be happy or full of gratitude? Or should I feel, 'Oh, I've done that before. There is nothing new?' I have never felt—and I don't think the Trio's ever felt—that we have dug to the deepest possible way that one can dig into these masterpieces. So, for us, a lifetime is barely long enough to dig, to find, and to renew that which makes our lives worth living as musicians."

Pressler seeks to share his insights, those things that have worked for him in practice and on the concert stage. He does not compromise his musical standards, and he demands the highest level of musical performance from himself and his students. As Mia Kim Hynes remembers him saying at her first lesson with him when she was only fourteen, "You are playing the Chopin *Ballade* today, and I will teach you as an adult."

Being selected into Pressler's class is a much-sought-after distinction, but that is when the work really begins. Pressler's students must dedicate a minimum of four to six hours to daily piano practice. Although the long-range goal may be a public recital, the immediate incentive is preparing for the next lesson. The nature of the lessons is demanding and uncompromising. No matter how prepared the student is for the lesson, Pressler uses that preparation as a basis for further study into the score, looking for more depth of musical expression, solving technical difficulties, and taking the performance to a higher level of achievement and understanding. Because Pressler is frequently away from campus, touring with the Beaux Arts Trio or playing solo recitals or presenting master classes, a student may receive a cluster of two or three lessons in the same week, which increases the demands of practice during this time.

As deadlines for competitions or recitals approach, Pressler's teaching style becomes less specific and detailed. At this stage, he may sing along with the melodies, perhaps conducting with his arms and body, striving for climaxes and insisting on a consistent tempo to ensure structural integrity of the performance. There may be discussion of how the acoustics of the hall will affect the listener's perception of the piece. Pedaling may become adjusted and the musical character more defined.

Once students leave his studio, they have learned to perform with confidence and security because they know what they have accomplished and understand how far they have come. They have observed Pressler's work ethic, and they have seen his example of a performer's life. They

Fig. 2.1. Pressler in his Indiana University studio

know what can be accomplished, how to achieve results from their practice, how to listen in depth to their own playing, and what to expect when they listen to others. They have learned a great deal of repertoire from their own studies and from listening to other students in performance classes and recitals. They have learned principles of technique that ensure looseness and flexibility. They know how to establish goals for learning repertoire. They have learned principles of musical expression that can be applied to all music, and they have learned how to play with color, how to shape a melody, and how to adapt to different pianos. They are indeed ready for whatever musical opportunities await them.

THREE

PRESSLER'S EARLY TRAINING

Times were uncertain in Germany in the early 1920s when Menahem Pressler was born to Moritz and Judith Pressler, owners of a clothing store in Magdeburg, ninety miles southwest of Berlin. But as Pressler recalls, he and his younger siblings, Leo and Selma, had a happy life at home as children.

"What I remember really is, the strongest part of the memory, was that there was always love. Yes, sometimes my father was very, how shall I say, rough. He would say, 'That has to be done,' or something like that. None of us children ever was rebellious or would think even in those terms, not to do what he had asked, and mother was as sweet and as kind as could be. And there was and is to this day very fine relations among the three of us."

The family worked hard and was, as Pressler says, "very, very religious." "We went to pray. We kept the Jewish holidays, which I, of course, became much less to keep them as I was traveling and playing. But I remember them, and I remember the prayers. And when I can, I like to go and pray. Yes, we were very, very much religious.

"Of course, when I came of age, I had a Bar Mitzvah, and my brother Leo had it. I remember that I had to learn the part of the Torah that I had to read, and that took at least six months, because you not only have to read, but you have to read and have to sing it the way it is marked in the Torah. You see, the Torah has little signs how to read it, how to sing it, and that's not easy. And I had to learn it, and I did. And I even remember what is my *capit* in the Torah, which was *Vayigash,* which means 'and he approached.' "

There were few concerts in Germany at the time, but the family loved music and enjoyed listening to records. Pressler remembers that his father "played very badly the violin," but at the age of six, Menahem began violin lessons, and his brother began piano lessons with a Mr. Kitzl, the

Lutheran church organist who came to the Pressler house. Leo didn't practice much and didn't really want piano lessons, but Menahem learned his brother's piano pieces just by having heard them during the lessons. Soon, at age seven, he was allowed to discontinue his violin studies and begin learning the piano.

Because he played by ear, "cheating," as he calls it, Menahem did not read music well. "I always asked the teacher to play the piece for me, and I would remember it. And then when I would play a wrong note, he would say, 'Now why don't you read the music?' And I barely could, until he discovered the problem, and then he taught me to read. He was a good teacher and he was very kind, and I would say that my physical ability and also my desire were much greater than my musical advancement at this stage."

Germany had come under the Nazis by this point, which made lessons difficult at times. Pressler recalls *Kristallnacht*, the "night of broken glass" in November 1938, during which mobs throughout Germany and Austria broke into synagogues, Jewish homes, and Jewish-owned businesses, including his parents' store, looting and destroying property and attacking scores of people. "But I also do remember something which is amazing. My brother was out on his bicycle and he fell and he broke his leg. The SS men, the ones in uniform, the Nazis, brought him to the house. They had kind of immediately set his foot, which later really proved to be of great help. So these were the murderers actually, but here on these terms they were marvelous, humane."

Germans, of course, were not supposed to associate with Jews, and certainly not visit their homes or teach them music. Pressler recalls, however, the courage of his teacher. "I do remember the great, great, great kindness of Mr. Kitzl. It was difficult for me to go on a tramway to his house, so he would come to my house and teach me. His whole attitude, the kindness that he showed me, was of help to me. You couldn't imagine what it would be like, when you wear the sign of Cain supposedly on your forehead. That's how they make you feel. But he didn't. He made me feel good."

Pressler remembers the first pieces he played with his teacher. "I only played classical pieces, but I remember an anecdote with my father. I played that little Schubert F minor *Moments Musicaux*. And when I finished playing for Kitzl, he said to me, 'The ending was wonderful.' So I told my father with pride, 'And the ending was wonderful.' He said, 'Well, what about the beginning?' He didn't understand what's with the rest of the piece, but I understood what [Mr. Kitzl] meant. Instinctively

I understood there is a difference between how you approach this and the other, and that *there* I succeeded more than with *that*."

Despite growing political concerns, Pressler was able to attend three special concerts during these early years. The first was in 1936 when he was twelve or thirteen and on a business trip with his father in Poland. The two took a side trip to Lwow so Menahem could hear the great Ignaz Friedman play a solo recital, an event that Pressler says had an enormous impact on him. He attended the second concert the next year, when Walter Gieseking played the Strauss *Burlesque* and a Mozart concerto with orchestra, and the third was an all-Chopin program presented in Magdeburg that included *majurkas, waltzes,* a *Polonaise,* and the *Bolero,* "a very interesting, thoughtful and creative program," Pressler recalls.

During his years of study with Kitzl, Pressler learned several Bach Preludes and Fugues, Liszt's *Hungarian Rhapsodie* no. 13, Beethoven's Sonata Op. 2 no. 3, a Mozart concerto, Beethoven's Piano Concerto no. 1, and Chopin works, including *Impromptus, Nocturnes, Mazurkas,* and *Waltzes.*

"To some extent," Pressler muses about that period of his life, "I was considered special [in the family] because I did what I did, which was playing music, and being successful quite early, so they all tried to help. If I had a recital, they all publicized it. They all tried to sell tickets. That's what I remember of home."

While Menahem studied the piano, his father, Moritz, kept watch on the political climate, thinking that the situation for Jews would improve. Preparations for the horrifying exterminations of Jews were just beginning, and Moritz waited almost too long to get his family out of Germany. In 1939, when Menahem was fifteen, Moritz applied for tourist visas for the family to visit Trieste, Italy, supposedly for a family vacation just weeks before World War II started. "That we *could* leave was a matter of luck," Pressler says. "The German border police let us through to Trieste, but they didn't have to." He remembers the "enormous act of kindness" of Mr. Kitzl forwarding to him in Trieste a copy of Debussy's *Reflets dans l'eau* with all fingerings marked.

Many years later, in 2005, Pressler returned to Germany to receive the *Deutsche Bundesverdienstkreuz* (Cross of Merit), which was presented to him in Magdeburg. "They had everything," he says of the event. "They even had a picture of my father's store which was destroyed. That was unbelievable to me. And [the presentation] was read by the prime minister [Dr. Wolfgang Böhmer] of the province. That was in my hometown, where they made me an honorary citizen and they gave me my graduation, which I had never had the chance to complete."

MR. ROSSI

While in Trieste, Pressler studied with a Mr. Rossi, who recognized Pressler's talent and offered him lessons at no cost. "I remember he was very nice, very supportive," Pressler recalls, "and I loved going to lessons. And one thing that helped me so much was my desire to practice."

After a few months, the family applied for travel visas to Palestine, which were granted only days before Italy joined the war. They traveled on the last ship allowed to leave the port of Trieste, which, as it turned out, was not allowed to return to Italy once it reached Palestine. While on the ship, Menahem played a recital for the captain's table, his first performance to have a printed program. His repertoire included the Beethoven, Debussy, Brahms, and Chopin pieces he had learned with Kitzl and Rossi.

ELIAHU RUDIAKOV

When the family arrived in Palestine late in 1939, his father worked first at a grocery store and then opened another clothing store, known locally as Pressler's Pants, that became quite famous. The family moved into an apartment on Hana Viem Street in Tel Aviv.

Menahem, sixteen, was advised to study at the Tel Aviv Conservatory (now the Tel Aviv Music Academy) with Abilea, a well-known piano teacher, but because he was in Switzerland at the time, Pressler began lessons with Eliahu Rudiakov, who taught Abilea's students in the master's absence. Pressler ended up staying with Rudiakov for four years. "Here again I met the most kind person who truly was wonderful and who taught me for free." Rudiakov, from a Russian background, had studied first in Germany with Max Pauer and then at the École Normale de Musique with Yvonne Lefébure, an assistant to Alfred Cortot. With Rudiakov, Pressler studied the Op. 110 Sonata of Beethoven, the Chopin A-flat *Ballade,* and the Balakirev *Islamey.* "I asked him, 'What is the most difficult piece in the repertoire?' And he told me it was the *Islamey,* so of course I had to play that in my first recital."

Each year in Palestine, Pressler performed a recital representing the best of the works he had studied during the year. For his second recital, Pressler played the extremely difficult Liszt Sonata. Another piece he learned during this time was the Grieg Concerto, which his teacher encouraged him to learn for the Palestine Symphony Orchestra (now the

Fig. 3.1. Eliahu Rudiakov, 1950. By permission of Ariel Rudiakov.

Israel Philharmonic Orchestra) competition. Pressler won first prize and the opportunity to perform the Grieg Concerto with the orchestra. It would be the first of his many concerto concerts. "It was a fantastic experience, first of all, because I had won this prize, and [secondly] to play with the Symphony Orchestra. It's like here playing with the New York Philharmonic. And I practiced like a maniac, and all I remember was that I loved doing it. I felt, 'That's what I want to do. That's how I want to spend my life.'"

LEO KESTENBERG

As a result of playing with the Palestine Symphony Orchestra, Pressler met pianist and educator Leo Kestenberg, the orchestra's general manager. Kestenberg had been the Minister of Fine Arts in Germany and had left Berlin when the Nazis came to power. He had settled in Prague for a while and finally emigrated to Tel Aviv. Rudiakov thought it would be good for Pressler to study with Kestenberg, who had been a student of pianist and composer Ferrucio Busoni in Berlin and had also studied with Franz Kullak, a student of Franz Liszt, who in turn had studied with Carl Czerny, a student of Beethoven.

Fig. 3.2. Leo Kestenberg. By permission of The Archive of Israeli Music.

Pressler studied with Kestenberg for three years, until 1946, when he was twenty-three and came to describe himself as being "a natural" at the piano. He remembers Kestenberg saying, "It's too *easy* for you. That's why you don't give it enough *thought*. That's why you don't look at the depths of these pieces. You just play." As Pressler remembers, neither Rudiakov nor Kestenberg actually taught technique to him, but each assigned *études,* such as Czerny, so that, as he progressed, he would be forced to develop the specific pianistic skills required for the next piece.

Pressler considered Rudiakov to be the finer pianist, but he later credited Kestenberg with influencing him to "read between the lines." "He was an extremely knowledgeable man and guided me, not just in piano playing, but in a philosophical approach to making music, helping me to understand it more as a way of life than just playing the piano." Kestenberg also helped him learn to listen for "beautiful sound." "He always said, 'This is harsh. This is harsh.' That in itself demanded of me to find something so he wouldn't say that. It created within me, not a technique of how to do it, but a technique of what sound did I want to hear? If once you have in your mind the sound you want to hear, you will find a way of handling your arm, your fingers, and your touch in order to achieve that sound."

With Kestenberg, Pressler learned Liszt's Concerto No. 1 in E-flat Major and the three Op. 31 Sonatas of Beethoven. Knowing that Kestenberg loved Beethoven's *Diabelli Variations,* he learned these on his own and played them for his teacher on his birthday.

Later, Pressler read in a newspaper about a new competition, the First International Debussy Competition, to be held in San Francisco. The competition required contestants to play much of the Debussy repertoire by memory. Pressler had studied only a few of these pieces, so Kestenberg helped him learn the repertoire, which became an important part of his life-long teaching and performing.

During this period, Pressler also studied harmony, counterpoint, and music history with another refugee from Germany, Dr. Riesenfeld. Riesenfeld taught harmonic studies and repertoire analysis using the German system that Pressler describes as "thorough, careful, conscientious, and very important," and he taught him musical structure and style, chordal relationships, and repertoire. "We studied analysis, music criticism, form, and harmony. He was very German in his attitude and his learning. He didn't like twentieth-century music and so I think, like many other Germans, he looked down on Debussy."

Riesenfeld became Pressler's good friend. The two spent time at the seashore in Tel Aviv, especially on days following performances, buying falafel or corn on the cob, and playing chess as a release from the pressures of performing. Meanwhile, Pressler continued to practice his usual eight hours a day in preparation for the upcoming Debussy Competition.

FOUR

THE DEBUSSY COMPETITION

PAUL LOYONNET

While preparing for the Debussy competition, Pressler met a musician who became a great influence in his life, Paul Loyonnet, a touring French concert pianist who had studied with Charles-Marie Widor and Isidor Philipp at the Paris Conservatory. Noted by Charles Timbrell to be "an important link to the traditions of the nineteenth century," Loyonnet was performing a concerto with the Palestine Symphony Orchestra and needed someone to play the orchestral part on a second piano.

Pressler began rehearsing with Loyonnet, which proved to be valuable to Pressler in two ways. The first was that Loyonnet was the first person ever to speak to him about technique. "That's what I learned with Loyonnet: to keep the fingers strong and have the arm relaxed and free." Loyonnet practiced the high-finger playing of the French School, which often caused tendonitis, but, according to Pressler, "he had a way of freeing his hand by keeping his arm loose, which is the best prescription to avoid tendonitis."

The second benefit Pressler derived from rehearsing with Loyonnet was the encouragement he received regarding Debussy and the competition in San Francisco. "He opened my ears and my eyes to Debussy with a few examples. That which he gave me was a concept. He played some for me, first of all, so I heard his use of pedal, where one sound mixed with another, not at all a German approach. I remember playing the first Prelude for him, and he showed me how to pedal exactly following the notation of the rhythm. I was only with him on four or five occasions, but he played a big role in my life. He was a completely unknown pianist to most of the world but a tremendous influence to me. Just by speaking, he opened many doors, and I walked through myself. I found the room that I walked through attractive, and so it helped me."

Every year, Pressler had played with the orchestra and every year he had played a recital on the radio in Palestine. "I actually became quite

Fig. 4.1. Paul Loyonnet. By permission of Université de Montreal.

known," he says, noting that he became great friends with Karel Salomon, the station's music director of its Hebrew section. "He was my mentor, and he had a very important role in my life. He was very, very good to me." But this year, Pressler was to keep a promise he had made to Salomon, whom he now called his "mentor," and that was to enter the Debussy competition.

"I did not think of winning a prize. I really didn't think that would be a determiner in my life or the one that created that change of direction for me, staying at home or moving to America. So I learned [the Debussy], and Salomon always had me play. It was he who also got me a seat on the plane to go to New York because that was very difficult at that time. And it had to go by way of Cairo. I had to fly to Cairo, and then that plane was delayed. I had to sit for two days in Cairo, and that was no fun as a young man alone, no fun at all. When you walked the streets, they would whistle after you like they whistle after girls here. It was terrible, and so I was hiding in my hotel room waiting [until] the plane [was to] leave. And then the plane left and of course it stopped everywhere, from Cairo to Geneva, Paris, Ireland, Newfoundland, and finally New York, where I had three days before taking the train to San Francisco.

Pressler was met at the airport by the music impresario Max Rabinoff, to whom he had been introduced previously in Palestine. The next morning Rabinoff took Pressler to the basement of the Steinway building to practice. Pressler recalls, "The piano tuner said, 'What are you doing here? This is for artists. What are you doing here?' And Rabinoff said, 'Let the boy play.' So the tuner listened for a little bit and said, 'This is the piano of Schnabel,' so I played some Beethoven. 'This is the piano of Rubinstein,' so I played some Chopin. 'And this is the piano of Casadesus,' so I played some French music. He said, 'Wait a minute.' He brought Mr. Steinway down, and Mr. Steinway said, 'Would you play something for me?' So I played. He said, 'What are you doing?' I said, 'I'm waiting here to take the train to San Francisco for the Debussy Competition.' He said, 'This place is your home away from home. You can practice to your heart's content,' which meant, after hours I could go to the basement.

"And the piano tuner who became such a good friend and admirer said, 'I want you to meet somebody special tonight.' And so I came and Byron Janis came. He was at that time studying with Horowitz, and he said to me, 'Don't go to the competition. The competition is fixed.' I said, 'What do you mean?' He said, 'The son-in-law of [E. Robert] Schmitz is going to win.' Schmitz was a famous French pianist in America who had received money from the French government to run the competition. But what Janis didn't know was, when you have [composers] Darius Milhaud and Roger Sessions [also Charles Cushing of the University of

Fig. 4.2. Pressler, with Darius Milhaud, after winning the Debussy Competition in San Francisco, 1946. (Ben Greenhaus)

California-Berkley] on the jury and [Major M.] Fisher, the music critic of the San Francisco Examiner, you cannot dictate who wins, yes? And I had promised to Karel Salomon, who had said, 'There will be many times you will be enticed or seduced not to go to the competition. But you have to go, because that is why you went. You went to find out how you stack up with the young pianists.' So I said to Byron, 'I am going.' And I went, and I'm glad I went."

In his preparation, Pressler had learned all but one, the *Hommage à Haydn,* of the required Debussy repertoire. He had not been able to obtain a score previously and finally found one in New York, just before boarding the train for his three-day trip to San Francisco. He taught himself the piece by sight during the train ride and arrived the day before the competition, then competed against sixty-four contestants. At great surprise to himself and his teacher, he won the coveted Debussy Prize, receiving $1,000 and many engagements as a result. After the competition Milhaud remarked, "The contestants played behind a screen. As a member of the jury I was struck by the qualities of real musicianship, deep piano tradition, [and] tenderness in sonority, of contestant Number Two. Without hesitation this mysterious Number Two was chosen for first prize."

Fig. 4.3. Pressler, with Eugene Ormandy, preparing to play with the Philadelphia Orchestra, 1947

"I remember among the twenty-seven required [pieces] was *Soiree dans Granade, Ce qu'a vu le vent d'ouest, L'Isle Joyeuse*, and the Etude in Fourths. I had practiced eight hours a day. I [had known] hardly any Debussy at all, but when I accompanied Loyonnet, he opened my eyes to how to read and my ears to hear. I felt a very natural affinity to Debussy's music. His music awoke in me a response, a very strong response. It was music that I, to this very day, I find magical, his and Ravel. It was magic."

The next significant contact in Pressler's life was when Rabinoff arranged an audition for Pressler with Arthur Judson, president of Columbia Artists and manager of many conductors. Pressler played for him and was accepted to the Columbia Artists' roster of performers, an association that continues even today. Judson, in turn, arranged for Pressler to audition with Eugene Ormandy, who engaged Pressler to make his debut with the Philadelphia Orchestra at Carnegie Hall playing the Schumann Concerto. Following this concert, the Orchestra's Board of Trustees invited Pressler back for the following three seasons, an invitation that has never been extended to any other soloist. His concerti for those reengagements were the Chopin F minor, the Beethoven Fourth, and the

Fig. 4.4. Publicity Photo

Fig. 4.5. Publicity Photo, 1946

Liszt E-flat Concerto. Following Pressler's performances with the Phila-delphia Orchestra, Judson was instrumental in securing orchestral en-gagements for Pressler to play with Szell, Stokowski, Masur, Paray, Solti, Dorati, Bernstein, Mitropoulos, and many more of the great conductors of the day.

FIVE

Opportunities in America

I S A B E L L E   V E N G E R O V A

Following the Debussy competition in 1946 but before playing the debut concert, Pressler began studying with Madame Isabelle Vengerova, a formidable teacher who was born in Russia and had studied in Vienna with Joseph Dachs, Theodor Leschetizky, and Anna Essipova.

"I was in New York, and I played the Chopin F Minor Concerto at the Metropolitan Opera House as a benefit concert for Hebrew University," says Pressler. "I was brought to her. She was at this time a teacher at both Juilliard and at Curtis in Philadelphia. She had Bernstein as a student and many others, Graffman, Lateiner, Rezits, Foster.

Fig. 5.1. Isabelle Vengerova. Courtesy of The Curtis Institute of Music.

"I had lessons with her for six months to a year at her apartment in New York. What she showed me, just in that short time—even if I couldn't do it at that time—revolutionized my thinking, because it was, for me, the discovery of the wrist. It is always something that goes with the key, that plays into the key, like you have a shock absorber on a car, providing cushioning. She, being a student of Leschetizky, taught me her exercises. I saw that and used it and organized it so that it would help me. Everyone who studied with Vengerova came out differently, understanding it differently, and then found his way through her opening of the door, his own way of doing it. Okay, we all do it differently, and we all expect something different out of it, but it has helped me. It has helped [her other students], and it has helped my students."

Studies with Vengerova came to an end when she heard, incorrectly, that Pressler was also taking lessons from Loyonnet. "I saw Loyonnet when he came to New York during this time, and he asked me to play for him and see what I had accomplished since I had last seen him in Palestine. And down in the basement of Steinway, I played for him. Someone must have told Vengerova about it, because she said, 'You played for another teacher.' And whatever I told her wasn't convincing enough, so she wouldn't let me continue lessons with her. She was famous for being difficult, but I really didn't notice it until then."

ROBERT CASADESUS

Soon after his break with Vengerova, Arthur Judson arranged for Pressler to study with the great French pianist Robert Casadesus at Fontainebleau in the summer of 1947. Though Casadesus was much devoted to performing the works of Debussy, Ravel, and Fauré, he also had wonderful insights into the German masters. Pressler's repertoire for the summer included Brahms and Schumann pieces and Beethoven's *Appassionata* Sonata, Op. 57. Casadesus loaned his score of the *Appassionata* to Pressler so that he could mark the fingerings, and Pressler remembers that the score indicated Casadesus had played the piece more than 100 times worldwide. Pressler studied with Casadesus during that summer and later the two became good friends through Daniel Guilet, who had attended the Paris Conservatoire with Casadesus's wife, Gaby. It was Casadesus's teaching of Beethoven that brought Pressler new understanding

Fig. 5.2. Robert Casadesus. By permission of Gréco Casadesus.

of that repertoire. And Casadesus's contribution to Pressler's career also included an original composition dedicated to the Beaux Arts Trio," a beautiful piece," recalls Pressler.

EGON PETRI

During the summer of 1948 following Pressler's debut concert in New York, the Steinway Company arranged for him to study with eminent concert pianist Egon Petri, a German of Dutch descent who was teaching master classes at Mills College in Oakland, California. Believed by many to be one of the greatest pianists of the twentieth century, Petri was described in Harold Schonberg's *The Great Pianists* as "a superb technician, a musician of intellect, refinement and strength." Petri had studied with Ferrucio Busoni and Venezuelan pianist Terresa Carreño, whose teacher, Georges Mathias, had been a student of Frédéric Chopin.

INFLUENCE OF EGON PETRI

STUDENT: I have an article for you about Egon Petri, who I know was one of your main teachers. Would you talk to us about him and any other teachers or musicians who had an influence on your career?

PRESSLER: Yes, Egon Petri was a great pianist, a tremendous pianist. It is interesting, I was just now in Oxford and a wonderful musicologist and pianist spoke about one of the last pieces of Busoni, the six pieces [*Elegies*] which are dedicated to six different pianists; and one is dedicated to Petri and one is dedicated to Kestenberg, two of my teachers. But Petri was a tremendous pianist. His technical ability was unbelievable, and he was a great musician. A great musician, that means he played anything up to Brahms: the complete Bach, all the Beethoven sonatas, Brahms, Tchaikovsky, nearly all the Liszt, and Busoni.

There was one great weakness in him, which was that he didn't like to play Schumann; it was outside his province. Petri was a great musician, but I didn't consider him a great artist. He was a great pianist and he was a great musician and therefore a great teacher, too, because he let you do things, although he always criticized them. He would say, "You can do it, but don't overdo it." He would always say something. At that time I was very young and I always played with my face close to the keyboard, and he said to me, "Menahem, tell me, what does it smell like?" At that time I couldn't get close enough.

But he was a great, great master of the keyboard, and he had these tremendous hands. The only other hand that I saw that was as beautiful and as great was the hand of Richter, that kind of a hand. But Petri was always secure, and he showed us six fingerings for the last movement of the *Appassionata*. It was amazing. And I said, "Don't you get lost when you have to perform?" No, he would not get lost. He was always absolutely clear about what he was doing. But he was telling us that his first great, great success was in Russia. He went to a tour of Russia and played in Moscow, and he had an enormous success. And so, after one recital, he played the second recital. A week later he played a third recital, and he played a fourth recital; he played a fifth recital. When it came to the sixth recital, he didn't have repertoire. And so he selected to play Schumann, the *Symphonic Etudes*.

So Petri sits down to play the *Symphonic Etudes*, and he forgets in the first variation. He started again, again it just disappeared out of his head. And he heard them yell the one piece which he played magnificently well, Schubert-Liszt, the Songs–he was famous for that. And so the public yelled, "Please play Schubert-Liszt." And he told us, "So my life was saved." He was a charming man, a delightful man, and he showed me, of course, many things that I learned and enjoyed. But, he could do everything. Therefore, if someone said to him, "How about rotation?" he would say, "Oh, that's a good idea," or "How about no rotation?" he would say, "Oh, that's a wonderful idea!" There were never any difficulties for him.

Fig. 5.3. Egon Petri

"Steinway provided me a practice room with a piano that was actually Stokowski's piano from Hollywood," Pressler says. "They sent it from his home to Oakland, so I had a piano I could practice [on], and I did, six hours, seven hours a day. I was very, very, very religious. Petri was very nice, very, very nice to me. The first thing he said to me—that was right after the debut—he said, 'What do you want to do here?' I said, 'I would like to study.' 'Well, what do you have to learn?' he said. 'You know it all.'

"He was a phenomenal pianist, and he would hear about this kind of a technique and then he would believe in that and he would do it, but it didn't really matter because he could also do the opposite equally well. He had a fantastic memory. I mean, a man who knew the complete Bach so well, all thirty-two sonatas of Beethoven, the complete Brahms, the complete Liszt, complete Busoni, who learned the Rachmaninoff Third Concerto as an exercise. His recording of Chopin's A-flat *Polonaise* sold well enough that he bought a house in California from the royalties.

"I studied the twenty-four *Etudes* of Chopin that summer, and all was in master classes. I came in with the Op. 10, no. 2, and I played it.

[27]

And he said to me, 'That was quite good. I would like it lighter and faster.' Okay, so I went once more through. Now he says, 'That's quite good. I would like it lighter and faster.' And of course at that time I was quite fresh, and I said to him, 'Master, would you show me?' And he sat down with his legs crossed, and he played the most fantastic *étude*. It was absolutely hair-raising. He actually gave me a great compliment in the end when he said, 'You know, Menahem, I sometimes ask myself when I'm onstage, "What am I doing here?" You never do. You always play the music, and you're so involved with it, and you're enjoying it so much.'"

During this period of his life, Pressler was spending as much time as possible in Israel between concert tours. Sara Scherchen, an Israeli girl of sixteen, asked Menahem to teach her piano. Although he turned her down at the time, he became interested in her and the two married in August of 1949.

"The nice thing was, at the time we were married, Israel was already declared a state, and we were married in Jerusalem by the Chief Rabbi of Israel, Isaac Herzog, whose son Chaim later became president of Israel. Isaac had been an officer in the army while Sara was a corporal at the headquarters in Tel Aviv with associations to the United Nations, because she was good in languages. Everyone was sure he wouldn't come but would send somebody else to do it. I used to play benefit concerts for his wife. You know, they would ask me, 'Will you play a benefit?' 'Of course!' As a young student, I was glad to have any opportunity to play. I played many benefits for Mrs. Herzog, the rabbi's wife, and for Mrs. Ben-Gurion, the prime minister's wife. So I thought somehow I could ask him. That he said 'yes' and that he came was a big surprise. And so, that's one of the reasons the marriage has held up so well!

"We got married in Jerusalem, which, of course, now it has even more meaning, great meaning for us. You know, for 2000 years, the Jews were praying at the Passover [seder], 'Next year in Jerusalem.' So when I asked Rabbi Herzog—the State had just been declared and he was Chief Rabbi of the State—if he would marry us, he said, 'Yes.' But everyone in the family and friends said, 'He won't come. He'll send a substitute.' You know, 'I'm busy this Saturday, I have something else to do. My assistant will do it.' No, he came himself in person. You see, the knot held."

Sara was born in Tel Aviv and brought up in the little town of Petach-Tikvah (which means Opening of Hope), and went to school in Ramat-Gan. She was the oldest of three and, according to Pressler, "the

Fig. 5.4. Wedding Photo of Menahem and Sara Pressler, 1949

Fig. 5.5. Wedding Photo, 1949. Menahem and Sara are seated on the right. Moritz Pressler is seated next to Menahem, with Judith Pressler third from the left.

brightest and the prettiest, and all her life, has lived up to the highest possible standard." "Sara started to study in Petach-Tikvah with a teacher who always said to her, 'Play with feelings,' even though she could barely read the notes, looking at every note. But she wanted to study, so she asked a friend who introduced her to me, and when I saw the way her fifth finger stuck out, and I said, 'No, you're not good for the piano.' So that's how it started, but I think she got even!

"We were married in Israel, but we left immediately for Holland. I had two recitals scheduled in Holland. I also had a concert with a fine orchestra and conductor in London, a benefit, I think, for the University, and I had concerts in Paris. So we actually lived for a few months in Europe."

The two settled in New York, and soon thereafter, Sara mentioned to violinist Isaac Stern that Pressler was looking for a teacher. Stern recommended Edward Steuermann.

INSPIRATION OF EDWARD STEUERMANN

The other man that I found very inspiring, who was also a student of Busoni, was Steuermann. He was the most interesting man, one of the finest musicians I've ever met. No one above him, not Richter, no one was a greater musician than Steuermann.

He was an immense, immense, immense musician; and I must say, one of the best lessons I had was when I was already teaching at Indiana, and I came to New York. He was teaching at Juilliard, and I met him at his studio at Juilliard to have lunch with him. And he said, "Menahem, I'm sorry. I still have a lesson to give. If you want, you can come in." And so I came in and he gave a lesson on the Schumann, *Humoresque*. It was a wonderful, magnificent lesson to a student who didn't understand the lesson. The student wanted to know, "Is it better with the third finger or the second finger? Shall I play louder here? Can I wait on this note a little longer?" He didn't understand that Steuermann really gave him the key into Schumann, which was absolutely beautiful.

And then I remember another thing. He was going to Israel to play the Schoenberg Concerto, so he had invited friends to his studio at Juilliard to hear him perform the piece. It was summer. It was hot, and there was no air conditioning. Now, if you know the Schoenberg Concerto, that is very difficult listening. It's even more difficult playing, but it's very difficult listening. So, Juilliard was hot like hell. Above, somebody practiced the organ, so there came the sound of the organ into the room. And here Steuermann was emoting with the Concerto, very deeply felt Concerto. And there was that organ, and it was hot, and you heard that music, and you thought, "It is living hell." Then he finished and he said, "I want you to hear it again." And I remember running away. I never told him that, because he was a difficult and very wonderful man.

EDWARD STEUERMANN

Pressler began taking lessons from Steuermann at the Juilliard School on Claremont Avenue and 122nd Street in New York City. By this time Pressler was touring regularly and his own lessons continued for several years, even after Pressler began teaching at Indiana University. Steuermann was a great pianist, who in Berlin had studied with Busoni, as had Kestenberg and Petri.

"He was one of the finest musicians I've ever met. No one, not even Richter, was a greater musician than Steuermann. Even more influential to Steuermann than Busoni was Arnold Schoenberg, with whom Steuermann had studied in Berlin from 1912 to 1914. Steuermann became the greatest disciple of that school, the most knowledgeable. It was Steuermann to whom Schoenberg dedicated his Piano Concerto, and Webern wrote his *Variations* for him. Steuermann played the piano part of *Wozzeck* for all the conductors in the beginning because only he could read that score. He was an immense musician who had

Fig. 5.6. Edward Steuermann, 1956. Photo by Fred Plaut. By permission of The Juilliard School.

deep insights. No one knew Schumann or Beethoven more deeply than Steuermann did. He always compared everything a composer had written to the work that you played, which meant he could call on a quartet, on a trio, on a symphony, on a song that would compare to it. He was a difficult man and a difficult musician because he'd convince you to play one way and at the next lesson tell you to play exactly the opposite! But for me, he was ideal because he freed me to find my own way.

"Always when I had a new work, I would play it for Steuermann. I remember the Schumann *Fantasie* and the *Kreisleriana*, Beethoven's Op. 111 Sonata, Chopin's Second and Third Sonatas, Busoni and Schoenberg works, the Berg Sonata, the Webern *Variations*. I mean, I wanted to learn from him. These works were really from the horse's mouth.

"But the thing was, he could never satisfy himself. He had great difficulties in his own performing, always forgot in a concert. He was very critical, enormously critical. And the one thing with him was, the better the student, the more critical he was; the less good the student, the more supportive he was. I mean, if you played well, it was very seldom that you heard, 'That was good,' because he always knew how it should and could be better. But then I knew some of the students that he was teaching who barely played decently, and he was the most supportive and would say, 'That was excellent. That was very good this time.'

"One time after a performance, he was very angry with me. He called me the day after I played the Chopin F minor Concerto with the New York Philharmonic with Mitropoulos and said, 'Menahem, I don't want you ever to come back for a lesson again!' Well, of course I asked him, 'What's the matter, Mr. Steuermann?' He said, 'You don't do anything I tell you.' I said, 'That is not the case, Mr. Steuermann. I mean, I may have done other things too, but I do what you say and I do what I feel and what I believe in.' Then I said, 'Did you like the performance?' And he said, 'Yes, very much.' So I said, 'In that case, can I come and play chess with you again?' He said, 'Okay, tomorrow.' And then I went back to play chess with him, and I lost. He was a very good chess player, but this time I wanted to lose, and we made up.

"I have never forgotten that because he was so rabid on the phone, but he must have felt—and I do feel even to this day—the deep admiration I had for him and for his knowledge and for the way he would show things. I learned from him, and I learned to understand, and I learned to look deeply into music. I really admired him, and now that I am a teacher, I admire him even more for his all-encompassing knowledge."

NEW YORK

New York became the Presslers' base. The couple had an apartment on Eighty-sixth Street and Central Park West at the Peter Stuyvesant Hotel, where Artur Schnabel also lived. Other friends lived in the same neighborhood. Steinway made sure Pressler had a piano at his home, and Menahem and Sara attended many concerts during this time in New York. "Horowitz, Schnabel, Alexander Brailawsky, Myra Hess, Rubinstein, Claudio Arrau, Heifetz, Simon Barere [the phenomenal technician who died on stage playing the Grieg Concerto], many, many concerts." Pressler and Sara enjoyed "many Saturday nights with friends, young artists, all of them. Seymour Lipkin, Gary Graffman, they all came to the house. We played, we talked and we discussed. It was a wonderful time to be in New York."

Sara traveled with Menahem much of the time for the first two years of their marriage. But after the birth of their first child, Sara stayed home. Each year, Pressler says, he questioned how the next season would be, how long he would be away. "The first seasons were fantastic, but then after a while, another young sensation comes along." Finally, the two decided to return to Israel, with plans for Pressler to teach at the Tel Aviv Conservatory (now the Tel Aviv Music Academy) and travel from there for concerts.

In America, Pressler had recorded many solos for MGM and in doing so had met violinist Daniel Guilet and cellist Bernard Greenhouse. The Presslers hadn't been back in Israel long before Guilet telephoned. "Menahem, can you come for nine concerts in America? And to make the trio record for MGM that you wanted? Columbia is willing to give us those concerts." "I said, 'Yes,'" recalls Pressler. "That was really a most important step in my life." So the two returned to America with their baby and resettled in a New York apartment.

U.S. CITIZENSHIP

It was while in New York that Pressler gained U.S. citizenship. "I am very, very happy and proud to be a citizen," Pressler says. "I love this country for the opportunity that it has given me, and that's why I have never minded to pay the taxes. It has always been a privilege to live in this country. It is a privilege to be protected in this country. It's a privilege to make friends in this country."

Though completely happy to have made the move to America and to have become an American citizen, Pressler says his feelings for Israel today are "as strong as they have ever been. As a country, it gave me an education, freedom, hope. It supported me, and I see that it has created dignity for all the Jews, if they like it or not, if they're Zionists or not.

"The love is very great, but it is enhanced by Sara's love. And also, even though we pay a great deal of taxes in America, we have taxed ourselves, or she has taxed me and herself, to support Israel but not to get any honors or be praised for it. She is always invited to recognitions, but she never accepts. She always selects things; she has many water projects, which are vitally important. She also supported the houses for children who come from North Africa and were mistreated and therefore had great psychological problems. She supported the poor children who needed books to go to school. She supported a clinic that helped them to learn how to brush their teeth and helped them with education and training, all that. She also planted trees, 500 trees to this one or that."

Pressler reiterates that he and Sara are extremely appreciative of what Israel gave them and that they both still have a passion for their homeland. "She always says, 'You have to be grateful, because they saved your life.' She was born there, therefore, she is grateful. She refused any luxury for herself. I didn't do that, not as much, but she did. It is a passion for us, a passion in our house, I must say. Sara spoke only Hebrew with our children. She had me only speak German, and of course, in school they spoke English. So they really learned to understand three languages."

Regardless of the couples' continued passion for their homeland, they remain thrilled to be in America. "And then, of course," Pressler says, "the greatest thing that happened in our lives was coming to Bloomington."

SIX

BLOOMINGTON

COMING TO INDIANA UNIVERSITY

Just as his concert career began to soar, Pressler's life took an unexpected detour. He received an invitation in October 1954 from Dean Wilfred C. Bain of Indiana University. "I said, 'No, I can't. I have concerts.'" "Bain wanted me to come to Bloomington, a great music school of course, and he had my name in his little black book because he had first invited Steuermann, my teacher. Steuermann had said, 'No, I am a city man, but I have a young colleague,' so Bain just wrote my name in his little black book, but didn't invite me yet."

Next Bain invited the pianist Willi Masselos to come to Bloomington. "Willi and I were part of a four-piano team and made recordings under assumed names playing things like *Night on Bald Mountain* just to earn some money. Willi believed in his stars. If the stars didn't tell him to go, he wouldn't go. And then one day, Masselos said, 'Menahem, should I go or shouldn't I?' I said, 'You must, of course.' He said, 'You wouldn't, would you?' In order to encourage him, I said I would, but I didn't have the slightest idea what Indiana University was like."

Masselos did take the position at Bloomington, and then enticed Pressler to follow. "When Bain called me, I said, 'I can't.' When he called me a second time, I still said, 'I can't.' So Masselos and Sidney Foster, who was already a professor here, called me, and Masselos said, 'You told me you would come,' so I accepted a position of Artist in Residence for one semester. That was in 1955."

"But Bain was, from the beginning, interested in getting the best. Willi Masselos was a fantastic pianist, and so was Sidney Foster. Then he got me. Pretty soon he got [cellist Janos] Starker, then [violinist Josef] Gingold, and it grew. Always the best."

When he arrived at Indiana, Pressler skipped a reception held by the university's president, Herman B Wells, who was renowned for remembering everyone—even those he had not met—by name. Instead,

Pressler left town immediately for a weekend concert tour. Winter weather set in during that weekend, and when Pressler found himself unable to make the drive home from the Indianapolis airport, he stopped to call his wife, still in New York, to let her know of his whereabouts. There in the airport stood Wells, who said, "Menahem Pressler, what are you doing here?" Rattled that Wells would recognize him, Pressler offered an explanation, and Wells said, "May I invite you to join me in my car? My chauffeur is coming." "And so he took me," Pressler says. "Wells became more and more interested in the School of Music, and every time I had a good notice in the *New York Times* or somewhere, I would get a little note from him. That this university is where it is was all his doing. He was a prince among princes."

Pressler's first years at the university did not pay all that well, though the position allowed him to continue his concerts. "I know that I got too little, because Bain knew how to divide up one salary check into two people in the beginning; and since there was a pool of so many, he could do it. Soon enough I got an invitation to another school with another salary offer and that helped."

The school allowed him to concertize, as long as his obligations to his students were satisfied. "Just so you give them all their lessons," he recalls being told. "And so if I was gone more than three weeks, I would sometimes bring in someone to teach them." More often, Pressler himself would offer to teach his students two or three lessons per week to make up the missed lessons. "[Bain] couldn't have attracted Starker and all these others if he hadn't let them play," Pressler says of the teaching and performance arrangements. He compares it to a School of Medicine: "The most honored teacher is the surgeon, not the one who doesn't do surgery anymore. Music is the same."

Pressler first lived in faculty housing on campus on the corner of East Third Street. "It was a nice apartment, small but nice." Sara soon joined him in Bloomington, "and soon enough, with a child, we looked for a place." He and Sara found the home in which they still live. "I have been happy that I bought that house—and then added to it. We enlarged the dining room and added two more bathrooms and enlarged the garage, too. It's really a beautiful, beautiful house. I love it there.

"My studio [at IU] was downstairs right next to the bathroom, and so many times people would run into my studio thinking it was the bathroom. And then as soon as the round building [the Music Annex] opened, I moved into this studio. I have cleaned it a few times, but you can see I am overrun like the Brazilian jungle—it grows!"

Beginning Teaching

And so Pressler began teaching. "During that first year I had some students who couldn't even read music. But first of all, I learned to see what each one needed, and I guess some people are more born to be a teacher than others. And that has nothing to do with their knowledge, but it has to do with their desire and ability to transfer knowledge, to understand the psyche of the person that you transfer the knowledge to, what he or she is capable of receiving, and how much that particular person even needs. Because to be a perfectionist with someone who doesn't need all that would break the spirit, and that little love for music would be killed."

Pressler had more than twenty students during his first couple of years at the university. During his third year when Sidney Foster suffered a heart attack, he and Masselos divided Foster's classes so that Foster could continue to receive a salary. "And every night after teaching and after practicing, we would go to Sidney's, eat something, drink a glass of wine, and talk. It was wonderful. Sidney and Bronya, his wife, they were the most wonderful friends one could imagine. So I started to have good students, because his class was good, and from then on I had only good students. I could choose my class. Today the class is full way ahead of time from all over the world.

"But I learned many things. I learned to hone my technique of teaching. I learned to understand my students more, and I learned to pace myself, because it's an enormous task to sit for six hours teaching and then to go practice, which was a must. So it is here that I grew to be a teacher. And I learned also to become a specialist in master classes. Now I have master classes all over the world."

Bloomington Colleagues

Pressler is quick to agree that he has had many wonderful colleagues in Bloomington, pianists as well as other musicians, who have been inspiring. "Absolutely. That's also what helped me, because when the other job offers came along—Rochester, Stony Brook, Juilliard, Texas, Cincinnati— what helped me decide to stay was two things: the faculty and the administration. To have a Webb [Charles H. Webb, dean emeritus] as a dean is wonderful, and that has continued now with Gwyn Richards. He's absolutely unbelievable, very, very special."

The colleagues have been extraordinary. "Sidney helped Abbey Simon to come here. He was a consummate pianist. And then Sidney and Abbey brought Jorge Bolet here because they had studied with him at Curtis when he was a graduate student, and of course they knew what he could do. I enjoyed Bolet immensely. And György Sebök was a unique musician. We've had fantastic people."

[37]

Master Classes

Pressler eventually become a specialist in master classes at Indiana University. "At first, Starker and I led the master classes in chamber music. Then he stopped and I took them alone. And then somebody dropped out of leading the piano master classes, so I had the chamber music master classes and the piano master classes and my studio with eighteen students. I mean, it was killing [me]. Sara began helping by selecting the students for the classes and eventually for my studio.

INTRODUCTION TO A MASTER CLASS

It's the sixteenth year [at Adamant, Vermont], and I'm delighted that we have so many new faces among our players, because, up to this point, no one would release his place in the class and I would never, never let one of my older students go for a new one, even if the new one is supposedly better.

Now that brings me to the point that I like to make before we start: we are here together, and the one thing that really brings us to be together is the love for music. And love for music is not exemplified only, or first, by how well you play. It is exemplified by how deeply you feel the music, and that can be exemplified by any one of us. We have had people who could not play very well but who learned something, and that in itself gave every one of us not only pleasure, but we were proud of that particular person's battle for getting better. And in a way, it really doesn't matter who the name of the player is. It is always the same battle to get a little bit better. Now I know one thing–and that comes with age–that you always pay a price, you get better in one way and you get less good in another, but better in a way you haven't had before. You enrich your all-around experience, and your regard for the composers becomes deeper, richer, and with a greater love for what they represent, for what they have given us.

So, here we are in the master class and we all learn how to control our emotions, especially the one emotion that we all experience: fear. And we have to control that and overcome it, and we do that by simply sitting down to perform. That in itself is an act of courage. There is no one who's trying to play badly; there is absolutely no one. So when we sit down to play, we would like to shine. We would like to be accepted as "Oh, you are wonderful." And at the same time, it is also that to which we have devoted our lives. We want our lives to be rich, to be something that is bigger and better than we are.

We hear today Beethoven and Debussy and Chopin. Whoever had such a dowry before? But we do, and so I don't want to delay the marriage. Let's start.

"The next classes were offered in Ravinia. Edward Gordon, the director, was a pianist, and he invited me once and from that time on until this day in Ravinia." Pressler has continued to offer master classes at many universities and musical centers around the world: in Germany, South America, Israel, Paris, Basel, Berkeley, Biola University, Adamant, "wherever I would say, 'Yes, I agree to go.'" A typical master class lasts three hours; some, especially in Spain, are four. "Most often there are four students in three hours so that each student gets forty-five minutes."

Judging Competitions

Pressler continues to judge several piano competitions. He has judged the Van Cliburn four times, the Queen Elisabeth of Belgium four times, and also judged for the Paloma O'Shea and the International Piano-e-Competition. "I have a letter from Leeds on my desk now," he says, "but I have never accepted it because it falls at the beginning of the school year. This next year in March [2008] I'm invited to a competition for competition winners in North Carolina as well as the Rubinstein Competition in Israel."

THE BEAUX ARTS TRIO

Pressler often says that he has truly learned the most about making music through his work with the Beaux Arts Trio, which he co-founded in 1955, not long after his first recording, the soundtrack for an MGM movie, *Song of Love,* about the life of Robert Schumann. Arthur Rubinstein had already recorded a soundtrack that had been released by RCA, and MGM was looking for someone to record the music for its own label. Pressler got the assignment, which eventually led to thirty more solo recordings for MGM.

Pressler had expressed interest in playing Mozart trios, and MGM encouraged him to find players for the project. He was introduced to Daniel Guilet, concertmaster of Toscanini's NBC Symphony who had formed the Guilet String Quartet after years of playing in the celebrated Calvet Quartet. Guilet then introduced Pressler to cellist Bernard Greenhouse, who was cellist with the Bach Aria Group, and thus the Trio was formed.

The first session of the Beaux Arts Trio resulted in a recording of Ravel and Fauré trios, followed by a recording of Mendelssohn and Haydn trios. The Trio originally had a limited tour of nine concerts,

Fig. 6.1. Beaux Arts Trio, 1955. Daniel Guilet (violin), Menahem Pressler (piano), Bernard Greenhouse (cello).

but on July 13, 1955, they substituted for the Albeneri Trio at the Berkshire Festival (now known as Tanglewood) and received praise from several noted musicians, including Festival conductor Charles Munch and soloists Zino Francescatti and Robert Casadesus. The debut was such a stunning success that a tour of seventy concerts was arranged. The Trio's third recording won the prestigious *Grand Prix nationale du Disque*.

Pressler admits to being the least experienced chamber player when the Trio was founded. "Guilet not only had studied with fine teachers at the Paris Conservatoire but also had experience in outstanding string quartets, learning how to play a masterpiece not just from section to section but truly how to structure the entire piece. Then Guilet was concertmaster of the NBC Orchestra under Toscanini, and you learn a tremendous amount from a conductor like that. Then he became first violinist in his own quartet, so he really knew music on all these different levels, great music-making. And then he came [to] the Beaux Arts Trio. So I was the beneficiary of his knowledge of music-making.

"He was very difficult, worse than Steuermann. It was not only that he was critical; it was that every second word in the rehearsal was seemingly like an insult. Bernie Greenhouse saw it as such, and so there were many battles there. I didn't see it as such, I must admit, until later. I only saw how much it meant to me to discover the extent to which one deepens oneself in the work and owns then the whole work, so that I, sitting at the piano, don't just play my part. I play every other part, yes?"

(The Trio's personnel has changed greatly over the years. Isidore Cohen replaced Guilet in 1969, and Peter Wiley took the cello position when Greenhouse retired in 1987. Violinist Ida Kavafian performed with the Trio from 1992 until 1998, when Young Uck Kim stepped in. The present players are cellist Antonio Meneses, who joined the group in 1998, and the newest member, violinist Daniel Hope, who began in 2002.

(At the time of this writing it has been announced that the Beaux Arts Trio will disband following the 2007–08 concert season with final concerts at the Tanglewood Festival in Massachusetts in August 2008.)

A CONTINUED EDUCATION

Pressler has maintained his search for excellent teachers and new influences throughout his life, seeking the best he could find, both in Europe and in America. The lineage of his various teachers reaches into history to Bach, Beethoven, Haydn, Mozart, Liszt, and Chopin and includes the Germanic, French, and Russian traditions. He was carefully schooled in the details of form, musical theory, and style. Through his conversations with Loyonnet and teachings of Vengerova, Pressler incorporated a relaxed technical approach into his playing and his teaching. He gained tremendous interpretative insights from Loyonnet, Casadesus, Kestenberg, and Steuermann and from his experiences with the members of the Beaux Arts Trio.

Pressler's desire for perfection has resulted in his being highly demanding both of himself and of his students, and his impulsive personality has led him to great spontaneity of interpretation. His amazing love for practicing as well as performing lends a quality of delight to his music making and his teaching. The ease with which he learns new pieces

Fig. 6.2. Beaux Arts Trio rehearsal, 2006. Daniel Hope (violin), Menahem Pressler (piano), Antonio Meneses (cello).

has allowed him to achieve an immense repertoire. And his personal drive and extraordinarily good health have enabled him to participate in a long and distinguished triple career of solo work, chamber music, and teaching.

When asked if these different aspects of his career were ever in conflict with one another or if they worked together harmoniously, Pressler replied, "I think they feed each other. I feel very strongly about each of them and have felt them feeding each other musically and even technically. You play chamber music in the most serious manner. You learn how to look at a work, you learn how to use your hands, and you learn the sense of balance. Then you play as a soloist. You learn to balance the two hands. You see the sense in which you bring a work from the first note to the last note to a really organic conclusion. And then you bring that knowledge, that inspiration, into the studio, and you have a relationship with a student who is wide open and can take that advice from you. And then, in a sense, the way he or she takes the advice and makes it work for himself or herself is a teaching to you. You learn something there too, so then you come back out of it with renewed pleasure in making music.

Fig. 6.3. Antonio Meneses, Menahem Pressler, Daniel Hope

"I have felt very, very much energized by those three activities and have been able to do them because it is not easy to 'dance at three weddings.' And I've been doing it and doing it with great pleasure and, I would even say, with great inner satisfaction. There is a saying from the Talmud: 'I learned a great deal from my teachers, I learned even more from myself, and I learned most of all from my students.'"

SEVEN

GENERAL ASPECTS OF
PRESSLER'S TEACHING

SELECTING STUDENTS

Menahem Pressler has instructed hundreds of students over his fifty-year teaching career, most of whom have been enrolled in masters or doctoral degree programs at the Indiana University Jacobs School of Music. Some have been undergraduates, and some have studied for their Artist Diplomas. In the earliest years of Pressler's teaching, students were routinely assigned to his studio. As the numbers of interested students increased, students would contact Pressler by phone or letter, indicating their desire to study with him, and Pressler would schedule personal auditions, at which time he would hear students play for ten or fifteen minutes and talk with them about their plans for the future. Students came to consider admission into Pressler's class as personal triumphs, affirmations of accomplishment, and guarantees of future success.

Pressler comments that what he looks for, first and foremost, in prospective students is their love for music and their desire to dedicate their lives to it "so that, whatever life brings, they will be happy. By that I mean, if they are in a certain place and they teach there, I want them to be happy they found an outlet for all they know, for their love of the works, and that they can transmit that love to others."

Pressler points out that he always takes on some students who he realizes will not be the best players but who might make good teachers. "I look for character, the attitude," which he describes as "a sense of inner discipline, a force that will help the student succeed. You have to come with everything, with the love for it, with the desire to really devote your life to it." He says he looks for coordination, to see that the hands are good. "And I look for intelligence, so that I know they will understand what I have to say to them. We must do anything to help a person find his maximum. How few do find it. I want them to be motivated and to continue after their degree, after getting a job, and so forth. I want them to keep their desire, no matter where they end up because that place where they are is the musical center for them. If you continue to live that way, you will make yourself happy and you will make others around you happy. You will not feel that you are just a poor pianist who makes a poor salary, but that you are a rich man."

Because of increasing demands on his schedule, the selection interviews in recent years have been conducted not by Menahem but by his wife, Sara, whom he calls "an innate psychologist who really understands people." After prospective students have passed entrance auditions into the School of Music, Sara interviews those who express the desire to study with Pressler. She does not hear them play but asks about their backgrounds and goals. Pressler says his wife "can discover in half an hour much more than I can by listening to them for ten minutes. She sees much further."

It is additionally important to Pressler that his students are supportive of one another and reflect the camaraderie he experienced as a student among young musicians in Israel. "There is a wonderful support system in my studio from one student to the other. It always has been, and that's what I feel is so vitally important. The outside world is hard enough, is difficult enough, and is supercritical very often without adequate knowledge. I have my students give master classes for themselves. They play for each other, and I want them to learn how to critique each other properly. We know what happens outside. We often see schools that are built like that, where one student speaks badly of the other, and it's as if the world outside has been transferred into the school. Instead, the students should be protected, at least during the years of study, so that you get strong because of the support you feel, like having good parents."

THE IMPORTANCE OF TEACHING

"Teaching is one of the most satisfying things one can do," says Pressler. "You teach things that you know to people who would like to learn, things that I have *tried* and they work. I have tried also to teach the technical system that has served me so well. Today, at my age, I've never had tendonitis. I never had anything where I had to stop practicing, even though it was difficult to sit down sometimes. That part was worn out sometimes, or the shoulders would hurt because I would sit there for four hours, very intensely practicing. The thing is, I was always relaxed or *free*.

Fig. 7.1. Pressler in the studio, 1970s

Let me put it like a good tomato: the right mixture of sour and sweet, the right mixture of tension and at the same time release. I have discovered a lot through teaching. I have even discovered things about the piece through the student's playing of the piece, not just because I knew it better but the student found a certain insight that I had not seen, and I was delighted. I really try to encourage what is in *their* personalities, their personal ways of expressing music, their strong points. And with that comes freedom."

Pressler realizes that every student is an individual. "When you have three students playing the same piece, they couldn't all play it the same because they're different. No, after a while you learn that each of the people that you teach has a fire inside them, that there are places that you don't touch because it hurts them and it will hurt you. But that is not a given. It is not written anywhere.

That is also one of the reasons I don't have any visitors in the lessons when I teach my students. Very often I get asked, 'Can we come in for one of your lessons?' I say, 'No,' because when you are alone with a student, that is different than when someone is there. You cannot say certain things in front of someone else because the student will accept from you like from a doctor. I may say, 'Look, this arm is bad here. We have to get to the wound in a different way.' Now when someone else is there, you can't say that. You leave the wound a little bit, and you give an aspirin, and you say, 'You will feel better tomorrow.' Now I don't do that in a lesson. It has to be between the student and me because there is a relationship that is built on trust, so you can really demand or say many things because the student knows the intention is for his good. That's what any teacher should remember. It's not a power play that you're better than the student or that the student is less than you are because you know a little more. No, there's always the belief that the student will be able to do it, to do something with the music and with himself, even though you have to criticize in order for him or for her to get that.

"What I pride myself with especially is that I taught my technical principles and the principles stay the same, but they are applied differently to different people because we have different physiques—long arms, short arms, big, small, heavy, no weight whatsoever. Besides that, we each have our own personality. And very often a teacher can be harmful—not that he wants to—but by demanding that all students do certain things, but this particular one cannot do it that way. You have to tailor your demands. You have to tailor your approach. With some I can yell, which I do, but with some you only speak very nicely.

"I think communicating with students is something you have naturally and something you develop. You love to speak to them, so that's a need. You have something to speak about. You speak, and what makes it so much more pertinent, of course, is that you speak to the student about what he or she is. So the student wants to hear that, because that's what he comes for. It's not that he has to please me with his playing but that he has to learn something. So I have to learn how to speak to students, yes? I've developed that by, you could say, on the job training, and you hope that the student will learn to transfer ideas from one piece to the next.

"Very often when you know how a piece goes, you don't actually have to make it clear to yourself in words because you already understand it. But when you have to say it to a student, you have to put it into words. You have to put your finger on it, and you have to explain, 'This is this and this is this.' And then, once you have expressed it in words, somehow you find a way of going a little further; and that's where teaching has helped you understand. It becomes deeper in you by making it clear to the student, yes? And what comes back to you is a deeper clarification for yourself. Also, you find out through students very often that pieces that you thought you did not like so much, you start to like. You hear it, you teach it, you like it, you play it, and it becomes your specialty, so to speak.

"In a way, it's what we have in a marriage with children. The children bring you immortality. So it is with my students. I give them, like a parent, the best I have found in the world of music. They open their hearts, their souls. They become my mental children. Through them, I will live longer, having given them the best to share."

THE DEMANDING NATURE OF HIS LESSONS

His students quickly realize the demanding nature of Pressler's lessons and master classes. Pressler gives his all, and students must come to lessons or master classes prepared to do the same. Pressler's daughter,

---

IN GRATITUDE tO TEACHERS

You know, we all know that playing is difficult; and the more gifted one is, the more you realize how difficult it is. And what gives music this wonderful impact and strength is that [pianists] feel that music has an enormous important function to make life worth living. We have many things: we like to live in a nice home, we like to be married, we like to have good children, we like to do all of those things.

But there is some part inside of each of our souls that is asking for some kind of nourishment. And nothing can give as much beautiful nourishment—well, of course, there are many, many things that will give people nourishment—but music does it without saying a word. It gives you these black dots, and these black dots give you a kind of fulfillment. And I find it very, very wonderful when people sit here and play in front of us and undergo the searing difficulty to play that and hear from me, "You have got to play all the notes!" Of course, he would like to play all the notes. I know that, and he practiced all the notes. But then, like all of us, you come in front of an audience and some of the notes seem to not want to be played.

A good teacher can find a way of coaxing students, of explaining, of encouraging. And, as a teacher, it is wonderful when one is able to help a student achieve something more easily. And I know that we all feel that gratitude toward our teachers, a kind of gratitude for being helped so that we will remember them always for good or for worse—and that better be for good!

---

[48]

Edna, describes the situation: "I have observed him teaching many master classes at Adamant, at Banff, or Ravinia, or in Germany at Kroenberg; and these have been professional pianists and non-professionals, senior citizens, and young people. One thing he requires is professionalism. Students must arrive on time, not a minute late, because he is always on time and he expects that in others. They must bring two scores, one for him and one for them. Even though he may have played the piece a thousand times, he still likes to look at the score; and it must be their own scores, not library copies. Also, they should bring their own pencils and a way of recording the lesson. They must know all markings. If he's working with an ensemble, the members must allow enough time to rehearse together as an ensemble, not just as three soloists, and each person must know the parts of all the other players. These are the basic requirements. If these requirements aren't met, then the lesson gets off on the wrong foot. There are times that I've wanted to warn someone so they didn't start out with a disadvantage."

The same applies for individual lessons as well. Pressler expects students to master every detail covered in previous lessons and to go beyond his instructions both in technical and musical preparation. He rarely gives praise during lessons: "If I don't mention something, then it's better!" A student can take pride in hearing Pressler say "not bad" following a performance.

The goal, simply stated, is technical and musical perfection. In Pressler's words, "Every single note should sound. [One mistake] is because we are human; twice is unforgivable." If students strive toward this goal, impossible though it is, students will be prepared for future opportunities. "Work and an opportunity will arise. But you have to be ready for it and capable of taking it. But very, very often we say, 'Oh, but if only I had that happen to me, I could have done such and such.' 'I could have' is a very lame excuse."

Pressler abhors what he describes as "the empty phrase." Jonathan Bass, former student and now on the faculty at the Boston Conservatory, says that Pressler "abhors a vacuum, so in other words, if you're not really putting anything in, he'll supply what's needed; but he'd rather that you bring in your own ideas." Pressler says, "I give you these ideas not so you will copy me but so you will develop your own ideas." Bass recalls, "There were times that he would say, 'I don't care if you do it this way or that way, but do something.'" Edna Pressler agrees. "He's thrilled when he hears something that he didn't come up with himself."

Paula Ennis, another former student, states that Pressler "is able to differentiate [among] five levels of accomplishment: good, very good, excellent, superior, and artistic. Many people cannot hear the difference between excellent and artistic, but he can and he wants you to." This push for excellence means that lessons are conducted on the highest level of professionalism. Pressler has a keen sense of what each student is able to accomplish, and he pushes and prods them to achieve their best. They see themselves growing and progressing from being exposed to his high level of concentration and discernment of sound and musical style.

THE TECHNICAL EXERCISES

Pressler describes his technical principles simply as "the free arm, the transfer of weight, coupled with a strong finger technique. That is the goal. Only the way it evolves in each person varies. Everyone is different—the length of the arm, the height of the body, the relationship to the keyboard." By collecting exercises from his teachers, both from the French way and from Vengerova, Pressler devised his own techniques to help others understand how to free their arms and so on. He also uses a circle-of-fifths scale cycle for single-note scales, octaves, and broken octaves. (See Chapter 8 for discussion of these exercises.)

For many of his students, Pressler requires that they practice exercises exclusively for two to three months before beginning to play repertoire. Usually, it is Pressler himself who has guided students through these technical drills, but sometimes he has relied on graduate assistants to teach the exercises, as much for the benefit of these individuals as for the student.

PRESSLER'S DEMONSTRATIONS

One of the tremendous benefits of study with Pressler is to be able to see and hear him demonstrate his myriad sounds and precise technique. Because of his many recordings, annual Indiana University performances by the Beaux Arts Trio, and occasional solo performances, it has been relatively easy to hear Pressler on disc and on stage. With approximately fifty Beaux Arts Trio recordings available, students can hear the master's energy, sonority, and stylistic understanding through virtually the entire chamber repertoire with piano.

Even more valuable to the student is the direct reinforcement Pressler provides in lessons by modeling the depth of tone needed for melodies, suggesting fingering and redistribution of the hands, shaping the desired inflection for musical lines, demonstrating the voicing of chords, and us-ing the pedals to create a multitude of effects. "When [Pressler] demon-strated," recalled Paula Ennis, "I heard the sounds that he could make. I noticed how he did it, and it was always a different touch, dependent upon the musical context. He would caress the key to make a beautiful sound, and I heard that there was a difference. I remember in teaching Ravel's 'Ondine,' he said to me, 'Silver.' And then I did it, so the technique was created by his mention of the word. I listened to his words and his metaphors and then my fingers and hands would just go there and try to create that sound I thought he wanted. He'd say, 'Do you hear that sound? Once you know you can do it, you can do it again.' So, what I remember about the creation of sound is hearing him play in the lessons. I'd listen very carefully, and then I'd try to re-create that; but I had to find my own way of doing it."

THE RECITAL

Pressler often reminds students that lessons and master classes are ulti-mately preparing them for recitals, chamber music concerts, or concerto performances before live audiences, which, he says, "provide a stimulus, provide inspiration, provide a response. There is an enormous impor-tance to a recital. A recital is somehow an end station in which, whatever the effort to learn those works, that effort has to come to a climax. But when it really comes into focus is when I feel that that particular student, through whatever I taught him, becomes himself. He gets his own face, yes? When I hear them perform, it's very difficult for me. I can't help but participate in the performance. I perform with them. I suffer. I have caught myself as if I were performing myself. I hear certain points com-ing that present problems for them, and I feel the problem very clearly; and if I can, I psych myself up so that the message goes to them."

SARA PRESSLER

Many students have commented on the important role Sara Pressler has played in their lives over the years, describing her as a "calm force," "a most cultivated and dedicated personality in whom Mr. Pressler seems to have found the ideal partner in life, musical affairs and his professional career," "a giver of advice," "always available to us, a friend, a mother, someone to listen, a beautiful heart, someone always in Mr. Pressler's shadow, but always present and so reliable and efficient!" Her role for the last twenty-five or so years has been as a sort of studio manager, not only interviewing each student who has expressed an interest in studying with her husband, but literally "making all the decisions about who will study with him and who won't." Pressler says, "Sara decides who gets in, but I decide who stays."

One former student, Stephen Mann, comments on Pressler's trust of Sara with that decision. "She's an excellent judge of character, and she has a really good feel for what types of personalities will work well with him, people who are teachable and yet strong, independent enough to take the pressures of being in his studio but yet are moldable, that don't come in with all their musical ideas completely formed."

In her time with each student Sara asks questions about practicing and personality, a process she describes as "completely extemporized. It's a kind of free-flow of ideas, starting, interrupting, coming back. It always depends on what we have in common at the beginning of the conversation, and then it keeps on going in a natural flow." Pressler says that Sara "understands personality and can see not only how a student will work with me but also how a student will fit in with the other students in the studio."

Additionally, when Pressler occasionally invites a colleague from another university to teach his students in his absence, Sara is usually the one to set up the teaching schedule. She also manages Pressler's summer master class schedules at the university, and when the couple hosts students in their home for dinners or receptions, she makes all arrangements, including those for food preparation. Pressler says, "I have been able to do many things because of the help of my wife who would take many things off my shoulders. She helped me because she felt that would make me happy. And it did—to a great extent."

Pressler has referred to Sara as his "rock" and described how important it has been to have someone he can "always trust and rely on." Pressler recalls that once, as he was leaving for a trip, he didn't want to awaken Sara, so he packed his own suitcase. When he arrived at his destination, he discovered that he had failed to pack any pants. "So that's the last time I did that!"

Another of Pressler's former students, Alvin Chow, who teaches at Oberlin Conservatory, says, "Mrs. Pressler was always very much involved with the students. We all considered her to be almost a second mother. We'd call her, check in with her, let her know how we were doing. She was always interested in our progress. I think also a part of it was that Mr. Pressler was traveling a lot, and I still remember that Mrs. Pressler, when she met my parents, said that she wanted us to consider them as our second family. And she said, 'I will be here to take care of them. I will look after them. Should they have any problems, they should feel free to call and just talk.' And I think that she made that offer to everybody." Angela Cheng, also on the faculty at Oberlin, recalls, "You definitely felt well taken care of from every standpoint, not just musical; and if you ever needed advice about how to deal with everyday life, you just had to ask Mrs. Pressler. It was wonderful."

INDIANA UNIVERSITY SUPPORT

A leading reason that Indiana University has been able to attract distinguished performers to teach in the Jacobs School of Music is its policy of allowing faculty members to continue their performance careers as well. "You know, in a sense, it is a wonderful school to which marvelous students came to study with me. It was a very fine place to bring up children. My wife loved the university surrounding and took many classes. And I also felt that the privacy it gave me away from business and away from the hustle and bustle all around that business was refreshing and needed. Over the years we saw this little school in the Midwest transformed to one of the best music schools in the world."

Pressler himself has been an important part in building the reputation of the school, in no small part for having invited other artists to teach there. Professor Glenn Gass says Pressler has made a powerful impact on the school: "[He] is one of the true giants who makes the IU School of Music such a special place, and we all get to bask in the glow created by having such a special artist in our midst. His presence and endless dedication to IU are a real source of pride for everyone connected with the school."

At Pressler's eightieth birthday celebration, former dean Charles Webb stated, "Thank you, Menahem, for changing all of us, for helping us reinvent ourselves as musicians and artists, for inspiring us through brilliant performance and the most perceptive teaching, and for leading us truly to the 'thresholds of our own minds.' We hope to be here when you and the world celebrate one hundred!"

EIGHT

THE TECHNICAL APPROACH

Any discussion of Pressler's approach to teaching must begin with an understanding of the technical principles essential to achieving precision, freedom, control, sensitivity, colors, and intensity. In considering how to begin to communicate technical ideas to students at their first lessons, Pressler says, "You must build a relationship first. You have to build a mutual vocabulary. You see, we must learn to understand one another, so that when I say, 'relax,' they know exactly what I mean." Former student William Goldenberg recalls, "It was common knowledge that the first thing [Pressler] would do at the first lesson was greet you with a handshake and talk about the strong grasp of the fingers and hand while keeping the arm relaxed."

Next Pressler leads students to the piano, where they experience the relaxed arm while playing single notes, and over the next several weeks Pressler presents various drills and exercises that help students understand proper use of the fingers, hands, wrists, arms, and torso. This process enables students to interact with the mechanism of the instrument in a natural way, as if the keyboard were an extension of their own bodies. The goal is that students learn to play in a relaxed manner with balanced arms, strong fingers, and flexible wrists, creating beautiful, sonorous, non-percussive sounds without harshness.

STRONG HANDS AND FINGERS

Of foremost importance is a strong finger technique. Pressler says, "If I had to choose between a relaxed arm or strong fingers, I would choose strong fingers because it is the strong fingers and hand that provide the platform to support the weight of the arm; and the weight of the relaxed arm follows the movement of the fingers and hand." Pressler speaks a great deal of the relaxed arm, but it is only by maintaining the hand's arch, coupled with the strength of the fingers, that the performer can support and apply the weight of the relaxed arm. Additionally, it is the weight of the arm applied through the hand and fingers that produces a rich, singing tone. Pressler frequently shows a student the exact hand position needed for a passage and may also check each note of a passage in slow motion to ensure that neither the knuckle of the finger nor the arch of the hand is allowed to collapse.

Pressler also emphasizes the role of the mind in preparing the hands for playing. Proper preparation ensures both note accuracy and tonal control. Coaching a student preparing to play the first chords of the Beethoven Concerto No. 4 in G major, he said, "Your hands must be prepared so that you cannot miss. You are assured every note will sound and the voicing will be just as you imagine it will be."

THE RELAXED ARM

Once strong hands and fingers are achieved, the arm must be loose and free. There can be no gripping of the muscles in the arms or shoulders because tightness inhibits freedom and control. Pressler often begins the first lesson by having the pianist sit upright with proper posture and freedom of breath, his shoulders loose and resting on the torso, and his arms hanging at the sides of his body. "Do you feel how heavy your hands and arms are? This is the weight of the completely relaxed arm." Though he insists on such relaxation, he admits that "there is really no such thing as a completely relaxed arm. It's a controlled relaxation."

Next, the hand is raised to the level of the keyboard, with the fingers resting on the notes of a five-note scale. Pressler gently pulls the elbow away from the body and then releases his hand, allowing the student's arm to swing back in place. Next, the student plays a single note and the arm is checked to see that it releases immediately upon impact and that it swings back freely. If Pressler sees tension, he may poke his index finger into the student's upper arm and say, "Release." Each note of the five-note scale is played and each time the arm is checked to see that all the weight is resting on each finger in turn, with the student all the while maintaining a relaxed arm. Pressler continues: "How does it feel? It should feel good, even pleasurable." Students describe the sensation as a "floating," "balanced," or "centered" arm, where any degree of the arm's weight is available at any moment to produce the needed musical effect.

To help students experience varying degrees of arm weight, Pressler often has them play series of eight repeated chords, beginning *pianissimo* and increasing to *fortissimo,* progressively adding more and more weight to the arms. Students then are asked to describe the feeling, realizing how the elbows and upper arms become increasingly involved as more weight is applied. Then Pressler explains, "When we remove the weight from the arm, where does it go? Of course, the weight is still there, but we are experiencing the muscles working together to provide a balanced platform for the fingers to do their work. The relaxed arm allows the fingers and hands to function properly."

Pressler's purpose of this technical training is to help students to teach their minds and bodies always to be conscious of the controlled weight of the arm and to enable the entire playing mechanism, the fingers, hands, arms, and torso, to be poised, balanced, and ready to come into contact with the keys. The exercises result not in a loose, floppy arm but one that is controlled, stabilized, and balanced, an arm that knows its role in enabling the proper activity of the hand and fingers.

TECHNICAL EXERCISES

Pressler has for years supplied students with photocopied pages of exercises that promote finger independence and proper action of the wrist, all the while maintaining the relaxed arm. "How did I get the technical exercises? I got [them] like a bee goes from this flower, takes a little bit, from this a little bit, and this one. And then I made my own honey, yes? What I learned from Loyonnet was to keep the fingers strong and have the arm relaxed and free. What Vengerova showed me was the discovery of the wrist, the transfer of weight, but the exercises I took from Dohnányi and Philipp and Hanon and other technical books. How do students find out what is a relaxed arm? That's why I do the exercises." So from the various exercises in his collection, Pressler picks and chooses, selecting those that meet students' particular needs. For example:

1. Sustain the whole note by resting the weight of the relaxed arm into the key. Play the triplets evenly. Practice hands separately and transpose to all other keys.

Ex. 8.1. Five-finger Exercise

2. Keep the same pulse for each bar throughout the exercise, while maintaining a relaxed arm throughout.

Ex. 8.2. Finger Independence

3. Trill exercise: keep the same pulse for each bar throughout the exercise. Continue with other fingers. Right hand 1-2, 2-3, 3-4, 4-5; left hand 5-4, 4-3, 3-2, 2-1.

Ex. 8.3. Trill Exercise

4. Major, minor, diminished, new key: continue the pattern through all keys and also play in reverse, starting on fifth fingers.

Ex. 8.4. Major, Minor, Diminished, New Key

5. Using the major, minor, diminished pattern of Exercise #4, play thirds and broken thirds through all keys. Play in both parallel and contrary motions.

Ex. 8.5. Thirds

6. Black-key exercise: play out two octaves and back.

Ex. 8.6. Black-key Exercise

7. Fifth-third exercise: continue up the scale, using a wrist "drop" to play the fifth and an "up" wrist motion to play the third. One gesture (the circle of the wrist's down and up motion) plays all the notes under the slur.

Ex. 8.7. Fifth-third

8. Wrist rotation: practice the pattern using both sets of fingers.

Ex. 8.8. Wrist Rotation

9. Ascend chromatically through all keys, then descend.

Ex. 8.9. Finger Security

10. Feel different accents as indicated.

Ex. 8.10. Changing Accents

11. Thumb turns: play the scale using 1-2, then 1-3, 1-4, and 1-5. Play the left hand with the same combination of fingers.

Ex. 8.11. Thumb Turns

ONES, TWOS, FOURS, AND EIGHTS

Pressler uses the first of the Hanon exercises to help students discover how to apply arms, wrists, and fingers to passage work. The student begins with a lifted wrist. Then the first note is played by suddenly dropping the wrist, while observing that the arm continues to hang loosely. The student again raises the wrist and then utilizes the sudden, forceful wrist drop to play the second note. The process continues very slowly through the exercise, playing one note at a time, while full attention is given to the action of the wrist. "No, don't raise your arm. The arm hangs. It's only the wrist that moves. The arm doesn't go forward. The arm doesn't go backwards. The arm just follows the wrist."

Ex. 8.12. Ones, Twos, Fours, and Eights

As this process is mastered, the student begins to play the exercise in groups of two notes, dropping sharply into the first note with a heavy wrist and then playing the second note very quietly with a light lifting of the wrist.

When the two-note slur is mastered, the student progresses to four-note groups, dropping the wrist on the C, then playing the E-F-G with the upward motion, then dropping on the A and returning G-F-E with an upward-moving wrist. There should be no visible finger motion during this upward movement but rather a unified gesture that plays all three notes. Pressler calls this "getting three notes for free." Hanon exercises #1 through #10 are played in this manner.

As students begin to understand the principle and apply it to their individual physical approaches to the piano, they progress to playing eight-note groups in one motion, with the first note of each pattern being played by the wrist drop and the following seven notes being played by the upward-moving wrist. The tempo increases throughout this process, with the circular motion of the wrist becoming smoother and less pronounced. The position of the fingers on the keys maintains the clarity of the notes, while the fluid motion of the wrist produces the sweep of the phrase, a release from tension, a *legato* touch, and a controlled gradation of tone color.

SCALE PLAYING

Scale playing actually begins with the finger motion learned in Exercise #4 in which the notes are played with the whole finger. Pressler clarifies, "But as we become the master of the hand, we play not only with the whole finger but sometimes with a slight pulling or scratching from the tip, especially while playing *pianissimo*." This motion is used for playing both single notes and chords. The hand remains as close to the key as possible and this subtle touch gives clarity to the sound and an intimacy with the note itself. "Some people believe this slight pulling motion can create tension in the hand, but it's actually the exact opposite. This touch helps the pianist create a strong grip. How can you play strong and fast if the hand is not strong? The fingers remain strong, but the arm is loose and free."

THE SCALE CYCLE

Close contact with the keys coupled with the circular motion of the wrist become important aspects of the scale cycle. Pressler has his students play all twenty-four major and harmonic minor scales in a continuous cycle, by means of turns. For example:

Ex. 8.13. Scale Turns

Keys of scale cycle: C–a–F–d–B♭–g–E♭–c–A♭–f–D♭–b♭–G♭–e♭–(d♯)–B–g♯–E–c♯–A–f♯–D–b–G–e–C

The student plays four octaves of a C major scale, ascending and descending, then the wrist drops into the lowest note of the scale followed by the upward motion of the wrist, which plays the five-note turn and takes the student to the next scale. Pressler frequently commands, "Now, twice as fast." The faster the student plays, the lighter he must play, and there should be less motion of the wrist and fingers. Eventually, each scale is played not only in four parallel octaves but also two octaves up, two out, two in, and then two octaves down, always using the five-note turn to progress to the next scale. And then in addition to single-note scales, Pressler requires students to play the scale cycle for octaves and broken octaves, an exercise that he considers to be foundational to his technical approach. "Scale playing is like brushing your teeth," he says. "It must be done daily!" And during all the exercises, the pianist's shoulders should remain relaxed and the arm free.

Another way Pressler has students practice scales is to play one hand in a regular tempo while the other hand plays at double speed. "That's to see that your ear is keen, that you hear absolutely that it is together, that you're absolutely conscious of having a unified touch, and that you know exactly where the fingers are. If I stop you, you have the corresponding finger in each hand. Play faster, now faster, now as fast as you can. That's as fast as you can?"

The student is constantly asked to investigate, "Why is this uneven? What is happening here? Why is this finger weak?" As Paula Ennis describes, "I would test different angles of my hand or wrist. I thought that was my job. This is a wonderful quality of a teacher: that they can inspire you to figure out what it is that you need to do."

OCTAVES

The scale cycle is used for octaves as well as for single notes. Pressler stresses fast, light octaves coming from impulses of the wrist, as well as heavier octaves that come from the arm. To sustain the hand position of the octave, the student is instructed to practice octaves while keeping the second and third fingers crossed. This allows the student to focus on the center of the hand so that the octaves become a unit rather than the student thinking about the extremes of the hand. "It's here, between the second and third fingers, that is the center of your hand. When you see a great octave player—Horowitz, for instance—they always have these two fingers very close. And so, what I would like you to do in the beginning to establish the feel of that in your hand is to cross those fingers when you play your octaves so that you feel the center of your hand. And play in slow motion. We choreograph the keyboard so that, when we need to get to a black key, we come a little closer to that black key; and when we need to go away, we go by small steps away from that so there is no zigzagging in and out. You always move in the direction of the keys."

BROKEN OCTAVES

Many students have reported the tremendous benefit of practicing broken octaves through the scale cycle. Says one student, "There is a little button in your upper arm. You unlock that button and you start feeling it, and that little button will go with you, will move with you, and then you will not get tired. But you have to unlock that button for yourself. When you have done that, you will have found the answer and you will have the endurance to play all the way through the cycle."

Former student Jill Sprenger remembers practicing the broken octaves. "Rotation of the elbow as a relaxation technique was practiced in broken octaves. [Pressler] had me raise my wrist up and rock back and forth, watching to see that my fingers and my hand would hang loosely. It's almost like windshield wipers with the elbow counter-rotating to the motion of the hand. What Pressler taught as the basis for advanced technique is whole-arm octave rotation and repeated octave playing from the wrist. These were the two octave techniques that he worked us all through."

APPLICATION TO REPERTOIRE

Following this technical study, Pressler assigns transitional repertoire, such as Weber's "Perpetual Motion," Chopin's G major *Prélude*, or one of Chopin's *Nocturnes* to begin the process of applying the technical principles to actual music. In particular, the student learns to use the wrist motions, dropping on strong beats and ascending during weaker beats to achieve technical freedom, *legato* touch, and proper rhythmic structure to the phrase. Constantly, Pressler is checking to see that the arms are "released," that the shoulders are free from tension, and that the fingers are not collapsing. At first the motions and resulting attacks are exaggerated, but as the student becomes more accustomed to the sensation of effortless playing and to the rich tone produced by the relaxed arms, and as Pressler becomes satisfied that no harshness is present in the sound, both the "drop" and the "lift" become more subtle.

Students are expected to continue practicing the exercises on their own so that the motions will become assimilated into their playing. Following this initial period of technical emphasis, Pressler rarely returns to the drills but provides frequent reminders such as "lean into the bass note," "release the phrase," and "that's an 'out.'"

As will be seen from the following chapters, Pressler's comments during lessons from this point forward in a student's development are highly detailed and consist of both technical and expressive guidance. The common vocabulary and the understanding of Pressler's ideas of touch and tone have been established.

NINE

PRINCIPLES OF EXPRESSIVE
PERFORMANCE

Recurring throughout Pressler's teaching are certain principles of expression that give insight into the multitude of "colors" that permeate his performances and those of his students. These principles of expression deal with all aspects of practice and performance, including integrity to the score, emotional involvement, quality of sound, phrasing, formal structure, pedaling, rhythm, fingering, and color.

INTEGRITY TO THE SCORE

Pressler believes that the first and most important consideration when learning a musical score is to follow the composer's indications. Audiences and music critics often hail Pressler's performances for their insightful expression, but he says, "All expression is based on the score. What does the composer expect? Let us satisfy him."

Pressler believes that only through thoroughly studying the score can one know accurately how to interpret a piece of music. "Very often the mistake is made that people think that, by playing the piece, they have the emotions. But what they do is, they just read the notes and repeat them. They have neither digested them nor internalized them. Of course, we are spoiled by some of the great pianists, Horowitz, Martha Argerich, the ones that take immense freedoms. And when they do it, one excuses it, one accepts it by virtue of their enormous ability. But we, as young pianists—like me!—we look at a score as our teacher." Pressler himself practices almost exclusively with music rather than by memory because, he says, "The score is the Bible. Ninety-nine percent of your effort should be directed toward the score." As he asked one student in illustrating this point, "Can we be more religious and do what the composer asks for?"

Devotion to the score means that, in addition to note and rhythmic accuracy, all markings regarding phrasing, articulation, and dynamics are followed and the performer must have knowledge of harmonic

relationships, melodic contour, unusual or unexpected features of an individual piece, and a thorough understanding of musical style. He or she
must know all the technical difficulties, the quality of sound that is called
for, and proper pedaling for the piece. Pressler adds, "Play the piece
through your own eyes, but your eyes must be open to the composer."

Pressler wants his students to "feel free and find their own way, if they
can. The one who is creative is going to look for it, and I will encourage
that. Not only will I encourage it, but if he finds something that even I
don't like but I feel it somehow opens in him a road to finding more
which is spontaneous and original, I will encourage it. The student may
ask, 'Why can't I do it this way?' and very often I will say, 'Yes, you can.'
But between that 'Yes, you can' and the laws of musicality, of style, and of
having integrity to the wishes of the composer, you must understand that
there are parameters; there are borders that are circumcised. It's not free
all over the place. You don't do everything that comes through your
mind. There are disciplines that have to be kept."

BECOMING EMOTIONALLY INVOLVED IN THE PERFORMANCE

A pianist who relies on his own emotions in performance while disregard-
ing details of the score risks sounding mannered or sentimental. As Pressler
commented in one master class, "What's missing? To begin with, what's
missing is a feeling that Tchaikovsky is more important than you are. I can
tell you don't feel that way, because, by the freedoms that you do, you feel
you are more important than Tchaikovsky. Now that's a bad beginning."
To another student playing Mozart's Piano Concerto in C Major, K. 467, he
asked, "When you have that B♭, where does it go? Yes, to the A. The lifeline
is B♭ to A, yes? But you wander around and make it sentimental." He says,
"There are no secrets here musically. It's plain on the face of the piece."

One of the benefits of such intensive practice and score study is a
heightened awareness of the character of a piece, a realization of what the
composer is trying to say. Pressler comments, "When you practice, the
music must take on a quality. It must be clear. It must say something." He
stresses that the pianist must feel inspired to communicate to the listener
through the music and not just repeat the notes. "Slowly, that work takes
on its own face within you so that you actually are part of the face. You are
not a Xerox machine following the score and what you see is all there is. It
is very often what you don't see, what is between the lines, that's important.
It is the beauty, and it is a great source of strength to find those things that

are between the lines. They force you to think; but since music is the language of the soul and of the ear, it is not knowledge alone. It is your sensitivity and sensibility that become aware of connections inside the works that may only be there for you. And I would go even a step further: that you may only imagine. First of all, you have to be interested and you have to be interesting. You have to be the one to make [the music] interesting.

"Sometimes we play a piece, such as an *étude*, to learn some particular thing, but generally, we play pieces because they say something, not just to overcome a technical problem." One student asked, "That's what I wonder: how you manage, after so many years, to keep your pieces so fresh?" Pressler replied, "You know, when you are in love as I am with these pieces, they are always fresh. They are always young. I remember the first time I was thrilled by them, and I am thrilled today by them." To another student, he said, "What is missing in the piece is an artistic attitude. You started it like it's a daily job. You start like, 'Let's go out to lunch. Let's go and have coffee.' But if you start the piece in a beautiful *pianissimo*, it's all of a sudden a kind of world that you pull yourself into and you pull us into it. So it is a way of touching, a very special way of touching it. The first one to be inspired by it is you—when you practice it, when you play it, when you touch it."

The challenge to the player is to continue to be inspired throughout the process of learning and performing. Pressler chided one student by saying, "It's good, but it's not magic." To another, he commented, "Why is it not yet good? Because if you just play it and you go about it and say, 'It's not important. It's okay,' it's like when you drive through the country and you see a restaurant sign that says, 'Come in just for food. It's quick. It's horrible. But it's just food.' But the food that Brahms serves up is for people whose taste buds are the most developed."

Another aspect of being emotionally involved in performance is finding the balance between technical control and musical excitement. When hearing a student play the third movement of Prokofiev's Sonata No. 7, Op. 83, Pressler tells him, "It's not so exciting that I can feel your life depends on it. That's what I want. One other thing: if the choice is to take the excitement of the performance or the clean note, take the excitement. If you hit it clean, how great, yes? If it's a 50/50 percent chance, go for it. If it's less than a 50/50 percent chance, you can't go for it because then you haven't got a chance of hitting it, yes? But if it's 50/50, take that chance of missing but having the excitement, yes? That's terrible advice from a piano teacher, but it's the advice I'm giving myself when I perform. That's how I live my life in performance."

PHRASING

Pressler believes that a piece of music can only communicate its character or message to a listener if the performer projects the phrasing of the
piece. To one performer, he remarked, "For you, it is enjoyable because
you conquered it, yes? For us, it can only be enjoyable if you tell us
something."

In teaching his many guidelines for good phrasing, he stresses that a
phrase is a complete thought, corresponding to a sentence that can be con-
veyed with one breath. Frequently, Pressler says to sing or speak the phrase
or he instructs the pianist to think of the idea as if presented by a singer or
an instrumentalist. He cautions one of his students, "To my way of feeling,
you played too slowly. I couldn't identify with you. I couldn't breathe with
you. I listened, but I didn't sing it with you. A singer would already be at
the end of her breath." Pressler also frequently speaks of shaping a phrase.
"When you have a line, you have to play it so that we see the outline."

The motion of the wrist and arm play an important part in shaping a
phrase. Rather than allowing the hand to drop as in playing a single note
or chord, the wrist stays as level as possible and the arm moves laterally
to unify the smaller motions of the fingers and wrist during a phrase,
creating a feeling of movement and flow to the phrase rather than a sense
of plodding. The only overt downward motion would be to apply weight
on the climactic note or chord of the phrase, which would be followed by
a lifting motion of the hand and arm at the end of the phrase to simulate
taking a breath.

Usually the dynamic inflection of the phrase is dictated by the contour of the musical line. "Now any time in music, unless the composer
asks for something else, when he comes down, you go down. If he falls,
you fall with him, yes? How does one hold a phrase together? One must
feel that you hear where the peaks of those valleys are."

The pianist must pay careful attention to the relationships of the
notes, such as observing the decay in volume of a long note and matching
the following note's attack to this decay. Pressler comments, "Between
notes, there's always a relationship, like between people," and he offers
examples: "Hear the decay resolving to the F♯" (Brahms, Sonata in
F-sharp minor, Op. 2, mvt. 1, m. 15); "Always, after a long note, start
softly. Otherwise, you accent" (Ravel, Piano Trio, mvt. 3, *Passacaille*,
m. 1); "Lean into the D♭, then resolve to the C" (Schumann, *Carnaval*,
"Chiarina," Op. 9, no. 12, m. 9).

And he reprimands a student: "Now, if someone plays the chords like
that, I would think he is a musicologist. It has absolutely nothing to do

with the music. He's just explaining to me the harmony. It could just as well be Czerny or his friend from next door who has written a composition. The chords must relate to each other."

Regarding *sforzandi*, Pressler says, "Now when Beethoven has one *sforzando* after the other, it, of course, means *crescendo*" (Beethoven, Sonata in A-flat Major, Op. 26, mvt. 4, mm. 136–138).

Another attribute of good phrasing is a feeling of motion. Pressler describes this in Liszt's "La Campanella": "The little bells, either they come or they go, depending on how you want the piece to start. They don't just stand still. First of all, you give the bells a color and a direction. That is the introduction. Those are the bells that are going to play." Regarding a Mozart sonata, Pressler says, "My question is, 'Is it going up or down, or is it staying on the same level?' It's going up, so fine, so let's do that. It starts from wherever you left off. Standing still dynamically does not exist in Western music."

The wrist and arm play vital roles in creating this sense of momentum. The wrist is positioned in varying degrees to drop weight into tones the pianist wishes to highlight. Then an upward motion provides a sense of motion away from this moment of color. In a similar fashion, the wrist drops into chord changes, and an upward motion unifies any repeated chords rather than allowing each chord to receive an equal attack. Frequently the dropping motion of the wrist may reinforce strong beats of the meter, but care must be given not to create a drumbeat effect so that the metric feeling will not overshadow the melodic shaping of the phrase.

In shaping a particular musical phrase, especially one that begins with less volume, builds momentum and volume toward a climax, and then resolves quietly, Pressler frequently uses the terms "start," "lean" (go deeper into the keys), and "resolve" in his instruction. "Start" is found countless times in scores of former Pressler students and is used not only at the beginning of a phrase but any time a new sense of shaping is needed, for example, at the beginning of an *arpeggio* or scale passage or to express short ideas within a *cadenza* or to begin a series of octaves or repeated chords. The term also can provide a point of rest before pushing a phrase forward again.

Pressler uses the terms "lean" or "lean in with the arm and the body" to describe a warmth of sonority at the climax of the phrase rather than hitting a chord and also to stress the harmonic relationship between two notes or chords. He uses "resolve" following a point of emphasis or at the conclusion of a phrase. Pressler emphasizes the organic nature of movement in explaining phrasing: a phrase progresses in a natural flow and then smoothly subsides, as do waves, leaves falling, a ball bouncing, or an automobile coming to an easy stop. Pressler also speaks of "grabbing" a chord, meaning to take hold of a chord with a strong grasp of the fingers, a technique used for "big, juicy chords, not fast."

Pressler helps his students find variety in phrasing. "Never say the same thing twice. Play it differently the second time. When [the composer] does it twice, he *needs* to say it twice, so *you* have to *need* to say it twice. He repeats it because it says in many ways so many things. There are so many varieties in which a fine pianist can tell us the story in so many ways that we don't say, 'Oh, we have heard that already and we are hearing it again.' It is always something special.

"You have many choices. You mustn't accent the downbeat every time. The thing is, you have the choices, and *you* must be the one to choose, not me. You are technically free. You have the memory and you have the sound, so inspire yourself." And the same principle applies, he notes, to passages of sequences in which each sequence should have a different color.

Another consideration about the organic nature of phrasing is that it is always changing, spontaneous. "You see, it's not natural," he criticizes. "You don't feel it fresh. You feel it like a recording. You repeat it, but you must experience it new each time when you play it. It has become a fossilized piece for you. You have to recreate it." He tells a student, "You compartmentalized it, and then you put the box away and it lost the flavor. It was not anymore a fresh flower. It was an old flower that has wilted but reminded you of the fresh flower."

Pressler offers specific suggestions as to enlivening a phrase. "There are many ways, of course, of doing this. This is one way, and the next time you bring it in, I will probably hear another way. But what it's supposed to show you is that you don't play it from one mold. Your inner ear must tell you how to play it differently every time." He tells a student, "You must plan your biggest places. And when you take your *ritardando*, you must be sure that the rhythmic values are in relation. Not too slow. The *ritardando* must be in proportion."

One student noted that Pressler focused greatly on comparing phrases, "pointing out similarities and differences between phrases and similarities and differences between entire sections. This helped me to present the music so that the listener can hear the architecture and logic of the music." Another student remembered that Pressler "saw every score as a totality in the sense of filling in all the details, which would include all the dynamic levels, the textures, and balances, so that you don't get just a sketch of a piece, but you see the whole piece, the form, the architecture, and all the colors within a piece. It wasn't just a matter of this or that. It was a matter of seeing the whole. He was brilliant with that."

RHYTHM AND METER

Essential to proper phrase structure is the underlying stability of rhythm and meter. The meter must be clearly felt and understood before beginning to play a piece. In teaching Schubert's Sonata in A minor, D. 845 (mm. 30–46), Pressler admonishes, "You don't play the meter. Everything is heavy. It must swing on the first note. Hear the relationship of the three notes within each beat." Referring to the first movement of Tchaikovsky's Concerto in B-flat minor, Op. 23, Pressler says of the composer, "Which note is it that is most important to him? It's the downbeat, and he confirms that with the orchestra's chords."

Pressler stresses that everything must fit into the framework provided by the rhythm and meter. "Yes, we must have feelings, but we must have them in time, without distorting the meter of the piece. Debussy says 'rubato,' which means, 'You take freedom,' but within the rhythm of the measure, yes?" In a lesson in which a student was studying Brahms' Piano Trio in B Major, Op. 8, Pressler sang the melody while tapping the beat and then said, "You heard this tapping, and with all the freedom I was singing, it stays steady. The motion must be within the framework. Okay, you can go a little bit faster, but not so much so there's no connection." Regarding syncopation, which can distort tempo when not played properly, Pressler says, "Syncopation works only when related to strict time. It's a beautiful piece, but it's too slow. You have to maintain the heartbeat" (Bach/Rachmaninoff, "Preludio" from the Sonata for Violin in E major).

He often refers to the heartbeat of a phrase or of an entire movement. Speaking of the first movement of Schubert's Sonata in G major, D. 894, Pressler says, "The inner timing, the heartbeat inside of him, continues. It never stops. You have to feel something. It has to relate. I would like you to practice with a metronome, going on the eighths. If the outside [meter] is not there, you cannot put everything else in. You have to have a rhythmic body in order to have a soul." In reference to Mozart, Pressler instructs, "Keep in mind the feeling of the tempo. It is not that we play like a metronome; but even with variety, we need to be consistent. That way, the heartbeat is alive and there is something that holds it together."

Of the *Appassionata* Sonata of Beethoven, Pressler says, "The rhythm has to be in that piece, whatever the tempo is, which means you have to be the one to decide the pulse and that pulse has to pervade the piece. You have to be conscious of and aware of the inner heartbeat." Often Pressler has students play or sing the beginning of various themes within a work to sense the tempo relationships among them. Or he might have them play one hand of the music while tapping the basic beat with the other hand, play one hand while singing the notes of the other hand, or play the skeleton chords of a passage while omitting any filigree notes.

For a piece of music which has multiple tempi within one movement, such as in Rachmaninoff's *Etude* in A minor, Op. 39, no. 6, Pressler suggests, "When you look at the beginning, he has one tempo, *allegro*. He gets faster and faster until he hits the *presto,* and so we've got to get to the *presto,* yes? So you have to know, what is your *presto.*"

Pressler warns students not to play what he calls false accents, overly stressed notes that fall between the beats, often created by the groupings of notes, such as might be played in the fourth movement of Beethoven's Sonata in E-flat major, Op. 27, no. 1, or the first movement of Tchaikovsky's Concerto in B-flat minor. Pressler cautions, "No false accents. The first note of each slur cannot feel like a downbeat." For Beethoven's Sonata in A-flat major, Op. 110, Pressler advises, "Play the right hand off the left hand. Don't have false accents" (mvt. 1, m. 26). And for playing the Barber *Fuga,* he says, "If you are so keen on the downbeat as he was, you shouldn't have an accent on the G♭ " (m. 1).

QUALITY OF SOUND

An important aspect of expressive playing is the quality of sound produced by the pianist. In addition to desiring a palette of colorful sounds and sonorities, most of the time the essential goal is a beautiful, non-percussive sound. The technical regime of Pressler's studio ensures a relaxed and free approach without physical tension, but a secondary product of this regime is that the hands and arms are synchronized with the key action to produce a beautiful sound. A pianist having come through Pressler's technical approach not only can adjust to the demands of different keyboards but also adapt to the demands of various repertoire.

Pressler is clear as to the particular sound needed for each composer. He tells his students, "Every composer must be played differently. You must have a 'Mozart' attitude." Or "When [Beethoven] says *con amabilita,* he means 'with great tenderness and love' but still with arm weight. It's Beethoven, not Chopin. There's more core to the sound" (Sonata in E major, Op. 109, mvt. 1). Referring to a Brahms *Intermezzo,* Pressler says,

"It's a singing *piano*. It isn't Haydn. It sings, but you don't have to hit" (*Intermezzo* in B-flat major, Op. 76, no. 4, m. 1). "The sound for Fauré," he says, "is beautiful, is rich" (*Nocturne* No. 6). And: "We don't play Haydn as loudly as Beethoven, although in this Sonata, close. But we still don't" (Sonata in E-flat major, Hob. XVI:52, mvt. 1). "Chopin is like Mozart but freer, romantic in the attitude and in the color of the sound." One student remembers Pressler saying, "The magic of playing Debussy is the ability to play from *pianissimo* down." Alan Chow, faculty member at Northwestern University, recalls, "He wanted us to discover first of all what the composer wanted—how he indicated it in the score, how does it fit into the emotional framework, how does that fit into the structure of the piece—and then make it happen."

Pressler's goal is to get the pianist to hear the sound in his mind before playing and to prepare rather than react automatically to the score. It is by using the inner ear that the pianist can be creative with the sonority and become an artist. Pressler tells a master class student, "No, first of all, you don't hear a musical sound. You react with your muscle. The muscle is not being led by the ear. No, you see a *forte*, and you jump, yes?" Pressler reiterates the point, "Sometimes I say to my students, 'You've got too many muscle spasms.' And many, many, many, many pianists, especially of today, are doing it that way. They think, 'It's a big hall. Therefore, you beat the piano.' But when you beat the piano, the piano beats back. You bite it; it bites back. What most pianists today do, they play to play clean, to play fast, and to play loud—the three virtues. But if they're not guided by that creative spirit, their playing doesn't mean much."

Pressler asks a student, "Can you feel that note in the bass or is it just a muscle action? You have to hear the note" (Beethoven, Sonata in A-flat major, Op. 26, mvt 1, m. 111). "That's too hard. What makes it too hard is that you play a loud note that has no relationship. You have to imagine that note. Go in with feeling" (m. 118).

Realizing the importance of the inner ear in creating sounds and effects, Pressler urges, "Can you come in without hitting?" (Beethoven, Sonata in A-flat major, Op. 110, mvt. 1, m. 112). "Now Brahms always gives us this *crescendo* on a note after we've already played it. That's very difficult to do! In reality, it's impossible. But it's not impossible to feel, so when you play that, you feel it" (*Intermezzo* in A minor, Op. 76, no. 7, m. 31). And also for Brahms, "Don't hit the downbeat" (Piano Trio in B major, Op. 8, mvt. 3, m. 67).

An important concept to Pressler is that the pianist be able to play with a transparency of sound, a non-percussive approach with no sound of the fingers hitting the keys and with the sound cushioned by the wrists and arms. Former student Madeline Bruser remembers, "Pressler was going for a transparent kind of sound, tender and gentle. To me, 'no hammers' meant that my fingers were in effect playing directly on the strings [so] that, through sheer mental focus, I was in contact with the place that actually made the sound."

Speaking of how to produce a beautiful, full-bodied sonority, Pressler says, "That is not a musical sound [the *fortissimo*]. Very often we have to think, 'What is a musical sound?' You can call it whatever you want, *fortissimo*, triple *fortissimo*. Yes, [Schubert] wants big power, and he wants bigger power when he has triple *fortissimo*; but it is a sound that comes from the body." Pressler demonstrates the chord with a hit sound and then with a body sound and continues, "So that it is a sound that makes music, yes? That is a musical sound. And you feel it coming out of you, and you lean against your left foot so that you have leeway to get that sound, that the body goes in, not just that the hand goes in" (Sonata in G major, D. 894, mvt. 1, m. 65).

Similarly, Pressler says, "You must back up every melody note with arm weight" (Schumann, *Symphonic Etudes*, Op. 13, mvt. 1, m. 262). He critiques a student, "What I object to is that there is violence in your sound, and there shouldn't be. It just doesn't fit the framework of the introduction" (Chausson, Piano Trio in G minor, Op. 3, mvt. 1). He reprimands another: "That's such an ugly sound. It screams. All of a sudden, the piano yells. Be careful with the register. That should be heavenly, not so hard" (Schubert, Sonata in A minor, D. 845, mvt. 2, m. 165). He adds that the Mozart should "have a presence, not less than *mezzo forte*" (Mozart, Sonata in D major, K. 567, mvt. 1, m. 57).

Pressler asks of each student a wide variety of touches and approaches to reflect specific needs of the repertoire. In many instances he suggests a specific way of producing a special pianistic color. He often speaks of the myriad of colors that can be produced by varying either the speed of attack or the weight of the arm:

For Barber:
Just float in with the weight of the hand. (Sonata, Op. 26, mvt. 3, m. 39)

For Beethoven:
Prepare the hands. Then you must descend slowly and gently into the keys to achieve a pure sound. (Concerto No. 4 in G major, Op. 58, mvt. 1, m. 1)

For Brahms:
Use your body, not just arms, for full sound. (Trio in C major, Op. 87, mvt. 1, mm. 363–367)

For Chopin:

Leggiero means scratch the surface of the keys. ("Polonaise" from *Andante Spianato and Grande Polonaise Brilliante,* Op. 22, m. 26)

That's ugly, ugly, ugly. That's such a glorious melody. It's not hit. It's warm and rich. It goes down so it can go back up. (*Barcarolle,* Op. 60, mm. 61–62)

For Debussy:

Pull the fingers away from the keyboard for a special sound. (*Etudes,* No. 1, m. 50)

The softer you play, the more you have to enter the instrument. Think inside the piano, very close to the keys, and soft, like you are wearing silk gloves. ("Soirée dans Grenade," from *Estampes*)

For Mozart:

When Mozart repeats it, what I want is a certain quality of sound. It does not have a sensitivity that will touch us, because by now we are ready to hear that closing theme. But give us something beautiful as far as the sonority is concerned. Vary it a little more. I wouldn't want you to play it my way, but what I like is that I make you aware there are ways. (Sonata in C major for four hands, K. 545)

You don't have to do much besides play it like a plaintive aria, a beautiful aria with a lovely sonority. Play with a free arm so you can lean in with your weight. (Concerto in C major, K. 467, mvt. 2, mm. 43–44)

For Prokofiev:

A sharp fast attack will give you the percussive effect you need. (Sonata No. 9 in C major, mvt. 1, m. 1)

COLOR

Perhaps the most remarkable facet of Pressler's teaching is the amazing abundance of images he creates to inspire his students. He seems to think of limitless ideas spontaneously as he teaches, frequently speaking of the need for the pianist to color his or her playing, and students always comment on how an image gives them a new direction for their practice and performance. One recalls Pressler saying, "Harmonies are to the ear as a kaleidoscope is to the eyes." Another remembers, "Be a painter" (Ravel, *Sonatine,* mvt. 1, mm. 24–25) and "A tremendous palette of colors is needed, so the hands must be sometimes loose and light, at other times very strong and forceful. Sometimes very slow attacks, as if stroking the keys; other times, very sharp attacks" (Ravel, Piano Trio).

Pressler uses vivid pictures to describe the music. In working with a student on the third movement of Prokofiev's Sonata No. 4 in C minor, Op. 29, he says, "What is missing is that you don't have any kind of a picture in front of you when you play the piece. Just now when I looked at the score and heard you play the piece, I can imagine an acrobat coming onto the stage [mm. 1–2], and he makes a somersault [mm. 3–5]. That's what I'm missing. We have really a character study there. And when someone hears you, he doesn't have to know what you're thinking of. It doesn't matter. But he will find his own picture in your playing. But if you play like you did, there is no picture for you, there's no picture for the listener, and there's no picture for anybody."

Pressler's goal, though, is not for students to mimic his ideas: "The reason I give you all these details is so you will develop your own ideas."

Pressler's coloring of notes and phrases come largely from the dynamics of a piece, which, he says, represent emotional changes or an increase in intensity and not just differences in volume. "Why so loud?" he asks. "*Forte* is an indication of emotion" (Barber, Sonata, Op. 26, mvt. 1).

Additionally, Pressler stresses that students become sensitive to differences in the various registers of the piano:

For Beethoven:

But a different register. (Sonata in E-flat major, Op. 31, no. 3, mvt. 1, m. 238)

This is like the voices of a choir. Hear the bass voice singing? (Concerto No. 4 in G major, Op. 58, mvt. 2, m. 6)

Feel the G♭s; don't just play them. (Concerto No. 5 in E-flat major, Op. 73, *Emperor*, mvt. 1, mm. 136–138)

For Chopin:

I want you to hear every register of the piano. You don't hear that the piano is lighter and darker. (Cello Sonata in G minor, Op. 65)

For Ravel:

Contrast of registers. (*Sonatine*, mvt. 1, mm. 11–12)

For Schubert:

Now he transfers it to the lower register. (Sonata in A minor, D. 845, mvt. 2, m. 172)

For Schumann:

Hear the register change. (*Faschingsschwank aus Wien*, Op. 26, mvt. 3, m. 3)

I would like to hear the different registers. (mvt. 5, m. 1)

Pressler reminds students to think orchestrally as if playing chamber music, considering separate musical lines and how they should balance and interact with each other. The student is cautioned always to be aware of the balance between the two hands and of multiple notes played in one hand.

Frequently Pressler suggests images of specific instruments, such as bells, brass, woodwinds, strings, and percussion to aid students' understanding:

For Beethoven:

The accompaniment is clear like woodwinds. (Sonata in A-flat major, Op. 110, mvt. 1, m. 5)

It's like on an organ. You pull out the stops, and it's loud. You push in the stops, and it's soft. (mvt. 3, mm. 81–86)

For Brahms:

The left hand represents horns. (*Variations on a Theme by Handel*, Op. 24, m. 105)

Tympani detached notes in the left hand. (*Variations on a Theme by Paganini*, Op. 35, Book 1, m. 121)

Like "*La Campanella.*" It must sound different from the rest. (mm. 296–299)

The left hand is like plucked strings. The right hand is sustained woodwinds. The right hand, although it is syncopated, is played with a great deal of expression, so you have to play with more *legato* in the right hand. (*Intermezzo* in A-flat major, Op. 76, no. 3)

For Chausson:

The *piano* must have a feeling like a harp. (Piano Trio in G minor, Op. 3, mvt. 1)

For Chopin:

It's a Polish Christmas song. The top is like bells. (*Scherzo* No. 1 in B minor, Op. 20, m. 305)

Hear the bells [the As]. (*Ballade* in F minor, Op. 52, m. 134)

Here you play the chimes, the children's bells, with a bell-like sound. (*Berceuse*, Op. 57, m. 35)

For Debussy:
Always play that B♭ like a gong. (*Images,* "Reflets dans l'eau," m.59)
Trumpets, French horns, tympani with low strings, then everybody [*tutti*]. (*Suite pour le piano,* mm. 259, 262, 263, 264)

For Prokofiev:
Clear, even, like a clarinet *glissando.* (Sonata No. 4 in C minor, Op. 29, mvt. 2, m. 83)

For Rachmaninoff:
Like a cello. (*Rhapsodie on a Theme of Paganini,* Op. 43, m. 676)

For Ravel:
Low accented notes, play like a plucked harp string; everything else is triple *pianissimo.* (*Sonatine,* mvt. 2, mm. 13–15)
Orchestrate. Horns [m. 37], bassoons and clarinets [m. 38], high winds [m. 42], Strings [m. 47], full orchestra [m. 51], horns [mm. 126 and 128]. (*Miroirs,* "Noctuelles")
Brassy chords. (*Miroirs,* "Oiseaux tristes," m. 33)
Cymbals. (*Miroirs,* "Alborada del gracioso," m. 76)

For Schubert:
I need three horns. (Sonata in A minor, D. 845, mvt. 2, m. 136)
The two notes in the left hand are a *tympani.* (mvt. 4, m. 529)

For Schumann:
Rich sound, like strings. (*Carnaval,* Op. 9, "Eusebius," m. 17)

Students from private and master class students recall other specific images Pressler suggested to help them achieve color.

For Bach:
Two priests conversing as they walk together. (*Goldberg Variations,* S. 988, Variation 3)
That's new; begin it *piano.* You have to have contrast in your life. (*Partita* No. 6 in E minor, S. 830, "Courante," m. 18)

For Balakirev:
Like a stride bass in jazz. (*Islamey,* mm. 13–16)

For Barber:
Dream-like, floating. (Sonata, Op. 26, mvt. 1, m. 127)

It's like an explosion. (m. 166)

It's a waltz, a crazy waltz. (mvt. 2, m. 47)

It's like a lion roaring. (mvt. 4, *Fuga*, m. 96)

For Beethoven:

Mysterioso. (*32 Variations in C minor,* WoO 80, m. 185)

Troubled. (Sonata in C major, Op. 2, no. 3, mvt. 1, m. 27)

The two trills are like butterflies. (m. 78)

Don't fall into the house. (Sonata in D major, Op. 10, no. 3, mvt. 2, m. 44)

A different mood, friendly, warm, gentle, *dolce.* (Sonata for Violin and Piano in G major, Op. 30, no. 3, mvt. 1, m. 8)

Not an echo, just a change of color. You mustn't change the character. (m. 29)

It's saying, "Goodbye," until the violin comes in, and he says, "Good-BYE!" You see how he laughs? It's Beethoven's humor. (m. 69)

You have all these G♭s; and then when you have the G♮, you play it like a G♭, like nothing ever happens in your life. The sun comes through! (mvt. 2, m. 57)

The trill is elegant, effortless, with a beautiful closure. (Sonata in F major, Op. 54, mvt. 1, m. 16)

Think "determination" on the *sforzando.* (m. 30)

Syncopations, like a jazz pianist. (m. 88)

And all the world. (Concerto No. 4 in G major, Op. 58, mvt. 2, m. 47)

At first the *sforzandi* are like sparks in the context of piano. (Sonata in E major, Op. 109, mvt. 1, m. 33)

Hang in the wind. (m. 105)

And here Beethoven says, "Everything is going to be all right." More like a vibrato than a trill. (Sonata in A-flat major, Op. 110, mvt. 1, m. 4)

A bell-like sound. (m. 38)

Don't let the left hand sound "oom-pah-pah-pah" like an accordion. (m. 65)

Taste each chord. (m. 95)

This is like a benediction, and it is the open fifth in the left hand that says that to us. (m. 104)

The thing that I miss that you should have is that you feel you are imperious. The emperor of Japan comes, yes? It is grandiose, that entrance; and when you play it, you must feel grandiose. (mvt. 3, m. 73)

A kaleidoscope effect with subtle changes. (Sonata in C minor, Op. 111, mvt. 1, mm. 6–8)

Drift away. (*Bagatelles*, Op. 126, no. 3, m. 24)

For Brahms:

It's like a choral society. (Sonata No. 1 in C major, Op. 1, mvt. 4, m. 107)

Suspend the sound, very light. (Sonata No. 2 in F-sharp minor, Op. 2, mvt. 3, m. 1)

The description for this would be the forest murmur. (Concerto in D minor, Op. 15, mvt. 1, m. 142)

Like a music box. (*Variations and Fugue on a Theme of Handel*, Op. 24, m. 214)

The bells of Rome ringing. (ending)

He uses head voice. Surprise us. A violinist would do a slide there. (Intermezzo in B-flat major, Op. 76, no. 4, m. 25)

Tenderly. (Piano Trio in C major, Op. 87, mvt. 1, m. 84)

When you spread your wings [C♯-C♯-B-A], take a little time. (*Intermezzo* in A major, Op. 118, no. 2, m. 69)

And whisper. (m. 76)

For Chopin:

The first chord is a cry for help. Now the way you play, you play loud chords. But it's not an outcry, because if you were in pain and you needed help, you would cry in a different way. And that's the way I'd like you to cry, as if it hurts. . . . Out of the kitten comes the tigress. (*Scherzo* No. 1 in B minor, Op. 20)

With abandon. ("Polonaise" from *Andande Spianato and Grande Polonaise Brilliante,* Op. 22, m. 133)

Whistle. It's like fireworks' colors. (*Nocturne* in D-flat major, Op. 27, no. 2, m. 52)

Say "goodbye" on the last two chords. (mm. 76–77)

And now they close their eyes. (*Prelude* in D-flat major, Op. 28 No. 15, last chord)

Chopin puts us in an emotional descent. (*Scherzo* No. 3 in C-sharp minor, Op. 39, mm. 494–497)

Evaporate. (m. 538)

A prayer. (*Fantasie,* Op. 49, m. 199)

Those notes are like *campanellas.* (*Ballade* No. 4 in F minor, Op. 52, m. 76)

Play that like a cello. (m. 91)

I would like you to imagine that outside of this building is a harp standing out there, and the wind goes through and whistles through it. Weightless, dreamy. (m. 134)

Triumphant. (*Scherzo* No. 4 in E major, Op. 54, mm. 601–605)

There's pain in that second. It's as if he were stuck by a needle, and then the pain is gone again. (*Berceuse*, Op. 57, m. 9)

I should be standing on a balcony looking out above Venice. With you, I see only Martinsville! (*Barcarolle*, Op. 60, m. 6)

Not quiet yet. He's still shaken by the excitement he's come through. It takes him a long time to calm down. (m. 103)

Settle on the E major. (*Nocturne* in E major, Op. 62, no. 2, m. 32)

A string of pearls. (*Nocturne* in C-sharp minor, Op. post., m. 58)

For Debussy:

Buddhist bells. (*Etude* No. 1, m. 48)

Raindrops. (*Etude* No. 11, opening left-hand passage)

Rays of sunshine. (*Images*, "Reflets dans l'eau," m. 57)

Whee! Like a *gliss.* (*Suite Bergamasque*, "Minuet," m. 50)

For Fauré:

Think of a falling leaf gracefully spinning to the ground. (*Nocturne* No. 6, mm. 85–86 right hand descending sixteenth notes)

You have to hear that this is an interruption. (m. 99)

For Haydn:

He's laughing, like the *basso* in the opera. You're too serious. (Sonata in E-flat major, Hob. XIV:52, mvt. 1, m. 115)

Clear, transparent, like fresh water flowing from its source in the mountains, like the mountains where Haydn lived. (m. 116)

For Liszt:

Make it whistle. (*Mephisto Waltz*, m. 187)

Let it soar, not walk. (*Paganini Etude* No. 3, "La Campanella," m. 120)

The B^7 is a hazy atmosphere. (Piano Concerto No. 1 in E-flat major, mvt. 1, m. 28)

Have you ever been to the Grand Canyon? In the Grand Canyon, you see all of a sudden the earth is opening up. It would be worth it to go to the Grand Canyon in order to play the Liszt Sonata, so that you see the earth opening up. (Sonata in B minor, m. 2)

For Mozart:

This is like you're climbing up and you're holding on, and the hands let go and you glide down. (Concerto in C major, K. 467, mvt. 1, m. 230)

Full of mystery. (mvt. 2, m. 37)

That's daring. It's a trapeze artist. (Piano Concerto in C minor, K. 491, mvt. 1, m. 125)

What kind of mood is that? It's happier and warmer. And what I need and what he wants is a warmer sound. It's a happier sound. It sings more. (mvt. 3, m. 104)

Can those be bright and shiny? And playful like a little laughter. (m. 194)?

Outwardly, it's a dance. After all, it's in $\frac{6}{8}$. But the words that he uses are not so happy. Give it a tiny bit of sadness that the chromaticism implies. (m. 221)

Play the last two chords with the orchestra. It's a tragic ending. It's as if a curtain goes down on a tragedy, a grand tragedy. (m. 285)

Can those octaves be a little more ominous? They have a little more drama than that. (Sonata in C major for four hands, K. 545, mvt. 1)

It's magic; paint a picture with those notes. The left hand is strumming, bowing. (Sonata in D major, K. 576, mvt. 2, m. 17)

Now, sparkle. (mvt. 3, mm. 40, 42, 49)

For Prokofiev:

Stormy, passionate. (Sonata No. 3 in A minor, Op. 28, mvt. 1, m. 1)

Dark and spooky. (m. 136)

Like a puppet show. Prokofiev says, "As if trumpets." (m. 213)

A new world. The curtain comes up. It's springtime. The flowers are beautiful. It's in a new key. Now open the curtain, something romantic. With you, it's just a day of work. (Sonata No. 4 in C minor, Op. 29, mvt. 3, m. 84)

"What's *precipitato*? Precipitate, rushed, dash. Just move! (m. 153)

For Rachmaninoff:

You know what makes roses so beautiful? It's actually the greenery around it that gives us the contrast. If you have little white baby breaths mixed in there, that makes the roses that much more beautiful. It's not just, "Here, red roses!" (concerning voicing in a concerto)

It's a dream sequence. (Concerto No. 3 in D minor, Op. 30, mvt. 3, m. 57)

"*La Campanella.*" (*Rhapsodie on a Theme by Paganini*, Op. 43, m. 823)

For Ravel:

Moths in darkness. (*Miroirs*, "Noctuelles")

Sinister. (*Miroirs*, "Oiseaux tristes," m. 7)

Play the C♭ a little bitter. (*Sonatine*, mvt. 2, m. 58)

For Schubert:

Let's try with metronome [at quarter note = 69]. That's better. The other is too much of a suffering tempo or an apologetic tempo. You must take no prisoners. (*Impromptu* in E-flat major, Op. 90, no. 2)

The octaves, although they are soft and subdued, they are clear, like a waterfall. Suggest freedom, singing on the water. You probably haven't had accompaniment class yet; but right here, you must learn how to accompany. (*Impromptu* in G-flat major, Op. 90, no. 3, m. 1)

A search for consolation. (m. 140)

You should vibrate inside with this theme. (*Impromptu* in A-flat Major, Op. 90, no. 4, m. 139)

Now it's happy. It should have a lilt in that register. (Sonata in A minor, D. 784, mvt. 1, m. 141)

Can't it have a much more silky sound? Subdued, soft. (Sonata in A minor, D. 845, mvt. 1, m. 1)

It's not light enough. It doesn't drop like rain from your fingers. (mvt. 2, m. 57)

The repeated notes: it runs out, like dribbling a basketball. (m. 135)

Very glittering light. (m. 184)

I will not insist on my way of doing it, but I hear it less. You have this sphere of air around you, as if the spirit is with you. You feel something that is unreal when you start? It is the way that you hear it. (Sonata in G major, K. 894, mvt. 1, m. 3)

For Schumann:

Mystery. (*Carnaval*, "Pierrot," Op. 9, m. 8)

Warmer sound. Color. (*Carnaval*, "Chiarina," Op. 9, m. 17)

You must be in a ball in Vienna, and you must be dancing cheek to cheek with your lover. (*Carnaval*, "Valse Allemande," Op. 9, m. 17)

Frightening, intense. (*Phantasiestücke*, "Aufschwung," Op. 12, no. 2, m. 40)

There's a mysterious quality in the tone. (*Symphonic Etudes*, Op. 13, mvt. 1, m. 296)

Like lava. (*Fantasie* in C major, Op. 17, mvt. 1, m. 53)

Think Marlon Brando in *A Streetcar Named Desire.* (mm. 299–300)

Can you get juicy chords? (*Faschingsschwank aus Wien*, Op. 26, mvt. 1, m. 1)

All of a sudden, you jump into something that has clouds. And then, when you go to the next chord [m. 402], it's clear [m. 404].

No, you're awaking. Start a little under tempo. (m. 490)

That is an exalted and excited ending. It's not all of a sudden sorrowful for having been at the carnival. (mm. 547–548)

For Scriabin:

Scriabin uses all those repeated notes to accelerate as if he shakes and shivers, like he's standing on a corner with a wet shirt. (*Etude* in B-flat minor, Op. 8, no. 2, m. 34)

The left hand is a carpet of sound on top of which the right hand enters. (Sonata No. 4, Op. 30, opening)

PEDALING

Another former Pressler student, Jeffrey Cohen, now a faculty member at the Manhattan School of Music, says of his teacher's pedaling instruction, "Sometimes Pressler would say the words 'slide' or 'glide' in referring to a *legato* of the hands and pedal, and I would think, 'He's trying to do something impossible on the piano.' But Mr. Pressler, if anybody, is the greatest magician. He's the Houdini of the piano."

Pressler frequently speaks of using "half pedals" or "quarter pedals," thus only partially pressing down the pedal, in order to achieve special color effects. Paula Ennis recalls, "I think I learned most about pedaling while studying Ravel. [Pressler] talked about fractional pedaling. I watched his pedal [right] foot and it was constantly gradating, constantly going up and down. Also, his left foot on the soft pedal was doing the same to get color."

Pressler instructs that pedal can be added to a particular chord to provide sonority or lifted slowly for a gentle release. He calls the damper pedal "the breathing organism of the piano. It can melt one phrase into another. The pedal must breathe. You give breath with your pedal. It assists you in breathing." He provides specific examples of its use:

For Beethoven:

Touch pedal on the bass notes. (*32 Variations in C minor,* WoO 80, m. 9)

Take two pedal changes to accomplish the *forte piano.* (Sonata in B-flat major, Op. 22, mvt. 4, m. 40)

One pedal. It must create a dust like a cowboy riding away. (Violin Sonata in A major, Op. 47 *Kreutzer,* mvt. 3, mm. 537–539)

After releasing the low B, keep the pedal through the scale. (Sonata in E major, Op. 109, mvt. 1, m. 15)

Can the foot be clear so it doesn't swim? (Sonata in A-flat major, Op. 110, mvt. 1, m. 19)

Lift the foot a few times after that G. (m. 55)

For Brahms:

This needs lots of pedal because you'll be playing in a big hall, even if it's too much for the practice room or the studio. (Sonata No. 2 in F-sharp minor, Op. 2, mvt. 1)

Keep your hands on the keys. Release the hands with the foot. (*Capriccio* in C-sharp minor, Op. 76, no. 5, m. 117)

For Chopin:

Touch pedal on each beat. ("Polonaise" from *Andante Spianato and Grande Polonaise Brilliante*, Op. 22, mm. 255–256)

Clear the pedal with small changes. (*Fantasie*, Op. 49, m.68)

Put the pedal down before you begin, and keep the pedal down into the second measure. Sustain the C♯ octave as long as possible. (*Barcarolle*, Op. 60, m. 1)

Use a pedaling so that the full *arpeggio* is the same under one umbrella. (Cello Sonata in G minor, Op. 65)

Pedal throughout the run. (*Nocturne* in C-sharp minor, Op. post., m. 58)

For Liszt:

When he turns it around, change the pedal. (*Paganini Etude* No. 4 "La Campanella," m. 13)

For Mozart:

You hear how wet that is that you play? I like it. But why is this section so dry? It's like in the desert all of a sudden. Desert wind has taken hold, and it's only the bones we hear. (Concerto in C minor, K. 491, mvt.1, m. 511)

For Prokofiev:

Change the pedal with the melody, generally twice per measure. If you touch the pedal lightly, it will not harm the harmonies. (Sonata No. 4 in C minor, Op. 29, mvt. 2, m. 25)

For Schubert:

You can't keep the pedal down when you play descending scales. It begins to swim. (*Impromptu* in E-flat major, Op. 90, no. 3, m. 20)

Do not keep the pedal down in the scale. You can change, change, change, change, change. (Sonata in G major, D. 894, mvt. 1, m. 4)

It should bother you when it swims. In a classic scale like this, it must bother you. You must be bothered by it. (m. 18)

For Schumann:

Touch the pedal on each lower note. (*Carnaval,* "Paganini," Op. 9, m. 1)

You have to change the pedal or the notes will bite each other. The A♭ and the G bite each other, and the B♭ and the C bite each other. (*Faschingsschwank aus Wien,* Op. 26, mvt. 1, m. 87)

Raise the pedal a little bit so we can hear the line. (mvt. 5, m. 47)

Pressler instructs further that the *una corda* pedal should be used "as a spice, not a regular ingredient." He tells a student, "You must not use the *una corda* so much. It's not like a pacifier. It makes the sound too dead, whispering, like you're talking under the breath." Regarding Prokofiev's Sonata No. 4 in C minor, Op. 29, Pressler says, "Yes, use *una corda.* The intention is the darkness" (Sonata No. 4 in C minor, Op. 29, mvt. 1, m. 1). "*Due corde,*" he explains, "means one half of the soft pedal" (Brahms, *Capriccio* in B minor, Op. 76, no. 2, m. 116).

Additionally, he helps students understand use of the *sostenuto* pedal to sustain bass tones:

For Brahms:

Just keep the G ringing with the *sostenuto* pedal. (Sonata No. 1 in C major, Op. 1, mvt. 1, mm. 250–260)

Catch the bass As with the *sostenuto* pedal until the return in m. 48. (Sonata in F-sharp minor, Op. 2, mvt. 3, mm. 42–48)

Use the *sostenuto* pedal for the C♯ octave until m. 204. (mvt. 4, mm. 197–203)

For Chopin:

Sostenuto pedal for the low Cs. (*Ballade* No. 4 in F minor, Op. 52, m. 202)

For Rachmaninoff:

Sostenuto pedal. (*Rhapsodie on a Theme by Paganini,* Op. 43, m. 411)

For Ravel:

Sostenuto pedal to open up the piano sound, first for the E [m. 64], then for the G [m. 66]. (*Gaspard de la Nuit,* "Ondine")

Sostenuto pedal. (*Miroirs,* "Alborado del gracioso," m. 13)

Sostenuto pedal. (*Miroirs,* "La vallée des cloches," m. 13)

TEN

GUIDES FOR PRACTICING

Practicing could be considered the most important part of a pianist's life since it is through practice that there is the gain of the confidence and security upon which a successful performance is built. During practice time, pianists study their bodies and apply technical principles to the repertoire in order to determine how to play comfortably and with beauty. Practice is a time of contemplation and appreciation of the great works of the repertoire, a time of exploring and experimenting, trying various fingerings, phrasings, dynamics, and articulations. It is a time for drilling the technical solutions and also for listening for beautiful sounds.

"What is practicing for?" Pressler asks. "Practicing is for creating within you how you would like the music to sound. And obviously, it is very seldom that we come to the ideal, but we come close because we create something that leads us toward that ideal."

PRESSLER'S PRACTICE ROUTINE

All pianists would do well to follow Pressler's example of practice. He has always made practice time a priority and readily admits that "to this very day, I have always loved to practice." He recalls a young pianist friend in Palestine. Pressler would practice for eight or more hours and then walk over the hill to his friend's house. Many times, upon hearing his friend still practicing, Pressler would return home to practice even more. In recent years, Melinda Baird observed her teacher's practice: "He gets here at 8:00 every morning, sometimes after walking forty-five minutes from his home to school, bundled up in his Russian hat and coat. He doesn't like to be interrupted. He gets in four hours every morning while he's fresh and doesn't schedule anything during that time unless it's something exceptional. He practices until his lunch break at 12:00 and then teaches from 1:30 PM until 5:00 or 5:30."

Pressler avoids distractions during his practice time and admonishes students regarding such. "Are you not strong enough to tell your friends to leave you alone and let you practice?" "My thing is, I would like to be able to do all the things I do. I teach, I play with the Trio, I play alone, I have master classes. So, in order to do all that, you have to find the time to practice. I mean, without practicing, there is nothing." Pressler even rearranges other parts of his life, including sleep, to get the necessary practice time. "There was a time, because I had so very much to do, that I would come home after teaching and go to bed and get up at ten o'clock and started practicing, then went to bed again at 1:30 AM, get up at 6:30 or 7:00 and start practicing just to get in the required hours that the repertoire demanded."

Pressler also organizes his practice time to fit particular technical needs of the moment. Sometimes he reviews the scale cycle or Hanon or other exercises to ensure that his arms and hands are relaxed and free. He spends virtually all his practice time using his score, believing that daily immersion in the score is the most effective means of strengthening the memory. "I would say I spend ninety-five percent of my time with the score. I firmly believe in that."

The master's practice process has changed over the years, however. "In the beginning, I would practice and practice while teaching the hands to do it. I would practice the difficult places, and I had all the confidence in the world to help me do it. But you can't be a teacher and travel and give concerts and still practice that much. You have to find a way to economize in practicing. And economize means exactly what it says. It means *less*. But it also means that you use an enormous amount of concentration, much more than when you had those plenty hours. The concentration is so keen that, very often, if I practice at home and my wife comes into the room and I don't hear her, I go right through the roof. I am 100 percent focused because I have to use every second."

Pressler usually begins his repertoire practice by spending time on passages that are the most difficult, asking himself questions and looking for solutions to technical problems. "You simply start to analyze first why it is difficult. I mean, does it demand too big a hand, this one place where the hand gets stuck? Am I too far away from the place? Is the fingering wrong? Is there a better fingering? Is there a better division of hands for the fingering? I mean, all of that is possible, yes?"

But one of his great skills is finding fingerings to make the music more comfortable and controlled. "There was a time that pianists believed that, if Beethoven wrote a particular fingering, you could not refinger it. But I found that, the more I thought about it, it seemed ridiculous because one doesn't *see* how you play; one *hears* how you play. Music is the language of the ear; it's not the language of the fingerings. So

I would take a place and would practice it until I found some kind of a solution of technique. Let's say I'm practicing the *Préludes* of Chopin. I will take the difficult ones first and practice them technically, conscientious of fingerings, arm weight, wrist, knowing what to do at which place, drilling again and again, especially the places where the jump makes it difficult or the fourth finger buckles under or whatever the difficulty is, yes? That is the way I will practice, incorporating all passages into an overall feeling of control."

Then Pressler combines technical practice and expressive practice, blending the challenges of each into one approach. "You see, if your mind is just set to watch the technical, it is a different difficulty than when at the same time it has to have all the mystery, all the great fire, or kind of expectation in the playing, or the *accelerando* or *diminuendo* or special *pianissimo*. If you just practice technique, it's only one aspect; so then the technique actually becomes much more difficult, because it's that which supplies the wood for the fireplace. But you've got to start getting that fire going. I believe firmly that you have to practice, not only the fingers, but the head and the emotions, the heart."

Slower movements take up a considerable amount of his practice time to ensure that they are full of expression, giving full attention to the depth of sonority, observing the relationships of entrances and balancing the hands and voices. "It takes so much more effort to practice a slow movement and to find its meaning than to practice something fast and agile. I mean, you must practice in such a way that you can become aware of such great beauty in a piece that you have to fight back the tears."

In the same way that he instructs his students, he spends ample time drilling technical passages and often practices the left hand alone, connecting his ear to the harmonic progressions. As if carrying on a conversation with himself, he is aware of entrances, harmonic resolutions, and possibilities of coloristic orchestration. And when practicing chamber music, Pressler also concentrates on making sure he knows the other parts as well as that of the piano.

Pressler speaks of using his practice to gain the confidence to perform. "Practice is about keeping confidence or gaining confidence, or if it's a new piece, establishing that confidence, yes? I remember a time when Indiana had a marvelous swimming coach, Doc Counsilman, who had Mark Spitz and Chet Jastremski. And they would have to fight for hundredths of a second to win. And that's only through trying again and again and again. I even remember asking him about it. I saw these swimmers standing on the block, and they were shaking their hands. And I said, 'Coach, what are they doing that for?' 'Oh,' he says. 'They psych themselves up.' We also have to do that, psych ourselves up. We do that by intense practice and by building the continuity of multiple run-throughs."

Pressler advises a student regarding multiple run-throughs. "You should play the whole piece through softly, and then practice it some more, and then play it again a little louder, and then practice it some more, and then play it again with full juice, so that you get three run-throughs in your practice session. And then you take apart the place where you know you are hesitating."

To memorize a piece, Pressler analyzes each section of it. "If I'm playing a piece by memory, I will play it without the music and I will see where the questionable places are. Those places I will mark in my music, and I will relearn them, rememorize it day after day so that place will be the most secure. I have advised students to number the phrases, then learn the numbers and play up to a certain point, then learn the bridge to get over that point and then play, beginning at different points within the piece. I consciously tell myself what the differences are between sections within a piece. The body doesn't like to accept changes, so you have to drill."

Because he is always simultaneously preparing repertoire for so many different solo and chamber music concerts, Pressler instinctively balances his practice to meet the needs of immediate concerts as well as future concerts several weeks away. "No, I don't write out a chart, but I don't usually practice the music for that day. I'm usually practicing music that's coming two weeks from now."

In addition to the inspiration of the music itself, Pressler has used the challenge of recitals, concerts, and recordings to keep himself inspired over the years of his long career. When he was preparing for his Carnegie Hall solo debut recital in 1996 (even though the Beaux Arts Trio had performed there more than a dozen times), he practiced many concerts, some in large halls in major cities and others in intimate halls in small towns.

PRACTICING MEMORY

Frequently, students comment that Pressler's chief means of helping them achieve memory security is by making the music become vivid in their minds. His images, colors, and phrasings provide a sense of security and control that usually results in a confident performance. Pressler encourages his students to memorize music by sections and to play separate hands by memory and analyze the areas that make one section different from another.

One student recalls, "He would have me begin to play a composition that I was to have memorized. Suddenly, he would begin to play and I would stop. Then, when he stopped, I would have to continue from that exact place. We continued to take turns throughout the composition."

"Strengthen your memory," another students recalls Pressler saying, "so that you can even play the left hand of the piece alone. You use any kind of help you can give yourself. In Mozart or Schubert, when he uses the same theme but with a little variation, you analyze. You consciously tell yourself what those differences are. Sometimes I will play a part of the Exposition, for instance, and then immediately play what it is in the Reprise in the different key. You have to drill in many different ways."

Another student remembers Pressler saying, "Every artist has memory problems, but the artist analyzes and can quickly find where to go. You have never analyzed why that passage is different from the first" (Beethoven, Sonata in F minor, Op. 57, *Appassionata*).

And still another remembers him advising, "You've got to make the effort, but do it the hard way. Do it four bars at a time, eight bars at a time. Redo it and redo it. And you'll see that a piece like this will come much faster than a piece like Mozart, which goes this way around and that way around. And as soon as you ask yourself, 'Which way is it?' It's too late. It's usually not that difficult once you have committed it to memory, memory of the fingers, memory of the ear, and memory of the mind, by which you know, 'Now I'm going to this key and now I'm going to that key'" (Prokofiev, Sonata No. 4 in C minor, Op. 29).

"I'm surprised at the memory difficulty," Pressler told one student. "You have to play it straight through at the end of your practice or at the beginning of it so that you know exactly what is strong and where you are weak, and then you study your score and you practice that particular part, memory-wise" (Schubert, Sonata in A minor, D. 845, mvt. 4).

PRACTICING EXPRESSION

Throughout all stages of learning a piece, Pressler incorporates suggestions for expression, constantly attempting to increase students' awareness of opportunities for making their music come alive with color. His use of metaphor plays a large part in this approach, as well as his attention to dynamic levels, melodic changes, differences in registers, and the expressive relationship of various keys. Pressler constantly reminds his students to listen to the quality of sound they are producing on the instrument. "Do you like that sound?" he will ask. "You keep making it!"

Frequent are his admonitions not to hit the keys. He expects students to be aware of the decay of the piano's sound and of matching notes to this rate of decay and stresses the importance of rests and long note values, saying that they must learn for themselves why the composer needed a specific amount of time for a passage.

Related to the concept of expression is the choreography of the motion of the hands and arms. Pressler encourages many approaches to the piano, both with hands and feet. He speaks of controlling the speed of finger attack and allowing the dampers to return to a position of rest without a percussive sound because all of these affect the look and sound of the performance and influence the attitudes of both the audience and performer.

Regarding emotion, Pressler comments, "When you play music, there must be something in you that starts to awaken certain feelings. If you are aware of what they are and if you can control them, that's wonderful. But let's say you can't control them. There were certain places in music where I used to feel like the bull feels when he sees that red cape. I was rushing every which way. I couldn't help myself. Inside me would be that soaring and desire and drive. And then I heard it on tape, and I thought, 'My God, how ridiculous.' And I had to learn to control it. Controlling does not mean suppressing but refining.

ELEVEN

TECHNICAL INSTRUCTIONS

Pressler's students receive an abundance of specific technical assistance to improve their playing. One learns how to apply technical exercises to the repertoire, how to work with the mechanics of the instrument, how to improve a passage with a new fingering or redistribution of the hands, and how to use the body efficiently and effectively in order to play comfortably and with beauty. Because Pressler's performing repertoire is immense, many students report that their teacher seems always to be able to demonstrate fingerings and phrasings from virtually the entire repertoire; and in doing so, he reminds students that technique is a tool for expression.

By practicing, the student experiences progressive growth over a period of time and learns to apply technical principles to all fingers and on black or white keys. The student learns to adapt to different pianos and how to blend movements of various parts of the body, from fingers to the wrist to the arm to the torso. Pressler challenges each student to discover what might be causing a musical passage to be uneven. Is it the position of the hands? The action of the fingers? A poor choice of fingering? Improper accent? Then he instructs in methods for remediation of the problem. Former student Sherri Jones describes Pressler's fingering suggestions. "Pressler's fingerings are, first and foremost, decided upon according to the intended sound color and musical content of a particular passage and secondly on comfort and expediency."

FINGERINGS

Pressler suggests fingerings and redistribution of notes between the hands in this manner:

For Barber:
  Finger redistributions. (*Excursions,* Op. 20, mvt. 4, mm. 8–11)

[93]

Ex. 11.1. Barber, *Excursions*, Op. 20, mvt. 4, mm. 8–11

Take the D and D♭ with the right hand. (Sonata, Op. 26, mvt. 3, m. 1)
Why not take the G with the right hand? (m. 13)

For Beethoven:
Divide between the two hands. (Sonata in C major, Op. 2, no. 3, m. 9)
The left hand takes the D after the *arpeggio*. The left hand takes F♯.
The left hand takes A♯. (Sonata in D minor, Op. 31, no. 2, *Tempest*, mvt. 1, mm. 93, 95, and 97)
Why don't you take that first F in the right hand so you have the others ready in your left hand? (Sonata in E-flat major, Op. 31, no. 3, mvt. 1, m. 44)
I would advise you to take that G in the left hand. (246)
3–2 in each hand on the repeated notes. Right hand 2–1. (mvt. 2, mm. 13 and 41)
Take the downbeats with the left hand. (mvt. 3, mm. 79–81)
Right hand 2–1–2–1. (m. 125)
Hand divisions for the *cadenza*. (Sonata for Violin, Op. 47, *Kreutzer*, mvt. 1, m. 36)

Ex. 11.2. Beethoven, Sonata for Violin, Op. 47, *Kreutzer*, mvt. 1, m. 36

It must bounce. Are you doing 2-1-2-1? Try once 3-2-3-2. The last one you take the 1, yes? (mvt. 2, m. 3)

The right hand takes the chord. (Sonata in C major, Op. 53, *Waldstein*, mvt. 3, m. 441)

Fingering from Robert Casadesus for m. 13: Alternate left hand, right hand, left hand, so that the hand is free. Fingerings for mm. 13–15. (Sonata in F minor, Op. 57, *Appassionata*, mvt. 1)

Ex. 11.3. Beethoven, Sonata in F minor, Op. 57 *Appassionata*, mvt. 1, mm. 13–15

The left hand takes the E [m. 174]; the left hand takes the F [m. 247]. (Concerto No. 4 in G major, Op. 58, mvt. 1)

The left hand takes the G, first beat. (Sonata in C minor, Op. 111, mvt. 1, mm. 2 and 4)

The left hand takes F-G; the right hand takes D; the left hand takes G. (Sonata in C minor, Op. 111, mvt. 2, mm. 1 and 2)

For Brahms:

There is a climb. It's not dynamically so much as emotional. Now the thing is, we do it with an easier fingering, which means, we use the right hand instead of the left. But do it once with the left hand. See how you have to stretch? So do it with the right hand and feel that stretch. (*Capriccio* in F-sharp minor, Op. 76, no. 1, mm. 1–2)

Ex. 11.4. Brahms, *Capriccio* in F sharp minor, Op. 76, no. 1, mm. 1–2

The right hand takes E-F; the left hand takes C-E♭. (*Capriccio* in D minor, Op. 116, no. 3, m. 98)

For Chopin:

The left hand takes the C-E each time. (*Etude* in A minor, Op. 10, no. 2, mm. 2, 4, 6, and 10)

Take the A in the right hand. ("Polonaise" from *Andante Spianato and Grande Polonaise Brilliante,* Op. 22, m. 89)

Legato left hand; use the 4 throughout this section. (*Ballade* No. 4 in F minor, Op. 52, m. 37)

Come in with the fifth finger on the low C, with the side of the hand. (m. 195)

The left hand helps. (m. 223)

Ex. 11.5. Chopin, *Ballade* No. 4 in F minor, Op. 52, m. 223

Finger redistributions. (*Ballade* in A-flat major, Op. 47, mm. 237–239)

Ex. 11.6. Chopin, *Ballade* No. 3 in A-flat major, Op. 47, mm. 237–239

Take the E♯ in the right hand. (*Nocturne* in C-sharp minor, Op. post., m. 63)

For Debussy:

The left hand helps with the lower notes. (*Images,* "Reflets dans l'eau," m. 3)

Finger the descending D♯ octaves with alternating third fingers, which makes a much better and freer sound. (*Préludes,* Book 1, "Ce qu'a vu le Vent d'Ouest," m. 51)

Finger redistributions. (Book 2, "Feux d'Artifice," beat four of mm. 2–5, 2, 7, and 11–14) (see Chapter 20)

Take the A with the right hand, and so forth. (*Suite Bergamasque,* "Prélude," m. 10)

For Haydn:

If this is the first piece in a recital, then I would suggest you play those thirds with both hands. Otherwise, you will always worry; and in the worry, the rest of the Sonata will suffer. It will relieve an enormous amount of worry for you. (Sonata in E-flat major, Hob. XVI:52, mvt. 1, m. 5)

Don't end the thirds with 1-2. Use 4-2 so that the hand is open. (m. 35)

Don't use 5-5-5 in the left hand. Replace the 5 with a 4. (mm. 44–45)

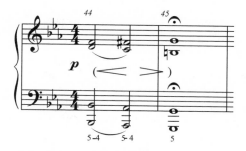

Ex. 11.7. Haydn, Sonata in E-flat major, Hob. XVI.52, mvt. 1, mm. 44–45

For Mozart:

I play both those Cs with the left hand. (Concerto in C minor, K. 491, mvt.1, m. 421)

Can I have more fingers? I would suggest you take two notes in the right hand and two in the left hand. (m. 470)

For Rachmaninoff:

Play the third with the right hand and then substitute the left hand. No pedal, so that the right-hand pattern will be clear. (*Etude* in E-flat minor, Op. 33, no. 6, m. 29)

Play the third fingers on the Bs. (*Etude* in A minor, Op. 39, no. 6, m. 97)

For Ravel:

Finger redistributions. (*Gaspard de la Nuit,* "Scarbo," mm. 102–108) (see Chapter 25)

Finger redistributions. (m. 389) (See Chapter 25)

Take the F with the left hand. (*Miroirs,* "Oiseaux Tristes," mm. 87 and 93)

For Schubert:

Let the left hand help. (*Fantasie* in C major, D. 760, *Wanderer,* mvt. 1, mm. 24–25) (see Chapter 26)

Actually, you can make it easier by playing the C♭ in the right hand, and then you can play the left-hand E♭s with 3–2. (Sonata in A minor, D. 845, mvt. 3, m. 58)

For Schumann:

Divide this up between the right hand and the left hand. (Sonata in F-sharp minor, Op. 11, mvt. 2, mm. 44–45)

Hand redistributions. (*Kreisleriana,* Op. 16, no. 3, mm. 137–140 and mm. 145–148) (See Chapter 27)

Hand redistributions. (Concerto in A minor, Op. 54, mvt. 1, mm. 32–33) (See Chapter 27)

For Weber:

Hand redistributions. ("Perpetual Motion," Sonata in C major, Op. 24, Finale, mm. 26–27) (See Chapter 29)

Hand redistributions. (mm. 30–33) (see Chapter 29)

APPLICATION OF TECHNICAL PRINCIPLES

Pressler frequently reminds students to use the concepts learned in their technical study to help them solve problems found in the repertoire. If mentioning a solution does not bring immediate results, Pressler may move a student's hand or arm to a better position or may demonstrate the passage at a second piano. If the student continues to have difficulty, Pressler will drill the student until the playing improves.

Relaxation

For students who are too tense in their approach, Pressler suggests the following:

For Beethoven:

You have to experiment with the fingering for the trill, or you hold the notes with the pedal and bring the hand with you so you're not bound. (Sonata for Violin in A major, Op. 47, *Kreutzer,* mvt. 2, m. 26)

Free the arm on the second quarter. (mvt. 3, m. 56)

Be completely relaxed. Be all ear and not all muscle. (Sonata in F minor, Op. 57, *Appassionata*, mvt. 1, m. 4)

For Brahms:

Relax the arm. Relax the body. And come in with all the weight. (Brahms, *Capriccio* in F-sharp minor, Op. 76, no. 1, m. 48)

Relax your shoulders. (m. 72)

Loose arm for the E resolution. (*Capriccio* in C-sharp minor, Op. 76, no. 5, mm. 90–91)

For Chopin:

To be relaxed is wonderful, but too much is not too good. No, the hand is not firm enough. (*Scherzo* No. 1 in B minor, Op. 20, m. 44)

For Mendelssohn:

I would like that the body is completely free. (*Rondo Capriccioso*, Op. 14, m. 27)

For Mozart:

The richness of these chords. Keep the shoulders loose. (Mozart, Piano Concerto in C minor, K. 491, mvt. 1, mm. 254–256)

Ex. 11.8. Mozart, Piano Concerto in C minor, K. 491, mvt. 1, mm. 254–256

For Schubert:

Relax your body, especially your neck. (*Impromptu* in G-flat major, Op. 90, no. 3)

To begin with, what is not good is that you don't free your hand. You don't free your arm when you play. Your wrist stays in one position. That should bring you from one to the next to the next. It's the most natural way of playing. And what is not good is that, when you play the same note, it's when you are at the low point and you come to the high point. [A♭ -A♭] and the long note is the resolution. No, you use the whole arm instead of just the wrist. Everything is free. It's loose. And the wrist gives you that note for free, but you don't get it for free. (*Impromptu* in A-flat major, Op. 90, no. 4)

For Schumann:

The arm must be relaxed to get a full sonority. You have to control the hand and the keys. Stay right in the keys. Everything is relaxed. (Sonata in F-sharp minor, Op. 11, mvt. 1, mm. 1–5)

For the right-hand octave passage, use a flat hand with a loose arm. (*Humoreske, Op. 20*)

Finger Motions

Much of Pressler's technical instruction involves close attention to proper finger motions. Following are examples of his instruction:

For Beethoven:

The right hand would go down, and the left hand closes ["out"]. But you're making a major operation [left hand]. Between fingers 2 and 1 is not a major operation, but your arm is going all over the place. The thumb pivots. The moment you play the second finger, the thumb is already there. (Sonata in A-flat major, Op. 26, mvt. 1, m. 57)

Ex. 11.9. Beethoven, Sonata in A-flat major, Op.26, mvt. 1, mm. 57

And you're right there. The arm, the ear, and your fingers are right here, and the left hand very light. (Sonata in E-flat major, Op. 27, no. 1, mvt. 1, m. 1)

You can't miss that, but your fingers are flying through the air instead of leading it from one position to the other. The fingers stay right in the key, and the wrist gets you from position to position. There is no reason to miss if you practice correctly. If you see how the hand is shaped, how the chords are shaped, and then it's right in the hand. The fingering is 4s and 2s, and the chord tells you what finger to play. (mm. 39 and 41)

Ex. 11.10. Beethoven, Sonata in E-flat major, Op. 27, no. 1, mvt. 1, mm. 39–42

For Brahms:

Use a close thumb. (*Variations on a Theme of Paganini*, Book 1, Op. 35, no. 1, m. 52)

For Liszt:

You have to anticipate when to continue, and the motion is smooth, especially when you take it from underneath. You must somehow make room. (*Paganini Etude* No. 2 in E-flat major, m. 8)

I would like for you to pull each finger out. You have to wait in a sense imperceptibly for the other hand to be there. (m. 5)

Very, very close. Not above at all. Completely within the key. (*Paganini Etude* No. 4, "La Campanella," m. 77)

For Mozart:

I like the scales very clear that you feel that the fingers are like little hammers. (Piano Concerto in C major, K. 467, mvt. 1, m. 97)

For Schubert:

And the right hand, the touch is very light, that you draw circles with your hand or with your arm. The fingers are close to each other. The hand goes up and down, over and over. But yours sounds like you are jumping over hurdles all the time. (Sonata in A minor, D. 845, mvt. 3, mm. 106–108)

Ex. 11.11. Schubert, Sonata in A minor, D. 845, mvt. 3, mm. 106–108

For Schumann:

Use the fingers to make the chords articulate. (*Carnaval,* "Marche des Davidsbündler," Op. 9, m. 248)

Close to the keys, working within the escapement, not from above. Combination of melody with repeated notes. (Sonata in F-sharp minor, Op. 11, mvt. 1, mm. 54–56)

Wrist Motions

To aid students in their wrist movements, Pressler suggests:

For Beethoven:

Loose wrist. (Sonata in B-flat major, Op. 22, m. 58)

The motion should be "down-down" [on the first of the thirds and on the downbeat]. (Sonata in A-flat major, Op. 26, mvt. 2, m. 17)

One motion [two eighths and quarter], then one motion [four eighths and quarter] and one motion [four eighths and quarter]. Goes to the end of each. The wrist goes in on each *sforzando.* Actually, you should enjoy that feeling. (mm. 26–29)

Ex. 11.12. Beethoven, Sonata in A-flat major, Op. 26, mvt. 2, mm 26–29

Now take that *forte* as a kind of energizer so that the wrist bounces. (Sonata in E-flat major, Op. 27, no. 1, mvt. 4, m. 139)

Use the wrist to run out. (Sonata in D minor, Op. 31, no. 2, *Tempest,* mvt. 3, mm. 398–399)

Rotate the wrist. (Sonata for Violin in A major Op. 47, *Kreutzer,* mvt. 3, m. 158)

You have the feeling that you do one motion and you get five more notes for free. (Sonata in F minor, Op. 57, *Appassionata,* mvt. 1, m. 143)

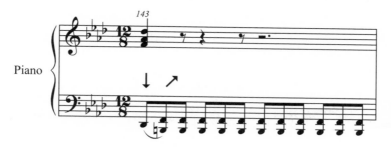

Ex. 11.13. Beethoven, Sonata in F minor, Op. 57, *Appassionata,* mvt. 1, m. 143

For Chopin:

Wrist rotation for the top note. (*Ballade* No. 4 in F minor, Op. 52, m. 191)

For Mozart:

Mozart has this in most all of his *concerti,* that the hands rotate. (Sonata in C major for four hands, K. 545)

For Schubert:

No, the wrist is up and the hand does like this, like you have a whip and that would be the end of the whip. No, you do this with the arm. The arm stays. It's done by the wrist. The arm doesn't do anything. You see how your arm does each motion? The arm has no motion, but you feel loose and hanging. That's right; keep the arm hanging and free. (*Impromptu* in C minor, Op. 90, no. 1)

Now the first thing is the position of your hands. Your hand must go up [turn toward] to the B♭. You see, when you would be in a pool and have to swim fast, you give a kick in order to push yourself into it; and this is that motion here, which pushes the hand into the direction in which you play [the "kick" away from the B♭]. (*Impromptu* in E-flat major, Op. 90, no. 2, m. 1)

Don't raise the elbow. Just raise the wrist. And make a circle. (m. 52)

Use 1-3-2 on the *mordent.* When you have the three notes, pull it with the wrist. (Sonata in A minor, D. 845, mvt. 1, m. 53)

The left hand is not good. Pull the wrist off the ornament. (m. 273)

For Schumann:

The notes are played not by the fingers, but by the wrist. (*Faschingschwank aus Wien,* Op. 26, mvt. 1, m. 87)

Use the wrist, "up" on the eighth note, "down" on the quarter. (*Carnaval*, "Pierrot," Op. 9, m. 2)

Use wrist on the eighth-note chords. (*Phantasiestücke*, "Fabel," Op. 12, no. 4, m. 15)

Arm Motions

Proper use of the arm is critical to freedom and tone production. Pressler advises:

For Beethoven:

Use the arm to help you get to the next position. As you play the G, your thumb is on its way to the D♭. (Sonata in A-flat major, Op. 26, mvt. 1, m. 37)

Now, the arm comes out on the *forte* chord [m. 15], and then you loosen all that up and come in with a relaxed arm [m. 16]. So when you play the chord, you feel the tension. And while it goes up, it releases itself. (Sonata in F minor, Op. 57, *Appassionata*, mvt. 1)

For Brahms:

Push out of the chord, and then fall into the next chord with the full arm weight. (Sonata No. 3 in F minor, Op. 5, mvt. 5, mm. 349–350)

Ex. 11.14. Brahms, Sonata No. 3 in F minor, Op. 5, mvt. 5, mm. 349–350

Stretch and open your arm. Make a curve with your arm there. (Piano Trio in B major, Op. 8, mvt. 2, m. 210)

What I would like is that you not jump so much around with your hands, but that you use the arm for each octave. For each octave, you have an arm motion, not just the wrist but with the arm, because it's heavy and it's not that fast. Use the whole body. And when you practice, go always to the next one [D-B♭, F-D, B♭-G, etc.]. Don't practice F-D, B♭-F, D-B♭, but D-B♭, F-D, etc. (Concerto in D minor, Op. 15, mvt. 1, m. 226)

Lean on the first note of the octave in both hands. (*Variations on a Theme by Paganini,* Book 1, Op. 35, no. 1, m. 77)

That F♯, sink in with your arm. (*Intermezzo,* Op. 118, no. 2, m. 23)

Lean into that chord [beat 3] so it can resolve. (m. 59)

For Chopin:

Bring the arm all the way down into the piano. That's the sound. (*Nocturne* in D-flat major, Op. 27, no. 2, m. 2)

For Liszt:

Keep the body moving toward the top of the keyboard. Stay in one direction for the octaves. (Concerto No. 1 in E-flat major, mvt. 1, mm. 5–6)

For Mozart:

Use your arm; you sound so lighthearted. (Concerto in C minor, K. 491, mvt. 3, m. 17)

For Ravel:

Grab the left hand chords. Play each one with a separate pedal. (*Sonatine,* mvt. 3, mm. 54–55)

For Schubert:

One direction through the four notes. The weight of the arm controls it. (*Impromptu* in G-flat major, Op. 90, no. 3, m. 3)

When you come to the lowest note, use the arm to push yourself out. (Sonata in A minor, D. 784, mvt. 1, m. 116)

Push yourself out of the chord with the arm. (m. 120)

On the first one, just let the arm sink in. (Sonata in G major, D. 894, mvt. 1, m. 3)

For Schumann:

From the forearm, not the shoulder. (*Symphonic Etudes,* Op. 13, mvt. 1, m. 167)

Use the arm on the left-hand scales. (m. 246)

Melody. Back up every note with arm weight. (m. 262)

Using the Body and Leaning into the Keyboard

If students have difficulty obtaining a loud *fortissimo,* Pressler suggests that they lift their bodies from the piano bench and put the upper body into the sound. For other uses of the torso, he suggests:

For Beethoven:
Use the body to go into the keyboard. (Sonata in F major, Op. 54, mvt. 1, m. 148)

Lean into the *sforzando* chords with the arm so they are not harsh. (Sonata in E major, Op. 109, mvt. 1, m. 33ff.)

For Brahms:
Lean in. Love it! (*Intermezzo,* Op. 118, no. 2, m. 6)

Full body weight for the last statement. (*Rhapsodie* in E-flat major, Op. 119, no. 4, m. 217)

For Chausson:
Use the weight that you have to get a chord that is rich. The body has to be in it [for sonority]. (Piano Trio in G minor, Op. 3, mvt. 1)

For Liszt:
But the E♭ must be juicy, rich, so the body must be ready to come into the chord. (*Paganini Etude* No. 2 in E-flat major, m. 73)

Light Arms and Hands

Many times a technical difficulty can be solved if the pianist will begin with an idea of light arms and hands. One student explains, "Pressler helped me discover how to take a miniscule amount of time and to know on which notes you can rest physically. And he said, 'Just pick one note, experiment with one that you can always know you're going to get and focus on, and then all the rest will work.' And that has always stayed with me because, if, in the middle of a jumbled passage, you focus on one of the middle notes and figure out which one works for you, then all the other ones come out right."

Examples of Pressler's suggestions follow:

For Barber:
Can you make a *diminuendo* going up? The hand must be light. (Sonata, Op. 26, mvt. 2, m. 164)

Just float in with the weight of the hand. (mvt. 3, m. 39)

For Beethoven:

The arm lighter. (Sonata in E-flat major, Op. 31, no. 3, mvt. 1, m. 184)

That's not difficult, but you tighten up so that everything becomes difficult. When you see people who water ski and the wave goes up, they use that wave. They don't need to fight in order to get up there. They use the wave, and you can use the pedal. That wave, that gives you the chord. That gives you power. (Sonata in F minor, Op. 57, *Appassionata*, mvt. 1, mm. 126–127)

Lightly. Think of keeping the weight of the arm back by the elbow. Be aware of the direction and movement of your arm. Allow the arm to move gently with the direction of the notes. (Sonata in A-flat major, Op. 110, mvt. 1, m. 12)

For Brahms:

Don't get stuck in the octave *glissando*. Don't stop the *glissando*. The thumb leads. Stay light. (*Variations on a Theme of Paganini*, Book 1, Op. 35, no. 1, m. 249)

Take time before the jumps in both hands. (m. 272)

Pull back as the octaves begin, starting lighter for relaxation as well as shaping. (m. 279)

Start the octaves much lighter and then *crescendo*. (Piano Trio in C major, Op. 87, mvt. 1, m. 155)

Right hand, free arm. (*Intermezzo,* Op. 118, no. 2, m. 45)

For Liszt:

Drop back after the accent and begin the *crescendo*. (Concerto No. 1 in E-flat major, mvt. 1, m. 5)

For Mendelssohn:

Now, for the octaves. What I would like is the arms very light, and lead with the left. Begin them very, very light. (*Rondo Capriccioso,* Op. 14, mm. 97–99)

For Schumann:

Lighter arm. (*Carnaval,* "Valse allemande," Op. 9, m. 239)

Avoidance of Stretching Hands

Pressler cautions students to avoid stretching their hands when playing by allowing the hand to move in and out, especially when moving back and forth between white and black keys. He further suggests:

For Beethoven:

I would suggest that you play 3–4. You can play anything you want, but it's always in and out and never hurried. You must practice that in such a way that it is always clear. (Sonata in E-flat major, Op. 31, no. 3, mvt. 1, m. 1)

You can take your thumb back so you don't stretch your hand so much, and don't try to hold onto all the notes. (Sonata in A-flat major, Op. 110, mvt. 1, m. 57)

For Chopin:

Use fingering that allows the closest hand position. Stretching is dangerous. (Concerto No. 2 in F minor, Op. 21)

For Schumann:

Different sound now! In and out. Your hand is not in. Your fingers should be right there. It can't be closer than a C to a B♭. In the left hand, what could be closer than an A♭ to a G? I don't understand why your hand has to go anywhere. I see a big traffic jam. In and out. To go out, you lift your wrist and relax your shoulders. (*Faschingsschwank aus Wien*, Op. 26, mvt. 1, m. 87)

VARIOUS DRILLS

Often during lessons Pressler assigns several types of technical drills a student is to continue in practice, expertly illustrating how to devise exercises out of passages. Many times he advises students to practice passages in a way opposite to that found in the score. By doing this, he says, students should become much more secure with the passages. He suggests, for example, that broken chords be practiced as blocked chords and vice versa or ascending or descending passages be practiced in reverse directions.

Pressler also instructs students to play passages with the hand opposite the one they are written for and to practice four-note chords as octaves alone and then to add the inner notes. Another practice, for the voicing of chords, is to play the melody note followed quietly by the other notes of the chord. Students also are encouraged to practice passages using various rhythmic patterns for evenness and control and to practice in various tempi, especially beginning with a slow tempo and only later progressing to a faster one. "Practice slow to fast. The head leads the hand, then it becomes hand, hand, hand."

Separate Hand Practice

Many times Pressler instructs students to practice hands separately, especially the left hand alone, to discover what is needed for each hand to feel completely comfortable and controlled. An additional benefit is that the player can focus attention on harmonic progressions. In a lesson on Ravel's *La Valse,* for example, Pressler had the student play the left hand waltz bass pattern while naming the bass notes of each measure. As former student Winston Choi reports, "He would sometimes have me play tricky passages, left hand alone, in lessons, not only for technical work but also to hear the harmonic progressions. His ears were extremely tuned into how harmonies are related, tension, and relaxation, as well as modulations. Thus, any technical work was meant to emphasize the structure of the piece by adding clarity, shape, and nuance."

Pressler also suggests:

For Balakirev:

The left hand is like a stride bass in jazz. Practice it alone and with the eyes closed. (*Islamey,* mm. 13–16)

For Beethoven:

Practice the left hand alone to hear the voicing. (*Bagatelles,* Op. 126, no. 1)

For Brahms:

Practice the left hand alone for security. (Sonata No. 2 in F-sharp minor, Op. 2, mvt. 4, mm. 71–92)

For Haydn:

Play the left hand alone for close fingers and careful articulation. (*Fantasia* in C major, Hob. XVII:4)

For Schubert:

Use the left hand to color the sound. You must practice the left hand alone. You don't possess the left hand. You haven't mastered that. (Sonata in A minor, D. 845, mvt. 3, m. 62)

Ones, Twos, and Fours

Often in lessons Pressler has students drill sixteenth-note passages using the ones, twos, and fours, learned in the Hanon exercises. Many students begin this practice in the Weber "Perpetual Motion" movement, but similar passages are the eighteenth variation of the *Rhapsodie on a Theme of Paganini* by Rachmaninoff and Chopin's *Prélude* in G major, Op. 28, no. 5.

Octaves

All Pressler students have experienced his drills for controlled octaves in which he asks the pianist to work the thumbs alone for close thumb motions, followed by practicing the fourth and fifth fingers, before putting all notes together again. He instructs:

For Brahms:

Can you play *legato* in the left-hand octaves? I would like you to play the left hand just with your thumb. Play the right hand; and, with that, play just the left-hand thumb. Now try it as an octave so that the ear hears a beautiful *legato*, so that, when the ear asks for it, you will supply it. The ear must ask for it. (Concerto in D minor, Op. 15, mvt. 1, mm. 157–158)

To make sure you get the octave, your hand must be strong between the thumb and the second finger. You must keep the octave distance between the thumb and the fifth finger, and you must keep the second and third fingers together. (m. 226)

Start the octaves much lighter, and then *crescendo*. (Piano Trio in C major, Op. 87, mvt. 1, m. 155)

For Liszt:

Drop back after the accent and begin the *crescendo*. (Concerto No. 1 in E-flat major, mvt. 1, m. 5)

For Rachmaninoff:

Drill first the thumbs, then the outer line of the octaves. (*Rhapsodie on a Theme of Paganini*, m. 816)

For Tchaikovsky:

Take the octaves apart and learn how the thumb must move. (Concerto in B-flat minor, Op. 23, mvt. 1, mm. 344–354 and mm. 583–599)

Isolating Problems

Another practice method is to divide passages into various segments to isolate a problem. Former student Jill Sprenger says, "For me, that opened a new world, because with any passage in any piece, you'd work on two or three notes and it would solve the problem of the whole phrase." As Pressler chastises a student, "It's a controlled trill, but it sounds terrible.

Always know the rhythm. 1–2 seems to be the best fingering for you. Do the trill exercise on these notes every day for ten minutes." In the same lesson Pressler had the student hold the second finger down while repeating the thumb and vice versa. (Schubert, Sonata in A minor, D. 784, mvt. 1, m. 22)

Skeleton Practice

Pressler also uses what he calls "skeleton practicing," in which the student plays blocked chords omitting any filigree, or harmonizes in one hand while playing the melody line in the other hand. Other specific skeleton practice suggestions:

For Beethoven:

Let's once leave out the spaghetti, just have the meat. No triplets, no sixteenths either. (Piano Trio in D major, Op. 70, no. 1, *Ghost*, mvt. 1)

Play just the skeleton, omitting the filigree. (*Bagatelles*, Op. 126, no. 3, mm. 36–44)

For Brahms:

Now we have more of these inner notes. Play the two melodies without the bass. (*Capriccio* in C-sharp minor, Op. 76, no. 5, mm. 41–44)

Practice blocked chords for security and for sonority, smoother, not so notey. (Trio in C major, Op. 87, mvt. 1, m. 309)

For Chopin:

Practice the left hand as written with the right hand blocked. (*Nocturne* in F major, Op. 15, no. 1, mm. 25–28)

For Haydn:

Practice just the skeleton to hear the chordal relationships. (Sonata in E-flat major, Hob. XVI:52, mvt. 1, m. 24)

Ex. 11.15. Haydn, Sonata in E-flat major, Hob. XVI.52, mvt. 1, m. 24

For Mozart:

Practice the skeleton chord progression. (Sonata in B-flat major, K. 281, mvt. 1, mm. 22–26)

Ex. 11.16. Mozart Sonata in B-flat, K. 281, mvt. 1, mm. 22–26

Without Pedal

Often a student is instructed to practice without pedal, so as to give full attention to finger action. "Both kinds of practice are important. First, you must wash yourself each day [no pedal]. Then it's also important to practice with pedal."

With Eyes Closed/Silently on the Keys

For practicing passages that have numerous leaps, Pressler advises practicing with the eyes closed to gain confidence and a special awareness at the keyboard. Similar results can be gained by practicing silently on the keys. "Practice the coordination of the hands without playing the notes," he says. "Don't rush." (Ravel, *Gaspard de la Nuit*, "Le Gibet," mm. 309–311)

With Metronome

Pressler instructs students to practice with a metronome in order to hear consistent tempi or to drill passages to a faster tempo. He tells a student practicing Schubert with a metronome, "When you come to the places that need to go faster, go a little faster, but come back to what that metronome is." (*Impromptu* in C minor, Op. 90, no. 1)

TWELVE

PRESSLER'S HUMOR

Pressler's humor and great wit has played an important role in his teaching. Though sometimes biting, his humor is a reflection of his good nature and optimistic outlook on life. Because lessons with him can be intense and students may at times feel intimidated, Pressler's humor has a way of lightening the mood and offering encouragement for students to continue study, to dig deeper within themselves, and to face further challenges of the repertoire. As Alan Chow describes, "He was very direct, and his vocabulary took a little getting used to: 'This is ugly,' 'You don't feel anything,' 'You play like a Xerox copy.' His comments were never intended to be mean or unkind. It was just his assessment, and once I got past the words themselves and understood the intent behind them, it was fine."

Other students offer examples of Pressler's wit and humor:

One of my favorite memories was of Menahem telling me that it doesn't matter how one gets the right sound, only that one gets it, then proceeding to demonstrate by playing a passage with his nose.

Returning from New Year's holiday, I hadn't touched a piano for more than two weeks. Naturally, he accepted no excuses and proceeded in listening to J. S. Bach's *Partita* in C minor, No. 2, with me as the perspiring soloist. After remarking that I had never played that well before, he asked me how long I had practiced it. I reminded him that I hadn't at all, and he replied in jest, "Well dear, stop practicing then!"

He told me at my last lesson, "You sound like the Salvation Army, 'Toot, toot, toot.'"

I remember at the end of the summer I would go off with my family for a week or so, and he was horrified with the whole notion of vacations. And I'd come back and I'd have a cold, and he'd say, "You see, you took a vacation and now you're sick." So, I couldn't win. It was impossible.

One time I was attending the Naumberg Violin Competition and I ran into him and he said, "Why aren't you practicing?"

"Your left hand sounds like . . . like . . . like an amateur bassoonist."

"Don't kid with me." This was said in disbelief when one of the students in the studio pointed out that Pressler had scheduled a studio class during the same time that Neil Armstrong was to make his historic first footsteps on the moon. Another student then suggested that perhaps we could take the class down to the faculty lounge and watch the historic event on the TV there. His response was, "There's a television in the lounge?"

He told me that the pedal is the breath of the piano. "If it's done poorly, it's as if it has asthma."

"Who was that?" This [he] said to me in the Green Room after a Beaux Arts Trio concert in Los Angeles. A friend and I came to the concert together, and before the concert started I told her some stories about Pressler. Sitting in front of us were Alan Alda and his wife. Alan turned around and said, "You know these guys? Wow, would you introduce us after the concert?" So, I swaggered backstage afterward with Alan Alda in tow. Everyone backstage was a-twitter when they saw him. I introduced him to Mr. Pressler, and when Alda left, Pressler uttered the now famous-in-L.A. remark.

A female student was waiting at the studio door for her lesson. Upon hearing the conclusion of a piece, she entered exclaiming, "That sounds great!"

"Don't tell him it sounds good! He still has very far to go!" Feeling very intimidated she replied, "Well, I was listening through a thick door."

"You see, I don't need marijuana. I don't need LSD. I have these inner wings that take me up."

I played one of the Schubert sonatas in a lesson. After the last note, Pressler sat there in silence for a moment. Then he said, "Ach, where to begin? I know I said that this finale is a garden, but with you it comes out a *rock garden!*"

"You play as if you're a bag of potatoes that has opened up and spilt all over the floor."

"Your fingers—they're like bananas!"

He shouted, "Clarinet, play in his ear. Wake him up!"

"You know, in your playing it is like you are inviting me over for dinner. And you say to me, 'Oh, you must come for dinner.' And then later on you insist, 'Oh, you must come for dinner.' And still later on, 'YOU MUST COME FOR DINNER.' So, I finally come. And what do you serve? A MCDONALD'S HAMBURGER!"

I was studying Mozart's Sonata K. 567, and he said, "You know, if you play those opening trills in that manner, I will have to pick up the phone and say, 'Hello.'"

Who could forget that his car featured a bumper sticker with a bust of Beethoven exhorting: DRIVE LESS, PRACTICE MORE!!!

One of the funniest things he would do is when he would imitate our playing by singing in an exaggerated manner. He would screech away in a hoarse voice to show us how pompous or thoughtless we were sounding.

"Well, it was good—and it was bad."

"I know I do bite—but not in public!"

I remember someone who was attending the master class saying they didn't like Schumann, and he screamed, very loudly, "It is because you have stone in your heart!"

My favorite story he ever told me was about a page turner in Buenos Aires, who, after *oohing* and *aahing* over his Trio concert that night, asked, "But what do you do for a living?"

Once, in playing the Liszt Sonata for him, I played a wrong accidental in the *cadenza*. He looked at me with those raised eyebrows and dryly asked, "And just HOW LONG does an accidental last?"

Mr. Pressler once or twice called me a Xerox machine.

"Don't play like a *hausfrau*."

After the dress rehearsal, he was very unhappy with my sound, and he said, "The people in the audience will need new batteries in their hearing aids!"

Only one time he said, "Bravo"; otherwise it was, "You play like an automaton!"

He was having me practice *glissandos* and go from C to G, C to A, C to B, and I was leaving a trail of blood, and I was waiting for some sympathy. And now it's getting kind of gruesome, and I'm thinking, "Am I going to get some credit here, or what?" And he said, "Keep going, G, A, B!" I'd take my own student to the Health Center if it happened in my studio, but he was like, "Are you going to stop in a recital? Well, why should we stop now?"

When we first played the Schumann Trio, he said, "It is decent. I can accept it. It is better than McDonalds."

"You sound too much like a teacher."

"Good is the enemy of better."

"Have you no love in your heart! It sounds so mechanical."

I was so nervous that I had to go to the bathroom right before our turn, and Mr. Pressler kept saying, "Where is the pianist? We lost the pianist."

In studio class a pianist was banging on a broken-octave passage, and Mr. Pressler said, "It sounded like a telephone."

In returning back to the A section in the Chopin *Etude,* Op. 25, no. 10, a student played rather mechanically. Mr. Pressler described it as [follows]: "After having spent the most romantic evening together, it is like saying, 'Good night!' and leaving."

I once mentioned to him that I don't taste when I cook. He said with an exaggerated expression, "That's like not listening while you are playing!"

After playing what was surely my most flawless performances of the first movement of Beethoven's Op. 110, I sat back, beaming, only to be met with, "Well, that was quite *glib!*"

"Believe me, as one who spends almost more of my life onstage than offstage, the public will always want to hear a person with a speech impediment *who has something profound to say* more than anyone who possesses a smooth, golden, radio voice!"

After an apparently lackluster first performance of the Schumann Concerto, Mr. Pressler was criticizing my performance. In desperation I said, "Well, some people liked it!" To which he retorted, "Some people like McDonald's hamburgers."

Once he told me, "Your bass notes all sounded the same, like potatoes falling out of a sack one at a time, bump, bump, bump."

A very striking example of his humor was when he described a wrong note as a horrible black blotch on a young girl's beautiful white dress.

There was a group that was playing a piano quartet in the master class, and at the end Mr. Pressler got up and said, "Do you know what your playing makes me want to do?" And he ran over to the door and pretended to vomit "Ehhh, ehhh, ehhh!" And he got everybody's attention, and he said, "You play so phenomenally well, but you phrased the recap the same way as the exposition. Why would you ruin something by just playing it the same?"

I told him I didn't have enough material for four lessons in a row, and he said, "Yes, I find everybody's reduced to whistling by the last lesson."

"I chose the Haydn E-flat Sonata for my Carnegie Hall recital. Haydn wrote it late in life, and it's full of adventure, it's full of virtuosity, it's full of beans. It doesn't show any age. I felt that it would be the right piece for me!"

After I finished playing Chopin's *Ballade* in G minor, Mr. Pressler looked at me and, pointing to the written rest in the score, said, "You are a stealer. You are stealing time from the rest!" A few days later, I met Mrs. Pressler and I mentioned to her Mr. Pressler's comment. In a playful tone, she said, "Oh, do not worry. As long as he does not call you a bandit, you are OK!"

"You overdo it. You put on so much make-up on the phrase that one doesn't recognize the face of the person!"

At the end of Brahms' F minor Sonata, Mr. Pressler commented that it was "too much, too obvious." Trying to defend my ego, I said, "I just wanted to introduce and prepare this beautiful modulation to the listener." He looked at me a little puzzled and said, "Yes, but you do not want to play like a musicologist, do you?"

"Play that a little tipsy."

When I was preparing for my doctoral exams, Pressler said, "I hope you have studied for your questions. They will be very hard. I mean, from my colleagues they will be very hard. Mine will be impossible!"

"You know there's a program in England which is called 'Desert Island Discs' where they ask you to take to the desert island the recordings that you love the most. Everybody gets to take the Bible, and some other things they like, but then when it came to the recordings, each one of us [members of the Trio] could take two records and one we could decide together. So the one we decided together was the Beethoven sonatas. But then Mr. Cohen, who was at the time in the Trio, he took Beethoven's String Quartet in E minor, Op. 59, no. 2, and Mahler's *The Song of the Earth*. Greenhouse took the Dvorak Concerto with Casals playing and the Schubert B-flat Trio with Casals/Cortot/Thibaud. And I chose the Beethoven Fourth Concerto with Schnabel, which I love very much. And then I was looking for a recording of the Ravel Trio, and I really looked everywhere, and I hesitated, and I thought it would be in terrible taste, dreadful taste, but in the end I said, "I'm going to take our performance of the Ravel Trio because it really is the best!"

"As a teacher I do not want any applause. As a performer, I cannot get enough."

Student: "You said that as we get better in some ways, we get worse in other ways, and I wondered if you would say more about that."

Pressler: "About getting worse? Or about getting better?"

"That's so weak. It sounds like you're suffering from tuberculosis!"

"Three pairs of ears are better than one, and [people say that] one person can't know all the answers—although I'm not of that opinion!"

Students also recall Pressler's humorous comments while working on specific pieces:

For Bach:
You are like a marionette that can only go 1-2-3, 1-2-3, 1-2-3.
Where does that G♯ go to? To the A. That D, where does it resolve? Yes, to the C. So why do you play like a Blind Man's Bluff? Isn't it amazing how blind you play these pieces? (*Partita* No. 5 in G major, S. 829)

For Barber:
You play like a blind man. I shouldn't say that. A blind man would be able to hear it. (Sonata, Op. 26, mvt. 4, m. 19)

For Beethoven:
You play it as if you're playing Scrabble. (Sonata in D major, Op. 10, no. 3, mvt. 2)
There's a pause that refreshes, but yours doesn't. There should be no pause before the final note. (Sonata in E-flat major, Op. 27, no.1, mvt. 4, m. 8)

You have all these G♭s. And then when you have the G♮, you play it like a G♭, like nothing ever happens in your life. The sun must come shining through. (Violin Sonata in G major, Op. 30, no. 3, mvt. 2, m. 57)

Your part is a commentary on hers. You sound like a parrot who doesn't know what is going on in the house, and he comes in and says a few nonsense words. You must find a reason for being there. You can't just come in out of the blue. (Sonata for Violin in A major, Op. 47, *Kreutzer*, mvt. 1, m. 63)

For Brahms:

The same is true of our orchestra. She very often played too loudly, but after all, she thinks she's 150 men, but she's only one woman! (Concerto in D minor, Op. 15, mvt. 1)

For Chopin:

You have to do like we all have to do. You have to count how much strength you have. We have to count how much money we have. We have to count how many friends we have. Always we have to count. (*Scherzo* No. 1 in B minor, Op. 20, mm. 570—*Coda*).

The arm must be in there at the top. No, yours is like a chicken whose throat was just cut. (*Nocturne* in D-flat major, Op. 27, no. 2)

Without waiting, just a *diminuendo*. When you wait, you go around advertising like someone with a sign, "Pleasure, enjoy!" (*Ballade* No. 4 in F minor, Op. 52, m. 42)

No, you're stopping all the time. The piece becomes like it's filled with plaster. Instead of seeing the arm, it's plaster here. It's wounded there; it's wounded all over the place. (Chopin, *Barcarolle,* Op. 60)

For Liszt:

Only a piano player could play like this (he sings with no expression), and that's not a compliment, yes? (Sonata in B minor, mm. 221–231)

Are the bass notes all the same? For me, this is tasteless. What do you achieve? The noise? If that's what you're looking for, you've achieved it. It's like an orchestra where the trombonist says to his wife, "Did you hear my solo?" "Wah, wah, wah—yes, I heard your solo!" (*Paganini Etude* No. 4, "La Campanella," mm. 131–133)

For Mendelssohn:

That's too much pedal. You practice so well and then you put on all that pedal. You have to go on a diet, a pedal diet! (*Rondo Capriccioso,* Op. 14, mm. 183–188)

Yes, pedal, but not like someone who is in a shipwreck and is holding onto a piece of wood! (m. 227)

How long have you got here? When you are at home and you have a little chapel, you go and say to Mendelssohn, "I took it. I won't repay you, but when I meet you later, I will repay you then." But when you are with me, you pay the price. (*Fantasy* in F-sharp minor, Op. 28, mvt. 4, m. 424)

Here it says *con fuoco* [m. 418], and then he says *fortissimo* [m. 426], and then here he says *fortissimo* [m. 432]. Do you have that much fire? Divide it up so that it lasts. Otherwise, the winter will be very cold! [mvt. 4].

For Mozart:

I don't know why you can't feel that, the A major. The sun must come out. The sky over the Prince Island suddenly opens, and it's no longer the Prince Island but the King Island, happiness in the most beautiful sense of the word. (Sonata in A minor, K. 310, mvt. 1)

You love every nuance and every phrase too much. It's as if you smother your children. (Sonata in C major, K. 330)

Live the pause. Let it be alive. It's the pause that refreshes. (Sonata in F major, K. 332, mvt. 3)

Why is this so dry? It's like in the desert all of a sudden. The desert wind has taken hold, and it's only the bones that we hear. (Piano Concerto in C minor, K. 491, mvt. 1, m. 511)

That B, do you only have two dresses? Then wear blue jeans so it's not always the same. Play so that one hand gives it to the other. But there's always a hole there. I think the stores are open. You can buy some new stockings, yes? (Mozart, Sonata for four-hands in C major, K. 545, mvt. 1)

For Prokofiev:

Your beginning starts off with some dust, and I always feel we should take something and clean it up. (Sonata No. 4 in C minor, Op. 29, mvt. 1, m. 1)

It was so fast and it was so loud that it couldn't grow from the B to the C to the C♯. That's what is missing. Of course, if you are twenty-one, you love to push the gas pedal down. (Sonata No. 7 in B-flat major, Op. 83, mvt. 1, m. 45)

For Ravel:

The trill is just a color. Not so self-conscious. It sounds like the left hand is the stepchild. It should be the lipstick, the glitter, the earrings that make the trills look good. But with you, it's such a dried out lipstick that, when you put it on, it has no more color. (*La Valse*, m. 557)

I think only the Salvation Army would play like that so that every chord is loud. (*La Valse*)

Wait for the climax. If the cymbal player enters at measure 33, he's fired! (*Sonatine,* mvt. 2, m. 35)

For Schubert:

I would suggest you use the thumb on the G. Your way sounds sort of like someone has been wounded in the war and has a scar, a sign of a handicap. (*Impromptu* in E-flat major, Op. 90, no. 2, m. 153)

Well, that's not bad, but it's not good. (*Impromptu* in G-flat major, Op. 90, no. 3)

The F is a note that, if you miss it, it's like seeing a person's underwear rather than his tuxedo. (*Impromptu* in A-flat minor, Op. 90, no. 4, m. 77).

I wonder, if that were orchestrated, how that person would feel, because you play with no inflection. He has to work for a living, too. As a conductor, I would throw him out! (Sonata in A minor, D. 845, mvt. 3, m. 37)

I get the feeling you are running from someone who is going to attack you. I get frightened myself, and I think I am looking on someone who is running away. It's not to be run away from. It's to be enjoyed. (Sonata in A minor, D. 845, mvt. 3, m. 241)

For Schumann:

Haven't you had a boyfriend before? *Passionato!* (*Carnaval,* Op. 9, "Chiarina")

THIRTEEN

PRESSLER AT THE MET: BEETHOVEN'S SONATA OP. 110

A Lecture Recital Presented at the
Grace Rainey Rogers Auditorium
The Metropolitan Museum of Art
New York City, New York

On one specific occasion at the Metropolitan Museum of Art, Pressler, ever the teacher, offered a lecture recital to the public, a setting in which he provided his audience with background about the piece he was to perform and the composer who wrote it. Then he worked through the piece, emphasizing areas that he especially wanted his audience to grasp. Pressler noted specific places that were of special significance and demonstrated how particular measures were to sound, explaining why they should be played and heard a certain way. In working through the piece, Pressler told the story behind or within the work, noted the mood(s) the composer was trying to convey, and then provided a brief analysis of the various musical, technical, practical, emotional, and often literary elements that worked organically to create the beauty and wonder of the music.

The following is a transcript of this rare event, which occurred on February 21, 2004.

Thank you for coming. It is something very beautiful that I would like to share with you, which is Beethoven's penultimate sonata. It's one of the most beautiful, in my opinion, and most direct works which he wrote where everything is organically derived and where, the more we know about it, the more we can really see how perfectly it was constructed. But the perfect construction is really only a very small part of what it shows us and what it means to us.

In music, loving comes first and understanding comes later. We find later why we love it. We must understand that, when he wrote it,

Beethoven had been a grand master and reinvented himself three times, had a career like everyone else at this time going up and coming down, and he had great successes and lesser successes. His works that were performed were very successful, like the *Victory Battle over Napoleon* that was really an occasional piece that was quite meaningless later. But he realized it, and so his writing became deeper and deeper into his insights. And he had the insights to go deeper for it.

Beethoven had a teacher for twelve years whose name was Christian Gottlob Neefe. This man, who was greatly influenced by Bach, had come from Chemnitz, very close to Leipzig. And that young Beethoven would play the complete *Well-Tempered Clavier*. It is very interesting that the older Beethoven got, the closer he actually came to Bach and Bach's influence over him became greater and greater. He used the fugue especially in this sonata. Not that he didn't use fugues before; but in this sonata the fugue became something that was not just a piece of work, but it became something where emotion and work became so closely intertwined that it is remarkable looking at it from every point of view, but especially listening to it. I will show you what it was that made one learn the piece. As I said before, you love it as a young man, and you begin this through your teacher. The teacher gave me the entrance to this sonata when he said, "You know, this sonata really represents Beethoven, the man, in every respect at all times in his life."

The first movement is that of an artist, an idealist. And I will show you very soon why that is true and why one can explain it that way. The second movement was that of a hedonist. Beethoven, like no other composer, could be vulgar. He is the one who could be vulgar and at the same time could rise to these unique places that on this earth we really only find in him. In the second movement he uses a very popular song at that time, which was sung in the bawdy houses of Vienna, and it's something like this [mm. 17–24]:

Ex. 13.1. mvt. 2, mm. 17–24

And it says, "Ich bin liderlich, du bist liderlich, wir sind liderliche Leute," meaning, "I'm a bum. You're a bum. We all are bums." Could have included us, too! Then comes the last movement, which consists of a slow introduction, the Recitativo, and a fugue, then another song and the fugue. In the song, the first one, one would explain that the hedonist is feeling the sorrow, the pain. Beethoven actually sets at the head of that movement. He calls it "Arioso dolente," "Song of Pain," something in which he complains about the pain that he feels or the sorrow that he feels about himself.

Now we actually also know that at that time Beethoven was nearly completely deaf. This is the most unbelievable thing that this man lived within the silences in the world and the sounds of his imagination. What imagination! Out of this comes a fugue, what I was referring to as Bach's influence and what the fugue means to him. The fugue is something that builds, that not only builds a musical emphasis, but in this case even rebuilds it. And it did. But this fugue is interrupted by the second Arioso where he, with a change in key, I will show you what it means to a listener. The distance is not important to the listener. E♭ minor or this is G minor, it is only what this key does to your insides. But he, when it comes to that second *Adagio,* he says, "*Ermattet,*" which means exhausted, and "*klagend,*" which means complaining, not complaining in that sense but feeling the difficulties. And out of this comes, in a sense, a rebirth, because all of a sudden he writes a fugue which is in a different key to begin with, just the opposite of the fugue. While the first one is this [mm. 26–30],

Ex. 13.2. mvt. 3, mm. 26–30

the second one [mm. 136–140] is just the opposite.

Ex. 13.3.   mvt. 3, mm. 136–140

And there he writes, which is so wonderful, "little by little come to life." And when he then returns to the key of the piece at the ending, it is a triumph of his spirit, and, I would say, of his life. And if there is anything we can do at that ending when it arrives, it would be to sing it like a chorale and to accompany him to the heavens where he goes.

Now let me show you what these different movements show me and how I relate to it. The first theme, which, as I said, is that of the artist, of the idealist [mm. 1–5].

Ex. 13.4.   mvt. 1, mm. 1–5

Beethoven describes the music with words that he has actually very, very seldom used, *con amabilita*, "with love," "loving." And then supposedly in his manuscript—he may have dictated it to someone else—he says, "*sanft*," meaning tenderly, so the feeling for this is with love [mm. 1–6]. And here for the first time actually, the new aria begins, and I will play that for you when I play the whole piece. But this aria, which is very beautiful, where he has it once in this key [mm. 5–8],

Ex. 13.5. mvt. 1, mm. 5–8

the second time when he comes to this aria [mm. 63–66],

Ex. 13.6. mvt. 1, mm. 63–66

you must feel what I feel when I play it: that the themes to where this aria is headed by the second time, it is so beautiful [mm. 5–8 and mm. 63–66]. I want you to feel this when you hear this. We speak in music very often about gestures, and there was no one really who was so imperious, whose gestures were so dramatic, whose feeling for a gesture was so strong than Beethoven. He starts a place like this [mm. 20–21],

Ex. 13.7. mvt. 1, mm. 20–21

and you hear that [mm. 19–23]. I don't think I know anywhere in music that's as pure as this [mm. 20–21]. And the variation of it [m. 22]

Ex. 13.8.   mvt. 1, m. 22

and out of that growing here [mm. 26–28].

Ex. 13.9.   mvt. 1, mm. 26–28

Can you imagine what it takes to do this [m. 28, beat 1],

Ex. 13.10.   mvt. 1, m. 28

to encompass this tremendous amount of tension, to build to this point [mm. 25–32], et cetera? But you feel it's been that tension how he's able to come from a point of [mm. 20–21] to the point that [mm. 27–28, right hand B♭ -G] that makes this enormous jump.

He has a moment here which is very beautiful which makes one have the feeling how he himself strives upward as does the player. He joins in the fight 50/50 with the player. It is this moment here [mm. 36–39].

Ex. 13.11. mvt. 1, mm. 36–39

Can you hear it? He doesn't permit a *crescendo*. He does a *decrescendo*. There is an intensification because it's going upward, it's striving upward. It goes here [mm. 36–38], and we reach this goal. Then he comes all the way down [mm. 39–40]. No other composer has been capable of creating between one note and the other a whole world of differences. It is something which through insight and inspiration will bring us to this point.

There's another moment which I'd like you to know of the first movement. There is, right in the beginning, the place like this [mm. 12–19].

Ex. 13.12. mvt. 1, mm. 12–19

This is a kind of bridge to that moment [m. 20], but when he comes to the Reprise, which means a repeat in the first movement, he comes to it and he shows you how organic it can be, because he comes right up to the theme. And we'll play that [mm. 56–57],

Ex. 13.13. mvt. 1, mm. 56–57

and the right hand [mm. 56–60, downbeat], and it's the same, as if it would be out of the same cloth. He builds that closeness, and there isn't a passage that isn't all part of the whole.

I'd like you to hear a point that to me is always very exciting and very interesting and very important when I play it, this place here. I have the feeling that a runner sometimes has when he runs and everything becomes very lucid and very clear and which resolves finally the pain and you are very happy within yourself, and this is the place. The theme is here [mm. 60–64].

Ex. 13.14. mvt. 1, mm. 60–64

That connection of this phrase, to me, is a miracle of writing [mm. 59–63].

Now let me come to the same point that I was just before when describing [mm. 36–38] when he does it the second time in the Reprise, where he does permit a *crescendo*. I think you may agree with me that here he comes to a point where he gives all of us a great opportunity. And that is what is great about this sonata, to strive in our insight for something that we can neither explain correctly nor touch, but we can feel. And that's his moment here [mm. 95–101].

Ex. 13.15. mvt. 1, mm. 95–101

And now he permits the *crescendo* [m. 97–100], and this time it falls slowly [mm. 101–104]

Ex. 13.16. mvt. 1, mm. 101–104

until here, where he gives the benediction [mm. 104–105, beat 1]. Can you hear what I mean [mm. 95–105, beat 1]?

Then, let me just show you how he finishes and how inventive the ending is. The triad going up [mm. 109–110], and he interrupts it [m. 111], the artist [mm. 110–116];

Ex. 13.17. mvt. 1, mm. 110–116

and you hear it. That is immense. After all, everything was [m. 111]. He opens a door [the E♭] [mm. 111–116 and mm. 1–3 of mvt. 2], and we come right into the second movement. In principle he does not say to stop. He doesn't give us an ending. The relationship, which up to this point was the idealist [mm. 115–116], to that [mm. 1–4 of mvt. 2]

Ex. 13.18. mvt. 1, mm. 115–116 and mvt. 2, mm. 1–4

is so perfect that we can't help but continue. And now we hear [m. 1–16],

Ex. 13.19. mvt. 2, mm. 1–16

and Beethoven, being stubborn as he always was, has to be his way. These accents in the left hand [mm. 11–16] are against the beat, so to speak, and so [mm. 9–15, and mm. 9–15] and then "Ich bin lüderlich, du bist lüderlich" [mm. 16–36], et cetera. So, you can hear the stubbornness. You can hear his being ordinary, being vulgar in some ways. And yet, at the same time [mm. 33–35], stopping it, then coming back [mm. 36–40].

Ex. 13.20. mvt. 2, mm. 36–40

Now this is the catch, for the Scherzo's in F minor; it's not a happy song. Yet he uses these words that are laughing at himself or at us or the world for that matter. Here he writes a trio which could be written by today's composer, could be someone like Webern [mm. 41–72].

Ex. 13.21. mvt. 2, mm. 41–72

Is this wild, going all over the place? And yet, when one analyzes it, as when we read it and learn it, it is really a counterpoint [mm. 40–72, played slowly]. Of course, at the same time, when you're young and you're learning it, you'd better learn how to say, "Peter eats the pickled peppers." The better you can say that, the better you'll play this place [mm. 40–75]. Can you say it?

Now, the finish of it. He slows us down from this very fast tempo, remember [mm. 96–98]? He ends it with the *coda* [mm. 144–158],

Ex. 13.22. mvt. 2, mm. 144–158

the climax [m. 154], and resolution [mm. 155–158]. And out of this comes Movement 3 [m. 1 to beat 1 of m. 2],

Ex. 13.23. mvt. 3, m. 1 to beat 1 of m. 2

one of the great moments in music [continuing through m. 3], and now the *Recitativo*. He gives us an enormous amount of "do this, do that," those values that are very, very difficult to realize, to be completely exact. But the more exact you are, the better you will express what he says here. And he uses something which no one had used before, which is called in German "*bebung*," which is a kind of *vibrato* [mm. 5–6, beat 1].

Now can you imagine this [m. 5 through the As]? You hear how that note vibrates in the air [continuing through m. 7, beat 1] and that he just made one stanza of that *Arioso dolente*? He starts it with a heartbeat, with an answer underneath [m. 7, beat 2 through beat 1 of m. 13]. Can you feel how he actually speaks to us, and for us? I mean, to hear this [m. 7, beat 2 through beat 1 of m. 8] and to imagine playing it, what it does to you [continuing to m. 12, beat 2]. And let me, before I come to the fugue, play for you what it comes back to when he is exhausted, when we actually hear his steps slowing [mm. 116–117].

Ex. 13.24. mvt. 3, mm. 116–117

You remember this [mm. 9–10, beat 2]? It's still strong, although he feels the pain. But here [mm. 116–120, beat 1], it's like we stop and we stay. We cannot go on [continuing until mm. 123, beat 3]. The despair is over now. But here, he was also the doctor who gave himself the right medicine to become healthy, to become strong again. And this is the first fugue [mm. 26—beat 1 of m. 29], built on pure fourths. It is the theme, but you will not recognize that you have heard it before [He plays mvt. 1, mm. 1 through beat 1 of m.5; then the top notes of m. 1, beat 1–2, then m. 2, beat 1–2, then replays mvt. 3, mm. 26–29]. So, even not knowing, we do feel the relationship, the deep relationship that comes when something is internally related like this [mm. 26–30]. Now it is a fugue in three parts, three voices. You have the first one [mm. 26–30],

Ex. 13.25. mvt. 3, mm. 26–30

the second one [mm. 30–36, beat 1], the third one [mm. 36–46, beat 1], et cetera. You hear how the fugue builds and how well we feel when we hear it, how wonderfully he expresses [mm. 26–39] something that is positive, that is well, that is healthy [mm. 39–40]. Now when he comes to the end of this fugue, building it to a climax, and it is interrupted with the *adagio* which had appeared earlier [Pressler plays mm. 106–116].

Now comes again the point where Beethoven speaks to us through ways that are as small as one can ask for. It's single notes that slowly become the chords that build in us that which we feel overwhelmed by. As much as the explanation will help, it is not that which will do it, because it was helped by an inspiration by the singular genius of Beethoven, coming here [m. 131, beats 1–3] when he finishes the *adagio* [m. 131, last note—m. 135] and the fugue, the inversion [mm. 136–149, beat 1]. And in this fugue, Beethoven uses all the means available to him. He uses the theme, he uses a diminution of the theme, he uses a *stretto*, he uses an augmentation of the theme, so that you have for instance this [mm. 152–153, left hand] [and again, left hand slowly], and on top you hear the augmentation [mm. 152–155]. You hear the *stretto* here [mm. 153–156]

Ex. 13.26. mvt. 3, mm. 153–156

[m. 160, beat 2—m.163]. And now he uses the same [mm. 167–175]. And then he arrives to that first theme, only this time really glorified to that point where I said to you before. Then it comes back, and he builds it to that triumphant moment [mm. 184–188].

Ex. 13.27. mvt. 3, mm. 184–188

And I hope you and I can follow him into the same feeling, grateful that he has given us something just close to the end of his life. I mean the Sonata was written in 1821. He died in 1827. The works with which he was concerned at that time were Sonatas Op. 109, 110, 111, the *Diabelli Variations* for the piano, the *Bagatelles,* Op. 126, the Ninth Symphony, and, of course, the great last string quartets.

I hope that, as I play it, you will be able to feel and follow with me through this piece, that you will have the same wonderful adventure that, as students of music, we each have when we play this piece.

Thank you very much.

FOURTEEN

Pressler at the TCU/Cliburn
Piano Institute

A Lecture Presented at Texas Christian University
Fort Worth, Texas
May 2005

Pressler is often asked to judge piano competitions, not the least of which is the Van Cliburn competition held in Fort Worth, Texas, every four years. He has judged the Van Cliburn several times and enjoys having the opportunity to address his audience of young players who are searching for the very nuances of performance and understanding of music that Pressler offers.

During his most recent visit to the Cliburn Piano Institute in May 2005, Pressler addressed an audience of music teachers and students, a forum in which he spoke about his training, his career, and his life-long love of music. He then took questions from the audience. The forum was recorded.

Tamás Ungar asked me to speak to you today. This is the year my Trio is going to be fifty years old, and I thought that would be a good thing to talk about because, in a way, it speaks about what my life is about, not just what the Trio's about but what my life is about and what music in my life is about. All of you who are coming here to practice, to learn, to listen, to participate are coming for a number of reasons. The very first one— and I hope the most important one—is the love for music, that which brings you here and that which actually nourishes you and that has nourished me.

The Trio started on the thirteenth of July 1955, so it has a few days still to go before fifty years. But, there was a lot before then. I was a young student who came from Israel to play in a competition, just like the one here. Only it was completely different at that time. At that time there were not that many competitions. This one which I came for was the Debussy

Competition in San Francisco, and I came not in order to win; I really came because my teacher sent me in order to find out "how good are you?" because I was in Israel. We were cut off from the rest of the world, and the only things that we knew about the rest of the world were an Artur Schnabel, a Vladimir Horowitz, a Rubinstein, a Casadesus from the recordings. And of course, none of us played that well. And anyway, whatever we played and whenever we played, we always felt it was not good enough. There must be a way to do it better.

I was sent, and I went to San Francisco, where we played in back of a screen, not like here, but in back of a screen so that no one who even knew someone in there could know who it was. We drew lots and in back of the screen you played, and there the judges had to judge. There were good judges at that time. There was Darius Milhaud, the great French composer. There was Roger Sessions, the great American composer. There was the critic [Major M. Fisher] of the San Francisco paper. When they called me on stage to tell me that I had won the first prize, it was a tremendous surprise to me, although from the second round on, I heard that I played as well as the others and that I knew the pieces as well as the others and that I was always asked for the more difficult pieces, which surprised me. And then, all of a sudden, they didn't ask me anymore and they asked two others to play. And when the two others played, I thought one girl played better; and I walked over to her and I said, "I congratulate you. You have won." And she started to cry and she said, "No, I think you deserved it more." And at that point, they called "number two," which was my number, to the stage; and I was told I had won the first prize.

Other things, of course, happened. At that time I was introduced to a great manager. I played for him [Arthur Judson] and he offered me a contract, and he gave me an audition to play for a great conductor by the name of Eugene Ormandy of the Philadelphia Orchestra, who said, "Next year you're going to make your debut with me." And I went home to my teacher and my friends and my fellow students, who said, "How was it?" "Well," I said, "I don't know really. I think it was very easy. You should all go!" It wasn't that easy, but one of my friends, one of my fellow students—he doesn't play right now anymore—by the name of Weissenberg, he did win also another prize in New York.

Anyway, I went home and I had now to clarify what is the repertoire. What is my repertoire? What am I going to play this next year? I'm making my debut with the Philadelphia Orchestra; and I had heard, while I was in America before going back, a magnificent performance of Willi Kapell playing the Khachaturian Piano Concerto. I heard Robert Casadesus. I had heard Arthur Rubinstein. I heard Horowitz. I had to find something which I could play, something which I thought I could play as well to belong into that category. Because to win a competition is one thing; you play against other young people. But to win in a hall like Carnegie Hall, you don't play against or in comparison with people like that. You play in comparison to Rubinstein, to Horowitz, to Casadesus, to Schnabel, to Myra Hess, to that which we all admire and love. Now on one hand, you feel you do not belong there. And it's true. You do not belong there. On the other hand, you would like to belong there. And on the third, "I think I can belong there."

So the consideration of which piano concerto to play, I decided on Schumann. Why did I decide on Schumann? I decided because I loved that composer. I still love him. I would say I love him even more today because I understand more. But I loved him because I felt that, with the words that Schumann spoke, I could speak those words and they would be mine, my own. I went to practice as you probably all do. I had the diet of eight hours a day. I started in the morning until noon and in the afternoon until late in the afternoon. And I had a very dear friend, a wonderful pianist, to whom luck did not play a role like in my life but who was at least my equal, if not more. I had great admiration for him. He was my age, and we always would meet at noontime after we each had four hours of practice, and we would walk on the seashore and get some respite and then go back to practice. His house was close to the seashore; and every time I got there and I heard him practice, I went right back home. I didn't knock on his door. When I saw he was still practicing, I didn't want him to get ahead of me. That's what you think, because you feel that every minute you practice, you may find the one elusive thing that you don't know.

I came back to America. I made my debut with Ormandy with the Philadelphia Orchestra, and I was fortunate to become the second in the history of the orchestra to get a four-year contract to play every year with them. I, during that year, played with Stokowski, with [Paul] Paray, with [Fabien] Sevitsky, with most of the great conductors. And at that point, of course, you think you can do nothing wrong. And that is a great mistake, because everybody does wrong things. And what you don't know when you're very young is that a career is not just ups, but it is ups and downs and sometimes never up, but up-down-up. At the same time, I started to do recordings for MGM, Metro-Goldwyn-Mayer. My very first recording was to do what Rubinstein played in the movie called *A Song of Love*, which was the life of Schumann. Rubinstein played "Dedication" of Schumann; he played *Carnaval;* he played "Mephisto." He played a number of things, but his contract as far as recording was with RCA Victor, and MGM wanted the same recording because it was their movie, so I got the contract from them. And I did the same things that Rubinstein did in the movie, and the record did very well.

And so they asked me for more records, and I started to make one record after the other until I had approximately thirty LPs from where I start from Mozart and Beethoven to Bartók, Berners, Lambert, the Piano Concerto of Shostakovich, Mozart Concerti. I did everything. And there I came to the producer, and I said, "I would like to do a trio record of Mozart." And he said, "Why not? Get yourself two people and make yourself a trio record." Now there I was a stranger in the world. I had not gone to Juilliard. I had not been in one of the schools in America where I would know people. I was just a young soloist who lived in a hotel apartment and practiced, had my concerts, would play, and would enjoy that. And I had actually a very, very nice life. But to make a trio takes two more people, so again luck played a big role.

In the hotel apartments where I lived, by the way, in the same hotel apartment Artur Schnabel lived too, and I never dared to say hello to him. Although I saw him in the elevator, I didn't even dare to say, "Good morning," because I was so in awe of him. There was the first of the second violinists of the NBC Orchestra, which was one of the great orchestras in New York, conducted by Toscanini. And he was very friendly with me; and I saw him socially and I played with him something, so I asked him, "Who do you think I should play with?" And he said, "You play with our concert master and our first cellist." I said, "But I don't know them." He said, "Come tomorrow to rehearsal with Toscanini and I will take you in and you can talk to them and I'll introduce you." So I went to the rehearsal, and he introduced me to Daniel Guilet and Frank Miller. And both of them came three days later to my hotel apartment to play with me a trio.

And there for the first time I got the knowledge of what does it do between one musician and another. Frank Miller said, "Yes, I'll play with you but not with Guilet"; and Guilet said, "I will play with you but not with Frank Miller." And so I was there in a quandary because Frank Miller was a phenomenal cellist and Guilet was a marvelous violinist. But then Guilet said to me, "You're playing this next week for the first time in your life the Schumann Quintet. I know that Quintet backwards, sideways, and forwards. Having been in a string quartet, I played it with every pianist. If you want me, I will coach you on it." I said, "That would be marvelous." So he actually stayed there the first night and we started to rehearse the Schumann Quintet. And he started to teach me about chamber music, and, I must say, I was in awe at his knowledge. I was enthusiastic about his passion, his passion for playing this music. He was so absolutely overwhelming with that passion that you could feel that was what he was living for. So therefore, my decision then was I would be playing chamber music with Guilet, not with Frank Miller.

As it turned out, we found one of the absolute great cellists that one could have asked for. That was Bernard Greenhouse, a great, great artist, a fantastic player, an interesting man who today, at the age of ninety, gives master classes all over the world. He just can't stop, and I hope he doesn't because he's great. He's a great inspiration; and to me as a colleague playing with him, it was the most wonderful thing to play. Certain pieces we would be playing ten times, twenty times, fifty times; and fifty times he would play that piece differently. Fifty times he had me on the edge of my seat, being observant to be able to play it with him so he doesn't say afterwards bad things to me. Actually, he never did. The only one who did, who was very, very, very difficult was Guilet, who in a rehearsal, not having the technique, not having the language, would be—every second word that he would use in a rehearsal would be—an insult. Now for many people that would be very hard to take. Greenhouse would be so upset that there would be a fight going on and I would be looking on, I must say, because I was young and not experienced and feeling that everything he said was actually opening my eyes to wonderful things. Why should we get upset? But he said it in such a way that it's very difficult to accept it. The only thing I have learned from him was not to do it that way, although I have had now the experience since I'm the only one playing after fifty years and keeping the Trio so that the Beaux Arts Trio is still the Beaux Arts Trio today. Actually, it is in a way better than it ever was or at least as good as its best times, because I do have great demands on my players. And this time I've got the most magnificent players to demand those things of. Our young violinist [Daniel Hope] just this last year was nominated for two Grammys; and if you get any of the magazines, the BBC Magazine has him on the front cover this month. And a great cellist is Antonio Meneses, who won the Tchaikovsky Competition when he was twenty-six. He is absolutely consummate.

Now we had only nine concerts to play the pieces, then to record, and then to say goodbye. But our very first concert, which was on the thirteenth of July in Tanglewood, was where we got a sudden invitation that the Albeneri Trio could not make the concert; and they invited our Trio to play because Charles Munch, the conductor and director, knew Guilet, and he thought, "If Guilet plays with these two people, it must be okay."

And so we got the invitation to play, and we really, I must say, worked tremendously hard on a very difficult and rich program, which we're playing by the way this year on the next day of the fiftieth year. Instead of the thirteenth, on the fourteenth of July, we'll be playing at Tanglewood that same program. That's Beethoven Op. 1, no. 3, Beethoven Op. 7, no. 1, which is the *Ghost*, and we finish with Beethoven Op. 97, the *Archduke*. Absolutely a test program, a program which one shouldn't play as a first program, but we did. We came to Tanglewood and Munch was there and greeted Guilet and greeted us and said, "I have to leave at intermission. I'm going to conduct the *Ninth* [Symphony] and I have a rehearsal in the morning. Therefore, I wish you good luck. All the best."

Casadesus was in the audience. Zino Francescatti—these names that probably mean nothing to you, but they were great, great masters—Zino Francescatti was a truly great violinist. We played the concert, and at the end of the concert Charles Munch came backstage and said, "I have not been able to leave. It was really something that I enjoyed and not heard in many, many years." And he even used the words that I like to compare it to which is the Trio of Thibaud, Casals, and Cortot. He said, "Okay, as long as I am director, you will be playing here every year." The management, which had given us nine concerts, all of a sudden decided, "We have found something in this Trio." And they gave us seventy concerts. That's an enormous amount of concerts for a group in small towns. And lucky they were small towns, because that way we truly learned to play repertoire. We truly learned to be a trio.

At the same time that this happened, I personally got a call from Indiana University, "Would you be willing to teach?" And the thing was, I had been playing under an assumed name in New York with one of the finest pianists in America, and we did so-called entertainment music under different names. We played *The Night on Bald Mountain*, we played *Swan Lake*, and all of these pieces. His name was William Masselos, a pianist for whom Copland wrote his *Fantasy*, the first one to play the Ives Sonata in America, a student of Harold Bauer who played the most beautiful *Davidsbündlertäanze*. Anyway, I had induced him to go after he was invited to Indiana, and he said, "All my stars are not aligned. I don't think I should go." I said, "Go." He said, "You wouldn't, would you?" In order to encourage him, I said, "Of course, I would." Anyway he went, and Indiana, I guess, needed a pianist, and they called me; and I said, "Of course, I can't do that. I can't come. I have too many concerts. I have seventy concerts. I can't come to Indiana." But that was a very persistent dean; and he called me three days later, and I said, "My answer is just the same. I can't accept." And that night Masselos and another pianist who was there, Sidney Foster, called and said, "But Menahem, you had told us you would accept. Come see what it is like. You can teach on Sunday. You can teach at night. You can teach early in the morning. You can do your concerts. You've got energy." When the dean called me, I accepted for one semester just to see what it's like; and this is fifty years later. I'm still there. So that was at the same time my life was going, I was going to teach and going to play.

Now the playing itself became something where, to learn a work, to play the work, to make the work part of you, so that, when you play it, people knew that this was Beaux Arts Trio. This was Greenhouse. This was Guilet. This was Pressler. And we achieved it. We did learn it. We played. We started to record. Our very first record that we made, which we made in three hours, was a record of the Dumky Trio and Mendelssohn Trio, which won the *Grand Prix du Disque* on a small label called Concert Hall. And then immediately a big label, Philips, took us. And we made one record after the other, the complete Haydn, the complete Beethoven twice, complete Schubert twice, Mendelssohn twice, Schumann Trios twice, Ravel three times, Ives, Rachmaninoff, Tchaikovsky, Shostakovich.

We did all of these things and listening to it very, very carefully because there was only one way in which a success can be guaranteed and which it can continue. It is that you stay, in a way, up on a level, which is your level, not as compared to someone else. You can say, "Oh, he is the best or that is the best." No, but a level that they recognize. And one thing which the Beaux Arts Trio had which I'm very proud of [was that] there wasn't a town that we played, not one, even the smallest one, that did not invite the Trio immediately to come back. The experience of all of us when we play is very often that people come backstage when we play and say, "Oh, we must have you back." And you never come back or you come back in a few years maybe. But with the Trio, it was always, always immediately. So that, as of today, when the Trio books the next season, there are towns where the Trio is playing, or I am playing, for the forty-fifth or the fiftieth time. That meant every year in Hamburg, every year in Paris, every year in New York. That is something very, very nice.

But believe me, all this does not come any other way but with blood, sweat, and tears. That is truly something which has a close connection to music-making. And in a way, I could say it has a close connection to learning. Learning, in principle, is not something that comes easy, because learning should not be sugar-coated. I know there is teaching that does only give compliments. I know there is teaching that makes a student feel very happy if he or she gets compliments, but they come out with actually nothing. The only way to grow is to recognize what is it that you need, what is it that you miss, and which way can you achieve it. With some people, it is one way. With other people, it is a different way. The first thing is that one must learn what one's own needs are. I know there are people who need to over-practice. There are people who, when they over-practice, become stale. So, everyone must know himself. When we speak about the great pianists, they do.

Music is an art, and it's the art of transmitting feelings. With muscles alone, music does not live. Sport is something that exists by muscles alone, and we all love sport, even the sport in music. We see our audience here. When it is faster and louder, we get up immediately and yell, but they know nothing. And then someone plays a Nocturne, and there's barely an applause, and that person played very well.

I met the wonderful magnificent artist in Holland by the name of Radu Lupu, who won here the first prize many, many years ago. Now here you have an artist who, when he won this first prize, did not accept it. He went away to study and then won the first prize in Leeds and then started to play. And to this very day this man practices, searches, compares, is not sure, and plays beautifully, magnificently, so to be one of the great Schumann and Brahms players.

And so, I do feel that I say about the Beaux Arts Trio, that I can say it today with two young people who do want and are able to make music and to accept and see the relationship that comes from the background that I come from all the way to them today. That music is a transmitting of that which we have learned throughout the time, that which we have gained the taste, although taste in music does change with the time.

Today one plays much different from the way which one played forty years ago, and certain things are much more acceptable today than they were then and vice versa. But there is one thing that has stayed always alive, and that one thing is that the person or the artist who is capable of giving someone else these strong emotions which make these great works in music stay alive until today. There is only one reason that a Beethoven sonata is still today as great as at the time that it was written and will be, because the true emotions, the greatest depths that are being given in these works, is gratefully accepted if there is an artist who transmits it. You hear lots of playing, and most of it is like a Xerox copy, and especially the fluid ones, who have no difficulty and manage less difficulties today than there ever were. But [playing] difficulties does not mean that the work has been played. To an amateur, it may mean that, but in reality, any great work, any great emotions are with effort. And if your ability allows you to use the vocabulary with ease, which means you can play with ease, then it is your duty to go as deep as you can into these works because it is only in their depths that you can find the answers and it's only in their depths that you find that which makes an artist great.

I was lucky the other day in California to look at this video *The Great Pianists* [*The Art of Piano—Great Pianists of the 20th Century*]. I don't know if you have seen that. It was wonderful to see the playing of Myra Hess, which we all here never experienced as much as they did in Europe, but to see her play and then to see the playing of Rubinstein at that time, to see the playing of a Backhaus, a great pianist, and to see the playing of a man like György Cziffra, whose fingers went so fast that really one could not believe one heard this piece that he was playing. Here was a gypsy, a musical gypsy, who had gained his fantastic fingers and could play anything. Life played a terrible role in his way and so he stopped rather early, but he was a magnificent pianist. And it was wonderful to see what could be achieved by nature, by people who come with natural ability, and what can be achieved by thought, and how much is achieved by devotion.

That is the decisive point in everybody, when you devote yourself. We have learned to accept pieces which are supposedly guarantees of success. We come to a competition and the piece that you see all along the line is the Second Sonata of Rachmaninoff. That means automatically, "Wow!" It means actually nothing unless it's played very beautifully, and only very, very few people play it very beautifully. And it is never the piece that is a success because people are always imitating. Horowitz had great success with the Barber Sonata; let me play the Barber Sonata. Horowitz had a great success with the Seventh Sonata of Prokofiev; let me play the Seventh Sonata of Prokofiev. No, Horowitz had a great success with the Seventh Sonata of Prokofiev first of all because he was Horowitz. What made him were his phenomenal ears, his enormous energy, his great technique, his understanding when he played a piece. Where is the great moment and where is the great climax? That was his success. And then you have another pianist who will take the Seventh Sonata of Prokofiev, a man like Sviatoslav Richter, and he sees it in a different light, and the sonata and he are equally great and we equally love him because, again, there is something in which we find the piece. Today we hear it quite often played, and the only thing that is similar to the normal sonata that we know is the noise level. That's even bigger than these great pianists.

So, before I finish, I just wanted to tell you that it is beautiful that you all come together in a place like here under the leadership of Tamás Ungar, who is a wonderful musician, who loves music, who loves teaching, and who loves young people and has created a keyboard institute. And I love to see people of advanced age who are teachers and music lovers and who, in a way, gain much more insight so that, when they hear a performance, the evaluation and that which they get out of it become more. I don't want to finish this little get-together with you without giving you the chance of asking me questions, if you have any.

Questions and Answers

T.U. (Tamás Ungar): I will moderate so I can see who has questions. Let me start off. I'm dying to know, because I've heard you with several members of the Beaux Arts Trio, in your heart of hearts, how much—it must have been difficult to change when Mr. Greenhouse left and you had to pick another cellist, oh, very, very—what happens to a trio, the chemistry of a trio?

M.P. (Menahem Pressler): Now from a pianist's point of view—and biased that we are, as pianists—when we talk about the Beaux Arts Trio, we think that you are the motor, you are the one, as I say, biased as we are. No, it's not bias. No, let me put it correctly. In a trio, the pianist is the most important because of the way the works are scored. He is the first among equals. In a trio, the score is sixty percent piano. We should be paid like that, too. I always ask, "I would like to be paid by the notes!" It's a very important question that you ask. A trio is, of course, the unit, a unit like you and your wife, and your wife dies. You don't want to be alone. You have to find someone, and especially as the pianist who know the works, who has seen it at their best, you can use Martin Luther King: "I have been on the mountaintop. I have seen it!" You have experienced it, so how do you look for someone?

Now, I have found the map. I have found that actually you don't look for it. It looks for you. You cannot audition for it, because the chemistry that happens during a performance cannot be experienced at any other time but in a performance. So when Guilet resigned, Cohen came in. But Greenhouse and I were both still in so it was easier. And actually, that began the golden time of the Trio. And when Greenhouse left, we brought in a new cellist [Peter Wiley] who was good, as a matter of fact. He is today the cellist of the Guarneri Quartet, very good, but it was not the right chemistry. So when Cohen couldn't continue—his health—there came in a magnificent violinist, Ida Kavafian, magnificent, but it wasn't the right chemistry.

So when it started again with Antonio Meneses and Young Uck Kim, he was wonderful, magnificent in every respect, but then he had this problem with his arm. And at that point I decided—we still had thirty concerts, fifteen in America, New York, Chicago, and Washington, and in

Europe, London and Paris—I would try to take somebody who has experience in chamber music, see if it fits and if it's good enough. I'll do the concerts and that will be it. And so the manager said, "You know, I know a young violinist [Daniel Hope]. He knows the Schnitke Trio." We had now recorded the Schnitke Trio. I said, "I don't care about the Schnitke Trio. I care about Schubert, Brahms, Beethoven." She spoke so highly of him [that] I said send him to my cellist. Let them compare and see. She sent him to my cellist, and he called me and said, "Menahem, I think he's the real thing!" I met them in Portugal. After the rehearsal, I had strength to practice five hours a day, six hours a day. It became a love feast. I couldn't get enough. They were tired, not me. So, that's why today I have the chance to continue.

A.M. (Audience Member): How much do you feel you—the word is not right, but let's put it bluntly—impose your terrific experience upon the strings?

M.P.: I would say, completely! I don't have to dictate because they are like sponges. They want to take it. Not that they don't say, "I think you are too fast" or "This is too loud" or "I think this is rhythmically not correct." No, they would say that.

A.M.: When are you going to write a book about your experiences? I'd love to read it.

M.P.: The book is nearly finished, but it's not me who wrote it but someone else.

A.M.: What is the key to successfully balancing your touring schedule and your personal life?

M.P.: That's a very important question, especially for a woman. The thing is this: if you are lucky, as I was, to find the right wife—don't laugh—who in every respect gave me a support system in which I was free to devote myself to whatever it was. She permitted me to give these concerts. She made it possible for me to travel. She made it possible for me to teach my students, to take care of the nitty-gritty of the house. She took care of my business. She took care of my bank account—I'm poor!

But if you ask me what does it take? It takes the right people together. And I would say it is especially difficult for a woman, of course. It is especially difficult for a woman. And we know some wonderful ones who didn't continue once they got married. And sometimes their husbands said that would be all right; and then, as soon as they were married, they felt, no, that is not a wife's work. It became a battle, and in most cases the woman gave up. So it is a problem because, to be successful, doesn't mean that you don't have any problems. You have plenty of problems being successful. But I tell you, they beat the problems when you are not successful.

A.M.: Mr. Pressler, I was your student thirty-eight years ago. I am absolutely in awe sitting here. My name is Nancy Munday. I've never felt I deserved being your student. It's just amazing, and I'm thinking how, anywhere you go, there has to be a student in the audience after all these years. Anywhere you go, anywhere you perform, you're followed by a wonderful family. Thank you so much.

M.P.: It's absolutely true. Students are a wonderful family.

T.U.: I want you to know that, at the Institute, the Academy, we've started a new chapter; and because it's so fresh, I didn't dare ask you. But in front of these people, you have to promise one of these days to come back and teach chamber music. We started this year with a quartet, and we had a string player coaching a pianist. We want to continue this, and, hopefully, when you are touring less—which I don't know if it's possible, maybe if we catch you in between two concerts—you'll promise me to come back. Most of all, we have a devil of a time to induce young artists to play chamber music; and I want to ask you, because all of these people here who are soaking your words up, to give us some guidance on the value. Maybe they would take it from you, of the incredible benefit as a soloist of playing chamber music.

M.P.: You know that everyone that you can think of—if it was Cortot, he had a trio; if it was Schnabel, he had a trio; if it was Horowitz, he played trios; Rubinstein, made recordings of trio with piano. To play chamber music is, in a sense, a must for any soloist, for any artist. I think it's a must; and all the great schools demand it, whether it's New York, Philadelphia, Indiana, Paris, or Berlin. They all demand chamber music, and it is needed. First of all, they find out that inspiration is a big important point that they don't really know what that is. A few do, but most of them don't. They think if you play clean, that is the inspiration. To find inspiration and get it through someone else and you give it back. I feel very strongly it's a wonderful idea you have. And congratulations.

A.M.: Just one more question, Mr. Pressler. I had the joy of hearing you and your colleagues just a few weeks ago in California; and I have to tell you, I was sitting in the fifth row observing the three of you, trying to see some evidence of the fact that you were the motivator, the father whose wisdom they soak up. All I saw—I'm actually moved when I think of it—all I saw were three fellow servants serving that music, and the result was magnificent.

M.P.: That's exactly what you should see. That's what I hope you would see.

A.M.: And that's what we all saw that night.

M.P.: Yes, three fellow musicians who are servants of Schubert. What else did we play that night?

A.M.: Schubert, Beethoven, and Shostakovich.

M.P.: Beethoven, Shostakovich and Schubert. Not bad.

A.M.: About practicing, Mr. Pressler, do you often come home and practice?

M.P.: You know that I do. You see, the first thing I said when I came was, "I have to practice because I'm going from here to a festival." And they said, "Of course, you can go to the hall." Bass Hall is right around the corner from the hotel. And then my host family picked me up, and I said, "I don't understand why there is not a piano in my room." And he said, "You will have one." And not only do I have a piano; I have a small concert grand, a small baby grand. So now if you ask me if I can practice, I say, "Anytime, and I do it nearly all the time." I was telling Tamás I was teaching in Italy three weeks ago at Lake Como where there is a famous pianists' academy where many of the winners of competitions go to school there, and actually two students who are semi-finalists played for me there. Now I had to find a time to practice over there myself, so I got up and at 5:30 A.M. I go to practice. Now the director, he started to practice, too. That was a good example. No, I am a firm believer in practicing because the best ideas come when you practice.

A.M.: Can you speak to a possible problem? Something I see in young people where, in duos and trios, they seem to be subservient to the string players, and perhaps they're being coached that way by string players sometimes, or perhaps they're feeling as accompanists rather than collaborators. Can you give us some ammunition as teachers of chamber music so that we can address this problem?

M.P.: Now I will tell you, the thing is that the first condition is to have a balance, and in most cases the pianist plays too loud, in most cases. So automatically a string player will object, "This is much too loud." And then the pianist becomes inhibited and plays too soft which [means], of course, the piece suffers. The string player may be happy, but the piece suffers. But unless you find the right way of balancing, and this is the first condition, that you hear a work in its entirety. The great chamber players play all the instruments the same.

The members of my Trio, they have to play the piano part, the violin part, the cello part. I have to play the violin, cello, and piano part to know which way it should sound. It is true, and that is what makes music absolutely so wonderful. There is no one way that is absolutely right, but one way that is absolutely right is that the balance is so that we hear it correctly.

Now the good pianist will do it. You know the famous story of David Oistrakh, when they came to play a violin sonata for him, and he said to the pianist, "Tell me. What happens when we put the violin on top of the piano?" She was thinking, and she said, "Nothing." He says, "Ah, and what happens when we put the piano on top of the violin?" (Laughter.) So that is the danger. That is the difficulty. You have to be able to get it right so that they hear it right. And that's where I'm very grateful to Guilet, because he insisted. He never wanted the piano to be soft, but he wanted the right balance. And we played at that time with the piano always on the small stick until Bobby Mann of the Juilliard Quartet heard

Fig. 14.1. Publicity photo

us and came backstage at the intermission and said, "Are you crazy? Open the piano! Pressler won't smother you. Even if he wants to, he will never do it." And I've never done it. I've defended my title as the softest pianist.

T.U.: On that happy note, let us all join in wishing you many, many happy anniversaries.

Part Two

The Music:
Transcripts of
Lessons and
Master Classes

FIFTEEN

JOHANN SEBASTIAN BACH

Bach appeals to that which we all need in living, which is a kind of order of things, whether an inner order or an outer one. Bach is on so many levels—the intellectual level—that you see how the voices are living with each other, next to each other, above each other, and somehow harmonize. Then when you hear his church music, his B minor Mass, or the Passions that he wrote, he becomes a religion in himself. You can be feeling, when you hear those Passions, that you are really communing with God. That's Bach. And there is no composer who did not appreciate that. Everyone, whether that's Beethoven or Mozart or Chopin, had to concern themselves at one point or another with Bach.

PARTITA NO. 2 IN C MINOR, S. 826

Each of the *Partitas* is a masterpiece in its own way, but this one is a favorite of audiences and performers because of the beauty and variety presented in the various movements. The grandeur of the *Sinfonia* is a wonderful way to open a recital and allows both performer and listener the opportunity to become accustomed to the sonority of the instrument. Too often the player approaches these pieces with too much emphasis on the top voice, without giving attention to all the voices. There must always be direction. Bach's lines are always going somewhere. There are sequences. There must be clarity of form, and the rhythm must be exact.

Sinfonia
M. 1. The *Grave* must be grandiose, not small. The first chord must have a sense of leading somewhere, to the chord on beat 3, then up to the chord on beat 2 in measure 2. Then it resolves again in C minor on beat 3. Use the pedal to open up the sound.
M. 3. Why is it so soft? That's so weak. It sounds like you're suffering from tuberculosis!

M. 4. When you go to the F minor, you make it sentimental. You lose the grandeur that a Bach *Grave* should have. Now less on beat 2; it's a single voice, but not slower. Beat 4, no accent on the G; go all the way to the C.

M. 6. It closes in the left hand on beat 3, but you are so loud in the right hand on the A♭ -G that the second voice takes over because you play too right-handedly. Don't stop the motion in beats 3 and 4; start less and then add. First it's two voices, then three voices, four voices, and five voices.

M. 7. It's grandiose coming to that G major; but with you, it's heavy, slow-poke. The F♯ goes to the G, and the A goes to the B with no *ritardando.* Your thirty-seconds are slow. Why is that? You must keep the same tempo all over.

M. 8. *Andante,* you have to feel the cadence to the first beat. Don't play with the left foot down; it's too soft. You're thinking *pianissimo;* think *piano.* All is health. Nothing sick!

Mm. 8–9. This is two bars without a stop, one line. It doesn't stop on bar 9. Each of these single left-hand notes has an intent, as if they are chords. He could have written all of these chords by name, I_4^6, IV, II, but he uses single words to tell you what the whole sentence is about.

M. 9. Why do you hit the B [beat 3]? Always separate the octaves [the Gs].

M. 10. To clarify the syncopation, I would like the note before the syncopation to have a dot [the C]. There's no waiting within the bar; it's continuous. And I would like more sensitivity when you go from the E♭ to the E♮ . Beat 2, it's how you bring in the D♭ and C. They make a circle; no false accents. And finish on the F.

M. 14. The D [beat 1] and the C [beat 2] are ornaments for the Fs.

M. 15. You don't feel a cadence in the left hand.

M. 16. Your detached notes are too short; they sound too cute, not serious.

Mm. 16–17. Be aware of the E♭ [beat 3] to the F [beat 1] to the D♮ [beat 3].

M. 18. The left hand is not strong enough; you have to give the right hand something to hang on to. The E [left hand fourth note] is too loud when you come back to it.

M. 19. Beat 3 comes too soon. Be conscious of the cadence, not only in the right hand.

M. 21. Here you should hear the difference in the right hand between going down [E♭ -D] and coming up.

M. 23. Not fast; resolve to the G [beat 3]. When the left-hand B♮ comes, come a split-hair late, because we expect the B♭. There is a turn in the road that lets us go on.

Mm. 24–25. Each time you reach for the G, it's a little more and a little more.

M. 26. We've had a C to a G, and a B♭ to a G, and an A to a G, and a G to a G. But this one isn't G to G; it's an A♭ [beat 1]. Isn't that surprising? But you are not at all surprised; you play as if it's going to a G. Play the A♭ less; it's a surprise.

M. 29. You have to lead us to that color note in the left hand [the C♯]. Why are you waiting?

Mm. 31–32. An oboe player could not play like that; their cheeks would fall off. Let it come down.

M. 33. You're so loud; you play like a player piano.

Mm. 42–44. Less and less as the sequences descend. Hear it winding down.

M. 46. That low D, there is new energy. You can't jump much more than an octave, but the theme is in the right hand.

M. 50. Follow the left hand line to the downbeat, B♭-C-D-E♭.

M. 64. No, finish it [on the downbeat]. Again you play like the player piano. You are like a marionette that can only go 1-2-3, 1-2-3, 1-2-3.

Mm. 68–69. Less and less as the lines descend.

M. 70. Be sensitive. Now it goes up; he turns it around.

M. 71. Now the left hand has the theme.

M. 74. The left hand finishes on beat 2 and the right hand begins. You don't finish, and then you go on with the same loudness and the same speed. It's off to the races again.

Mm. 77–78. The trill closes on the downbeat, then you have time to breathe. And start in *piano*.

M. 80. Not weak.

M. 84. It finishes loud [on the downbeat], then it starts.

M. 87. That finishes [on beat 2]; it's like an ornament.

M. 90. Not much *ritardando*. And since you already have the C, you don't need to start the trill on the C.

Allemande

M. 1. Remember this is a dance, so the left hand starts with a dance step.

M. 2. Hold back on the cadence [beat 3].

M. 5. Why does it stop? No, it doesn't start new in the left hand on beat 3.

M. 6. But finish! [on beat 4].

Mm. 9–10. Make it a line; it grows. Hold all the sequences together.

[157]

M. 16. Broaden only on the dominant chord; he's taking a bow.

M. 17. The left hand has no expression. It's too loud when the right hand comes in [beat 4], because it never changes in dynamics.

M. 22. Let me hear it cadence in the left hand [beat 3].

M. 26. Finish. Bring out the left hand [beat 3].

M. 27. The right hand is too loud; it's killing everybody in sight!

M. 31. The trill finishes on the G [beat 3].

M. 32. The left hand finishes.

Courante

When you practice something like this, it must take on a quality. What you do is you practice the notes, and so you get the notes, more or less. But it doesn't make any sense to you, and you certainly don't make much sense to anyone else. It's one note after the other, and there's no phrasing. You know that this is a dance, so it must have phrasing. It would be beneficial to play the left hand alone, just the single notes, until they make some sense to you, until it's like a picture for you. Before you play something like this, it must be clear. It must say something.

M. 2. Come down from the C to the G [left hand]. The scale has to start on a lower level and then take us all the way up to the A♭.

M. 3. The fingers are like little hammers. Match how the right hand played the scale.

Mm. 4–6. Practice the lower two parts with two hands so we hear the independent lines.

M. 12. Personally, I would not repeat the right hand G [beat 3].

M. 24. And likewise, I would not repeat the C at the end. And do a bow; it's a dance, yes?

Sarabande

You have to find many ways to express the mood, many colors. Every note is in relation to all the others.

M. 2. Relate the line to m. 1.

M. 4. Finish on the G.

M. 5. The left hand goes up, then it falls.

M. 6. Now it's less.

M. 10. Everything should bring you to that B♭ [right hand].

M. 12. Finish it [on beat 3], but not with a *ritardando*. You have to play it in such a way that you anticipate the B♭.

M. 14. It doesn't stop on the A; it goes to the C [right hand, beat 2].

M. 15. Don't hit the A♭. It's part of the line.

M. 16. And finish [on beat 3].

M. 23. Don't accent the right hand two-note figures; make a line.

Rondeaux

There's a joy and pain in there. It connects; it doesn't stop.

M. 8. Play the scale as if it's in one hand.

M. 16. Finish on the C.

M. 24. That's a finish on the F.

Mm. 26–29. Hear the cadences.

Mm. 26–32. It must sound natural, like you are singing it.

Mm. 31–32. Come down [*decrescendo*] from the G.

M. 32. The last G is too short.

M. 48. Finish there on the C. The first three left-hand notes belong to the finish; the other notes begin the next phrase.

M. 65. It finishes in the left hand [on the E♭]. Then don't *accelerando* in the right hand.

M. 72. Don't bring out the B [downbeat]. By itself, it doesn't mean a thing.

M. 81. The E♭ is new; it's different from the C [m. 80].

M. 88. The way you play that F♯, it's like you've been stung by a bee. It's ending. Come down from the D [m. 86].

M. 89. No bump on the G [left hand downbeat].

M. 111. All the time, he gives you a long note on the downbeat, but this time he gives you two notes. Let us hear the difference.

Capriccio

M. 4. That C is an ending [tenor line].

M. 5. Nine out of ten people would play G minor just the same as C minor. I want to hear G minor, so bring the top part down so we can hear the tune.

M. 8. Finish on the downbeat.

M. 2. Finish it there.

M. 32. You play the C so loudly we can't hear the G [beat 2]. The G is the theme.

M. 40. The top line is too loud. The C has to ring [beat 2].

M. 50. No, the lower voice is too loud. Sustain the C.

M. 58. The first one goes up to a C [m. 56]; the second one goes to a B♭ [m. 58]. But you play them the same way.

M. 60. Play the left hand D–G short-long. Then in mm. 61–62, you have it in the right hand.

M. 64. I would suggest you don't play those thirds *legato*.

M. 65. The first one goes to G and resolves. The second one goes to F [m. 67] and resolves.

M. 69. I wouldn't play the eighth notes so short. It takes away from the first voice.

M. 70. That F♯ is an ending [alto part].

M. 71. That B♭ is so loud; you play it like a player piano.

M. 72. The primary line is in the middle [B♭-G-C-A], and they're always short. When you play that A-F♯-G that loudly up on top, you can forget any other voice. You can play "America the Beautiful," you can play anything you want, because we don't hear anything else but A-F♯-G.

M. 73. Now the top voice has the tune [G-E♭]. Then it's in the middle voice [C-F♯ in mm. 73–74].

M. 76. Make a *crescendo* going to G [downbeat].

Mm. 89–90. The E♭-C [middle part] answers the C-G [top part].

M. 95. Put your left hand 5 on the C to bring out that line, and feel the Gs bringing you to the C.

SIXTEEN
BÉLA BARTÓK

Fig. 16.1. *Out of Doors*

Béla Bartók created a signature in his writing which is clear to all of us. You cannot help but recognize Bartók immediately, because his face in his music is very clear. Who liked Bartók at the time? The quartets you couldn't give away; but today you put Bartók on a program, and it's one of the things people love. The Sonata, the *Rumanian Folk Dances,* the *Out of Doors,* these are all popular pieces because they are colorful, innovative even today, and appeal to our basic need for excitement and drama. Here is a composer who understands structure and knows how to write music to fit the hands.

Out of Doors gives us five character pieces, with the bass clusters representing drums, swirling figures in multimeters, reminding us of the gondola moving through the water, bagpipe effects in 'Musettes,' mysterious night sounds, and a perpetual motion race to the finish. Sometimes people say they want to hear more melody, but to me there's melody everywhere in these pieces. The challenge is to take pieces with such obvious primitive elements and present the subtlety, the simple charm, and beauty.

OUT OF DOORS

No. 1 with Drums and Pipes
Mm. 1–5. Start heavy and slightly slower until the melody enters.
Mm. 2–3. Make these off-beat drums meaningful.
Mm. 5–6. Not so loud; these Es introduce the melody.
M. 7. The melody begins. Keep it *non-legato.*
M. 11. Lead with a *crescendo* to the *sforzando.*
M. 13. Softer Es again.
M. 19. Lead again to the *sforzando* with a *crescendo.*
Mm. 25–30. Still *non-legato* until the *legato* in m. 31.
Mm. 26–29. Maintain the two- and three-note groupings of the right hand, not necessarily coinciding with the left hand.
M. 41. Hear the two parts within the left hand.
M. 63. Play a heavier left hand into the *sforzando.*
M. 67. The *sforzando* is an ending; take time before beginning again.
Mm. 77–80. Steady.
Mm. 86–88. Keep the tempo steady. Don't be influenced by the off-beats in the left hand.
M. 105. The eighth-note rest means one more time.
M. 105–106. Lead upward to the B♭.
M. 109. The two-note groupings give you a G-G-F♯ melody.

No. 2 Barcarolla

M. 1. Hear the waves. Inflect the line.

M. 11. Still waves. The sixteenth notes are *pizzicato*, shorter and passive.

M. 32. *Cantando*. A higher level when the theme is presented in octaves.

Mm. 49–61. These continue to be waves. Lead to each *sforzando*.

M. 62. *Agitato* is not *molto accelerando*. Just push and continue to sing.

Mm. 71–74. Listen to the falling fifths in the right hand.

Mm. 83–85. Transfer the line smoothly from hand to hand.

Mm. 111–114. The C♯s are still passive and short. Pull the final one to elongate just a bit.

M. 112. Pull back before the G of m. 113.

No. 3 Musettes

M. 1. This represent bagpipes. Swing to the A each time.

M. 8. Not so measured. The wrists move in to begin the trills and out with the rest.

M. 36. The two-note slurs are the bagpipes.

M. 41. The bagpipes continue the left hand with a free melody.

M. 47. Delay the *sforzando*.

M. 53. Aim with the thumb to play the right-hand octave.

M. 60. A new melody starts. Dance with it four times.

M. 81. Start. *Crescendo* to a *forte*.

M. 87. A new idea.

M. 116. As if the C interrupts.

Mm. 125–126. Connect the thirty-second notes to the C in m. 126. Take the Cs with *sostenuto* pedal.

Mm. 127–128. Not so loud on the octave melody.

No. 4 Musiques Nocturnes

Hear three staves, Debussy-like. Hear the difference between the G, A♭, F♯. Color the changes of register.

Mm. 7–15. The *sforzando* of each group is important, like a bouncing ball. One impulse.

M. 17. Starts a long-line melody. Not fast.

M. 38. It's a flute melody, far away in the night.

M. 49. Softer than before.

No. 5 The Chase

This movement builds to a giant climax to end the whole suite. Therefore, the other movements are not so loud. Save the real strength until the last statement.

M. 4. Play the last chord louder with pedal.

M. 5. Play the right hand *non-legato*.

M. 8. Starting from this point, sweep the left hand to emphasize the Es. Not notey groups.

M. 14. Drop back in dynamics to begin the melody.

M. 43. Touch the pedal to each chord.

M. 51. Roar!

SEVENTEEN

LUDWIG VAN BEETHOVEN

Fig. 17.1. Concerto No. 5 in E-flat major, Op. 73, *Emperor*

Beethoven is the Bible. That is the first thing you think of when you say Beethoven. I mean, the greatness of that music is overwhelming. You play it, and at no time should you not be aware that, to live up to the piece, takes all you've got and more, so that you actually can never live up to the piece. It is enormously difficult physically. It is difficult emotionally, it's difficult intellectually, and it is difficult stamina-wise. Beethoven mirrors the universe, to my feeling. He always speaks for us, to us. He always addresses the world. It is beautiful to be able to say that you have devoted your life to his music because the only one who gets richer from it is not Beethoven, but you. And there is something very, very magnificent about that one man who had that many variations of emotions, his coarseness and depth and virtuosity. There is no one else who had that breadth of emotion, from the most esoteric, from the most philosophical, to the most vulgar. He has it all, and he is as human and as divine as a man can ever be. He is made in the image of God, yes?

When we see all thirty-two sonatas, we see that he was looking and going further and further, and you have him grappling, fighting to find answers. He elevated himself continuously, and that is not an easy thing to do. We know that if we have anything we would like to do, if it is a bigger challenge than what happened yesterday, we try to postpone it. And we think, "No, maybe next week we'll try for that." And then we forget about it, and after a month we say, "You know, I intended to do that. I always wanted to do that." But he went through this struggle, which in a way becomes more meaningful to all of us as we see what life does to us. And we look at his music and it is such a mirror of everything that has ever happened to any of us that we can all identify with this music.

Look at how Beethoven kept the discipline of form. Yes, he breaks it, but he creates a new form and the form is still there. There's an exposition. There's still a development. There's still a reprise. In every sonata, he does it in a somewhat different way, yes? The first sonata is very catholic, very exact. Then more and more the great master and the dreamer and the phenomenal philosopher in music found that dream. Other composers found other freedoms, but not of that sublime order from Op. 1 to Op. 111 or Op. 121.

What you have to do is to sensitize yourself so that your emotions are up to what Beethoven is asking for. Very often the mistake is made that people play that piece and they think that, by playing the piece, they have the emotions. But what they do is just read the notes and repeat them.

On Getting Better (on Hearing Dame Myra Hess)

STUDENT: I have one question about something you said the first day [of the master-class]. You said that, as we get better in some ways, we get worse in other ways, and I wondered if you would say more about that.

PRESSLER: Let me say, to get better means we hear more. To get better means we feel more. To get better means we are less concerned with ourselves. We become more and more the messenger. The really great artist is the messenger. He brings the message of the composer as he sees it, and he delivers it to us and he enriches our lives by that. What we do when we are young is, we play the piece and we say, "Look at me. Who plays the octaves like me? Who plays as loud as I can? Who plays as soft as I can?" But there is something to that, because that has a daring in it which is wonderful to keep. Now when we get older, when we know more of the danger, we don't dare so much. We take it a little easier when it comes to daring. We do feel more deeply and we hope we give the message more clearly, but we don't dare as much. Or we're blind and we dare so much that everything gets lost, and that happens to us, too. So when we get older, I would say surely the body is not as elastic as it was.

But I remember one of the greatest evenings that I've ever heard a Beethoven pro-gram [was] when it was played by Myra Hess in Indianapolis. She was quite old. This was very soon before she retired. When she retired, she had that terrible arthritis. She couldn't play at all, not even for herself a few notes.

On that night she played the most magnificent Beethoven program. I had just come back from tour, and my students said, "Couldn't we go and hear her?" And so I said, "Okay, let's fill the car and let's drive there." She had the music in front of her, and she started with the Op. 34 *Variations*. And then she played the D-major Sonata with the wonderful *Adagio*. And then she played the Op. 110–Intermission–the *Appassionata*, and it got better and better and more wonderful and deeper. And in the *Appassionata*, she had, in a way, more strength than the best *Appassionata* that I ever heard, which was Richter when he lost complete control at the end. He got so fast, he couldn't play any notes. He played so fast the fire came out of his head and not out of his hands. But she had all that fire and everything was there. That was remark-able because you wouldn't expect an older woman to be like that. So I saw what her strength was, not by the force of her hands, but her strength was the depth of her feel-ings and her passion for the music. And so, that's what I think we can get better at.

What I'm afraid of is that we won't play as well Rachmaninoff and the *Don Juan* by Liszt [when we are older]. We will still have to go through it–every fine pianist at one point in his career has to start with those pieces–because they give you, how shall I say it, the money to pay for your livelihood. I remember myself coming to my teacher and I said, "What is the most difficult piece for the piano?" And he [Rudia-kov] said, "Balakirev, *Islamey*." I said, "I will play that for my first recital!" And I did. And I worked, and I worked, and I worked, and I worked–many hours.

Today, I love to listen to *Islamey* when it is well played; but ask me if I would want to play that or play a Beethoven sonata, and I would rather play a Beethoven sonata. It is also because I wouldn't play it as well as I did then.

They have neither digested them nor internalized them. But for those who can hear, his music is very, very meaningful.

CONCERTO NO. 5 IN E-FLAT MAJOR, OP. 73, *EMPEROR*

Mvt. 1. Allegro

M. 2. Pedal before playing the first note. Relate the recurring E♭-G motive [the seventh and eighth notes]. Play with more intensity as you reach the top. Then climb down from B♭ to G, etc. Take extra time before the trill. Swell the trill. Then *crescendo* again.

M. 4. *Crescendo* to the last C. Then *crescendo* each four-note group. The last two eighth notes move to the downbeat of m. 5.

M. 6. Start slower and in *mezzo forte*. Voice the left-hand B♭ as it begins. *Crescendo* to the top and push faster.

M. 9. Broaden before the trill. More intensity at the top. Show the top C-B♭. In playing the descending scale, feel the pulse so as to *decrescendo* organically. Slur the B♭-A to the A♭⁷ chord. Play the octave B♭ with the left hand.

M. 107. The right hand can help by playing the first four notes of the scale.

M. 108. Lean into the F♯ downbeat.

M. 109. Begin the trill on F.

M. 115. After the downbeat, begin a phrase. Be careful with pedal.

M. 121. Hear the F-G-A♭-B♭ line.

M. 125. Continue the *crescendo* all the way to the top.

M. 134. Color that first F♭.

Mm. 136–138. Hear the G♭s in different registers. Feel the G♭s; don't just play them.

M. 140. Hear the two-note slurs

Mm. 146–148. *Sforzando* two times per bar, not four.

M. 149. The *sforzandi* represent intensity.

M. 150. Start.

M. 151. Color the B minor.

M. 154. The A major is transparent.

M. 157. Decrease to the downbeat of m. 158.

M. 158. *Crescendo* as the scale ascends.

M. 159. A release of the confinement of the previous section.

M. 176. *Decrescendo* as the *arpeggio* descends.

M. 182. Don't rush. Touch the pedal to each low note.

M. 183. *Crescendo* during the fourth beat.

M. 184. *Crescendo* to the *sforzando*. *Crescendo* the left hand during the last beat.

M. 187. Use the wrist in the left hand on each beat along with the orchestra.

M. 195. Start.

M. 196. The left hand should use the wrist on the fourth quarter.

Mm. 199–200. Start *mezzo forte*. Then inflect downward.

M. 201. Play only *mezzo piano*.

M. 206. Use the last two beats to get to m. 207.

M. 208. Lean on the low E♭.

Mm. 209–210. No *crescendo*.

M. 211. Start *piano*.

M. 225. Start. *Con pedal.*

M. 226. Use the arm on the right-hand C♯.

M. 264. Start the scale without an accent.

Mm. 266, 270, 274. Hear the trills moving from G to B♮ to C.

Mm. 268–269. Descend and then climb back up.

M. 280. The right hand plays the last sixteenth note.

M. 292. Pedal two times per measures. It's not an exercise. Show the skeleton.

Mm. 306, 308–310. Use full body on the chords.

M. 313. *Crescendo* to the *sforzando*.

M. 332. Play *legato* from the F♮-F♯ to the G of m. 333. Make it melodic.

M. 336. The left hand continues the even triplets.

M. 340. Play more trill notes.

Mm. 348–349. Change the slurring to begin with each accented note.

M. 351. Lean on the D, then on the F [m. 353], then the A♭ [m. 354].

M. 371. Play with pedal in the higher register. After the trill, reach out as you climb to the high C, and then lean on it. Accent the low B♭ and pulse the scale to help the orchestra reenter.

M. 380. Play very close to the key. Hear the beginning D.

M. 381. A *nachschlag* [F-G] after the G trill.

M. 382. Drill the left hand for evenness.

M. 384. Echo.

M. 388. Begin increasing the intensity.

M. 407. Phrase the last four sixteenth notes into m. 408.

M. 433. *Decrescendo* as the line descends.

M. 438. Pedal changes on each low note.

M. 455. Lean into that right-hand B♭.

M. 467. Take full time on the last beat.

M. 482. Take time to begin the scale. The left hand also *crescendos*.

M. 483. *Con pedal.*

M. 490. *Crescendo* to the top and play the top note with an accent.

M. 499. Start.

M. 501. Push forward.

M. 502. *Crescendo* to an accent on the downbeat of m. 503.

Mm. 515–516. Let us hear the A♮, A♭, and G♮.

M. 525. *Decrescendo* to the bottom of the scale.

M. 560. The D [downbeat] leads to the last E♭.

M. 568. *Decrescendo* to m. 569. Then *poco a poco crescendo.*

Mvt. 2. Adagio un poco moto

M. 16. Play the grace note on the beat. Phrase the right hand, not single notes.

M. 19. Use the last beat to reach the D♯, then *decrescendo* and slur to m. 20.

M. 20. The D♯ has a double function as the end of one phrase and the beginning of the next.

M. 22. Play the turn on the beat.

M. 23. Play both the sixteenths and the triplets evenly, and *crescendo* all the way to the G♯ of m. 24.

M. 24. The fourth beat moves slower to the G♯ of m. 25. Then ease up, coming away from it.

Mm. 32–33. Each three-beat gesture opens and closes in one breath. Don't segment.

Mm. 35–36. A *cadenza,* play *grandioso.* Use arm weight. Play closer to the keys in the left hand than in the right hand. Push to the top, then play rich sixths at the bottom.

Mm. 37–38. Hear different Gs as the passage diminishes. Broaden before the trills of m. 39.

M. 38. The left-hand chords answer the trill note.

M. 44. You reach ecstasy on this F♯. Then *crescendo* to the G♯ and play it richly with arm weight.

Mm. 45–47. The orchestration becomes increasingly thicker.

M. 48. Take time with the thirds.

Mm. 49–52. One continuous phrase.

Mm. 54–56. Spin a line all the way over the top.

M. 60. Hear the melody and always relate to it.

M. 64. Swell the measure.

Mm. 76–78. Climb down using the lower note of each beat.

Mm. 81–82. Keep it in a cocoon. *Diminuendo,* if anything.

Mvt. 3. Rondo: Allegro ma non troppo

M. 1. Play a clear triplet in the left hand. Practice the slurrings of the right hand.

M. 3. Release each chord. The rests are important.

M. 4. Release the third to play the trill. Let the trill's *diminuendo* close the phrase.

M. 9. *Piano.* The right hand reacts to the left hand.

M. 14. No pause into the D, and end only *mezzo forte.* It's continuous into the orchestra's entrance.

Mm. 42–44. Follow the melodic notes of the scale [E♭-G-B♭-E♭]. *Crescendo* as the line ascends.

Mm. 47–48. *Con pedal.* Swell a little into the C before coming down. Have steel fingers getting into the new theme.

M. 49. Singing, but not hard. Don't beat time. Play at least two-measure phrases.

M. 69. A huge *crescendo* with an accent on the top Gs.

M. 70. Make a line [C-D-E♭] to the downbeat of m. 71.

M. 72. The left-hand sixteenth notes are playful.

M. 78. Begins two-measure swells according to the chord progression.

Mm. 86–91. Huge sonority. Use pedal.

M. 94. Contrast the *forte* to the *piano.*

M. 111. The left hand can play the last two notes of the measure.

Mm. 112–114. A *non-legato* scale. Relate the motives [A♭-F-A♭, B♭-G-B♭, C-A♮-C].

M. 119. *Crescendo* into m. 120.

Mm. 128–137. Maintain the meter. Don't emphasize the pattern of the notes. *Con pedal.*

M. 137. Depress the pedal before beginning in the new key.

Mm. 147, 153. *Crescendo* to the top.

M. 154. *Fortissimo.*

M. 162. The new A♭ key is magic. Use a new approach to the key.

Mm. 165–172. It's contained. Feel the swells, but not hard.

M. 172. Use the last beat to get to the A♭ of m. 173.

M. 176. *Decrescendo* into the A♭.

Mm. 191–198. Yodel, but *pianissimo.*

M. 201. Push to the *sforzando* of m. 202.

Mm. 244–245. Have inflection within the scale. Bring it down and back up.

Mm. 305, 307. Hear the top note.

M. 386. Start *piano.*

Mm. 403–404. Speak with both the left hand and the right hand.

Mm. 406–407. *Crescendo* through these two measures.

DID YOU KNOW BEETHOVEN?

STUDENT: Did you know Beethoven?

PRESSLER: I have his cellular telephone number! The only thing is, from here, from Adamant, there is no connection!

STUDENT: Can you give us some advice on how structurally to organize this kind of style—slow-fast-slow-fast [Op. 110, mvt 3]?

PRESSLER: In a sense it's very easy. I mean, writing a *fugue* after the slow movement, everything is easy, form-wise, because he forces you into a form. You cannot do anything with a *fugue*; you must follow it. That is why, in principle, most people don't play a Bach *fugue* badly. It's like a corset. There are only very few who play it really well so that it is the masterwork it is, but generally speaking, for me sitting in Brussels and listening to the young pianists playing *Preludes and Fugues* of Bach, nobody plays badly and nobody plays well. Because when you follow it [the form], you get from Burlington to Adamant; you can't miss. But that you see the beauties on the road, you know, for that you have to have open eyes and so, a special gift for it.

But you don't have to organize in this part. It is really organized for you. What you do have to do is, you do have to sensitize yourself so that the emotions are up to what Beethoven is asking for. Very often the mistake is made that people play that piece and they think that, by playing the piece, they have the emotions. But what they do is, they just read the notes and repeat them. They have neither digested them nor internalized them. So that when you do hear someone play the late Beethoven sonatas wonderfully, that even today when we hear the slow movement played by a Schnabel, you are stunned. How could he dig so deeply into that music? Nobody knows how, but he did. And of course, for the ones that can hear, that is very, very meaningful.

Mm. 419–422. *Crescendo* to the *sforzandi. Con pedal.*

M. 424. *Crescendo.*

M. 425. Use thumbs for full sonority.

SONATA, OP. 81A, *LES ADIEUX*

Mvt. 1. Das Lebewohl (Les adieux): Adagio/Allegro

M. 1. The Introduction begins with a definite entrance of two horns. The melody must *decrescendo* to the E♭ of m. 2.

M. 2. Surprise us with C minor. Start the new phrase by taking over the same level of the E♭'s decay. Play exact thirty-second notes.

M. 4. Close the phrase without *ritard.* Then imitate in the higher register. Think bright.

M. 5. Phrase to the second beat without *ritard.* "In time" can be just as expressive.

M. 6. Hear the left-hand D moving to the D♭ of m. 7.

M. 10. Glide down from E♭ to D.

M. 11. Play the E♭ minor chord a little late with an *agogic* accent.

M. 16. *Decrescendo* the two chords.

M. 17. Play the chord with arm. Energy. Then start a new phrase.

Mm. 17–18. The arm goes up on the second eighth and down on the quarter.

Mm. 17–20. Work on the *legato* thirds.

M. 19. The *sforzando* is the climax of the phrase. End the phrase on the D octave. Then begin again.

M. 20. Right hand: work both the thumb line and the top fingers.

M. 22. Sustain. The dotted half note must sound longer than the previous quarter notes.

Mm. 21–25. The left hand must flow, especially during the long melody notes.

M. 24. *Decrescendo.* Color the C♭. Contrast this phrase with the next one. Work the *legato*.

M. 26. Suffer.

Mm. 27–29. The phrase is G-E♮-F-C-E♭-D.

M. 30. *Legato* thirds.

M. 31. Enjoy the changing registers. *Decrescendo* to prepare for the *crescendo*.

M. 32. Start on the F♯.

M. 33. Start the *crescendo* with the fourth eighth note where the hand position is set.

M. 34. Arm chords.

Mm. 35–38. "Le-be-wohl, le-be-wohl."

M. 35. Pain.

Mm. 36, 38. Play even trills. Orchestrate. Hear the difference between the G♭ and the G♮.

M. 38. Sing.

Mm. 39–44. Follow the melodic and harmonic outlines.

Mm. 47–48. Close each phrase.

Mm. 48–49. *Tenuto* marks over G-F-E♭. Reach a peak.

M. 50. Lean into the left-hand C♯-E♮. Relate this to m. 51.

M. 51. The left hand should resolve the G♭ to the F.

Mm. 52–53. Melody projection. In octaves.

M. 58. Hear even eighths from the right hand to the left hand.

M. 59. Not such a *crescendo*.

M. 62. *Subito piano*. Even right hand to left hand. Hear right-hand D-C-B♭, followed by left-hand D-C-B♭.

Mm. 63–64. Speak the line. *Legato.* Hear the register changes.

Mm. 65–69. Horns again.

M. 70. Follow the left-hand line.

M. 72. A breath after this measure, but relate the fourth-beat chord to the next measure—it's not Schoenberg.

M. 73. The F goes all the way to the E♭ of m. 75.

M. 75. The right hand is a woodwinds entrance. Be definite; lean into the chord with emphasis on the E♭. This is a sliding motion, but stationary on the keys rather than a percussive striking. The left hand should move toward the thumb. Not loud.

Mm. 75–76. *Decrescendo* the E♭ to the D♭. Both hands coordinate the release with an up motion.

Mm. 79, 83. Relate the chords with the common As. Lean into the chords with sonority below.

M. 80. Descend from C to C♭. No *crescendo.*

M. 87. Surprise.

M. 88. Still *piano.*

M. 94. A breath after this measure.

Mm. 95–108. Find a form. Try four-measure phrases.

M. 113. No *crescendo.*

M. 123. *Decrescendo.*

M. 134. Stretch from the B♭ to the C♭ of m. 135.

M. 149. *Decrescendo.*

M. 150. No gross *crescendo.*

M. 158. The *coda* begins.

M. 161. No *crescendo.*

M. 170. *Legato* octaves.

M. 173. *Decrescendo.*

M. 180. A breath after this measure.

Mm. 181–191. *Decrescendo* each three-note figure.

M. 197. Sing the left-hand *legato* line. Follow the shape up to A♭, then down to E♭, a smooth *arpeggio.*

M. 201. The right hand must still be heard as the left hand was before [m. 197].

M. 222. Broaden. Ask a question.

M. 223. The same tempo.

Mm. 235–238. Smooth from top to bottom.

M. 238. *Legato.*

M. 239. Rustic.

M. 247. A special triplet. The whole line is a dream.

M. 251. Go to heaven!

Mm 254–255. Full chords, and out.

Mvt. 2. Abwesenheit (L' absence): Andante espressivo
Prepare the hands for a gentle descent into the keys. Be aware of the hands' weight throughout this movement.

M. 1. Hear the left hand as an echo to the right hand.

M. 2. Play differently than m. 1.

M. 9. Reach up to the B♭.

M. 11. Start the *sforzando* as *mezzo forte* and then increase.

M. 12. Play eight-note groups over the bar line.

M. 13. No accents. A smooth line. Let the last note of each group bind to the next.

M. 14. Sensitive last beat.

M. 15. The call.

M. 16. Play the trill as indicated [as thirty-second notes]. Not fast.

Mm. 19–20. Play the left hand full as if octaves with some easing to the fourth beat.

M. 31. *Piano.*

M. 39. Less E♭ than in m. 1.

Mm. 41–42. *Decrescendo* as each hand climbs upward.

Mvt. 3. Das Wiedersehn (Le retour): Vivacissimamente
Mm. 1–4. Begin with an explosive chord. Then begin *mezzo forte. Crescendo* through m. 4. Loosen the arm. Use the wrist.

M. 5. *Forte.* Then m. 6 is *mezzo forte,* m. 7 is *mezzo piano,* m. 8 is *piano.* Then play *subito forte.*

M. 10. *Crescendo* as the scale ascends.

M. 11. *A tempo,* repose. Two-measure phrases. Don't emphasize the triplet.

M. 16. Finish.

Mm. 17–22. Long lines here, too. Do not push the right hand.

M. 28. Pull back; prepare for the *fortissimo.*

M. 29. Move forward.

Mm. 45–48. Shape the phrase.

Mm. 49–52. Again, shape the phrase.

M. 59. Whistle over the top.

M. 61. Left hand not jerky. More pedal sound. Light trill in the right hand.

M. 68. Clear even right-hand chords.

M. 77. Save to lead to a *fortissimo.* This is No. 1.

M. 78. This is No. 2. *Crescendo* through m. 79.

M. 79. This is No. 3.

M. 82. Rhythm, rhythm, rhythm.

M. 84. Lyric.

M. 99. Descend to a *piano* to start m. 100.

Mm. 104–108. Hear the *decrescendo* from G major to C major to A♭ major. Much pedal. Remember the sound of the theme.

M. 107. Resolve the E♮ to the E♭.

Mm. 110–111. Be sure the hands are exactly together.

M. 163. Clear left hand.

Mm. 172, 173, 174. *Crescendo.*

Mm. 175–176. One pedal, but begin clearing the pedal during the *sforzando.*

M. 176. The *poco andante,* it says, "I forgot to tell you what it's really about!" Don't punctuate so much. Too many pauses. Hold it together.

Mm. 178–181. *Crescendo* from E♭ major through F minor to G minor; then decrease to E♭ major.

Mm. 181–183. One voice, then two voices to four voices.

M. 185. A variation.

M. 189. A variation.

M. 192. Pull back. *Decrescendo.*

Mm. 193–195. Push forward to the top and then play the chords in time.

EIGHTEEN

JOHANNES BRAHMS

Fig. 18.1. Piano Sonata in F-sharp minor, Op. 2, from *Piano Works In Two Volumes* by Johannes Brahms, Edited by E. V. Sauer

Brahms, actually, is our language today. I would say he's the most popular composer in that sense. And that which he himself felt as a weakness—not being as varied and as profound as Beethoven—to us doesn't mean anything. To us, he is very profound, he is very varied. And so we play his works, and each time we feel absolutely fulfilled, and it doesn't matter if it is a symphony or his piano concerto or an *intermezzo,* quintet, quartet, trio, sonata. He has been one of the great ones, yes? His lyricism, the variety of his harmony, the form are all sublime. Of course, he couldn't compare himself to Beethoven. And why should he? And why would we? I mean, Beethoven, Mozart, Bach, they are incomparable, and Brahms is incomparable.

PERFORMING BRAHMS' CONCERTO NO. 2 IN B-FLAT MAJOR

Let me tell you how that is performed. I have heard many, very good performances, many excellent performances. I was talking about the performance of Mr. Serkin, who was playing in New York with the Philharmonic, and it was one of those performances when you feel that it could have been created just at that moment. And he was playing it like Parsifal; he was defending the Holy Grail. And he was hearing Brahms the way it should be, and it was so wonderful to see him when he played those octaves. He was so wild that his cufflinks were hitting the keys and [one] heard people laughing, but not me.

To me the performance was absolutely unforgettable because he expressed all that is in that music, where a young composer takes on the whole world. And it's wonderful that we know that Brahms played the first performance. When you play in Leipzig at the Gewandhaus, . . . you take that terrible walk to the stage, and you see the picture of the program, Brahms premiering his Concerto in Leipzig with the Gewandhaus Orchestra. It was not a success. It was absolutely a disaster. The public didn't like it, and the critics were horrifyingly bad. And even Clara [Schumann] said to him, "You've got to change it." And you know, he didn't change one note, although he always listened when he couldn't play anymore, and they tried to honor him. He played both concerti in Leipzig. He said, "Oh, I played terrible." He probably did, because he didn't practice. But he played both and it was a big success. So perseverance counts for something.

SONATA IN F-SHARP MINOR, OP. 2

Mvt. 1. Allegro non troppo, ma energico

M. 1. Roll the left hand, but play the right hand as a solid chord with a strong accent. *Crescendo* to the last octave, while leading with the thumbs.

M. 2. Play the chord the same as in m. 1.

M. 3. Play the chord with a *sforzando*. Use two or three changes to clear the pedal.

Mm. 4–6. Climb up melodically C♯-D-E♯-G♯-D-E♯, etc.

Mm. 6–7. Broaden and emphasize the last D. Begin the octaves less.

M. 8. A very big *crescendo* at the end of the measure. And broaden into the downbeat. Hear the A-G♯ going to the F♯ of m. 9.

M. 9. Have a clear pedal on beat 3.

M. 11. Start again after beat 3. Phrase toward each beat.

M. 15. Hear the chord decaying and resolving to the F♯ in m. 16.

M. 30. Use the last right-hand note of each measure to measure the leap.

Mm. 38–39. Play as *pizzicato* notes.

M. 40. Arm octaves, then use the wrist into m. 41.

M. 42. The low E is important, and lean into the right-hand octave Bs.

M. 45. Emphasize the low G♯.

M. 51. The left hand *crescendos* into the downbeat C♮ of m. 52.

M. 60. Color the C♮ in the left hand.

M. 62. A special color for the C major chord.

M. 69. This measure may push faster, but m. 70 is *a tempo*.

M. 73. Pull back after the downbeat. Then push forward as the line descends.

M. 77. Restart after the downbeat, then push downward to m. 79.

M. 82. Broaden into the *sforzando* of m. 83.

M. 83. *A tempo.*

M. 84. A contrast of dynamics, harmony, and length of line.

Mm. 93, 95. Hear the resolutions of the chords.

M. 99. Color the chord.

Mm. 101–102. Resolve the inner line [A-G♯].

M. 108. *Tempo giusto.*

M. 111. Broaden this measure [before the *dolce*].

Mm. 121–122. Drill the *arpeggio* leading to the Recapitulation.

M. 125. Continue the pedal until beat 2.

M. 128. A pedal change on each chord.

M. 153. Broaden to the E♮.

M. 161. Either pedal each left-hand octave or use no pedal.

M. 162. Bring out the lower line.

M. 164. Continue bringing out the lower line. And color the C♮.

M. 179. Begin with only one *forte*. Use the second finger to lead to the left-hand octave.

Mm. 182–184. *Crescendo* and push forward.

Mm. 184–185. Broaden; have a strong attack for each cadence chord.

Mm. 185–186. Push forward again.

Mm. 187–188. Broaden and accent each chord.

Mm. 193–194. Maintain an even tempo. No rushing.

Mm. 197–198. *Diminuendo.* Each chord is an "out."

Mvt. 2. Andante con espressione

Mm. 1–8. These are four-measure phrases.

M. 5. Shape the two-note gestures as "in-out."

Mm. 7–8. Left hand: play *legato* F♯s [play within the escapement].

M. 13. Shape to the E♭ in m. 14.

M. 19. The right hand is all "up" arms.

M. 20. Intense upper part. No silence following this measure. Try for as much contrast between *piano* and *pianissimo* as one would between *forte* and *piano*.

M. 28. Play the first two B♭s with the left hand.

M. 31. Pedal each left-hand octave.

M. 33. "Up" chords in the right hand.

M. 36. No silence following this measure.

M. 37. Deep sonority for the left-hand melody [D-E-F♮-C♯].

M. 38. Then the left hand plays "away."

M. 43. Keep it moving to the downbeat of m. 44.

M. 44. The right hand plays the F♯.

M. 46. *Con moto.*

M. 50. *Legato* top part. Shape the measure.

M. 56. The left hand prepares the low grace notes as a "down." Then plays the chord as an "up."

M. 58. Shape the motive.

M. 66. Full of pedal. Not too short on the chords.

M. 68. Shape the measure dynamically and with momentum.

M. 74. Hear beats 1 and 3 resolving.

M. 84. The accented chords are resolutions.

M. 86. Play the G♮ full of color.

Mvt. 3. Scherzo: Allegro

Shape four-measure phrases.

M. 1. Suspend the weight. Play very lightly.

M. 5. Touch the pedal.

M. 8. End *fortissimo.*

M. 19. No *ritard.*

Mm. 20–21. Each is *pizzicato.*

M. 22. A little more weight in the left-hand melody.

M. 25. Be careful with the *legato* slur.

M. 31. Start the measure still in *piano.*

M. 37. Color the B major key.

M. 42. *Crescendo.* Catch the bass As with the *sostenuto* pedal until the return in m. 48.

M. 59. An echo. Slightly slower.

M. 63. Still a richness to the tone.

M. 77, 78. Touch the pedal.

Mm. 82, 84. Take time to prepare the chord.

M. 87. Think a tiny break after beat 2 to prepare the right-hand F♯ octave.

M. 95. Prepare before the right-hand A♮ octave.

Mm. 105–106. Touch the pedal each half measure.

Mvt. 4. Finale

M. 1. More left-hand melody for richness.

M. 7. Think a *fermata* over the trill. Take the first four notes of the scale with the left hand. Every note in the scale must be heard evenly.

M. 15. Play the first five notes of the scale with the left hand.

M. 16. Close the passage with a *diminuendo* to the D.

M. 21. Close the trill with an F♯ -G♯ before the B♮ .

M. 22. [Pressler plays an E♮ on the last triplet.]

M. 23. Maintain the tempo with the left-hand eighths.

M. 26. Shape the B♯ -B-A♯ .

M. 28. Pedal each beat.

M. 41. Direction to the *forte* of m. 42.

Mm. 55–56. Very fast graces. Stay steady, not faster.

M. 71. Phrase the left hand to the low note using the thumb each time.

Mm. 76–77. *Secco* left hand.

M. 79. *Decrescendo.* Then *forte.*

M. 80. Right hand: have a close thumb for B-C♮ -B.

Mm. 88–89. More pedal as the *crescendo* begins.

M. 97. The left hand must hold the keys on the last Gs.

M. 107. A slower *arpeggio* [the F$\sharp^7$ chord] for color.

M. 111 (after 2nd ending). Play the B major chord with a strong accent in each hand.

M. 145. Pull the chord in the right hand [beat 2], emphasizing the syncopation.

Mm 164–165. Accent the left-hand chord on the second beat of each measure.

M. 166. Pull the chord [beat 2] in the left hand.

M. 169. A clean break.

Mm. 175–177. Left hand: use 1–2 for each slur.

M. 180. Close the slur as everywhere else.

Mm. 181–182. Quieter than mm. 179–180.

Mm. 185–186. *Pesante,* but no accents.

M. 194. Maintain the meter. Therefore, pulse the left-hand D$\sharp$s.

M. 195. Broaden into m. 196.

M. 197. Use the *sostenuto* pedal for the C$\sharp$ octave until m. 204.

M. 225. More short pedals [beats 1 and 3].

Mm. 258–260. Make the left-hand theme clear.

M. 267. Count, in order to *ritard* evenly.

M. 270. Play the left-hand B-D$\sharp$ after the octave as a dotted quarter.

M. 272. Emphasize the low F$\sharp$ as the last note of the theme.

M. 280. Play the right hand as a solid chord.

PIANO TRIO IN B MAJOR, OP. 8

Mvt. 1. Allegro con brio

M. 1. Prepare mentally. You have to know exactly the sound you want to produce. The hands must be ready.

M. 4. Come down [*decrescendo*] for the cello entrance, then be under the cello.

M. 9. Lean into beat 2.

M. 14. Cello, come down from F$\sharp$ to B.

M. 16. Cello, come down from G$\sharp$ to B.

M. 28. The last F$\sharp$ is a pick-up to the next measure.

M. 29. More sound, but not faster.

M. 35. Lead with beat 4 to the downbeat.

M. 51. It doesn't have a feeling that you have arrived. First of all, you have to rehearse it; and secondly, you have to rehearse it; and thirdly, you have to rehearse it. But after all the rehearsing is done, then you have to really play it with all your imagination and awareness.

M. 56. Piano, *decrescendo* with the cello.

Mm. 68–69. The piano is a continuation of the other instruments. Listen to the last note of each triplet and don't let there be a hole between the strings and the piano.

M. 72. Cello, finish it [on beat 3], but don't take time. Show that there's a change of direction.

M. 74. Violin, don't you have a *staccato* over that B♭? You have to honor it somehow, but you dishonor it.

M. 75. Without that chord, their notes don't mean a thing. You play it so unimportant, so meaningless.

M. 77. Not slow.

M. 87. Piano, come down.

M. 91. The C♯ resolves to the B♯.

M. 121. No waiting for the chord, just play it so that out of B major comes G major. You go from a B top note to a G [m. 123] and to an E [m. 125].

M. 127. Loud, but only one *forte*.

M. 135. This, of course, is the climax.

M. 137. Same tempo. Cello, you're playing clean and you're playing well, but I can't identify with your playing. More intensity.

M. 153. Not *forte*.

M. 176. Beat 4, not so loud. The violin has the melody.

Mm. 176–179. Violin, would you play G♯-B the same as F♯-A and E-G♯? Then, piano, whatever he does, you have to play that way, too.

M. 195. It sounds so spastic, so jagged.

M. 214. Finish. Then begin beat 4 with a different sound.

M. 252. More left hand.

M. 254. *Tranquillo,* cello. It is slower; you did that. But it is also a kind of summation, so it is not a kind of *vibrato* that wakes up. It is a kind of *vibrato* that goes to bed, yes? It's a kind of closing, a kind of summing it up after you have told the story. Piano, he needs to play off of something. He must hear your left hand. And the left hand, of course, needs the right hand.

M. 260. Cello, find time within the beat to finish the phrase. That was better, but you gave a wrong accent.

M. 262. When the violin plays that F♯ [downbeat], the piano must play a different color on that chord. It's better, but it's still not good. Why is it not yet good? Because you just play it and you say, "It's not important. It's okay." It's like when you drive through the country and you see a restaurant that says, "Come in just for food. It's quick. It's horrible, but it's just food." But the food that Brahms serves is for people whose taste buds are the most developed.

M. 264. Brahms writes a swell in the piano part. It's not possible, but you can feel it.

Mm. 264–267. You have an F♯, an E, a D♯, a C♯. It's a composed *diminuendo,* but he also asks for one.

M. 268. That's a *subito pianissimo* following a little *crescendo.*

M. 274. Cello, I would like you to slide the last two notes. It is a *diminuendo* without accenting the last note. On the contrary, the last note should disappear. Basically, you should not play a *ritard.* You relax.

Mvt. 2. Scherzo

M. 4. Cello, go away on the last note. Piano, it is lighter. You take over from the cello. Answer in the same character.

M. 7. Piano, the left hand goes to the center of the phrase, then away.

M. 9. The first one is too loud. You are entitled to a little swell, but no heavy accents. And actually, the part you should listen to inside you is the left hand.

M. 17. Here you play second voice under the strings. And play 2-1.

M. 21. Violin, when you have the G♯, it is less than the A.

M. 24. Piano, on the last C♯ you play an octave in the left hand.

M. 25. Very light, very *legato.* It's always two bars together, the right hand followed by the left hand. Each chord gets a pedal, but be sure that the low notes are clear.

M. 26. Play the C♯-A♯-G with the right hand.

Mm. 29–32. Divide the *arpeggio* into two hands [second ending]. The left hand takes the last three notes each time.

M. 32 (first ending). It's a question mark, yes?

Mm. 34–35. Change the foot so that it clears up.

Mm. 36–44. Piano, the left hand is always a trumpet, yes?

M. 44. Finish on the downbeat. In the left hand the wrist plays one motion but gets two notes.

M. 48. Not a long note; don't sit on the downbeat.

M. 60. No pedal; there are rests.

M. 64. Piano, that's such a mess. You're in too much of a hurry getting back up.

M. 67. The G resolves to the F♯ [m. 68].

M. 77. Brahms has a pedal there, four bars, more or less.

M. 99. Piano, too loud. The strings are above you.

M. 103. For once play an F♯ instead of the E♯, so you see the F♯ is very special. Obviously it was done with great deliberation to get that feeling of suspense, of something that somehow asks us to be afraid for a second.

M. 124. Finish the phrase.

Mm. 129–132. That's so lame, like a lame duck because of 5-5-5-5. Practice the right hand alone and change the fingers.

M. 132. Here the violin finishes very softly, so the piano has to play softer still, yes?

M. 136. Close it.

M. 137. Can you play *piano* in the right hand and *pianissimo* in the left hand?

M. 138. Play the octaves *molto legato*. The C♯ dies down and the A [beat 2] starts where the C♯ has come down to.

M. 145. Light, light.

Mm. 152–153. Hear the difference between the major and the minor.

M. 155. Be conscious of major going to minor in the left hand.

M. 159. A maximum of *piano*. If he had wanted you to build up to something, he would not have had the strings come in *piano* [163]. Practice so that it gets lighter than that. Not fast.

M. 165. That chord, feel that your body becomes a sounding board. Is that as nice as you can play that? I hope not! This is a waltz by Brahms, and it shows that he lived in Vienna, the charm. And the left hand stays steady [Pressler sings the melody while tapping]. You heard this [the tapping]. With all the freedom I was singing, this stays steady.

M. 170. Going up takes a hair of time longer than you're doing.

M. 173. Don't hit the downbeat. Do you see where he starts the *crescendo*? That would be a good idea.

M. 178. Piano, they are not *staccato*. Very little space between the notes. Use some pedal. Not slower. The strings can't connect to you and everybody goes to sleep.

M. 180. Strings, you have to respond to whatever she does. If she slows down, you must catch up the time.

M. 181. Strings, it must be beautiful.

M. 197. Piano, change the fingers in the left hand.

M. 202. Brahms gives you a *decrescendo* on the higher note. It's exceptionally beautiful because the other way is ordinary. But this is special.

Mm. 203–204. The right hand sustains and gives us the illusion that you are still pedaling.

M. 210. Now you need to spread the wings. If you look at the violin part, you see he is going all the way to *forte*. So he needs time, and you need time. The piano part must match and become one with the violin part, yes? Can you make a *legato* there [on the downbeat]? I play fifth finger, and I go to the second finger just at the last second. Stretch out and make a curve with your arm there.

M. 212. These three dots under a slur—it talks in there. Then you go down and you make that last swell [downbeat, m. 214].

M. 215. Here you give the tune to the cello. Let the cello be above you, yes?

M. 217. But you play the chord [downbeat] so perfunctory. You play it, but you're only interested in getting down there for the bass notes.

M. 219. The left hand is a tympani.

M. 227. You have to pedal in such a way that the chords in the left hand don't disappear. All these chords are long chords. You have to be a virtuoso with your foot. You have to pedal it so that you dry it a little bit and we can hear those tympani going, yes?

Mm. 241–244. Make a line out of it. You play one measure at a time. You have to connect it with your hand, so use 5-3 or 5-4.

M. 243. You leave that to the cello. That high note is hazardous. And if he hits it clean, he gets complimented. And if he doesn't hit it clean, you play loud and you get the compliment, yes?

M. 259. That is the last note of the phrase. Close it.

M. 434. That E is a continuation of what just happened in the strings.

Mm. 439–445. The pedal is all the way until Brahms gives you the change of the pedal, even through the rests. Make a *decrescendo,* not a *crescendo.* The arm is too heavy. A light arm floating over the keys.

Mm. 446–448. I take only the first note in the left hand and then I play everything else in the right hand. And why does it get louder when it goes up? Play very close to the keys, very close.

It's not Mendelssohn. Mendelssohn's are wine-drinking Alps, or champagne. These are heavier Alps, beer-drinking Alps. These are German with potatoes and sausages, but they have to be as light as they can. It's fantastically composed.

Mvt. 3. Adagio

It is soft, illuminating, like a prayer, like a church. I think you can hear him talk to himself. It's an innocence, as close as one can come to an audience. The middle section is more alive where the cello has that marvelous solo. And at the return, the piano is, so to speak, improvising and the strings have the melody.

M. 1. *Pianissimo* and loose arm. That's too slow and has no beat. The two quarter notes go to the next measure with a very slight *crescendo.*

M. 4. Strings, that's so loud and too much *vibrato.*

M. 8. Help it to move. The beats continue. They don't stop.

M. 13. You play with no control of your arm. Prepare the arm, and the weight goes right into the key.

M. 15. You must hear the E. It must ring. Then it resolves to the D♯ [m. 16].

M. 16. Violin, I would like that the eighth notes have more meaning. With you, they're just a bridge to the next note.

M. 20. Piano, that's too loud. You must take over from what they do.

Mm. 23–24. I want more sound. Emotionally, I want more.

M. 26. Strings, that's too much *vibrato*! As small as possible. Very beautiful. Piano, come down. Each chord must relate to the one before it. And very *legato*.

M. 29. Here it's the cello. And here it's the violin [m. 30]. And here it's the piano [m. 31]. But not loud, just present.

M. 33. The left hand must support.

M. 42. Now the cello goes all the way to the top.

M. 43. Close it [beat 3]. There's no hitting. Can you lean into the piano so that you don't hit [beat 4]?

M. 48. Piano, what are you waiting for? There's no hole there.

M. 54. Piano, the right hand is too loud. The solo is in the violin. You just have an accompaniment.

M. 62. Cello, they play off of your downbeat.

M. 67. Piano, resolve to beat 2. And don't hit the downbeat.

M. 69. You have to play *legato*. It's not just that he has the slur, but he also uses the word. And how do we play *legato*? You have to phrase it. It has to be going somewhere.

M. 71. That finishes on the downbeat.

Mm. 79–80. There's no rhythm in you. Even when you don't play the eighths, you must feel them. Your heart should beat those eighths.

M. 90. Don't separate so much. There's a slur over the dots.

M. 93. Piano, let me hear the high B.

M. 95. Hear the cello A.

M. 96. Hear the violin E.

M. 97. Now hear the piano chord.

M. 98. A resolution on the B major chord.

Mvt. 4. Allegro

M. 1. Pedal is marked, but you should use very little.

M. 3. Cello, the E♯ is less than the G [m. 2].

M. 9. Piano, see how Brahms holds the left hand? He creates a sort of pedal.

M. 15. Can we be a little bit more religious and do what he asks for? It's not that you play it too loudly, but you play it in sunlight. It should be darker.

Mm. 18–21. Piano, it sounds so *staccato,* like "Chopsticks." Play it *pianissimo* with some pedal, and catch the left hand in the pedal. Each measure descends. Violin, not so ringing. Have more air in the sound. And piano, you never play the last triplet of the bar. Which sin is bigger? If it's too loud or if it's not played at all? For both you go to hell. I mean, you certainly won't be invited to where Brahms is. No, you will be only invited to where the players are who don't play him well, yes? So there is no excuse to say, "I don't want to be too loud." Of course, you don't want to play too loud, but not playing the notes is not better.

M. 45. The *ritardando* cannot always be the same. The piano has to follow the strings, and it depends on how the phrase goes.

M. 46. With some pedal. It's the same mood.

M. 64. Have a feeling of *Appassionato.* Cello, Greenhouse plays it all with up bows.

M. 87. Strings, more of a break after the first beat.

M. 101. Resolve it. The F♯ goes to G.

M. 106. No, it doesn't *crescendo.* Just the contrary. It's obvious, wouldn't you agree?

M. 112. It's one instrument divided into two.

M. 129. It's *pianissimo* and *sotto voce.* My God, how far can this man go? All the way!

M. 142. Yes, it's a syncopation, but you must still play it in a three.

Mm. 151–152. Not faster.

M. 184. Play the last octave with the right hand.

M. 199. Play that A♮ [the sixth note] with the right hand.

M. 205. *Con passione.*

M. 241. Cello, play that D with a little accent.

M. 242. Hold the pedal all the way until the next bass note [m. 246].

Mm. 253, 261. Play these first three notes with the left hand.

M. 263. It's only *mezzo forte.* There's your *forte* half an hour later [m. 266].

Mm. 263, 265. Play the sixth note with the left hand.

M. 304. Start less.

M. 309. Hold back. Broaden. And then *a tempo* [m. 310].

Mm. 319–320. Cadence in the left hand. We need that F♯ .

NINETEEN

FRÉDÉRIC CHOPIN

I always loved how Chopin was so personified by the touch of Rubinstein, how he entered the key fully and deeply with such beautiful tone and the piano just soared. And I will always remember studying Chopin with Vengerova because she showed that very beautifully. I love the way that the harmonies are often very original, like in the *Fantasie-Polonaise* and the marvelous way in which the harmony supports a melody. I was in Warsaw and I passed by the church where Chopin's heart is, and I passed by it a few times because, after all, he's a composer who touches all of our hearts and who has given us some of the most beautiful things that are written for the piano. And there is no other composer for whom the piano opens up in the way it does for Chopin.

SONATA NO. 3 IN B MINOR, OP. 58

Mvt. 1. Allegro maestoso

M. 1. A daring descent to the F♯. *Crescendo* the chords to m. 2. Left-hand *legato*.

M. 2. Listen to the rests. Start the chords *piano* and pedal each one.

Mm. 3–4. Continue the *crescendo* until m. 4. Accent the chord on beat 3.

M. 5. *Crescendo.*

Mm. 6–8. Continue the *crescendo* to the *forzando*.

M. 8. Have a small break after the *forzando*. Then an extreme contrast. Think *pianissimo*.

M. 9. The B is gentle.

M. 12. Another start following the rest. Play the Es as a right-hand octave.

M. 13. *Diminuendo* to beat 3. Play the F♮s as a right-hand octave.

M. 17. Majestic. Not harsh.

M. 18. *Decrescendo* before the *sforzando* of m. 19.

M. 19. Delay the *sforzando* chord. Play the F♯ with the left hand.

M. 21. Resolve to beat 4.

M. 22. Each beat resolves [D to C♯, etc.] within the *crescendo*.

M. 23. Play the first chord sweetly. Then sing the eighth notes.

Mm. 23–24, 25–26, 27–28. Each phrase *diminuendos.*

M. 28. A slight *ritardando.*

M. 29. Start *mezzo forte.* Then *crescendo* to the top of the line.

M. 30. *Decrescendo* as the line descends.

M. 31. Begin less with a gradual *crescendo.*

M. 33. More *orgel* point [the A].

M. 38. Lean into the notes with more weight as the line ascends.

M. 44. The A resolves to the G. One pedal for the entire measure. Take the last G with the right hand.

M. 54. Arm weight in the high C♯.

M. 55. The bass C♯ cadences to the F♯ of m. 56.

M. 57. Not suddenly faster. The left hand phrases from each fourth sixteenth note.

M. 61. Lean in with the arm. Rich and juicy! Not too slow. Keep it flowing.

M. 63. Richer. Juicier.

M. 65. *Sforzando* on the downbeat.

M. 66. *Grazioso.* Shape the top line's three-note figure F♯ -F♯ -E, etc., resolving to the third note.

M. 69. Not fast. Don't rush.

M. 73. Rich tone as the sixths begin.

M. 76. Tenderly. Evenly-flowing.

M. 84. Hear the D *orgel* point. *Con passione.*

M. 87. Resolve the A to G♯.

M. 90. Resolve the D to C♯, then to the B, then to the A.

M. 92. Accent the left hand's second C♯.

M. 96. Not too fast.

M. 99. Hear the drama of the octaves.

M. 100. Take beat three with the right hand.

M. 104. Play the final E with the right hand.

M. 105. Sing the left-hand C octave.

M. 108. Start again after beat 2. Play the line *legato* with less bite to the sound.

M. 112. Play the E♭ and D♭ with the right hand.

M. 114. Broaden going into m. 115.

M. 115. Play the sixteenth notes not so hurried.

M. 116. Begin the phrase *piano.*

Mm. 117–118. *Crescendo* the line from the D♭ up to the B♭.

M. 121. The left-hand melody is clear, warm, *legato.*

M. 122. The left hand resolves to the B♭ [in m. 123] with a *decrescendo*.

M. 126. Smooth repeated A♭s. Very close to the key.

M. 131. Resolve the initial F♮ to the E♮ .

M. 132. Resolve the B♯ to the C♯ of m. 133.

M. 133. Resolve the right-hand E♮ to the D♯ .

M. 135. Grand.

M. 140. *Dimenuendo* the F♯ to G♯ and A♯ .

Mm. 146–147. *Decrescendo* all the way to the downbeat of m. 149.

Mm. 152–153. Hear the left-hand G♯ -A♮ -A♯ .

M. 157. *Diminuendo* the right hand from the D♯ .

M. 164. The left-hand sixteenth notes are only a murmur.

M. 171. Play the right hand smoothly.

M. 174. Play with charm.

M. 179. Play the third sixteenth note with the left hand.

M. 180. *Diminuendo* each group of two beats.

M. 189. Beats 3 and 4, vibrate the pedal. Shimmer the sound.

M. 192. Play the right-hand line passionately.

M. 196. Start a *crescendo* that continues until the last measure.

Mvt. 2. Scherzo: Molto vivace

M. 1. Hear the turns within the passage. Use these to shape the phrase.

M. 8. *Diminuendo* to the bottom of the line.

M. 17. Think minor for this phrase. Sad.

M. 31. *Diminuendo* as the line descends.

M. 58. "Out" on the chord. And let the arm fly.

M. 61. *Crescendo* from the D♯ to the E.

M. 66. *Crescendo* from the G♯ to the B.

Mm. 77–80. Begin the sequence D♯ -E-B.

Mm. 81–84. This is the second statement.

M. 85. This is the third statement.

M. 93. This time as if from far away.

M. 101. A horn call.

Mm. 103–108. This phrase is like memories. Spooky.

M. 109. Suddenly hopeful.

M. 125. The sunrise.

M. 145. Float the arm; no accents.

M. 154. Go to sleep.

M. 157. The wind blows. Shape each two-measure group.

M. 186. Accent the left-hand chord.

M. 187. *Diminuendo* to the G major in m. 188.

Mvt. 3. Largo

Mm. 1–2. *Crescendo* the line. Go to the second note of each slur [the long note].

M. 4. No left pedal for this theme.

M. 11. Play the sixteenth notes *liberamente*.

M. 12. Pull back as the B resolves to the A♯.

M. 13. Push the phrase forward.

M. 17. Play the right hand as a duet.

M 29. Play the line with wrist rotation. Impressionistic.

M. 35. Resolve the A♯ to the G♯ of m. 36.

M. 46. Sing the left-hand line.

M. 67. Play with generous sonority.

M. 69. A relaxed cadence.

M. 88. Play the line without accents.

M. 89. A slight break before the D♯s.

M. 96. Broaden into the downbeat of m. 97.

M. 110. A color change on the E, but not a *diminuendo*.

M. 116. Resolve the G♯ to F♯. Begin a *crescendo* on the last beat.

M. 117. Broaden before m. 118.

Mvt. 4. Presto, non tanto

M. 1. Extroverted. A *presto* in one.

M. 8. Each chord with an accent.

M. 9 and following. Restless. Begin *pianissimo*. The left hand is not accented; it makes circles.

M. 15. Don't accent the right-hand chords.

M. 19. *Decrescendo.*

M. 20. *Crescendo* from the F♯ to the D.

M. 22. Resolve the inner line E to the D.

Mm. 25–26. Play the line smoothly without accents.

Mm. 28–51. The left hand makes circles. The right hand as smoothly as possible. No galloping horses!

M. 37. *Decrescendo* beat 1 to beat 2.

M. 41. Maintain a loose arm.

M. 44. Climactic. Begin a gradual *decrescendo.*

Mm. 48–52. Bring out the inner chromatic line descending from F♯ to B.

M. 52. The two chords are "out-in."

Mm. 52–54. Grandiose with rich sonority.

Mm. 54–56. The left-hand melody answers the previous *forte* statement.

M. 60. With presence. *Legato.*

Mm. 64–66. Think the left-hand resolutions.

Mm. 74–75. *Decrescendo.*

M. 100. Begin *mezzo forte.*

Mm. 111–113. Answer the previous phrase. Don't bark.

Mm. 117–118. A strong left hand.

M. 126. Don't hit the downbeat.

M. 143. The E♭ major is a surprise chord after the B⁷.

M. 172. Whistle over the top.

M. 183. Hear the counterpoint of the bass line in relation to the right hand.

M. 187. Begin *piano.*

M. 191. Don't slam the *sforzando* chord.

Mm. 207–210. Grander but not harsh.

M. 214. Take the A♯ and D with the right hand.

M. 226. Play as if an intense whisper.

Mm. 238–240. Shape the inner phrases of the line [D-F♯ -D♯ -G-E, B-D♮ -B-E-C♯].

M. 242. Play the downbeat with a slight *fermata.*

M. 250. Start the C♯ as a *subito piano.* Lean into the thumb to project the line.

M. 253. Broaden going into the *fortissimo.*

M. 254. Play the sixteenths clean and articulate.

M. 262. Start. Begin *mezzo piano.* Follow the bass line.

M. 273. Play the last eighth as the last note of the phrase. Not accented.

Mm. 277–280. Each F♯ -B is a *diminuendo* two-note phrase.

Mm. 282–286. *Crescendo* to the last chord.

NOCTURNE IN E MAJOR, OP. 62, NO. 2

This is a very beautiful and unusual piece for E major. Be aware of the three layers: right-hand melody (use flatter fingers for rich sonority), the left-hand bass line, and very quiet but colorful chords. There is great optimism in the upward motion of the melody and great melancholy in the beauty of the chords Chopin has chosen. One must be very sensitive to the way in which every note of the right hand balances with the left hand, being aware of the distance between the hands as well as function of the right-hand notes in relation to the chords.

Play the left hand alone, as if that's all Chopin had given us, listening to the relationship between the bass line and the chords. One should also practice the bass and tenor lines with two hands.

M. 1. Begin with the pedal down for full sonority of overtones. The up-beat B is rich, but not allowing the full weight of the arm. The A starts lighter with the wrist rotating in the direction of the melody [A-B-D♯-E-C♯-B]. The left-hand C♯ resolves to the B. Then the fourth-beat chord is very light.

M. 2. Play the right hand's F♯ with an upward motion of the wrist. The left-hand B [beat 4] leads to the C♯ of m. 3.

M. 3. Hear the E as part of the C♯ minor chord. Play the F♯ very lightly, matching the point to which the E has decayed. Shape this four-measure phrase with a sense of momentum and dynamic coloring.

M. 6. Sneak the A♯ in with a light, relaxed arm.

M. 8. Match the D♯s. The right hand can help on beat 4 by playing the A.

M. 9. The *dolce* colors the variation of the phrase. Slower as the line reaches upward and then drift faster as the notes descend.

M. 12. Color the G♮.

M. 15. Use fingers 4–3 for the G♯s; not hard.

Mm. 15–16. Relate the four left-hand chords.

M. 17. Hear the color changes within this measure. Color the D♮ and the A♮.

Mm. 17–21. The chromaticism builds the intensity.

M. 22. Lean into the A. Use fingers 2–3 for the repeated D♯s.

M. 23. Catch the right-hand E in the pedal. An expressive trill in the right hand.

M. 24. Use the left-hand line C♯-B to pace the return of the theme.

M. 25. A *pianissimo* return. The arm follows the fingers in the *leggiero* passage.

M. 27. Color the deceptive cadence; take time.

M. 29. The C♯ begins leading us back. Sneak in with the D♯-E-E♯. *Crescendo;* don't accent individual notes.

M. 31. Color the top note [G♯]. Swell the trill.

M. 32. Pull back before the downbeat. The left hand comes out of the darkness, never notey, always shaped. Magical, soothing; use flatter fingers.

M. 33. Lean into the left-hand D♯ dissonance and resolve to the C♯.

M. 37. Lean into the downbeat.

M. 38. Resolve on beat one, then push forward, pulling back before the downbeat of m. 39.

M. 40. Three layers begin, then four layers in m. 43. Point out each entrance as they occur. Practice each hand's part with two hands.

M. 47. Take time into the downbeat.

M. 48. The left-hand chromatic line leads to the restatement in C major.

M. 49. *Agitato* again. A bigger statement than before, a third higher.

M. 51. Lean into the D [beat 4].

M. 55. Descend through the repetitions to m. 56.

M. 57. Linger over the top A; it's a magical moment.

M. 58. The tune reemerges, but tinged with melancholy because of the B bass note.

M. 59. Color the D major chord. Taste the difference; it's a "heart" moment.

M. 65. Biggest point of the piece with climactic G♯ -F♯ -F♯ , as high as m. 60 is low, but it falls away quickly.

M. 71. Point out the differences from the first statement: the full chord [m. 71], the grace note [m. 73], and adding more voices [m. 74].

M. 78. Cadence on the E [beat 2], then no accents to the top.

Mm. 79–80. Hear three different Bs.

M. 80. No accent on beat 4; it leads to the downbeat of m. 81.

M. 81. Use fingers 3–5 on the final Es with a slow release of hands and pedals.

TWENTY

Claude Debussy

What makes Debussy unique is his world of sound, the contours, [and] the magic of light in music that he has from time to time. You really see a moon. You really can feel it, in a French way. To me, it always has some perfume in it. After all, the country that made perfume famous, yes? It is Debussy that has this wonderful, original way of sounding that you smell it and feel it and taste it. Yes, you taste it. Debussy lives by shadows. There is little light and lots of shadows. When I am in Paris and I sit there in a café, I really feel he's part of that, or at least he made that part of it for me, yes? I can't think French without having a note of Debussy in my ear. And it is something that touches you on one side of your emotional *scala*. After all, we do all have a feeling *scala*, and you have a point where it touches your scale of feeling. And you are conscious of what this chord does to you. You really can taste the chord.

A thousand things come to mind to describe the physical mechanism to play Debussy. The first thing is the touch, the ability to play from one *pianissimo* down, yes? It is not so much to play up. It is to play down. And the mastery of the pedal in a way that demands very much more than the clear-cut pedal that you have in classical music. You actually have to make an exercise so that your foot doesn't get tired, so that you learn to do, let's say eighths, then you do sixteenths, and triplets, then thirty-seconds, slight, very slight. And in the end you know you can do it when you feel it in your toes. Somehow it comes through your shoes, yes? That you feel how the pedal slightly moves, but very slightly. And you hear it, you feel it, and it satisfies something when you play and therefore can continue playing and keeping that mood, not going out of that mood.

PRÉLUDE, "LES COLLINES D'ANACAPRI," BOOK 1, NO. 5

This is an enchanting piece, painting a picture of the beautiful island of Capri.

Mm. 1–2. Distant bells. Use a very light brush stroke of the alternating hands.

Mm. 3–4. The tune is heard in the distance. Use a pulling away motion of the fingers, the left hand helping with the E.

M. 4. The left-hand chord is less active and less sharp than the right hand.

Mm. 7–9. The tune is coming closer.

M. 11. The wrist goes "down-up" on the two-note slur figure. The left hand is within the key, undulating.

M. 14. Enjoy the arrival notes of the tune, the C♯ [m. 14] and A♯ [m. 15]. Who could imagine a more lighthearted joyful tune?

M. 21. Inversion. The right hand has the *vibrato*. The left hand has fragments of the tune.

M. 24. A chromatic melody begins, leading to m. 31. A popular tune is presented in left-hand octaves. Pedaled, but *non-legato*.

M. 49. Orchestrate, like a combo; hear the clarinet and string bass. Shifting rhythms, with each line voiced independently.

M. 74. Practice the left hand taking over the right-hand line. It should sound like one hand.

M. 81. The wrist applies full arm weight into each melody note.

Mm. 82–83. Two pedals per measure.

M. 92. One big *crescendo*. Create swirling circles of sound.

Mm. 94–95. Like a harp.

M. 95. Alternate hands for better, easier sound [L-R-L-R-L].

PRÉLUDE, "FEUX D'ARTIFICE," BOOK 2, NO. 12

The swirling patterns are played principally with finger motions, using slight wrist rotation to make circles out of the pattern. Suppleness of the hand is needed along with firm but gentle fingers. Practice at a slower tempo to feel individual finger security and independence, and then allow the hands and wrist to move to the left and right.

M. 2. Finger redistribution in beat 4 of mm. 2–5, 7, 9, and 11–14.

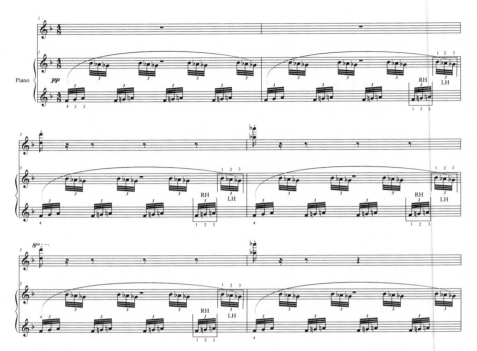

Ex. 20.1. m. 1–6

M. 3. Touches of pedal on each right hand octave, which is played with a slight arm rotation [elbow releasing to the right], providing a light, clear attack to each octave.

M. 17. *Crescendo* through the *glissando*. Use fingers 2-3-4 braced.

M. 18. A "down-up" motion.

M. 19. An "up."

M. 20. Practice finger drills. Find left-hand fingers, either 3-2 or 2-1, that balance best between the two hands. Drill the hands blocked together. Tilt the hands slightly toward the right. Train the body to remember stances, direction, and the attitude of being ready to move.

M. 25. Begin with an accent.

M. 30. At the top of the run, practice D♯-F♯-E♮-D♮-C♮ for security and control. Use a slight arm accent on the top note to signal the change of direction.

M. 32. Drop into each top right-hand note. Hear three beats, not six.

M. 36. Use arm weight in the right hand.

M. 44. Left hand, *decrescendo*. Right hand, clear.

M. 48. Each beat is less.

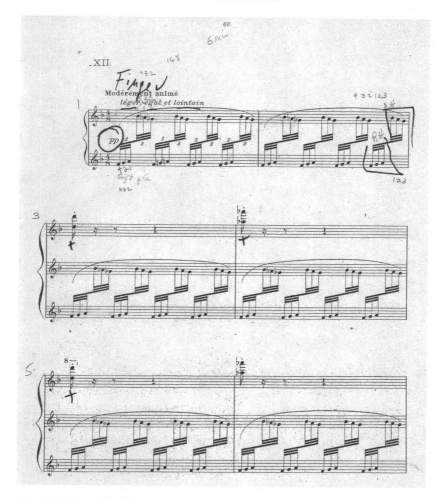

Fig. 20.1. Feux d'artifice

M. 53. An arm strike with braced fingers.

M. 57. Hear the three layers: the left-hand notes played with arm weight, the top right-hand notes played with the arm, and the sixty-fourth notes played with a pulling away of the fingers.

M. 61. Prepare the chord and sink into the keys. Voice the top of each chord for color.

M. 63. Use a flatter hand for the black keys.

M. 65. No accent with the E run.

M. 67. Shape the *cadenza*. Begin slower, then push to the end.

M. 79. Gestures. *Crescendo*. Shocking.

M. 81. A very exact *toccata* effect, both ascending and descending.

M. 82. The high Gs are an upward arm motion, hooking the note. A sharp upward attack on the left-hand E.

M. 87. A long pedal with slow pedal release.

M. 89. Play the last three notes with a finger *staccato* and light hand.

M. 91. Smear the grace notes. Not too articulate.

Mm. 91–92. Prepare for the Gs. The arm releases to the right on the downbeat.

M. 94. The inner part is an echo.

Mm. 96–97. The right hand is two "up" motions.

M. 97. Dying away to the end.

M. 98. A slight accent on the last note.

L'ISLE JOYEUSE

M. 1. Start the first trill from no place, as softly and as slowly as you can, as if from far away, with the fingers very close. Develop the trill, and when the *crescendo* is at its maximum, play the descending notes and help yourself with the left hand on the C♮. Release the arm, then start again.

M. 3. Play the three-note motive over the trill as *legato* as possible, like the mating call of a big bird on the island. The two notes are an answer from another bird. The five notes are like a *glissando*. Play these notes in the left hand.

Mm. 4–5. Still less; everything comes down. It doesn't *crescendo* anymore.

M. 6. The *sforzando* is in *piu piano*.

M. 7. Sneak in with the A. This is the first time we know what the key is; it could have been any key. [Pressler plays different chords coming in under the trill.] It's the beginning of the dance. You feel the swing, but it should barely be heard. You could try playing the top E with the right hand.

M. 11. Use the right-hand thumb on the Es because you have to hold the A.

M. 12. The left hand has *pizzicato,* and the top would be horns if it were orchestrated.

M. 14. Have a little pause at the end of the measure.

M. 20. Bring it down. He's coming to a new world.

M. 21. Now stay very quiet. It's like in a very thick fog, as quiet as humanly possible. Keep the left-hand fingers on the keys with very little articulation. A completely different color; lift the arm to remove the weight.

M. 24. Now he's coming closer.

M. 25. At the end of the measure, use the thumb on the lower notes [F♯ - F♮ -E] so that you control the tune. Use fingers 1-4-2, 1-4-2, 1-3-5.

SVIATISLAV RICHTER

Now let me tell you a story. When I heard Richter the first time live was on the Italian Riviera. The Trio was playing in Menton on the French Riviera, and Richter was playing in Italy, right across the border. He was playing a big concert and it was magnificent. The *Symphonic Variations* of Schumann was wonderful, and then he plays Debussy *Images,* Book I. And he comes to "Mouvement" and he comes to [Pressler sings mm. 89–91], and he forgets. And he goes looking and looking. Somehow he got to the end of the piece, and then he played–I don't remember–I think he played Rachmaninoff, something at the end. And of course the audience gave him a very big applause, and then he went to play an encore and he played "Mouvement" again, and he comes to the same place and forgets. And he finished.

I was fortunate; I came with the manager of the concert in Menton who was a friend of Richter. So, after the concert we ate together, and he was dreadfully unhappy. I mean, no matter what you said to him, he was just sitting there. I spoke with him in German, because he spoke only German or Russian, neither English nor French.

This was Friday night and we were playing on Sunday, and he said to us, "Ah, I would love to go to France for the weekend, but with my passport, it is impossible." So, I said, "Why don't you come with us? In the big car, you sit in the back and fall asleep. And when we come to the border and the man says, 'Passport,' we'll show him our passports and we'll say, 'He has the same. Let him sleep." That's exactly what happened. And so, he came across the border.

And then when I said "Goodnight" when he was leaving to go to his hotel–it was 2:00 in the morning or something–I said, "Do you know the Trios by Schumann?" He said, "No." I said, "You will love that. It is exquisite music," which it is. "And if you would honor us with coming to the concert. That would be very special, for me especially, but it would be very special for the Trio." And he did come to the concert, which was for me surprising because he had a shirt on and he had a little cross, which to a Soviet artist seemed not possible actually. But he did, and he came to the concert, and thirty years later I read in his memoirs about the night of that concert. It was not supposed to be published, but he wrote about that night hearing the Trio.

But I do remember hearing him playing "Mouvement" and getting lost at that place; and then [when] he played it the second time, my stomach was in such disarray. I was so worried, and he again forgot. But it shows you only one thing: he suffered. Most of the audience didn't even know it. I suffered because I felt for him, but the rest was so marvelous, so magnificent. It can happen, but it shouldn't happen to a dog.

M. 26. No accents, as if suspended in the air like a cloud.

M. 28. This is a waltz, very dance-like. Hear the contrary motion. Practice only these two parts.

M. 28–29. If you swell these measures, it must be barely perceptible, only known to you. And use the thumb as before.

M. 36. Barely hear it. The left-hand notes are like overtones.

Mm. 40–41. Reverse the dynamics. Go to the G, not the E.

M. 52. The accents should be sharper, much more than the trills.

M. 55. The left-hand chords are *legato* and filled with desire.

M. 66. Hear the B to B♭. The second time is less to prepare for that entrance. Resolve the B♭ to the A [downbeat] in m. 67.

M. 67. It's never loud; it doesn't yell. You have to find the right sound. It's never naked; it always has a veil over it. Practice only the octave melody, and color the thumbs. Then add the quiet chord notes, and you will have a balance between the chord and the melody. After you have learned where all the notes fit, it must sound completely free. It's *molto rubato;* he gives you all the rights. It is an island with no law; you can be dressed or not.

Mm. 73–74. Color this differently. Lush.

Mm. 79–80. Use your body when you play chords in that register so there's weight in the keyboard and you're not hitting.

Mm. 85–86. More body in the right-hand chords.

M. 99. The top E is long, and the bottom one is short. The left hand plays 1–3. [Pressler plays just the melody notes, E-C♯-E-C♭-D-F♯.] This must sound clear like water. Count, play steady, and hear the difference between the E [more] and the C♯ [less].

Mm. 105–106. Contrast these *pianissimo* measures, which should sound immediately like a cloud, with the *piano* measures, which have a little bit more rhythmic energy.

M. 115. These white-key chords are a surprise.

M. 120. Hear the horn [the G].

M. 121. The A♭ descends to the G [m. 123].

M. 123. Do something magical here. These notes are like muted horns.

M. 132. Listen for the A♭. The right hand mustn't be too loud.

M. 141. Let the chord ring.

M. 158. The trill doesn't run; stay exactly in tempo.

M. 159. The pause is very small; it's a *fermata* over nothing.

M. 160. Sharp rhythm here.

M. 166. Come down; you have a long way to go.

Mm. 182–185. Like two harps. Roar by the end of it.

M. 186. Very soft, tiny pulse of sound from nowhere.

M. 196. Start again.

M. 200. Listen for the trumpets; they're still at a distance.

M. 216. Begin a long *crescendo* to m. 220.

Mm. 237, 239. Tympani notes [C-F and F-B♭].

M. 244. Hit that C♯ and go down to a *mezzo forte* before coming up again. That leaves room for the left hand to come out.

M. 252. Again, hit, come down to *mezzo forte* and then go all the way up. Count [1-2-3, 2-2-3, 3-2-3, 1], and be as close to beats 3 and 1 as you can [mm. 254–255]. Practice just the As. Be conscious of the notes you're aiming for.

M. 253. The last gesture is one motive played as quickly as possible.

TWENTY-ONE

JOSEPH HAYDN

Haydn, I think, was the most original of his time, a gigantic figure in music, and is still a very much unexplored treasure, the master of the last movement. No one could write last movements like that; he always has a surprise for you. While the others—Brahms, Schumann, Beethoven included—were struggling with the last movement from the formal point of view, Haydn never did. I'm glad that the Trio learned the forty-three trios and recorded them all.

In Haydn you are very sparse with pedal, although you don't think of the harpsichord when you play him. You think of what he sounds like to you, and of course you often have to adjust to the acoustics of a big hall. What you give when you play Haydn is his character—noble, grand, and more sophisticated than young Beethoven was at that time.

SONATA IN C MAJOR, HOB. XVI:50

Mvt. 1. Allegro

M. 1. A special sound. The theme has inflection. Come down from the C.

M. 9. Left hand *decrescendo* with the first sixteenth notes. Then *crescendo* with the second group.

M. 13. Beat 2 is a start.

M. 14. Intensify the second half of the measure.

M. 15. Sing to the top. Use the left hand to help the thirds, starting on the A.

M. 19. *Decrescendo.*

M. 20. Don't rush.

M. 25. Resolve the G to the F♯ .

Mm. 26–27. *Crescendo* as the line ascends. Hear left hand, right hand, etc.

M. 30. With charm in the left hand.

M. 32. The beginning of the measure is a surprise, as if a variation of the previous. Think the tops of the thirds. The right hand can help the thirds with last C.

M. 42. Play the contrasts with charm.

M. 46. The G major chord is a surprise. Phrase the right-hand D-B-G to the A. Then *crescendo* the left hand.

M. 48. Right hand *crescendo* up the scale.

M. 51. Contrast of dynamics and register.

Mm. 57–59. Bring out each entrance of the canon.

M. 65. Open up with the F-A.

M. 72. *Decrescendo* to the beat 4.

M. 83. A very light left hand.

M. 91. *Decrescendo* to the downbeat of m. 92.

M. 96. *Decrescendo* to the downbeat of m. 97.

Mm. 99–100. *Crescendo* to the *fortissimo* chords.

M. 108. Beat 4 not too fast.

M. 115. Continue the same tempo. Don't rush.

M. 116. The A♭-C diminishes to the G-B♮. Sing the right-hand B♮-D-C-B♭.

Mm. 117–118. Careful pedal on the descending passage.

M. 119. *Crescendo* to beat 4.

Mm. 120–121. The C♯ resolves to the D. The B resolves to the C.

Mm. 126–127. Follow the contour of the phrase dynamically.

M. 128. Restart and *crescendo*.

M. 150. Arm release on each chord.

Mvt. 2. Adagio

M. 1. Follow the contour of the line, whether in left hand or right hand. *Crescendo* when ascending; *decrescendo* when descending.

M. 2. Sing the turn, not too fast.

M. 3. The right-hand line is played with arm weight. Pedal with each left-hand chord.

M. 6. Rich sound for the C♯.

M. 12. *Decrescendo* the first and second beats.

M. 14. Close the phrase.

M. 17. Land on the D. Take time with the trill and decrease to the C.

M. 18. A loose arm, *staccato*. The articulation becomes progressively more *legato* to m. 19.

M. 24. Start the right hand less, then have motion over the stretch.

Mm. 25–26. Less of the inner parts.

M. 32. Divide the passage between the hands. Play five notes in the right hand; then four in the left hand, four in the right hand, and four in the left hand.

Mm. 33–34. Resolve E to the F.

M. 43. Voice the tops of the thirds.

M. 45. The top line is most important.

M. 47. No pedal on the last beat.

M. 51. Close the phrase on beat 2.

M. 59. Treat this flourish as a little *cadenza.* Then *mezzo forte.*

Mm. 60–62. Relax on the F of beat 2. It is a finish each time.

Mvt. 3. Allegro molto

More "offs"! Light-hearted in mood.

M. 1. The left hand is *legato* to m. 3.

M. 4. Don't rush.

Mm. 4–7. Choose whether you want to swell these measures or build to the last note.

M. 10. No *ritardando.* Not sentimental.

M. 11. Not a long *fermata.*

Mm. 71–72. Hear the resolution of the B♮ to C and of the D-F to C-E♮.

M. 89. Push forward to m. 90.

M. 104. "Out" on beat 3.

Mm. 116–119. Voice the tops.

Mm. 134–135. Even eighths.

Mm. 152–155. Swell these measures, with the downbeat of m. 154 being the climax.

M. 159. *A tempo.*

M. 161. Pull back; it's asking a question.

Mm. 165–166. No pause between these measures. Play as a contrast to m. 161.

M. 168. Less than m. 166.

Mm. 170–172. *Crescendo* these measures.

M. 173. Bright and shining. It's a concluding statement.

Mm. 181–182. *Crescendo* to the C major chords.

TWENTY-TWO

FRANZ LISZT

I think Liszt was a grandiose man. He was what you call a showman in the best sense of the word. His emotions were varied and rich. His interests were so great about literature, the *Sonetti del Petrarca* and *Après une lecture de Dante,* looking at the beauty that he saw, *Aux cypress de la Villa d'Este, Années de Pèlerinage.* He became an abbé. Look at the pieces he started to compose, such as *St. François d'Assise.* He was a deeply religious man, although he sometimes lived a sinful life. But he was generous, and you have that in his music. And he elevated the piano to this tremendous height. But he was generous in spirit, receiving Grieg and reading his music and was kind to him; and he taught for free, always for nothing. And of course, because of my training and my upbringing, he played an enormous role in my life. For Busoni, Liszt was the greatest of the masters, and, therefore, Busoni patterned himself after Liszt. Because Liszt was interested in everything, so Busoni was. Kestenberg even wore his hair like Liszt.

Liszt created the songs of Schubert for the piano, not to show himself but to make the songs heard. He transcribed the Beethoven Symphonies. At that time, not everyone knew them. He publicized these pieces; he played them. He's remarkable, absolutely remarkable. He has a great place. He wrote a lot of pieces that are not so good; but at his best—his Sonata, his *Dante,* his *Mephisto Waltz,* his *Etudes*—he's fabulous. He has an important place in the history of the piano, of pianists, of music.

APRÈS UNE LECTURE DU DANTE

Mm. 1–2. Very energetic and bold. Always a sharp attack to the second of the repeated octaves—ta-da! Hold back in the first measure; then push to the bottom of the phrase.

M. 2. Use two or three changes to clear the pedal.

M. 3. Start the line with less arm weight.

IMAGES AND INTERPRETATIONS

STUDENT: Do you want to say anything about the relationship between the *Wanderer Fantasy* and the Liszt Sonata?

PRESSLER: No, we don't have so much time. There is certainly a big relationship. I mean, Schubert, when he wanted to be a virtuoso, tried in the *Wanderer Fantasy,* but it was not one of his most successful pieces. That's the most interesting part. It's a great piece because, with Schubert, what he has to say in the slow movement is magnificent, but the whole piece is not his best.

Liszt here is at his best. I mean, everything that he represents is in that piece: the amorous, the religious, the showman, the influence, the example, the role model, everything is in that piece and is held together, unified. I mean, this piece can have an enormous impact on a musician, not just for an audience. When they hear fast octaves, they're always impressed. They cannot do it, so that is okay with them. But that is not the point. The piece is really a great piece and makes enormous demands, but it takes time, it takes thought. All your good practicing will help, but there is so much more to be found. And so much more variety to be expressed, because he, as you can see, expresses so much.

STUDENT: I wonder if you would just say something about what it would mean to you to interpret a piece. I feel like, between the demands of the composer and the demands of the instrument, then for me to put in more of myself seems to be where I always go wrong.

PRESSLER: No, no. First of all, before you put yourself into it, see whatever his demands are and what you can do with them. You only become personal after you have exhausted your maximum and when you know you have done everything the composer has asked you to do. Then you can say, "Now let me make sense of it, in my way." And then you try to make sense of it. And then you listen to yourself and then you find, "Can I like it? How can anyone else like it if I don't?" So you do have to find a way of liking it, yes? That's difficult. And as I say, this is a piece that can very, very easily seduce you to many wrong things. It can inspire you to many right things. It's a grandiose piece, and we can study to find out if he was influenced by Wagner or if Wagner was influenced by Liszt. What's great in Wagner? We love Wagner. What's great in Liszt? We love him, but in principle, we don't care if he was influenced or not.

STUDENT: When you're learning a piece with such a vast canvas as this or when you're learning a piece with a tiny canvas that has a program to it, do you think it's helpful to study or imagine the programmatic aspects, like the fate, before learning it, or is it better to get the craft and count it right, and so forth?

PRESSLER: That's absolutely the must.

STUDENT: So get that first before you get into the program.

PRESSLER: Absolutely. And then, actually, everybody can have his own program. I have a student who's very religious. He is Greek Orthodox. He travels throughout the country trying to show the salvation of people through that sonata. He shows how the devil was tempting, and he shows many other things. It's wonderful. I listen to it with pleasure. I'm not Greek Orthodox, so I don't think that way; but he thinks that way, and he finds his answers that way. And he comes to these conclusions, and these chords become very meaningful to him; and he comes to that end, and he feels salvation, and people love when he talks about that. And when he plays it, it's lovely. So, he found his way of doing it, and Horowitz found a different way. I don't know what his way was or what stories he told himself, but the story Horowitz tells us is devastating, great, magnificent, controlled, and wondrous, absolutely wondrous.

STUDENT: Would you recommend that the student needs certain literature of this period to stir the imagination after they've learned the piece?

PRESSLER: I will tell you, after he learns the piece and it didn't stir his imagination, don't give him anything. It won't help him! It's like somebody looks up into the moonlight and says, "Isn't that beautiful?" Of course, it is beautiful. You see it, you feel it, but who can explain the beauty? Now, the more you are erudite, the more you know about things, then, of course, the more you see it, the more you recognize it, and the more you put into it. But a great deal comes spontaneously. I mean, G-E-B♭-D, G-E-B♭-C; I don't think that needs to be explained.

STUDENT: I just want to make sure that you're differentiating between the idea of a program and the idea of an image, right? Because very often you use fabulous imagery in order to get a touch, a certain quality of sound. So that's very different from having a program.

PRESSLER: Yes, I'm trying to use some kind of a picture for the student to understand what would explain that particular place. Now, he can visualize the Grand Canyon, or he can see [an image] in Switzerland. I don't know where he sees it or what does it, because I don't know if they told me these things when I studied the Sonata. I mean, when you play music and you do it, there is something in you—or is supposed to be—that starts to awaken certain feelings. If you are aware of what they are and if you can control them, that's wonderful.

But let's say you can't control them. I mean, there were certain places in music when I used to play them, I felt like the bull feels when he sees that red cape. I was rushing every which way. I couldn't help myself. And then I heard myself on tape and I thought, "My God, how ridiculous," and I sought to get a distance. But each time I came to play it, inside there would be that soaring and desire and drive, and then I had to learn to control it. Controlling doesn't mean to suppress it but means to refine it. It means to express emotions in a way that one can live with them. Your emotions have to be in the service of something; and if it is only in your service, you minimize the significance of the piece. Because however big you are, you're quite small next to [the Liszt Sonata]. And imagine how small you are next to Schumann. Even Liszt would acknowledge that. Actually the Sonata is dedicated to Schumann. There couldn't be a greater compliment than that.

M. 5. Sustain the right hand.

Mm. 14–15. Touch pedals on the two chords.

M. 20. Full body weight in these *fortissimo* chords; they have meaning.

M. 28. Pull back slightly as the line descends.

M. 29. Begin *pianissimo* and *crescendo* slightly in m. 31.

M. 34. Delay the As.

M. 47. Begin again with the last sixteenth of the measure.

M. 52. Accent the A downbeat.

M. 64. *Decrescendo* to beat 4 to close the phrase.

M. 66. Start.

M. 76. Clear.

M. 77. Start the octaves. A clear accent on the Ds [beat 3]. Show the meter.

M. 79. Clear accents on the bass notes.

M. 80. Push to m. 81.

M. 81. Push to m. 82.

M. 83. Broaden the tempo on the octaves.

M. 85. "Out," then "in" on the E♯ octaves.

Mm. 88–89. Pull back after the E♯ ; then push forward.

M. 102. Broaden leading into m. 103.

M. 103. Create the sonority with full body weight.

M. 128. Color the chord.

M. 136. Depth of tone, very rich.

M. 140. Push forward.

M. 147. The two-note slurs are sighs.

M. 150. *Sforzando* on the D downbeat.

M. 153. *Crescendo* to the A♭ .

Mm. 154–156. Inflect following the shape of the line. Decrease all the way to the C♯ of m. 157.

M. 167. Sing the left-hand tenor line.

M. 175. Start again.

M. 178. Broaden before the D major chord; then begin a sweep. *Crescendo* all the way to the top, and play the last interval with the right hand.

M. 181. Go forward; don't hold back so much this time.

M. 187. Resolve to m. 188.

M. 202. Save. Don't begin the *agitato* too quickly.

M. 213. Broaden into the *più mosso*.

M. 214. *Sforzando* on the downbeat.

Mm. 231–233. Phrase beats two and three into the downbeat.

M. 235. *Crescendo* to m. 236.

M. 303. Start the octaves *mezzo forte*. Push the tempo each time to the top.

M. 315. Broaden into m. 316.

Mm. 327–328. Push forward.

M. 329. Broaden.

M. 339. Start *mezzo forte*.

M. 341. Come down to *mezzo piano*.

M. 342. Stay close to the key for great control.

M. 352. Start again.

M. 356. Start slowly in *pianissimo*.

Mm. 364–368. Leave room for an overall *crescendo* throughout the phrase.

M. 372. This D major chord is the arrival point.

TWENTY-THREE

WOLFGANG AMADEUS MOZART

Mozart. When we speak his name, the smile immediately comes to the face because he meant so much to everyone. He meant so much to Beethoven, yes? Mozart is heaven on earth, especially when you play his piano concerti. And some of the chamber music, like the Quintet for woodwinds, is as heavenly as that. He is in direct contact with your heart, because his music is supposedly—you have to use quotation marks—"simple."

But if it's so simple, why don't other people write it? Wonderful music. But in this simplicity, he, in two or three notes, expresses his feelings, and his feelings are going direct to your feelings. And he is romantic, in a classic sense. He is brilliant, a virtuoso in a classic sense. He creates for each concerto a new form, which is wonderful when you look at K. 271 or how he created in the very last, K. 595, that sense of resignation.

I'm glad we have a Mozart. I was once asked, "What would you do without Mozart?" And I said, "We could live without Mozart. After all, there's Beethoven and there's Bach and there's Handel and there's Brahms. But without Mozart, we will have to *walk* through life. But with Mozart, we can *fly*."

SONATA IN B-FLAT MAJOR, K. 281

Mvt. 1. Allegro

M. 1. Be sure the trill connects into second beat. Ease out of the trill with a decrease of speed. The line must be full of color. Let the wrist follow the curve of the melody, and add color to the passages.

M. 3. The two chords must relate to what's come before. Full sound on the G and F. Touch each chord with pedal. The thirty-second-note figure must be played with a relaxed hand following the pattern of the notes. Keep the wrist free to move.

M. 7. Strum the chord. The *forte* is not such an extreme contrast with the *piano*. Think emotional change rather than volume. Full arm weight is never used.

M. 14. A slight break before bringing in the ultimate B♭ -D-F-D.

M. 16. Bring each hand to a close with no extra space within the octave leap.

M. 17. Move the phrase forward through the Cs.

M. 20. This measure answers m.18.

Mm. 22–26. Practice the skeleton chord progression through this passage. Not so brittle-sounding.

Mm. 23–25. Use the wrist on beat 4 to synchronize the hands.

M. 29. *Diminuendo* as the line descends.

M. 35. The D is the resolution of the E♭. It must relate; not so short.

M. 35–37. Stroke the left-hand notes.

M. 41. Place the graces on the beat.

Mm. 48, 50, 52. The left-hand starting notes are not so loud. Play the scales with some freedom, rhythmically and dynamically.

M. 68. The second figure is an echo and slightly slower.

M. 69. This figure descends slightly broader and leads back to the return.

M. 109. Close the phrase.

Mvt. 2. Andante amoroso

M. 1. Swing to the downbeat of each measure. Feel the meter.

M. 7. *Diminuendo* to m. 8.

M. 12. Only *mezzo forte*. Press into the right-hand E♭.

Mm. 14–15. The chords are not short.

Mm. 16–20. Hold it together in four-measure groups. Don't take time to breathe between every two measures.

M. 17. Grace notes on the beat.

Mm. 25, 33. These grace notes are played as even sixteenth notes.

M. 27. Think *mezzo forte;* not so loud.

Mm. 45–46. Close the phrase; resolve.

Mm. 47–48. Connect the octave B♭ leap.

Mm. 48, 50, 52. Different B♭s each time, according to what follows.

M. 53. From the key, not harsh.

Mm. 99, 101. *Decrescendo* each measure.

Mvt. 3. Rondeau: Allegro

M. 1. Maintain an even tempo throughout. Relax the arms.

M. 3. *Decrescendo* with the descent of the line.

M. 7. Graces are played on the beat.

Mm. 7–8. Connect the trill to the B♭ with no holes.

M. 17. Close the phrase.

Mm. 39–42. Closing notes for the trill each time.

M. 43. These figures should not all sound the same.

Mm. 52–59. The left hand is smoother, not so *staccato* nor accented. The accents belong only to the right hand.

Mm. 68–69. Voice the outer lines.

M. 70. Roll all the way from the bottom to the top; open the door.

Mm. 75–76. Shape the three-note left-hand figures.

Mm. 113 and 118. Even sixteenth notes, not smears. Lead into the trills easily.

Mm. 157–159. Each measure is colored slightly differently and should sound spontaneous.

Mm. 159–160. Time is needed to close the entire movement. Play the cadence slower.

TWENTY-FOUR

SERGE PROKOFIEV

Fig. 24.1 Sonata No. 7, Op. 83, *Complete Prokofiev Sonatas* © Kalmus Editions.
All rights reserved. Used by permission of Alfred Publishing Co., Inc.

Prokofiev has had an enormous, enormous impact on me and on the piano repertoire. To begin with, by learning his works and playing his Third Piano Concerto, which I did a number of times, and playing all the sonatas, which I recorded for MGM, and editing the ninth for publication by Leeds Music, I thought he was an enormous composer, and now I think so even more so. His music has an excitement and the special colors of folk tunes and marches and many playful elements. His sonatas reflect his varied moods from romantic to rhythmic and percussive. I feel his music is incomparable.

SONATA IN B-FLAT MAJOR, NO. 7, OP. 83

Mvt. 1. Allegro inquieto

M. 1. *Non-legato.* Driving, intense.

Mm. 7–23. One large *crescendo.*

Mm. 12–20. *Crescendo* to each accented B♭.

Mm. 20–23. *Crescendo* to the *fortissimo.*

M. 24. Pedal each first beat.

Mm. 40–41. No false accent on the right-hand G♭s.

M. 44. Downbeat like a *sforzando.* Then a new start after the downbeat.

M. 50. The F-E-D-C like a *glissando.*

Mm. 59–60. More pedal.

M. 64. Still *fortissimo.*

M. 65. A new mood. Horns.

M. 69. A different orchestration.

Mm. 81, 83, 85. Swing into the high Bs.

Mm. 87–89. Swing into the left-hand downbeats.

M. 89. Climb to the A♮.

Mm. 103, 106, 110. Start lower than the accent each time.

Mm. 103–105 and mm. 106–109. *Decrescendo* as the line ascends.

M. 119. Make it more important [*mezzo piano*]. Hear the bass A up to E♭ [m. 20] and back to A again [m. 124].

Mm. 124–128. Hold together better.

M. 129. Do not rush.

M. 143. *Decrescendo* as the line descends.

M. 147. Take the E♭ and D♯ with the left hand.

M. 148. Take the C♯ with the left hand.

M. 149. Resolve the A♭ to G.

Mm. 153–154. A suspended low level.

M. 155. A suspended high melody.

M. 181. *Crescendo* the bass line D-E♭-E♮-F.

M. 189. Use the pedal to help create the *tumultuoso* effect.

Mm. 218, 222, 226, 230. Start each phrase softer.

Mm. 224–225. *Crescendo.*

M. 236. Sustain the Cs.

M. 257. Not so soft. It should rattle.

M. 260. Take the final D with the right hand.

M. 263. Take the final A♮ with the right hand.

M. 274. Sing the left hand with the right hand. Still brittle.

M. 333. Hear the bass B up to F [m. 334] and back to B again [m. 338].

Mm. 334–335. Play the C♯-D like a *glissando.*

M. 359. Like coming awake. Start *pianissimo.*

M. 363. Take the A with the left hand.

Mm. 392–393. Get mad!

Mm. 395–396. An extreme *crescendo.*

M. 404. Take the A♮ with the left hand.

M. 411. And away. *Decrescendo;* like "smoke."

Mvt. 2. Andante caloroso

M. 2. *Decrescendo* from the A [beat 3] to the G♯ of m. 3.

M. 3. *Crescendo* to the D♯ of m. 4.

M. 10. *Decrescendo* to F♯ of m. 11 [resolve].

M. 25. A new mood at the *dolce.*

M. 32. Work with each phrase of the variations. Follow the curving line. Be freer, although not very much faster.

M. 40. Like a melody; hear the canon.

M. 44. Hear the canon. Reach out to the D♭.

M. 51. *Crescendo* the last beat to m. 52.

M. 52. A very big chord.

M. 53. Church bells start here.

M. 60. Follow the right-hand line with its underlying doubling in the left hand.

M. 63. Take the A♯ with the left hand.

M. 73. Come down.

M. 87. Come up again melodically.

Mm. 102–107. Stretching the interval and the sonority to C♯, to G♯, to G♮, and to E.

Mm. 106–107. *Decrescendo* to the final chord.

Mvt. 3. Precipitato

M. 1. Work with the repeating chords in the right hand to achieve a clear melody. Not loud. It's like a driving piston power that will run over you.

M. 45. B♭ is the first big moment.

Mm. 70 and 71. The left-hand G ends the motive.

M. 83. The *espressivo* is a relief from the driving character of the piece.

Mm. 119–126. Go to the accent.

Mm. 125–126. Use pedal.

M. 127. Big for the second time in the movement.

M. 171. This chord is a goal, so save for three lines before it.

M. 172. *Crescendo* to a big accent on the downbeat of m. 173.

Mm. 175–176. *Crescendo* to the last octaves.

TWENTY-FIVE

MAURICE RAVEL

Ravel and also Debussy were influenced by Liszt, Rimsky-Korsakov, and Balakirev, but their point of departure is indirectness of rhythm, form, and emotion. Ravel is cooler than Debussy, not as humorous or sensual, but often more erotic. Both are very, very special, and I immediately react if I hear a piece by Debussy or Ravel; I guess you have to be so inclined. The demands on the pianist are enormous, and perhaps the inside rewards are greater rather than the outside.

Ravel was not a performing pianist. He wrote difficulties for us to solve, so it is often necessary to find the best fingering to fit the hands.

GASPARD DE LA NUIT

You know, when you are in love with these pieces as I am, they are always fresh and they are always young. I remember the first time I was thrilled by it, and I am thrilled today by it.

"Ondine"

M. 1. Put the pedal down before beginning to play. Present a clear design, not too soft. At the end of the measure prepare for the entry of the melody. Experience it. Don't teach it.

M. 2. Create a magical sound. Use the side of the thumb [left hand] for a gliding effect. The phrase says, "On-dine." The right hand keeps going. Don't slow down. The left hand has no accent on G♯. Play *legato* to m. 3.

M. 3. Color the D♯. Not the same as in m. 2.

M. 4. *Decrescendo* the D♯ to the C♯. The B♯ must pass the C♯. Not hurried on the last two eighths.

M. 5. Color the B.

M. 6. No accent on the A♯.

M. 7. Not hard on the E♯. The last E♯ continues to sing. The right hand cannot play so softly since it is preparing for the color change in m. 8.

M. 8. Right hand, a new color. Feel the A♮ in beat four. Play the left-hand E and C♯ as a two-note slur with a slight change of pedal.

Mm. 8–9. Play A♯ -C♯ -D♯ -E♯ -C♯ as a phrase. Less right hand on the last beat of m. 9.

M. 10. Hear the register change for the left-hand melody. The right hand is like a silver thread.

Mm. 11–12. C♯ -F♯ is the first time to reach the F♯ . D♯ -F♯ is the second time.

M. 13. In the right hand, relate the A♮ to the G♯ of m. 14. *Decrescendo* the B♮ -C♯ in the left hand.

M. 14. In the right hand, play more of the middle and less of the extreme registers. Slur the D♯ -B♮ in the left hand. Then *crescendo* the G♯ - B-C♯ to the D♯ of m. 15.

M. 14. Right hand: use 4–2 on the G♯ -E. Play the top downbeat D♯ with the right hand. *Decrescendo* the G♯ -B-C♯ and connect tenderly to the next measure.

M. 16. Begin the right hand much lighter than the level of the left hand in the previous measure. Focus on D♯ -C♯ -G♯ . Practice the left hand like Scarlatti.

M. 17. Press the right-hand chord. Use a brush stroke on the thirty-second notes.

M. 18. Listen to the left hand.

M. 19. Lightly press the chord.

M. 20. In this instance, *piano* means more. *Crescendo* the last three thirty-second notes.

M. 21. It never comes out in the sunlight. Play the left hand more crystal-like and shimmering.

M. 22. Play the left hand like a *glissando*. And don't stop before the A♯ of m. 23.

M. 23. Don't play this as an exercise. The thirty-second notes should shimmer.

M. 24. The right hand takes the first third [C♯ -E♯].

M. 25. When you have the octaves [right hand], I would love to hear both the thumb and the top note. Play the lower A♯ of beat 3 with the left hand. Sing the last right-hand chord.

M. 26. Not loud. It doesn't go to a *forte*. Hear a richer second within the chord. The right-hand D♯ comes together with the left-hand B♯ .

M. 27. Quicker graces. Color the chord.

M. 28. Voice the top B♯ . Play the last G♯ to the C♯ of m. 29 like a *glissando*.

M. 29. Too much *retenu;* it's not natural. You don't feel it fresh; you repeat it like a record—you must experience it each time when you play it.

This is the height of sensibility, but you accent the notes. I hear a loud melody; I hear an arrangement by Liszt; I don't hear the sensibility and beauty of Ravel.

M. 30. Be very subtle when you play the inner line B♮ to B♯.

M. 32. Play the right hand very clear. Play the left-hand *legato* with no accents. Phrase to the A♯. Then G♯-D♯ to the D♯ of m. 33. Have a new pedal for each measure.

M. 33. Phrase four notes to the D♯ of m. 34.

M. 34. Phrase five notes to the C♯ of m. 35. Then *decrescendo* the B♮ to the D♯ in m. 36.

M. 36. Reach to the high note of the right hand.

M. 37. A slight *fermata* on the A♯ [beat 3]. Play the D♯ [the 15th of the thirty-second notes] with the left hand.

M. 38. No false accent on the C♯ octave. Stroke the C♯-F♯-E♮ melody.

M. 41. Left hand, be aware of the left-hand line. Play the A♯-D♯ with reversed hands [the fifteenth of the thirty-second notes]. At the end of the measure, prepare the entry of the melody.

M. 42. No pedal on the last beat of the measure.

M. 44. Caress the keys *pianississimo* over the top of the right-hand passage. Be sure to hear the melody. Close the left-hand D♯. No *ritardando* into m. 45. Only a slight hesitation.

M. 45. Play the left hand as an expressive *legato*. On beat 4, color the octaves between the hands.

M. 46. I would make a *diminuendo* going up. Thin out the texture in each register change.

M. 47. Phrase the left hand like the opening.

Mm. 49–50. Hand redistributions. The left hand takes the fourth, seventh, and eighth thirty-second notes. The left hand takes the high G.

M. 52. The right hand is like spurts of water. The left-hand melody is *legato.*

M. 54. No *ritard.*

M. 55. A delayed downbeat. The first beat is like a harp. Then don't hesitate before the next measure. It's going there!

M. 56. At the end, the right hand thins out to nothing so that when you get to the top, the ear of the listener goes to the left hand and he hears the melody.

M. 57. Voice the bottom of the right-hand passage while the left hand voices the top of the chords. Change the pedal according to the bass notes. Hear the E and the D in both the left hand and the right hand.

M. 58. This is the second time for the E-D.

M. 59. At the top of the *crescendo,* use every note.

M. 60. Color the second beat [left hand]. On beat 4, hear the C♯-B♮ between the hands.

M. 61. Hear the left-hand D going to the D♯ of m. 62.

M. 62. Beat 2, not too slow so as to relate to the downbeat.

Mm. 63–65. In the right hand, begin voicing the tops, and then add the thumbs [m. 63]. Then add the inner notes [m. 64], and then add the left-hand [m. 65].

M. 64. Use the *sostenuto* pedal to open up the sound.

M. 66. Practice the right-hand melody in the thumbs and the fifth finger. You haven't practiced the separate hands. It has become a fossilized piece for you. You have to re-create it. Voice and hold the right-hand melody notes. Color the E♯ [beat 3] warmer. Use the *sostenuto* pedal for the bass B and then the G♮.

M. 68. There's no *ritardando,* but there's sensitivity galore. Not too softly.

M. 69. Color the A♯. No *ritardando.*

M. 70. No, it isn't Liszt; it's what Heifetz does—it goes right through the heart. It's not a piano player "plink, plink." This is the most beautiful *glissando* that you can imagine [G♯-G♯-F♯-D♮-A♯]. It shouldn't have this roughness; it's quiet going up. I need to hear the A♯, but you come a half-hour late in the left hand. It's the downbeat, but you don't get there. There are no secrets here musically; it's plain on the face of the piece.

M. 72. Now you do really a bad sin for which you have to go to church. You played a *glissando,* and he said, "*le plus piano possible.*" But you did it "Reyeaaaahhhh!" Just caress the piano. I play the *glissando* with my whole hand; shape the hand, so that the thumb supports the second finger. No pressure; use little arm weight.

M. 73. Come down; whatever became loud comes back. Hand redistributions.

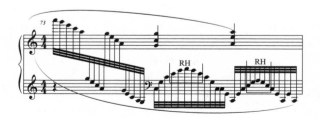

Ex. 25.1. m. 73

M. 75. Hand redistributions.

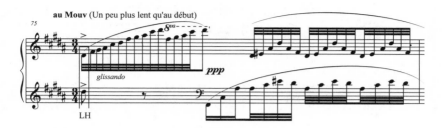

Ex. 25.2. m. 75

M. 79. Color the A♯ darker.

Mm. 80–81. Slurrings in the left hand to beat 2 of m. 80, then to the downbeat of m. 81.

M. 82. Play the left hand expressively.

M. 85. A deeper B.

M. 87. The A is a teardrop. Pass by the B [of m. 86], and then resolve the G♯ to the A.

M. 88. Start *mezzo forte,* then more *virtuosic.* After the first high C, it's less and less. Then start coming down from the high B♭.

M. 89. Hear G-F, G-F, G♯-F♯, C♯-D♯. Then hear C♯-D♯ in m. 90.

M. 92. Not nervous. Not so active. *Diminuendo* each one.

M. 92. Like waves.

M. 93. *Diminuendo* to the top and no hit on the last note.

You compartmentalized it. You put it into compartments, and then you put the box away and it lost the flavor. It was not any more a fresh flower. It was an old flower that has wilted but that reminded you of the fresh flower.

"Le Gibet"

M. 1. The repeated B♭s are "in-out," and the thumb stays.

M. 3. The right hand plays the first F. The melody is in the left thumb.

M. 7. The F♭ is sensitive, soft, like a threat.

M. 10. Hand redistributions. Voice the right-hand thumb.

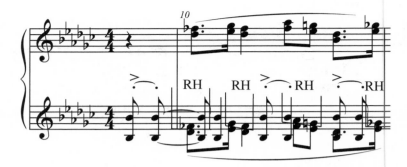

Ex. 25.3. m. 10

M. 12. Not such thick sounds in the right hand. More tops. Color the chords. Keep the bass in the pedal.

Mm. 15–16. No voicing in the middle line.

M. 20. Play the bottom two notes of the right hand together with the top two notes of the left hand. Then the top two right-hand notes with the left hand's upper note. The middle line is bells getting angry.

M. 21. Beat 3 is the first G♭.

M. 22. Beat 1 is the second. Beat 3 is the third. Color each one. Play the last two beats freer.

M. 29. Swell to the downbeat [right hand].

M. 31. Melody is doubled, richer.

M. 32. Change the color, but still *pianissimo*.

M. 34. Color the chord.

Mm. 35–36. Bells in the top line.

M. 38. Sensitive beats 1 and 2. Then expressive going to m. 39.

M. 40. The low B♭ octave is nothing. Use flatter fingers in the right hand.

M. 45. Maintain the pulse.

M. 51. Play the last B♭s [beat 4] with the left hand.

"Scarbo"

M. 1. Don't begin too quietly.

M. 2. An exact eighth rest. The right-hand chord is more important that the repeated notes. Sear the chord. Relax the left arm.

Mm. 4–5. No holes in the *tremolo*. Just *vibrato*. Always *diminuendo*.

M. 5. Voice the chord.

M. 6. Release the right hand, and then lift the pedal very slowly.

M. 16. Voice the chord.

M. 22. Have a breath following this measure.

Mm. 23–29. Play the *tremolo* regular and even.

Mm. 32–33. Phrase out on the E [m. 32]. Don't hit the third chord, but grab it. Hand redistributions.

Mm. 35–36. Ring the third chord. The right hand helps with the sixteenths.

Mm. 37–41. Hear "Scar-bo" [A♯ -E♯].

Mm. 50–51. The G♯ resolves to G♮ and the C♯ to the B.

M. 52. Use 2–1–2–1–2 right-hand fingering.

M. 65. Color the thirds. *Espressivo.* More on the E♯ .

Mm. 73–74. Right hand, close to the keyboard, not from above. Hand redistributions.

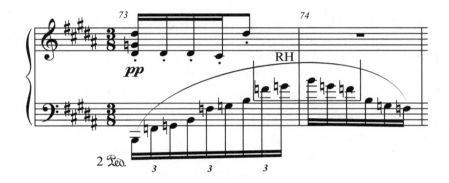

Ex. 25.4. mm. 73–74

Mm. 80–81. Swell these measures.

M. 93. Like a *glissando.*

M. 94. A relaxed chord.

Mm. 94–98. Fingerings for repeated notes.

Mm. 102–108. Hand redistributions that make the passage secure and climactic. Have less *accelerando* and more sound.

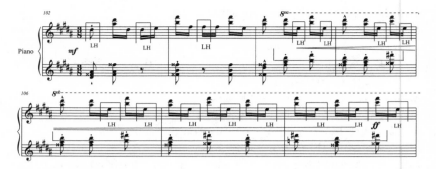

Ex. 25.5. mm. 102–108

M. 113. A warm sound.

Mm. 116–119. Fade the D♯s into nothing.

M. 121. Not too high off the keys.

M. 122. Relax the right arm. Redistributions.

Mm. 122–130. The right hand takes the E [the fourth sixteenth note] every time.

M. 133. In time; color the chords.

M. 142. In time; color the chords.

M. 155. Love the note [G♯]. Voice the chord.

M. 168. Right hand, from far away. Use 4-2-1, 5-3-1 fingering.

M. 174. Come back in sound.

M. 179. A higher level.

M. 190. Think of swelling the chord as if it's alive.

M. 195. Left hand, each one more.

M. 202. Begin building.

M. 204. More. Play with the whole arm.

Mm. 205–207. Hear the different registers.

Mm. 212–213. Left hand passive, not active.

M. 214. Right hand "out."

Mm. 232–234. Hear three bars. Don't lose the meter.

M. 235. Right-hand fingerings [3-2-1-2-3].

M. 244. Voice the tops of the chords.

M. 256. This is Scarbo being a gentleman. A freer tempo, it's beginning.

M. 268. From far away.

M. 271. No *crescendo.*

M. 272. Hear the register change. Less sound.

M. 278. Color the G♭ -B♭.

M. 291. The beginning of the phrase, not the end.

Mm. 309–311. Practice the coordination of the hands by tapping without playing the notes. Don't rush.

Mm. 314–317. Schizoid character.

M. 318. Contrast. A different character.

M. 323. A different character than before.

Mm. 325–326. Relate to the first entrance of the theme.

M. 328. Warm.

M. 333. More sound.

M. 334. The low A is a gong of sound.

M. 339. Accent the low G.

M. 346. More expressive. Ring the left-hand chord.

M. 348. The right-hand chord rings.

Mm. 353–357. Hand redistributions.

Ex. 25.6. mm. 353–357

M. 367. Like a tympanist.

M. 380. Less active.

M. 382. Stand still. This is the low point.

M. 389. Hand redistributions.

Ex. 25.7. m. 389

M. 395. It asks a question.

M. 398. *Decrescendo.*

M. 418. Feel the meter of each bar.

M. 427. It's dying away. Don't show the changes of register.

M. 430. The left hand plays the D♯s. Feel quarters, not eighth notes.

M. 431. Sing the melody.

M. 433. The left hand plays the upper notes.

M. 436. The left hand plays D♮ -E.

M. 437. Expressive thirds.

M. 441. Color, like a harp.

Mm. 445–447. As if time stands still.

M. 448. A low point. Show the shape of the seconds. More left hand.

M. 460. Keep the B in the bass.

M. 475. Use less pedal as you descend.

M. 544. Hear the chromatic line between the hands.

M. 592. Not too loud.

M. 593. *Legato* right hand.

M. 620. As if a halo over the F♯ .

M. 623. Right hand, not too comfortable.

M. 627. An "out" gesture.

LE TOMBEAU DE COUPERIN

Prélude

Mm. 1–2. Continuous right hand to left hand. Pluck the left-hand Es with fingers only.

M. 2. Play the crushes more like an accent than five notes. The left-hand G-As are very quiet.

M. 5. The melody begins, therefore, no accent.

Mm. 5–6. The tenor has two-note slurs.

M. 8. Softer, as an echo, since it is the repetition of the group.

M. 9. The third time begins a longer phrase.

Mm. 14–15. No inflection. Resolve the right-hand C♯ to B and the A to G. Relate the melodic content of each one-measure phrase.

M. 21. Leave room with a slight *decrescendo* for the new melody. Relax the tempo slightly.

Mm. 25–28. A richer left hand as it steps down followed by the final E.

M. 28. "Whistle over the top." Let the momentum carry you.

M. 29. Return down with a little slowing. Resolve the B [middle of the measure] to the A of m. 30.

Mm. 29–30. Hear the V-I cadence.

M. 34. Hear two different left-hand Ds. Color the chord.

Mm. 58, 63. No inflection in these measures.

M. 66. Hear the V-I cadence to m. 67.

M. 77. A higher level than m. 28.

Mm. 79–80. The left-hand long-note As are not harsh.

M. 83. No accents.

M. 87. Begin the line.

Mm. 88–89. Try alternating the hands [left hand plays A-B-A-D]. Hear E-B, E-B.

Mm. 91–92. Like a *glissando*.

M. 93. The hands shake within the key for the trill effect. Sustain all notes in m. 94. Then release all but the chord notes.

Fugue

Dispassionate, like three monks singing in a monastery. There are only two *fortes* in the entire piece.

M. 57. Right hand, let it run out. Settle.

Forlane

M. 1. Full of style and color. It's a dance.

M. 64. *Decrescendo* to m. 65.

M. 66. *Crescendo* to m. 67.

M. 68. *Decrescendo* to m. 68.

M. 81–82. Not dry.

Mm. 91–92. A swell in these measures.

Rigaudon

M. 3 and following. Finger pluck the low notes.

M. 23. *Crescendo* to the accent.

M. 25. With pedal.

M. 66. Color the B♮.

M. 85. Mix the sonorities with pedal.

M. 117. *Con pedal.*

Mm. 127–128. Sharply defined.

Menuet

M. 1. The phrase floats in. Think a long line.

M. 56. Surge [*crescendo*] to the *fortissimo* of m. 57.

Mm. 124–125. Play the lower part deliberately.

M. 125. A gentle accent.

M. 126. The trills are like a flutter.

Toccata

Practice all repeated notes. Pull the fingers to get out of the way.

M. 1. No matter how fast, it is never hasty, always even. One pedal for the first two measures.

M. 3. From the E sneak into F♯-E-D-E. Don't inflect the B.

Mm. 4–5. Practice with a very free wrist. The right hand is just a wrist throw, not the arm.

M. 5. The theme begins. Tap the pedal on first beat.

M. 21. Reach for the left-hand D-A. Don't jump. Make it part of a four-measure phrase. Touch the pedal on the downbeat.

M. 33. Color the new key. Hear all the keys you move through.

Mm. 35–37. Play the D, C, and D with the left hand.

Ex. 25.8. mm. 35–37

Mm. 40–42. Use alternating hands on the repeated notes.

Ex. 25.9. mm. 40–42

Mm. 53–56. The left hand changes touch. Start short, becoming longer. Close the phrase with a slight *rallentando*.

M. 57. A Ravel touch. Not dry, but with pedal. Slower. Practice the left hand alone, very close to the key. Hear every note. Make a long line. Practice together for the octave melody.

M. 58. The right-hand B is an upbeat.

M. 66. Both hands *crescendo.*

M. 70. The left hand plays "out-in." The right hand is a clangy effect.

M. 71. Hear a clear top line.

Mm. 78–80. Practice the repeated notes with close fingers.

M. 94. *Diminuendo* and pull back slightly to make room for the melody.

M. 96. Practice the left hand for a Ravel touch, like a silk glove.

M. 103. Begins a variation of the preceding. Give clear shape to the melody.

Mm. 105–106. *Diminuendo.*

M. 113. Begin again.

M. 121. Pull back slightly.

M. 122. *Un pochissimo meno mosso.*

M. 126. Less than m. 122.

M. 147. A new start. It's the lowest point.

M. 154. Practice the repeated notes between the hands.

M. 155. How proud Ravel must have been to discover how to play the melody and the *toccata* together. Lean into the top, but hear all notes.

M. 181. A slight "phraselet" before this measure; a mental breath.

M. 190. *Crescendo,* then play m. 191 with arm weight. No noise, just pure sound.

M. 227. The E tympani has waited 200 measures for this entrance. Start *mezzo forte.*

M. 230. Slightly less to be able to build.

M. 243. Broaden slightly.

Mm. 246–247. The E chords begin. Build from here.

M. 249. *Crescendo* to the chord in m. 250.

M. 250. No *ritardando* and no extra time.

PIANO TRIO IN A MINOR

The Ravel Trio is certainly a masterpiece of the twentieth century. As a trio it is unique because it is so integrated that each movement is written for an instrument called "trio." One would really do well to study the integration because the writing for each instrument, where balance plays an immense role, is unique. There is no other trio that I know that is written as completely where at one point or another you shouldn't hear the individual instruments. Yes, you can hear in the opening that the piano plays, but as soon as the three play together, it should be really like one. I have played it many, many times, and recorded it many times, but when I start the piece, it hasn't failed for me not to feel an awareness of something very special running cold down my spine. To me it speaks in

Fig. 25.1. Piano Trio in A minor

very direct terms of how beautiful that piece is. Technically, it is a challenge and will always remain a challenge, no matter how great the player, because you must concentrate on the other players, not just on yourself. So, the Trio is really something truly special, and even within the works of Ravel, it plays a very special role.

Mvt. 1. Modéré

A transparency is needed so all parts can be heard. Also, a tremendous palette of colors is needed. The hands must sometimes be loose and light and at other times very strong and forceful. Sometimes very slow attacks as if stroking the keys, at other times very sharp attacks. Perhaps play a little slower than a usual *modéré,* to give the depth of feeling and to hear all the colors. Ravel's metronome marking gives the dance-like feeling he wants, but, on the other hand, there is a mood of nostalgia that is so touching and beautiful.

M. 1. Very gently lift the first chord and drop on the second. *Diminuendo* the three left-hand Es.

M. 4. *Diminuendo* before the strings' entrance.

M. 10. *Diminuendo.*

M. 31. Piano, follow the strings' dynamics. *Diminuendo.*

M. 37. Violin, *crescendo* to the B. Then play *diminuendo.*

M. 38. Piano, time the downbeat to match the cello entrance.

M. 52. The harp-like figure must *diminuendo.*

M. 53. Piano, not late on the downbeat. Otherwise, the strings don't know where you are. Strings, less on the F♯. Time must stand still.

M. 61. The piano is harp-like. The violin is too naked, too crass.

M. 67. All parts hold the tempo leading into m. 68.

Mm. 81–82. Piano, continue to bring out the top Es.

M. 83. Cello, listen for the violin's G and join. Very light on the A. Otherwise you make us listen to the A.

M. 84. Cello, slide from the E down to the G.

M. 89. Piano, be sensitive on B-C♯-E but in tempo. Without *ritardando.*

M. 104. Violin, *crescendo* to the F of m. 105.

M. 105. Violin, give a sign when to move on beat 7.

Mvt. 2. Pantoum

Very steady piano accents are needed to hold it together.

M. 31. Play the downbeat with an accent.

M. 38. Cello, no *ritardando.* You sound like you're running out of gasoline.

M. 47. Piano, be steady to hold it together.

M. 61. Piano, more.

M. 70. Piano, *diminuendo.*

M. 73. Cello, less than m. 74 for the contrast.

M. 85. Piano, don't sit on the third beat. It's less. Release the chord.

M. 124. Piano, I'm not pleased with your sound. Not "dah!" Hear the harmonies, not just the melody.

M. 130. Violin, each two-note slur is less.

M. 132. Strings [at Square 12], play toward each other. Be aware.

M. 138. Piano, the low E♭ is *piano*. Leave room for the strings.

M. 140. If there is a *ritardando*, it must be within the framework of the piece. [Pressler sings how it should be.] Do it more with the *diminuendo* than with the time.

M. 140. A new kind of sound from the strings [at Square 14], one we haven't heard before in the piece. We had it in the piano at m. 124 but not in the strings until now. And there it should be especially beautiful. Greenhouse, who was my cellist for thirty-two years, used to say, "Menahem, here's your song." It could even take a little more time. What I would like is that you take time to change the color, time to feel what you're doing. Violin, don't accent any notes. Go from the low to the high, and don't accent the high open string so that we don't hear an open string. At one measure after Square 14, a little *diminuendo* between the G and the F and between the E and C [two measures after Square 14]. Can we somehow coordinate our *vibrato*? Vibrate in the same place, in the same amount.

M. 143. The piano must be less. Leave room for the strings.

M. 166. The piano is less also.

M. 173. The *glissando* must *diminuendo* to match the strings.

M. 187. Cello, you must always have something left over when you are on your own. You must play with some voice so that you have room to come down.

M. 198. Strings, lean on the triplet but don't accent.

M. 217. Start the *crescendo* from a *piano*.

M. 226. Strings, why do you play a longer note on beat 3? The same length, only with an accent. [The player asks about the down bows, which are indicated. Pressler says that this may have been suggested by the ones who played the premiere who were very fine players. It's more natural sounding. It gives a better accent.]

M. 235. Piano, you are so loud!

Mvt. 3. Passacaille

M. 1. Piano, too loud. Start on the key so that you pull the note out. Don't hit. Use a *legato*, overlapping sound. When you play, can you have this heartbeat inside you? And always, after a long note, start softly. Otherwise, you accent.

M. 12. Still *pianissimo*.

M. 13. Cello and piano *decrescendo* to beat 2.

M. 23. Violin, in order for you to resolve better, give more on the A. Lean on it, then you can release the B.

M. 33. Piano, breathe before this entrance.

M. 36. The piano must strengthen in response to the cello in the previous measure.

M. 49. The piano chords are *legato,* not separate accents.

M. 53. The cello is important.

M. 57. Listen to each other for the timing of the downbeat.

M. 80. Cello, don't come down so far. Leave some room for the piano to enter.

M. 81. Piano, leave yourself some room to still go down.

Mvt. 4. Finale

When you practice, listen for the places where you continue each other. [Pressler interrupts the group many times, insisting on correct rhythms, correct triplets, and all the chord notes from piano and strings.]

M. 1. Violin, play the notes clearly so the piano knows where to come in.

M. 6. *Diminuendo.*

Mm. 9–10. Piano, never fast on the eighths.

M. 11. Violin, not a Russian player like you do, but French, not heavy. Cello, more of the chords. A richer sound.

Mm. 24–25. Violin and cello, use the grace note to create a kind of accent.

M. 29. [Pressler believes the right-hand beat 4 is C♮, not C♯.]

M. 30. A little *ritard* and then at least two beats for the *glissando* so there is a *fermata.*

M. 42. Piano, no accents in the line.

M. 45. Cello, no accent when changing trill notes. In principle, it's behind the theme. It's a kind of mystery that's added.

M. 49. Have a *poco ritard* leading into Square 6. Start from nothing, no accent. Cello, not too active because at m. 54 the piano takes up the same figure behind the cello theme.

M. 58. The piano solo beginning at the end of the measure [the trumpet fanfare] is *pianissimo.* It's difficult, but you must try very hard.

M. 66. A *slight ritardando* leading into the *fortississimo.* Then a clear downbeat together.

M. 72. Go down so far [to *pianissimo*] that you don't hear the notes anymore. It murmurs.

M. 83. Like a piano solo. And never fast on the eighths.

M. 84. Violin, listen to the cello so that she can get her four notes in. She is close to it, but sometimes she has trouble getting them in, so don't hurry.

Mm. 98–99. Piano, *decrescendo* each slur.

M. 120. Reinforce. It's the symphony. It's everybody, the whole orchestra.

M. 123. Piano, let them hear the five As so they know where you are. Keep one pedal until the end.

TWENTY-SIX

FRANZ SCHUBERT

Schubert—again the smile comes to the face, because he is divine. It is the combination of a Mozart and of a song master and of a man who cannot stop seeing beauty. He can't stop, so his pieces become long, longer, and longer, yes? He is the endless song. But, when you have the patience, I mean the inner patience to go through the piece and really live it along the way, you become older than you are. His pieces are tremendously rewarding, and the listener, the one who is open to it, is rewarded deeper than from anyone because he's more direct going to the heart. You need less brain, you need less of anything but an open heart. It is probably not apparent that he is that innocent, but there is that innocence like in Mozart that comes out. It's not the perfection of Mozart but the amount of beauty that he heaps on his music. It's a garden with so many flowers that you look to the left and it's green, and to the right it's yellow, and there it's blue, and this one is full bloom, and this is half bloom. It's enormous. It takes such great control to play Schubert's music. The timing has to be just right; the understanding of the harmonic relations must be right. And the inner timings, the heartbeat inside of him, continues, and it holds the whole piece together.

FANTASIE IN C MAJOR, D. 760, WANDERER

Mvt. 1. Allegro con fuoco ma non troppo

M. 1. Relax the body before beginning. The hands must be well positioned to support strong fingers. All other notes, though not as forceful as the top line, should sink to the bottom of the key bed. The eighth notes are lighter and played with an upward motion, moving to the quarter notes, which are played with a downward motion.

Mm. 2–3. Voice the top line B-C-C-C♯ -D.

M. 3. Separate the two chords. And "out" with the arms.

M. 4. Play these chords slightly less, due to the relationship of the V^7 chord to the tonic of m. 1.

M. 6. Play the first three sixteenth notes with the left hand.

Ex. 26.1. m. 6

Mm. 8–10. Let the left hand help as in m. 6.

M. 13. *Crescendo* this measure. Then a breath, an air space.

M. 14. Lean into the E, then into the D♯ [m. 15].

M. 15. *Crescendo.*

M. 16. Press forward during the repeated chords to the climactic E major chords in m. 17.

M. 18. *Pianissimo.* Maximum contrast with the opening, whispering.

M. 20. *Decrescendo* the first two chords. The half-note chord is like woodwinds. Wait and place it.

M. 24. There is a sweetness to this measure.

Mm. 24–25. Let the left hand help.

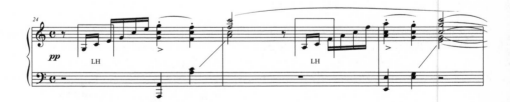

Ex. 26.2. mm. 24–26

M. 25. Place the F chord. Now it begins to awaken.

M. 26. Place the C chord. It is slower, later, a different color than the F chord of m. 25.

M. 27. Start the sixteenths *a tempo,* but not as loud as in m. 29.

M. 32. Lean in. Take time to prepare the chord. Don't hit. *Crescendo* up the line.

M. 34. In a state of suspended sound; don't pump the rhythm. Hear the E going to D [m. 35].

M. 36. *A tempo;* not slow. Rotate the hands to bring out the thumb melody; don't just poke at it.

M. 44. Pull back slightly for a clear cadence.

Mm. 45–46. Feel the change from *portamento* to *legato* and the difference in mood that results.

M. 46. Lean into the C and glide down to the G♯. Don't accent the syncopations; it's like a lingering on each note.

M. 47. *Pianissimo.* A new color, private. Sustain the lower Es.

M. 48. The left hand answers the right hand.

M. 50. The E-F♯-G♯ opens up in sound leading to m. 51. Work on fingering.

M. 51. The flower blooms.

Mm. 51–52. Gracefully. *Decrescendo.*

M. 52. Pull back on the last three eighths.

M. 57. Lean into the E; don't just hit.

M. 58. Color this E differently from m. 57.

M. 59. Phrase the octave groups C-A-G and B-G-F♯.

M. 61. Hear the difference in register.

M. 62. Hear the mode change, mysterious, quiet, ominous. Sneak in with the left-hand octaves.

M. 63. The left-hand octave motive B-D-C♯ has the same shape as when it appeared in the right hand.

M. 65. Open up the sound. Contrast A♯-C♯-B with the B-D♮-C♯ of m. 63.

M. 66. The fourth-beat chord and bass note D♮ must be clearly heard.

Mm. 68–69. *Crescendo* for maximum contrast. No *ritardando.* Hear the line [E-C-E-G-C-E] going up.

M. 70. Grand.

M. 71. A daring descent.

M. 75. Start the sixteenths less.

M. 83. Don't just hit; give it meaning. Hear the A and then the B [m. 85].

M. 86. Swing into the left-hand chord.

M. 88. Hear the right-hand top notes.

M. 99. Resolve the C to B.

M. 102. Allow time for the left hand to *crescendo* to the *sforzando* chord. Then have a *subito piano* that descends to m. 103.

Mm. 107–108. Allow more time to reach the surprise B♭⁷ chord.

Mm. 108–109. Hear the shaping within the scale [m. 109]. Be sensitive to the B♭ -A♮ -A♭ and give each note meaning.

M. 110. Constant changes of color and articulation. The last beat slows slightly.

M. 111. Play the octaves with two hands. Beats 3 and 4 *ritard* slightly and *decrescendo*.

M. 112. This is the bottom of the *decrescendo*. Without a care in the world. Don't rush the last three eighths. More spacious.

M. 113. The last three eighths move upward, so *crescendo*.

M. 114. The last three eighths descend, so *decrescendo*.

M. 120. Go to the right-hand G. Place the bass G.

M. 121. Take time to place the low E♭.

M. 123. Don't rush the three eighths [G-A♭ -B♭]. Maybe a hair slower.

M. 124. Hear the bells in the upper voice.

M. 126. Design the three eighths differently each time.

M. 132. *Crescendo* to the downbeat of m. 133.

M. 133. Sweep the *arpeggio* down and back up.

M. 136. Play with a richer sound.

M. 137. Start the sixteenths lighter.

M. 140. Come back in sound.

Mm. 142, 144, 146. Shape each left-hand scale: *crescendo* the last beat of the right hand to the next bar.

M. 142. The last chord is an upbeat.

M. 143. Come back in sound.

M. 144. A two-note resolution. Reach to the high chord. Then the others are close to the key.

M. 150. Begin a two-measure *crescendo*. Don't let octave displacements interfere with the long line.

M. 152. The left hand should use the last G to relax the hand for the sixteenths of m. 153. *Crescendo* the right-hand scale to m. 153.

M. 152. Come back again. Then *crescendo* to m. 153.

M. 153. Leave room to move forward in sound.

Mm 157, 158. The last three eighths *crescendo*.

M. 160. Broaden.

Mm. 161–162. Don't start too loudly. Build up to the climax. The right hand's last two chords in each measure are an answer. The left-hand thumb leads in the sixteenths.

Mm. 161–164. Slower. Not a race. Work the thumbs.

M. 165 and following. Continuous forward motion to each quarter note.

M. 177. Left hand, pull the fingers on the keys. More *legato*.

M. 179 and following. No right pedal.

M. 188. Lean into the A. Then resolve to the G♯.

Mvt. 2. Adagio

You must be able to give it a variety of touches, of expression, of moods. Each new variation means a new emotion. You must be a poet to give the piece a sense of continuity so that we will want to hear it. You have to have a certain amount of freedom to push the tempo but then to come back.

M. 1. The mood is hushed, magic. Suffer; feel the pain. Pull on the keys. Use the natural weight of the arm. Create movement into beat 3 of each measure.

M. 2. An even roll to the top G♯.

M. 3. Vibrate the chord on beat 3.

M. 7. The chord on beat 3 should not be rolled in the same manner as the chord on the downbeat of m. 8.

M. 9. New. Move with simplicity. Sing with relaxed inner voices. Make music out of the weaving inner lines. Practice inner lines by themselves. Follow the contours.

M. 11. *Decrescendo* the sixteenths at the end of the measure.

M. 12. Voice the tenor line, then the soprano, then the tenor, then the soprano again. *Crescendo* until the *diminuendo* begins. The fourth beat is *diminuendo* within *pianissimo*. Hear the resolution to m. 13.

M. 13. Color the sixteenths in beat 1. Beat 2 is *diminuendo* within *pianississimo*. The last eighth is a teardrop.

M. 15. *Crescendo* to m. 16.

M. 16. The last beat is magical.

M. 19. Hear the different chord color under the same melody.

M. 20. Not too much *crescendo*.

M. 21. Not too much *accelerando*. Left hand, hear the melodic changes.

M. 22. Only one *forte*. No pedal.

M. 24. Now it is *forte*.

M. 27. The new key is a new world, a little brighter and more hopeful. There is a feeling of solace and inner peace.

M. 31. The sound is darker than before. Be aware of the G♯ pedal and sensitive to the E♮.

M. 33. Swell to the C♯, then resolve to the A.

M. 35. A little more sound.

M. 39 and following. The first chord of each repetition is the theme, so lean in. The scales must have a sense of elegance and the notes are like water drops. Come out with the wrist so there is no accent at the end.

M. 47. Rotate the wrist. Throw the weight. Hear the change from C♯ to D♮ . Come out of each second chord to prepare for the next.

M. 49. Use a flutter pedal. The *tremolo* starts from nowhere. Ride the keys. Feel the chilling wind, icy cold. A foreboding, fearful. You're shivering, out in the cold with a wet shirt.

M. 50. The melody louder than the previous *tremolo*. A beautiful singing melody with a chilling accompaniment. *Decrescendo* the melody.

M. 56. Light first chord [a resolution]. Hear the register change and dark mood of beat three. Take time to hear the change to C♮ .

M. 57. Practice an octave *tremolo*. Then add the other notes. No big *ritard*. Clearer pedal, but not a true E major.

Mvt. 3. Presto

With enthusiasm and with abandon. Let us feel that you're very happy when you're playing this movement. The wrist and arm must follow the fingers, and the arms must be loose. Don't get stuck.

Mm. 1–2. The first two measures lead into m. 3. There is a sense of movement so that it swings and it doesn't run away.

M. 3. Get hold of the rhythm. The third chord is an "out" motion. The first chord is an "in."

Mm. 3–5. Least, more, most, then *decrescendo*. The left hand takes last C [see many similar spots].

M. 15. A different sound, lower and wider.

M. 19. The wrist moves down, then up.

Mm. 27–29. Drive forward.

M. 30. A question.

M. 31. The answer.

M. 47. Imitation in the lower voice. Don't rush.

M. 53. Start.

M. 58. Less.

M. 59. Serious.

M. 65. Start.

M. 79. Dance. Keep the wrists loose.

M. 87. More linear. Take the time needed for the left hand.

M. 95. Not too loud. This the first time. Then m. 99 is more, and m. 103 is the most, so that when *he* insists, *you* insist.

Mm. 127–130. *Decrescendo*. A little *ritard* for transition.

M. 131. Start fresh.

Mm. 157–158. The first chord is *sforzando,* not the second.

Mm. 177–178. Rich chords.

M. 179 and following. As many colors of A♭s as possible.

M. 186. *Diminuendo.* The last A♭ belongs to the next phrase.

Mm. 193–194. *Decrescendo.*

M. 197. Play the D♭ with the left hand.

Mm. 215–216. *Legato* left-hand octaves.

Mm. 217–218. *Decrescendo* to the C.

M. 225. A different color for the G♭s.

Mm. 247–248. Less than mm. 245–246.

Mm. 251–252. Less than mm. 249–250.

M. 257. More.

Mm. 267–268. Bring to a close.

Mm. 269–277. One voice, then two, and so forth, until six voices.

M. 279. Play the C [beat 3] with the left hand.

M. 308. Start anew.

Mm. 328, 330, 332. Color the bass octaves.

M. 336. Throw the arm into the last note. Then push off.

M. 346. Drop back in volume.

Mvt. 4. Allegro

This movement is the easiest musically but gives a sense of greatness, of strength.

M. 4. The E is more than the D in m. 2.

M. 6. The C♮ is less than the C♯ in m. 5.

M. 8. More sustained sounds in the *crescendo* in contrast to the shorter eighth notes.

M. 11. More going to A♯.

M. 25. *Crescendo.*

M. 26. Most.

Mm. 30, 31. *Crescendo* to beat 3.

M. 33. Resolve to beat 4.

M. 34. Maintain weight in the right-hand fingers. Help with the wrist. A gradual *crescendo.*

M. 38. *Crescendo.*

M. 43. Use wrist rotation for the sixteenths.

M. 44. Heavy, sustained chords.

M. 52. Less, only *mezzo piano.*

Mm. 56–57. Not heavy.

M. 57. The last two eighths are detached.

M. 58. Hold the first notes just a bit. Then begin the *tremolo.*

M. 61. Full value, even a bit of extra time.

M. 62. Use wrist. Relax hand and follow curves of the *arpeggio* [*decrescendo,* then *crescendo*]. Shape the left hand as in the beginning.

M. 63. Take time on beat 4 and keep the elbow very loose.

M. 66. The right hand is quiet and close to the key.

M. 70. E major is a surprise. Listen for the D [beat 3].

Mm. 71–72. Smooth; don't pulse the rhythm.

Mm. 81–87. Be aware of various levels of sound. Use the wrist; follow the curves, shaping.

M. 90. Bigger chords must have a bigger sound.

Mm. 95–96. Dramatic. Pull or grab the chords. Beat 1 is dissonance; beat 3 is resolution.

M. 97. Start. *Crescendo.*

M. 103. Drop back.

Mm. 105–106. *Crescendo.*

Mm. 107–112. Two-measure phrases. Feel the underlying excitement.

M. 108. Hear the C resolving to B.

M. 114. Pull or grab the chords. Lead the *arpeggios* with the right hand.

M. 115. Regenerate.

M. 122. Beat 3 is an "up" motion. The final chord [m. 123] is a "down" with full arm sonority.

TWENTY-SEVEN

ROBERT SCHUMANN

I think Schumann speaks to me very specially, and so I listen to him very specially. And he means something very special. What is it? It is young and truly romantic, but romantic in a way that is always fresh, that cannot be warmed over. You start playing him, and the romantic feelings are the ones that you had at 18. No matter if you are 80, you feel 18 when you play his music. It is so direct and so personal when you play Schumann. That's why there are very few Schumann players today.

There used to be great Schumann players and even today you do have a Radu Lupu who plays beautiful Schumann or Perahia who plays beautiful Schumann, but very few play really beautiful Schumann. The ideas just tumble out with Schumann. His texture changes and his whimsical approach, I would say his lack of mastery. He was not a Brahms or a Beethoven, but when he speaks to you, you know that you have to respond. He addresses you personally, and he addresses your feelings. And when you play him, you build a technique to meet his needs, how the fingers quickly enter the keyboard and exit, like little "lightnings."

Schumann is very, very special, feeling-wise, the really romantic approach. You see, Schumann you can play every day. Tchaikovsky you cannot. You play Tchaikovsky one day and the second day, and then you need a few days rest to come back. You will always love him; he has so much beauty and drama and romanticism in a way, but his romanticism, grand romanticism, is not the beauty of a Schumann. It doesn't touch the soul as deeply. Tchaikovsky touches the feelings, like a good dinner, like a good wine, that kind of a feeling, but not the feeling with which you identify, as I say, that touches your soul.

KREISLERIANA, OP. 16

No. 1. Äuszerst bewegt

M. 1. Start the line *mezzo forte*. Play faster, with more fury and with much pedal. Connect the left-hand octaves and chords with pedal throughout.

M. 4. A pedal change for the right-hand E.

M. 8. Build to the *sforzando*. And play the top note with a wrist snap.

M. 11. Play the inner line poetically [G-F-E-D].

M. 17. Begin again.

M. 25. The first note should never be automatic.

M. 37. Play a lower level than in m. 33.

Mm. 45–46. This is a high point. Play two-measure groupings here.

M. 57. Emphasize the *sforzando* in the left hand, not the right hand.

M. 65. Begin less again.

M. 72. The last chord is only an eighth note.

No. 2. Sehr innig und nicht zu rasch

M. 2. Play the chord as a *sforzando*.

M. 4. Play this second chord full but not *sforzando*, then begin
  pianissimo.

M. 5. Play the inner lines with direction.

M. 8. Close the inner lines with a clear triplet.

M. 11. *Diminuendo* the left-hand trill to close the phrase.

M. 12. Hear the line of the A♭ and G.

M. 13. As the G *decrescendos*, match the F to the point of decay.

M. 15. Color the G in contrast to m. 13.

M. 16. Start a long line.

M. 25. Play the tenor note late in each rolled chord.

Mm. 29–30. Pedal beats 2 and 3.

M. 36. Play the chord *sforzando*.

M. 38. Very alive. Play two equal contrapuntal voices. Play four-measure
  phrases.

M. 41. Close the phrase.

Mm. 47–48. Repeat the phrase with less sound [E♭ -B♭ -C-D♭].

M. 80. Pedal each eighth note.

Mm. 92–93. Faster and in phrases. Hear the imitation in the bass. Swell
  to the left-hand A [of m. 93].

Mm. 96–99. Build the repetitions of the motive. Try short Ds in the
  bass.

Mm. 103–105. The bass notes C, D, and E♮ build as a support.

M. 106. Not so loud. Save for the culmination in mm. 109–110.

M. 110. The hands starting together. Richer.

Mm. 120–123. Play one long phrase. Like a last breath. More poetic.

M. 134. Roll the G♭ -B♭ to contrast the F♯ -A♯ of m. 132.

M. 141. Roll the G⁷ chord to a beautiful sound on the top G.

M. 142. *Forte* on the downbeat. This is the culmination of the *ad libitum* of m. 141.

Mm. 159–165. Full pedal here, since it's in the treble.

No. 3. *Sehr aufgeregt*

M. 1. Faster, but clear. Play four-measure phrases, each one beginning with an important pickup note. The wrist must bring out the right hand's G-A-B♭.

Mm. 2–4. Pluck the bass notes.

M. 4. The F♯-D must be very clear.

Mm. 19–21. Building the A-D and A♭-D to the final A♮-D.

M. 33. Freely passionate. The after-note Ds must be light breaths.

M. 35. The *sforzando* must be reached.

M. 50. Play the left-hand grace note longer and supportive.

M. 68. Pause for the right-hand D♭.

Mm. 79–83 [second ending]. Reiterate each measure.

M. 129. Start from here.

M. 137 to the end. "Double time."

Mm. 137–140. Play the lower right-hand note with the left hand.

Ex. 27.1. mm. 137–140

M. 145. Resolve to beat one, then go on.

Mm. 145–148. Use fingering of mm. 137–140.

M. 152. *Crescendo* to m. 153.

M. 153. Start the long *crescendo* on beat two.

M. 156. Pull back. Broader for the final chord.

No. 4. *Sehr langsam*

M. 1. Match the last chord to the point of decay of the previous chord. Listen for a true *legato* of all lines.

Mm. 5–6. Play the thirty-second notes *liberamente*, as a *cadenza*. Begin slower.

Mm. 12–23. Practice each line for *legato* phrasing.

M. 27. The *adagio* does not need to be played slower. The *ritardando* is already enough.

No. 5. *Sehr lebhaft*

Mm. 1–2. The last sixteenth note moves to the following measure.

Mm. 1–5. Group these five measures together. They must all be under the same roof.

M. 5. Multi-voices. Hear gnomes from all directions.

M. 14b. Even though it's impossible, the B♭ must swell.

Mm. 15–16. The dotted patterns should sound jerky; then the even eighths will sound smooth. Have variety in the way that you play recurrences of the phrase.

M. 25. Sweep over the top of the line.

M. 37. The left hand should run out. Not a *crescendo.*

Mm. 42–43. Resolve the bass F♯ to the G.

Mm. 44–45. Resolve bass A to the B♭.

M. 55. Pull back. Take time, but come back to the tempo.

M. 67. Prolong this B♭, but then no *ritardando.*

M. 70. The sixteenth note is within the *ritardando,* so it is not quick.

Mm. 81, 83, 85. Play wrist chords [beats 2 and 3] that lead the line forward.

M. 87. Broaden into m. 88.

M. 95. *Decrescendo.*

M. 111. Play the left hand slightly less so it easily joins the right hand.

M. 112. Hear the octaves between the hands.

M. 120. *Decrescendo* the cadence.

M. 147. Resolve to the right hand's G [beat 2].

M. 160. The D major chord can be plucked. *Decrescendo* to the G minor chord.

No. 6. *Sehr langsam*

M. 1. Keep the phrase moving.

M. 3. *Mezzo piano.* Not *pianissimo* each time.

M. 5. The G^7 chord opens the door.

M. 6. *Crescendo* to beats 2, 4, etc., but don't rush the thirty-second-note entrances. These show the influence of Bach.

M. 9. Take a little time into the G♭ [beat 3].

M. 10. Even more time than the previous measure.

M. 11. Let the left hand be clearly heard.

M. 15. *Crescendo* the graces.

M. 19. An awakening.

M. 20. A♭-G answers the B♭-F.

M. 24. Relate the E♭ to the next D [m. 25]. Keep all this quiet.

M. 35. Roll the chord, crossing the left hand over to play the top F as a beautiful note.

No. 7. *Sehr rasch*

M. 1. Start *mezzo forte*. Use wrist into the top right-hand notes as well as in the left hand.

M. 8. Left-hand *sforzando* with the side of the hand.

Mm. 17–18. Phrase two measures together.

M. 32. Snap the wrist on the high C to close the section.

M. 40. Close this section before beginning the scale.

Mm. 41–52. Shape the lines and make room for new entrances. Start the *fugue* in one *forte*. Save for m. 48.

M. 60. Use the repetition to build to m. 61.

M. 65. Broaden to prepare for the richness of mm. 66–67.

M. 89. The *sforzando* in left hand closes this section.

M. 90. A remembrance of what has occurred.

M. 106. Not too much *ritardando*.

M. 110. Play the grace note quickly, but clearly.

No. 8. *Schnell und spieland*

M. 1. Quick and playful. Think long phrases. These are elves, not elephants! Work on wrist motion until natural. The upbeat F♯ is "in"; the G is "out," et cetera.

M. 15. Left-hand *legato* octaves.

M. 26. Shape the left hand. It can be a freer tempo. The right hand continues the "blip, blip."

M. 74. This theme is played with the arm. It can be a little slower. Pedal measure to measure, not as marked.

M. 81. Climax on the Cs. Then start less.

M. 113. Fade the Gs with flutter pedal. Wait for three pedal changes.

M. 129. A little more sound on the left-hand Fs.

M. 139. This is the last time. Pause after the treble G-D before continuing the phrase.

M. 141. Come down only to *piano*, then fade to the end.

M. 145. *Ritard* between the last two notes.

CONCERTO IN A MINOR, OP. 54

DEBUT WITH THE SCHUMANN CONCERTO

STUDENT: How many times have you played the Schumann?

PRESSLER: Many times. That was my debut concerto with Ormandy, that was when I was for the first time in the Academy of Music, in the rehearsal, sitting on that stage, with the Philadelphia Orchestra playing. And the celli play (Pressler sings the second movement theme A-G, E-C, A-G). I never heard such a beautiful sound ever in my life. So I was seated there. It's the rehearsal, I was playing, and there comes that moment, and I just sit there [Pressler mimics with wide-mouthed amazement], and Ormandy looks at me, and I jump in with my part. I still remember.

And after the rehearsal, Ormandy says, "Can't you look at me?" I didn't even know that I had to look at him because I thought that he would look at me, but I remember that sensation. First of all, it started with [Marcel] Tabuteau playing the oboe. Such oboe playing doesn't exist today. There is nobody that plays that theme like that. Okay, that was beautiful and I played the theme right after him. I tried to imitate him as much as I could. But then the celli started (A-G); and since that time, I have never had that sensation ever again. I mean, I still enjoy it, but that kind of a sound, that was really unexpected. I had never thought that on earth you hear that kind of sound.

Mvt. 1. Allegro

M. 1. *Crescendo* to the *sforzando.* Then start from the second group and *crescendo* all the way to the *sforzando* in m. 3.

M. 2. With energy.

M. 12. A quick grace note. Take the left-hand [beat 1] C with the right hand.

M. 14. Resolve the E to the D.

M. 15. Resolve the C to the B♭ and the B♭ to the A.

M. 20. The right hand is the accompaniment to a song. The left hand is *legato.*

M. 25. Close to beat three. Then less.

Mm. 32–33. Play the lower treble line with the left hand. The C♯ -D and B♮ -C not too hazy.

Ex. 27.2. mm. 32–33

M. 34. Hear the C♯-D and B♮-C in a new register.

Mm. 35–36. C major cadence.

Mm. 51–52. Hear the harmony change to G minor.

M. 52. Bring out the canon of D-D-C-C-B♭-B♭ between the hands.

M. 56. Tops.

M. 58. A new color.

M. 65. Relate the C [last note of turn] to the B♭.

Mm. 65–66. Whisper sweet nothings: "I love you."

Mm. 69–70. Very even and clear all the way to the bottom.

M. 88. Close the phrase.

Mm. 112–114. Shape the phrase.

Mm. 128–130. Take the left hand's 1st- and 3rd-beat top notes with the right hand.

Mm. 132–133. Not too dry; use some pedal.

M. 133. Loose arm. Brilliant. Don't rush.

M. 156. Depth of tone, fullness, generous with weight and depth. Use the best finger to apply the arm weight.

M. 157. Use the right hand this time. It should be perfectly even, and we shouldn't be able to tell when the left hand takes over.

Ex. 27.3. mm. 156–157

M. 164. Play the melody *mezzo forte,* still clearly projected.

M. 183. More.

M. 185. Surprise. Start and build from the D♮.

M. 189. More energy.

M. 197. *Legato* octaves.

Mm. 198–200. Each one grows.

M. 201. D♮-E♭-C takes longer [than m. 197] because you have a much bigger jump to play.

M. 205. Play "up-down." That gives it leverage. Playing the repeated note is one thing, but when you play the other notes, it causes you to play

3–3, and that is very difficult. Your finger is not there. You make a motion with your hand before the finger has reached the key. You should work on this without the triplets. Then play the melody with the chords. Joyful, passionate throughout this entire section and more dynamic variety.

M. 207. Each time you have that long note, free your arm. Free everything around it.

Mm. 208, 212. Breathe. Change to a more natural phrasing.

Mm. 209–210. Voice the bass line while the flutes and violins play the tune.

M. 214. That's the first *sforzando*.

M. 229. Start *piano*.

M. 238. The E is a new entrance.

M. 242. The D♯ in the left hand reacts to the *sforzando* and gives impetus to the left hand.

M. 245. *Passionata! Fortissimo!*

M. 295. Accented eighth notes.

M. 311. Play the left-hand A-B-B♯ -C♯ bass line *legato*.

M. 315. Less. *Decrescendo*.

Mm. 318–319. Hear the left-hand line, D-C♯ -B-D-B, as a cello line.

M. 343. A color change to D minor [beat 3].

M. 365. Sing. Each left-hand group leads to the next melody note.

Mm. 381–383. The left hand can help.

Ex. 27.4. mm. 381–383

M. 399. You hit that E♭ by itself. You can take a little time, but it is E♭ -C. You can play the E♭ with the left hand.

M. 401. *Ritard,* but without *diminuendo,* to start the *cadenza* out of a rich bass with full sound and expression. There are so many ways of doing it to make it easier for you, such as L-R-L-R-L.

M. 402. Very full. Hear the quarter equal to the half note of the preceding.

Mm. 404–405. Less and less.

M. 406. We have to hear the A♭ -G. Start shorter and slower.

M. 410. And more.

M. 411. It is *stringendo*, but you can pull back a little for the C minor [beat 1].

M. 415. Keep going.

M. 417. Those are eighths in the left hand. Don't land on beat four.

M. 418. A deceptive cadence. Then surprise us. Begin less; it starts.

M. 420. You have an open phrase and a closed phrase [m. 421]. These are horns; hear the tops.

M. 421. Out on the downbeat. Hand redistributions.

Mm. 421–425. Hand redistributions.

Ex. 27.5. mm. 421–425

M. 426. With strings added.

Mm. 426–429. You have to be careful that the repeated notes are played. It's question-answer, question-answer.

M. 430. Start.

M. 432. *Piú piano.*

M. 434. The trills are on the beat, not before. A crisp trill. Voice the tops of the left-hand chords.

M. 436. The E goes down to D.

M. 439. Out. Don't land on those notes. *Leggiero.* The left hand is lighter each time.

M. 441. Take the E [beat 1] with the right hand's first finger.

M. 445. Take the G [the left hand's seventh note] with the right hand's first finger.

Mm. 446–451. Hear the progression from F♯ to D.

M. 448. No accent on the G♯ [beat 3].

M. 451. You only stretch to get to that B♭. The rest is in time. Then *espressivo.*

M. 452. Less on beat 3.

M. 454. Darker in mood.

M. 455. A surprise chord. The left hand should be *legato*.

M. 483. Play the B♭ [beat 2] with the left hand.

M. 492. Clear eighths [the triplets].

M. 496. The left hand is *legato*.

M. 500. Clear sixteenth chords.

M. 504. *Espressivo*. Feel the intervals.

M. 510. Less sound this time. Hear the left hand.

M. 516. Don't let the pedal accent the As. The left hand must sound the same all the way through. Use the *una corda*.

Mm. 522–528. *Diminuendo* to nothing.

M. 528. Left hand, play the second finger on the single-note As.

M. 537. Don't accent notes that Schumann doesn't accent.

M. 540. You can play that downbeat as a right-hand octave.

Mvt. 2. Intermezzo

M. 68. *Diminuendo* together with the strings and keep it hanging in the air a bit. The right hand takes the E.

M. 91. Relate the C♮ to the B♭ [m. 93] and the G♯ [m. 96].

M. 94. No swell here, so don't do anything extra. No extra expression or weight.

M. 97. Here you can do a little swell.

M. 106. A special moment.

Mvt. 3. Allegro vivace

M. 2. Start less after the *sforzando* and then *crescendo* toward the next *sforzando*.

Mm. 120–123. The four bars in *diminuendo*. The *staccato* notes between the syncopations should jump. Fresh and light.

Mm. 161–164. Follow the left-hand line down.

M. 166. Use the wrist for fluency and to bring out the downbeats.

M. 173. Begin a *crescendo* by following two-measure groups.

Mm. 181 and 183. Accent the tops of the *arpeggios*. Careful coordination of beats 2 and 3 with the right hand.

M. 185. Start.

Mm. 231–236. *Virtuoso*. Take over during the orchestra's rest.

Mm. 231–233. "Out-in," "out-in."

M. 248. Close beat 1, then start again on beat 2.

Mm. 252–255. Four-measure phrases.

M. 256. Give the grace notes bite.

M. 334. Start *mezzo piano*.

M. 771. Hold the tempo. Don't stop every two bars. Practice the left hand alone for technical and memory security and for four-measure phrasing.

M. 786. Punctuate the cadence with a separation in the left hand. Have a *diminuendo*.

Mm. 878–879. Vary the C♯s.

M. 919. Enjoy it.

M. 944. Push forward.

PETER ILYICH TCHAIKOVSKY

Tchaikovsky's first concerto, which uses the complete armor of a pianist, is one of the grandest in the repertoire. The beautiful melody of the second movement really touches the soul, but it is a different soul than the soul that Beethoven touches. It's as different as a beautiful novel that inspires and delights you compared to reading a treatise like Goethe's *Faust*. Beethoven will ask of you the depths, the penetration, the metaphysical, like those trills in the Op. 111, almost a meditation. In Tchaikovsky it is a direct approach like Verdi is to the opera. It is a wonderful piano concerto, and I've learned to love it more and more because the use of the keyboard is magnificent. And what an inspiration that beginning, how powerful! It's a completely different attitude from Beethoven or Brahms. It's a different person who plays a great Beethoven from the person who plays a great Tchaikovsky, but the person who plays a great Tchaikovsky will also play a great Prokofiev which comes out of Tchaikovsky.

PIANO CONCERTO IN B-FLAT MINOR, OP. 23

Mvt. 1. Andante non troppo e molto maestoso
You have everything it takes to play this concerto. You have drive; you have a feeling for the music. What's missing? To begin with, what's missing is a feeling that Tchaikovsky's more important than you are. By the freedoms that you take, you feel you are more important than Tchaikovsky. Of course, we are all spoiled by some of the great pianists, Horowitz, Martha Argerich, the ones who take immense freedoms. And when they do it, by virtue of their enormous ability, one excuses it and accepts it. But we as young pianists—like me!—we look at a score as the teacher.

What was missing in your playing first of all was *legato*. All the octaves were *non-legato*. He takes all that trouble to write all that under one slur [mm. 94–95], and then he writes all the two-note slurs [mm. 96–97].

You play very well at m. 108 [the second theme]. Why do you play it so much faster and louder when it comes back and both hands take it [m. 168]? It's the same. He just translates it so there is more variety in his approach.

M. 6. Let each measure grow.

M. 16. Build to this point to lead back to the return.

M. 25. Begin *mezzo forte*. Shape the phrase. *Crescendo.*

M. 26. Sing the chord [beat 2].

M. 27. The octaves are *legato,* not just dah-dah-dah-dah-dah-dah-dah [Pressler plays bouncing octaves]. It's a beautiful melody. Just because we heard it in the movies and on every sound track in the country and on every elevator, you renew it when you play the piece because it's not just for the display. It's for the beauty. It's for the power and the pianism, which is wonderful. It's really marvelous to have a Ferrari, isn't it? Play the octave passage with just the thumbs. The thumb is very close. And now add to it the top, so it sings.

M. 29. Start *mezzo forte* again.

Mm. 36–39. Then a place like this, even a person like me who knows the piece can't recognize it, because you play it so fast. There are bars. There is rhythm. Yes, we have freedom. Yes, we can go faster. After all, the best example is Horowitz, who is the greatest pianist who ever played that; and he goes tremendously fast. But there is always a rhythm in it. And hear the sequences in it.

M. 41. Then that first *cadenza.* Everything's on the same level. The first one must be less, then more, then the most [leading to m. 44], and then start again. And don't snap those single notes. You must be certain that you play them exactly. You could even play them with alternating hands. A missed note here is like you're going out to conduct and your suit opens up in the back. Everybody laughs at you. And if you could see yourself, you'd laugh, too. You'd say, "How silly! I took my old suit that doesn't fit anymore." Watch when you play those notes. In a concert your hands will sweat and be cold. And when you see any famous person in the house, you will shake. Even if you sweat and are cold, those notes you cannot miss. And the last sixth must end together. That's why it is probably better to use one hand for the sixths so that no matter what happens in the chord itself, the ending will be exact. And don't sit there on the top note. [Pressler demonstrates, taking time to wipe his forehead on the long note.]

M. 78. Can you make those top notes like little bells? Use your wrist, but with the pedal.

M. 81. Close the phrase.

M. 95. Play the first G octave with the left hand.

Mm. 96–97. More declamatory.

M. 100. Play the D♭ and C octaves with the right hand instead of the left hand.

M. 108. This is like the *Gopak,* the Russian dance.

Mm. 115–116. Play the F octaves in the left hand.

M. 117. *Crescendo* to the top with an accent.

M. 118. Play as two-note slurs.

M. 133. Hold back just a little before the orchestra returns.

M. 142. *Crescendo* to the top.

M. 160. Lead with the left hand. Shape the line.

M. 163. Begin adding more pedal.

M. 183. Less; close it.

M. 192. After the long A♮ , the B♭ is less. Release.

M. 196. Release the phrase.

M. 198–199. When he does it twice, he *needs* to say it twice, so *you* have to *need* to say it twice.

M. 204. End *pianissimo.*

M. 218. Now with all the notes, it's the same thing. Shape it the same; phrase exactly as Tchaikovsky asks. Just because it is familiar to us, you still have to phrase.

M. 234. The left hand starts again.

M. 240. You have to give us the changes [the inner notes B♮ -C-B♮ -D, C-E♭ -D-F]. Now build it. To my ears, your biggest *crescendo* is at the beginning, and then there is not enough at the top.

Mm. 244–246. Hear the chords. [Pressler plays the right-hand chords only.]

M. 260. Play that place so that the cup runneth over. He says *molto espressivo.*

M. 263. He dissolves it out. Keep the pedal down; and when you hear dirt, shake it out a little.

M. 275. Like a harp.

M. 346. Settle deep into each note.

M. 352. Broaden over the top.

M. 357. Not so quiet; *mezzo piano.*

M. 362. Appreciate the different registers.

M. 370. It's all one phrase; interlock the motives.

M. 434. Don't rush.

Mm. 436–437. Strike the tops [right-hand, beats 2 and 4].

M. 443. Start again.

M. 470. *Decrescendo.*

M. 491. With pedal.

M. 512. Start.

M. 518. Slur from C♯ to D.

M. 546. Here again, close the phrase.

M. 568. It should have the charm of a music box.

M. 578. Less and less; let it run out.

M. 584. Wrist octaves.

M. 591. Release the pedal on beat 3, and shape the two-note slur to m. 592.

Mm. 599–600. The way the left hand talks, the right hand answers.

M. 605. A *fermata* over the first chord, then begin the line.

M. 606. Stress the long note, then resolve it. Play *mezzo piano,* not *pianissimo.*

M. 609. Slower; it's a deceptive resolution.

M. 610. In the descending run, try playing the black notes in the right hand and the white notes in the left hand.

M. 615. Start a little slower.

M. 634. Slur the right-hand top G to the C [less on the lower note].

M. 662. The orchestra plays all the downbeats. You make a line out of it. Begin *mezzo forte* and then *crescendo.*

Mvt. 2. Andantino semplice

M. 13. Project with tone. *Mezzo piano.*

Mm. 29–30. Close each measure.

M. 35. *Crescendo* to a *mezzo forte.*

M. 42. Flutter the pedal.

M. 48. Relate to the trill that's coming.

Mm. 50–51. Stay in tempo.

Mm. 63–64. *Crescendo.*

Mm. 100–101. In time.

Mm. 168–169. Close the two chords with a *decrescendo.*

Mvt. 3. Allegro con fuoco

M. 32. Less.

M. 36. Build to the downbeat of m. 37.

M. 66. Lean into the sonority.

Mm. 77–78. The left-hand A♮ is less.

M. 80. Begin pushing forward.

M. 102. *Crescendo* into m. 103 [C-D♮].

M. 104. *Crescendo* into m. 105 [D♮-E♮].

M. 113. Wrist octaves, then use the arm at the top of the *crescendo.*

M. 138. Lean in again.
M. 188. Use wrist on the accents.
M. 213. Broaden into m. 214.
M. 248. Start again. Then a huge *crescendo.*
M. 284. No false accents.

TWENTY-NINE

CARL MARIA VON WEBER

For many years most of my students played Weber's "Perpetual Motion." It applies the technical principles learned in the exercises and brings endurance, like the perpetual motion that Paganini has for the violinist. I learned it in my youth, and I was encouraged by the generation before mine. A man like [Benno] Moiseiwitsch would play it with great charm and elegance. Hofmann would play it, and the endurance would be astonishing. I say we play it for endurance, but it is also a very beautiful piece. I remember that when I found one could use the wrist in order to relax, one could more easily get through it. I felt it was a wonderful *étude* for strengthening the hand, infusing the wrist principle as helper in overcoming tiredness in many places and having that endurance which we need for bigger, longer pieces.

"PERPETUAL MOTION": SONATA IN C MAJOR, OP. 24, FINALE

Mm. 1–4. The entire piece is practiced first with the four-note wrist groups, with the right hand eventually playing long lines of unaccented notes. The left hand stays very close to the keys.

M. 4. Take a little time before the *piano* of m. 5.

Mm. 5–7. The left hand plays the thirds with an upward release.

Mm. 7–8. Close the cadence in the left hand. Have a slight breath before beginning the theme again.

Mm. 14–15. *Decrescendo* to the line before the *fortissimo*.

Mm. 16–17. Phrase in two-measure groups.

M. 19. Have a slight break before the chord.

M. 21. *Decrescendo* as the line descends.

Mm. 26–27. The left hand plays the lower Gs.

Ex. 29.1. mm. 26–27

Mm. 30–31. The left hand plays the Gs.

Ex. 29.2. mm. 30–31

Mm. 34–36. The left hand plays the lower Ds and Cs.

Ex. 29.3. mm. 34–36

Mm. 43–44. The left hand takes the low F♯s.
Mm. 65–68. Build.
M. 69. Start.
M. 72. *Decrescendo* to the downbeat of m. 73.
Mm. 75–76. Use several changes to clear the pedal.
M. 90. *Decrescendo* as the line ascends to the *dolce*.
M. 94. *Decrescendo*.
M. 102. The left hand takes A♯ .

Mm. 107–108. Play two-note slurs in the left hand.

M. 112. Right hand, play an A♯ grace note to the high A♯. Resolve the chord to B major [m. 113].

M. 115. Play the high D♯ with the left hand.

M. 132. Play the ascending line elegantly.

M. 152. Wrist rotation for the right-hand broken chords.

Mm. 162–163. No pedal.

Mm. 168–169. Swell these measures.

M. 170. Sing the quarter-note line, which is doubled in both hands.

M. 179. A slight pulling back and *decrescendo*.

Mm. 180–181. *Crescendo* as the line ascends.

M. 183. *Decrescendo* as the line descends.

Mm. 188–191. Keep the hand turned in one direction.

M. 192. The left hand takes the E♭.

Mm. 208, 210, 212. The left hand takes the low note [B♮].

M. 214. The left hand takes the low note [E♮].

M. 226. *Leggiero.*

Mm. 230–232. The left hand takes the offbeat notes.

Ex. 29.4. mm. 230–232

M. 241. "Out" after beat 1 to begin the scale.

M. 245. Lean into the G, then start again.

M. 269. Accent the bass G octave.

M. 273. Start.

Mm. 274–277. Play the second, third, and fourth notes an octave lower than written.

Ex. 29.5. mm. 274–277

M. 279. Left-hand wrist octave, not plodding.

M. 288. A slight broadening on beat 1.

Mm. 296–300. Add a grace note as in m. 295.

Mm. 300–301. Play out [*decrescendo*].

Mm. 302–308. Hear the left-hand line [G-C-E-G-C] and build.

M. 312. Phrase into the G [B-C-G]. Then start *mezzo forte.*

M. 317. Have a slight break before the left-hand C octave.

Mm. 324–327. Phrase from the last eighth into beat 2.

Mm. 327–330. Play the passage in double octaves.

Mm. 329–330. *Crescendo* to the last chord.

APPENDIX A.
MENAHEM PRESSLER'S
MUSICAL ANCESTRY

Through his various teachers, Menahem Pressler's musical ancestry can be traced back to Bach, Beethoven, Mozart, Chopin, Liszt, and many other significant pianists and musicians. During his youth and early concert career he sought out the world's finest teachers–mentors who expanded his pedagogical training to include the German, French, and Russian heritages. Pressler's own teaching, therefore, is a blending of all his varied influences and traditions.

The following chart places Pressler in the center surrounded by each of his teachers, then traces their ancestry back through history.

Pressler's Musical Ancestry

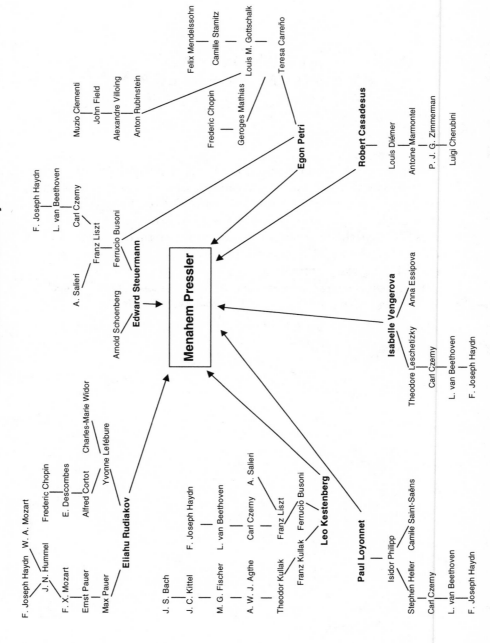

APPENDIX B. LINEAGE OF PRESSLER'S PIANO TEACHERS

The following outline illustrates a more complete lineage of Pressler's musical ancestry than the chart found in Appendix A. Thus we can see that influences coming from Germany, Austria, Italy, France, Hungary, Poland, Russia, Israel, and many other countries became part of Pressler's musical background and influence.

I. Kitzl
II. Rossi
III. Eliahu Rudiakov
  A. Max Pauer
    1. Ernst Pauer
      a) Franz Xaver Mozart
        (1) Franz Xaver Niemetschek
        (2) Sigismund Ritter von Neukomm
          (a) Franz Xaver Weissauer
          (b) Michael Haydn
          (c) Franz Joseph Haydn
        (3) Andreas Steicher
        (4) Johann Nepomuk Hummel
          (a) Wolfgang Amadeus Mozart
          (b) Franz Joseph Haydn
        (5) Antonio Salieri
        (6) Georg Joseph Vogler
          (a) Giovanni Battista Martini
            (i) Angelo Predieri
            (ii) Giovanni Antonio Ricieri
            (iii) Francesco Antonio Pistacchi
          (b) Francesco Antonio Vallotti
            (i) Ignazio Donati
        (7) Johann Georg Albrechtsberger
          (a) Leopold Pittner
          (b) Marian Gurtler
          (c) Joseph Weiss
    2. Vincenz Lachner
      a) Franz Paul Lachner

(1) Anton Lachner
(2) Simon Sechter
    (a) Leopold Koželuh
    (b) Franz Dussek
        (i) F. Habermann
        (ii) Georg Christoph Wagenseil
            (*a*) Johann Joseph Fux
    (c) Joseph Peter Emilius Hartmann
(3) Abbé Maximillian Stadler
    (a) Johann Georg Albrechtsberger
        (i) Leopold Pittner
        (ii) Marian Gurtler
        (iii) Joseph Weiss
B. Yvonne Lefébure (most likely)
  1. Charles-Marie Widor
  2. Alfred Denis Cortot
    a) Émile Descombes
      (1) Frédéric Chopin
        (a) Adalbert Zywny
        (b) Joseph Eloner
    b) Louis Diémer
      (1) Antoine-François Marmontel
        (a) Pierre-Joseph-Guillaume Zimmerman
            (i) Luigi Cherubini
            (ii) François-Adrien Boieldieu
                (*a*) Charles Brocha
            (iii) Jean-Baptiste Ray
            (iv) Charles-Simon Catel
                (*a*) François-Joseph Gossec
                    (*i*) André-Joseph Blavier
                (*b*) Thomas Gobert
IV. Leo Kestenberg
  A. Franz Kullack
    1. Theodor Kullak
      a) Carl Czerny
        (1) Ludwig van Beethoven
            (a) Christian Gottlieb Neefe
            (b) Franz Joseph Haydn
            (c) Johann Georg Albrechtsberger
      b) Sichter
      c) (Carl) Otto Nicolai
      d) Albrecht Wilhelm Johann Agthe
        (1) Michael Gottard Fischer
            (a) J. C. Kittel

(i) Johann Sebastian Bach
2. Franz Liszt
  a) Carl Czerny
    (1) Ludwig van Beethoven
      (a) Christian Gottlieb Neefe
      (b) Franz Joseph Haydn
      (c) Johann Georg Albrechtsberger
  b) Antonio Salieri
3. Karl Wehle
  a) Ignaz Moscheles
4. Henry Charles Litolff
  a) Ignaz Moscheles
    (1) Johann Georg Albrechtsberger
    (2) Antonio Salieri
B. Ferruccio Busoni
  1. Wilhelm Mayer
    a) C. F. Pietsch
V. Paul Loyonnet
  A. Charles-Marie Widor
  B. Isidor Philipp
    1. Georges Mathias
      a) Frédéric Chopin
        (1) Adalbert Zywny
        (2) Joseph Eloner
    2. Camille Saint-Saëns
      a) Charlotte Masson
    3. Charles-Wilfride de Bériot
      a) Sigismond Thalberg
        (1) Johann Nepomuk Hummel
          (a) Wolfgang Amadeus Mozart
          (b) Franz Joseph Haydn
        (2) Johann Peter Pixis
          (a) Johann Georg Albrechtsberger
        (3) Frédéric Kalkbrenner
          (a) Louis Adam
          (b) Nicodami
        (4) Ignaz Moscheles
          (a) Johann Georg Albrechtsberger
          (b) Antonio Salieri
    4. Stephen Heller
      a) Franz Brauer
      b) Carl Czerny
        (1) Ludwig van Beethoven
          (a) Christian Gottlieb Neefe

(b) Franz Joseph Haydn

(c) Johann Georg Albrechtsberger

c) Anton Halm

5. Théodore Ritter

a) Franz Liszt

(1) Carl Czerny

(a) Ludwig van Beethoven

(i) Christian Gottlieb Neefe

(ii) Franz Joseph Haydn

(iii) Johann Georg Albrechtsberger

(2) Antonio Salieri

VI. Isabelle Vengerova

A. Joseph Dachs

B. Theodor Leschetizky

1. Carl Czerny

a) Ludwig van Beethoven

(1) Christian Gottlieb Neefe

(2) Franz Joseph Haydn

(3) Johann Georg Albrechtsberger

C. Anna Essipova

1. Theodor Leschetizky

a) Carl Czerny

(1) Ludwig van Beethoven

(a) Christian Gottlieb Neefe

(b) Franz Joseph Haydn

(c) Johann Georg Albrechtsberger

VII. Robert Casadesus

A. Louis Diémer

1. Antoine-François Marmontel

a) Pierre-Joseph-Guillaume Zimmerman

(1) Luigi Cherubini

(2) François-Adrien Boieldieu

(a) Charles Brocha

(3) Jean-Baptiste Ray

(4) Charles-Simon Catel

(a) François-Joseph Gossec

(i) André-Joseph Blavier

(b) Thomas Gobert

VIII. Egon Petri

A. (Maria) Teresa Carreño

1. Anton Rubinstein

a) Alexandre Villoing

(1) John Field

(a) Tommaso Giordini

        (b) Muzio Clementi
          (i) Antonio Buroni
    2. Georges Mathias
      a) Frédéric Chopin
        (1) Adalbert Zywny
        (2) Joseph Eloner
    3. Louis Moreau Gottschalk
      a) François Letellier
      b) Charles Hallé
        (1) George Osborne
      c) Camille Stametz
        (1) Frédéric Kalkbrenner
        (2) Felix Mendelssohn (-Bartholdy)
          (a) Ludwig Berger
          (b) Marie Bigot
          (c) Carl Friedrich Zelter
            (i) Carl Friedrich Christian Fasch
B. Buchmayer
C. Felix Draeseke
D. Ferruccio Busoni
  1. Wilhelm Mayer
    a) C. F. Pietsch
IX. Edward Steuermann
  A. Vilém Kurz
  B. Ferruccio Busoni
    1. Wilhelm Mayer
      a) C. F. Pietsch
  C. Arnold Schoenberg

APPENDIX C.
TRIBUTES TO PRESSLER

Colleagues, friends, students, and audiences find Menahem Pressler to be such a remarkable human being and such a strong force in music that the natural response is to express their appreciation to him and attempt to put into words the significant impact he has had on their lives. But as his daughter, Edna, notes, "He doesn't want to take time for tributes. He values getting right to the instruction." Nevertheless, it seems appropriate to include here some of the many laudatory comments received from the numerous people whose lives Pressler has touched over the course of his unparalleled career.

Pressler's joyful smile, sparkling eyes, and eager encouragement when I got it right were contagious and danced their way through my week between lessons. From him I learned about imagination and creativity that were almost childlike in approach, full of joy, poignancy, and even spirituality. He was spontaneous and effervescent. His detailed attention and enchantment with color, touch, visual imagery, and emotion opened a new world to me. In studying the Schumann *Papillons*, I remember the intensity of Pressler's search for meaning and [the] individual character of each of those delightful pieces and their individual sections. His amazing sense of timing, balance, contrast, and color in the Chopin *Andante Spianato and Grand Polonaise* invited a rainbow of emotions and technical tools to be explored and transferred in future repertoire.

–Jane Abbott-Kirk

What can I say about Mr. Pressler? Mentor, friend, establisher of taste, arbiter of standards, unending source of inspiration, and one who made self-expression and self-discipline synonymous.

–John Adams

Pressler is one of those master teachers [who is] rare in our today world. He holds that great tradition of reading the score with a certain care, of rhetoric, of a deep, first-hand understanding of the classics. And his care of the sound itself is remarkable. In our lessons, we often talked about great performers, such as Stokowski, Leschetizky, Szell, Paderewski, and I was always mesmerized, because I felt he had drunk from that water, that Pressler had received some of that information first-hand from the great masters.

Studying with Pressler is different from studying with any good, knowledgeable, practical piano teacher. His aim is not the everyday struggle of the young musician, such as winning this prize, this competition, or getting that one contract. The practical victories should happen as part of the process, as a symptom, a consequence of a much higher goal. He makes you look very far, in a life-long search, for a very high ideal. He is very able to teach the practical things, the pedal, the sound, the trill, the exercises (he had so many!), but all of these things are part of a broad concept. This way, he was looking for proportion, for the organic balance in a piece of music. The little pieces should hold together, with no room for superficial show, for extravagances with no meaning. Studying a certain piece with Pressler did not only enable me to play that particular piece on a better level but to understand better all of the pieces of that same composer.

–Fernando Araujo

A very knowledgeable pianist about the history of his *métier* and always interested in what was going on in the world. He would bring into our discussions such diverse names as Schnabel and Cortot, Horowitz and Rubinstein, Lupu and Pollini, Tureck and Kissin, or Keith Jarrett! His five decades of teaching experience allowed him to form a different approach with each student, something that we all knew, despite the fact that we didn't attend each other's lessons. In fact, numerous students from other classes would knock on his door constantly in order to ask permission to attend his lessons, and he would offer a most patrician but firm reply: "This is a private matter between me and my students, dear." What strikes one the most, however, is his dedication in the pedagogical process and his passion to nurture and refine the abilities of young performers, whether in his elite class in Bloomington's Indiana University or in master classes throughout the world.

–Konstantine Athanasakos

The first time I'd had a private lesson with him was at Adamant, and it was a completely different experience, like nothing I had ever had in a private lesson before. It was so intense, and I came away thinking, "What am I doing?" I've never had anyone talk to me that way. He was just so direct, and it sort of hurt my feelings, you know, because he would yell and say, "Why do you play that note so badly? Why do you play like 'eh, eh, eh'? Why do you not play like 'oh, oh, oh'?" He was just so finely tuned in to listening to every single note in such an intense way, and I had never had anybody who was so critical. But what made it so hard is that he was always right, and that what he said really worked.

I think he's extra hard on his students their first year because he wants to make sure they understand what his standard is. And it doesn't matter what else is going on out there, what you're getting in the studio is harder than anything you're going to encounter. And he'll tell you that very openly. He'll tell you, "It is my job to prepare you for what's out there. And so, if you can get through what's in here, you can get through anything out there." He says exactly what he thinks on the spot. It's very honest. That's one of his best qualities.

–Melinda Baird

I remember, when he taught me the Brahms, he said, "I'm showing you these things so that when you teach others. . . ." And I remember also being inspired by this whole idea that there was a future there, there was a life. It wasn't like "Either I'm going to be Van Cliburn or nothing." It's "You can be a teacher and a teacher is a noble profession, and you pass these things along," not to mention chamber music and all these other things. That was an important lesson, I think. And the other thing that was really great for me was that, even though he put a lot of magic into music for me, he took a lot of the mystery out of it, in a good way, because I was very hungry for good, solid musicianship. Detailed, that was what I was really hungry for.

I don't think that he's known to be such a patient person because he has very high and exacting standards and he's not a pushover. But when he knows that you're trying your best and that you're really giving it all you've got, he has infinite patience. He's a chameleon. He can play many types of styles. And I think he helped me with that, too, to see the specific style of these composers and the specific sounds that they have and the particular language of each composer. It's a very strong trait with him, and he's able to convey that very well.

–Jonathan Bass

I think having even the smallest exposure to Pressler's own love, respect, and, dare I say, obsession with music creates an immediate desire to care for something as much as he does, to care for the piano sound one produces, for the practice time one allocates oneself, for thoughtful programming, for the sensitive resolution of a chord. His utter dedication to music is at once humbling and inspiration.

–Alasdair Beatson

I worked hard for Pressler because he inspired me so much but also because he was kind, sweet, warm, and encouraging. From my perspective today, I feel that much of his ability to be this way came from his high degree of personal fulfillment as an artist. He was not frustrated in his own musical endeavors, but rather his childlike joy and his artistic fulfillment naturally spilled over in the lessons he taught. He was completely consumed with the joy of making music and sharing it with his students as well as with his audiences. He set an extraordinary example in that way, which I still view as a great lesson in the nature and art of generosity.

I played Chopin's *Impromptu* No. 2, and he said, "You play it very square." He then played the opening of the piece for me. It was the first time I had heard him play. And I cried, because I had never heard anyone play so beautifully [and it was the first time I had] been in the presence of an artist who connected so deeply to the magic of music. I still remember not only how he played but how he looked as he played, with a far-away look in his eyes, as though he were seeing a vision that the music created. His face showed his complete immersion in the world of music, and I felt he actually lived in that intangible world. It was always completely clear that the primary value he held as an artist was the ability to create magic through the imagination and through an intimate, sensuous relationship with the piano.

–Madeline Bruser

With his demands and expectations from all of us, Mr. Pressler taught us all what it was to achieve and maintain excellence. Learning to set priorities and to craft technique and musical analysis that would pass his muster are skills that could be applied to anything else, whether it be [as] a surgeon, painter, chef or pilot.

–Mark Cappelli

He seems to have an incredible amount of energy, which I believe is an important asset to his success; and I really liked his detailed instruction in many areas such as tone, direction, emphasizing certain important notes to bring out the texture and meaning in the music. I remember him asking me repeatedly what the music meant to me. He was extremely loyal to the score.

–Susan Chan

I can't express in words how grateful I am to have worked with [Pressler]. I feel that every little accomplishment that I have is because of my studies with him. He has completely molded the way I think, the way I feel, the way I play music, and the way I teach. Everything is according to what I learned from him in my seven years with him, so I am just so grateful. I mean, I can't tell you how every part of my musical being is because of him. From his playing, his teaching, and how he cares about all his students, it's just so inspiring. And if I could be just one percent of what he could be, it's just amazing.

Rarely would he come from a physical standpoint. It was always trying to stimulate the imagination, stimulate the hearing, and stimulate your own way of creating that expression and finding your own way of expressing what that composer has in mind. And so, I think that's why I don't think any Pressler students sound alike. I mean there are certain qualities that they have, of course. There's that care of sound. There's that care and respect for the score. But there's no formula that everyone follows because everything must be alive and must be created for the moment. And I think in that way, as we all come out, we all have his stamp; but somehow he leaves enough room for us to be able to make it our own with his guidance.

–Angela Cheng

In my own practicing, I can always vividly imagine Mr. Pressler's presence next to me. The richness of what he has passed on rings constantly in my ears as his system of musical thought was so clearly defined. Much of my time I was studying was spent thinking, "What would Mr. Pressler say about this?" I think that he wanted us to find something personal to say with the music. By helping us build the piece, pace climaxes, experiencing the emotional ups and downs within a piece, opening up our imaginations, widening our sense of color, instilling a basic common sense of finely nuanced phrasing, as well as constant attention to touch and a beautiful tone, he gave us all the tools . . . to be able to offer an intellectually and emotionally satisfying personal performance in our studying of a piece.

–Winston Choi

Every time I see Pressler play or hear him play, it's larger than life. It's not just him. It's everything about him, his life experience and the way that he deals with people, and the way that he just loves life. And you always hear that and sense that in his playing. And I think that's why, fifty years later, the Trio is still there and getting amazing reviews and he just seems continually energized. Studying with him becomes a way of life, because when someone asks you to listen that way, you can't go back and hear music in any other way. It affects everything from then on, and you enjoy music more, I think, because of all the things he's opened your ears up to.

–Alan Chow

Pianists have to be magicians for us to play a *legato* line, and certainly Mr. Pressler is the greatest magician. He's the Houdini of the piano. And he's also like the Kreisler of the piano because the way that he would describe connecting tones in a melodic line would be the way that a violinist might think of connecting the tones. Music is a life's study, or many lives' study, but he basically gave us the vocabulary and the foundation to play anything. You know, it's like you have a toolbox; and as you're learning and hopefully your whole life, you're filling this box with tools and . . . have [them] there whenever you play *any* piece of music. He really gave us that. He filled our toolbox and enabled us to spend our life in music meaningfully.

The thing that strikes one is the question that probably everybody would ask: "How in the world do you do this?" But I guess I could answer the question. As amazing as [Pressler] is, it's about his spirit, the strength of music in a person's life. It's serious business to be a musician. It's nothing to scoff at. It's the most incredible responsibility when you have great talent, and he takes that responsibility to the utmost, almost like he's on a mission to teach that much and to play that much. It's like he's on a life mission to show us that the importance of music in our lives is everything.

–Jeffrey Cohen

The miracle of his teaching is that our studio was chock full of wonderfully talented pianists, and they all sounded different because he knew how to accentuate and augment each individual's strengths. No one was ever compared to anyone other than him/herself but rather to that person's ideal performance of that piece. The feeling was that, when your lesson was not so great, he always looked so hurt, as if it was a personal injury. It made you feel guilty. And when it was good, he rarely complimented you, so that there was always a search for a higher level, no matter how good it may have been. When he did actually say it was good, it was like a miracle occurring.

–Henry Doskey

What he encouraged me to do was to play from my heart with all the passion and the feeling and the fire. That's what he loved and encouraged. If he saw it was moving you, he was very happy. I think this is a wonderful thing, not just in playing the piano but on the human level, how to relate to people, to have confidence in what you say, to believe in what you feel, and to have confidence that what you feel and believe is important and really counts. This is what he encouraged in me, and I think that's the greatest gift you can give to a student.

He demonstrated so much in my lessons, more in my undergraduate than in my graduate. And I thought, "Oh, my God, that sound is so beautiful." I watched every movement, and I saw how his touch was. Sometimes he would strike a note downward and sometimes with an upstroke, and I thought, "This works in making sound. This must be a secret. He's not telling me this, but I see it, so I've got this secret of the touch. Sometimes he's caressing the key, or sometimes he's going in, or sometimes he's getting the finger straight." I thought it was wonderful and very inspiring, and it made me very curious about things.

–Paula Ennis

His playing is a model of eloquent, exquisite beauty. He is incapable of playing a meaningless note, and he makes every passage come alive with sparkle and charm. His vision of what music is and the spiritual depth behind every note reaches deeply into one's soul and become a permanent part of everyone fortunate enough to experience it.

–George Fee

Mr. Pressler has such an impressive palette of touch and sound . . . from the most delicate *pianissimo* to the most powerful *fortissimo,* but never hard and never meaningless.

–Anne-France Fosseur

He's the only teacher I've ever encountered who teaches true mastery of the pedal, one of the aspects which I think sets his students apart from the rest.

–Charlene Harb

Mr. Pressler made no bones about making value judgments concerning my music making. I was told that what I was doing was "bad." And this is a good thing. I came to see that something that does not strive after the inherent truth of the music, the inherent joy and love and beauty in it, is bad. I know that my love for music was indeed made purer and stronger in the fire of our lessons. It was hard not to worship the man, truly! He is still my favorite pianist on earth, my ideal as a musician, for his integrity and incredible beauty and joy and sound. And in terms of his teaching, he never gave me less than one hundred percent of what he had to give in every lesson.

–Christopher Harding

Without him–I'm sure all his students say this–I would not think the way that I do, I would not see the world in the colors I see the world. I would never trade my years there. Sometimes my friends will say, "How could you stand that? My teachers were always nice to me." I say that prepared me for the world, so that when things didn't go the way I thought they should or I didn't get something, I don't have to take it personally, because he taught me, "It's all about the music. It's between me and Mozart. If you don't like it, that's your problem, not mine." And that's priceless.

–Mia Kim Hynes

He taught me how to be musically and emotionally involved while paying attention to every detail in phrasing, tone, balance, and pedaling. I have been able to teach very young students how to build up strong fingers, use wrist and arm motion for sound, and become relaxed, based on the exercises I learned from Mr. Pressler. What I have received from him has been the basis of my musicianship and my teaching, and I feel good that I can give back to three younger generations what Mr. Pressler had given me.

–Julia Lam

He taught me to try to explore every facet of a work and approach it with intense involvement in order to maximize one's expressive capabilities.

–David Lyons

Mr. Pressler has taught me to find the love, the joy, the humor in everything. He gives full and utter respect to the composer and for people. If he ever said, "It's not bad, but . . ." that was a very great compliment from him.

–Stephen Mann

It's still amazing how he used to come to his studio directly from the airport, with his suitcases, to make up lessons.

–Tongsook Han Park

His love of music and upbeat attitude were infectious to all. To my ears, his biggest message was that music and love, health, and happiness are closely connected. It was a wonderful and important truth to learn.

–Rebecca Penneys

Mr. Pressler's highly evocative language was a breath of fresh air. What I took away was the freedom to use my imagination in new ways to communicate musical experience to students. I also came to realize the importance of inspiration, for Pressler's excitement, enthusiasm, and affection for each moment in great music was highly contagious. And I worked *much* harder because of his boundless energy and the living example he set before us.

–Lynn Raley

Menahem Pressler was always a master of metaphor and could instantly translate an important point into colorful and poetic expression. His intense blue eyes flashed with fury if mistakes continued, but he was warm and generous with a chuckle if pleased and would often demonstrate during the lesson. He enlarged and enriched my repertoire of beautiful sounds from *ppp* to *FFF* and taught by example how to produce and scale these sounds. I particularly remember how he told me that every pianist has an individual "box" and that to play above one's natural sounds is to force. He helped me to find my own individual voice of expression.

–Ann Saslav

He's amazing. I don't know where he gets all this energy. I tell him he's like the Energizer Bunny, keeps beating that drum, just never stops. It's amazing. He would get off a plane and come in directly from the airport in those days, probably still does, you know, come in and teach all his lessons and stay until midnight practicing. I mean, he's an incredible bundle of energy, and he's literally consumed by music. And I think that's what gives him his love of life and gives him this energy. I think it's that love for music and that all-consuming effect that it has on him.

–Karen Shaw

What I appreciated about Mr. Pressler was that he was so kind. While he could go for the kill and you never wanted to be under his scrutiny if you weren't prepared, but his ego–he was so confident of his own playing. I remember before he went out on stage in Vienna, he was just laughing and joking backstage, and I said, "Don't you ever get nervous?" And he said, "I've never gotten nervous. Ever since I was little, I couldn't wait to get out on stage and play." But while he was so confident, he never had an ego that got in the way of his being a human being and kind.

–Jill Sprenger

Studying with Mr. Pressler has been one of the most gratifying and inspiring musical experiences I ever had. His musical vision, feeling, and understanding are almost magical. He was, and still is, a constant influence and reference in my interpretation of the piano repertoire. From him I learned to always go to the heart of the music, to make everything absolutely transcendental and meaningful.

–Rámon Tamaran

He changed my approach to the piano and helped me understand that weight to the pianist is as breath to the singer. Through his extraordinary use of color imagery, poetic lyricism, and profound sense of the dramatic, he challenged me to hear beyond the obvious and opened my ears to interpretative possibilities I had not yet imagined. I now also realize how much I learned from him by example. Being in his presence taught me that an artist's life requires deep commitment, rigid discipline, steely determination, boundless energy, and above all, finding one's own musical voice and following one's own passion. No matter where I go, the mention of his name to other musicians creates an immediate smile and musical kinship. Using his name is like having a musical American Express card: you never leave home without him. His pianism and artistry are legendary throughout the world, and having been his student always fills me with enormous humility and pride.

–William Tucker

I think what distinguishes Mr. Pressler from all others is his unique intuitive and uncanny ability to penetrate and capture the essence of the music; to describe the exact image, character, mood, and color representative of the work; and to pinpoint the pianistic technique needed to re-create the music. He is also a master psychologist and has a remarkable sensitivity to the human response.

–Sandra Webster

When he demonstrated a passage that changed from major to minor, I could see that he really felt the color change in his heart and was able to express it through the touch of his fingers. He taught me how to make the music more colorful by creating layers of sound by varying the touch of the fingers on the keyboard.

–Mary Wong

APPENDIX D. PRESSLER'S
STUDIO ROSTERS, 1955–2008

Note: some records, particularly the early years, are incomplete.

1955–1956

Gabel, Harriet
Henry, Jacqueline
Hoop, Elsie
Mayshoff, Renee
Ross, Johanna
Youngblood, Joseph

1956–1957

Brill, Hadassah
Burton, Joyce
Carnes, Ted
Chang, Predenc
Dike, Joy
Hichels, Paul
Jensen, Sandra
Major, Mariah
Wilson, Sharon
Youngblood, Joseph

1957–1958

Carnes, Ted
Green, Rhoda
Haddad, Diana
Hotard, Earny Pierre
Jaulman, Donna
Jensen, Kayleen

Moore, William
Pippin, Partricia
Shirley, George
Stokan, David
White, Marilyn

1958–1959

Basa, Teresita
Birmingham, Hugh
Carnes, Ted
Edelstein, Martha
Fulbright, Ercy Glenn
Green, Rhoda
Haddad, Diana
Jensen, Kayleen
Shirley, George
White, Marilyn

1959–1960

Basa, Teresita
Bogdan, Gordon M.
Cohan, Jack Gordon
Elledge, Carol Anne
Fjerstad, Helen
Garner, Nancy Sylvia
Goodman, Martha
Green, Rhoda

Haddad, Diana
Haddad, Loretta
Hermann, Herbert
Hotard, Earny
Jensen, Kayleen
LaBounty, Edwin
Levin, Nilly
Lewin, Harold
McCoy, Marie
Nielsen, Mary Ann
Peck, Judith C.
Prince, Priscilla
Ritter, Dorothy
Schenkman, Walter
Shirley, George
Sinclair, John
Thornburg, Judy
Tobin, John
Vatcharakiet, Saisuree
White, Marilyn

1960–1961

Baird, Frank
Bechtel, Ben
Bogdan, Gordon M.
Brown, Suzanne Swain
Compton, Kathryn
Deluca, Maria

[283]

East, Elizabeth Jane
Elledge, Carol Ann
Fjerstad, Helen
Gaume, Mary Matilda
Goodman, Martha
Green, Rhoda
Haddad, Diana
Haddad, Loretta
Harnisch, Beverly
Hermann, Herbert
Levin, Nilly
Lewin, Harold
Maier, Connie
Marberger, Nola
Peck, Judith C.
Prince, Priscilla
Schenkman, Walter A.
Shirley, George
Tobin, John
Trickey, Robert H.
Vatcharakiet, Saisuree
Ward, Sarah
Woodle, Jimmy O.

1961–1962

Abbott, Jane
Adams, John P.
Baird, Frank
Bechtel, Ben
Compton, Kathryn
East, Elizabeth Jane
Erisman, Zoe B.
Gaume, Mary Matilda
Globenski, Anna Marie
Haddad, Diana
Haddad, Loretta
Harnish, Beverly
Hermann, Herbert
Knappenberger, Shirley
Levin, Nilly
Peck, Judith C.
Romanio, Steven A.

1962–1963

Cohan, Jack Gordon
Erisman, Zoe B.
Haddad, Loretta
Harnish, Beverly
Levin, Nilly
Orvis, Joan Eleanor
Saslav, Ann H.
Webb, Charles H.

1963–1964

Cohan, Jack Gordon
Edwards, William Pope
Emanuel, Jerry Franchot
Ennis, Paula
Erisman, Zoe B.
Goan, Charles William
Haddad, Loretta
Harnish, Beverly
Hays, Phyllis J.
Levin, Nilly
Moody, Carol
Niermann, Priscilla
Orvis, Joan Eleanor
Pientka, Kenneth
   Charles
Saidenberg, David
Saslav, Ann H.
Seulean, Kathryn Ann
Shimazaki, Kiyo
Suppan, Leonore
Thomas, Linda
   Elizabeth
Valiquette, Jeannete
Wennerstrom, Mary
Zandmeer, Arlette

1964–1965

Alpher, David B.
Andrews, Craig
Burnett, John Walker

Buttars, Jane Lurene
Davis, Merelyn
Dyme, Saralyn
Emanuel, Jerry Franchot
Ennis, Paula
Erisman, Zoe B.
Farmer, June Marie
Gold, Edward Michael
Gray, George Branson
Hansen, DaWayne Harry
Horn, Carolyn Ann
Horsley, Pamela Kay
Kohn, Laurie
Mafit, Martha Louise
Moody, Carol
Niermann, Priscilla
Paschall, Peggy Williams
Pientka, Kenneth Charles
Renkous, Carol
Robertson, Sandra Lee
Rutledge, Jane
Shaw, Karen
Suppan, Leonora E.
Thomas, Linda Elizabeth
Voois, Jacques C.
White, Rachel Frances
Zendmeer, Arlette

1965–1966

Ahuvi, Uriel
Alpher, David B.
Bruser, Madeline
Burnett, John Walker
Burton, Betsy Bowles
Buttars, Jane Lurene
Dyme, Saralyn
Ennis, Paula
Essers, Louis N.
Gold, Edward Michael
Gray, George Branson
Griffel, Pamela K.
Hansen, DuWayne Harry

Hersh, Alan Bruce
Horn, Carolyn Ann
Horsley, Pamela K.
Jackson, Kathleen Louise
Kohn, Laurie J.
Lamb, Linda Lou
McGreer, Dennis
  Maynard
Paschall, Peggy Williams
Pientka, Kenneth Charles
Riley, James Kent
Robertson, Sandra Lee
Roddey, B. Gatewood
Schmitt, Jacqueline Jo
Thomas, Linda Elizabeth
White, Rachel Frances

1966–1967

Adams, John P.
Ahuvi, Uriel
Alpher, David B.
Bruser, Madeline
Burnett, John Walker
Burton, Betsy Bowles
Buttars, Jane Lurene
Callander, Ruth Marion
Covington, Kate R.
Duerk, Judith Burhop
Elliott, Pamela Kay
Ennis, Paula
Essers, Louis N.
Evans, Dane Edward
Feninch, Sarah E.
Globenski, Anna Marie
Goan, Charles William
Gold, Edward Michael
Graham, Edward
Gray, George Branson
Griffel, Pamela K.
Hansen, DuWayne Harry
Harb, Charlene Alice
Hirt, Linda

Jackson, Kathleen Louise
Keisling, Connie Lea
McGreer, Dennis
  Maynard
Orvis, Joan Eleanor
Paschall, Peggy Williams
Paulus, Sharon
Pientka, Kenneth Charles
Robertson, Sandra Lee
Romanio, Steven A.
Schmitt, Jacqueline Jo
Shaw, Karen
Stokan, David S.
Taslitt, Marc Shalom
White, Rachel Frances
Yoshida, Akiko

1967–1968

Ahuvi, Uriel
Alpher, David B.
Bold, Barbara L.
Bruser, Madeline
Burnett, John Walker
Burton, Betsy Bowles
Buttars, Jane Lurene
Callander, Ruth Marion
Cameron, Gayle Ruth
Ennis, Paula
Evans, Dane Edward
Globenski, Anna Marie
Gold, Edward Michael
Gray, Frances Muir
Greenspan, Judith Elaine
Griffel, Pamela K.
Hansen, DuWayne Harry
Harb, Charlene Alice
Hotard, Earny Pierre
McGreer, Dennis
  Maynard
Merrill, Zoe Erisman
Oden, William Charles
Orvis, Joan Eleanor

Paschall, Peggy Williams
Pienka, Kenneth Charles
Schmitt, Jacqueline Jo
Stokan, David S.
Taslitt, Marc Shalom
Uragami, Yoko
Yoshido, Akiko

1968–1969

Adams, John P.
Bailey, Betty Anne
Barela, Margaret Mary
Bold, Barbara L.
Burnett, John Walker
Buttars, Jane Lurene
Callander, Ruth Marion
Cameron, Gayle Ruth
Cameron, Richard G.
Cohan, Jack Gordon
Davis, Mary Adell
Eaton, Jack
Evans, Dane Edward
Globenski, Anna Marie
Gray, Frances Muir
Griffel, Pamela K.
Hagopian, Robert A.
Hotard, Earny Pierre
Mundy, Nancy Catherine
Ngan, Amy
Oden, William Charles
Orvis, Joan Eleanor
Paschall, Peggy Williams
Rucker, Mary M.
Schoen, Sallie Warth
Schutt, William Joseph
Shaw, Karen
Stokan, David S.
Swedish, Stephen John
Taslitt, Marc Shalom
Whiddon, Lester R.
Yoshida, Akiko

1969–1970

Adams, John P.
Bailey, Betty Anne
Barela, Margaret Mary
Bold, Barbara L.
Brown, William Paul
Burnett, John Walker
Buttars, Jane Lurene
Callander, Ruth Marion
Callies, Benjamin James
Cameron, Gayle Ruth
Cameron, Richard G.
Cohan, Jack Gordon
Ellison, Linda Lee
Globenski, Anna Marie
Goan, Charles William
Gray, Frances Muir
Griffel, Pamela K.
Harbottle, Nancy
Hogopian, Robert A.
McDonald, Charlene
 Harb
Mundy, Nancy Catherine
Nagai, Megumi
Ngan, Amy
Orvis, Joan Eleanor
Peters, Susan Martha
Petersen, Katrine
Rucker, Mary M.
Schutt, William Joseph
Snow, Pamela H.
Stokan, David S.
Swedish, Stephen John

1970–1971

Adams, John P.
Bailey, Betty Anne
Barela, Margaret Mary
Blisch, Susan
Bold, Barbara L.
Brown, William Paul
Burnett, John Walker

Cameron, Gayle Ruth
Ellison, Linda Lee
Ennis, Paula
Fischer, Ruth Andrea
Globenski, Anna Marie
Hagopian, Robert A.
Jones, Hugh A.
Macpherson, Gordon
Mayerovitch, Robert
 Mark
Nagai, Megumi
Ngan, Amy
Peters, Susan Martha
Rucker, Mary M.
Schutt, William Joseph
Stokan, David S.
Swedish, Stephen John
Webster, Sandra
Wood, Betty Pai-Tee

1971–1972

Auh, Mijai Youn
Barela, Margaret Mary
Brown, William Paul
Cameron, Gayle Ruth
Crossen, Janet Sue
Doskey, Henry C.
Ennis, Paula
Fischer, Ruth Andrea
Gipson, Ronald Earl
Globenski, Anna Marie
Hagopian, Robert A.
Hoogland, Philip
Lam, Julia Tieu-Wong
Macpherson, Gordon
Mayerovitch, Robert
 Mark
McComb, Gayle R.
Nagai, Megumi
Penneys, Rebecca A.
Peters, Susan Martha
Planes, Alain M.
Redekopp, Karin

Rucker, Mary M.
Schillin, Scott
Schutt, William Joseph
Stokan, David S.
Swan, Andrea
Swedish, Stephen John
VanBoskirk, Roe A.
Webster, Sandra
Wood, Betty Pai-Tee

1972–1973

Brown, William Paul
Crossen, Janet Sue
Doskey, Henry C.
Ennis, Paula
Evans, Dane Edward
Gipson, Ronald Earl
Lam, Julia Tieu-Wong
Macpherson, Gordon
Mayerovitch, Robert
 Mark
McComb, Gayle R.
Schillin, Scott
VanBoskirk, Roe A.
Webster, Sandra

1973–1974

Ahmad, Rosemary
Broome, Cherie Michele
Brown, William Paul
Crossen, Janet Sue
Doskey, Henry C.
Ennis, Paula
Evans, Dane Edward
Gipson, Ronald Earl
Hatten, Robert S.
Jones, Sherri L.
Lam, Julia Tieu-Wong
Lehman, Dawn
Macpherson, Gordon
Mayerovitch, Robert
 Mark

McComb, Gayle R.
McDonald, Charlene
  Harb
McGreer, Dennis
Melendez, Evelyn E.
Sawamura, Chieko
Schieber, Claudia
Stipelman, Rena
Tucker, William Stanley
VanBoskirk, Roe A.
Vogel, Ronald Brian

1974–1975

Ahmad, Rosemary
Asch, Cathy
Broome, Cherie Michele
Brown, William Paul
Cappelli, Mark
Crossen, Janet Sue
Doskey, Henry C.
Evans, Dane Edward
Gienger, Eugene A.
Gipson, Ronald Earl
Globenski, Anna Marie
Gray, Frances Muir
Hatten, Robert S.
Heiberg, Tania
Jones, Sherri L.
Knox, Roger
Lam, Julia Tieu-Wong
Lehman, Dawn
Macpherson, Gordon
Martin, Pauline
Mayerovitch, Robert
  Mark
McComb, Gayle R.
McDonald, Charlene
  Harb
McGreer, Dennis
Pro, George H.
Reynerson, Rodney
Sawamura, Chieko
Snow, Pamela H.

Stipelman, Rena
Stokan, David S.
Stowell, Patricia
Terada, Etusko
Tucker, William Stanley
VanBoskirk, Roe A.

1975–1976

Broome, Cherie Michele
Capelli, Mark
Cheek, John A.
Fee, George D.
Friedman, Marian
Gburek, James Bernard
Geinger, Eugene A.
Goter, Arlene
Grippe, Kerry
Heiberg, Tania
Jones, Sherri L.
Martin, Pauline
Mayerovitch, Robert
  Mark
McComb, Gayle R.
McGreer, Dennis
Reynerson, Rodney
Siebech, Silvia
Snow, Pamela H.
Stipelman, Rena
Street, Eric
Street, Paul
Terada, Etsuko
VanBoskirk, Roe A.
Watanabe, Etsuko Terada
Wilkie, Christine

1976–1977

Cappelli, Mark
Cheek, John A.
Doskey, Henry C.
Ennis, Paula
Evans, Dane Edward
Fee, George D.

Friedman, Marian
Gburek, James Bernard
Gienger, Eugene A.
Globenski, Anna Marie
Goldenberg, William
Grippe, Kerry
Jones, Sherri L.
Kim, Young Sook
Lorati, Linda
Lortie, Louis
Martin, Pauline
Mayerovitch, Robert
  Mark
McGreer, Dennis
Reynerson, Rodney
Siebeck, Silvia
Snow, Pamela H.
Stipelman, Rena
Street, Eric
Thomas, Diana
Watanabe, Etsuko Terada
Wilkie, Christine

1977–1978

Cappelli, Mark
Carr, Nadine
Cheek, John A.
Conroy, Mark Lyndon
Ennis, Paula
Evans, Dane Edward
Fee, George D.
Friedman, Marian
Funahashi, Lily
Gburek, James Bernard
Gienger, Eugene A.
Globenski, Anna Marie
Goldenberg, William
Green, Philip Edward
Han, Tongsook
Kim, Young Sook
Komasa, John
Kovshik, Walter
Lorati, Linda

Macpherson, Gordon
Malson, Eric
Martin, Pauline
Mauchley, Jay
McDonald, Charlene
  Harb
McGreer, Dennis
Moyer, William Fredrick
Reynerson, Rodney
Rutland, John Randall
Smukler, Amy
Snow, Pamela H.
Stipelman, Rena
Street, Eric
Summer, Averill

1978–1979

Arner, Lucy
Cappelli, Mark
Evans, Dane Edward
Fee, George D.
Gburek, James Bernard
Gienger, Eugene A.
Globenski, Anna Marie
Goldenberg, William
Green, Phillip
Griffitt, Lorna
Han, Tongsook
Kawashima, Nobutatsu
Kikkawa, Yuka
Komasa, John
Kovshik, Walter
Mahonske, Adam
Malson, Eric
Moyer, William
  Fredrick
Otten, Gregory P.
Packer, Lori
Ratner, Richard
Reynerson, Rodney
Rutland, John Randall
Rybak, Alia
Smukler, Amy

Street, Eric
Sullivan, Mark Hallum
Summer, Averill
Trudgeon, Jill
Weinberg, Alan

1979–1980

Blaisse, Muriel
Cappelli, Mark
Fan, Felicia Sum Mei
Fishman, Lenore
Fournier, Michel
Gburek, James Bernard
Globenski, Anna Marie
Goldenberg, William
Griffitt, Lorna
Han, Tongsook
Hashimoto, Kyoko
Higbey, Julie Anne
Kikkawa, Yuka
Kim, Young Sook
Mahonske, Adam
Malson, Eric
Otten, Gregory P.
Packer, Lori
Ratner, Richard
Reynerson, Rodney
Rybak, Alia
Shank, Nadine
Smukler, Amy
Street, Eric
Sullivan, Mark Hallum
Trudgeon, Jill
Wampler, Cheryl
Weinberg, Alan

1980–1981

Blaisse, Muriel
Doskey, Henry C.
Fishman, Lenore
Globenski, Anna Marie
Goldenberg, William

Hinson, James H.
Kikkawa, Yuka
Malson, Eric
Morgan, Katherine
Moyer, William
  Frederick
Packer, Lori
Ratner, Richard
Shank, Nadine
Smukler, Amy
Street, Eric
Sullivan, Mark Hallum
Tinfow, Bradley
Toews, Heather Dawn
Wampler, Cheryl

1981–1982

Barak, Ida
Byrne, John P.
Chow, Alan
Chow, Alvin
Clasquin, Deborah
Doughty, Dorina
Doyle, Rebecca
Fabi, Marie
Fishman, Lenore
Fournier, Michel
Griffitt, Lorna
Higbey, Julie Anne
Hurwitz, Sheila
Hurwitz, Teresa
Kikkawa, Yuka
Lecuona, Rene
Leutou, Vladirmir
Malson, Eric
Morgan, Katherine
Muller, Marie-Laure
Nee, Elizabeth
Otten, Gregory P.
Packer, Lori
Ratner, Richard
Rhee, Yung-Mee
Smuckler, Amy

Street, Eric
Sullivan, Mark Hallum

1982–1983

Alitowski, Liane
Beckouche, Muriel
Cheng, Angela Mai-Lin
Chow, Alan
Chow, Alvin
Clasquin, Deborah
Dahlberg, Susan
Fabi, Marie
Fishman, Lenore
Frohnmeyer, Michael
Harbottle, Nancy
Higbey, Julia Anne
Hurwitz, Sheila
Hurwitz, Teresa
Jonove, Marjorie
Kikkawa, Yuka
Labe, Tom
Lecuona, Rene
Malson, Eric
Nakata, Atsuko
Packer, Lori
Ratner, Richard
Rhee, Yung-Mee
Shafer, Timothy P.
Shank, Nadine
Sharpe, Kevin Michael
Street, Eric

1983–1984

Alitowski, Liane
Bass, Jonathan David
Cheng, Angela Mai-Lin
Chow, Alan
Chow, Alvin
Clasquin, Deborah
Cohen, Jeffrey
Fabi, Marie
Fee, George D.

Fisch, Asher
Fishman, Lenore
Glazier, Richard
Hanson, James
Hayashi, Ririko
Hurwitz, Sheila
Hurwitz, Teresa
Kawai, Keiko
Kikkawa, Yuka
Ratner, Richard
Rhee, Yung-Mee
Segger, Joachim
Shafer, Timothy P.
Shank, Nadine
Sharpe, Kevin Michael
Street, Eric

1984–1985

Alitowski, Liane
Bass, Jonathan David
Cheng, Angela Mai-Lin
Chow, Alan
Chow, Alvin
Clasquin, Deborah
Cohen, Jeffrey
De Grado, Andrew
    George
Fabi, Marie
Glazier, Richard
Griffitt, Lorna
Hanson, James
Hayashi, Ririko
Hurwitz, Sheila
Hurwitz, Teresa
Koivisto, Veli
Rambo, Deborah
Ratner, Richard
Rhee, Yung-Mee
Sabransky, Philip
Sharpe, Kevin Michael
Street, Eric
Tal, Michal
White, Miriam

1985–1986

Alitowski, Liane
Banados, Anibal
Bass, Jonathan David
Cheng, Angela Mai-Lin
Chiu, Lorraine
Chow, Alan
Chow, Alvin
Clasquin, Deborah
Cohen, Jeffrey
De Grado, Andrew
    George
Fabi, Marie
Franzen, Elizabeth
Glazier, Richard
Jackson, D. D. Robert
Kim, Adrienne
Mort, Barbara
Piitz, Lori Ellen
Rambo, Deborah
Ratner, Richard
Roudier, Alain
Sabransky, Philip
Sharpe, Kevin Michael
Uetake, Sakae
Wogaman, Stephen Neil

1986–1987

Alitowski, Liane
Banados, Anibal
Bass, Jonathan David
Cheng, Angela Mai-Lin
Chiu, Lorraine
Chow, Alan
Chow, Alvin
Clasquin, Deborah
Cohen, Jeffrey
De Grado, Andrew
    George
Fabi, Marie
Glazier, Richard
Jackson, D. D. Robert

Kim, Adrienne
Piitz, Lori Ellen
Rambo, Deborah
Ratner, Richard
Roudier, Alain
Sabransky, Philip
Sharpe, Kevin Michael
Uetake, Sakae
Wogaman, Stephen Neil
Yamamoto, Grace
Zohar, Asaf

1987–1988

Alitowski, Liane
Banados, Anibal
Bass, Jonathan David
Cheng, Angela Mai-Lin
Chiu, Lorraine
Chow, Alvin
Cohen, Jeffrey
De Grado, Andrew
   George
Fabi, Marie
Jackson, D. D. Robert
Kim, Adrienne
Piitz, Lori Ellen
Rambo, Deborah
Ratner, Richard
Sabransky, Philip
Sharpe, Kevin Michael
Uetake, Sakae
Wogaman, Stephen Neil
Yamamoto, Grace
Zohar, Asaf

1988–1989

Alitowski, Liane
Barnes, Paul Edwin
Bass, Jonathan David
Cerovsek, Katja
Cheng, Angela Mai-Lin
Cho, Cecilia Chinsoon

Chung, Hee Sun
Cohen, Jeffrey
De Grado, Andrew
   George
Fabi, Marie
Fritz, Conroy Gordon
Huter, Steve R.
Kim, Adrienne
Kim, Joo Youn
Kim, Mia Mikyung
Lee, Tania Ko-Wen
Levit, Cindy Elaine
Murphy, Kevin
Naoe, Manami
Piitz, Lori Ellen
Rosenwald, Eva
Sharpe, Kevin Michael
Siemers, Robert Mark
Sunago, Mika Kitamura
Tschudy, Lynn
Uetake, Sakae
Wogaman, Stephen Neil
Wong, Mary Ki Yan
Zohar, Asaf

1989–1990

Barnes, Paul Edwin
Bass, Jonathan David
Cerovsek, Katja
Cho, Cecilia Chinsoon
De Grado, Andrew
   George
Huter, Steve R.
Kim, Adrienne
Kim, Elisa Soyon
Kim, Joo Youn
Kim, Mia Mikyung
Linhardt, Cynthia Susan
Lyons, David Paul
Miranda, Julianne M.
Naoe, Manami
Piitz, Lori Ellen
Sharpe, Kevin Michael

Siemers, Robert Mark
Wei, Yu-Mei
Wong, Mary Ki Yan

1990–1991

Ahn, Soojin
Aznavoorian, Marta
Barnes, Paul Edwin
Cerovsek, Katja
Chang, Angelin
Cho, Cecilia Chinsoon
Choi, Mikyung
De Grado, Andrew
   George
Huter, Steve R.
Jeanney, Helene
Kim, Elisa Soyon
Kim, Joo Youn
Kim, Mia Mikyung
Linhardt, Cynthia Susan
Lyons, David Paul
Piitz, Lori Ellen
Siemers, Robert Mark
Wei, Yu-Mei
Wenaus, Grant Edward
Wogaman, Stephen Neil
Wong, Jerry Tang

1991–1992

Barnes, Paul Edwin
Chang, Angelin
Chen, Han-Yin Judith
Choi, Mikyung
Chung, Hee Sun
Cochrane, Lynda
   Catherine
De Grado, Andrew
   George
Fritz, Conroy Gordon
Hashizumi, Yuko
Hsu, Gloria Y-Chu
Jeanney, Helene

Kim, Elisa Soyon
Kim, Joo Youn
Kim, Mia Mikyung
Lyons, David Paul
Ozolina, Agija
Seil, Richard David
Shin, Sukyung
Siemers, Robert Mark
Subotic, Vedrana
Suzuki, Haruko
Topfer, Aaron L.
Wenaus, Grant Edward
Wogaman, Stephen Neil
Wong, Jerry Tang
Yoo, Hye-Young

1992–1993

Auler, Robert Marshall
Chan, Susan
Chang, Angelin
Choi, Mikyung
Garcia-Tessier, Ramón
Harding, Christopher
Hsu, Gloria Y-Chu
Kim, Elisa Soyon
Kim, Joo Youn
Kim, Mia Mikyung
Ohno, Saori Sarina
Poon, Christina Ching-Y
Shin, Sukyung
Subotic, Vedrana
Suzuki, Haruko
Topfer, Aaron L.
Wogaman, Stephen Neil
Wong, Jerry Tang
Yamada, Kyoko

1993–1994

Choi, Mikyung
Garcia-Tessier, Ramón
Harding, Christopher
Hsu, Gloria Ya-Chu

Kim, Joo Youn
Mikkola, Laura Imola
Moon, Suzanne Sayang
O, Sorim
Ohno, Saori Sarina
Poon, Christina Ching-Y
Sheikh, Zaiba Yasmin
Shibatani, Naomi
Shin, Sukyung
Subotic, Vedrana
Suzuki, Haruko
Wong, Jerry Tang

1994–1995

Bolt, Anne Rosemary
Cassidy, Robert L.
Choi, Mikyung
Dessuane, Ana Paula da
    Matta
Garcia-Tessier, Ramón
Harding, Christopher
Hsu, Gloria Ya-Chu
Kim, Joo Youn
Kim, Moon Jung
McVey, Roger Dale
Mikkola, Laura Imola
Moon, Suzanne Sayang
O, Sorim
Poon, Christina Ching Y
Scow, Gina Marie
Sheikh, Zaiba Yasmin
Shibatani, Naomi
Shin, Sukyung
Suzuki, Haruko

1995–1996

Choi, Mikyung
Choi, Winston
Ferguson, John Murray
Harding, Christopher
Kim, Joo Youn
Kim, Moon Jung

McVey, Roger Dale
Moon, Suzanne Sayang
Scow, Gina Marie
Suzaki, Haruko

1996–1997

Choi, Winston
Cilliers, Jeanne-Minett
Ferguson, John Murray
Harding, Christopher
Jones, Paul Steven
Kee, Soyoung
Kim, Joo Youn
Kim, Moon Jung
Larin, Nicolas
McDonagh, Orla Olive
McVey, Roger Dale
Moon, Suzanne Sayang
Scow, Gina Marie
Suzuki, Haruko

1997–1998

Araujo, Fernando
Choi, Winston
Cilliers, Jeanne-Minett
Fosseur, Anne-France
Frochot, Ludovic
    Emmanuel
Gales, Carl Edward
Ho, Sarah
Huang, Wen-Ting
Hwang, Veronica Jeong
Iwaasa, Rachel Kiyo
Kim, Joo Youn
Kim, Moon Jung
Kwak, Sung-Ok
Larin, Nicolas
Martellotti, Patricia M.
Planes, Vincent B. D.
Scow, Gina Marie
Tang, Zhihua
Viljanen, Hanna Katja

1998–1999

Araujo, Fernando
Chirico, Amanda
  Suzanne
Choi, Winston
Cilliers, Jeanne-Minett
Ferguson, John Murray
Fosseur, Anne-France
Frochot, Ludovic
  Emmanuel
Gales, Carl Edward
Hanus, Michael
  Thomas
Ho, Sarah
Huang, Wen-Ting
Hwang, Veronica Jeong
Iwaasa, Rachel Kiyo
Kim, Moon Jung
Kim, Sai Hii
Kwak, Sung-Ok
Martellotti, Patricia M.
Oliveira, Barbara
  Doria
Planes, Vincent B. D.
Suh, Jung Won
Tang, Erica
Tang, Zhihua

1999–2000

Araujo, Fernando
Cho, Anna
Cho, Soo Hyun
Choi, Min-Ju
Choi, Winston
Cilliers, Jeanne-Minett
Ferguson, John Murray
Fosseur, Anne-France
Frochot, Ludovic
  Emmanuel
Hartman, Maya
Ho, Sarah
Huang, Wen-Ting

Kim, Moon Jung
Kim, Shinah
Liu, Yi-Heng
Ming, Kristine Leinani
Oh, Jiyoung
Planes, Vincent B. D.
Rajmilchuk, Esteban Ari
Seedman, Joshua Leon
Simon, Sabine
Suh, Jung Won

2000–2001

Athanasako, Konstantin
Cheng, Tong
Cho, Anna
Cho, Soo Hyun
Choi, Winston
Hartman, Maya
Huang, Wen-Ting
Kim, Moon Jung
Kuijken, Pieter
Liu, Yi-Heng
Ming, Kristine Leinani
Planes, Vincent B.D.
Savvides, Christos
Seedman, Joshua Leon
Sokoloff, Larissa
Suh, Jung Won
Wei, Mei-Huei
Xiao, June

2001–2002

Baird, Melinda
Choi, Winston
Chun, Jane Minjin
Cocchiarella, Nino
Fang, Jeanette
Hartman, Maya
Huang, Wen-Ting
Kim, Shinah
Kuijken, Pieter
Lavandera, Pablo Luis

Liu, Yi-Heng
Min, Ahlin Lee
Ming, Kristine Leinani
Planes, Vincent B. D.
Savvides, Christos
Seedman, Joshua Leon
Sokoloff, Larissa
Van den Bercken, Daria
Wei, Mei-Huei
Wong, Sau Ting Stella
Xiao, June
Xu, Grace Enhua
Yu, Grace Chung-Yan

2002–2003

Baird, Melinda
Beatson, Alasdair Roy
Briere, Jimmy
Chun, Jane Minjin
Cocchiarella, Nino
Fang, Jeannette
Fosseur, Anne-France
Hellmann, Mary E.
Ho, Grace Szewai
Honik, Inti Sebastian
Huang, Wen-Ting
Lesniak, James Robert
Liu, Yi-Heng
Mann, Steven Kenneth
Min, Ahlin Lee
Ming, Kristine Leinani
Park, Eun-Shik
Planes, Vincent B. D.
Savvides, Christos
Seedman, Joshua Leon
Sommer, Pamela
Wong, Sau Ting Stella
Xiao, June
Xu, Grace Enhua

2003–2004

Baird, Melinda
Beatson, Alasdair Roy

Briere, Jimmy
Cocchiarella, Nino
Erice Calvo-Sotelo, Leo
Gorgojo, Raquel
Hartlieb, Tobias Manfred
Hellmann, Mary E.
Ho, Grace Szewai
Huang, Wen-Ting
Ljung, Philip
Mann, Steven Kenneth
Ming, Kristine Leinani
Park, Eun-Shik
Peh, Alex L.
Wong, Sau Ting Stella
Xiao, June

2004–2005

Adam-Murvitz, Batia
Baird, Melinda
Bernard, Maxim
Chou, Susan
Gorgojo, Raquel
Guntren, Alissa J.
Huang, Wen-Ting
Keller, Ingrid P.
Koo, Abigail Bonkyung
Mann, Steven Kenneth
Min, Ahlin Lee
Park, Eun-Shik
Reeder, Joy Paula

Takei, Ligia Lyka
Xiao, June

2005–2006

Abromovich, Ruti
Adam-Murvitz, Batia
Baird, Melinda
Bernard, Maxim
Chiang, Emily
Chou, Susan
Gleiser, Kati
Hackmey, Efi
Keller, Ingrid P.
Koo, Abigail Bonkyung
Mann, Steven Kenneth
Meek, Scott
Park, Eun-Shik
Reeder, Joy Paula
Xiao, June

2006–2007

Abromovich, Ruti
Becque, Helen
Bernard, Maxim
Chan, Sze Yau
Chiang, Emily
Chou, Hsiao-Tung
Gleiser, Kati
Hackmey, Efi
Kammerer, Benjamin

Kawaguchi, Haruka
Keller, Ingrid P.
Kim, Jayoung
Ma, Carlin
Mann, Steven Kenneth
McQuay, Michael
Meek, Scott
Park, Eun-Shik
Reeder, Joy Paula
Xiao, June

2007–2008

Abromovich, Ruti
Achar, Sonia
Bernard, Maxim
Beus, Megan
Chan, Sze Yau
Chou, Susan
Cubas, Aymara
Gleiser, Kati
Hackmey, Efi
Hartnett, Owen
Keller, Ingrid
Kim, Jayoung
Lau, Shine Shine
Lysack, Chris
Ma, Carlin
Marrs, Andrew
McQuay, Michael
Meek, Scott
Park, Eun Shik

BIBLIOGRAPHY

Baird, Melinda, "The Eccentric Professor and the Learning Experience: A Look at the Teaching Techniques and Standards of Menahem Pressler." Unpublished paper, 2003.

Buechler, Mark. "The Hunger Within." *Indiana Daily Student.* May 14, 2004.

DeBrunner, Mary. "Former/Current Students to Celebrate Prof's Birthday." *Indiana Daily Student.* December 15, 2003.

Delbanco, Nicholas. *The Beaux Arts Trio: A Portrait.* New York: William Morrow, 1985.

Doyle, John. "An Interview with Menahem Pressler." CBC Arts National, Windsor, Ontario, Canada. 1985.

Duchen, Jessica. "Lucky Charm." *International Piano.* May/June, 2005.

Fine, Larry. "Irrepressible Pianist Pressler Going Strong at 80." *Reuters.* January 2, 2004.

Gelfand, Janelle. "A Master Class with Menahem Pressler." *Clavier.* July/August 1993.

Glazier, Harriet. "Menahem Pressler: *Belle Musique.*" *Arts Indiana.* October 1988.

In the Heart of Music, directed by Andy Sommer. Bel Air Media and the Van Cliburn Foundation. DVD. 2005.

Jacobi, Peter. "At 80, Pianist Menahem Pressler Looks Back–and Forward–at Life and Music." *Bloomington Herald-Times.* December 14, 2003.

Knudson, Erika. "Playing It Forward: Teaching, Performing, Are Senior Faculty Members' Gifts to Future Teachers, Performers." *IU Music.* Spring/Summer 2003.

Leo Kestenberg Project. http://www.Leo-Kestenberg.com

Logan, George M. *The Indiana University School of Music: A History.* Bloomington: Indiana University Press, 2000.

Namer, Dina Michelson. "Pressler at Adamant." *Piano Quarterly.* Spring 1991.

Oestreich, James R. "A Pianistic Quarterback Passes to a Younger Generation." *New York Times.* November 30, 2003.

O'Riley, Chris. "An Interview with Menahem Pressler." *From the Top.* WGBH, Boston. April 23, 2000.

Pressler, Menahem. "Beethoven's Op. 110." Lecture-Recital presented at the Metropolitan Museum of Art, New York. February 21, 2004.

———. Interview. January 6, 2004.

——. Interview. June 28, 2004.

——. Interview. August 21, 2004.

——. Interview. May 26–27, 2006.

——. Interview. April 20–21, 2007.

——. Interview with Mark Sullivan. March 2, 1996.

——. Lecture presented at the TCU/Cliburn Piano Institute, Texas Christian University, Fort Worth, Tex. May 25, 2005.

——. Master classes. Adamant Music School, Adamant, Vt., August 17–21, 2004.

——. "Preface." *Sonata No. 9, Op. 103 by Serge Prokofiev.* New York: Leeds Music, c. 1955.

——. "Suggestions for Performance." *Brahms, Fantasias, Op. 116.* Vienna: Schott/Universal edition. 1981.

——. Unpublished technical exercises. Bloomington.

Rezits, Joseph. *Beloved Tyranna: The Legend and Legacy of Isabelle Vengerova.* Bloomington, In.: David Daniel Music Publications, 1995.

Schonberg, Harold C. *The Great Pianists.* New York: Simon and Schuster, 1963.

Slonimsky, Nicolas. *Baker's Dictionary of Musicians.* 8th ed. New York: Schirmer Books, 1992.

Street, Eric. "Tracing Our Musical Ancestors." *Clavier.* December 2001.

Stryker, Mark. "Once More with Feeling: Pianist Shares Expertise." *Detroit Free Press.* October 20, 1995.

Sullivan, Mark. "The Beaux-Arts of Menahem Pressler." *Piano & Keyboard.* September/October, 1996.

Timbrell, Charles. *French Pianism: A Historical Perspective.* 2nd ed. Amadeus Press. Pompton Plains, N.J.: 2003.

Wagner, Jeffrey. "Menahem Pressler: Multifaceted Musician." *Clavier.* May/June, 1982.

Where Music Lives, written and directed by Robert Albers. WTIU, Bloomington, May 18, 1987.

INDEX OF COMPOSITIONS

Page numbers in italics indicate musical examples.

INDEX OF NAMES AND CONCEPTS

Page numbers in italics indicate illustrations.

William Brown is a frequent recitalist and chamber musician who earned his master's and doctoral performance degrees while studying with Menahem Pressler at Indiana University. Brown is a professor of piano and dean of Music, Arts and Letters at Southwest Baptist University. A past president of the Missouri Music Teachers Association, he has received the Parkway Distinguished Teacher Award and has contributed to *Piano Guild Magazine* and *PedalPoint*. He has had additional piano study with Marie Whiddon, Susan Baker, Roger Keyes, Walter Robert, Dmitry Paperno, and Dorothy Brandwein.

ALSO BY ROBERT EVERSZ

ZERO
TO
THE BONE

A NINA ZERO NOVEL

Robert Eversz

SIMON & SCHUSTER
New York London Toronto Sydney

SIMON & SCHUSTER
Rockefeller Center
1230 Avenue of the Americas
New York, NY 10020

For information about special discounts for bulk purchases,
please contact Simon & Schuster Special Sales at
1-800-456-6798 or business@simonandschuster.com

DESIGNED BY LAUREN SIMONETTI

Manufactured in the United States of America

1   3   5   7   9   10   8   6   4   2

Library of Congress Cataloging-in-Publication Data

Eversz, Robert.
Zero to the bone : a Nina Zero novel / Robert Eversz.
        p.   cm.
1. Zero, Nina (Fictitious character)—Fiction. 2. Los Angeles (Calif.)—Fiction.
3. Women photographers—Fiction. 4. Tabloid newspapers—Fiction. 5. Ex-con-
victs—Fiction. 6. Paparazzi—Fiction. I. Title.

PS3555.V39Z34 2006
813'.54
2005054467

ISBN-13:   978-0-7432-5017-7
ISBN-10:   0-7432-5017-6

To Nina Zero's readers:
thanks for sharing the wild, bumpy ride.

The strong men, the masters, regain the pure conscience of a beast of prey; monsters filled with joy, they can return from a fearful succession of murder, arson, rape, and torture with the same joy in their hearts, the same contentment in their souls as if they had indulged in some student's rag.

—Friedrich Nietzsche

ZERO
TO
THE BONE

1

A DAY HIKER found her body beneath the thorny skirts of a man-zanita bush in the Santa Monica Mountains just north of Malibu, her skin white as sun-bleached bone against the baked earth. She did not look dead to him at first glance and he thought she might be taking sun, but where she lay was not a spot for sunbathing and her clothes lay twisted in the brush rather than folded within reach.

From a distance her body still retained some of the beauty it had possessed in life and so the hiker expected her to stir at his approach but she didn't move, not at all. When he dropped down from the trail and into the brush he saw the bruise circling her neck and death's terrible vacancy in her face.

He grasped her wrist between his thumb and forefinger, hoping to track a faint pulse of blood. Her skin felt less alive than stone. He called 911 and hiked back to the trailhead to wait for the responding officers, out of sight of the body, because the woman was so young and beautiful, even in death, that the only way he could prevent himself from crying was not to look at her.

Later, when questioned by a reporter from a supermarket tabloid, he described in photographic detail the body's pose on the ground and the ruin strangulation had visited upon her face, sordid details expected by the readers of tabloids but ones I'll omit in this telling because I knew the woman, and the brutal manner of her death will haunt me for the rest of my days.

The last time I saw Christine she wore a glittering silver strap-dress to the hanging of my show of photographs at Santa Monica's Leonora Price Gallery, the Betty Boop tattoo on her bared shoulder winking suggestively at the muscular boy in cutoffs who mounted photographs on the near wall. She planned to wear the dress to the opening party two nights later and claimed to want to know whether I liked the style. The photographs were staged tableaux carefully composed to look culled from the pages of the *National Enquirer,* the *Star,* or the paper I freelanced for, *Scandal Times.* Several of the images depicted a blonde bombshell caught by a tabloid-style camera in scandalous scenes involving cars, sex, drugs, and guns. Christine played the role of the blonde bombshell, her wholesome looks shaded at twenty-one with a complicated sexual awareness, the lens capturing little-girl innocence and anything-goes depravity in a single, flashing glance. The depravity made her visually compelling, but in many ways she was far more innocent than depraved. She didn't want my opinion about the dress—I realized that the moment I saw how assertively she wore it. The dress clung to her with the fierce grace of a tango dancer. She knew she looked stunning. She simply couldn't wait for the show to open. She wanted to see what she looked like as a troubled movie starlet, unaware that I cast her in a role she played well enough in real life.

The evening the show opened I was working late in the offices of *Scandal Times,* trying to suppress my anxiety about exhibiting my so-called serious work, when Frank pitched a padded manila envelope onto the desk. Frank was the tabloid's crack investigative reporter, author of such seminal stories as "The Truth about Two-Headed Sheep" and "James Dean's Body Stolen by Space Aliens, Worshipped as God," practically required reading for every budding tabloid reporter and true aficionado of the form. He'd been in the parking lot, having a smoke, and the scent of cigarettes wafted from his hair like a stale aura.

"Since when did you start getting mail here?" he asked.

I glanced at the envelope, addressed to me care of the tabloid, with no return address and twenty Walt Disney commemorative Mickey Mouse stamps pasted down the right side, as though the sender had neither a clue how much postage the envelope required nor the time to get it metered.

"I get mail here all the time." I dipped into the side pocket of my camera bag for a Swiss army knife and slit open the envelope's top flap. "Most of it's from people peddling information, you know, the four Ws of tabloid journalism: who's doing what to whom, and where." I shook something that looked like a CD loose from the envelope.

"I get mail too," Frank said.

"What kind?" I asked.

"Death threats mostly. Last week, Steven Seagal's PR girl threatened not only to kill me but to make sure I was reincarnated as a leech." He fingered the edges of a candid I'd taken of Ben Affleck walking out the door of the Brentwood Starbucks, fingers wrapped around his morning latte. The image was set to run with a story about celebrity caffeine addicts. It had been a slow news week, Hollywood scandal-wise.

"Affleck's easy," he said. "Can't pay more than two hundred for him, plus a hundred bonus points for the coffee. You got anybody else?"

I showed him Owen Wilson in a geeky bucket hat and dark sunglasses, shot through the window of Kings Road Café as he inhaled the fumes wafting from a large porcelain cup. The disguise was effective enough that we argued back and forth about whether Owen Wilson sat beneath the hat or some look-alike, until I settled the argument by tracing the baby-arm-on-steroids contours of his nose, which even the modern miracle of plastic surgery can't duplicate, should it want to try. I walked the CD to the boom box on the shelf behind Frank's desk and pressed play. Nothing happened. Frank pulled open his petty-cash drawer. I forgot about the CD, thinking someone had sent me a blank disk by mistake. He paid five large in advance for the Wilson, plus three for Affleck.

It had been a tough couple of months, financially. I needed the cash to bail my car out of the garage and to finance the black cocktail sheath of a dress I planned to wear to the gallery that night, when friends, models, and art collectors would gather to drink wine and gossip while pretending to look at the so-called art. High art is a low-pay occupation, and I'd pretty much invested—or sunk without trace—the last of my money in producing and then printing the photographs to be exhibited. Then, two weeks before the show was to open, an idiot in a BMW rear-ended me in traffic, sending my beloved 1976 Cadillac Eldorado into the shop for bodywork and a two-hundred-thousand-mile makeover. His insurance was covering the bodywork but not the makeover. The mechanic had offered me a loaner while my car was in the shop. I couldn't afford to say no.

This explains why I pulled into the gallery's parking lot on the biggest night of my life in a six-year-old Chevy Metro with a four-cylinder, 1.3-liter hamster cage for an engine, my toothless Rottweiler riding shotgun, resplendent in a red bow tie and his usual goofy grin. Unlike me, he didn't feel humiliated to be seen in such a car. My Goth-girl niece waited out front, leaning with calculated teenage sullenness against the passenger-side suicide door of a 1967 Lincoln Continental. Cassie had flown in the night before from Phoenix, where she lived with her foster parents, and spent the day shopping for vintage clothing on Melrose Avenue, accompanied by the owner of the Continental, Nephthys, a woman who looked like a punk Barbara Stanwyck. Cassie had met Nephthys and Christine six months before, when they modeled together for several photographs in the show, and since then she clung to them as her new role models. Her lips scrunched as though she bit into something sour when I stepped from the car and she said, "Since when do you wear mini-skirts?"

It was the first time she'd seen me in a dress, even if I'd accessorized it with a pair of Doc Martens, a rhinestone nose stud, and a black leather motorcycle jacket. Cassie had just turned fifteen. I was twice her age. To her eye, I was a dinosaur. I gave her a friendly shove and asked where Nephthys was. She shrugged and pointed her chin toward the gallery, its brightly lit picture window framing an exhibition hall more packed than I had a right to expect. When I asked her why she remained outside she sidled up and bumped against my arm, her wary interpretation of a hug. "You're late," she said. "I was afraid you weren't going to show."

I kissed the side of her head. Cassie didn't show sentiment often. I wanted to reward it. Something shoved me from behind—the Rott, eager to bull his way into the party. Cassie broke away from me to kneel and give the dog a bigger hug than I'd ever seen her give a human being. I tossed her the leash and a moment later we swung open the gallery door to a D-list Hollywood arts crowd, not a single true celebrity among the young and trendy who dressed, talked, and gestured like movie stars in training, as though fame awaited them as certainly as age. A half dozen in the crowd had modeled for the faux-tabloid photographs that lined the walls, and all had invited their equally young and beautiful friends. Leonora Price—the sixty-something doyenne of L.A. arts photography—called my name when I pressed through the door and glared at me from behind rhinestone-flecked cat's-eye glasses. She cleaved the crowd, big red-bead neck-lace swaying above the bodice of her lime green dress, to wrap a withered arm over my shoulder, scold me for being late, and swing me face-to-face with two of the few people in the crowd not wearing black, a doctor and her doctor husband, who announced that they'd just purchased two of my photographs.

"Hold on to them," Leonora advised. "My girl is queen of the tabloids, the first serious photographer to cross over since Weegee." I shook their hands solemnly, embarrassed by such high praise. Leonora promptly slung me toward two men in gray Italian suits, maneuvering me with a hand on the nape of my neck as deftly as a puppeteer. The two men wore black shoes that gleamed with the high shine only the professional classes can achieve, their smiles polished to match. Personal injury lawyers, Leonora whispered, who had just purchased three images for their Century City offices. The lawyer on the left said how much they loved the photos, their jaundiced take on celebrity, and we talked a minute about what it's like to work as a tabloid photographer. "If Leonardo DiCaprio ever breaks your nose while you're snapping his candid," one said, "give us a call, we'd love to represent you." They cawed with laughter and I barked back, two personal injury lawyers and a tabloid photographer, fellow scavengers recognizing each other across the species barrier.

Leonora steered me close to the wall, the long, bony forefinger of her right hand curling toward a red dot beneath the nearest photo-graph, signifying the work had been sold. She painted her fingernails red to match the sales dots; red and green were her good-luck colors. "The photographs, they look wonderful up, don't you think?" She flicked the nail toward the next photo, and the one framed beyond that, all three marked with red dots. Still gripping the nape of my neck, she turned my head to plant a loud kiss on my brow, her milky blue eyes fierce and gleeful. "Be proud," she said.

The emotion vented through me like scalding water seeking a fissure, and I turned away because I didn't want to burden her with a sudden burst of tears. Two weeks earlier I'd gone alone to see the comic-book flick *Spiderman,* where the sight of Kirsten Dunst lifting enough of Spidey's mask to plant a wet one on Tobey Maguire's lips provoked such a surge of Eros and sorrow that I'd bolted for the bathroom, locked myself in a stall, and sobbed through a half pack of tissues. Since the deaths of my sister and mother I'd been increasingly unable to control my emotions, prone to jagged crying fits at moments that once would have provoked no more than a smirk of irritation. I'm not a photogenic crier, and the only thing that prevented tears from sizzling down my cheeks and snot dripping from my nose was the sight of the Rottweiler towing Cassie through the crowd, Nephthys one step behind.

"Have you seen Christine?" Anxiety thinned Cassie's voice to a whine. "We've been calling her, like, all day. We even stopped at her apartment."

"She'll show." I deflected the Rott with my knee and told him to sit. "She's already seen the photographs, so she's probably planning a big, fashionably late entrance."

"Christine, she's late to everything," Nephthys said, then wrapped me in a congratulatory hug, not oblivious to the fascinated stares of both men and women in the crowd. She wore a thin black halter and stretch shorts, showing as much of her tattooed body as possible in public without getting arrested. She was insanely proud of her tattoos, precise re-creations of the hieroglyphics and pictographs depicting her namesake, the Goddess of the House and Friend of the Dead in Egyptian mythology. She gave the hug full body contact, then pulled her head back to drop a lip kiss on me, unexpected at that moment but not so bad really, in a nonlesbian girlfriend kind of way. "You rock, girl," she said. "The photographs are killer."

"Cindy Sherman meets Weegee," someone said behind me and I turned to see who, because those were exactly the two traditions I intended to cross when I began composing the photographs in my head. The man who had spoken turned to look at me over his shoulder and then this really weird thing happened to time, the glittering hum of voices ground down and vectored out to silence, the crowd at the peripheral fringe of my vision spun into a centrifugal blur, and if I knew I had a soul, I'd say it broke its moorings and lurched momentarily free of my body.

I'd never seen the man before, but still, his face looked strangely familiar, and I would have sworn I knew him in a previous life if I believed in such things, which I don't. Yes, he was handsome in a black-haired, blue-eyed, and black-leather-jacketed way, but I wasn't that conscious of his face; I felt as though I'd found something I wasn't particularly looking for and never thought I needed until that moment, and now that I saw it, I didn't know whether to grab it or run headlong in the opposite direction. I floated toward him, not consciously moving my feet at all, and then the sensation of timelessness wavered and broke, because I'd walked right up to a strange man without an idea in my head about what to say, and that made me feel uncomfortably self-conscious.

"You're the photographer, aren't you?" He turned to a photograph of Christine on the nearest wall. "I can't tell you how many times I stepped into the grubbier version of this scene."

I'd taken the photograph at night off the Pacific Coast Highway a few miles south of Malibu, a white-gowned Christine hitchhiking in the headlight glow of a Mercedes convertible stopped on the shoulder, a little chrome automatic pistol dangling from the forefinger of her opposite hand. The driver's door to the Mercedes wings open into the center of the image and the body of an elegant young man in a white dinner jacket sprawls toward the pavement, his legs and hips still inside the car, the back of his jacket stained with vivid blossoms of light gray, the color of blood in black-and-white photography.

Frank stuck his shaggy head between us and introduced the man I'd been speaking to as Sean Tyler. We shook hands, his palm leathery smooth, like a good work glove. "Let's go out to the car for a sec," Frank said, and hoisted toward Sean the laptop bag slung over his shoulder. "I got something I want to show you." And then they were gone, just like that, Sean's big shoulders gracefully creasing the mob, leaving me face-to-face with Terry Graves, my parole officer, who pinched the muscle between my neck and shoulder and said photographs weren't her thing but these wouldn't be so bad if she could drop a neutron bomb in the middle of the room to eliminate the poseurs. I told her I needed a glass of wine and pressed toward the door, curious about Sean and what kind of business he had with

Frank. He didn't look like the kind of scamming tipster Frank usually met in alleyways and other dark places.

Out in the parking lot they stood hunched over the open trunk to Frank's Honda, a silvery light illuminating their faces from beneath, the blue-black of Los Angeles night blanketed around their shoulders. Frank had parked at the far end of the lot, near the street and away from the casual glance of passing eyes. When he heard my footsteps, and glanced to see me walking toward them he reached down into the trunk and shut off the light.

"There's really nothing you want to see here," he said, and I realized then that the source of light had been his laptop.

"Maybe I should be the one to decide that," I said.

In the washed-out streetlight his face looked flush and his eyes glazed. "The disk somebody mailed you?" He cleared his throat. "It wasn't music."

"If it was sent to me, then I should see it," I said. "In fact, if it was sent to me, you shouldn't even be looking at it."

Frank stared at me like I really didn't get it.

"No, it's all right, she probably needs to see this," Sean said. "I mean, you're not sure, right? She'll know better than you."

Frank reached into the trunk, pressed something, and moved aside. "This was supposed to be a good night for you," he said.

I stepped up to the rear bumper and looked into the mouth of the trunk, where Frank's laptop played a high-resolution amateur bondage video already well in progress. The scene depicted what I imagined to be a routine S&M scenario: a young woman, semiclad in red latex and bound at her wrists to a metal rack, was mounted from behind by a man in a black latex suit and ski mask–style hood. A similar hood covered the woman's head, slits cut for her eyes. A rubber ball was wedged into her mouth, held in place by a strap. With strips of latex disconnecting her features, the woman's face could have been any young woman's face. The eyes were listless. She didn't seem to mind being tied to a rack.

"Ruffies," Sean said.

"Rohypnol," Frank added. "The date rape drug of choice."

I wanted to ask Sean how he knew she was drugged, but before I could speak the man slung a rubber strap around the woman's neck and jerked it taut. Her head snapped back and she twisted her shoulders, trying to pull away. The man strangling her stood over six feet tall and pinned the woman to the rack like a butterfly. I looked away because I didn't want to watch, but then I felt Sean's hand gently supporting my back. The light from the screen illuminated his face from beneath, as though by theatrical stage light, the lupine curve of his lips and miss-nothing intensity of his eyes sadly predatory. I knew then what he was doing there, what he did for a living, and what was happening in the video. When I glanced back at the screen, the latex suit had been unzipped at the back and my eye met the mischievous wink of Betty Boop, tattooed along the upper curve of the woman's right shoulder.

2

I DROVE BACK to Venice Beach trying to convince myself the woman in the video didn't have to be Christine. An early summer inversion had settled over the city, smog condensing with beach fog to form a swirling yellow mist in the spears of light thrown by the Metro's headlights. In the passenger seat, Cassie vied with the Rott to see who could lean their head the farthest out the window. Cassie knew nothing about what might have happened to Christine. When I'd returned to the gallery after answering Sean's questions the crowd had thinned to a few friends, my models, and their hangers-on. I pretended nothing had happened and proposed a toast first to Leonora Price for taking the risk of exhibiting my work, and then to my models for being so photogenic. When I started to cry, everyone thought the emotions of the moment overwhelmed me in a good way. They all seemed happy, both for me and for themselves, like fireflies burning bright for one brief night against the greater darkness that awaits us all.

I'd shot Christine's first set of photographs just before Thanksgiving, and we'd gotten along so well she'd accompanied me to the airport to pick up Cassie, who was flying in from Phoenix, released to my care for the holiday by her foster parents. The idea to stage a photographic scene that involved them both had sprung from Cassie's insistent complaints that I didn't appreciate her talents as an actress or model, begun no more than a minute after she wheeled her suitcase from baggage claim. We talked about it over dinner that night—pasta and pizza at Angeli Caffé on Melrose—and the next day I rented a bungalow at the Beverly Hills Hotel for the shoot, Nephthys pitching in to help with set design and makeup. We'd scoured Cassie's face of Goth-girl makeup, secured a curly blonde wig over her purple hair, slipped her into a white dress, and photographed her as a contemporary adolescent Shirley Temple shooting junk amid a zoo of stuffed animals, Christine as her movie-star mom talking on the phone in the background, back turned, clueless.

Film and photo shoots promote a quick and easy camaraderie among participants, and during ours Cassie bonded instantly with Nephthys and Christine. We drove to Chinatown for Thanksgiving dinner that night, substituting Peking duck for turkey, and then over the weekend rode the bike paths of Venice Beach and watched films together. The experience seemed formative to Cassie, who was short on noncriminal role models just then, and she studied both Christine and Nephthys with the voracious curiosity of a young girl watching those a few years older to figure out the woman she might become. Christine and Nephthys may not have been the most wholesome role models, but by the age of thirteen my niece had already involved herself in criminal enterprises that would have sentenced her to a juvenile detention facility for the remainder of her youth had she been caught; any corrupting influences were likely to pass both ways. That Christmas we met again, and though I kept in touch with Nephthys after that, calling her every couple of weeks and meeting occasionally for coffee, Christine and I drifted apart, not from any conflict or lack of interest, but because we had little to talk about except what each of us was doing at the moment. We rarely talked about our pasts or personal issues. She was always a cipher to me, though a lovely one, a woman whose chatter captivated me even if, after a moment of reflection, I didn't find much meaning in it.

I didn't really know much about Christine's sex life, what turned her on. Some people found strangulation erotic, their partner throttling them a few seconds shy of brain damage and death, making the orgasms that much more intense. The video had ended violently but not conclusively, the woman unconscious but not necessarily dead. Maybe the sex had been consensual but had gone a little further than either partner intended. Christine could have been hiding somewhere, her silver dress hanging in the closet while she recovered from a bruised throat. The woman didn't even have to be Christine. More than one woman bore a tattoo of Betty Boop on her right shoulder.

I glanced over at Cassie. The Rott stretched across her small body, his head out the window, snapping at the wind as though one night he might catch it. I worried what the polluted air was doing to her young lungs but knew she'd scream if I insisted on raising the window.

"Why did you start crying tonight?" Cassie asked, aware I watched her.

"I just felt like it," I said. I didn't want to tell her, not then, not until I knew something more definitive.

"I hope it wasn't from happiness," she said. "I hate it when people cry from happiness. It's so *Miss America.*"

"Maybe you'll grow a heart some day, find out what it's like." It does little good to remind teenagers they're cruel, but Cassie didn't seem to mind. She peered at me from the far side of the passenger seat, her face a shining darkness in the night.

"If I had a heart, I'd just suffer," she said.

Cassie voiced few complaints about going to bed that night, tired enough by the show and her day of shopping to curl under the covers in my bedroom soon after we returned to the place that passed for home. I lived then in a one-bedroom apartment on the second floor of a twelve-unit teardown a half mile from the Venice Beach boardwalk. The landlord accepted all species of living creatures, from ex-cons with big dogs to illegal immigrants packed ten to a room, though cockroaches formed the largest population by far. Not many landlords are willing to rent to ex-cons, and those who are compensate for the risk by doubling the price.

In my line of business the phone often rings at two in the morning with a rumored sighting of one A-list actor or another snorting cocaine off the back of a naked model or some other routine paparazzi photo op. Cassie slept in the bedroom because I didn't want my work to wake her. I pulled the futon from the IKEA sofa and laid it flat on the floor, thinking I might try to sleep, but the images from the video still flickered through my mind and I got no closer to bed than kicking off my shoes. I pulled a bottle of Jack Daniel's from the kitchen cabinet, poured three fingers into a tumbler, and sat at the kitchen table to explore the digital camera I'd purchased a few months before at the insistence of *Scandal Times.* The tabloids are catching up to technology, Frank said. From now on the paper would be looking for photographic content in digital form. Get used

to it. I still took my most important shots on film but when the subject and conditions allowed I used the digital camera, a Canon SLR
as complicated to navigate as a computer, something else I needed to
learn to use.

Just past midnight the cell-phone display lit with a call from an
unfamiliar number in the 818 area code, originating from the San
Fernando Valley. My network of tipsters, finks, and quislings covers
most of the 310 area code—the West Side of Los Angeles—but every
now and then a tip comes from the hills on the Valley side of Mulholland Drive. I took the call. A voice asked if Ms. Zero was speaking and it took me a moment to place the voice as Sean's. "The
night's turning out slower than I thought," he said. "Any chance you
can get her photo to me? I might be able to start work on this right
away."

I didn't have anything in the apartment larger than a thumbnail
image from a proof sheet. "I know an all-night darkroom in Hollywood," I said, and told him I'd meet him there in an hour.

I collected the negatives I'd need from the hall closet, thought
about changing from the dress to a more utilitarian pair of jeans, but
decided I didn't want to risk waking Cassie by hunting down clothes
in the bedroom closet. The Rott was slow to understand that his job
was to stay behind and play guard dog, but after I whispered Cassie's
name a dozen times, pointing his nose toward the room in which she
slept, he curled up at her door, sighed, and watched me go. I didn't
want her to wake and feel abandoned.

Sean was waiting for me when I pulled into the mini-mall parking
lot, sipping a cup of take-out coffee as he leaned against a pole sign
advertising discount dry cleaning, a Korean nail parlor, video rental,
an optician, a Thai restaurant, a postal store, a photo and camera
shop, and the all-night donut shop that sold him the coffee. Many
people in Los Angeles hated the garish ubiquity of mini-malls—there
seemed to be at least one at every commercial intersection, and often
two on dueling corners—but where else were you going to get a
frozen yoghurt to go while you mailed a package and picked up the
dry cleaning? In a city increasingly blenderized by corporate fran-
chises, mini-malls were thriving shrines to the small businessman and
the best places to find exotic but cheap cuisine, from Argentinean to

Vietnamese and most every nationality in between. I slid the Metro between the chalk in front of the photo store and shouldered my camera bag.

A confused look must have clouded my eyes when the door snapped open without my touching the handle; it had been so long since a man had opened the door for me I momentarily thought it somehow opened itself. Getting out of the car in a short, tight dress presented another problem, particularly in such close proximity to a man, but I think I managed it with little flash and some grace.

"Did you get a chance to talk to any of Christine's friends?" Sean asked. "Anybody tell you anything that can help us find her?"

I'd asked Nephthys and a few other models, I told him, but nobody had seen her in the past twenty-four hours. He hadn't wanted me to mention the video to anyone, not yet.

"Any idea where she works?"

"Some call service center," I said. "The graveyard shift, I think."

"Did she report for work yesterday?"

"I'll check with another friend," I said, thinking of Nephthys. "I don't know where she works, not exactly. Actresses don't usually go public about their day jobs, even the ones they hold at night."

"Anything else she does every day?" he asked. "The thing about work, it can help us establish when she went missing, if that's what happened."

I told him I'd ask around. I knew she had a roommate, though I'd never met her. Christine came from a small central California town she couldn't get away from fast enough, but I didn't remember which one. When it came to facts, I knew little more than her address and telephone number. A hipster-technician with curly hair and a patch of scrub on his chin appeared behind the photo-shop glass, flipped the security locks, and swung open the door to let us in.

We followed the technician to the darkrooms down a back hallway. Like most darkrooms this one had the square footage of a closet, and when the door shut behind us the environment felt a little too intimate. I asked Sean how long he'd been interested in photography. He stood no more than a foot behind me while I unpacked negatives, proof sheets, and photographic paper from my camera bag, so close I could feel his breath on the back of my neck. I knew it was a stock question. I didn't care what we talked about. He could have been reciting the names of horses running at the track that day and I would have been content, because silence in that small room would have been too powerful.

"I've always liked it," he said. "You ever take photos in color, or just black and white?"

"I took color photos in a studio for a while." I flipped through the proof sheets of the photographs I'd taken of Christine, looking for an image that caught her in an unguarded look, and found a shot in which she sat before a dressing-table mirror, staring at some un-fixed point beyond the glass. "A long time ago I worked in a baby-portrait studio called Hansel & Gretel's, like the fairy tale. All the employees, we had to dress like characters from the fairy tale."

"The wicked witch, too?"

"No, she was considered too scary for little kids."

"It's a scary story. You remember how it goes? A starving wood-cutter and his wife—the wicked stepmother—abandon their children in the forest."

"I don't remember that part." I shuffled through the negatives and found the one that matched the image on the proof sheet. "I only remember the breadcrumb trail, the candy house, and killing the witch at the end."

"That's what everybody remembers."

I loaded the negative into the enlarger and switched off the lights. The safety light cast so faint a red glow that Sean's black leather jacket disappeared and his face hovered in the darkness like the face of a ghost.

"If you go back to the original," he said, "it's a story about felony child abandonment and a serial child killer that ends in justifiable homicide."

"Gretel burns the witch to death, right?"

"She shoves her in the oven and slams the door."

"My kind of girl," I said. I flicked on the enlarger light and fo-cused it onto an eight-by-ten photo, then clicked it off. "Two years of taking photos of screaming babies convinced me that birth control is not a bad thing."

I liked the warm sound of his laughter in the dark. He slid around the room to watch over my shoulder. I flicked on the enlarger light and counted to three, burning the image into the photographic paper, then slipped the paper into the developing tray. Immersed in liquid developer, Christine's image surfaced, the shadows surrounding her like dark clouds to frame the blank purity of her face. Sean leaned over my shoulder to watch the image develop, his face so close I smelled the coffee on him, fused with the light scent of his sweat and the oils in his black hair. When the shadows ripened to a dense black, I tonged the photograph into the stop bath to halt the changes in the image and eased it into the fixer to seal the results.

"You know what I love about this?" Sean asked. "It's like an investigation. You start with a blank and you end up with an image of what happened." He gracefully slipped aside as I turned to the sink to wash the print beneath running water, the final step before drying. "Homicide investigation, it's black and white, too. I'm not talking about moral issues here, I'm talking about how it feels. Things happen in my work that don't happen in the real world, the world of color. Sometimes I think I live and work in a shadow world."

I turned to him, my interest sharply focused because I'd thought the very same thing about my work in the tabloids, that I lived and worked in a world that shadowed the real world but really wasn't the real world at all, in the same way that most people who work graveyard shifts and long nights feel distanced from the daylight world of sun and color. Space in the darkroom was cramped and Sean had been hovering over my shoulder to watch me work, and so when I looked up at his face glowing beneath the safety light, our lips no more than a breath apart, what happened was my fault as much as his; I kissed him as much as he kissed me. Even though I considered it a little odd that a homicide investigator was so willing to talk to me about abstract feelings for the work he did, I hadn't even been conscious of our flirting, in the same way that I wasn't conscious of the terrible and wonderful consequences of kissing him. Yielding to the impulse to kiss him was like the first step toward falling together downhill, all tumbling-forward momentum, our limbs entwined as though the swift exhilaration of our coupling required an even tighter embrace to hold us together, his tongue in my mouth tasting as rich and fertile as earth, and when he penetrated me I launched into free fall, clutching his leather shoulders, my legs wrapped around his waist and my teeth dug into his neck.

He made a sound like weeping when he came, as though he released his pain with his seed. I stroked the back of his head and kissed his brows and it wasn't until I thought about his pain that I thought about anything except pleasure. Wild sex had been far from my thoughts when I entered the darkroom. It had been over a year since I'd made love to a man. Sean and I had coupled with such spontaneous passion that I'd neglected some unpleasant but essential realities. I hadn't asked him to wear a condom and he hadn't volunteered. I had to trust that he'd been surprised by the encounter no less than I, that his sexual history was clean enough that he hadn't infected me with anything, and that I was late enough in my cycle not to get pregnant. That was a lot of trust to place in fate and someone I'd just met. I broke away from him and pulled down the hem of my dress.

He wiped his face with both hands and stared at me above his fingertips. "Have you ever been walking fast," he said, "your mind on something that takes all your attention, so you're not really looking where you're going, and then, bam, you run straight into somebody, and you both go sprawling, wondering what hit you?" He glanced down and saw that he'd kicked himself free of only one pant leg, the other clinging to his ankle. "That's how I feel right now."

Water still streamed over the print in the sink. I closed the faucet and loaded the wet print into the air dryer, turning my back to give him a moment to pull up his pants in dignity. How much did he know about me? Had Frank told him that I was an ex-con paparazza on parole? I packed the negatives, proof sheets, and photographic paper back into my camera bag, wishing I could sort and pack my feelings as efficiently. I'm accustomed to getting screwed by the cops, but this was a first. I gave him the print, said, "This is quick and dirty, not really up to gallery standards, but it should serve your purpose."

I opened the door, letting our eyes adjust gradually to the light spilling in from the hallway. Sean swung the photograph toward the light to examine it. "It may be quick and dirty, but it's beautiful, too." He sounded as though he spoke about our sex as much as the photograph. "I'll make photocopies and return this to you,"

"You can keep it," I said.

"Would it offend you if I asked you to sign it?"

I flipped the print image-side down to sign my name on the back, then slipped the photograph into an oversized envelope to protect it.

Outside, in the mini-mall parking lot, he looked at me strangely but said nothing when I gave him my hand to shake rather than a kiss goodbye.

Among the loneliest places in the world is any street in Los Angeles at 3 AM, where the stray headlights of automobiles skitter past each other like the wary survivors of an apocalypse and every few miles the swift descent of flashing police lights on one car or another demonstrates that no one roving about at such an hour can be up to much good. Los Angeles defines itself by day, a city of sunlight glinting sharply from the glass, metal, and chrome of rushing automobiles. Past midnight, the city extinguishes itself in the absence of the very things that define it, and roaming its streets is like roaming a wasteland. Until that night I hadn't thought myself lonely. I had my dog, my work, and a few close friends, and even though I sometimes missed the comfort and pleasure of another body next to mine, I didn't really see the point. The cool, smog-tainted emptinesses of the city by night harmonized with my spirit far more than the glare and bustle of daily life, as though I felt more at ease with the negative image of things than with the things themselves.

To attach any significance to what happened in the darkroom that night would be a mistake, and given Sean's profession, an error that could only lead to grief. What had he said? That he felt like he'd been looking in the wrong direction while rounding a corner and knocked into somebody. What do you do when you run into somebody without looking? You apologize and move on. Sure, I felt more passionate in those few brief moments than I had in years, probably because I'd been caught so completely unaware, but a moment of spontaneous passion was nothing to build a relationship on, except one of the most casual kind. The problem was, I didn't believe I wanted a serious relationship either. If I disallowed myself casual flings and serious relationships, that left me with the sole possibility of sleeping with like-minded friends I found sexually attractive, a phenomenon so rare I may as well have converted to Catholicism and taken vows.

I keyed the top deadbolt to the door of my apartment and when I didn't hear the thumping gait of the Rott coming to greet me, I dismissed my foreboding with the thought that he liked his sleep too much to get up. Careful not to wake Cassie, I pushed quietly into the apartment and shut the door behind me, listening for the sound of the Rott's limbs stretching on the carpet, his regular prelude to rising from sleep. The door to my bedroom, where Cassie slept, yawned open. I crept to the door frame and peeked inside. The covers to the bed lay flung aside, the bottom sheet indented where my niece had slept not so long ago. I called her name and turned to the bathroom, hoping to see a sliver of light or hear the toilet clatter and flush. I called her name again, louder, and leapt to flick on the lights, fearing what I might find but fearing more the dark and silence.

A sheet of paper, anchored in place on the kitchen counter by an empty glass, caught my eye. I recognized at a distance the unruly scrawl of printed letters as my niece's handwriting. "Baby and I gotta go somewhere to do something," she wrote. "I'll call tomorrow. Don't worry." I crumpled the note and flung it across the room. Don't worry. Right. Might as well shoot me in the gut, tell me, don't bleed.

3

THE VENICE BEACH boardwalk gleams like a carnival during daylight hours, tarot and palm readers competing with merchants and political cranks for the tourists crowding the boardwalk, but after the sun sets the merchants and mystics pack up and the crowds dissipate, leaving the trash behind. Violent crime escalates, and though most of it is perpetrated by drunks and druggies on other drunks and druggies, I did not always feel safe walking the neighborhood after midnight, even when accompanied by the Rott, and this intensified my worries about Cassie. I searched the beach and boardwalk until dawn, asking the drunks, drug addicts, skate punks, and homeless if they'd seen a teenage girl walking a Rottweiler that night. I called the dog as I searched, certain he'd come if he heard my voice, but the only replies sprang from those so deep into one mind-fogging substance or another that any claimed sighting of my niece or dog would be hallucinated.

Cassie had proved capable of taking care of herself on the streets, and that helped me pass the night a little easier. She'd been running wild the year we met, one of a gang of runaways sleeping rough in an abandoned Nike missile base. I hadn't even known she existed until a couple of homicide detectives from the Hollywood station picked me up late one night to identify the body of her mother—my older sister. She had been an even stranger child then, harmless enough to look at but wild and unpredictable, like a feral kitten. She could take care of herself well enough. What I didn't know was how well she took care of others. She and the dog got along, I knew that. Cassie shied from contact with me but didn't hesitate to hug or pet the Rott. I knew the Rott would be fiercely protective of Cassie, but I didn't know how fiercely protective Cassie would be of the Rott.

The cry of the cell phone woke me a couple hours past sunrise, curled in the cramped front seat of the Metro, parked on a residential side street in Los Feliz. I glanced at the call display, hoping to see the unfamiliar number of a public phone box where Cassie might be waiting to be picked up. The display registered a name instead, Nephthys, returning my call from late the night before. After abandoning my search of the beach, I'd driven across town to park and wait for her to wake.

"She didn't say anything to me about it," Nephthys said when I told her about Cassie. "You know what it's like at that age. It's hard to find anything good to say about the people trying to take care of you, but she seemed happy to me, excited to be staying with you. But she's not your average fifteen-year-old. She does what she wants and damns the consequences."

While we were talking I locked up the car, crossed the sidewalk to a 1920s bungalow complex, followed the concrete path toward a rear unit set behind a screen of palm fronds and birds-of-paradise, and knocked on the door. "Wait a minute, someone's at the door," Nephthys said, and a moment later her eye blackened the peephole on the opposite side. "Holy crap! It's you!"

When she snapped open the door I half expected to see hieroglyphics painted on the walls of her apartment to match the tattoos on her body, but Nephthys's fetish for things Egyptian pretty much ended at her skin. She invited me into a tiny, cluttered kitchen, the sunlight streaming onto bright yellow walls. "Don't worry about Cassie, that girl is fifteen going on thirty-five," she said, pouring me a cup of coffee. "She was smart to take the dog with her. The dog will protect her."

"Sure, but who's going to protect my dog from Cassie?"

Nephthys took my comment as gallows humor. "They're both going to be okay, don't worry." She put her hand on my shoulder and looked up at me—she didn't stand taller than five foot two—her Egyptian-lined eyes crinkled with concern.

I was crying again.

"No, it's not that, it's something else, it's Christine." I wiped the sleeve of my jacket across my eyes and told her that someone had sent me a video depicting Christine in an S&M scene that featured strangulation, that it probably wasn't anything serious but I had to find her as quickly as possible. "She told me she worked as a call service representative," I said. "Do you know the name of the company, how to get in touch with her boss?"

"Call service representative? That's what she told you?" The corner of her mouth curved in a wise-girl smile. "That's not exactly accurate."

"You mean she didn't have a job?"

"She had a job, but I think 'call service representative' might be a euphemism." She touched my elbow as though sharing a secret. "She works at one of those 1-900 places."

I must have looked confused.

"Phone sex," she explained.

No wonder Christine hadn't told me the strict truth.

"Do you know which one?"

"Sweet Lasses, I think it's called, but that kind of work, you never leave the house, the calls are patched to your phone line. I have the number stored on the computer." She edged past me, careful of our cups of coffee, into a dimly lit living room furnished with a thrift-shop aesthetic, mix-and-match furniture from different eras and styles existing in happy harmony, brightened by colored fabrics from India and South America draped across the chair backs and hung from the ceiling, flag style. "Christine is another girl who can take care of herself; believe me, she's not as innocent as she looks. But if you're worried, we can take a look at her journal, see if she wrote anything that might explain what's going on."

"Do you have the keys to her apartment?" I asked.

"No," she said.

"Then how do we get her journal?"

"It's online." She plucked a red batik covering from an egg-shaped iMac. "Christine is a Suicide Girl."

"I can't believe Christine wanted to kill herself," I said.

"Suicide Girls isn't about killing yourself." She poked the computer's start button and the thing chimed to life. "It's an online community where Goths, punks, and alts show off their tats and body mods."

"Alts?"

"You know, people into alternative culture." She cracked her knuckles over the keyboard. "For example, I'm a post-post-feminist Egyptologist and body performance artist who reads science fiction and listens to old bossa nova records, and that's just to start. It's easier to say 'alt' and move on." Her fingers clattered over the keys and a website loaded onto the screen, thumbnail jpegs of pierced and tattooed young women on the left, some kind of Internet message board on the right, interviews and weird news stories down the center. The women weren't entirely naked but they didn't wear a lot of clothes either. A logo in the top right corner depicted the letters *SG* and an illustrated woman posed before a background of stars. On closer inspection, a shirt I thought a woman wore turned out to be a tattoo.

The screen flashed purple as the page shifted and Christine's face appeared in the upper left corner, above her personal profile, which listed her age (*21*), body mods (*tongue, nipple, ear, tattoo*), favorite bands (*Bowie, Yeah Yeah Yeahs, The Cure, Sonic Youth, Pixies, Portishead*), favorite films (*Amélie, Chocolat, Boogie Nights, Edward Scissorhands*), favorite books (*Harry Potter*), and the five things she couldn't live without (*chocolate, Veuve-Clicquot, pain, laughter, latex*). To the right of her profile, sentences from her online journal staggered across the page:

my hair crisis is finally solved and I'm closer to my dream of looking like a 1950's movie star for that show I've been writing about.

i wanted to go platinum, like marilyn monroe.

so i went to the all nite drug store to get the die and started fooling around with a pair of scizzors and i woke the next morning my hair like a haystack, just dry and all over the place ugly.

i thought i'd have to wear a bag over my head but boyfiend the bastard treated me to a day at the stylist and now i look bootifull.

tonite i see the guy says he's johnny depp's producer. probably just another cum on.

hey, any of u going to the show nite after tomorrow? if u do the bootifull christine will kiss ur face.

The journal entry was dated the day we'd hung the show, not quite seventy-two hours earlier. She'd dropped by the gallery to model her dress in the afternoon, returned home to type her journal entry, then later that night, if her journal was credible, she'd met the man who claimed to be Johnny Depp's producer. "This so-called producer, how do you think she met him?" I asked.

Nephthys said she remembered Christine had written about him before and tapped at the keyboard again. The previous day's journal entry popped onto the screen:

> i don't know if this is just more elay bullshit but some guy claims to be a producer on one of johnny depp's films (from hell, not his best) wants to see
> ME!!!!???!!!
> this is his line—he said he needed people who could be cool around johnny, said i sounded like somebody might be good to hang with, maybe cast in the picture but no, he wasn't going to lead me on, make promises.
> this means he just wants to screw me, right? whatever. if that's all he wants, no effing way, but i'm not gonna tell the boyfiend . . .
> tg he won't read this, he thinks sg is crap!
> don't don't don't forget two nights from now the show.

I asked when she'd last seen Christine.

"I didn't. I mean, we communicated here on the site but I haven't actually seen her this week." She scrolled down the page to a series of comments made in response to Christine's journal entry that day. A few of the comments were marginally pervy, but most were touchingly supportive messages. *Ur soooo Hawt!!!* One comment read. *I can't believe ur not gonna be a ****. And then, further down the page, I saw a thumbnail close-up of Nephthys next to her name and the exhortation, *U Rock Grrrl!*

"You wrote this?" I asked.

"We all post messages to each other's journals." She darted the cursor to her thumbnail image and clicked. "I can't tell you how excited I was when the first photoset of my tats went online. That's how I met Christine and a bunch of my friends. Here, let me show you . . ."

I dug my address book from my camera bag while she loaded a page that contained her thumbnail photo, personal profile, and journal. She clicked another jpeg at the top of the page and a photograph surfaced onto the screen, Nephthys standing at a brick wall, legs pressed tightly together but arms stretched wide, her hieroglyphic-tattooed body like a canvas framed in red. I took my eyes from the screen long enough to show her the address I listed for Christine and she confirmed it was the same as the one in her book. "I keep calling her cell but I don't get an answer," I said. "Do you know her room-mate?"

"Tammy."

"Another Suicide Girl?"

"No, she's an aspiring actress." Nephthys's mouth crinkled as though wrapped around something sour. "Tammy's a real girly-girl. She's on location right now, somewhere in Canada I think, shooting some made-for-dreck movie."

"What about the boyfriend?" I asked.

"I don't want to betray any confidences, but the video you mentioned?" She turned in her chair and looked up at me, her face small and compact as a child's but the look in her eyes not childlike at all. "It doesn't surprise me. They were into some really twisted shit."

Christine's supposed boyfriend, the self-help author Dr. James Rakaan, practiced past-life regression therapy on a dead-end street in the hills above Sunset Boulevard, just east of the Beverly Hills border. I remained a little fuzzy on the underlying theory, but as I understood it past-life regression therapists uncovered a patient's memories of past lives through hypnosis, sometimes because it was just a cool thing to do but most often because some memories were so terrible that they influenced the patient's present life. One case history I read on the Internet described a man with chronic phantom back pain who discovered he'd taken a Roman spear to the liver in the second century while trying to save his family from slaughter. Once he remembered and dealt with the trauma, the pain disappeared. According to the promotional information on his website, www.RakaanHeals.com, Dr. Rakaan was not only one of the most revered practitioners of the exciting new science of past-life regression therapy, but also the author of *New York Times* best-sellers such as *Healing the Past-Life Child Within* and *Soul Mates: One Love Through a Hundred Lifetimes,* plus one title that stayed twelve straight weeks on the self-help bestseller list, *You're Not Crazy, You Really Are Napoleon: How to Unleash the Power of Your Past Lives*.

In his private practice, Dr. Rakaan charged hundreds of dollars an hour to a star-studded list of studio executives and celebrity clients, but almost anybody could afford the price of a book, the website quoted him as saying, and he was happy to make his techniques available for the benefit of the general public. Most impressive of all, Dr. Rakaan not only elicited past-life experiences from his patients—any second-rate past-life regressionist with half his credentials could pull that off—but with certain talented subjects he could invoke future lives as well, telling patients what shapes their reincarnations would take up to six lifetimes from now, something he called future-life progression, or FULP.™

While I drove toward Beverly Hills I called the phone number Sean had left with me, and when his voice mail picked up I left a detailed message about Christine's journal and the name of her employer. When I finished giving him this information I nearly said something sappy about our encounter the night before but restrained myself, instead suggesting he could call to let me know he'd received the message. I figured he wouldn't mind my talking to Rakaan. I tracked people for a living, if celebrities can be called people and photographing them a living.

I parked the Metro in a free slot across the street from Rakaan's office and walked down a winding flagstone path to a garden complex housing an herbal tea shop, an acupuncturist, a practitioner of holistic medicine, and a carved wooden signboard announcing the offices of Dr. James Rakaan, C.H.T. The heady scent of sandalwood greeted me when I stepped across the threshold into the reception area, a junglish room decorated in palm fronds and rattan furniture. The receptionist, a young woman with opaque gray eyes and a nebula of auburn curls framing her pale skin, serenely tilted her chin toward the ceiling and asked if I had an appointment when I said I wanted to talk to Dr. Rakaan.

"Tell him that I'm worried about Christine," I said.

The receptionist advised me that Dr. Rakaan was with a patient at the moment but if I would please have a seat, in a few minutes she'd be able to take a message to him. While I waited, I glanced through a brochure touting a Caribbean cruise to the Panama Canal and spiritual enlightenment, in that order, cohosted by Dr. Rakaan and Thomas Van Voorhees, a renowned medium who claimed he could convey detailed messages from deceased family members in the spirit world. I had barely talked to my family members when they were alive, didn't see what good it would do to chat with them dead, but I figured I was probably in the minority there. The door behind the receptionist's desk eased open and a woman in dark sunglasses, white dress, and floppy hat emerged, looking like an aging movie star who didn't want to be recognized. She succeeded. The receptionist slipped into the gap and a few minutes later Dr. Rakaan himself emerged.

You might think that someone hailed as a revered figure in an exciting new science, even one so unexacting as past-life regression therapy, would be a nerdish gentleman of a certain age, balding at the top and dumpling at the middle, a man given to stay-pressed slacks and half-tucked shirts, his abstract but kind gaze obscured behind thick eyeglasses he likes to clean with the bottom end of his mismatched tie. Not Dr. Rakaan. Not even the photograph on his website prepared me for the striking image of the man himself striding into the reception area, long black hair as sleek as a flag waving to his shoulders, the stout bridge of his nose like the stem of a Y connecting the flying wedge of his massive brow, his glance as piercing as phaser fire set to stun. I didn't doubt he treated a star-studded list of celebrity clients. He looked like a movie star himself.

I asked if he'd seen Christine lately.

"Are you talking about one of my patients . . ." He made a show of trying to pluck the name from memory. "Christine Myers?"

"I'm talking about your girlfriend. That Christine."

Dr. Rakaan stepped aside, the tips of his fingers brushing toward the open door to his office, a gesture I took as an invitation to enter. His office looked like something Dr. Freud might have imagined if he took Prozac instead of cocaine and lived in Beverly Hills instead of Vienna. I avoided the rattan couch and selected a club chair set casually beside a weathered teak desk.

"I'm sorry, but I don't have a girlfriend named Christine," he said. He settled into the swivel chair behind the desk and clasped his hands below his chin, his wide shoulders framed by a window overlooking the back garden.

"I don't care how you characterize your relationship. I just want to know if you've seen her in the past three days or know where she is right now."

His eyebrows puzzled together, narrowing his eyes to slits, an expression no doubt meant to convey his confusion but instead gave his face a cagey look. "And you are . . . ?"

I gave him my name.

"You're the photographer." He nodded as though watching things fall into place. "She was very excited about that, the exhibition I mean, on the verge of euphoria, really. It gave her a tremendous boost of self-esteem, something she needs very much."

"Why would Christine say you're her boyfriend if you're not?"

"Therapy can be an emotionally intimate experience, even more intimate than sex." His face angled into the soft light from the garden window and a smug smile creased his lips, a smile he thought better to contain a moment later. He was not a man unaware of his own handsomeness. "It's one of the hazards—of any kind of therapy actually, not just past-life regression. Even relatively well-adjusted patients form a strong bond with the therapist and sometimes that bond is misinterpreted by the patient to be a romantic one. When a patient is deeply troubled, with a past-life history of abuse . . ." He raised his hands and held them palms up, a gesture of disarming helplessness. "She can fantasize a romantic relationship when none in fact exists."

"Is that what happened to Christine?"

"I can't really tell you without violating the confidentiality between therapist and patient. But what's this about Christine being missing?"

"She didn't show for the exhibition last night. I've asked around and nobody has seen her for three days, not since she was supposed to go on a date with some guy she thought was Johnny Depp's producer."

"A date?" His voice cracked in the middle, as though torn between surprise and skepticism. "She mentioned nothing to me about it. But she missed her appointment two days ago, I can tell you that much. And her karma is so unpredictable this isn't the first time I've worried about her."

"What's wrong with her karma?"

"She was murdered in her most recent past life and in the life before that as well." He spoke as though these events had taken place just days or weeks ago and winced as though he regretted having to divulge a confidence. "Christine loves pain. That's what her sessions are about. Her love of pain. So naturally I worry about the kind of company she attracts. But really, the most likely thing is that she and this producer hit it off and they're somewhere in Vegas, Hawaii, or Mexico together. From what I understand that kind of behavior isn't unusual with her."

He stood and apologized that he had another appointment scheduled and couldn't spare more time. I allowed myself to be goaded into standing but instead of moving politely toward the door, I thought about the jealousy in his voice when he spoke and said, "I don't doubt she's your patient, but you're having sex with her, aren't you?"

Dr. Rakaan pushed past me and opened the door.

"Sure," I said. "She's young, blonde, beautiful, and like you said, liable to have romantic feelings toward her therapist. You may as well sit a man down to a gourmet meal and ask him not to eat. Of course you're having sex with her."

"I'm not sleeping with Christine," he said.

"I'm sure Christine is nothing special to you. I'm sure she's not the only patient you're having sex with. And I didn't say you were sleeping with Christine. I said you were having sex with her."

His fingertips darted to his temples as though his head was about to explode and he said, "You have incredibly filthy karma, I can't believe I didn't see it when you first walked in. Is it possible that you're . . . ?" His face slackened in stunned awe, then he shook his head, revolted. "I'm sometimes hit with moments of clairvoyance. In some cases, I don't have to take someone through past-life regression to discover who they once were. I already know. Do you have any idea who you were in your past life?"

"I hope you're not going to tell me I was Napoleon."

"You were Lizzie Borden," he said. "Now, please, get out of my office."

4

I SHOULD HAVE laughed when Dr. Rakaan claimed I was the reincarnation of Lizzie Borden, the young Massachusetts woman accused of hacking her father and stepmother to death with an axe in
the late nineteenth century. Nothing like being called a reincarnated
axe murderer to make you feel good about yourself. Particularly if
the call might be accurate. While I coasted down the hill toward Sunset Boulevard my cell phone chirped, flashing a familiar-looking
number that took me several seconds to place. I'd grown up with
that number. I hadn't received a call from my parents' house since
my mom died. Pop and I hadn't talked for six years, and it would
have been just the same to me if we didn't talk for another sixty. I
couldn't imagine why he'd be calling now, and because I couldn't
imagine a single compelling reason, I took the call.

"Hi," Cassie said. "I'm kinda stuck. Can you come pick me up?"

"Sure," I said, shocked to hear her voice coming from that
number.

"I'm at Gramps's house."

"Gramps?"

"You know, your pop. I'm at his place. In Canyon Country."

"Since when do you call him Gramps?"

"He's my grandfather, isn't he?"

"Your mother hated him."

"He's not so bad." Her voice sounded almost cheerful. Her voice
never sounded cheerful. "He came out to visit me. In Phoenix. And
we've been talking on the phone. So I thought I should go see him."

"Pop drove to Phoenix to see you?"

"A couple of times."

A car turned into traffic in front of me as I neared the bottom of the hill. I hit the horn, hard, but resisted the temptation to flip off the driver when he glanced in the rearview mirror. That didn't, however, stop him from flipping me off.

"Why didn't you tell me?" I asked.

"Because I knew you wouldn't like it."

"Is the Rott with you?"

"He's right next to me." She turned her face from the phone and pitched her voice singsong high to tell the dog she was talking to me. "That's why I need you to come get me. People aren't so fast to pick up somebody hitchhiking with a big dog."

"You hitchhiked to Canyon Country last night?"

A distance of thirty miles.

"Of course not. Somebody I know, he gave me a ride."

"At midnight."

"He could only go at night, because he had to work the next day."

"Without saying a word to me."

"I was gonna tell you but you were gone. I left a note."

Helpless and innocent are not two words I would use to describe my niece. Her stepfather was currently serving a ten-year sentence in Oregon for bank robbery. Her mother had been a con artist at the time of her death and worse things before that. The kid knew how to look out for herself.

"So are you gonna come get me or not?"

"I'm not going inside that house," I said. "I'll honk outside, three times."

For once in my life I obeyed the speed limit as I drove the Golden State Freeway north toward Canyon Country, in no hurry to get where I was going. My feelings toward my pop had mellowed considerably over the years. Used to be I wanted to kill him. Then for a long time I would have settled for a painful, crippling injury. Whenever he hit my mom I went back to wanting to kill him. After her death, when I watched him collapse from something like grief at her funeral, I stopped wishing him violent physical harm. Since then I merely wished never to see him again.

He hadn't been the worst father, despite the beatings he dispensed to one family member or the other with near sacramental regularity.

He despised physical weakness and considered it his duty to demonstrate by example how to defend ourselves from everyone except himself. Had he not decided to instruct us during moments of capricious rage, tindered by alcohol and sparked by unpredictable reactions to words or gestures that struck him as disrespectful, beating the hell out of us one moment and declaring how good it was for us the next, I could have accepted—eventually—the slaps, punches, and kicks as educational.

I don't want to disparage his accomplishments. He taught me many things, more things of true value in life than anyone else. His beatings taught me discipline, how to walk quietly and be silent, how to tune into the moods of your opponent and hit him before he hits you or to run before he strikes. Above all, he taught me how to watch. I'm a photographer because of him, because of my fear of him. I learned early how dangerous it could be to talk, how the wrong word could summon the beast in him with savage speed. I learned to sit silently and watch, my eye like a camera engaged in distant action. These skills have served my career well. And if nothing else, I owe to him my ability to throw a killer left hook and to take a punch without crumpling in pain or intimidation.

Pop was never one to garden much, preferring to spend his free hours tinkering with his pickup truck, but as I looked at the one-story tract house where I'd been raised, the height of the weeds growing from the lawn startled me. Our lawn had always sprouted equal amounts of dandelions and crab grass, but thistle, foxtail, and ragweed now grew a few inches shy of being declared a fire hazard. I circled the block and parked across the street from the house, tapped the horn three times, noticed the paint looked more weathered than ever and the asphalt-shingle roof needed patching. Pop was letting the place run down, not that it mattered to me. While I waited, I searched for Sean's number on my cell phone and called it. His voice mail picked up. I left a message detailing my conversation with Dr. Rakaan and disconnected. If he wanted to call me, he'd call me. I pocketed the cell as Cassie stepped out the front door, without the Rott. She shrugged and turned her palms up, making the gesture theatrically big so I couldn't fail to notice it, then curled her hand toward her shoulder, motioning me to come to her.

I stuck my head out the window, shouted, "What?"

"Baby! He won't come!"

"Grab his collar and pull him!"

"I can't! He's too big!" She drew out the words when she shouted, emphasizing her relative helplessness against the size of the dog.

I vaulted out the driver's door and strode across the street, my patience finally down to the bone, and even though I didn't like to yell at my niece, preferring instead to discipline her with a minimum of anger—not that she listened—this time I planned to tell her exactly how I felt about getting ditched in the middle of the night and then dragged out to a house I considered hell on earth, but the second my Doc Martens brushed the weeds beside the front walk the sweat burst from my skin in a dozen places and my throat constricted as though wrapped by a snake.

"What's wrong?" Cassie asked, no doubt afraid that her attempts at manipulation had irrevocably pissed me off.

I couldn't allow myself to lose my temper with her, not there, where I'd suffered so much from Pop's anger that I had a panic attack just approaching the door. I asked her where the dog was.

"Under the bed in the back bedroom." She took a step toward the door to encourage me to follow. "He won't come out for me."

I shouted for the Rott, heard his bark in response but not the thumping gallop of his paws racing to greet me. Cassie pulled at my arm, her voice rising an octave in fear or frustration, I couldn't tell which. "I told you, he won't come, he's stuck under the bed. You have to come inside and get him." I allowed her to lead me up the steps and across the threshold into a house that had been both a sanctuary and a place of terror for me. The smell wrapped me as my eyes adjusted to the dark, the stale odors of old man, smoke, and fried food as heavy as cloth. I glanced at the rust-colored couch and brown recliner in the living room, both positioned at angles favorable to watching the television set in the corner, the heavy oak coffee table still chipped in evidence of the things Pop had broken against it, a smooth path worn in the beige carpet leading toward the kitchen, where Pop himself sat framed in the doorway, hunched over a mug at the table, staring at me like an animal from its den. I nodded once, slowly. He nodded back and raised his right forefinger from the top of the mug.

The Rott barked again, his paws scratching against the bedroom door. Cassie scuttled down the hall. "Listen," she said, a false cheer running through her voice. "It sounds like he's come out now." She opened the door before I could get to it, the Rott bulling through the gap as it widened, bumping Cassie aside to get to me. I dropped to my knees and we collided, chest to shoulder. I turned with the blow, landing on my back, the Rott thrilled to find me pinned to the floor, squirming to escape his fat, wet tongue. I rolled onto my stomach, his tongue flicking at my ears from behind, the high-pitched squeals of my niece's laughter resonating in the narrow hallway. I'd never heard her laugh before. I struggled to my knees and glanced into the room where the dog supposedly had been hiding. The bed frame stood about six inches above the carpet, barely high enough to give clearance to a cat.

"The dog is bigger than the bed," I said. "No way he could fit under there. And even if he did get stuck, how was he going to open the door? If you're going to lie, at least try to make it believable."

When I saw her cheeks crimson above a pleased smile I realized she had lured me inside the house for some other reason. I'd shared the room with Cassie's mom, Sharon, until she ran away from home at age sixteen. The sight of my childhood room didn't make me sentimental. Except the bed and dresser, everything of mine had long since been thrown out or given to Goodwill. Maybe Cassie was searching for some kind of context. She'd been placed in foster care after her mother's arrest for bank robbery. Before that, the years they'd been together had been troubled. Maybe my presence helped her visualize how her mother lived as a girl.

I told the Rott to sit and then stood behind him, stroking his head down to his haunches, physical contact that bound us and prepared him to obey. Cassie held his head in her hands at the same time, the Rott in dog heaven between us. Then I commanded him to heel.

"That's a fine dog you got there," Pop called. He stood at the threshold between the kitchen and living room, backlit by sunlight streaming through the kitchen window. "Why don't you sit down a bit, have a cup of coffee with your old man."

I understood then that I'd been tricked into this meeting for reasons mystifying enough to hook me into staying. I suspected it would turn into an ambush, some recounting of his grievances against me.

Not that I feared him. When he turned into the light, heading for the kitchen cabinet where he stored the coffee mugs, I noticed his barrel chest now slumped toward his waist and what remained of his hair grew in sparse gray tufts around the balded crown of his head. He was too old to fear. I was more concerned with what might happen to my heart if I turned him down and walked out the door. He was my father; even though we had thirty years of sometimes violent history behind us, to refuse a simple request to talk would be heartless. I'd listen to what he wanted to say and then I'd leave. I didn't have to talk if I didn't want to.

When I sat at the table, the Rott settling next to me on the floor, I realized it was the same chair I'd been assigned as a child, that I'd unconsciously reverted to my traditional place in the family. I'd always been the appeaser, the only one in the family who, when I sensed it coming, could sometimes calm the beast in my pop. I'd stroke his arm, telling him what a good poppa he was, until he calmed, or didn't. I'd been so terrified of him as a child that I'd changed myself to fit his ideas of how I should act, think, and dress, in hopes that by appeasing him he wouldn't hurt me. I took to styling myself like a girly girl, blonde hair flipped at the shoulder or worn in pigtails, fuzzy sweaters and knee-length skirts, open-toed pumps, toenails buffed like paint on a Corvette. Maybe I even wanted Pop to love me. I still don't have that too clear. Looking back, I think he might have loved me more than his other children— not that he loved any of us much—and so when at last I snapped, rebelling violently against him and the false image of myself we'd created, he'd all but disowned me. While Pop fiddled with the coffee, I thought about taking his chair, his place at the table, but decided it was a spiteful impulse I'd best ignore.

"Cassie and me, we had quite the time, didn't we Cass?" He looked over his shoulder at his granddaughter, who stood in the kitchen doorway, uncertain whether her presence at the table would help or hinder the conversation. "She didn't even tell me she was coming last night until just past eleven. Then she gets here and tells me you didn't know she was going, that she took your dog and wrote you some note." Pop set a cup of coffee onto the Formica tabletop in front of me and sat, facing the entrance to the kitchen. "Time was, a child of mine pulled a stunt like that."

"If you ever hurt Cassie, give her a black eye or a split lip, I'll break your leg with a baseball bat."

It had to be said, and it didn't make much sense to delay saying it.

He stared at me, wrinkled skin hooding the expression from his eyes, and I counted, one-two-three, waiting for the familiar signs of his transformation from man to beast: the baleful glare, the flush of blood and sweat across his brow, the clenched jerking of his muscles signaling the moment before scales broke through the skin covering his face and he flung a mug of scalding coffee at my head.

But it didn't happen. He just shrugged and smiled.

"Still the hard-ass, I see," he said.

I stared at him, waiting.

"Don't get me wrong. I'm proud of you. You want to break my leg, fine, just don't forget who taught you how to swing the bat."

Had he thrown his coffee at me, I would have ducked and flipped the table on him, but I didn't see the compliment coming and it caught me flush in the face. "You did," I said. He'd taught me how to throw and catch too, didn't even seem to notice I was a girl until my T-shirts began to strain against what would develop into an unspectacular set of breasts. He'd been the first to insist I put on a bra and stop acting like a tomboy, then whipped me like a boy when I rebelled.

"I been following your work in the papers." He pulled a copy of *Scandal Times* from the chair next to him. "You gotta be persevering to do the kinda work you do."

I nodded.

"You really stand up for yourself, I'll say that much. Sure, you let things get away from you there for a while, got into a little trouble, but strong character showed you through, and you set yourself right." He sipped at his coffee, eyes cagey above the rim of the mug. "I'm no friend of the law's. Never have been. Somebody hits you, you hit them back. That's what I always taught you to do. Doesn't matter if you get in trouble. You do it because you gotta stand up for yourself. You weren't out there robbing banks like your sister." He looked up at Cassie, standing in the doorway, his expression anxious. "Sorry Cass, don't mean to speak bad about your mom."

"It's okay, Gramps," she said. "I know my mom was a lying, thieving bitch."

"Well now, that's a little harsh," he said, genuinely shocked. "I look at your beautiful face and I see your mom did at least one thing right. And you shouldn't swear like that. It's undignified."

"Okay, Gramps," she said.

Where she found her patience with him I had no idea, just as his seeming blindness to her Goth-girl rebelliousness perplexed me. Had I attempted a style like that as a teenager, he would have thrashed me.

"We all get our heads screwed on backwards every now and then, you, your mom, even your aunt here, that's the chief thing to remember." His face split with a sudden laugh and he said, "Hell, sometimes I get my head screwed up my ass, pardon the French. That's what happened between me and Mary here."

Mary Baker, my birth name.

"You mean Nina," Cassie said. "She likes to be called Nina now."

Pop pulled at his face, the subject of my name change still a source of confusion and irritation to him. "She can call herself any damn thing she wants, no skin off my back. Thing is, before, I was wrong. I took it too personal. Thought she was rebelling against me personally, when she was rebelling against everything in the whole damn world, maybe mostly herself."

"I'm not the one needs to hear this," Cassie said.

When Pop shifted in his chair to face me I knew this was in no way spontaneous, that the two of them had talked about this moment some time before, either on the phone or the night before, in person. "I never shoulda turned my back on you like I did, after you got arrested that first time." He sighed so heavily the table shifted, and the sound of that sigh had more sadness in it than anything he'd ever said to me. "Sure, you did some things no father would be proud of, but I raised enough hell when I was young that I shoulda known you were going to raise your share of it, too. But I didn't see it coming, that's why it shocked me so much. You were always a willful little girl, but I thought you'd settled down, didn't understand you'd just delayed your hell-raising. So when you started to do those things you did, it was like somebody punched me, and so I did what I always do when someone hits me. I lost my temper and I hit back every way I knew how."

"You always were good at losing your temper," I said.

"That was wrong of me." He pulled again at his face. "I don't regret being tough with you, don't get me wrong there, I don't regret giving you a little needed discipline. But those times I got mad at you and went a little too far, I'm sorry about that. My temper, you're right, that's never been one of my best qualities. But I guess you know a little about that yourself. I guess you know what it's like to lose your temper, do things you regret later."

"It's true, I lose my temper," I admitted. "But most of the things I've done needed doing and I don't regret them."

"You think you woulda been able to do those things you say needed doing if I'd coddled you your whole life?"

I flinched when the cell phone went off in my pocket and yanked the thing out by the antenna. Frank's name flashed on the display. I didn't want to answer Pop's question because once I started, it would take me six weeks to finish. Let him think I was rude, that I thought the call more important than our conversation. What did he want me to say? That it was okay? That I forgave him? I didn't. I took the call. Some hiker had found a woman's body in one of the canyons north of Malibu, Frank said, the connection breaking up as he drove in and out of coverage. He was checking it out, wanted photo backup. Could I make it? I told him I could and disconnected the call.

Pop watched me carefully, both curious and, it seemed, a little afraid.

"I don't hate you as much as I used to," I said. "Don't feel the need for it."

Pop smiled like I'd just kissed him.

"Well, I guess that's a start," he said.

5

THE SUN HUNG white-hot in the scalded blue sky as we climbed the coastal canyons toward Malibu, the Metro's hamster-powered engine whining on all four treadmills at each rise in the road. Cassie fiddled with the radio while I drove, the signal for college station KXLU fading to static as we wound deeper into the canyons, her bitten fingernails purple on the dial. We didn't speak for miles, but I knew by her dreamy smile she was pleased with herself, her small hands resting on the Rott's massive neck, lost in her own world. I hadn't wanted to take her with me on this assignment, but she was scheduled to fly back to Phoenix early that evening. She had set me up cleverly, I thought, tricking me into the house to get the Rott. I didn't want to lecture or yell at her, but I didn't want her to think I was unaware of her manipulations. "I understand why you wanted to see your biological grandfather," I said. "I understand everybody wants to know something about the family they come from, but why did you have to take my dog?"

"Because if I took the dog, you'd come and get me," she said.

"I would have come to get you. I love my dog but I love you, too."

She worked a purple fingernail between her teeth while she thought about that. "No way you would have come inside the house. The only way to get you inside was the dog."

We crested the ridge at Mulholland Highway, the first breath of cool ocean air brushing our faces. Cassie didn't seem the type to want to promote peace in the family, but then, she had so little family left, maybe she thought it a good idea to get us together again, not understanding that if I was going to bury the hatchet with Pop, I'd be just as likely to bury it in his head. Past Mulholland the road traced the ridge line, the horizon opening to vistas of the coast loping north toward Point Dume, the white-tufted waves in the distant ocean like chalk marks on a vast, blue board. For a few moments, I felt good about myself, about being alive in the world amid so much natural beauty, but then I spotted the patrol car blocking access to Edison Road and the hiking trail leading into the Santa Monica Mountains National Recreation Area. I braked hard and swept to the side of the road, muscles tensed to confront a familiar tableau, dead body in the mountain brush, a staple of *Scandal Times*'s incisive, hard-hitting news coverage, a story I'd photographed a half dozen times in the past year. Though we rarely got close enough to photograph the body, I always disliked the assignment. What we found this time might not turn out to be the anonymous victim of an act of murderous rage but someone I knew, someone I'd worked and dined with and whose face graced some of the best photographs I'd ever taken. I usually felt detached when called upon to photograph victims but this time I felt angry.

"Why are we stopping here?" Cassie asked.

"I have to do a quick job," I said. "Do me a favor and stay in the car, watch the dog for me."

"What's to shoot out here?" Her purple lips carved a mischievous smile. "You get a report Mark Wahlberg is skinny-dipping? I'd see that."

"You'll stay near the car." I pulled my camera bag from the backseat and took a moment to stroke the Rott's head. "It's a body-in-the-hills story. I need to grab a shot of some eyewitness, shouldn't take me more than thirty minutes. Take Baby for a walk if you like, but don't go far or we'll miss your flight."

As I walked away from the car, it occurred to me that my niece might very well intend to miss her flight. She had already proved herself to be a master of manipulation. She might take the Rott for a walk and lose track of time or deliberately lose herself in the hills, returning too late to make her flight to Phoenix. I glanced back as I strode toward the entrance to Edison Road. She stood beside the loaner car, her hand on the dog's head, watching me go. I rounded the corner, certain she was bolting into the brush the moment I disappeared from view.

"Sorry, area's closed for the afternoon," the sheriff deputy said when I approached the patrol car.

I flashed my press badge.

"It's even more closed to the press." He pointed across the road. "You can get some good hiking that way. I heard there's a trail over there that'll take you all the way to the beach."

Or to hell. It was his polite way to tell me to get lost. I spotted Frank's Honda tucked into the brush up the road. I thanked the deputy for his help and flipped open my cell phone while I walked. When the call connected, Frank told me he was interviewing an eyewitness and directed me to take the footpath beside the car; I could find him in the meadow over the hill. Frank needed to lose about twenty pounds to be considered merely overweight and wasn't capable of running any distance greater than to the bathroom without losing his breath, but he always showed remarkable endurance when pursuing a story. I wasn't surprised to find that the switchback trail carved a steep incline into the hill, leading to the top of a ridge that dropped to a meadow studded with wildflowers and fringed in oak.

Frank stood just beyond the tufted shadow of the nearest tree, the eyewitness's face in the sun. Like a television news reporter, Frank always knew where the camera would be positioned and staged his interviews accordingly. I selected the digital camera from my bag and snapped off a sequence of telephoto shots. The eyewitness looked legit enough through the lens, a late-thirties nature boy whose neatly trimmed black beard, ruddy complexion, and green-on-green hiking attire gave him the appearance of an aspiring park ranger. *Scandal Times* didn't generally run large photographs of noncelebrities; at most, his candid would be boxed in miniature within a larger photograph of the crime scene to establish that we weren't making it all up.

Frank greeted me in mock surprise as I kicked down the hill and turned to ask the eyewitness if he minded having his photograph taken, conveniently failing to mention that I'd snapped a dozen images from the ridge above. I didn't ask Frank what he'd been told. I didn't want to know just then. I wanted to do my job. I directed the eyewitness to stand on the slope and stretch out his arm as though pointing at the body in the brush, a style of shot favored by *Scandal Times* that has grown no less hokey since it began to appear regularly in the tabloids of the 1930s.

I took the shot and bagged the camera.

"Just one question," I said. "The body, did she have any tattoos?"

"Did she ever." He tapped his shoulder. "She had a tattoo of that old cartoon character, Betty Boop, right there. Just what I told your colleague. She must have been a beautiful girl, I'll tell you, the sight of her lying there, it brings you to tears. A helluva shame." He scratched his throat at the beard line, started to ask something, stopped himself, then went ahead and asked anyway. "You mind me asking how you knew about the tattoo? Is this some kind of serial thing?"

A shout from the ridge turned me to the sight of the Rott galloping down the hillside, Cassie carefully stepping down the trail as though she'd never walked off-pavement before. I veered away from the eyewitness and snapped my fingers at the Rott, following with a sharp, pointed gesture at the ground, but the dog was too excited and moving too fast to obey at first, running past me before bringing his bulk under control in a holding pattern, his truncated tail wagging him in circles. I gave him a few strokes along his flanks and told him to sit. He did. Cassie approached slowly, uncertain of her footing on the uneven ground.

"I thought I told you to stay near the car," I said.

"Don't blame me." She pointed at the dog. "I'm just following him. He got away from me when I was trying to put the leash on him." She held up the leash, rolled in her hand, as evidence.

I wanted to ask why I hadn't heard her calling him until the last moment, or point out that it was just as likely that she'd led the Rott over the ridge and then unleashed him, knowing he'd run straight to me with little encouragement, but such concerns seemed petty under the circumstances. Cassie peered around the meadow and focused for a moment on Frank, who asked a few meaningless wrap-up questions to the eyewitness. "Where's the body?" she asked. "Anywhere close?"

"Do you know who the body is?" I asked.

She shook her head, purple-limned eyes gleaming.

"Christine," I said. "This is why she didn't show at the gallery last night. Somebody raped her, strangled her, dumped her like trash."

Cassie blinked, shielded her eyes from the sun, asked, "Christine?"

"Sorry, I gotta go." I strode toward a grove of oaks at the edge of the meadow, heeling the Rott to my side. I'd delivered the news to

Cassie too brutally, but I knew no other way to talk about acts of brutality. Despite my rage I worried about her, how she'd handle the death of a woman she'd taken as a role model, like Nephthys, cool and sexy and all screw-the-world attitude. The oak grove spread from the meadow up the flanks of the ridge, the sweet, woody scent not enough to soothe me. Not nearly enough. I walked deep into the screen of trees and picked up a weathered branch as thick as a table leg. The Rott, sensing my temper, scouted the grove far to my right. I stepped up to an oak split by lightning, its bark charred black, and slammed the limb against the stump, the contact jarring me to the bone. And then I lost myself to my rage, flailing at the tree as though I battled a circle of demons, my face flushed as I struck again and again, the tears steaming from my eyes as though vented from a superheated core. When I slipped to my knees, muscles trembling with exhaustion, I realized I was done, the rage burned clear. I wiped the sweat from my forehead and the tears from my cheeks, then glanced at my hands, black with soot, my face now streaked with ash, the ancient mark of someone in mourning. I was feeling eye-for-an-eye and tooth-for-a-tooth just then.

"Are you okay?"

Cassie stood a dozen yards distant, the Rott clutched to her side, her expression both serious and afraid. When I nodded she edged closer, carefully, as though approaching a wounded but still dangerous beast.

"You really lost it," she said.

"No, this isn't losing it." I stood, my thigh quivering with the effort, and tossed the branch aside. "This is just exercise."

"Better a tree than someone's head, I guess." She took another step closer, the carefully drawn line around her eyes unbroken by grief, her arms wrapped around her thin chest and her mouth held tight in a thin, straight line.

"You're crying again," she said.

"Of course I'm crying. Normal people cry when someone they like dies."

"Normal people," she said and paused, thinking it over, "don't go around beating the crap out of dead trees."

The Rott crept close enough to touch, head low and tail wagging cautiously, and when I reached to stroke him he banged against my leg. I told her she had a point and hiked toward the ridge, the strength returning to my legs with each step, my momentary exhaustion emotional as much as physical.

"Who do you think killed her?" Cassie walked closely behind, taking each step as though the ground might drop out from beneath her.

"I have no idea, not yet."

"Are you going to look for her killer?"

"That's the police's job."

I'm sure she noticed my shrug, as though I wasn't sure of my answer.

"You'll follow the story? For the paper?"

"A story like this, a dead-body-in-the-brush story, normally it's one issue and out because, really, who cares? Once the girl is dead, she's dead. We'll only do a follow-up if the police publicly point to a suspect or arrest somebody."

"Who do you think killed her?"

Her morbid curiosity unnerved me.

"How do I know who killed her? This shit happens all the time. Every month somebody finds a body in the mountains or desert around here, every week some kid riding a bike or playing on the lawn gets gunned down by gangbangers, every day somebody beats, stabs, or shoots somebody to death, bodies stuffed in closets, suitcases, the trunks of cars, people shot down in their own bedrooms or stabbed in their kitchens, assaulted on the street by total strangers, beaten, robbed, raped, crumpled up and tossed aside like trash in the gutter, and those are just the fatalities; that doesn't even count the dozens of people who don't die, who survive their wounds to linger on in one pitiful shape or another."

Cassie called for me to wait up, trailing so far behind I doubt she heard much of what I'd said. I paused at the crest of the hill, the canopy of oaks billowing down to the meadow. She stopped a dozen feet below and looked up at me, bone-white forearm shading her eyes from the bright blue sky.

"I was thinking you might know someone more specific," she said.

"That's the whole point. How can I be specific when death is everywhere? Christine was wild but she wasn't stupid, no more than other girls. Do you think she realized the guy who asked her out was going to kill her? That's why you have to be careful. What happened to Christine? That's the price of running wild in the world."

"Some guy asked her out? Who?"

"Somebody who claimed to be a producer."

"So you do know a little more than you're saying," she observed, and stepped up the hill as though she hadn't heard anything more than what she wanted to hear.

Frank was gnawing on a foot-long sub, scribbling notes on a legal-sized pad propped on the hood of his Honda, when I hiked around the curve. Cassie dawdled far behind, lost in her own Gothic, death-obsessed world. "I'm sorry it was Christine," he said as I heeled the Rott. "I didn't know her, of course, but I'm sorry for you."

"You want the flash card?" I asked, referring to the removable memory chip that stored the digital camera's photographs. "Or would it be okay if I stopped in tomorrow to transfer the images?"

"Tomorrow will be fine." He turned his back to the car, leaned against the front fender, said, "We could hear you banging on that tree a hundred yards away. You scared the shit out of our eyewitness, thought you were a crazy woman."

"That was nothing," I said. "That was just my normal homicidal PMS rage. You should be glad you don't have to deal with hormones that make you temporarily insane."

"I count my blessings every day."

I thought about whether or not I should ask about Sean, whether it would clue Frank something was going on between us, then decided I should just go ahead and act as though nothing had happened.

"You mean Detective Tyler?" Frank jutted his chin toward the access road. "He's up there. "

"His case?"

"Jurisdictional issues. This is LASD turf." He narrowed his eyes at me. "Since when did you get to be on first-name basis with a cop?"

"Why does LASD get it?" The Los Angeles Sheriffs Department patrolled the coastline between Pacific Palisades and the Ventura County border. "The video wasn't shot out here. I mean, where she was killed, that's who gets jurisdiction, right?"

"But where was she killed? The video doesn't show one way or another. It's just a room." His eyes tracked over my shoulder. "A case like this, cross-jurisdictional conflicts, possession of the body is nine-tenths of the law."

Cassie collapsed against the Honda's passenger door as though worn out by the hike and stared up at Frank. "Nina says you're going to drop the story. Why would you want to do that? It's a great story. Beautiful dead girl, bloodsucking killer rapist, I'd think readers would eat that up."

Frank stared her down, asked, "What do you care, you little ghoul?"

Cassie beamed as though she'd just been called the most beautiful young woman in paradise. "I care a lot, you fat fuck," she replied. "Christine was my friend."

"First of all, 'fat fuck' is cheap alliteration. You should be writing headlines for *Scandal Times*." Frank crossed his arms over his chest and leaned forward, scowling. "Second, I never said I was going to drop the story."

"Don't encourage my niece to swear," I said. "She doesn't need it."

"You were swearing yourself just a minute ago," Cassie said.

"No, I wasn't. I never swear."

She looked at me like I'd lost my mind or lied, or maybe both.

"I don't think Christine was this guy's first," Frank said.

"You think it's a serial killing?" Cassie asked. "What makes you think that? Is he collecting trophies?"

"I didn't say serial killing," Frank said, wagging a corrective finger. "I said he probably wasn't her first. A couple of weeks ago a girl with bruises on her throat was found wandering naked in the desert near Palmdale, with no idea how she got there."

"How does that connect?" I asked, not getting it.

"The cops suspect ruffies."

"Rohypnol, that stuff is nasty," Cassie said with too much authority.

"How do you know?" I asked.

"You think I'm not supposed to know stuff like that? That I'm too *little*?" She crossed her arms over her chest, offended. "I started seeing that stuff in the seventh grade, all the date-rape drugs, particularly Vitamin K."

"Vitamin K?"

"Slang for Ketamine," she said. "Kids use it to get high."

"So maybe she took it recreationally, or one of her so-called friends gave it to her," I said. "Isn't that more likely?"

"You're right, probably doesn't mean anything." Frank smiled, suddenly cheerful. "But it's almost summer, readers are going to want a story they can take with them to the beach, and when you can cross genres like this, movie starlets and murder, it makes great beach reading."

6

FRANK'S INTENTION TO continue following the story animated
Cassie during the ride south to the airport, the loaner car rolling with
the curves along Pacific Coast Highway as she calculated the possibility that Christine had been victimized by a serial rapist and the
certainty that Frank wouldn't let her killer get away with it, declaim-
ing in a thin, high voice that the press coverage would pressure the
police to catch the bastard if she didn't find him first, as though she
planned to join the *Scandal Times* staff as a combination research assistant and amateur sleuth. Her reaction worried me. Frank could be
a crack investigative journalist when the desire moved him, but I
didn't think his interest was all that genuine. He wanted a hot story
to sell newspapers, not the truth. Cassie gave far more credence to
his interest than experience and common sense warranted. If the
story didn't develop over the next day or two, he'd drop it. That
would disappoint her, but life is full of disappointments. I didn't
worry about her disappointment. Her emotional detachment and
morbid curiosity, that worried me.

"I don't get it," I said. "The way you reacted when I told you
Christine was dead, I never would have guessed you knew her."

"What do you mean?"

"You didn't cry, you didn't even look shocked. You went from
hearing she was killed to wanting to find out who killed her without
any of the emotional steps in between."

"Like what steps?"

She was curious. She really didn't know.

"Like grief. I'm not sure you really care. Don't you feel sad?"

"I'm not like you." She leaned back hard against the passenger seat, offended. "I don't beat the crap out of dead trees and think it solves anything."

"Maybe it didn't solve anything, but I feel better."

"Maybe this makes me feel better." She bit at the edges of her purple thumbnail. "Are you going to look for the guy who did this to Christine?"

I shrugged.

"It's like you get angry and then you forget about it. What's the good in that? And you tell me I don't care? At least I care enough to want to do something."

"I'm a tabloid photographer, not a detective."

"You think the cops should handle this? Is that what you think?" She made a face to let me know what she thought of that idea. "You used to be hard core."

"What happened to Christine is terrible," I said.

"She was your friend!" Cassie shouted. "She modeled for your photographs and took care of your niece! We have to avenge her death."

"You have to go back to school," I said.

She made a sound in the back of her throat, sounded like a growl.

"Do I want to find whoever did this?" I nodded, once. "Frank wants to follow the story. That's a good start. We'll follow the story."

We rode a while in silence, the sun firing bright orange as it arced toward the sea. The Rott, made uncomfortable by the tension between us, stirred at Cassie's feet and attempted to clamber onto her lap. She pushed him back onto the floorboard, then remembered to give him a scratch as consolation. "Do you remember when we first met?" she asked.

"Sure," I said. I'd tracked her to an abandoned missile base north of Los Angeles, hoping to convince her to leave, and when she refused, I hit her with a right hook and dragged her out.

"You were really hard core then," she said. "You really kicked ass."

"I'm trying to mature a little."

"If you mature any more, I'll think you're dead."

I glared at her.

She gave me a big, smart-ass show of teeth. "If I find the asshole who killed Christine?" She mimed a pistol with her right hand and pulled the trigger. "Bang!"

I tried to remember how I'd felt about death at her age, hoping it might help me understand her reactions, but I was far more innocent at fifteen than my niece—or her mother. My sister had run away from home at sixteen, uncertain of what awaited her on the road but knowing she couldn't live with the old man's violence anymore. She'd hoped for a little excitement, I guess, and got it quickly enough, landing in the Las Vegas hooking scene, where her youth made her a prime commodity until her eighteenth birthday turned her legal but far less exotic. She stayed in the trade for several more years, moving on whenever the cops busted her for soliciting, from Vegas to Phoenix to Houston to Dallas, until she hooked up with a con artist who saddled her with Cassie and introduced her to a drug dealer who married her, convinced Cassie was his kid. A couple of years later, the dealer decapitated two of his slow-pay accounts with a ceremonial samurai sword and left enough evidence at the scene to make his arrest, conviction, and execution a simple legal formality. My sister had acquired a taste for the con by then, mostly small-scale sleight-of-wallet jobs involving drunken men, and she drifted up and down the coast, Cassie in tow, until one night in Portland she met Hank Bogle, a man accustomed to taking what he liked and he liked her. They lived in larcenous bliss for a little more than three years before a bungled bank job sentenced her to three to five years in Coffee Creek Correctional Facility and strapped Hank Bogle to a ten-year ride in the Oregon State Penitentiary.

Cassie entered the terminal at LAX oddly cheerful, but as we wound our way through the long lines to the Southwest ticket counter her chatter ceased and she fidgeted with her hair, sweeping it back or twisting it in knots, checked and rechecked her ticket and student identification, and rifled through her overnight bag for one thing or another, a constant flutter of seemingly meaningless activity. I figured she suffered from anxiety, her jitteriness no more than a case of pre-flight nerves, but after she collected her boarding pass from the ticket counter she said, "I'm moving in with Gramps."

"Nice fantasy," I said, not taking her seriously.

"I've almost got it worked out with my caseworker." She nodded emphatically. "Gramps is filing for custody here, too. Says he'll adopt me if that's what it takes. Says the courts will grant him custody because he's a blood relative."

"You can't move in with him," I said. "Your mother ran away from him because he beat her. Wait until your caseworker hears that."

"He's changed. He's not like that anymore."

"He'll always be like that," I said.

"You won't adopt me, so you got no say."

She clutched her boarding pass like a badge and scurried into the line snaking toward the baggage x-ray machines, aware that no one without a boarding pass was allowed past that point and our argument would end.

"You know I can't adopt you." I said.

"Why not?"

I couldn't figure why she asked. She knew the answer.

"Because I'm on parole," I said.

The man before us in line glanced back over his shoulder.

"You mean you're a criminal," she said, stating a fact. "Like my mother."

I glowered at the man in front of us, told him to mind his own business. His head snapped forward like it was attached to a string.

"You know all the shit you accuse me of?" she asked.

"Don't swear," I said.

"Like swearing, that, too." Her voice scratched higher, like nails on chalkboard. "You lecture me about running wild in the world, getting myself into some dangerous shit, but you did the same things yourself. So you got no right to criticize me!"

I didn't know whether I was dealing with typical teen rebellion or something deeper, her reaction to Christine's death connected to the death of her mother and feelings of abandonment. "I'm not criticizing you," I said.

"You were just telling me I couldn't go live with Gramps!"

"I warned you about him. Nothing more."

"And you criticize my language!"

"Have I ever told you I was perfect? Of course I criticize your language. Swearing is ugly. Sorry if that offends you. It's not like I'm saying you're a bad person."

"You fucked up your life so you think you can tell me how to run mine?"

"That's kind of the point of being your aunt, isn't it?" What she said hurt me but I kept my voice low and level, refusing to play to her emotions in that public place. "I'm older. I've made lots of mistakes. And so I want to protect you from making the same mistakes I made. I'm not trying to criticize you so much as warn you what's likely to happen. Swearing makes you look cheap and vulgar. Running wild in the world can hurt or kill you. You're fifteen years old. The things I did that got me into so much trouble? They happened when I was over twenty. I didn't have anybody advising me what could happen. I'd like things to turn out a little better for you."

"But I don't want to run wild anymore!" She grabbed my arm, panicked now because only one passenger remained between her and the x-ray machines. "I'm tired of running away from foster homes. That's why I want to live with Gramps."

The security officer directed her to set her bag on the conveyor belt, place any metal objects on her person into the plastic tray, and step through the metal detector. "I'm going back to Phoenix just long enough to collect my things," she said, as she dropped her pack onto the conveyor belt. "Then I'll come back and spend the summer with Gramps."

The metal detector bleeped when she passed beneath the arch. A matron stepped forward to wand her down one side and up the other, the detector emitting a high-pitched whine when it passed Cassie's stomach. The matron scowled in puzzlement and placed her hand flat on my niece's black velvet blouse near the abdomen.

"I've got a pierced belly button." Cassie lifted the tail of her blouse to show it. "Sorry, I should have guessed it was gonna set the thing off."

The matron nodded and pointed her toward the back of the conveyor belt. My niece grabbed her pack and ran, turning once on her way to the gate to wave goodbye.

7

I BAILED MY Cadillac out of the garage the next morning, engine tuned, lubricants and filters changed, rear bumper replaced, right rear fender mended, and a new money-green paint job shining from hood to trunk. A twenty-something punk in a BMW Z3 had rear-ended me two weeks before as I braked for a yellow traffic signal outside Beverly Hills. The driver wore a cell-phone headset as good as surgically implanted into his ear when he stepped out of the car, and as he strode to inspect the damage he complained to the headset—presumably he was talking to someone—that a stupid bitch had slammed on the brakes in front of him and now he was going to be late to his meeting. The Caddy was a vintage '70s Eldorado, five thousand pounds of rusting steel and pitted chrome, and the Z3 had crumpled like a bird against bulletproof glass. When he saw the damage up close, he jabbed the stubby antenna of his cell toward my chest and screamed, "It was a fucking yellow light! Nobody in L.A. brakes on yellow!"

At the garage I bid farewell to the four hamsters powering the Chevy Metro, bent to kiss the Caddy's laurel-wreath hood insignia, happy to have a real car again, and drove to the converted sewage-works warehouse that served as the corporate offices of *Scandal Times*. While I joined Frank in his office the Rott stayed outside to play a little ball with the security guard, something they both liked to do. I plugged the digital camera into the back of Frank's computer and watched the downloaded images in a silence broken by his loud sighs of disappointment. He didn't blame me for the unimaginative framing and ho-hum staging, he said, certainly aware that such a statement was a backhanded way of blaming me. He knew I'd been shocked by the death of my model. But the results spoke for themselves, and they spoke badly. The images might work for mid-paper, continuation-of-story visuals but didn't have enough zing for the first three pages, and if they dared put one of them on the cover, the entire *Scandal Times* readership would fall asleep in the supermarket checkout line from sheer boredom.

"We'll run a vidcap for the front-page visual," he said. "Blow up just the image of her face, play the angle that the killer sent you the video. That ties the murder directly into *Scandal Times,* makes us look like a central player in the investigation, even if the cops are ignoring my calls at present."

I unplugged the camera and packed my gear. The thought of running an image from the video sickened me, but Frank was right; the photographs I took in Malibu weren't dramatic enough to sell the story. Every issue hit the stands with a photograph of a celebrity or some type of mayhem, and preferably both. If the story didn't get to the front page, someone who had seen Christine in the company of her murderer would be less likely to notice. Front-page publicity was essential to collecting casual eyewitness evidence like that. And I was going to be part of the story whether I liked it or not.

"Why did he send the disk to me?" I zipped the camera bag and thought about it. "Why not send it to the *Times*?"

"Publicity. The *Times* wouldn't put it on the front page."

"How does that matter to him?"

"I'm a tabloid journalist, not a psychologist."

"So make something up."

"I'm good at that, right?" He groped toward a box of donuts, looking for a sugar rush to help him think. "Let's say Christine isn't his first, let's say he assaulted that girl out in Palmdale. You know the details of that?"

"None."

"A hiker found her near a popular trail, half naked and her neck bruised. She couldn't remember how she got there. Loss of memory, that's one of the effects of Rohypnol. Her larynx was crushed. She couldn't even speak. Whoever assaulted her came within a few seconds of killing her but stopped."

"Do the police think it's the same guy?"

"Too early to tell. But let's speculate."

"He's not the spontaneous type," I offered.

"You're right there," Frank said, nodding. "He doesn't pick up some girl hitchhiking, strangle her on a whim and dump her in the desert, not this guy. If Christine is typical, he mounts a production. He scouts a location and sets up his bondage and video equipment like a director or film producer."

"Maybe he even pretends to be one," I said, and told Frank about Christine's plan to meet someone who claimed to be Johnny Depp's assistant.

"Depp's assistant? What a headline! And she believed it?"

"Actresses are desperate, you know that."

"Maybe he comes on like somebody important to gain just enough of her trust to slip a ruffie into her drink, or even better, maybe he is somebody important, though certainly not Depp's assistant." He yanked open a desk drawer organized like a garbage dump and rifled it. "You saw the video. Do you think he could be a pro?"

"No idea."

"Would it help to see it again?"

"I thought you gave the disk to Sean."

"I burned a copy first—that's how we'll grab the vidcap." He pulled a plastic CD sleeve from the back of the drawer, shook loose a disk, and fed it into his computer. "Imagine going to all that effort. Location, lights, camera, stirring performances, and nobody notices. The girl in Palmdale, she's just another victim to the cops, a sad and tragic story but nothing they don't deal with fifty times a year. Her story makes the front page of the *Antelope Valley Press*—a box in the lower right corner, no headline—but the *L.A. Times* and *Daily News* bury it in the journalistic equivalent of where the sun don't shine. It's like he released a film into an empty theater. Nobody even noticed. So he decides to do it again, and this time, send a copy to the press. No way he's going to be ignored a second time."

I drifted behind Frank to stand and watch the parts of the video that I could stomach, too uneasy to pull up a chair. A small, black box popped onto the screen of Frank's computer. He pressed a few keys and the video zoomed full screen, Christine already chained to the wall, sheathed in latex, a black ball strapped into her mouth. From the angle and steadiness of image, the camera looked to be mounted on a tripod in the corner of the room. The lens framed her in long shot, no sound, the frame wide enough to show a section of cream-colored wall and a wide swath of ceramic-tiled floor, the white of each tile enclosing a gold, Walk of Fame–style star. Her arms hung slack against the chains, hips thrust back as she stooped slightly forward. She glanced over her shoulder toward the camera as though she watched someone behind the lens, even though the man who assaulted her entered the frame from the opposite side of the room.

I mentioned the discrepancy in her eye line.

"Someone on ruffies, they don't know up from down," Frank said. "She may be looking but I don't think she's seeing much of anything."

The man approached Christine with a strutting confidence, a black latex suit stretched taut over a tall, athletic frame that matched Rakaan's and a hundred thousand others. His lips protruded like obscene fruit from a slit cut at the mouth of his hood, and twists of latex cowled his eyes in a nightmare image of man as Minotaur. I couldn't distinguish man from beast behind the mask. She flinched when he first touched her from behind, perhaps not expecting someone to come from the opposite side. She bucked away, once, as he mounted her, but he was big if not particularly strong, and Christine was a small girl, drugged and bound to the wall. She didn't have much of a chance to resist. He outweighed her by more than fifty pounds. But still, she seemed resigned to the act, and if I hadn't seen the violent end, I could have mistaken it for a harmless game of bondage captured on home video.

"Whoever shot this left the sound off," Frank said, fiddling with the sound control at the base of the player. "Or maybe he purposely exported the video file without sound before burning the disk."

As I watched the scenario play out I tried to remove any thoughts of Christine from my mind, and above all from my heart. I didn't need another excuse to break down in tears. I needed to watch the video for evidence of the identity of the killer, and so I told myself that this wasn't Christine being violated, this wasn't how she spent her final moments, gagged and raped on camera, drugged so far out of her mind that she may not have been all that aware of what was happening to her, but when the killer looped the strap around her throat and jerked her head back so sharply it could have broken her neck I couldn't keep my eyes on her approaching death and glanced away the moment a ghosted image flitted across the corner of the screen.

"Stop, go back." I grabbed Frank's arm so fiercely he nearly jumped out of his chair in fright.

"What is it?" He lurched forward to pause the video.

"Can you play it back in slow motion?"

He hadn't seen it, his eyes focused like Sean's two nights before on the act of strangulation, not on the periphery. The action reversed looked not much different from the action in forward motion, just a little more hellish.

"Where's the light source?" I asked, and when Frank guessed it came from somewhere in the ceiling, out of frame, I traced the way the shadows from the chains binding Christine slanted right to left on the wall. "Light from directly overhead, the shadows would hang straight down, and you'd get subtle hot spots on the black latex here." I pointed to a small, glinting reflection of light on her right shoulder, then traced a closely observed line to the upper right corner of the screen. "From the angle of the shadow and the positioning of hot spots on the latex you can track the source of the light, probably a portable film light on a stand, mounted maybe eight feet high. Look, see the way the wall is brighter on the right side of the screen than the left?"

"Okay, I'm convinced," Frank said. "But so what?"

"So watch the lower right corner of the screen, the floor there."

The action moved forward again, the killer unbuckling a strap that circled his chest and looping it around Christine's neck, and when he jerked the strap taut, crossing his wrists behind her neck to increase the killing power of his hold, a shadow crossed the floor in the lower right corner of the frame. "See it?" I said, gripping his arm again. "Go back and freeze the image if you can."

Frank inched the action backward and stopped. The shadow hovered from right to left on the floor, a gray ghost on the white and gold tiles, squat head and shoulders clearly defined on a curiously compressed torso—the type of shadow cast by a strong light placed above and behind a man.

"They aren't alone in the room," I said.

8

WE DROVE THE Antelope Valley Freeway out of Los Angeles late that morning, top down on the Cadillac, the Rott banished to the back to make room for Frank, who huddled with the cell phone in the passenger seat, his forefinger plugging the opposite ear to block the wind noise while he made one call after another, tracking down leads to the Palmdale assault. The Caddy's air conditioner had expired long before I bought her, and as we approached the 25,000-square-mile hot plate of the Mojave Desert, the dry, hot air whipping over the windshield did no more than wick away the sweat like a combination fan and blast furnace. As I drove, I thought about why the killer had sent the video to me care of *Scandal Times*. Frank had said he wanted publicity. That raised a question that made me even more uncomfortable than the heat: Why Christine? Enough people had died around me that I sometimes felt like a modern Typhoid Mary, an unwitting carrier of death to those I touched. I didn't want to think about it anymore. I noticed Frank checking his notes between calls and asked, "How do you know Sean?"

He said something I couldn't hear above the noise of the road, something about a club. At speeds above forty-five miles per hour, holding a conversation in the Cadillac was like shouting into gale-force winds.

"I met him in a strip club," he repeated, this time shouting.

"What was he doing there?"

He looked at me like I'd just asked a particularly stupid question.

"Okay," I said. "What were you doing there?"

"Same thing Sean was," he said and laughed. "He used to work undercover. This was before you started shooting freelance for us, before he got promoted to Homicide."

"What station?"

"North Hollywood now. Van Nuys before that."

"He was working undercover when you met him?"

Frank put his cell phone away and pulled down the bill of his baseball cap. "I thought he was just another sleazeball in a strip club, like me, even if I was working on a piece at the time."

"A piece of what?" I asked.

"Journalism, wiseass. We were doing a series on amazing identical twins, you know, one case study a week, each written up by a different reporter, and I drew stripper siblings from Scandinavia, Fawn and Dawn Svedenson."

"Their real names?"

"Hardly. Try Cristina and Krisztina Szegedi from Budapest." He smiled as though remembering something pleasant. "They didn't quite have the Swedish accent down but I think I was the only one in the joint who noticed, besides Sean."

"So he was working undercover," I said.

"What do you care?"

He stared at me with a little too much curiosity.

"Because I'm trying to figure out how you knew he was a cop."

"I interviewed him after he got his transfer to North Hollywood, remembered drooling next to him at the strip-club bar. We're both from the north side of Chicago, originally." He pointed to the Cubs logo on his baseball cap. "When we were at the bar he asked me why I wore the cap and I told him because I was a rabid Cubs fan suffering from premature male-pattern baldness. We talked baseball—this was the year Sammy Sosa and Mark McGwire were breaking Maris's record—and when I mentioned I worked for a newspaper he vanished like a vampire. I thought he was a drug dealer at the time, because, you know, what do drug dealers do for entertainment except go to strip clubs? And he looked like one."

I thought I should just drop it there, knowing any more questions would tip Frank something was going on, but I couldn't help it, I had to know. "Did you tell him anything about me? That night, I mean, when he came to the show."

"Why? Did he make a move on you? And more important, did you knock his teeth out?"

"Did you tell him anything about my history?"

He settled into the wedge between the seat and door to watch me while I drove, looking for signs of embarrassment or dissimulation. I adjusted my sunglasses and draped my wrist over the wheel to conceal the fluttering in my stomach.

"That was fast," he said.

I glanced down at the speedometer, said, "I'm barely doing seventy."

"You just met and already you're banging each other?"

"Just answer the question."

"No, I didn't tell him you're an ex-con on parole." He pursed his lips and whistled a high note. "When he finds out it's gonna be like a dog discovering he's sniffing the tail of a cat in doggie drag."

We met Charlotte McGregor near the student cafeteria at Antelope Valley College, a flat desert campus of concrete buildings huddled low to the ground against the heat, students picking their way from shade tree to shade tree along the concrete paths. Charlotte waved to us from the trunk of a poplar tree a few steps from the cafeteria entrance, wearing a champagne-colored cotton jacquard dress that fell just above the knee and a gold silk scarf tied loosely around her neck. Even at a distance her beauty was striking, her hair the color of weathered brick and her pale skin an act of defiance against the desert sun, but like a trick of perspective she didn't get much bigger as we approached, her height about eight inches short of fashion-model regulation, reminding me of a young Holly Hunter. She studied acting in the Theater Arts Department, Frank told me, and hoped to be admitted into UCLA for the coming fall semester. Charlotte extended a shy hand, and when she spoke her voice rustled and creaked like the broken reed of a clarinet.

"I'm sorry," she whispered, high cheekbones flushing a vibrant pink against her pale skin. "My voice hasn't recovered yet. Maybe we should get started? I'll fill you in while we drive out to where I met him."

Charlotte began communicating with the man who claimed to be Brad Pitt's assistant through Hotornot.com, a dating website devoted to the game of rating sexual attractiveness on a scale of one to ten. He'd been one of hundreds to respond to her photograph and bio— she'd scored a 9.8, she said—and they e-mailed back and forth for a week before agreeing to meet. She'd thought posting on the website would be a good way to hook up with people in L.A. She wanted to become an actress and spoke of the same kind of discovered-in-a-drugstore dream most young actresses have—a small but significant role in an independent film or television show that would launch her career. Los Angeles can be cruel to aspiring actresses.

The Starbucks where they initially met was separated from campus by a few barren miles of landscape notable for the lack of anything in particular to look at, the broad streets laid out on a grid and named after numbers or famous letters in the alphabet, as though something a little more distinctive might ruin the minimalist effect of the place. Outside, the Starbucks offered a drive-through service window for those who had been permanently grafted to the seats of their vehicles. Inside, it looked like just about every other outlet and the coffee tasted the same, which is what most people accept as the charm of the place, if such a thing can be said to exist. I leashed the Rott to a handicapped parking sign near the shaded entrance and followed Charlotte and Frank up to the service counter. The coffee shop's air conditioner had been set to stun, the effect of walking in from the hot desert like jumping from a sauna into a cold pool.

"What made you believe he was Brad Pitt's assistant?" Frank asked.

"He sent me a snapshot of him and Brad hanging out together at some event, a film premiere maybe." She paused at the baked goods counter, staring at her reflection in the glass. "I mean, why wouldn't I think he was legit? Sure, maybe he could be exaggerating about the assistant thing, maybe he'd show up and say he'd worked as an assistant on a film that starred Brad Pitt, sorry for the misunderstanding. But you have to understand, where I am now?" She turned her head from the glass to give us a look both grim and self-disparaging. "Even a gofer seems glamorous. Anybody connected to the film business is a step up from Palmdale. Of course it turned out the picture was a fake." She stepped up to the counter to order a cup of Nepalese tea from the *barista*.

"What did he say his name was?" Frank asked.

"Tyler Durden."

"Tyler Durden? *Fight Club,* right?"

"The movie? Wasn't it incredible?" She smiled and for a moment she seemed transported, one memory connecting to another, until the smile abruptly dropped from her lips. "He played Tyler Durden. Brad Pitt. In the movie. That was his character name." She brushed a strand of hair from her face, hand trembling. "He used Brad Pitt's character name as his own and I didn't even recognize it. I'm too stupid to live."

She picked up her tea and walked toward a window table lacquered in sunlight, hung her purse by its strap on the chair back, and sat down facing the front. I liked the look of the sun slanting across her face, tinting her skin gold and lighting the tips of her long, red eyelashes, but I didn't want to pull out my camera, not yet. A photograph of the teary-eyed victim might sell to the readers of *Scandal Times,* but I didn't want to traumatize her. I didn't normally care so much about these things. Maybe her lack of size inspired the kind of compassion I felt for children. Maybe I felt that through her, the one who lived, I could soothe Christine's ghost. I again observed how small she was, her wrists the size of a champagne flute. Christine in heels didn't reach five foot seven, and she'd weighed less than 110 pounds. Maybe Christine and Charlotte had been stalked and seized not just for their beauty but for their size; small girls are easier to physically control and dominate.

"You told the cops the name, of course." Frank took a chair at the two-seater next to her table. I wasn't surprised he'd caught the reference to *Fight Club;* trivia like that stuck to his mind like pasta to a wall.

"They didn't say anything about it one way or another," she said.

"That doesn't mean they didn't get the reference. I'm a big fan of the police. Most of the time they do a great job, given the resources at their disposal, particularly homicide detectives. But they aren't exactly open about sharing information." He popped the top of his medium-sized coffee to let it cool. "What time were you scheduled to meet Mr. Durden?"

"Four. But then he didn't show and I started to feel incredibly anxious, you know? Like wondering if he'd set me up as some kind of joke, this hick girl from Palmdale." She glanced out the window, her fingers cupped around the tea like a prop, though she showed no intention of drinking it. "Sometimes I get myself so emotionally wound up about things I make myself sick, you know? I mean, like, literally. I thought it was that, at first."

"You started to feel, what . . . sick . . . drugged?"

"I didn't know what I felt like, to tell the truth. I don't do drugs, not really, just a joint every now and then." She stared at the ceiling and bit her lower lip. "Don't print that, okay? About the joint."

Frank shrugged, said, "I think I can forget I heard that without losing my journalistic integrity. But you knew something was wrong."

She nodded and rotated the cup in her hands a half circle, the bottom rim scratching softly on the table top. "When it kept getting worse I thought I was having an allergic reaction to the tea. But a few minutes later, I really didn't care. I didn't feel anxious anymore. I felt really good, kind of heavy and super relaxed, like I didn't want to move but that was all right, I could just sit there and watch the sun set and it was all good."

"Do you remember leaving the café? Or did you black out?"

"Wait a minute, let's back up here." I drew a flicking, annoyed glance from Frank, who didn't like to be interrupted when interviewing a subject. "Did you notice anyone in line behind you? Someone who might have reached across the counter while you were picking up your tea?"

The shake of her head was quick and tight, as though she'd already been asked this question. "The store was pretty empty. I mean, I wasn't the only one in here but there wasn't a line. But I think I know why you're asking. The cops wanted to know the same thing, after they gave up on the idea that I'd taken the drug 'recreationally,' as they put it."

"They said that?"

"They were real assholes when they first picked me up. Thought I'd been out raving the night before, got so stoned I passed out, implied the whole thing was my fault. But the doctor who examined me, she was good, she knew I'd been strangled, and . . ." She compressed her lips tightly and took a deep breath. ". . . that other thing, the rape, she saw that, too. When I told her how I couldn't remember what happened, she asked me to pee in a cup, and the whatchacallit, the urinalysis, showed positive for Rohypnol."

"Can you remember anything that happened between the time you ordered the tea and when you started to feel different?" I asked. "Did anyone approach or talk to you?"

She touched the scarf at her throat, a quick gesture to check its position, and nodded. "Less than five minutes after I sat down, this guy? He came toward the window, and it was like he wasn't watching where he was going, he bumped into me." She lifted her tea and wobbled the table. "You can see, the tables aren't so stable, so he reached down, like immediately, to hold it, and of course some of the tea spilled, so he got a napkin to wipe it up."

I didn't notice a dispenser on any of the tables.

"Where did he get the napkin?"

She pulled her head back an inch, surprised by the question, and it took her a moment to remember. "He had it with him. Had to. He was mopping up where the tea spilled a second after he bumped the table." She pushed her tea forward and folded her hands carefully in front of her, the pressure of her grip reddening the tips of her fingers. "Do you think he was the one who drugged me? You think he put something in my tea?"

"No way the *barista* does it," Frank said, glancing toward the service counter. "Unless he leaves the country the next day. The guy who bumped the table, what did he look like? Can you describe him?"

"I can try." She closed her eyes and tilted her head toward the ceiling. "He wasn't big or small, kind of average in height. About my age. I can't describe his face in detail because he wore sunglasses and one of those floppy hats guys like to wear. You know what they look like?"

"Bucket hats," Frank said. "Like a fisherman's hat."

"Exactly. This one was sky blue, with a red band. What else?" She tapped her index finger against her knuckle and nodded. "Right. A faded red sweatshirt turned inside out, his jeans fashionably baggy, but not hip-hop baggy, more surfer baggy. I got the idea he was posh."

"Why posh?" Frank asked. "A lot of young guys dress that way."

"But only someone who comes from money, serious money, knows how to put it all together so perfectly. It's like they all go to some fashion school for rich kids, learn how to get the perfect slumming look." An expression of pure class awareness lodged in her eyes, as though she so keenly felt the differences in class that she'd become expert in spotting them, something I'd noticed in those with money and in the less advantaged driven to achieve financial and social success. "It was in his voice too the way he talked. He had that lazy, laid-back kind of voice, like he didn't have to bother with things like money or achievement because he'd been born with his, you know what I mean? He wasn't from around here, that's for sure."

"Did he stick around?" Frank asked.

She shook her head. "He went into the bathroom, I guess to wash his hands or something, and then he took off."

"How long before you started to feel funny?"

"About twenty minutes, I think. Long enough to drink my tea, and worry that the guy I was supposed to meet wasn't going to show. After that, I don't remember things so clearly."

"Do you remember how you got out of the café?"

She shook her head and said, "Vaguely. I remember somebody came up, said he was Tyler Durden. I remember hearing his voice, hearing him say his name, but I can't remember what he looked like. Wait a minute!" She nodded, remembering. "He was standing behind me. That's why I couldn't see him. He was standing behind me, asking if I was okay, and then he helped me up, out of the café, and into a car."

"Do you remember what kind of car?"

She cupped her hands to her face, hiding a grimace. "It gets really blurry after that. I see shapes, colors, light, but it's all like a ghost world. The car?" She shook her head. "Black. We took a drive, then I remember a room somewhere. I think he must have kept drugging me because I blank out completely after that. I can't even remember him, you know, doing things to me. Not really. All I remember after that is coming out of it, sitting in the desert, half my clothes flung around me, the other half just gone."

Charlotte tugged at the loose knot tying the scarf around her neck, her lips drawn into a tight, defiant line. The scarf slipped away to reveal a faint bruise the width of a purse strap circling her throat and two thumb-sized blotches of purple on opposite sides of her larynx. "The doctor can't tell me when I'll be able to regain my voice." She nodded as though coming to some decision with herself and swiftly unclasped the hook at the back of her dress, pulled down the zipper, and turned in her chair to show us the cross-hatching of faded red welts between her shoulder blades. "I asked the doctor about these. She said it looked like somebody whipped me."

She zipped up the back of her dress but couldn't locate the clasp.

When I reached over to help her she thanked me, her voice cracking right down the middle, and she bit her lip, hard, to keep from crying. "How can I be an actress with a voice like this?" she croaked. "How can I play to the back of the theater if the audience can't hear me in the front row?"

9

THEY BURIED CHRISTINE about a hundred feet from U.S. Highway 99 in Cherokee Memorial Park just outside of Lodi, the pastor's portable sound system dueling with the diesel roar of produce trucks plying the lettuce route between Stockton and Sacramento. I stood outside the immediate ring of mourners, more interested in witnessing the service through the lens of my Canon than aligning myself with Christine's old friends from high school, her new friends from Los Angeles, or the members of her family. I didn't know her as well as the others who gathered for the funeral and I hadn't driven three hundred miles just to mourn her passing. My motives were more complicated.

The pastor eulogized Christine with platitudes that sounded to my ear more predictable of a small-town girl than accurate of a big-city one. I knew little about her life except that it had been short, and remarkable mostly in the brutality of her death. She had been born in Lodi twenty-one years before they buried her, the third child of five. Her mother served in the local Methodist church as a secretary and her father worked as the manager of a chain supermarket. She hadn't excelled in school except for the theater arts classes she took in her junior and senior years. Even though she'd been dragged to church every Sunday, she never had been particularly devout. At the age of sixteen she had—to the dismay of her parents—simply refused to go anymore, except for Easter and Christmas services. On her eighteenth birthday she took a Greyhound bus to Los Angeles.

I wasn't the only one who felt more comfortable standing away from the cluster of family and friends. Dr. James Rakaan stood several steps beyond the fringe of the crowd, eyes cloaked behind Dolce

& Gabbana wraparound sunglasses, his long black hair waving dramatically to the shoulders of a black suit. The suit tapered to his waist in a way that only the finest tailoring can provide and a single white lily dangled by its stem from his clasped hands. If *GQ* ever decided to come out with a special funeral style issue, he was ready to model for it. Though I hesitated to take photographs while the pastor spoke, a man sitting in the passenger seat of a sedan parked on the fringe of a nearby service road wasn't so timid, taping the crowd with a video camera. I traced the line of his lens. He thought Dr. Rakaan looked as photogenic as I did. I wondered if the cameraman worked for the local police department or had driven north from Los Angeles.

A flutter of white in the cemetery beyond Rakaan caught my eye and I shifted a step to get a clearer view. The tissue wrapping a bouquet of flowers flapped in the breeze, lightly held by a man in a sport coat who squatted over a distant headstone as though he'd come to pay his respects to a dead relative. I caught my smile before it surfaced and forced it back down. Sean. He noticed when I raised my camera to look at him and blew me a kiss. Very funny.

A good documentary photographer sees not only through the lens but also to the side of the frame, a difficult trick to master but critical in catching a more arresting image to photograph or a rock hurled at her head. While I watched Sean through the viewfinder my opposite eye caught a glimpse of a young man at the back of the crowd looking away, as though trying to keep his face out of the shot. Like Rakaan, he wore a black suit and black sunglasses, and though his hair was blond he too wore it long, in the style of young Kurt Cobain, a combination surfer-grunge look. He stood so far to the side of the frame the movement wouldn't have diverted my attention for more than a moment had he not looked out of place. None of Christine's friends from L.A. dressed like him; most wore oddly matched clothing of various colors, including red and yellow, as though they wanted to celebrate her life more than her death. Her local friends dressed more traditionally, the young men in sport coats and slacks but nothing so obviously Italian. He looked like he'd stumbled across the wrong funeral, as though he hadn't known Christine well enough to have met her friends or family.

He might be her secret lover, I speculated, or just a casual one who'd fallen for her more than she cared for him, someone who still carried a bright enough torch to see his way to her funeral. And he was rich, I thought. Like Charlotte, I had an eye for the telling differences between the rich and the rest of us, particularly those born into money. I saw it in his clothes and the way he stood, and I'm sure if I'd been able to get close enough I would have seen it in his hands.

I lowered the camera and strolled clockwise around the back of the crowd, looking for a better shooting angle like a wolf looks to cull a herd, and when he glanced back to see where I'd moved, what I was doing, I took his photograph. He looked young, no more than nineteen or twenty, the wisps of hair on his chin as thin as cigarette smoke. I lowered my head when the pastor spoke in prayer and I added my own to go along with the official one, nothing poetic, just rest in peace and all that, and when he said amen the crowd broke apart.

Nephthys stood arm in arm with two young women, one with long, blonde dreadlocks and the other with home-chopped hair dyed red and black. As I walked toward her someone touched my elbow from behind, as though trying to catch me, and I turned to a petite young blonde in a long-sleeved black blouse and iron-gray skirt, her makeup tracked by dried tears.

"I'm Tamara, Christine's roommate; we haven't met yet." She hooked her hair behind her ears and stared at me with granite-gray eyes both curious and a little afraid, her immaculately pinked lips twitching as though smiling came so naturally to her she needed consciously to repress it. "You're Nina Zero, right? The photographer? I just got back from location yesterday, I can't believe what's happened, I'm just in like total shock. Total."

"Like everybody," I said. "You were where, Canada?"

"Toronto. That's where we were shooting. It's cheaper up there— at least, that's what they tell me."

"It must have been hard on you."

She looked confused.

"Not to be here, when your roommate was murdered," I said.

"Oh yeah, totally." She shrugged, a gesture she meant to convey helplessness. "We talked on the phone, like, every couple of days, so it's not like I felt out of touch. Christine was so happy she was going to be in your show. She was struggling, you know? Going to auditions, doing a small part here or there, the typical struggling actress life, but nothing that made her feel good about herself, and when she saw I was starting to get work, it was like really hard for her. I know what it's like to struggle, believe me. 'You're going to be next,' I'd say, you know, trying to get her to believe in herself." Her smile finally broke through, unrepressed, a bright and shiny show of teeth and lips. "But the photos? She thought they were way cool. Believe me, I was sad I couldn't break away from shooting to fly down, attend the premiere." The recognition of something horrible flew across her face like a shadow. "Of course, she was already dead by then, at least, that's what I've been told."

"Can we talk about this later?" I asked. "Not here, not at the funeral."

"Of course." She stepped quickly back, thinking she'd offended me.

"We'll meet in L.A.?" I reached out and touched her arm. "I want to talk to you, not like this, but really sit down and talk."

"Christine was into some wicked dark stuff," she whispered. "But she had a great heart." She crossed her arms over her chest and moved toward the chapel, her steps long and careful around headstones set flush in the ground. She knew I worked for a tabloid. Her comment about Christine hadn't been malicious, but she was letting me know she had a story to tell and assumed I'd already heard enough to understand the reference to dark stuff. She looked back, once, to mime a phone with her thumb and little finger and mouth the words, "call me."

Further on, Nephthys walked toward the chapel with a group of L.A. friends. Between the growls of trucks on Highway 99 I heard the sweet sound of their singing, "If I Ever Leave This World Alive," a song I recognized from an Irish band, Flogging Molly. Nobody like the Irish to celebrate the dead. I knew I'd start crying if I listened to more than a verse and struck out across the cemetery, spotting the distant figure of the young man in the black suit. He strode casually beside a group of locals who headed for their cars as quickly as they could without breaking into a sprint.

I veered across a short stretch of verdant lawn, rounded the back corner of a massive concrete mausoleum, and ran, out of sight of the others, for the length of the building, intent on reaching the parking lot in time to see if the kind of car he drove matched my expectations. At the far end of the mausoleum a circular fountain sprayed water in long, pulsing arcs, and beyond that stretched the parking lot, studded with cars. I skidded to a stroll. The young man in the black suit hurried across the asphalt and stopped improbably to key the door of a vanilla Hyundai Sonata, a car so plain even suburban dads thought it too conservative. I crouched behind the fountain and maxed out the lens to full telephoto, framing the rear bumper as the Hyundai lurched away.

At the sound of footsteps behind me I glanced over my shoulder. Sean jogged toward the fountain, his hands swinging free. He'd left the flowers behind. A dozen yards distant he stopped and caught his breath. "If you don't want to talk, just say so. You don't have to run away from me."

"What are you talking about?"

"You didn't hear me?"

I raised the camera and took a quick candid, his hand on his hip, doubt in his eyes.

"Not since I gave you Christine's photograph."

"I was just calling your name, back there," he said, ignoring the dig.

"Didn't hear you."

I kept the camera to my eye, aware that it distanced him, and snapped the shutter on his wry smile. He stepped forward, forcing me to lower the lens when his face blurred the lens, too close to focus.

"You see something interesting?"

"Did a second ago." I turned away from him, toward the parking lot. "Young guy in a black suit, expensive cut, didn't look like he knew anybody here. You notice him, too?"

"I was looking at other things, mostly," he said, looking at me. "You already got the pictures you need? You mind if we take a walk?"

I capped the lens and slung the Canon over my shoulder, stomach jittery in a way that I'd never before experienced in my many and varied experiences with the law. I always felt uneasy around cops, particularly when they wanted to talk to me. The act of passion we'd committed earlier that week only made it worse and as we stepped away from the fountain the fluttering in my stomach turned to nausea, the result of combining my fear of the I-don't-think-we-should-see-each-other-again speech with my dread of the I'm-going-to-have-to-arrest-you lecture. "Did you get my messages about Christine's diary and her so-called therapist, Dr. Rakaan?" I asked, seeking distraction.

"Yeah. I passed it on," he said.

"Passed it on? To who?"

"To Parker Center," he said, referring to the administrative center of the Los Angeles Police Department. "They probably shared it with LASD but it's their case now. Nobody's contacted you yet?"

"You're not working on it?"

"It's not like the news business, it's not like I get the exclusive because a source handed me some evidence." He pointed us toward an older section of the cemetery, behind the mausoleum, where the funereal style changed from mower-friendly headstones set flush in the grass to the granite rectangles, arcs, and spires of traditional memorials. "Every department works from a certain geographical region. Christine lived in Los Feliz, that's in the Northeast Station. I work out of North Hollywood. And her remains were recovered by LASD—an entirely different jurisdiction. Right now it's been kicked over to the big dogs working Robbery Homicide out of Parker Center. You know those guys?"

"Not personally," I said.

"Good thing," he said, as though he hinted at something else. "Anything that crosses jurisdictional lines, it's their bone. And when I say big dogs, I mean they growl and I back off. Right now RHD and the Sheriff's Department are, quote, cooperating, unquote, with each other. I'm just as happy to stay clear of it."

"RHD, they also take on high-profile cases, serial killings too, right?"

He looked at me as though he suspected I knew more than he

thought I did. "O. J., Blake, Spector, RHD gets all the big ones. Some guy stabs his wife because she burnt the toast, I get the call."

"So what are you doing up here?"

"It's a personal thing." He stared down at his feet as we stepped onto the grass of the old section. "Whenever there's a funeral in a case that involves me, I go."

I knew investigators attended funerals to observe and often video-tape the results—hence the guy with the camera in the parked car—but Sean didn't talk about it like police procedure, like just another part of the job. "The flowers," I said, momentarily touched by his compassion. "They were for Christine."

He paused at a waist-high white marble tombstone set on a pedestal, braced himself against its arched top, and watched me as though carefully preparing what he wished to say.

"Why didn't you tell me you were on parole?"

"When did I get a chance to talk to you about anything?" I walked to a granite headstone with a pitched roof, like a little house, and stood behind it, braced like Sean for an argument. "You have my phone number. You want to know anything about me, all you gotta do is call the number."

"I'm not the most by-the-book cop in the world," he said. "I thought I could deal with the tabloid stuff. Sure, somebody might get their boxers in a twist, warn me about compromising an inves-tigation by talking to you about one case or another, but cops and reporters have dated before, and you're a photographer, not a writer, so you'd be even less of a threat. And North Hollywood, it's not exactly jam-packed with the kinds of stories *Scandal Times* likes to print. So what was anybody going to say, in the end? I can deal with rumor and innuendo, done it my whole career. If we don't talk about cases, nobody could say anything." His hand shot to the Windsor knotting his tie and pulled it loose so fast and hard he nearly popped the top button. "I hate ties," he said, angry now, at the tie, at the situation, at me. "I always feel like I'm going to stran-gle when I wear one. I think I must have been hanged in a past life."

When he pulled the tie from his collar I noticed a dark bruise on his throat, and while I was wondering if he'd worn the tie to conceal the bruise I realized that was where my lip had fastened to him the night we'd lost ourselves; I'd marked him.

"You said something about dating," I said. "I don't remember being asked out on a date."

"A euphemism." He stuffed the rolled tie into the side pocket of his sport coat. "Do you know what happens to me if we're caught dating, or whatever it is you want to call it? It's against regulations for a cop to be romantically involved with a parolee. Maybe they won't take my badge for it but they'd punch my ticket to someplace like the Pawn Shop Unit, where I'd spend the rest of my career checking swap meets for stolen watches. They'd slaughter me."

"Who said anything about romantic involvement? You don't even return my phone calls. You think I'm going to let myself get involved with someone doesn't even have the common decency to call me back? Why are we even talking about this?" I turned and walked away, got as far as the next headstone before I stopped, circled back around to face him. Why didn't he simply pretend nothing had happened? That would have been the easy way out. To argue about our relationship as though we had one was ridiculous. We'd never appeared together in public. No one saw what happened in the darkroom. To my knowledge, then, no evidence existed of our lovemaking. If all he wanted was to protect his career, he'd stonewall me. Why make himself even more vulnerable by admitting to me the risk he faced? Did he suspect I'd hidden a camera somewhere in the darkroom and filmed our encounter? "Do you think I'm going to blackmail you? Is that what you think?"

He looked up at me from beneath his brows, eyes screened by the angle, then back down to his hands. "No," he said. "I don't think that."

"Because as far as I'm concerned, nothing happened."

"I'm glad forgetting is so easy for you."

"Easy?" I wanted to knock him onto his smug behind. "I did not plan what happened in that darkroom. I didn't set you up. I didn't even come on to you. The last thing I expected was to be overwhelmed by passion while printing a photograph for a homicide detective. When did I have the chance to say anything to you? It was over before I even knew what hit me. I'm supposed to tell you my entire life history the moment we shake hands hello? Maybe you should have made your intentions clear at the start. Maybe you should have told me the photograph was just a pretext for something else on your late-night agenda."

"I didn't know what was going to happen that night," he said. "Not consciously."

"You're an ex–undercover vice detective. You've lived half your life with your left hand not knowing what your right hand is doing."

He drew his head back like a hammer and a surprised laugh shot from him. "Your aim is lethal, you know that?" He spread the lapels to his sport coat, as though baring his heart to a firing squad. "You want to shoot me dead, here I am."

"I don't want to shoot you. I want to know your intentions."

"I don't know what my intentions are." The sport coat draped shut and he leaned one hand against the tombstone, the other cocked on his hip. "I know how I felt the night I met you. I know that much. And I know how I felt when I learned you were on parole."

"What do you want me to say, that I'm sorry I am who I am, that I've done what I've done?" I stepped away from the headstone, let him look at me head to toe. "I'm not. You can't pick one part of me, throw away the other. And the fact that you even want to try means you don't know me."

"And you? Do you know anything about me?"

I walked toward him, the pained and wary expression on his face like the look of an animal with a trap-caught paw. Then I reached out and pushed him, just hard enough to move him off his spot. He laughed, surprised, but he didn't push me back. "This thing blind-sided both of us," I said. "Maybe we should look at it like just another L.A. moment, nothing more than a late-night traffic accident, a fender-bender, no one seriously hurt, nothing more significant than an exchange of phone numbers and a few minutes lost by the side of the road."

The muscles at the hinge of his jaw flexed like something alive beneath the surface of his skin and he nodded, once, obviously unhappy and just as obviously relieved. I resisted the temptation to raise my camera and capture that look on film, instead glanced down at the shoebox-sized marker at my feet. A cursive script carved into granite the name of the person buried below, followed by the dates *October 30, 1932–October 31, 1932.*

The poor child had lived a day and died.

An appropriate epitaph for my relationship with Sean.

10

MY PAROLE OFFICER decided Monday morning at seven o'clock was as good a time as any for an unannounced search of my apartment, her stentorian knock startling the Rott into a fit of barking that didn't stop until I crawled out of bed and creaked open the door. When I complained about the hour she tartly suggested I look at the parole agreement I signed upon release from prison, and then she proceeded to cite the relevant section in the event I'd forgotten. "You, your residence, and property can be searched any time of the day or night—" She glanced over the shoulder of her gray blazer as she attacked my kitchen cabinet, emphasizing the word "any" as though I should be thankful she hadn't come knocking a couple hours earlier, before continuing, "—with or without a search warrant and with or without cause. While on parole, you must obey the conditions of parole. If you do not obey, you can be—"

"I know, arrested and returned to prison," I said. "You mind if I make a cup of coffee while you tear apart my kitchen?"

"Help yourself." She turned to face the living room, separated from the kitchen by a waist-high counter. "I see you've done your usual crack-up job of interior decorating." She showed her teeth, midway between a smile and a snarl. She was being funny. Most of what I owned tumbled in and out of fruit crates I'd rescued from the back of the local supermarket, with the exception of a fold-out futon that served as a couch, and tacked to the wall, a museum poster of a Diane Arbus photograph depicting a strange-looking child holding a toy hand grenade. Graves lifted the corner of the futon with the black toe of her stub-heel pump. "I guess I don't have to waste a lot of time searching in here." She moved into the bedroom. "I'm sorry about your model, what happened to her," she called. "What was her name?"

"Christine," I called back. I didn't want to witness her going through my things. I stayed in the kitchen, watched the coffee stream black into the pot. I didn't have much to search. She banged around in the bathroom cabinet for a few minutes, then walked back into the kitchen and leaned against the counter, arms folded over the size .38 bulge under her left shoulder, her pistol six points bigger than her bra size. I offered to pour her a cup of coffee. She shook her head, and watching my reaction closely, asked, "Did you have any involvement in what happened to her?"

She had to ask the question. I'd been convicted on charges of manslaughter and I was on parole. It was her job to ask me the question. When I told her that yes, I thought I did have something to do with it, she stilled like a dog on point. "Tell me exactly how you're involved."

"Someone sent me a video of her murder, care of *Scandal Times*."

She nodded, once, her glance charged with authoritative focus.

"The reporter I work with, he thinks whoever killed her wanted publicity. Why else send a recording to a tabloid? He knew we'd give it front-page treatment."

"So would the *L.A. Times*."

"No way. The front page is for national and political news unless a celebrity is involved. And the *Times* doesn't offer national coverage. *Scandal Times* does."

"So he sent the video to you." She shook her head, her lips taut. "That doesn't mean anything. You said yourself, it made sense to send it to *Scandal Times*."

"But why Christine, except for me?"

"I see what you're saying. You don't think she was a random victim."

"What if he chose her because she modeled for me?"

"You don't know that, so maybe you should just calm down a little bit." Graves brushed past me to open the refrigerator door. "When you said you were involved, that's what you meant?"

"What else?"

"In my job, it could be a lot else, trust me."

She stooped in front of the refrigerator and rearranged the cartons of milk, juice, and eggs, then dug open the meat and cheese drawers.

"What are you looking for?" I asked.

"Drugs. A lot of parolees, they store them in the fridge."

"I've just told you one of my models maybe was murdered because of me and now you're accusing me of using drugs? You know I don't use drugs."

She glanced over her shoulder, steel-gray eyes annoyed.

"A stick of dynamite, then." She rattled the drawers shut and stood to peer inside the freezer compartment. "From what I've heard, nothing that's happened so far is your fault. I'm not saying you're not capable of doing something stupid, but what happened to your model was just bad luck. You can't hold yourself responsible for it, do you understand? You had nothing to do with the crime, no more than any other victim."

"I feel like I victimized Christine just by knowing her."

"That's nonsense. Everybody dies in the end, whether you know them or not." She pulled a carton of Häagen-Dazs ice cream from the freezer and stared at the label. "I knew I'd find something if I looked hard enough. Chocolate Chocolate Chip. Do you know how addictive this stuff is?"

I opened the flatware drawer and offered a spoon.

"Absolutely right. How do I know it's the real thing unless I give it a taste test." She set the carton onto the counter and pried off the top. "A homicide detective from North Hollywood called me a couple of days ago, told me a little bit about what happened."

"Sean Tyler," I said.

"Detective Sean Tyler to you," she corrected. "The investigation got kicked automatically to Parker Center, so I was wondering why he was bothering to call me, particularly when he asked about your marriage history."

"What did you tell him?"

"The truth. That you once had a green-card husband."

"He was more than that and you know it."

"You still have a perverse attachment to the idea that you were in love with him, that's what I know." She dug a spoonful of ice cream from the carton and held it up for inspection. "You knew him for a couple of days, he treated you badly, and then he died. Move on with your life. Anything I should know about your relationship with Detective Tyler?"

"He liked my photographs," I said. "But considering my legal problems, that's about all he likes."

"Smart career move." She slid the spoon into her mouth, held it there for a moment, and when she pulled it free the thing was so clean it could have been pulled from a dishwasher. "This stuff is deadly. Maybe I should confiscate it for your own good." She grinned, pleased at her joke, and tossed the spoon into the sink. "How much longer she on parole?"

"Six months, I think."

"I know that." She returned the ice cream into the freezer. "I was repeating what he asked me. Detective Tyler. He wanted to know how much longer you were going to be under direct supervision of the California Department of Corrections." She strolled to the front door, where she stopped long enough to scratch behind the Rott's ear. He sat absolutely still beneath her hand, even more intimidated than I was. "Do me a favor. Don't do anything stupid the next six months, okay? I've put a lot of work into keeping you straight, and I'd hate to lose it because you did something dumb."

She showed her teeth again, waited for my submissive nod, and left.

When I walked the Rott to the Cadillac later that morning I wasn't particularly surprised to see someone had slashed my ragtop. Angry and depressed, but not surprised. My apartment bordered gang turf held by the Venice Shoreline Crips of Oakwood. Someone had tagged the right rear fender months before, a compressed black scribble left by the same moron with a spray-paint canister who tagged every neighborhood surface in reach. For a brief moment I was thankful the Caddy's money-green paint job hadn't been tagged. It would be easy enough to mend the ragtop with a sail needle and some canvas thread, then reinforce it with duct tape. I reached for the door, peering through the driver's-side window as I pressed the thumb-latch. A copy of the current issue of *Scandal Times* lay on the driver's seat, front page facing up. I didn't remember leaving it there. The Rott sprang forward as the door swung open, intent on leaping over the frame and onto the shotgun seat. I lurched to grab his collar and kneed his shoulder to keep him out. He barked and strained forward, trying to sniff beneath the newspaper. I gave him a sharply voiced command to sit and he obeyed, a single bark of protest to signal his reluctance.

I pulled the door open until the hinge caught and then kneeled on the pavement beside the door frame. The video image of Christine in a bondage hood ran on the front page of that issue, in the lower right-hand corner, prime real estate by tabloid standards because it encourages the reader to turn the page to read the story, or, if that's above their particular skill level, to look at more pictures. The issue didn't lay flat or follow the contours of the seat. Instead, it mounded upward. I glanced at the Rott, who licked his snout, something he did when excited about something, usually food. I turned back to the driver's seat and carefully lifted the corner of the paper to reveal a long, black tail, then the gray, short-haired hindquarters of a rat.

I lost my temper and shouted. The Rott broke out of his command to sit and stuttered back on all four paws. I told him to sit again and leaned into the passenger compartment. A yellow packet lay on the passenger floorboard, bearing the illustrated image of a rat and the skull and crossbones. Rat poison. I broke out my cell phone to call the police, then Frank, and last of all Christine's roommate, Tamara, to postpone our breakfast date. I didn't figure a neighbor was expressing his displeasure over the loudness of my stereo. I didn't have a stereo. The rat had to connect to our story about Christine's murder. Whoever left it thought the rat and poison would serve as a warning. But a warning against what? If the killer sent me the video, why would he drop a dead rat in my car after the story ran?

I locked the Rott in the apartment and shot a series of digital images of the slash in the convertible top and the objects left on the front seat, fudging the position of the rat for greater dramatic impact. When I got the shots I needed, I sat on the curb and found myself wishing someone would invent a fast-forward drug, something I could take in the morning to get the bad days over with fast, because this was showing all the symptoms of being a real tit-trampler of a day.

An LAPD squad car rolled up to the Cadillac's rear bumper a little more than a half hour after I called, the two black-uniformed officers inside taking last sips of take-out coffee before cranking out another call response. The dispatcher had probably reported a code 594, vandalism of a motor vehicle. The officers—a baby-faced Latino and a husky white woman with curly blonde hair—expected to verify the damage and tell me to contact my insurance company. When I told them someone had left a dead rat on the seat of my car, the Latino looked at the female officer as though either I was nuts or this was going to be one of those days. He wedged his hands into a pair of latex gloves, lifted the corner of the newspaper, and verified that it was indeed going to be one of those days. I explained that my name was mentioned on the front page of the paper draping the dead rat and suspected it had been left as a threat. They absorbed the information slowly, then the Latino poked around the interior of the car looking for other items of evidence while the curly-haired blonde spent her time in the squad car, working the computer.

Frank pulled his Honda to the curb some minutes later and emerged from behind the wheel proffering a business card between two sausage-sized fingers. He made a joke about the dead rat that the Latino officer did not find particularly funny, and it took a minute of careful explanation to convince him that Frank belonged on the scene because he'd written the article that featured my name. The offense was no longer considered an act of vandalism but a death threat, the officer said, and they needed to secure the crime scene. In a few minutes someone from the detective bureau would be out to interview me. When Frank tried to interrupt him, he said, "Why don't you wait over by your car until someone asks to talk to you?" He was polite but firm. Like most cops, he was accustomed to dealing with assholes.

"I called the investigator assigned to Christine's death," Frank said as we walked to his car. "A detective out of Robbery-Homicide named Robert Logan. He's coming over from Parker Center, though I can't say he sounded very happy about it. You get photos of the rat?"

"While I was waiting. Couldn't get him to smile, though." I lifted my camera bag onto the hood of Frank's car and slid an eight-by-ten from an envelope containing photographs I'd taken at Christine's funeral, printed from a flash card hooked directly into a printer. The image of the Hyundai Sonata's back bumper was awkwardly framed but clear enough to make out the plate numbers. I asked him if he knew someone who could trace the owner.

"It costs money to trace a plate. Who's paying?"

I pulled a photo of the young man in the black suit from the envelope, told Frank that he'd attended Christine's funeral looking like he didn't know anybody, then gave it a little extra spin by mentioning the police seemed as interested in him as I was.

Frank turned the print toward the sun, said, "He's the right age group, isn't he? We should show this to the woman up in Palmdale, see if she recognizes him. He doesn't look like the guy from the video, though. Too short."

"Three people were in that room, plus Christine," I said.

"Three?" Frank puffed his cheeks, thinking about it. "Where did you learn to count, the school for the mathematically impaired?"

"The latex suit, the shadow that passes through the frame—"

"That's two," he said, flashing two fingers.

"—and the person behind the video camera," I said, rolling right over him.

"You don't know that." He looked at me like I was cheating.

"Maybe not, but I've spent most of my life behind a camera so I know how the world looks through the lens. The guy in the latex suit did not set up that camera. From the way he glanced at the lens it looked to me like he was taking directions. And not from the shadow, because when you shoot anything, you stand behind the camera, not way off to the side of the frame."

A beige Crown Victoria slid behind the squad car. I sheathed the photos in the envelope. Frank turned, cued by my glance, and waved to the figure stepping out of the Crown Vic, a mid-forties man with side-parted hair and a dark mustache that gave him a retro, 1970s look. The detective buttoned his dark blue blazer and strode toward the officer taking prints off the glass of the Cadillac's side window. Frank gave a friendly shout of his name and ambled forward, hoping to get a quote, until the detective leveled his finger like a sidearm and ordered him to return to his vehicle.

"Hard-ass?" I asked.

"That's the one place he doesn't need body armor, that's for sure." Frank took the envelope, tossed it onto the passenger seat, and lit a cigarette, making the most out of the wait. "They could take a skin graft off Logan's ass and use it to grow Kevlar vests."

The detective spoke with the uniformed officers at length, then broke huddle to strap on a pair of gloves and stoop beside the driver's seat. He examined the evidence with quick, efficient gestures and craned his neck to an awkward angle to read the text of the front page of the paper blanketing the rat. The way he shook his head, I don't think he liked the article. He stripped off the gloves and walked toward me.

"Your car?"

I contemplated a half dozen smart-ass replies to such an obvious question but kept my mouth shut and nodded. He slipped the gloves into his jacket pocket and leaned one hand against the roof of Frank's Honda, subtly trapping me against the side panel. "I gotta tell you, if this is some kind of publicity stunt, I'm gonna be really ticked off."

"My name's Nina Zero." I extended my hand. "Nice to meet you."

He looked at my hand, then at my face, and cracked his mouth in a smile that looked like he'd trapped a piece of beef jerky in his back molars. "Bob Logan, Robbery-Homicide Division." He grazed my hand so briefly I suspected he wished he'd kept on the gloves. "I don't mean to be rude, but that rat isn't the only thing that smells here, so if either of you planted the damn thing you'd better tell me now before you face criminal charges. How many years are you looking at if you violate parole? I know I saw it in the file but I forgot."

"Oh please, if you're not going to take this seriously, bag the rat and let me get on with my day."

"Bag the rat! I like that." He bared his teeth to a sharp exhalation of breath that might have been a laugh and shifted his shoulders toward Frank. "You didn't get an idea to play a funny prank on your photographer pal here? Except she doesn't get the prank, instead she gets hysterical and calls the cops. Is that what happened?"

Frank shook a cigarette out of his pack and stuck it into the corner of his mouth, trying to figure out where Logan was going with this. "Don't forget I called you, suggested you come down and take a look at this. I don't know what your criminal profiling textbooks tell you but that doesn't sound like a prankster to me."

"Sure it does. If you get me to fall for your prank, it becomes news, just the kind of so-called news you like to print."

"Why don't you give us a little respect here?"

"Because your paper isn't fit to wipe my ass."

"What exactly don't you like about our coverage?" Frank thumbed open his silver Zippo but didn't strike the flint. "We played by the rules. We handed over the disk the same day we got it. We didn't print anything you told us we couldn't print. Hell, I even tithe my income to official LAPD charities. I don't see why we have a problem here."

Logan stared at Frank, no less angry than when he first approached us but curious about something. "Were you aware Charlotte McGregor was arrested at a rave in the desert this spring, five tabs of ecstasy in her purse?"

"Why should I be?" Frank asked. It was a legitimate question but it sounded too glib, even to my partisan ears.

"Because you just printed a story suggesting McGregor and Christine Myers were assaulted by the same party." Logan leaned in so close to Frank's face he could have bitten his cheek. "Have you met Ms. McGregor's sometime boyfriend?"

"Don't believe I've had the pleasure," Frank said.

"A twenty-six-year-old repeat offender convicted four years ago on charges of assault and battery. Guess the sex of the victim."

"Female?"

"That was easy, wasn't it? Care to guess the nature of the assault?"

Frank clicked his Zippo, said, "No idea."

"He throttled her. And if we get enough evidence to arrest him, your article is going to be presented as the Holy Bible in court, because he has an alibi for Myers. Investigative reporter, my ass. If you were a cop, I'd bust you down to meter maid." He pulled a black leather notepad from the inside pocket of his blazer and leaned forward to get in my face like he had Frank's. "I'll take your statement now, if you still care to give it."

11

CHRISTINE'S ROOMMATE, TAMARA, sat hunched over our sidewalk table at the Fig Tree Café, her long blonde hair tenting the mug of green tea she cupped in both hands as she stared at the sea. The fog had burned off early that morning, leaving bright sunshine and the smell of salt water in the air. A beautiful late spring day brings out the crowds no matter what day of the week, and a parade of bicyclists, Rollerbladers, power walkers, and joggers plied the bike path just beyond our table. With a fresh cup of coffee and the prospect of good food, the bad start to my day had started to burn off with the fog until Tamara looked at me for a brief moment and said, "I don't know if this is such a good idea, talking to you."

I resisted the impulse to remind her that she'd suggested we meet. If she really didn't want to talk, she wouldn't, but I suspected she just needed a little gentle prodding. "So don't say anything. We'll have a nice brunch together, maybe take a walk on the beach." I caught the attention of a passing waitress, a young retro-hippie in a flowing skirt who held her notepad six inches from her face while she took down our order.

After the waitress hustled to the kitchen, Tamara said, "The police interviewed me, you know, when I got back from the funeral." She wore sunglasses to shield her eyes from the glare of the late-morning sun, the color of the frames matching the blue of her cling-wrap jeans. "Talking to the police about the death of a friend, that's a scene I never thought I'd have to play."

"Did they tell you not to talk to me?"

She shrugged, said, "I don't think they like tabloid reporters."

"Some do, some don't. Depends on the cop. No different than

some actresses. You, for example, when I met you at the funeral, I thought you were the type to want a little free press."

She turned to me as though I'd just kicked her under the table. "I'm not going to profit from Christine's death, okay? What happened to her was horrible. I don't want my name mentioned in the paper. I want to see the person responsible suffer."

Actors are ciphers by profession, and the sunglasses made her even more difficult to read. I slipped my napkin from beneath the flatware and worried it between my fingers, trying to balance Tamara's reluctance to talk with the idea that she had approached me. "Then why do you want to talk to me if you don't want to talk to me?"

"I do want to talk to you, that's the point. But I don't want to talk to the tabloid photographer. I want to talk to the person who knew Christine and cares about what might have happened to her."

"If you want to talk off the record, that's fine with me. But you have to understand I'll probably use whatever you tell me. I'm not going to hold your hand and tell you how terrible it is, because I'm past that point."

"So it's just a story to you," she said.

I couldn't tell if she was disappointed or relieved.

"More like a quest."

She cocked her head to the side. It wasn't the answer she expected. "What kind of quest?"

"It's the way I approach things. If all I wanted was to take pictures of movie stars, I'd get myself certified to work the red carpet at events like the Oscars. That doesn't interest me. I think truth has a private face. And the only way to capture that private face on film is to wait long enough for the subject to give it to you, to catch it by accident, or to hunt it down and take it. The photographs I took of Christine were consensual. She trusted me enough to give a little bit of her true self, in the disguise of the role she played. To see the true face of whoever killed her, that's something I have to hunt down and take."

"Is that what you're going to do? Try to find out who killed her?"

"I'm not a cop," I said. "I can't arrest anybody. But whoever killed Christine has already involved me."

"It involves me, too. It involves everyone who knew her."

"It's more than that." I looked down at my hands, saw that I'd torn my napkin to shreds. "What happened would be bad enough if her murder was some random event. But what burns me is that somebody sent me a video they'd shot of her, moments before her death, and ever since, I haven't been able to figure out why. Were they playing me for the publicity? Or was it a taunt?" I sat back in my chair, thinking I talked too much.

"What kind of video?" Tamara asked.

"You didn't see the paper?"

"You mean the one you work for?" She shook her head. "I'm sorry, I haven't gone grocery shopping yet."

"It involved Christine chained to a rack."

I shut up when the hippie waitress arrived. She set a salad and more hot water in front of Tamara and slid a three-egg omelet and whole-wheat toast onto my half of the table.

"How can you eat that and not get fat?" she asked, like I'd just gotten away with robbing a bank.

"Easy," I said. "I'll just go into the bathroom twenty minutes from now and throw up." When she looked ill I assured her I was kidding and we talked about dieting for a while, or rather, she talked about dieting and I talked about running and weight lifting. She asked me to show her my muscles so I did, pulling my arm from my jacket to flex a biceps that wasn't bad for a girl. She thought that was impressive and funny at the same time and asked if I was gay. I told her I preferred men but most of the time I wasn't anything.

She looked at me for several seconds, sucking on her lower lip as though she wanted a more definitive answer, but when she spoke again, it was about something else. "It was a bondage video, wasn't it?"

"Something like that."

"Who else was in it?"

"Hard to tell," I said.

She picked at her salad, head down, and shrugged. She thought I knew and wasn't willing to say. I thought she knew and wasn't willing to say either.

"They wore latex suits and hoods," I said. "I didn't even know it was Christine until the back of the suit got unzipped and I saw her tattoo."

"Betty Boop?"

I nodded.

"She loved that tattoo." Tamara held her napkin to the bottom rim of her sunglasses and seemed ready to break into tears but sighed instead and blew her nose. "We went down to Hollywood one night three months ago, drank tequila shots at the Viper Room to screw up our courage and got work done at Tattoo Mania on Sunset. Want to see mine?" She stood from the table and bent to roll the cuff of her jeans to reveal a multicolored hummingbird etched into the skin just above her ankle. "It hurt like hell. The skin's really sensitive there. But I'm glad I got it done. Do you have any work done?"

"Nothing so beautiful," I said. "Who do you think was in the video?"

Tamara rolled the cuff down again, sat, and pulled her hair away from her face. "Do you know where she worked?"

I shrugged, maybe yes, maybe no. I wanted her to tell me.

"She did phone sex, you know, one of those 1-900 numbers."

"Sweet Lasses," I said.

"Not Lasses." She shook her head. "Lashes. Sweet Lashes."

"You mean whips, that kind of lashes?"

"She worked for a service that specialized in S&M; you know, I've been a bad boy, whip me while I kiss your feet." She scrunched shut her eyes and stuck out her tongue as though spitting out something bitter. "It was really gross. She said it was making her a better actress, you know, a role-playing exercise. I listened to her do it a couple of times and sure, it's acting, kind of, but so is pornography. I mean, it's not as bad as that because she's not, like, doing anybody but still, just to be pretending while the guy on the other end is, you know, I don't even want to say it, I mean, yuck, it's just disgusting."

I plowed into the eggs while Tamara talked, thinking how a single shifting consonant not only changed "Sweet Lasses" to "Sweet Lashes" but made what seemed an embarrassing and sleazy job into something far more sinister. "At the funeral, when you said Christine was into some dark stuff, that was what you meant?"

Her hair fell back to her shoulders when she released it and she nodded as though coming to a difficult decision, the kind of nod someone might make before deciding to take a running jump over a chasm. "I was thinking, what if she met someone that way? I mean, on the phone. It was a bondage video, right? What if someone offered to meet her in the flesh and she said yes?"

"Did she?"

"That's what I'm asking you."

I shook my head, confused. "Sure, it's possible."

"Will you check it out?"

"Do you have any reason to think that's what happened?"

"You mean, like, evidence?"

"You lived with her. Did she meet anyone else that way?"

"There was so much she didn't tell me." Tamara pushed her salad away, more pecked at than eaten. "I know for a fact she was having at least one secret affair, maybe more."

"Did she ever talk to you about Dr. Rakaan?"

"Her therapist?"

"I heard they were more than doctor and patient."

"Who told you that?"

I shrugged, not wanting to betray a source.

"Were they?" I asked.

"It's possible." She made a face as though she smelled something spoiled and tapped the table three times with the lacquered nail of her right forefinger. "I loved Christine but sometimes it was hard to keep up with her, because she wasn't exactly chaste, you know? The work she was doing with Dr. Rakaan involved how she felt about sex, I know that much, I know it dealt with her past-life relationships, and let's face it, she was pretty hot. Any guy not dead below the waist is gonna respond if she comes on to him and Rakaan is not dead below the waist." Tamara's hand shot to her mouth and she stood so abruptly I thought she was going to be sick. "Christine was a slut. Maybe something did happen between them. But that's the thing about sluts—it usually doesn't mean anything." She excused herself and clipped the table with her hip as she darted toward the bathroom, an odd reaction to our conversation that made me feel guilty I'd joked about bulimia.

12

THE SAN FERNANDO Valley is to the pornography business what Hollywood is to the feature film industry: a dark star whose sheer mass of production draws actors, producers, and technicians from around the world. When I suggested to Frank that we locate and interview the owner and manager of Sweet Lashes—this was one assignment I did not have the courage to attempt alone—he obliged with an enthusiasm and promptness I'd rarely seen in him before, producing the name of the holding company and its address within the hour. Sweet Lashes was only one of several 1-900 numbers the company operated spanning the gamut of human sexual tastes—and tastelessness. By the time we pulled up to the address, attached to a courtyard building that looked like it might have housed medical professionals in more reputable days, Frank had managed to set up an interview with the owner, who was surprisingly willing to talk.

I expected to meet a slovenly man with untucked shirttails and crumbs in his beard, whose busty, big-haired secretary polished her nails over a dusty keyboard, hired more for her oral than typing skills. I expected to open the door to the musty smell of unidentifiable stains on old carpets and cigarette smoke tarring the walls, scents I associated with losers who couldn't get a real girl and so resorted to varying forms of fantasy ones. My expectations were not fulfilled. Frank opened the door to a small but tidy lobby decorated in fresh flowers, one bouquet on a coffee table set before a blue couch and another spraying blooms above the desk of the receptionist, a blonde-haired man in his early twenties with lacquered nails and a sweet, nervous smile. My gaydar is not the most sensitive instrument, but he pinned the needle. He notified the owner we'd arrived and waved us through, asking if we wanted coffee or mineral water as we passed by.

The owner of Sweet Lashes was hovering over the open drawer to a filing cabinet when Frank and I entered the office, a pencil clenched between her teeth and a manila file folder in her hands. "Christine's employment records," she said, then remembered the pencil in her mouth and tossed it onto a desk cluttered with papers, cups, pens, and computer gear. "My name's Anabelle Lash."

"I'm a big fan, Ms. Lash," Frank said, the skin at his scalp line tingeing pink in an unexpected blush. "I wasn't sure it was you when I saw the name on the corporate records but I'm delighted to see it is. I'm Frank Adams, feature writer for *Scandal Times*."

The woman shook his hand briskly, her black hair falling in waves around a face all the more striking for not being classically beautiful, her prominently ridged nose curving above lips so full I suspected collagen injections to match the silicone implants ballooning her breasts. She wore just enough makeup to cover time's weathering marks on her skin but not so much that it reduced her face to a mask. I guessed her age at mid-forties. I introduced myself as the cameraperson and asked if she minded my taking a few photographs while Frank interviewed her.

"Not at all," she said, her voice surprisingly husky. "One of the first things I learned in the adult film business was to make love to the camera, if not the camera operator." She wagged her finger playfully. "The only thing you can do wrong with a camera is to make me look ugly."

"Impossible," Frank pronounced.

I slipped the digital camera from my bag while Frank chatted her up, gleaning from the conversation that Anabelle Lash had been one of the most celebrated adult film actresses of her time, which surprised me because it never occurred to me that something like that would be celebrated. She'd won not one but multiple AVN Awards, pornography's equivalent of the Oscar, for her performances in films whose titles could not be printed in a family newspaper, even a family newspaper as dysfunctional as *Scandal Times*. I surveyed the lighting conditions as she talked, and fiddled with the curtains to use the light coming from the window as a key light and the lamp on her desk as fill light.

"Christine came to work for us six months ago," Lash said, following every adjustment of the lights without changing the angle of her face. "I have to tell you she was a natural. It wasn't my idea to cast her with Sweet Lashes. I originally wanted her to work the Wet and Wild number, which is our soft-core surfer-girl fantasy line, but she insisted on Sweet Lashes, said it would be more fun for her." She smiled, polished teeth gleaming, as sincere as any sales manager. "That's really important to us. Our people, they have to enjoy the work. If you don't like what you do, do something else, that's what I tell people. And Christine? She enjoyed the work. You remember what she looked like? The girl next door, right?"

Frank nodded, seemingly so enthralled his eyes bugged out. He always fawned around film people, complimenting their most recent projects and hailing their older ones as classics of whatever genre fit, but his personal servility never encroached upon the articles he wrote, a Dr. Jekyll in the art of the interview and a Mr. Hyde behind the pen.

"We called her the Mistress of Kink. She could work both sides of the aisle, so to speak, but she excelled as a dominatrix. I mean, nothing was too wild for her." She shook her head as though such a thing was to be both pitied and admired. "She could have been a star in the adult film business if she wanted. Christine was really special."

That struck me as odd because from what I knew, Christine had played the submissive role in her relationship with Rakaan. Frank decided to go in a different direction with the interview, asking instead about Christine's experience in adult films.

"Christine was all talk," she said. "I know for a fact she never worked in adult films. It's a small world and news gets around. I don't think she even modeled topless. But the girl had a mouth on her that could boil dirt."

Frank sat up and looked over his shoulder. "The calls, are they routed through here?"

"This is just the business office. We'll screen applicants, meet employees when necessary, but the calls are processed through a call center off the premises, a service we contract out. And the employees, of course, all work at home, where the calls are forwarded."

"Do you ever monitor the calls?"

"That would be an invasion of privacy." She placed her hand flat on her desk and arched her back, a theatrical gesture meant to convey indignation. "I don't know about you, but most people would not want someone uninvited listening to their private fantasies of licking the boot of a dominatrix—unless of course that was part of their fantasy."

"Nice reply," Frank said, smiling, charmed by her performance. "But it doesn't answer the question."

"I can monitor any call I want, but do I want?" Lash glanced at the ceiling, shrugged, and then fixed a darkly blunt look on Frank. "Do I really want to hear another freak shout 'beat me baby, eight to the bar?' I mean, excuse me, this is what I do and I'm not ashamed of it—the career choices of adult film stars of a certain age are shall we say limited—but it's like I'm a fertilizer salesperson, maybe I sell bullshit but I don't need to take a bath in it. I listen only when training someone, and taking live calls is the last step in the training process, so I listen just long enough to make sure she's got it."

"So if a girl, say, wanted to meet someone who called her through the service, you might not know about it?"

"Stop right there," she said, flashing her palm. "This is not a front for prostitution. No way, no how. If one of my girls or boys tries to set up a date with one of our clients outside the service, they're gone. They can't have so much as a cup of coffee, and if they do, they're fired." Lash flipped open the cover of the file on the desk and brandished a document several pages long, stapled at the top left corner and signed on the last page. "It's all in the standard contract everybody signs, including Christine."

"I take it this means your answer is no," Frank said.

"No, what?"

"No, you wouldn't know about it."

He met her glare with a calm smile.

"The front-for-prostitution angle, I don't really care about that." He shifted in his chair and leaned forward, his shoulders slumped and baseball cap tipped high. "I'm a tabloid writer, not a cop. But Christine met someone dressed in latex who chained her to a rack and then strangled her to death. Given that she worked an S&M hotline, I have to think it's possible she met the killer through a call routed from your service. This can't be a surprise to you. I'm sure the cops already talked to you about it."

"Talked?" She flung her hands in the air. "I feel like a grilled cheese sandwich. My business is one hundred percent legal. The cops don't like it, I don't give a flying fuck." Her head dropped into her hands and she looked out the window through the grate of fingers splayed over her eyes. The way the light spilled over her, she looked lost.

I took the shot.

"They threatened to subpoena our records yesterday," she said. "We'll fight it, of course. I can just imagine the cops calling every one of our customers, asking why they called Christine and what they talked about."

"Don't you think it would be worth it," I asked, "if one of your customers is Christine's killer?"

"Christine wasn't a whore," she said. "If the police investigate her murder like she was, then it cheapens her memory, ruins my business, and wastes everyone's time." She stood, nodded toward Frank, and stared at me. "And speaking of time, yours is up."

Los Angeles and the San Fernando Valley are twinned economically and politically, part of the same metropolitan area and ruled by the same mayor, but the two regions are divided by more than the high hills that obstruct the view of Hollywood from Burbank. The dozen communities that comprise the San Fernando Valley burst from the razed orange groves in less than twenty years, asphalt, concrete, and steel fertilized by the economic miracle of water piped over the mountains. They rolled the cityscape across the valley like a rug, the streets straight and flat and the blocks largely distinguishable from each other by street numbers more than landmarks. Though not particularly scenic, the San Fernando Valley is a driver's paradise compared to the jammed streets of Los Angeles, surface traffic flowing steadily along the wide avenues even during rush hour. We lowered the Caddy's ragtop and reveled in the late-afternoon warmth, Frank jotting notes of our meeting onto his pad while I drove.

"How's your love life?" I called across the seat.

"The only thing worse than my love life is my sex life." He pocketed his notepad, lowered his Cubs cap over his eyes, and leaned against the passenger door. "If I called Anabelle Lash, do you think she'd go out with me?"

"That's a little like asking if you went up to the counter at Mc-Donald's, would they take your order," I said, trying not to sound catty. "The woman all but had a sign sprouting from the top of her head reading 'Billions Served.'"

"Lucky for me I like McDonald's," Frank said.

I hadn't laughed in a week and that gave me a good one.

"You knew Christine better than I did," Frank said. "Maybe she wasn't a full-time pro but did you ever get the feeling she wouldn't turn down a little money for sex on the side?"

"That wasn't Christine's style. She was more into fun than money. I can see her maybe trying it once just to see what it was like, but to turn it into a regular gig?" I shook my head. "No way. She had too much going for her."

"What if it wasn't a paid gig?"

"You mean, what if she was doing it for fun?"

"I don't know what I mean, I'm just throwing it out there."

I felt something warm and wet on the back of my neck—the Rott's nose. He'd clambered onto the seat back to rest his head on my shoulder. He normally rode shotgun. Just because he was a good sport about giving up his seat didn't mean he didn't need a little attention.

"I guess that depends on the dynamics of the conversation," I said, stroking the Rott's muzzle with my free hand. "If she liked someone enough to want to meet him for one reason or another, the threat of losing her job wouldn't stop her."

"What if the caller said he was Depp's assistant?"

"She'd meet him, no hesitation at all, if she believed him."

The Rott lifted his head from my shoulder and shifted toward Frank. He's a sociable dog and isn't happy until everyone in the immediate vicinity pays him some attention, as though he considers himself the glue that holds our little pack together. Frank pushed him away. The Rott considered that a good game and bulled forward again and again until Frank relented and stroked his head.

"Unless we can come up with a better angle," he said, "we'll play up the Sweet Lashes connection as the most likely way she met the killer."

"I'd like to talk to Nephthys first."

"You mean the tattooed babe?"

As good a way as any to describe her. I nodded.

"Does she have a boyfriend?"

I took my eyes off traffic and stared at him.

"She's hot," he said. "And it's not just the freak-show appeal of the tattoos, either."

"I don't know whether she's got a boyfriend—or a girlfriend."

"Girlfriends are fine as long as she shares."

"You dream," I said.

"Dreams are all I have, so I may as well enjoy them."

He rubbed his knuckles on the Rott's head, giving him a noogie. The Rott rewarded Frank with a wet one to his stubbled cheek.

"Just wanted to warn you," I said, "if you go with the Sweet Lashes connection, it's going to ruin your chances of getting Anabelle Lash to date you."

"I hate it when professional ethics get in the way of opportunities for cheap and meaningless sex, particularly when I have so much of one and so few of the other." He pushed the Rott away and lifted the cell phone from his shirt pocket. "I'd better ask for that date now, before we run the article."

13

NEPHTHYS CURLED HER small body onto a plush red lounge chair in the back room of the Chinese-themed Good Luck Bar, gold silk pajamas flowing from her limbs and bead-embroidered black slippers adorning her feet. Surrounded by her friends, she looked like the habitué of an opium den, a blue drink served in a bowl-shaped glass instead of a pipe balanced on her knee. She called the Good Luck her local bar, and with a postmodern decor of Chinese lanterns, latticework, and lacquered screens mixed with thrift-shop furniture, it was the kind of bar only someone from a Bohemian neighborhood like Los Feliz could call local. Her friends did not dress so extravagantly—two in jeans and bare-midriff blouses and the third in bicycle shorts, calf-high lace-up boots, and boy-beater T-shirt—but judging from the pierced eyebrows, tongues, ears, and noses, they all shared a similar aesthetic of the scarified body beautiful. Everyone had been inked, either along their arms or stomachs or legs, the designs sometimes playfully macabre and other times fantastic; a green dragon flew up one girl's arm, background clouds billowing from her skin like waves.

Nephthys lifted her drink so I could better appreciate the deep blue color and asked in a stage-loud voice, "You want one of these?"

"What is it?" I asked.

"A Yee Mee Loo."

"What does that mean?"

"Blue drink."

Everyone laughed in the spirit of an old gag pulled on someone new. Their faces looked familiar, and after a few minutes of conversation, I realized they had come as a group on the night my photographs were first exhibited. They knew each other from an art school over the hill in Pasadena and were trying to make the transition from studying the arts to the more difficult task of making a career. I pulled up a chair next to Nephthys and ordered a Jack Daniel's neat from a passing waitress. They talked so fluently about the Los Angeles arts scene that I felt like a fraud, not an unusual feeling when I'm around other people in the arts.

I picked up the digital camera to tune out the conversation and found myself the sudden center of attention. The girls were not camera shy; they made faces, kissed each other, and showed off their tattoos, mugging playfully—and sometimes shamelessly—for the camera. The digital revolution has put the world onstage, making us all actors in the theatrical performance of our lives. We're all on camera all the time and more vain than ever. This can be a disaster for a photographer seeking the quiet truth of an unguarded moment. When I want to be ignored, I pull out a film camera. Film takes too long to be developed for anyone to care what you shoot. After I bagged the digital camera the conversation drifted to job opportunities, a topic that didn't interest Nephthys so much. She worked as a set decorator for mostly independent films, work that she liked and paid her well. I told her about my talk with Christine's roommate, Tammy. Nephthys had identified Dr. Rakaan as Christine's boyfriend, something Tammy disputed. "I get the feeling you two don't see everything the same way," I said.

"Just because I think she's a two-faced, lying bitch?" Her lips, painted the color of dried blood, spread in a happy smile. "Nothing wrong with her that a total personality transplant wouldn't cure."

"What does she lie about?"

"She lies about herself to herself. Like she thinks she's going to be this big movie or television star but the roles she's cast in? Bimbo of the week." Nephthys growled like an angry cat and laughed. "Tammy's okay, I'm sure, she's just not my kind of girl."

"Christine must have liked her."

"Christine was a complex girl, more complex than she looked." She raised the drink to her lips, blue against red, and sipped. "Part of her was this conventional, small-town girl, superficial and boring, not much different than Tammy. That's why they got along so well."

"And the other part?"

"Unpredictable. She could light you on fire with her smile but sometimes when you looked deep inside her, the darkness you saw could freeze you. She was wild, incredibly sexy, and . . . what?" She sipped at her drink and nodded, as though alcohol fueled her thinking. "Not immoral. She had a conscience. She never willingly harmed anyone that I know about. But she liked to be a daredevil, to try things other people might find shocking."

"You told me she was into some twisted stuff, with Rakaan."

Nephthys chewed at her lower lip and when she opened her mouth to sip at her drink, she revealed that lipstick had stained the tips of her front teeth red. She shook her head, not to contradict what I'd said but to signal her reluctance to talk about it.

"When I met Rakaan, at his office, it seemed clear to me that you were right, he was sleeping with Christine." I put my heels on the edge of the chair, curled my arms around my knees and stared at her, hoping she might respond to the intimacy of eye contact. "He denied it, pretty strongly, in fact so strongly it was like an alarm going off, you know, *liar, liar, liar.*"

"It wasn't that they just slept together," she said, making it sound like sleeping together meant nothing at all. "And it wasn't that they were lovers either. Christine had more than one lover."

"Were you one of them?" The question popped from me unconsidered. I lifted my hands in apology. "Sorry, none of my business."

Nephthys smiled a small, sad smile and shrugged. "You'd have to put chains on Christine to tie her down and that's what Rakaan did to her, but she slipped loose every now and then."

"You talking metaphorical chains or real ones?"

"Both." Her lips tightened and she leaned forward, coming to some decision, her forehead less than the span of a hand from mine. "Christine told me that she was working out her past-life karma with Rakaan, that her sessions with him began with hypnosis and deep, probing conversations but quickly evolved into bondage scenarios."

"You mean, they'd talk about it."

"No. I mean they'd do it. Not in his office but later, at his house."

I pulled my head back and tried to read her face for signs that she was kidding or trying to deceive me and saw none.

"He'd tie her up?" I asked.

"That was just one of the things he did, with her permission. They'd take turns doing things to each other—whipping, slapping, spitting, hot candle wax, you name it."

"Strangling?"

She bit her lip and nodded. "Choking is supposed to be a big turn-on. That's why, what happened, it wasn't such a big surprise for me. But the way she talked about it, she wasn't doing it just for kicks. The bondage scenarios were an important part of her therapy."

"Her past-life regression therapy?" After a moment of sheer incredulity, I realized my mouth hung open. "Just so we're absolutely clear on this, he would tie her up and do stuff to her, whip her, have sex—whatever—and he did this to her because . . ." I tried to think of a good reason but my imagination failed me. "Why?"

"She said it helped her work out some emotional issues she had about sex and it didn't hurt that the sex was incredible. Rakaan said she got off because she was connecting with her past lives."

I remembered my brief interview with Rakaan, how he'd said their sessions were about Christine's love of pain. "He told me she'd been murdered in her past life," I said. "He made it sound like it happened not just once but a couple of times."

"She told me the same thing, that it was like this thing she had, this violent history with men from one lifetime to the next." She gripped my arm with her free hand. "She gave me one very specific example. In the nineteenth century she was a young widow working in London, as a milliner's assistant she said. She had some health problems and the doctor who treated her fell in love with her. The doctor, he liked rough sex and one day he went too far and killed her. Do you know who the doctor was?"

I shook my head, expecting Jack the Ripper.

"Dr. Rakaan," she whispered. "They were lovers in at least one past life, you see? Christine said when he strangled her to death back in England it was an accident, he didn't mean to kill her. The therapy aspect is, they have to relive in this life what ruined their lives in the past."

"Meaning he ties her up and strangles her," I said.

"Except this time, he was supposed to bring her back, he wasn't supposed to seriously hurt her. That was how it became therapeutical. They were supposed to see how her death in the past lifetime had been an accident and learn how to trust again."

"Except he screwed up again and killed her," I said, feeling sick to my stomach. "What's he going to tell her in the next lifetime, *Oops*?"

Nephthys released my arm and settled back into the lounge chair, the plush fabric haloing her in red. "I don't take this reincarnation stuff so seriously. I mean, it's fun to think about but I don't really believe it. I can't even tell you for sure whether Christine believed it either but it unlocked some serious demons inside her. She really got off on the things they did together."

"Have you talked to the police about any of this?"

She hid behind her blue drink, then slowly lowered it to peer above the rim of the glass, regarding me as though she felt guilty about something, then shook her head.

"Why not?"

"It's not so simple." She released a little tension with a sigh. "If Rakaan killed her, it was an accident. Should he spend the rest of his productive life in jail because he went too far?"

I nodded, said, "Sure, if he killed Christine."

"Look, you can cross an ethical line and get away with it—people do it all the time—but when you cross the line habitually you sometimes forget where the line is, and one day you don't just cross it, you break it, you shatter it to pieces. I think maybe that's what happened to Christine. They just kept crossing the line, venturing further out each time, and they just went too far." A tear spilled from her eye and tracked a black line down her cheek. "I'm trying to figure out what Christine would want. If she and Rakaan finally broke a line they crossed every time they were together, would she want to see him punished?" She wiped her face and saw the mascara on her fingertips. "Crap, I hate it when I cry. Now I gotta spend the next half hour in the bathroom, repairing the damage."

"Why are you telling me this if you don't think he should be punished?"

"You know what I think?" She sat up straight and pressed at her eyes, drawing concerned looks from her friends. "I think he should be hung by his balls, that's what I think. Maybe I didn't go to the police but that doesn't mean I wouldn't be thrilled to see him exposed on the front page of *Scandal Times* for the unethical pervert he is."

"Then the cops will end up knowing anyway," I said.

The next morning, Nephthys told her story to the police.

14

DR. RAKAAN LIVED in a modest million-dollar French chateau in the Hollywood hills—if any French chateau costing a million can be considered modest—on a ridge above Beechwood Canyon. At the top of the ridge the sky cracked open to a vista that on windswept days curved with the earth to the milky-blue band of the Pacific, but on most days terminated in a curtain of smog just past the tar pits at La Brea. Million-dollar views on the ridge were just that; real estate prices began at seven figures and went up from there, depending on the size of the lot and the age of the house. Rakaan's house had been built in the 1920s by one of Los Angeles' many eccentric architects. Back then the area was known as Hollywoodland, the real estate development that gave the world the Hollywoodland sign, later shortened to just Hollywood, which towered above the brush-choked hillside at the dead end of Rakaan's street.

I scoped the weave of hillside streets in the Thomas Guide and decided I wouldn't risk a drive by. Earlier that afternoon I'd tried to stake out Rakaan's office, but the lack of clear sight lines for a telephoto lens and the presence of an unmarked surveillance unit on the street convinced me to try his house instead. At Christine's funeral the surveillance cameraman considered him someone of interest, and Nephthys's testimony probably shot him to number one on the list of suspects. The police would certainly have a unit down the street from his house but I hoped the mixed suburban and wild hillside terrain would provide camouflage. If the evidence and my instincts were accurate, Rakaan would soon be practicing past-life regression therapy out of his cell in the Twin Towers, the city's futuristic jail complex. We had an image from Christine's funeral to run in the event of his arrest but I wanted to take a photograph that clearly implied his guilt, something furtive and hurried and just a little bit sleazy. I let the Cadillac drift to the curb on a side street a half mile down the hill, calmed the Rott with a few strokes to his head, and went to collect my gear in the trunk.

The trunk space of a 1976 Cadillac Eldorado is bigger than some apartments. Mine functioned as a roving closet, office, kitchen, and bathroom cabinet while I drove around town, hunting down one shot or another, sometimes for twenty-four hours a shift and longer. I pulled a running outfit from my change-of-clothing case and loaded a day pack with extra clothing, water, food, and camera gear. The Rott jittered on his front paws and barked to hurry me along while I changed clothes in the front seat. We ran the hill at an optimistic clip, cramped from too much sitting, but the Rott was a sensible dog and when he started to tire he went on patrol. I scanned the street while I waited, running in place to keep my muscles warm, and spotted the surveillance sedan parked across the street and three houses down from Rakaan's. In a neighborhood of fifty-thousand-dollar automobiles and two-thousand-dollar gardening trucks, the sedan—a five-year-old Chevy the color of dirt—didn't qualify as covert surveillance; if Rakaan knew he was being watched, he couldn't miss spotting it.

We took off again when the Rott had left his mark, setting our pace to a seven-minute mile, fast for an uphill run. As we approached the Chevy I reminded the Rott to heel; we wouldn't remain anonymous for long if he decided to mark the cop's tires. Any cop other than Logan would see us as a jogger and her dog, a common sight in the hills. I figured Logan would be out working the case, not warming his butt in a surveillance vehicle. At the end of the street the pavement yielded to a dirt fire road, blocked from traffic by a gate. I glanced at the scrub-brush hills above Rakaan's house as we ran, scouting out a suitable blind. We skirted the gate unchallenged. Fifty paces beyond the gate I knelt to unleash the Rott and studied the hillside, searching for a path through the chaparral and scrub oak. The terrain broke sharply uphill to the left, boulders exposed during the excavation of the road jutting from the brush. Another twenty yards from the road the hill sloped up a cut made by runoff water. I hit the hillside near the cut in full running stride, the brush tearing at the skin of my legs as momentum carried me up the steepest few yards of slope. When I stalled out, I grabbed a stalk of chaparral and pulled myself to a lip of earth that marked a more gradual incline. The Rott followed me part way, then dropped back down to the road and barked. Big dogs aren't great climbers, particularly Rottweilers, and he clearly thought I was crazy. I slapped my side to encourage him and he came bounding up. When he slowed near the lip, I grabbed his collar and helped him over.

We cut diagonally up the hill until the terrain curved to a view of Rakaan's house, well within telephoto range on the street below. I didn't expect to run into any police surveillance in the hills and didn't. I grew up hiking hills like the one above Rakaan's house, felt as much at home there as anywhere. I chose a scrub oak as our photo blind and settled into the hillside for a long wait. The Rott wasted little time in nosing around the day pack. I zipped it open, pulled out a small aluminum bowl, and filled it with water. While he lapped it up I snuck out a pound of hamburger wrapped in butcher paper, his expression turning mournful when I pretended I was going to eat it all. I couldn't torment the poor creature for long, broke it into his bowl and watched him gum it down.

The blind I'd chosen angled down the hillside to a three-quarters profile of Rakaan's house. I planted a telescoping aluminum tripod into the dirt, mounted a 500-millimeter telephoto lens to the Nikon, and screwed the tripod into the camera's base plate. The Nikon came loaded with high-speed Tri-X black-and-white film, and in the event clouds veiled the moon I'd brought along a roll of infrared film, capable of exposing the face of Benjamin Franklin on a hundred-dollar bill in the darkness of a locked safe. Then I leaned back against the scrub oak and waited, reading from a book I'd bought the day before, *Transcending Anger: How to Harness the Power of Rage for Positive Change*. After the first few passages I decided the book wasn't going to help me much, but reading it was as good a way as any to pass the time.

I heard Rakaan's vehicle before I saw it, a new Porsche Cayenne SUV, eight turbo-charged cylinders in full throaty roar as he powered up the incline. It was a beautiful car and he drove it like he might never get another chance behind the wheel, whipping into the chateau's circular drive and stopping with such quick precision that I nailed only one shot before the driver's door flashed open. I reframed the telephoto, left hand gently cupping the lens and my right shoulder pressed like a sharpshooter's against the tripod mount, and when Rakaan's head emerged from the cabin I pinned the shutter release. The Nikon's auto-advance motor hummed in rapid fire, 2.5 frames per second as I followed Rakaan to the front door, where he fumbled his key into the lock and glanced over his shoulder as though he feared something might be gaining on him.

I double-checked my shutter speed and F-stop for accuracy of exposure, noted that I'd burned over twenty frames of film, and decided to reload. I threaded a new roll of Tri-X into the camera and snapped closed the back, satisfied that I'd lensed at least one usable image of Rakaan looking furtive. Arrows of light flashed from the glass facades of the city's midrises as the sun arced toward the sea. I returned to reading my book about anger management. A blood-red mist settled over the city, smog reflecting the last rays of the sun. When the light faded to darkness and the air cooled I slipped into sweatpants and rested my eyes, the Rott snuggled against my side. Like film work, gotcha photography requires moments of intense activity spaced between hours of waiting, and in my experience, the best gotchas almost always occur at night.

The Rott woke me when he stirred, his ears twitching forward like birds on a limb. I traced by sight the line of his hearing to the back of Rakaan's house, where a wall-mounted lantern threw a half-circle of light onto the descending hillside. I tucked the Nikon and tripod under my arm and crept through the brush toward a clearer angle. Like most houses on the ridge, Rakaan's had been partially built into the descending hillside, the structural supports invisible from the street. A figure cloaked in black clipped down a set of stairs at the side, a bag slung over its back. At the base of the stairs the figure paused, facing the abrupt slope below the house. The bag reflected light—probably a plastic garbage bag. I jammed the tripod into the earth, opened the aperture wide, slowed the shutter to a thirtieth of a second, and put my eye to a telephoto image of Dr. Rakaan's flowing black hair. He stepped cautiously off the landing, the slope steep and slick with gravel over packed earth. No more than thirty feet from the back of the house, the hill dropped sharply to rock and canyon. Rakaan stooped over the bag, as though making certain the contents were securely bound, then swung it over his head. He let it go like a rock from a slingshot, and after four seconds of silent free fall it crashed into the deep brush near the bottom of the canyon.

The Nikon's motor hummed in auto-rewind as Rakaan climbed the stairs back to his house—I'd shot out the roll. I didn't think I'd just witnessed the nightly ritual of taking out the trash. The cops had clearly spooked Rakaan. The contents of the bag made me curious but not curious enough to goad me into doing something stupid, like prowling through the canyon brush at night to retrieve something that would be tainted evidence in a murder case if I touched it. I planted the tripod in front of the scrub oak, dug out another roll of Tri-X, and while I reloaded called Detective Tyler. When he picked up the call I said, "A source tells me Dr. Rakaan just threw a stuffed trash bag into the brush behind his house."

"Who's your source?" His voice sounded distracted, as though I'd just pulled him from a task that required concentration.

I yipped and softly howled into the mouthpiece.

He laughed, his voice brightening.

"Your source is a coyote?"

"My source is anonymous and hoping to stay that way."

"And what about you? Are you on record for this if I pass it on?"

"Logan already hates me. He hears my name with this, he'll want to stick me in a cage."

"So the tip I'm supposed to give him is, an anonymous source of an anonymous source says Rakaan is illegally disposing trash behind his house."

"Maybe you can simplify it, say an anonymous source."

"You being the anonymous source who saw the bag in question."

"I can see why you made detective. You're sharp."

He told me to hold for a second and I heard voices in the background, muffled by the palm of his hand. He came back on line, his cadence more hurried. "I haven't heard anybody say Rakaan's the one yet, but remember it's not my investigation."

"What are you working on now?"

"Twelve-year-old kid. Gunned down in a drive-by."

I told him I was sorry.

"Nothing to be sorry about, it's what I do for a living." His voice slowed and softened. "Maybe when you've completed your parole agreement we could meet for a cup of coffee, take up where we left off that night in the darkroom."

I broke down my camera gear and packed it in the bag, wondering how someone could so effortlessly make meeting for a cup of coffee sound like a euphemism for sex. I'd spent enough fruitless nights camped out on hillsides or slumped in the Cadillac, waiting for a shot, not to take Sean's hint that a bust wasn't planned for the night. I liked hanging out in the hills but that didn't mean I wanted to sleep rough. The surveillance cop didn't give me a second glance when I ran back down the hill, the Rott heeled beside me.

Most of the night remained ahead of the clock. I sponged the sweat from my skin in the front seat of the Cadillac, changed into my street clothes, and drove down the hill into Los Feliz to meet Nephthys for a drink at the Good Luck Bar, thinking I might as well drop by while I was in the neighborhood. Maybe I wanted to celebrate getting a photograph that implicated Rakaan and maybe I wanted to feel more like a normal human being. Normal people meet friends for drinks after work. Nephthys and her friends didn't fit anyone's definition of normal, but at least they celebrated their nonconformity together. I missed that in my life. I missed friendship, particularly with other women.

Then again, maybe I just wanted a drink.

Past 10 PM a young arts crowd packed most of the chairs and tables in the Good Luck Bar, the clash of shouted conversations nearly overpowering the chill-out music blasting through the sound system. The Los Angeles club and bar scene divides mostly along the lines of sexual orientation but the vibe at the Good Luck Bar wasn't gay or straight; even though the clientele seemed as sex-obsessed as any other group of twenty- and thirty-year-olds clustered together, sexual orientation wasn't the draw. The girls around Nephthys welcomed me like a friend, and the one who liked to wear boy-beater T-shirts bought me a drink. She'd been interviewed that morning by an abstract painter who needed an assistant, one of the few jobs available to young artists in their actual field of study. Whether or not she got the job wasn't the point to her; she was happy enough just to get the interview. Some time later she and the girl with the green dragon tattoo spotted a couple of wild-haired boys they knew at the bar and drifted over to talk. I told Nephthys about Rakaan tossing a bag into the brush behind his house. She listened from behind the rim of a margarita, the green contrasting nicely with her red silk blouse and black slacks. I was beginning to think she chose her drinks by color rather than taste or alcohol content.

"What do you think was in it?" she asked.

"His dirty laundry."

"You photographed him?"

"It was pretty dark out but yes, I think I got him."

"Maybe I'm not a regular reader of *Scandal Times* but I'll buy that issue, I promise. I only met him once—twice now counting the funeral—but I'll be happy never to meet him again." She flashed a happy, acid smile. "And if he's in jail, I won't have to meet him again."

"You met him just once?"

I'd assumed they'd been well acquainted, if not friends.

"He didn't like being seen in public with her."

"Why not?"

"Because the public considers sleeping with a patient unethical."

"Some people are so narrow-minded."

She smiled at the joke and sipped at her drink, remembering.

"They were eating at this sushi place on Olympic. She asked me to drop by, pretend it was a coincidence. Rakaan wasn't happy to meet me. In fact, he buried his face in the menu like he'd been caught cheating on his wife."

"Why did they continue to hide?" I asked. "Sure, I understand he could get into trouble if it gets around he's boning his patient, but once they formed the connection why didn't they just drop the patient-doctor relationship and come out as lovers?"

"They liked the deception." She glanced behind her, not wanting to share the conversation with a casual listener, and pressed her mouth closer to my ear. "The bondage was only one manifestation of what was going on between them. The idea of two people tying each other up and having sex isn't so wicked, not anymore it isn't, but the idea that two people are murderous lovers through multiple lifetimes, that they've murdered each other before and might very well do it again, that's wicked. I think they both got off on the idea that their sex could end in death, that one could kill the other."

"I thought Christine was the victim." I shifted my stance, aware that such conversations should not be shouted, and spoke in her ear like she'd spoken in mine. "In her past life, I mean. I thought the whole point of the so-called therapy was to relive the past-life experience that's screwing up the present."

"That's like saying you're healed the moment you admit you have a problem. That's only the first step. After that comes the cure." Nephthys pulled back and faced me, her black, scythelike eyebrows arching high to dramatize the idea she wanted to get across. "The scenario evolved from sexual reenactments of past-life murder to her taking revenge in the present life. You understand what I'm saying? Christine became a dominatrix toward the end of their relationship. Their roles reversed. She tied, whipped, and strangled him."

I remembered what Anabelle Lash had said, that Christine had excelled in playing the dominatrix to her phone-sex clients. That Christine enjoyed deception made sense; Nephthys may have known about her relationship with Rakaan but knew little about her phone-sex work. Tammy, who knew about her job with Sweet Lashes, was ignorant of her twisted sex life with Rakaan. "If Christine liked deception in her sex life, do you think she also liked to deceive her friends?"

"I don't think anybody saw all sides to her," Nephthys said. "I think part of her appeal was that she was a little like a chameleon, able to transform herself to meet the fantasies of the person she was with, no matter what the relationship."

"How well does Tammy know Rakaan, you think?"

"About as well as any patient knows her therapist."

"Rakaan was treating Tammy?"

Nephthys stepped back, surprised that I hadn't known.

"Of course. How do you think Christine met Rakaan?"

Nephthys put her hand on my shoulder and turned to say hello to the two boys from the bar her friends were swinging our way. The conversation splintered into fragments, nobody saying anything of much importance but everyone enjoying the diverse company. Nephthys began to flirt heavily with one of the new arrivals, a tall and pale-skinned boy with a wounded look—maybe it was the pierced eyebrow—who said he played guitar in a band. I'd heard of the band so I supposed he was vaguely famous. I hung around long enough to finish my drink and kissed everyone goodbye, apologizing that work intervened.

Frank would want to see the images of Rakaan the next morning and I was far too curious to wait to see how the exposures worked out. I drove to the all-night darkroom in Hollywood, where I developed the negatives and printed the corresponding proof sheets. Four of the shots looked promising, despite the lack of light. I set up the enlarger and went to work printing eight-by-tens. One of the photographs caught Rakaan's unshadowed face in clear focus the moment before he released the bag. I tried enlarging the sweet spot, eliminating the foreground, and dropped the resulting print into the fixer just as my cell phone rang.

The call was coming from Frank's phone. I checked the time; the only stories that break at 4 AM are big ones. Frank sounded wide awake when I picked up the call. A source monitoring the emergency services scanner reported the police were raiding Rakaan's house. I packed up and drove across town as fast as I could risk, but by the time I reached Beechwood Canyon a police barrier stretched across the road a half mile down from Rakaan's house. Journalists and photographers were not invited.

I'd missed the shot.

15

OLD-TIMERS—DEFINED by local standards as anyone over forty—have told me that rush-hour traffic once moved in predictable directions, from San Fernando, San Bernadino, and the beach communities toward the center of Los Angeles in the morning, the flow reversing in the afternoon, with routine and predictable slowing in local commercial hubs like Long Beach. Traffic now jams in all directions, the roads resembling long and narrow parking lots for three hours in the morning and four hours in the afternoon, with almost as many people trying to get into the beach communities most mornings—particularly Santa Monica—as those trying to get out. I did the sensible thing; I found a quiet, tree-canopied street and a level parking spot off Beechwood Canyon and curled up in the backseat, the Rott slumbering on the floorboards just below my side.

The heat woke us well before noon, inland temperatures rising toward the mid-80s, a beautiful late-spring day if you like it hot. I fed the Rott some kibbles softened with water, stretched out the kinks, and drove the Hollywood Freeway north to the *Scandal Times* building, stopping once along the way. I found Frank reclined in his workstation, feet up on the desk and his head cocked back against the headrest of his chair, oblivious to time. Like me, he worked odd hours and was prone to napping during unguarded moments. I pulled a sugar donut from the box I'd bought on my way to the office and held it under his nose until he woke enough to lift one eye to see what was giving him such sweet dreams.

"Too late?" he asked, referring to the bust from the night before.

"Way late," I said, and propped against the computer monitor the proof sheet of thirty-six images I'd taken of Rakaan throwing the black bag down the hill behind his house. "But maybe this will work for you."

He grabbed the donut, dropped his feet from the desk, and pressed his nose to the proof sheet, looking at the images while he ate. I handed him a viewing loupe and a cup of take-out coffee and told him how I'd climbed the hill behind Rakaan's house the evening before, intending to get a tabloid-worthy shot. Frank pressed the loupe against his eye and hovered over the proof sheet, scattering crumbs with each bite. "Why did he panic?" He mumbled, mouth full. "I understand why he didn't think anybody could see him, why he thought he could get away with it, but why didn't he just hold on to whatever he had in the bag? Why take the risk of dumping it?"

"Maybe he noticed an increase in police surveillance, figured he was about to be busted."

"That hot tattooed girl, she talked to the police?"

"Yesterday morning."

"What she said must have made an impression." He lifted a grease pencil from the coffee cup that served as his pencil holder and tapped it against the proof sheet. "Last night, you call Logan about these?"

"Not Logan, no. I called someone else, a mutual friend."

"Tyler?"

"He suggested I was wasting my time with Rakaan."

"It didn't take him long to screw you, did it?"

"What do you mean by that?"

"Not literally. Figuratively. He suckered you into leaving the scene."

I didn't know if Sean intended to betray me, but that was the way it turned out. When you don't know the heart of someone, results matter.

"So you missed the bust shot. A bunch of cop cars in front of a house. So what? Bust shots are overrated." He circled an image of Rakaan, feet braced against a clump of brickellbush and arms extended above his head, the moment before he flung the bag into the canyon below. "This is the image I'll pitch to go with the story. How do you think it's gonna print up? Will you see enough of his face to know it's him?"

I dug the print of that same shot I'd enlarged the night before and tossed it onto his desk, Rakaan's face as bright and clear as a mug shot. Frank craned his neck to look at the print and smirked with satisfaction; the print gave him a front-page image to sell the story.

"How are we feeling about the cops these days?" he asked, lifting the print toward the light. "Should we say screw 'em—figuratively speaking only—or should I fax the print to Logan?"

"If they bother to look for the bag, the photograph is evidence."

"And withholding evidence is a crime. That's a parole violation, isn't it?"

"I forget to flush, it's a parole violation. Maybe you can trade the photo for information about what's in the bag."

If nothing else, my gullibility managed to give Frank a good laugh. The police did not like to trade information, particularly not with tabloid reporters. They gave you what they wanted to give you and never anything that could remotely compromise their investigation. While Frank photocopied and faxed the print to Logan, I flipped through the sheaf of photographs I kept in my camera bag until I found the one of the license plate I'd snapped at Christine's funeral.

"You find out about this license plate yet?"

"Why do you care?" He tossed the print onto his desk and rooted around for something in the drawer next to the printer. "We're already running with Rakaan in the next issue. If he's good enough for *Scandal Times*, he should be good enough for you."

"He's only one guy," I said. "The video suggests two more."

"You can't seriously tell me you think Rakaan isn't guilty for this." Frank yanked the drawer to the end of its pull and stuck his head into the gap. "Past-life regression therapy that includes sado-masochistic practices with a patient? What a slimeball! I've never even met the guy and I hate him."

"Did you run the plates or not?"

"They're rental car plates." He pulled his head from the drawer, eyebrows twitching as though something completely confused him. "Registered to Budget out of LAX. Anybody could have driven that car."

"What are you looking for?"

"My Nicorettes!"

"You're trying to quit?" I asked.

"No!" he shouted the denial, as though the idea terrified him. "I work in a smoke-free office. What, I'm gonna light up in here, get fined by OSHA, and then fired by the paper?"

A fresh-air fan is one of the benefits of driving a convertible. I told Frank that I'd let him smoke in the car, all the encouragement he needed to grab his gear and accompany me to the airport. He worked his cell phone while I drove, blowing smoke into the wind and tipping his ashes into an empty can of Diet 7 Up. In addition to the Rakaan story, he was writing against deadline on the Komodo dragon attack of Sharon Stone's husband, new medical evidence linking dieting with depression, and a story provisionally headlined "Why the FBI Murdered Elvis," the tabloid defining murder loosely to mean the FBI knew Elvis was addicted to various drugs but did nothing to help him. "All the news that's shit to print," Frank liked to say, and he was neck deep in it as usual.

I drove into the desolate grid of remote parking and air-freight warehouses east of the airport, following the car rental signs until I spotted the Budget pole-sign floating over a flat-roofed building. Frank wrote something on a sheet of paper and stuffed it into an envelope while I parked in one of the few spaces reserved for the drive-in trade—almost all of their customers took the shuttle from LAX.

I told the Rott to stay in the car and followed Frank inside a one-room customer service area with flanking counters and a switchback rope line near the entrance. We arrived between shuttles, the rope line empty and only one of four sales representatives busy with a customer. Frank skirted the ropes, scanned the faces of the waiting reps, and walked up to a mid-thirties Latino with swept-back hair and a broad face whose brass name tag read "Frank."

"Hi, Frank, what a coincidence, my name's Frank, too." Frank smiled and bobbed his head as though genuinely delighted. "I think coincidences like this bring luck. What do you think?"

The man's brow wrinkled toward his eyes and he smiled, a little confused but wanting to be friendly. "I think we're in luck, then," he said. "Do you have a reservation today?"

"No reservations, no, but we're definitely looking for a car."

"What kind of car are you looking for?"

"Kind of car?" Frank asked, as though he didn't understand.

"Compact, midsized, full-sized . . ." He gave us a dubious look. "Maybe luxury?"

Frank leaned back and looked at me for the answer.

"We want a white Hyundai Sonata," I said.

The rep nodded as though I'd just made a perfectly reasonable request. "That would be a midsized vehicle." He shifted to face his computer screen. "Are you looking for a reservation beginning today?"

"We've written down our full itinerary right here," Frank said, sliding the envelope onto the counter.

The sales rep reached for the envelope without taking his eyes from the screen, confirming the current availability of white Hyundai Sonatas, then glanced down to finger out the folded sheet of paper. A clear look of understanding buzzed his eyes when he spotted the fifty-dollar bill, as though the whole thing made sense to him, good sense. He slid the envelope containing the fifty under his keyboard and unfolded the sheet of paper, which listed the license plate number and the date of Christine's funeral. I'd wanted Frank to accompany me to the agency because he excelled at this type of operation; he'd marked the guy he thought would be most flexible and set him up to expect something a little unusual, so the sight of the money was a pleasant surprise rather than a shock.

"I'm sorry, the car for the dates you've requested are completely booked," the rep said, jotting down information from his reservations screen. "Can I help you with another reservation?"

"I think that's it for today, thanks."

"Don't forget your itinerary," the rep said, and handed the folded sheet of paper back over the counter.

Frank played a little game with the paper while we walked to the car, pretending to offer it to me then snatching it away when I reached for it. "I did all the work here," he said. "I should have the right to first look." He carefully unfolded the sheet of paper, put his nose to it, and then thumped his hand against his chest as though he'd just been hit with a heart attack.

I plucked the note from his hand and read the name, birth date, address, and driver's license number the rep had written beneath the plates. The kid's name was Stewart Starbal and he lived in Beverly Hills. I did the math. He was only nineteen years old. "How did he rent the car?" I asked. "I thought you had to be, what, twenty-something to rent a car."

"Not if your daddy is one of the top power brokers in Hollywood." Frank recovered from his heart attack and lit a cigarette. "Our friend didn't give us the credit card info but I'll bet my last smoke that it's an American Express Platinum in daddy's powerful name."

"You mean the guy who did the space vampire films?" I tried to remember the titles, big-budget action films with more computer-generated imagery than live action. The vampire, a wicked female wired and implanted with biocompatible weaponry, worked as a covert assassin, killing in various imaginative ways a diverse array of intergalactic bad guys, most of whom had drinkable blood.

"Each of those space vampire films grossed more than two hundred million," Frank said, shaking his head at the casual way I'd summed them up. "We're up to number five in the series and Jason Starbal not only produced every one of them, he owns the original copyrights."

I opened the door for the Rott, looked at the name again. "But this says Stewart, not Jason Starbal. What makes you think he's related?"

"Look at the address."

The driver's license listed a number on Trousdale Place.

"North of Sunset," I said.

"Not just north of Sunset. Trousdale Estates."

Originally part of the largest private estate in the history of Beverly Hills, owned by the oil-rich Doheny family, Trousdale Estates wasn't developed for residential use until the 1950s and quickly became the address of choice for Hollywood's celebrity elite, from Marilyn Monroe to the great Elvis himself. Strict building codes limited the height of residences to a single story, and each estate was so completely walled and lushly landscaped many houses weren't even visible from the street. Celebrities value privacy and security almost as much as fame and money, and Trousdale Estates offered both, backed by a 24/7 private security patrol. I'd tried to photograph subjects on those streets before and failed. The neighborhood was a paparazza's nightmare.

I located the Starbal estate easily enough on the map and after dropping Frank at the office parked across from its heavenly-white gates, the Thomas Guide on my lap and my eye on the clock. The gate stood seven feet high, keeping a solid line with the brick security wall, also painted white but embossed with gold stars and partially screened by a row of evenly spaced camellias. To see beyond the wall I'd need to vault it or wait for the gate to open. A stakeout wasn't an option, not there. I commanded the Rott to stay and jumped the door frame, leaving my camera gear behind. Near the security wall I broke into a running start and leapt, grabbing the top ledge to pull myself high enough to see over the top. The drive cut through a loping green lawn and circled a fountain centered by a famous nude man, painted gold—a larger-than-life-sized replica of the Oscar award, symbolizing either Starbal's ambitions or unfulfilled career expectations because the Academy had yet to nominate his films for anything. Behind the arcing jets of water sprawled a white neoclassical mansion with glistening marble colonnades. Two vehicles were parked at the garage end of the drive, a new BMW M3 and a more modest PT Cruiser. I released my grip and dropped back to the ground. Something about the wall bothered me and I glanced back as I walked away, noticing I'd left black scuff marks on the immaculate white surface. Oops.

Ten minutes after I'd parked, a private security sedan rolled to the curb in my rearview mirror. The security guard who sauntered toward the Cadillac sported a mustache like a real L.A. cop but not the talk-back-to-me-you-die attitude. His job was to keep order in the neighborhood, not arrest people. When he neared the driver's door I glanced over my shoulder as though surprised and braced the Thomas Guide against the steering wheel. He glanced from my face to the map and back to my face. I tried to look helpless—hard to do when you have a nose stud and multiple ear piercings above the collar of a leather jacket, not to mention a hundred-pound Rottweiler in the passenger seat—and asked him for directions to a street on the other side of Coldwater Canyon Drive. He was happy to direct me and we parted good friends.

Most of the estates in Beverly Hills lie nestled into the Santa Monica Mountains north of Sunset Boulevard and because the roads are relatively few, residents leaving the enclave must funnel down the canyons to less than a dozen streets crossing Sunset; only a couple streets in Trousdale Estates led to Sunset, and of these two, Loma Vista cut the more direct route. Parking on the street north of Sunset is punishable by immediate deportation by the Beverly Hills Police Department. I cut across Sunset and spun the Cadillac into a two-hour parking spot facing north, toward the hills, where I raised the canvas top and set up camp. Lensing the face of every driver rolling toward Sunset from Trousdale Estates was going to be tedious, but I didn't see any other way to do it.

An hour and over two hundred cars into my wait the distinctive grille of a Crown Victoria slid into the spot behind mine, signature police lights folded toward the windshield. I lowered the Nikon into the camera bag, afraid Logan would emerge from behind the wheel and not much comforted to see Sean instead. I zipped the bag with one hand while I watched him approach in the rearview mirror.

"Do you have a minute to talk to me?" he asked.

I half expected him to tell me to put my hands behind my head and step out of the car, a more typical request when I'm approached by a cop from behind, but that was no more than my usual paranoia. I leashed the Rott, figuring this would be as good a time to take him for a walk as any.

"How did you know where I was?" I asked.

"Your colleague told me." He kneeled to take the Rott's head in both hands, wearing the same black leather jacket as the night I met him despite a late-afternoon temperature approaching the high 70s. He was as hard core about his leather as I was.

"You could have just called," I said.

"I wanted to surprise you." He stood and glanced around the street, the homes large but not palatial, a respectable upper-middle-class neighborhood with views of the obscenely rich on the other side of Sunset. "What are you doing parked here?"

"I heard a rumor Madonna was in the neighborhood."

We both knew it was a lie, just like we both knew the reason he hadn't called wasn't because he wanted to surprise me. When he caught me trying to peer through the dark barrier of his sun-glasses he folded them into his breast pocket, revealing a glance as warily curious as a coyote's. He'd missed his shave that morning, maybe two mornings straight, the stubble matching his jacket and the color of his hair. He looked pretty hot to me, I won't deny it, but I wasn't going to burn my lips on that flame, not twice. I gave the Rott the lead and followed him down the street, away from the traffic on Sunset.

Sean walked at my side, matching his stride to the Rott's stop-go rhythms, and asked, almost formally, "Did I say or do anything that led you to believe Rakaan was the chief suspect in the murder of your friend Christine?"

"Are you trying to play me?" I asked.

His head cocked to the side. "What do you mean?"

"I mean you lied to me last night, so are you lying to me again?"

The Rott stopped to sniff the skirts of an azalea bush as though they held some promise. I looked at Sean, trying to figure him out. He kept his head cocked to the side and he remained silent.

"You convinced me Rakaan was nothing special. I believed you when you said nothing was happening the night of the bust. I packed up and missed the shot." The Rott lost interest in the azalea and nearly pulled my arm from its socket when he bulled forward.

"I didn't lie to you about last night," he said when he caught up. "Sure, I may not have been completely forthcoming about Rakaan but I didn't know they were going in for the kill. From what I understand, the decision to move came in a hurry, possibly because someone tipped them that he was trying to dispose of evidence."

"My tip, you mean," I said.

"Officially recorded as an anonymous tip." He gripped my elbow to make sure I listened. "An anonymous tip that suddenly wasn't so anonymous after a certain reporter faxed a photo of Rakaan disposing of evidence."

Sean wasn't going to tell me outright what he really meant; he was going to make me work for it. I tried to read his eyes. Something both worried and irritated him. "You phoned Logan to report a tip from an anonymous source," I started.

He nodded. I was headed in the right direction.

"The next morning he gets a photo that identifies the source as me. He knows you know who I am. You know what I do. If I called you on the phone, you'd recognize my voice."

"'How the fuck is she an anonymous source, Tyler?'" Sean said in Logan's voice. "'You knew who she was. You lied to me about my own fucking investigation. Maybe it's a two-way leak. Is it?'"

I winced. I never saw it coming. Neither had Frank. I heeled the Rott and stood over his shoulders, holding him in place with my knees. "He thinks you fingered Rakaan for me?"

Sean nodded.

"I talked to Rakaan before Logan did," I said.

"I'm not the one who needs to be convinced."

"Logan is playing a mind game with you," I said, seeing clearly what was going on. "He didn't even consider Rakaan a suspect until I convinced one of my friends to talk about Christine's so-called therapy sessions. He knows people are willing to talk to me and it ticks him off. And Rakaan? A hypnotherapist with a Hollywood A-list clientele? It's like you couldn't invent a more tabloid-ready suspect. He's trying to back you down, that's all."

"Back me down or throw me off."

"We didn't send the video to him, we gave it to you. He's jealous already. Then the tip that leads to Rakaan's arrest comes through you. If he wants to take credit, he has to slap you down."

"That's the way I figured it too but that doesn't make life much easier."

The Rott squirmed between my knees. I told him to heel and walked him back toward the car, trying to figure why Sean needed to tell me this. Maybe he was telling me not to call him again and being far too subtle about it. "What was in the bag, the one Rakaan threw?" I asked.

Sean puffed out his cheeks, stressed by the question. "I don't know if I can tell you that."

"I told you it was there. The least you can do is tell me what was in it."

"I can't tell you that, not on the record."

"Then off the record."

He stared at me while we walked, and I thought he wasn't going to answer, but as usual I was misreading him, or maybe just reading him half right. "The bag contained bondage gear."

That didn't surprise me.

"His DNA showed on her body, didn't it?"

"Not just his," he said, and followed that stunner with silence.

"Rakaan isn't the only one involved."

"Hard to say what it means."

I spotted the high, sloping profile of a PT Cruiser speeding down Loma Vista—the same car I'd seen in Starbal's drive. I judged the distance to my car as I watched it veer left onto Sunset, headed toward the Strip. I'd need a helicopter to catch him. I turned back to Sean, who watched me with the same anxious interest I'd taken in the PT Cruiser. I forgot about Stewart Starbal for a moment and asked, "Who sent me the video? Not Rakaan."

"The maid," he said. "Nobody can find her. She came in once a week to clean. They think she found out what was going on, mailed you the copy because you were connected to Christine."

"Watch the video. Rakaan wasn't alone in that room. If you look in the corner of the frame while Christine is being strangled, you'll see a shadow cross the floor. I don't think it was the maid."

"I'm not going to watch the video because it's not my case to work. I didn't even keep a copy to look at. It's not my concern. It's Logan's."

I'd figured Sean had bigger eggs than that, and to hear him worry about case protocol disappointed me. I'd thought he was a little bit of an outlaw, like me.

"If you don't care one way or another, why did you come here?"

Sean crossed in front of me and stopped, his look sliding to pure worry. "If Logan is willing to slap me down, I figure someone like you he's willing to take off at the head. So be careful. I know you tabloid types are aggressive by nature—"

"I'm not aggressive," I said. "I'm persistent."

"You want to call it persistence, fine, the end result is the same. If you irritate Logan so much he thinks you're a problem, he's not going to show you any mercy. Trust me, he's capable of setting you up and cutting you down."

"I trust you," I said.

The single line that creased his forehead relaxed and he smiled like a male Mona Lisa. "I came for one other thing," he said, and when I asked him what, he slid into my arms and kissed me with such a fierce tenderness that I nearly felt too stunned to respond. Nearly. But not quite.

When he walked away I wondered if the kiss was off record, too.

16

WHEN I LEFT the apartment with the Rott that evening to run the wet sand at low tide I felt as though someone watched me from a distance, a feeling I imagine I inspired in others who felt no less uncomfortable about it than I did. While I ran, I wondered who would take the trouble and why. I thought about the rat that had been left on the seat of my car the morning before and whether I should consider checking into a motel for the next few days. I quickly decided against it. The Rott and I had faced down scarier situations than a dead rat. I'd installed new security locks the first week I'd moved in and the front windows were protected by quick-release security bars. I'd be easy to find at *Scandal Times* if someone wanted to get me badly enough. At the Santa Monica pier I broke the run to do stomach crunches and push-ups in the sand, then pushed myself a little harder than normal on the run back. Too many thoughts skied through my mind. Pain blotted them out.

Less than an hour after we returned to the apartment, the Rott alerted me with a bark that someone climbed the stairs. He hadn't quite learned the footsteps of everyone in the building—a difficult task considering the transient population—and I figured one of the half dozen illegal immigrants who lived next door had caught his attention, until the doorbell rang. I stuffed down the last bite of a Trader Joe's microwaved enchilada and walked to the door. The bullet shape of my father's skull lurked on the other side of the parabolic peephole lens. I opened the door too shocked to say anything except, "What the hell are you doing here?"

He dropped his head as though it shamed him to appear on his daughter's doorstep, asked, "Is this a bad time?"

"It's never a good time." I lacked the heart to block the door and stepped away to let him in. "Just curious, were you outside earlier this evening?"

He nodded, said, "I was getting ready to come up when you went out for your run, then when I saw you come back I thought I should give you a little time to wash up." He looked me up and down, edging toward the center of the room. "You sure took off like a jack rabbit outta hell. You in fighting shape?"

"Hope I don't need to be, but yeah, I am."

He smiled as though that pleased him and I half expected him to test my reflexes with a punch like he used to do when I was a tomboy, before adolescence turned me into a girl and he only tried to hit me when he was serious about doing damage. I'd never imagined him visiting me where I lived, and the sight of him in my apartment so spooked me I couldn't have aimed a camera without shaking the lens. "I don't keep beer around," I said. He liked beer, one of the reasons I couldn't stand the sight of it. "But I can pour you bourbon if you want."

"That would be good," he said.

"On the rocks, right?" I moved to the kitchen cabinets, where I pulled down two tumblers, put three cubes in his glass, one in mine. I hadn't meant to be polite but I couldn't think of any other way to pour myself a drink without being rude, which I also didn't mean to be. He was looking around the room like he was lost when I turned to hand him the drink.

"I thought you were making money." He glanced pointedly at the stained carpet and then reached to finger the splintered edge of the kitchen counter. "Maybe you could spend a little of it to move someplace decent."

"Tough to find a place willing to take an ex-con with a dog." I didn't tell him I'd been burned out of my last apartment and the landlord would rather shoot himself than provide a reference. I pointed to the dining table, cluttered with proof sheets and camera equipment, told him to have a seat. I wanted to ask him what he thought he was doing there but I kept my mouth shut. He'd tell me soon enough.

"Cassie told you she was coming to live with me?" He reminded me where I get my drinking habits by downing his drink in one pull. "I'm sure you don't think that's such a good idea."

I got the bourbon from the kitchen and refilled his glass, then left the bottle on the table. I didn't answer him one way or the other. Just because he had something to say didn't mean I did. He shook his head when the silence grew long, then stared at me for a clean sweep of the second hand, but he'd come to me for a reason and the days had long passed when he could force me to do anything. I finished my drink and poured another, just enough ice left in the glass to cool the bourbon.

"She needs family and she doesn't have any other choices," he said, watching me as carefully as I watched him. "Her stepfather? He's in prison, the no-good son of a bitch. From what Cassie tells me, he's not the kind of man wants to raise a kid anyway." He pointed his glass to the futon-couch on the floor of the living room and the bareness of the walls. "You'll admit this isn't a good environment for a kid, if you could take her, and the way I understand things, you're a single woman with a criminal record, you can't. Don't take offense now. I'm just tellin' the truth."

"Why do you want her?"

"She's my granddaughter," he said, astonished at the question.

"Her mother was your daughter and you didn't want her. I'm still your daughter and you don't want me either."

"That's not true. I may have been hard but I—"

"You don't like kids," I said, cutting him off. "You liked us well enough when we were too small to rebel. I'd even go so far as to say you weren't a terrible father, except for those moments you lost your temper. It didn't help that you lost your temper at least once every damn day."

He shrugged his shoulders, said, "Mary, I'm not here to—"

I banged the bottom of my glass on the table. Mary was the name I'd been born under, Mary Baker, a name I'd changed long ago. "My name's Nina," I said. "Call me by my name."

As we glared at each other over the table I watched the pupils of his eyes compress to pinpoints of rage, and I began the count to a beating I'd learned in childhood. I planted my feet on the floor and squared to face what had always followed his rage, as inevitable as the gravity behind a falling rock, but instead his eyes dulled and the rage subsided.

"Okay. Nina," he said, without irony.

"Cassie is fifteen years old. When Sharon was fifteen you slapped her around so much she ran away." My hands flew in unfettered gestures, hands that normally lay quiet no matter how great my agitation. "You did the same thing to me; the minute my body started to change you changed, too. Not that you didn't hit us when we were younger. Of course you did. But the way you hit us changed. You hit us like you really meant it. You hit us like you used to hit Mom."

"You think you're the only one who got smacked a little when you were young?" He wiped his eyes. No tears there. Just frustration. "My dad beat hell out of me when I was growing up."

"And that makes it right," I said. No comment. Just said it flat.

"No, damn it, it doesn't make it right, but it makes it what it is. I turn on the damn TV and all I hear is somebody whinin' about how much they suffered because their daddy did this or their momma did that and nobody loved 'em enough when they was growin' up. In the end it doesn't make a damn bit of difference, you play the hand you're dealt with, you just play it out, and sometimes you look back and you don't like the way you've played it, don't like the way you've done some things and it's too damn bad." He stared down at his hands cupped around the glass, machinist's hands cross-hatched with scars blackened by grease that never washed entirely clean.

Cut open his chest, I imagine his heart looked the same way.

"I didn't mean to be hurtful," he said, staring at his hands. "Sharon, I could never figure out how to handle her and so I did what I was trained to do, what I'd been told was the right way to raise kids, the way I'd been raised myself. When she started acting up I beat hell out of her. And you're right, I got harder on you when you turned teenagers, because the consequences in life change when you stop being a child. It's a lot easier to screw up your life at sixteen than nine."

"Sharon, she turned prostitute at sixteen and died a violent death before her fortieth birthday. All that beating, it sure stopped her from screwing up her life, didn't it?"

"I couldn't figure out how to do it any different." He blinked rapidly, as though dirt had been thrown into his eyes. "I thought she was just bad, she woulda turned out the same way no matter what I did. I knew I had a temper. Of course I knew that. I lost my temper and did some things I was sorry for, even then. But then both you and your brother, you grew up pulling in harness and so I thought I was doing things right. Sure, you were headstrong and didn't always mind but damn it you didn't give me one-quarter the trouble Sharon did. You were a good girl, right up until the time you snapped, went crazy on the world."

"What did you do then, Pop?" I asked.

He pulled his head back and shook it, confused.

"What did I do?" he repeated.

"I was a good girl." I stood from the table and backed toward the kitchen counter, taking deep breaths in a vain attempt to calm down. The Rott whined, like he sometimes did when I raged around the apartment. "I couldn't even breathe in the house without worrying you were going to lose your temper and start hitting someone. Of course you thought I was being good. You tie somebody up, stick a gun in their face and tell them to be quiet, you know what? They're going to keep their mouth shut. You keep someone that way their whole life, you think they're gonna have any idea who the hell they are? Of course you thought I was good. You thought I was good because I wasn't even there! The person you were looking at? That wasn't me. That was a hostage, a hostage to your rage and my fear."

"Mary—I mean Nina—I think you should—"

"Shut up!" I shouted, and the Rott barked in response. "You know the worst thing about it? About being held hostage like that? I actually loved you for it. Every day I breathed I knew I was alive because you decided you weren't going to kill me. And I felt grateful. I learned little ways to please you, things to say and do that would calm you enough so that you wouldn't hurt me or somebody else. Sometimes those little things didn't work and you beat somebody, but once you'd hurt us good you'd stop and then I'd be grateful again because I knew it could have been worse, a lot worse. When you gave me a split lip I saw that as you being merciful because you could've broken my neck."

I walked to the bottle and refilled his glass first, then mine. Maybe he was smarter than I gave him credit for. Maybe he knew what I needed to do. Because he didn't move. Not even after I poured his drink. He stared forward and down, at a fixed point on the table just beyond his hands.

"No wonder I went a little loco, eh?" I drank the bourbon I'd poured and made sure to leave the glass on the table when I backed again to the kitchen counter. I knew myself well enough not to leave a weapon like that in my hands. "This gets us back to the original question. What did you do? When I stopped being your good little girl and started to become the person I am. When I lost control of my life, my self, my anger."

He glanced from the fixed spot in front of his hands, looking like he didn't know the answer or was too afraid or ashamed to say. I waited, a step away from flinging open the door and throwing him out.

"Everybody sins and is sinned against in this world." He let go of his drink and turned in his chair to face me head on. "I sinned against you and I'm sorry for that. I ask for your forgiveness."

"I can't give it that fast. I'm sorry, I just can't. One apology doesn't change years of abuse. And one apology doesn't mean you've changed."

"I'm not going to insult you by claiming I've changed. But I've learned some things about myself these past months, since your mother died. Those things I've learned, they don't change who I am, but I don't see myself the way I used to. I've lost my pig-headed certainty about some things. I've changed that, at least. I used to think I was the strong one in the family." He lifted the glass to his mouth and breathed the whiskey before he drank it. "I was a real tough son of a bitch, the toughest guy on the street for thirty years straight, smacking around your mother and anyone else I felt like. What could be tougher than that?"

He looked at the palm of his right hand like he'd never seen it before and slapped himself so hard the bourbon splashed from his glass. I stepped quickly back, startled by the speed of the blow, and before I reached the kitchen counter he pulled his right hand into a fist and punched himself in the face, his neck snapping to the side with such force that he spun off his chair, the glass rolling from his hand onto the carpet. "Damn me," he said and hit himself in the face again, a left hook this time, then followed it with a right cross and another left, chanting "Damn me," with each blow, hitting himself the way he'd taught me to hit others, in a timed combination of punches, each one setting up the more devastating blow to follow, cursing himself as he hit his face again and again, the beast in him finally eating itself with the same brutality it had devoured others.

A good daughter would have rushed to stop him.

I let him go.

He stopped beating himself and wept, hiding his red and swelling face in the crook of his elbow. "I'm not so tough after all," he said. Blood streamed from a ring-cut above his right eye. "Your mother, she was the tough one in the family. All those years, she stuck it out. We had ourselves some good times, I'm not saying we didn't, and she knew I loved her. But I wasn't worth the spit in her mouth, the way I treated her. She could have left me but she didn't." He pulled the bloodied sleeve from his face and stared at me. "Why didn't she? Do you know?"

"No, I don't," I said.

I got rubbing alcohol and bandages from the medicine cabinet.

17

LONG AFTER THE alarm rang the next morning I remained in bed, my limbs like sand and blood, so heavy not even the Rott's nudging licks could rouse me. I counted the drinks I'd consumed the night before, thinking I might be suffering from a hangover, but I'd stopped drinking at three shots of bourbon, and even though I knew the world was not a fair place, I'd never suffered the indignity of a hangover without a good drunk preceding it. If what I felt was the effects of a hangover, it was a strange one, my breasts so tender they felt like they'd spent the night at a soccer match, playing the ball. I rolled into a sitting position and told the Rott to leave me alone while I summoned the energy to stand. My breasts always hurt the day before my period. I stumbled into the bathroom to flush my face with cold water.

The events of the day before still echoed through my head and I winced through a series of self-recriminations as I recalled the visit from Pop. Maybe my fatigue came not from an abuse of alcohol but an abuse of emotions, my hangover emotional rather than physical. Pop had left the apartment with neither my blessing nor my condemnation of his plan to bring Cassie to live with him. Most people would not consider a grown man beating the crap out of himself to be a successful demonstration of fitness to care for his granddaughter, but it convinced me of the depth of his pain and the sincerity of his remorse in a way that words never could. Pop was a man of action more than words. I trusted what he did more than what he said. I'd never seen him weak before and though it disturbed me, it didn't frighten me nearly as much as when he abused his strength. Cassie was going to move in with him no matter what I said. She was far tougher than I'd been at her age. I decided I'd roll with it. Maybe after the first few weeks she'd be the one beating Pop.

And what was Sean's kiss about? I dragged through the morning rituals of face, toilet, teeth, and hair wondering what he'd meant by it. He knew involvement with me was career suicide but he put the gun to his head anyway. Sean had worked undercover, Frank said. Most police officers lead dual lives, the often brutal world of law enforcement balanced with the more tender necessities of family life. Undercover officers added another layer of complexity, working and partying with those they intended to arrest. Maybe Sean was working undercover even now and the kiss had been given to inspire false trust. Deception was probably part of his nature. Sure, that's a good trait to have in a boyfriend. Based on my love history, Sean was just my type of guy.

Whoever drove the PT Cruiser I'd seen at the Starbal estate the day before was even slower than I to get started and it wasn't until midmorning that I spotted the car rolling down the hill from Trousdale Estates. I ordered the Rott to the floor and pulled out behind, pitching down onto Sunset Strip two cars back in the flow of traffic. The driver wasn't in much of a hurry. The Whiskey A-Go-Go slipped by on the left, Book Soup drifted past on the right; two blocks later the driver wheeled left and parked in the lot behind Sunset Plaza. I made him as the guy I'd seen at Christine's funeral when he stepped out of his car. I swung around to the back of the lot and parked. He locked the Cruiser and ambled across the lot, dressed in baggy jeans, red sweatshirt, and blue bucket hat.

Sunset Plaza is a favorite haunt of celebrities slumming incognito, a mile-long stretch of high-rent boutiques where the traffic on Sunset gears down to gawk and tables and chairs spill on to the sidewalk from ersatz European cafés with Beverly Hills prices. I played tourist with a telephoto lens and snapped a few shots at a safe distance. The green-and-beige awning of a Coffee Bean and Tea Leaf franchise hung over the sidewalk midblock. When the guy veered beneath it, I bagged the Nikon and followed him in.

I took a sidewalk table near the door and watched him order at the counter, wondering why he'd risked attending Christine's funeral if he'd been complicit in her death. Maybe his father's wealth, fame, and power gave him a natural immunity against fear. His size didn't match that of the assailant captured in the video. He better fit my image of the voyeur, the shadow flitting across the corner of the frame or the eye behind the camera. Or maybe he'd met Christine in a club, enjoyed a brief romance that he'd never fully given up, and now mourned her as his great, unrequited love. Maybe his resemblance to the man Charlotte McGregor had described at Starbucks was coincidence. The only way I'd find out was to ask. When he carried his coffee and a slice of cake to a dark corner table, I strapped my bag to the back of the chair across and asked if he minded sharing the table.

He checked me out, his eyes dilated and his smile tilting so dangerously over his perfectly dentisted teeth I thought it might fall off, an expression made even goofier by the bucket hat. Beneath his lower lip he was trying to grow a soul patch, and his blonde hair drifted toward his shoulder a little too unevenly, as though he'd instructed his hair stylist to give him a cut that made him look like he wasn't getting haircuts. He wasn't a bad-looking kid, just a little vacant, and I thought he'd probably been smoking something that morning that explained his appetite for chocolate cake.

"You're Stewart Starbal, right?"

He nodded, said, "Sure, whatever, sit down."

He reacted to things with the offbeat timing of someone going through life on a two-second time delay. He still didn't have a clue what I was doing there and was just stoned enough not to care.

"You don't recognize me," I said.

He peered at me and grunted as though slapped on the back. "The funeral. You were the one taking pictures."

"That's me, a camera wherever I go. Christine modeled for me. I took some photographs of her for a show hanging right now in the Leonora Price Gallery."

He fumbled off the lid to his coffee to let the liquid cool enough to sip, looking like he wanted to be awake for this. "You're her? The one who works at that tabloid? I remember she was talking about it. The show, I mean."

"You knew her well?"

He shrugged, meaning I could come to my own conclusion.

"I didn't see you at the opening."

"Yeah, whatever; I hope to catch it, maybe this week."

"I don't remember her talking about you. How did you meet?"

"At the house," he said.

"You mean your dad's house."

He shrugged. Whatever.

"What was she doing at your dad's house?"

"This is boring, man."

He closed his eyes like he was sleeping.

"Just think about how bored Christine is right now." I refrained from calling him a little twerp. "She's dead, remember? Strangled to death while drugged out of her mind on ruffies."

His eyebrows furrowed. I'd upset him. The lid to his coffee skittered away from his fingertips, and when he tried to snare it he nudged the cake with the back of his knuckles. "If I didn't care about her, I wouldn't have gone," he said, meaning the funeral. He pressed the lid back onto the cup, noticed the chocolate, and sucked on his knuckles before backing his chair from the table. "Sorry, gotta go. You want the cake, it's yours."

"You want to be famous?" I asked.

He gave his head a little shake and said, "What?"

I slid a fake mock-up of a *Scandal Times* cover story next to his coffee, a card with my numbers paper-clipped to the top right corner. "Starbal Spawn Mourns Strangled Starlet," the headline ran, above a telephoto black-and-white image of Stewart Starbal at Christine's funeral. Frank had composed the story based on the little we knew about his involvement. The text mattered little, Frank said. The Starbal name would sell the story.

"Arts photography doesn't pay the bills so I moonlight as a paparazza." I pointed at the cake. "You sure you don't want that?"

He looked at my finger, then the cake, said a stunned, "Go ahead."

I could have asked for his shirt and gotten the same response. The cake tasted delicious. I shoveled it down, suddenly ravenous. "You ever been to Palmdale?" I asked, my mouth full of cake.

He shook his head. "Not to stay."

"Ever flirt with somebody online from Palmdale?"

"Who knows where anybody's from online?" He continued to stare at the *Scandal Times* mock-up. "Do you mean they're actually going to publish this? In the paper?"

"Do you know a girl, Charlotte McGregor?"

"No. Why?"

I pulled the newsstand issue of *Scandal Times* from my bag, folded to Charlotte's photograph. I'd taken it in the desert after our interview, the late-afternoon sun setting her skin aglow. "She was given ruffies, raped, and strangled, like Christine. But she was lucky. They didn't kill her."

"No, I don't know her." He didn't look happy about being asked. "But I thought the cops, I thought they already arrested a guy? This Dr. Rakaan?"

"Get this." I leaned across the table like I was delivering secret information. "The killers filmed her rape and murder and the video contains evidence that at least two people were involved, not counting Christine, maybe three. Then somebody sent me a copy of the video as a way to brag about it. Can you imagine anything so stupid?"

I'd never seen someone more likely to melt under the table.

"Maybe they didn't want to brag about it," he said. "Maybe they had some other reason."

"Like what?"

"Whatever. I don't really know. I'm just speculating."

"Of course they were bragging," I said. "What else could it be?"

"Maybe they wanted it to stop."

He appeared so diffident that I doubt he convinced himself.

"I'm just curious." I stuffed the last bite of cake into my mouth and polished the fork. "Why did you go to the trouble of renting a car to drive to Christine's funeral? Why didn't you take your own car?"

He thought about that as though considering the question for the first time. "It wouldn't start," he said. "It was the battery or something."

"So you cabbed all the way to the airport to rent a car to drive to the funeral of a woman who . . ." I shook my head, not believing a word of it, but letting him know I was trying to stay open-minded. "I'm sorry, how did you know Christine? Did I forget, or did you not tell me?"

He didn't answer.

"Wait, that's right, at your dad's house. Was it one of those big Hollywood parties I'm always reading about?"

"I didn't say it was my dad's house, I didn't say anything, and if I did say something, I lied. I didn't know Christine, I'm just a vulture likes to go to funerals, okay?" His eyes, already reddened by whatever substance he'd been abusing, looked like they bled when he cried, the tears pouring from him like blood from a wound. He lurched to his feet, knocking aside the chair next to him before regaining his balance. "I gotta go."

"If you go, I can't stop them from printing this."

"You can print anything about me you want. It doesn't matter." He took a step toward the door and bumped into the table, then swung wide around the back of my chair, shoulders hunched as he stumbled out of the café.

18

NOTHING SELLS LIKE fame, the reasons for celebrity far less important than the fact of it. Since Charlotte McGregor's appearance in the pages of *Scandal Times,* two film agents had approached her about representation and casting people from three different productions had called to encourage her to audition. The phone hadn't been ringing off the hook, she said, only because modern phones don't have hooks. She'd driven into the city from Palmdale that morning to interview with one of the agents and to audition for a small part in a low-budget horror flick. She'd be happy to talk to us again, she said, because we'd brought her so much luck. When she emerged from her casting session, held in the office of a tiered, red granite and green glass building near the *Variety* headquarters on Wilshire, she appeared to glide across the paving tiles. A young man with stylishly tousled hair and a rumpled suit, worn without the tie, held the door open for her, grinned winningly when she thanked him, then wandered toward the courtyard fountain as though waiting for her to finish with us.

"Is that your boyfriend?" Frank asked. He butted his cigarette and returned the unsmoked half to the box, a frugal but disgusting habit that made his clothes reek like an ashtray.

Charlotte glanced back at the boy and smiled.

"Just someone I met at the audition."

"Big part?" I asked.

"Two lines and a scream when I get hacked by an axe." Her fingers traced the contours of the scarf around her neck and adjusted it's position. "I couldn't do the scream because of my throat, you know, it's not healed yet, so I'm not sure I'll get the part."

"If your boyfriend sees this guy," Frank said, the forced casualness of his tone a sure sign of something nasty to come, "won't he beat the crap out of him? I mean seeing that he's a violent criminal who's done time for assault. Or are you thinking he might beat the crap out of you instead?"

"You mean Randy?" Her voice cracked a higher octave at the mention of the name, as though she couldn't believe he'd intruded upon her new reality. "I haven't seen him in months."

"Is that why he tried to strangle you?"

"He never did that to me," she said, her hand again rising to her throat.

"Oh, you mean it was just other girls he strangled, not you."

"It wasn't other girls. He got into a fight with his girlfriend when he was, like, under a lot of stress."

"So he only strangles girls he likes, is that what you're saying?"

"Oh my God, you sound just like the cops." She glanced at me as though deciding whether to stay and fight or turn and run.

"He sounds like the cops because they just blindsided him," I said.

"The blindsiding, that was no big deal," Frank said. "It was the threat to throw us in jail that bothered me."

"So, what, it's my fault you didn't ask me about my ex-boyfriend?"

"No, it's my fault for being such a sucker." He didn't have his notebook out, jotting down her replies. He was angry and being a bully about it. "It's my fault because I believed you were being shafted by the cops. Because you looked like someone had victimized you. And because you look so completely innocent and believable I gave you the star treatment in the pages of *Scandal Times*."

"I am innocent," she said, the blush of indignation firing color to her cheeks. "I was victimized."

Frank tapped his thumb and forefinger together, mime for a running mouth. "Everybody's an actor in this town. What about the hits of ecstasy in your purse? You told us you didn't do any drugs."

"They weren't mine," she said.

"I'm sure the cops believed that when you explained it."

She crossed her arms over her chest, her mouth wrinkling to a sour turn. "Of course they didn't believe it. Not even I could believe the little fucker set me up like that."

"You mean your ex-boyfriend, Randy," I said.

"We were at the rave together and when the cops raided he dropped his stash in my bag." She tossed her head back and her auburn hair jumped from her shoulders. "I didn't even know it. He told me later he couldn't risk getting busted, because of his record. Can you believe anybody could be such an asshole? I was like, sure, just drop it on the ground then."

"But he didn't think they'd search you, right? Because you were a girl." I put on a boy voice, said, "'So what's the big deal, babe? I didn't know they were going to look in your bag.'"

"You read my statement? The one I made to the police?"

"No, but I've been around enough low-life characters in my life to know how it works. You wouldn't be the first woman to take a fall for her boyfriend."

"I hate it when you do this," Frank said.

"Do what?"

"Play the gender card." He fingered the half-finished cigarette from the pack in his pocket and flicked his lighter. "Men are shits. Women are abused innocents."

"It's true," I said, laughing.

"That's why I hate when you play it." He exhaled the smoke like a sigh of exasperation. "Show her the photographs, not that I'll believe a word she says."

I lifted a folder from my bag. I'd pulled a sheaf of random eight-by-tens from the trunk and stuffed them into the folder with a single shot of Stewart Starbal, the same way the cops show suspects in a mug book. "Tell us if you recognize anyone," I said.

Charlotte shuffled through the first few, squinting as though near-sighted or just serious about getting it right. "This one," she said, holding up a photograph of a sunglassed man holding a cup of coffee. "Ben Affleck, isn't it?"

Frank rolled his eyes at me, his way of calling me a moron.

I photographed celebrities for a living. No surprise one had slipped in by mistake. I told her to go through the photographs from beginning to end without commenting, then to go back and identify anyone she recognized. I watched her carefully, looking for the light of recognition and dreading it might be sparked by another misplaced celebrity.

She completed her pass through the sheaf of photographs and said, "Him." She flashed the telephoto image of Stewart Starbal. "This looks like the guy who bumped into my table, the day I was drugged."

"Looks like or is," Frank asked, blowing smoke.

"He's got the same hat, that's for sure, and it looks like the same sweatshirt, except not turned inside out. How can that be a coincidence?" She pulled the photograph closer to her face, then flipped it toward us and pointed to Stewart's soul patch. "He didn't have one of these things below his lip, at least I don't think he did."

"You don't think he did, or he didn't," Frank said. "Those are two different things."

"I spent thirty seconds with the guy," she said, and stuffed the photograph into my hand as though glad to be rid of it. "And after that, I was drugged out of my mind. He looks like him, but with different facial hair. I can't get any more certain than that."

"Easy enough to grow a soul patch," I said to Frank.

"Easier to grow the patch than the soul," he answered. "But I don't feel comfortable going to print with this." He thanked Charlotte for taking the time to talk to us. "I'm sorry if I offended you but I had to see where you're coming from," he said, the closest I'd ever heard him come to an apology.

The art of acting teaches how to lie with the seamless ease of the truth, and the pressures of trying to make a living at it can make its students masters of manipulation. Charlotte was polite enough to thank us before she clipped away, toward the fountain, the boy, and her new life. I believed her performance but didn't so certainly believe she told the strict truth—not that I disbelieved her either. That was my problem with actors. With the good ones—and Charlotte was good—I couldn't always tell when they weren't acting. If she'd told the straight and strict truth, we'd managed to further traumatize a woman who'd been victimized enough.

"If you're not doing anything, I know this convent nearby," I said to Frank. "Maybe we can go, beat up a few nuns."

"Hell no, nuns are tough," he answered, stubbing out his cigarette. "I went to Catholic school. The nuns, they kicked my ass plenty of times."

"What can you tell me about Stewart Starbal?" I asked.

"Second of four kids, born to Jason Starbal and . . ." Frank flipped back in his notebook until he found the relevant entry, ". . . Minnie, maiden name Minnie Mapes; her first marriage, his second. She was an actress when they met, nothing more distinguished than the usual cute girl roles, sacrificed her career to raise a family. She broke her neck in a slip-and-fall accident six years ago."

"Starbal the elder never remarried?"

"Dedicated his life to being a single dad, lots of high-profile dating, low-profile rumors before his wife died of being one of the names in Fleiss's little black book."

"You mean Heidi Fleiss," I said. She'd been arrested in the mid-'90s for running a call-girl ring to the stars. "No big deal there, half of Hollywood was in her book. But that's ancient history."

"So what if he had a wife and four kids at home, right? I'm not commenting on the man's morality here, just pointing out that if he was active as a married man we might speculate that as a long-term widower he's either found God or someone to replace Ms. Fleiss."

"You're so cynical. How old are the other kids?"

"Jagger, the oldest, he's a product of Starbal's first marriage, already has his own film production company called Illusterious Productions, oddly spelled."

"Oddly spelled how?"

"With an *e,* like a cross between *illustrious* and *mysterious.* Stewart is the second child. He's got a younger brother, Redford, who's already entered one of his student films in a festival, and a baby sister, Dalí, who plays piccolo in the youth symphony."

"Dolly?" I asked, not quite hearing it. "As in baby doll?"

"Dalí, as in Salvador," he corrected. "C'mon, I'll walk you to your car." It was an offer of convenience rather than courtesy; he'd parked his Honda on the street, his front bumper nestled against the Cadillac's rear. "You met Stewart. How does he look to you?"

"Stoned, clueless, and guilty. I figure he's the shadow in the video."

"A shadow, that fits. He hasn't made much of an impression so far." He jangled his car keys as he walked. "You do any kind of search for him and you come up with little more than references to his famous dad. Graduated from high school with grades that wouldn't have gotten him into USC, except Starbal senior is one of the school's most famous alums and biggest benefactors. Rumored to like video games and playing guitar, not supposed to be particularly good at either. No arrests, no trophies, no known girlfriends."

"He could always play for a slacker revival band," I suggested.

Frank stopped at the Honda, not quite making good on his promise to walk me to my car. "You're right, he's the perfect shadow. The kid, he casts no light at all."

19

NEPHTHYS ANSWERED THE door to her courtyard bungalow that night wearing a red kimono draped over black silk pajamas, an Oriental motif that complemented her Egyptian pageboy hairstyle and charcoal-lined eyes. She looked so beautiful, framed by the exotic fabrics that hung on the walls of the living room behind her, that I felt an admiring kind of envy, wishing I was the type of woman who felt comfortable lounging around the apartment in a kimono and silk pajamas and thought interior decorating involved more than tacking a poster to the wall. I carried a sack of Thai takeout from Chan Dara in the crook of my arm, the scents of spices and meats pinning the Rott to my side like a magnet.

"Is it okay if the dog comes in?" I asked. "He gets lonely in the car."

"You're both welcome." She tugged me into the kitchen by the sleeve of my leather jacket. Brightly glazed flowerpots stood in the wood-framed windows and in the few days since I'd visited she'd hung an entire community of Mexican Day of the Dead figures from the ceiling, the costumed skeletons dancing overhead like spirits. Halloween was months away; she'd hung them for reasons that had nothing to do with a seasonal celebration.

"Your apartment is so beautiful." I set the food down onto the counter and laughed, too self-conscious. "Listen to me, next I'll be asking where you bought your dishes."

"At thrift shops and flea markets, if you want to know. That's where we set decorators find a lot of our stuff." From the cabinet beside the sink she pulled out a mixed set of Fiestaware plates, bowls, and platters. "When I work on a film, I try to get inside the characters' heads. I think someone's personal environment says a lot about who they are."

"You just stuck a knife in my chest," I said, and turned to unpack the curries, rice, and noodles from the bag.

"Why? What's your apartment like?"

"A minimalist slum."

"I'm sure it's not that bad."

"It is. I don't decorate. I don't own things to decorate with. I used to, when I was, you know, before I went to prison."

"You're like a nun or monk." She hovered over the curry, her mascara-lined eyes widening at the promise of spice. "I noticed that about you right away. You wear your leather jacket like a habit, you know? Maybe I'll start calling you the warrior nun."

"I don't think I'm that moral," I said, a little offended.

"What I'm talking about has nothing to do with morality in any conventional sense of the word." She dished the curry into small bowls and set them onto the table, next to a larger bowl for the rice. "I'm an epicurean. I surround myself with beautiful, exotic things because I like them. They're my weakness. Not the beauty of gold and diamonds. I prefer a more occult beauty, the beauty of strangeness. If I had to choose between truth and beauty, I'd take beauty half the time. A beautiful lie sometimes is more attractive to me than an ugly truth—particularly in love affairs. You're more the Stoic type. You'd never choose beauty over truth."

"I don't think truth can be separated from beauty."

"Then how can you explain Christine? She loved the lie, loved to tell one, loved to live one, and that made her mysterious and oh so beautiful."

And it got her killed, I wanted to say, but didn't. I removed my leather jacket and strung it over the chair back. When she noticed the scars on my arm, she hit me with a questioning look that I quickly deflected. We toasted to the memory of Christine and devoted ourselves to the rich, red Panang curry and the complimentary tang of pad thai, a noodle dish leavened by bean sprouts, lemon, and crushed peanuts, the meal and our conversation lubricated by a supermarket Chardonnay. We talked about our childhoods—Nephthys had been raised in a middle-class neighborhood near Madison, Wisconsin, the daughter of an English professor and a failed performance artist—before we drifted inevitably to the subject of our toast. "It's hard to remember she's dead, sometimes," Nephthys said. "I'll sometimes have this thought, like, call Christine, and I have to check myself."

I didn't have that problem. When the people in my life died, they died. I didn't imagine them alive again, though I sometimes imagined avenging their deaths. "Do you remember, at her funeral, seeing a young guy, about twenty years old, wearing an expensive suit and looking like he didn't know anyone? Wait a minute, I'll show you." I zipped open my camera bag and pulled from the portfolio of photographs the shot I'd taken of Stewart Starbal wearing baggy clothes and a bucket hat at Sunset Plaza. "This is the same guy, probably the way he dresses most of the time."

She tipped the photograph toward the candlelight and nodded. "Sure, I remember seeing him there."

"Do you know him?"

She shook her head and passed the photograph back to me.

"Did she ever mention the name Starbal to you, Stewart Starbal?"

"Not that comes to me right away." She tilted her head and looked to the far corner of the room as she thought back. "Any relation to the movie guy? Those vampire-in-space movies?"

"His son. Any chance she met him through Rakaan?"

"If she did, she wouldn't have told me." She lifted the rim of the glass to her lips, eyes darkly luminous above the golden wine. "A lot of famous people were on his client list. He insisted on confidentiality and she kept it. It may sound weird to you, but they trusted each other."

"If you're strangling each other unconscious for sex play," I said, "I hope you trust each other."

"Why do you want to know about him?"

I told her about the shadow moving across the corner of the frame in the video of Christine's killing. She stood and carried the dishes to the sink, and when I bumped her aside to get to the dish soap she said we'd take care of the dishes later. "Grab your chair," she said. "We'll hunt back through her diary, see if we can find any kind of mention."

Nephthys carried the bottle of Chardonnay and our two glasses into the living room, where a length of red batik draped her computer.

I pulled a chair from the kitchen and placed it next to hers. While the computer powered up I refreshed our glasses with wine and caught her staring at the scars on my right forearm, one of the reasons I'm partial to my leather jacket and long-sleeved shirts. She softly gripped my wrist and examined in the monitor's cathode-ray light the rough-edged holes that crater my skin from forearm to biceps.

"What happened?" she asked, simply and without pity.

"An asshole burned me with a cigarette," I said. I let her take her time. I knew she'd have to ask, eventually, once she'd seen them. "He tied me to a chair. He'd smoke, ask me questions, and when I didn't answer or said something he didn't believe, he'd stub out his cigarette on my skin. Burning me with a cigarette, that was just one of the tortures he had in mind. The other wounds, they pretty much healed, but I'll carry these to my grave, along with the memory."

She kissed my arm once and let it go to navigate her browser to Christine's online diary. "Is that the one you killed? The one you went to prison over?"

"This wasn't the guy, no. This one was already dead when I shot him."

The screen flashed from page to page, Christine's quirky biographical data boxed on the left, her diary entries running on the right, each entry accompanied by snippets from those who read her diary and wrote comments, mostly compliments and expressions of support. Nephthys scrawled the cursor to an entry dated two weeks before her murder.

The bootiful christine got the guided tour of a bev hills manse today—I'm under blood oath not to give out the name but if I whisper in your ear Father of Intergalactic Bloodsuckers you'll know who I mean.

While my friend made a (wink-wink nod-nod) professional visit I got surprised by the bloodsucker spawn and their posse, they weren't even supposed to be there, but it ended up pretty cool cause they gave me the grand tour.

The place was effing HUGE, room after room, two pools, game room, private screening room, it's like, their walk in closets are bigger than my entire apartment. The boyz already have their own production company, maybe they noticed what a great poisonality I have, they'll make me the next great whatever when they get rich and powerful like daddy.

Too bad they were such spoiled brats.

One was kinda sweet. I gave him my phone number. When he called I told him I was already seeing someone but stay in touch. I'm such a slut/tease.

But at least I'm gonna have some fun.

"She didn't use real names in her diaries, so everything is in a sort of code." Nephthys highlighted the first sentence. "I wouldn't have guessed this without your hint where to look, but the Father of Intergalactic Bloodsuckers has to be Jason Starbal."

I reread the text, fitting the details to the little I knew about Starbal. Nearly every big-time producer who didn't have a place in Malibu lived in Beverly Hills, so that meant nothing. Stewart and one or more of his brothers could be the bloodsucker spawn, but then, Starbal wasn't the only producer to have kids. "The friend making the professional visit?" I asked.

"Has to be Rakaan," Nephthys said. "She usually calls him the boyfiend but she's coming really close to violating their confidentiality agreement so maybe she's just being coy."

"Impossible to prove," I said.

"Let's cross-check her screen name with the site's discussion threads to see if she mentioned it anywhere else. The threads are like the diaries, they don't disappear. So what we'll do is check the threads that were active then." She tapped at the keyboard and the screen flashed to a page containing fill-in boxes for keywords and member names. She typed *bloodsucker* in one and *Christine* in the other. A message appeared stating no results for the search. She typed in a different search term and asked, "When you said the guy who burned you was already dead, did you mean literally, figuratively, what?"

"Dead as in dig-a-hole dead. Somebody I knew, he shot him first. He was dead by the time I grabbed the gun, but that didn't stop me from emptying the cylinder into his chest." I refreshed Nephthys's glass and finished off the bottle in mine. "The guy who ordered me tortured, that's the one I killed."

She tried another search term and hit return.

"How'd you do it? You mind me asking?"

"He drove into a gas pump."

"How was that manslaughter?"

"I was on a Harley at the time, chasing him with a handgun."

"Did you shoot him?"

"Never got close enough. The gas pump blew up. He fried to death." I sipped at the wine, wondered whether I'd do things any differently if I could go back in time. "I was a lot angrier then, more desperate, too."

"Maybe this is one of the reasons you won't let Christine go, what happened to you." Another search term failed. She growled at the screen and tried again. "Most people would back away, let the police handle it. But look at you, you're actually trying to chase down whoever did this to Christine, just like you chased down the guy who had you tortured."

"I work for the tabloids," I said, not agreeing with her at all. "This kind of thing, it's my job."

"You choose your job." She whooped and pointed at the screen with the red lacquered nail of her right forefinger, having found something under the search term *brats*. "This is the day after she wrote about visiting the mansion, a thread called the daily rant, where people vent about things that piss them off."

The threads ran the opposite of blog style, oldest entry at the top and newest at the bottom, member names on the left and their comments on the right. Most people ranted about the daily annoyances of urban life, like bad drivers and people who don't clean up after their dogs, the screen names of the ranters more original than the rants. Someone ranted against Republicans for being rich and a poor Republican ranted against being ranted against. Christine's rant appeared near the bottom of the page.

anybody born not just with a silver spoon but a dinner service for twelve in his mouth. I just met some of these a**holes, and it's not just that they carry daddy's credit card, not just that they haven't worked a day in their collective lives, it's the arrogant attitude they have, that sucksess is their birthright. look in the mirror, a**holes, see the < l.a. bratS > written on your foreheads.

The passage revealed what Christine thought of the people she'd met—assuming they were the same ones she'd mentioned in her diary—but it didn't tell me who they were, not definitively. Nephthys gave me a little dig with her elbow.

"You don't see it, do you? Look again."

"What am I looking for?"

"Look in the mirror, that's the clue."

I knew the asterisks were used to write a swear word without actually writing it, but it wasn't until I considered the way another set of punctuation marks bracketed "l.a. bratS" that I saw it.

Write "la brats" on someone's forehead, stick him in front of a mirror.

It spells Starbal.

20

I DRAGGED THROUGH a beach run late the next morning, my pace on the hard, wet line of sand above the receding tide as slow as a jog on dry beach, the Rott racing far ahead, then charging back to urge me forward. I wasn't surprised at feeling tired. Nephthys was a champion nonstop talker, not someone who dominated conversation as much as pushed, prodded, and goaded it into movement whenever the words slowed; I hadn't navigated the roving traffic cops back to Venice until well past midnight. After the run I lay in the sand to stretch and do stomach crunches but fell into a light doze instead, luxuriating in the heaviness of my flesh on the warm sand. Losing a few hours of sleep didn't usually bother me, but my energy levels had been so low that week I was beginning to believe fatigue was my normal state. When the Rott stirred beside me I woke and sat up with the distinct feeling of being watched. The Rott felt it too, his attention divided between the gulls he thought it his genetic duty to chase and a man who had settled into the sand ten yards behind me.

On late May weekdays the beach at the end of my street attracts a scattering of sunbathers, mostly serious sun junkies and out-of-towners who don't have the two weeks to wait for full summer temperatures, and the beach offers wide stretches of open sand between bodies. The man behind me sat fully clothed, but that wasn't remarkable. People came in all styles of dress to sit or walk the sand. He did not look all that different from most of the denizens of Venice Beach, a mid-thirties man dressed in worn jeans and an old T-shirt. I might have figured he was on his lunch break had he been eating something, had he not selected a spot ten yards away from me when he could have settled another twenty yards distant and still remained thirty yards from the nearest person, and most of all, had he not been staring at me with all the obviousness of a hungry man a piece of meat.

I thought about staring back, one of the power plays allowed to women with big, ferocious dogs, decided I didn't need the trouble. I hugged the Rott and stood, but made the mistake of turning toward instead of away from him.

"That's a nice dog you have," he called, in that aggressive way some men have of making a comment about the weather a challenge.

I looked at him long enough to be polite, nodded, and walked toward the boardwalk. He had the dry, furrowed look and stringy hair of a long-term meth abuser, someone thirty-five going on sixty. Maybe he thought complimenting my dog was a good pickup line.

"I'd take extra good care of that dog, if I were you," he said.

The line and its implicit threat stopped me in the sand and I looked at him again, noticed the lightning bolts home-tattooed into the webbing between his thumb and forefinger. He'd done time, the tattoo said, and he'd done violence while doing time. I'd been an angry person when first released from prison, and had he said something like that to me in those first months I would have taken serious offense. He wasn't me. He needed to mind his own business. I'd matured since then. I thanked him for his concern and ran instead, calling the Rott to heel in a forceful tone he obeyed without hesitation. The guy didn't look in good enough cardiovascular shape to chase me more than a hundred yards, but tired or not, I took the long route back to my apartment, doubling back to make sure I wasn't followed, proud of my newfound maturity and self-restraint but not so mature I didn't fantasize kicking what remained of his teeth down his throat.

After I showered and dressed I worked on a shrine to Christine I'd begun after her funeral, tacking photos to the wall, one by one, as the mood struck me. Earlier that week I'd stopped in a church and bought a half dozen devotional candles in the style popular with Mexican Catholics, the ones in glass holders bearing the appliqué images of saints and the sacred heart of Jesus. I'd arranged the candles on a few upended fruit crates propped against the wall below the photographs. I planned to light them one night and say a prayer for Christine and all the others I've lost. I've always respected the atmosphere of belief if not the text preached from the pulpit. I guess that makes me half pagan.

When my cell phone rang I answered in a meditative mood, staring at a candid shot of Christine laying across Nephthys's lap. I didn't recognize the calling number or the caller, who, without giving his name, asked, "Where do the lost people go when they slip through the hole in the center of everything?" The voice reminded me of some of the drunk or stoned boys who used to call me when I was in my teens and early twenties, so slurred by one intoxicant or another that I struggled to separate the words from the ellipses.

"If they're Catholic, they burn in hell for eternity," I said.

Laughter keeled over the line.

"That's funny. I'm not Catholic."

"But you're lost."

"So lost I don't know the way home."

The silence at the end of the sentence made me think he'd severed the connection.

"What's going on, Stewart?" I pushed a tack in the wall, securing the top two edges of an image of Christine applying a sheath of red lipstick to her lower lip. "I know you didn't mean to hurt Christine. Where are you now? If you want to talk to me about it, maybe I can help."

"You don't know anything," he said, pain spiking through whatever substance numbed him. "The cops, they don't know anything, you don't know anything, everybody's wrong about what happened to her and so it's like, kick the shit out of Stewart time, you know? And who do I think maybe might understand what I'm trying to do? My family, everybody in my family hates me. My friends, they want to soak me in gasoline and burn me alive. And you, Christine's friend, the one person I thought might understand, even you want to beat the shit out of me. I didn't mean to hurt her? You know what I say to that? Fuck my family! Fuck my friends! And fuck you!"

The line closed like a stone door with me on the wrong side, staring at the cell phone in my hand and wondering if the call had been a hallucination inspired by Christine's shrine. From the sound of Stewart's voice he'd taken the kinds of drugs that dulled the emotions rather than excited them, but still he'd lashed out, unable to control his anguish and anger. Why did he think I'd understand? I'd done nothing to help him. Instead, I'd threatened to brand his name into the headlines of a tabloid newspaper. I looked at the return number left on the cell's call display—another cell phone by the look of the digits. In my experience hallucinations didn't leave evidence. I pressed call, let it ring a half dozen times, hung up, then called again after a two-minute wait.

The line connected to the sound of a sigh.

"Tell me where I'm wrong," I said. "You're right, I don't know anything, but I can't help you if I don't know what's going on."

He didn't answer.

"Where are you? I'll come over, see if I can help you out."

"It's too late," he said, his voice no more than a whisper.

"Too late for what? For Christine? Hell yeah, it's too late for her."

"Are you going to publish that story, the one you showed me?"

"It's negotiable," I said. "You need to give me something that points the story in the right direction if you want me to keep your name out of it."

He said nothing, the sound of his breath progressively slower and deeper with each inhalation, as though he was calming down or drugging out.

"Did you ever check out Christine's online diary?" I asked.

A sigh rustled through the line.

"She wrote in code about visiting your house, meeting some people there, maybe you and your brothers."

This time I didn't even get a sigh.

"She wrote you have a film production company. What kind of films are you interested in making?"

The high-pitched strangling sound he made might have been a laugh but it just as easily could have been a cry. "It's not my production company. It's my brother's, his friends'. I have nothing to do with it."

"Christine gave you her phone number, right? Said to call her when she broke up with her boyfriend. She didn't mention your name online, but I think that was you she was writing about."

"She was playing with me."

"No, she wrote you were pretty hot; I mean, why else give you her phone number? Where are you now? We should talk. I can help you. The police may be slow but they're not stupid. They'll figure it out sooner or later, however you're involved."

"See if you can find me . . ." he said, fading away, then snapping back, "I'm in the Marmont, third floor back."

"You're there now?"

"Mickey Mouse stamps," he said. "Remember those?" He made the strangling sound again. "Just wanted you to know my intentions were good."

The line banged and crackled as though he'd dropped the phone. I jumped into my boots, shouldered my camera bag, and nudged aside the Rott, who guessed the moment I picked up the bag we were rolling and bolted for the door. Chateau Marmont lay at the foot of the Hollywood Hills, a thirty-five-minute drive from Venice Beach in light traffic. Over a dozen Mickey Mouse stamps had paid the postage on the DVD depicting Christine's murder. Stewart may have lied to me about other things but he wasn't lying to me about the stamps. He'd either seen the envelope the disk had been mailed in or had mailed it himself. I called Frank and told him about the conversation while I drove toward Hollywood.

"Maybe he heard about Rakaan," Frank said.

"What about him?"

"They just arraigned him on charges of murder two."

"How is it second-degree murder? Accidental death during sex-play strangulation, that sounds more like involuntary manslaughter to me."

"Maybe they're hoping to start high and plead him down," Frank said. "How savvy is this kid, you think?"

"I'd say more clueless than savvy."

"Then he probably licked the stamps."

"And stuck them on with his thumb," I added.

"You want company at the Marmont?"

"I think you'd spook him."

"I could hang out in the bar."

"A tabloid writer in a celebrity bar?"

"I'd be as popular as spit in a sauna, wouldn't I?"

We agreed that he'd drive in from the Valley and wait in the lobby while I talked with Stewart. I couldn't imagine why a Starbal would be willing to go on record, but the story was worth the possible waste of Frank's time. The crime scene technicians would have dusted the envelope for prints and checked the stamps for traces of saliva that contained the licker's DNA, but these techniques wouldn't help the police track down a suspect unless his prints and DNA sample were in the database from a previous arrest. DNA alone wouldn't lead the police to Stewart.

Ahead of me, Chateau Marmont rose above Sunset Boulevard, a 1920s Hollywood imitation of the French Chateau style, it's faux-stone walls and black-tile mansard roofs scaling the steep hillside in multiple tiers. Other hotels in town offered more luxurious digs at comparable prices but none approached the debauched gentility of the place, like a shabby aristocrat with a nasty vice up his frayed silk sleeves, and you'd have to check into one of the meth-and-hooker motels branching off Hollywood Boulevard to find a more partying clientele. The Marmont had the rarest quality of all in a city as devoted to amnesia as Los Angeles: a sense of its own history, the legends of those who frequented the place not so much the supernovas of the present but those whose fame shot across the sky decades ago, from Greta Garbo through James Dean to Johnny Depp. I cruised past the hotel entrance—garage parking was for guests only—and found a two-hour parking spot on the street up the hill. I told the Rott the hotel didn't allow dogs, news he accepted with his usual resignation, settling down in the backseat with one of my old running shoes as companion and chew toy, to await my return.

I'd stayed in the Chateau once before, a splurge that lasted one night because of the narrow difference between the room rate and my life savings at the time. I molded a pair of sunglasses to my face, swept past the registration desk, and climbed the stairs like I belonged there. On the second-floor landing a tall and broad-shouldered guy tried to avert his face behind a curtain of flowing black hair as he clipped past, heading downstairs in a hurry, and at first I thought he might be a nouveau rock star who didn't yet realize nobody played incognito at the Chateau. I watched him round the staircase turn, and then climbed on toward the third floor.

Stewart hadn't specified the room number. Hotel management might not appreciate my visit if I knocked at every door, said, oops, wrong room. I slipped the cell phone from my jacket pocket, hit redial for Stewart's number, and listened at the nearest door while the line connected. Nothing. I moved my ear from door to door until I heard the chirp of an answering phone from a distant room at the very end of the hall, a half-inch crack of light between the edge of the door and the frame. The door had been left ajar. Nobody leaves their door ajar in a hotel. The doors close automatically. I glanced behind me, suddenly cautious of witnesses, and crept forward, the fight-or-flight injection of adrenaline already coursing through my body. A face towel lay wedged beneath the corner of the door, near the frame, as though it had gotten tangled beneath the door as it shut. I gently pressed my elbow against the wood and nudged into the room.

Stewart Starbal lay on the bed, propped up by a mountain of pillows at the headboard, the television across the room playing a syndicated episode of *Cheers* with the sound off. A bruise spread beneath his left eye like a storm cloud, and his upper lip swelled around the cut that split it. His cell phone lay chirping on the floor beside the nightstand. I severed the connection on mine and called out Stewart's name. He didn't move. The plunger of a syringe poked from beneath the corner of a hotel towel draped across the bed—his works. I hadn't figured him for a junkie. A dull blot of blood on the skin at the crook of his elbow marked the spot of the fix. I called his name again and leaned across the bed to touch cool skin at his throat. While I felt for his pulse I thumbed 911 into my cell phone. The bruises on his face looked less than twenty-four hours old, the blood pooled beneath the skin purple and not dried black, but he'd certainly been beaten before he talked to me. His pulse eluded me. I didn't think he was dead. The pulse on an overdose victim is often too faint to detect.

I remembered the young man I'd passed in the hall as I was climbing the stairs. The overdose didn't have to be accidental. Maybe Stewart had been dumb enough to mention that he'd been talking to someone who worked for the tabloids. I sprang out of the room and sprinted toward the stairs, telling the 911 operator a young man lay dying of an overdose in the Chateau Marmont. She could hear me running and told me to stay on the scene. They knew my identity the moment they picked up the call but I didn't care. I hung up and shouted to the lobby desk receptionist that they had a medical emergency in Stewart Starbal's room. His voice chased me down the stairs and out the door that led to valet parking. I dodged a couple waiting for their car and dashed toward the street in time to see a black

Corvette speed from a distant curb, far too fast to catch sight of the plates.

As I watched it go the phone rang in my hand. I checked the number. Frank's. He was driving in from the Valley, probably approaching the hotel at that very moment. I connected and didn't wait to hear his voice, shouting, "Quick, a black Corvette is leaving Chateau Marmont, can you see it?"

He didn't speak for a second, then cleared his throat.

"I'm waiting in the lobby," he said. "You ran right past me."

21

FRANK WAS SAVVY enough to distance himself the moment the staff descended. Luxury hotels may not appreciate guests inconsiderate enough to die in their beds but they've become accustomed enough to the ritual that most have protocols for handling it, and because part of the historical richness that made the Chateau Marmont a destination hotel involved the overdose of one celebrity or another, the staff had more experience than most. Suicide is one of the dirty realities of the hotel trade. Given that price is no object to those who plan to check out permanently, few with a valid credit card will choose Motel 6 over the Ritz. Once the staff ascertained that I was not a close relative of the victim, they shuttled me off to a spare room next to the office. The room served as a catch-all storage space, containing a bed, stacks of spare linens, extra file cabinets, and one reluctant eyewitness to an overdose. They were good enough to bring me a room-service carafe of coffee but refused my request to let me get my dog to keep me company.

Frank called a half hour into my vigil to report that the emergency medical technicians had packed up and left without a stretcher. When a homicide investigator named Mike Dougan from the LAPD's Hollywood station poked his head through the door, nobody had to tell me Stewart was dead.

"I was afraid it might be you." He flashed a name written on his notepad—mine. "Not too many people out there named Nina Zero."

"Nice to see you again, too," I said.

"Still got that toothless Rottweiler?" he asked, in a not unkind voice. I'd met Dougan the year before, during the investigation of my sister's death. The circumstances of that meeting hadn't been conducive to building any kind of friendship, but he treated me as fairly as his job allowed. With his push-broom mustache and a chest and belly so massive it made him look like he was always falling forward, he reminded me of a human walrus. I was even remotely happy to see him. I'd been dreading a conversation with RHD Detective Logan. Logan didn't yet know how Stewart connected to Christine. The Chateau was Hollywood's turf, so it made sense that Dougan answered the call.

"The kid, is he dead?" I asked.

Dougan mimed giving himself a shot in his forearm.

"Overdose. Nothing the EMTs could do for him."

"How long?"

"How long what?"

"Has he been dead."

Dougan stared at me, trying to read why I wanted to know.

"He called me an hour before I found him." I clicked open my cell phone and navigated to the number Stewart had called from—his cell phone—and the time he'd called.

Dougan crooked his neck to read the display, flipped back in his notebook to a number he'd scrawled on the page, and asked if it was mine. It was. He'd found my number on the call list of Stewart's phone. I wondered if Stewart called anyone after me but didn't have the courage—or audacity—to ask.

"I didn't see more than the one track mark on his arm," I said. "I figured him for a pothead, not a junkie. Maybe it was his first time."

"Shooting junk is like Russian roulette," he replied. "Sometimes once is all you need. And if the dose is hot enough, you're pulling the trigger on a fully loaded gun."

That implied suicide—or murder.

"Did he leave a note?"

"Junkies don't write notes, not even when they intend to overdose. Most of them, they start to commit suicide with the first fix, and it just takes them a long time to die."

"I didn't see other track marks," I repeated. "Just the one."

"If you know what a track mark looks like, then you should also know junkies can inject into the legs or hands."

"Did you check?"

His stare turned aggressive. None of my business.

I decided to impress him with my domestic virtues and poured him a cup of coffee. "I'm only asking because I was thinking he didn't administer the hot shot," I said. "Or if he did, somebody prepared it for him."

Dougan's mustache twitched and he pulled down on his face with the palm of his hand, exasperated. "I'd forgotten how much trouble you were. Maybe you should tell me how you met . . ." He glanced down at his notes for the name and his mouth drooped open. "Oh shit, it's not *that* Starbal, is it? The movie guy?"

"His son," I said. "I first saw him at the funeral of Christine Myers, a girl who modeled for me. After the funeral I tracked him down. I wanted to know why he'd gone, because nobody else there seemed to know him."

He absently accepted the cup when I pressed it forward.

"You recognized him?"

"We tracked him by his license plate."

"Why go to so much trouble to find a stranger at a funeral?"

"Because Christine Myers was murdered."

Dougan looked like a man standing upright in a landslide, nothing he could do about the earth sliding beneath his feet except try to ride it out and hope it didn't get worse. "This is the girl they found near Malibu, isn't it?"

I said it was.

"I should have known."

"A lot of murders in L.A.," I said. "You can't keep track of them all."

"I don't expect to. But seeing you is like seeing a buzzard circling overhead; you figure something's dead close by." Beneath his mustache his lips twitched in a failed smile, as though he half regretted the remark, then he dropped his head to sip at the coffee. He knew the comment wounded me and was decent enough to feel guilty about it. "He called you before you called him, right? Did he say why?"

"He wanted to know what happens to the people who slip through the hole in the center of everything," I said.

"What did he mean by that, you think?"

"That he was lost. At least that's what he said."

"How did he sound? His emotional state."

"Depressed and very stoned."

"Did he say anything or indicate in any way he wished to take his life?"

"He kept saying it was too late for things," I said, remembering the conversation. "But I'm not sure I buy this as suicide."

"Why not?"

"As I was coming up the stairs, I saw someone maybe come out of his room."

"You saw . . . somebody . . . maybe . . ." He drew out the words to emphasize the uncertainty of my statement. "Did you see someone come out of the room or not?"

"I can't be sure, but you saw Starbal's face, the bruises. Looks pretty obvious to me somebody beat him up last night."

"And decided that wasn't enough punishment?" His voice spiked with disbelief. "So he comes a second time to kill him?"

"I'm not saying that's what happened, just that it could have."

"Can you give me a description?"

"About six feet, broad shoulders, long and wavy black hair, mid-twenties. He turned his head away from me when he was coming down the stairs, so I didn't get a good look at his face."

"You know what I can do with this?" Dougan flashed his notepad to show he'd doodled a fat *0*. "Zero, like your name."

I decided not to tell him about the black Corvette. He'd ridiculed me enough. A guy leaves the hotel and drives away. So what? Even if he'd been in Stewart's room, that didn't mean he'd murdered him. Dougan was right, it looked more like a suicide than a murder, but the probability that Stewart had killed himself unsettled me far more than the idea that he'd been murdered.

"Here's what I don't get." Dougan flipped back in his notebook. "A guy you barely know, he's getting ready to give himself a hot shot, and out of all the people he can call to share his final moments with, it's you. I'm not hearing why."

The true answer to that was more complicated than I wanted to admit, at least to a homicide detective, no matter how much he was willing to tolerate me. "He knew I worked for a newspaper. I'm pretty sure he knew something about Christine's murder and wanted to tell me about it."

"Why you?"

"Because I knew Christine."

"But inconveniently someone murders him just before he can talk to you, doggone it." He wagged his head again, his smile tight and unbelieving. "I believe you're sincere. It's not your fault you have a hyperactive imagination. But from what I see so far, I also think you're wrong. Of course, if a strange thumbprint shows on the plunger of the syringe, I'll call you a genius." He flapped his notebook closed and tapped me on the shoulder with his fist, just lightly enough to be friendly. "Stick around while I check a few things out, will you? Shouldn't be too long."

Dougan lumbered out the door, slapping his notebook against his thigh. I watched him go with some reluctance. He'd left me alone with my thoughts, and my thoughts weren't good company just then. Whatever Stewart had wanted from me, I'd failed him. I'd been so emotionally focused on Christine that it never occurred to me to care what happened to him. Did someone set him up with a hot shot or had he shot up intending suicide? Judging by the timing of his call, a lethal dose flooded through his veins while we spoke. Maybe he'd expected to be found in time to be revived, the dose a way of tempting death rather than an irrevocable leap into it. Why else mention that he was staying at the Chateau Marmont? Then again, he might have figured he'd be dead by the time I arrived, the call less a cry for help than a final, damning comment on my lack of humanity.

Maybe I stuck to the idea that he'd been murdered because if he'd killed himself, I was complicit in his death. I'd threatened to publish his name in connection with Christine's murder, a final shove to someone already falling down. Maybe by calling me during his last moments he intended to let me know I'd driven him to suicide. I backed toward the bed and sat, feeling pretty rotten about myself. Certain things he'd said during our conversations jutted out at me. Even when I first met him, in the coffee shop on Sunset, no more than a mile away from the Chateau Marmont, he'd said it didn't matter what I printed. Maybe he knew even then that he was going to kill himself. Maybe he'd been going back and forth about it, trying to work up the courage, and I'd showed up with my smart little threat to expose his connection to Christine, hoping to pressure information from him, and I'd pressured him right over the edge. What else had he said during that first meeting? That whoever sent the disk of Christine's killing hadn't been bragging about it. He'd wanted it to stop. But if he knew who did it and wanted them to stop, wouldn't they kill him?

Dougan swung the door open and stared down at me with what looked like suspicion and pity, as though he'd overheard me talking to myself, a bad habit I'd picked up in prison.

"The bad news is I've been ordered to accompany you to Parker Center."

Parker Center. The administrative center of the LAPD.

"What's the good news, you'll loan me a quarter to call my lawyer?"

"You're not under arrest, that's the good news," he said. "Can you get your partner to come out from behind his potted palm in the hotel lobby, take care of your dog for you? We'll go in my car."

22

DURING MY LONG and varied career as baggage in the Los Angeles legal system I'd never been treated to an escorted tour of the Parker Center, the stone-and-steel administrative heart of the Los Angeles Police Department, eight stories of concentrated law enforcement rising from the eastern border of the Los Angeles Civic Center. Dougan led me up the elevator and through corridors to an interview room where all the chairs had seats and the table wasn't scarred by thirty-year-old cigarette burns. Most LAPD station houses are dives, not only unfit for the recently arrested, but overcrowded and decrepit places for the beat cops and detectives who work there, crammed into facilities designed for fewer than half their number. Though tarnished by the sun and smog, Parker Center was an aging beauty with good bones, built in the 1950s by the same architect who designed the Capitol Records building in Hollywood. Dougan asked me if I wanted coffee. I was experienced enough with cop coffee to say no. I expected the subtle humiliation of being made to wait and looked forward to the opportunity to lay my head on the table and nap, but before I could drift off Robert Logan broke through the door, a file under his right arm and a cup of coffee from Starbucks in hand. Dougan stepped in behind and waited for Logan to choose a seat before taking a chair on the opposite side, where he lifted the lid of his cup to let the coffee cool.

"If I knew Starbucks had a franchise in the detective's squad room," I said, "I would have asked for a cup."

"You had your chance," Dougan said, his smile so tight it looked braced by rubber bands. Under the circumstances, he didn't want to make the mistake of being too friendly. "Could you state your name and address for the record?"

Logan opened the file and glanced through his notes while I answered those and other basic questions, his left hand fidgeting with his tie, tugging at the lapel of his blazer, then brushing back and forth along the bottom fringe of his mustache until it finally anchored itself to the coffee cup.

"You have the right to remain silent and refuse to answer questions," Dougan said. "Do you understand?"

I recognized the phrase like the opening line to a familiar movie. "Wait a minute, why are you giving me the Miranda treatment?"

Dougan glanced up at Logan, who merely nodded.

"Simple precaution," Dougan said. "In consideration of your record and your current parole status."

"You told me I wasn't under arrest."

"You're not."

"Not yet," Logan interjected, and turned a page in his file.

"So I'm free to get up and leave," I said.

"I wouldn't advise it," Dougan said. "Anything you say or do can be used against you in a court of law. Do you understand?"

I glanced around, spotted the video camera not-so-covertly hidden in the upper right corner of the ceiling, realized they'd be taping this in the event I confessed or said something incriminating. "Of course I understand, but I haven't done anything."

"You have the right to consult an attorney before speaking to the police and the right to have an attorney present," Dougan said. "If you cannot afford an attorney, one will be appointed for you. Do you understand?"

"What's the phrase? No good deed goes unpunished? I can't believe you're reading my rights. I've cooperated with you from the start."

"Do you understand?" he repeated.

"Yes I understand, and I also understand that if I decide to answer questions now, I can change my mind and talk to an attorney anytime I want, and the way this interview is starting out that's going to be pretty darn soon."

Dougan double-clutched, realizing at the last moment that I'd already answered the next question on his pro-forma list, and asked,

"Knowing and understanding your rights as I have explained them to you, are you willing to answer our questions without an attorney present?"

I rolled my eyes. "I'm willing because you made it pretty clear it would be in the best interests of my continued freedom."

Dougan shook his head. He didn't like the answer but he could live with it. "I take that as a yes," he said.

Logan cleared his throat and looked up to catch my attention, his glance as friendly as a slab of concrete. A surveillance photograph of Stewart Starbal taken at Christine's funeral lay face up in the file spread open before him. "I've asked around and from what people tell me you're not a total scumbag, so I'm going to make the effort here to work with you on this. Don't screw up the chance. If you screw up, I'll make sure your parole is revoked. Is that clear?"

"I haven't done anything wrong and that's twice you've threatened me. I'm beginning to think you'll have my parole revoked no matter what I do." I winced, hearing myself speak. Just another self-pitying ex-con who can't get a break in the world.

"Do you know how to operate a video camera?" Logan asked.

"No," I said.

"I find that hard to believe, you being a hotshot photographer and all."

"What you find easy or hard to believe is none of my business," I said. "I can only tell you the truth and let you work it out for yourself."

He snorted at my mention of truth and decided to try again.

"Have you ever operated a video camera?"

"No."

"Have you ever met Dr. James Rakaan?"

"Once."

"Can you tell me about that?"

"I went to his office the day after I got the video of Christine's murder in the mail." As I detailed my encounter with Rakaan I tried to guess where Logan's line of questioning headed. He wasn't asking random questions. He'd arrested Rakaan and presumably was trying to build a case against him.

"You never met him before that?"

"Never," I said.

"If you're lying, I'll find that out."

"I'm not lying."

"Of course you're lying. The only question is where and how. Did Christine Myers ever mention Dr. Rakaan to you?"

"Never."

"I understand why you don't want to talk about it."

"Talk about what?"

"You're a photographer, she's a model, she and her boyfriend like to have sex together on camera . . ." He settled back in his chair and let his glance roam about the ceiling, as though imagining a scenario. "Sure, I can see how that would happen. The two of you get together, have a couple of drinks, she suggests you shoot some video of the two of them having sex together. Isn't that what happened?" He dropped his voice and leaned across the table. "It's not your fault Rakaan went too far. How were you supposed to know he'd kill her? It was supposed to be a harmless little game, dress up in sexy costumes and screw each other, something you could videotape for them—maybe you were even invited to participate when things got really hot. Only they didn't get hot, she got dead. Again, that's not your fault. You couldn't know that was going to happen."

"That's not only insulting, it's stupid," I said. "Obviously you've tripped to the fact that Rakaan and Christine weren't alone in the room, if indeed it's Rakaan underneath the rubber suit."

"How would you know they weren't alone if you weren't there?"

"It's obvious to anyone with a little camera experience, though it might have taken you some time to notice it," I said, letting him sort out the insult implied in that.

"Didn't you just say you never operated a video camera?"

He cocked his head to an ironic angle.

"A frame is a frame," I said. "Video or photography, same difference."

"So you could use a video camera, if you found one in your hands."

"Just like you could use your eyes, if you opened them."

To my right, Dougan sucked in his breath. I didn't worry about going too far. If Logan had any cause to arrest me, he'd do it no matter what I said.

"Toward the end of the video a shadow falls across the corner of the frame. Look closely enough, you'll see the shadow corresponds to someone moving in front of a light set for taping the action." I pointed to the photograph of Stewart Starbal so aggressively Logan leaned sharply back. "And I'm guessing the person who cast that shadow is staring up at you right this moment."

"Meaning you," Logan said.

"Meaning Stewart Starbal."

Logan picked the photograph from the file, glanced at it, and shook his head, his lips a terse blue line beneath his moustache, blue from repressed anger. "What did you say to Mr. Starbal that drove him to suicide?"

"I didn't call him. He called me."

"Did you threaten to publish his name in the paper?"

If he was looking for the hook to hang me on, that might be it.

"He called to tell me that he sent me the video," I said. "The video of Christine's murder."

"Sure he did."

"The dose that killed him was already in his veins when he called me," I said. "Check the time of the call."

"Looks to me like he called you and . . ." The snap of his fingers sounded loud as a firecracker. "Bang, he kills himself. No test will prove different. The timing is too tight. Were you trying to blackmail him? Said you'd splash his name across the headlines if he didn't give you what you wanted?"

"He called to tell me the cops didn't know anything," I said. "He told me nobody knows the truth about what happened to Christine, and then to prove it he identified the stamps on the envelope the video was sent in, Mickey Mouse stamps, something only the sender would know."

"And something he told only you, conveniently, before he died." He shook his head as though he regretted having to say it. "I'm sorry, but you're just not a credible witness."

"Did you find any DNA evidence on the envelope?" I asked.

"The envelope passed through the U.S. mail system. Of course we found DNA evidence. Some of it yours." He gave me a shrewd look, like he was setting me up for a right hook. "Your fingerprints were on the DVD, on the envelope, too. Did you see or touch that disk before it was mailed?"

"How could I possibly see it before I got it?" I asked. "You think I mailed the video to myself?"

"Interesting idea." He snapped his fingers at my chest. "Did you?"

"Of course not."

"Then why volunteer the idea, if you didn't do it?" He tilted his head toward Dougan, who sipped his coffee, watching the interrogation play out. "Did you hear me suggest that Miss Baker mailed the envelope to herself?"

"No, I didn't," he said, playing the straight man.

I stared at Logan, stunned. I'd walked right into it. But it wasn't a right hook. It was more like a head butt or rabbit punch, a reminder that he could play with the rules however he wanted, because for now he was both opponent and referee. "I think this is the point where I suspect you're trying to set me up and decide to ask for a lawyer to be present," I said. "I've cooperated from the start and you've rewarded me with nothing but outrageous allegations. Just do your job. Check Stewart Starbal's DNA against the samples found on the envelope. He's a twenty-year-old kid, not a criminal mastermind. He probably licked the stamps, and if he didn't lick the stamps, he left a strand of hair inside the envelope."

"He was a twenty-year-old kid," Logan corrected. "Now he's just a dead kid. And I gotta think part of the reason he's dead is because of you. And I'd love to just *do my job,* as you suggested, but everywhere I turn you're there, pissing all over everything. Reporters, they're bad enough as a breed, but tabloid reporters, they're scum, and yes, I do mean to include the paparazzos in that comment." He hunched over the table and motioned me forward, his tone changing from outright hostile to gruffly paternal. "So we're going to make a little deal, you and me, something that will probably keep you from punching the return ticket on your parole agreement. I say probably because I don't know what the current investigation is going to turn up. If you've lied to me, I'll find out, so you'd better tell me now."

I kept my mouth shut and my eyes open.

"Good," he said, accepting that as complicit agreement. He stared pointedly at Dougan for a moment. "A few people have spoken up for you and that's the only reason I'm willing to go this far. You're going to stay out of my way from now on. I don't want to hear your name in connection with another incident, not one. I don't want you talking to witnesses—or victims—and I don't want you taking their photographs, and if you do, I'll charge you with obstruction of justice. Do you understand?"

"Where's the mug book you want me to go through?"

He blinked, looked down at his file, shuffled some papers. "You mean the guy you think might have come out of Starbal's room, the one you supposedly saw on the stairs?" He looked up at me, almost couldn't hold back a smile. "We'll get back to you later if we come up with anything."

"I'm not talking about that," I said. "I'm talking about the other mug book."

"What mug book?"

"You know," I said. "The mug book of those you suspect cut the canvas roof of my car and dropped rat poison and a dead rat onto the front seat. I know you didn't ask me in here to threaten to violate the First Amendment rights of the newspaper I work with, the right to a free press, and my own personal First Amendment rights to free speech." I glanced directly into the video camera in the upper right corner of the ceiling. "And I know you wouldn't be stupid enough to threaten my First Amendment rights with videotape rolling. Because the newspaper I work with is very aggressive about protecting the rights of its journalists. I know, I'm only a paparazza scum, but the newspaper's lawyers insist I'm paparazza scum with constitutional rights, and believe me, you get sued by Elizabeth Taylor enough times, you become very good at protecting those rights. So I have to think you were just kidding around, we're all going to have a big laugh any second now when you explain it's all a joke, you really invited me here to inform me about the progress you've made in identifying the person who threatened my life."

Logan squared his collection of notes, forms, and photographs and closed the file. Some time ago, had a cop bullied me around like that, I might have hidden under the bed for a week. He backed away from the table and stood.

"If you're talking about the code 594 misdemeanor vandalism of your car, that's not being investigated by this division. I suggest you direct your questions to the front desk at the Pacific police station. Maybe they'll be able to help you." He turned for the door, remembered his coffee, and reached back for it. "Oh, and Detective Dougan here will escort you back to your vehicle."

I looked at Dougan, who stared straight ahead until the door closed with Logan on the other side of it. He shook his head, took a last sip of his coffee, and glanced at me over the rim. "Really? Someone stuck a dead rat in your car?"

"A dead rat, a box of rat poison, and a copy of *Scandal Times*," I said. "The rat was left under the story about Christine Myers, to make sure I got the message."

"I'll make a call to the squad room at Pacific, see if I can find out for you the status of the investigation." He stood and tossed his coffee cup into a trash can in the corner. "Come on, I'll call while I take you to your car."

Once out of the room, Dougan took a deep breath and winked at me, a gesture he wouldn't have dared while in sight of Logan or the video camera. "You're really a pistol, you know that?" He led me down the corridor toward the elevators that would take us down to the parking garage. "I thought Logan really had you on the run until you started firing back there at the end."

"I should feel lucky he didn't beat me with a rubber hose," I said.

Dougan laughed and stabbed a finger at the elevator call button, as pleased as I'd ever seen him. "Don't think that won't happen if you continue to get in his way. You're a helluva lot of trouble, but personally I think you're good people. You've always played things straight with me and I like your dog. I'm one of the last guys who wants to violate your First Amendment rights." He laughed again and shook his head. The elevator door whooshed open and he ushered me inside. "So please don't treat me to a speech on the Constitution when I suggest that if you have any vacation time coming up, now's a good time to take it."

23

ON THE MORNING Stewart Starbal died, Dr. James Rakaan was arraigned in Los Angeles Superior Court and formally charged with second-degree murder in the death of Christine Myers. Though precious little information is divulged by either side during an arraignment hearing, Frank heard from sources in the coroner's office that the severity of damage done to the victim's trachea, combined with the graphic video evidence, convinced prosecutors that a charge higher than manslaughter was both justified and winnable. The judge sided with the prosecution during the arraignment, and citing the defendant's financial resources, set bail at one million dollars, off the top end of the scale for second-degree murder. It could have gone far worse for Rakaan. The district attorney could have filed charges of first-degree murder, presenting the video as evidence that he'd tortured his victim before her death. Torture is murder with special circumstance, a crime that eliminates the possibility of bail and qualifies a defendant for the death penalty.

Hollywood relishes the fall of the rich, famous, or powerful—if only because it makes for more room on the ladder—but after a decent interval has passed they're more than likely to welcome the offender's return, because even more than a fall-from-grace drama, the town loves a good comeback story. You can be disgraced and loathed, but infamy is still fame, and once you're famous you're famous. Like death, fame allows no regress.

Rakaan could have called any number of former friends, clients, and supporters upon posting bail. A few even might have answered his call. But his voice was the last one I expected to hear when I answered the cell phone as I walked toward my car, parked on the hill behind Chateau Marmont.

"We need to meet, off the record," he said.

"Why would I want to meet you if it's off the record?"

"Because I didn't kill Christine."

"Right," I said, meaning *wrong*.

"I need to know more about the video," he said. "You're the only one who's seen it. I need to know why they think I killed her."

"Maybe it's because you were tying, strangling, and screwing her for fun and profit."

"Please," he said, his voice cracking. "I need help."

"Try consulting another past-life regressionist," I suggested. "Maybe you got away with murder in a previous life and it's catching up to you now." I severed the connection with a sense of satisfaction that soon deflated to regret. I didn't need his photograph for *Scandal Times* and I sincerely doubted he'd tell me anything that would lead to a major story, not when he insisted that our conversation be off the record, but he might let slip something that I could throw to the cops or into the paper. I definitely wanted to question him about his relationship to Stewart Starbal. Maybe Rakaan already knew Stewart had talked to me and the meeting was no more than an elaborate ruse intended to trick out what he'd revealed to me before his death.

I wouldn't learn anything by avoiding him.

When the phone rang again I answered it.

"I didn't kill Christine," he said, no beg in his voice this time.

"Next thing, you're going to tell me you really loved her."

"No, I won't tell you that. I was obsessed with her, yes, and in a not completely healthy way. She was my personal demon. And my relationship with her has not only very nearly destroyed everything I hold dear but soon will put me on trial for my personal and professional life."

"Don't be so dramatic," I said, getting angry at him again. "Christine is dead. You're not. Count your blessings. At the worst, you can plea bargain down to voluntary manslaughter, do your time, and get your freedom back in five years."

"Easy for you to say."

"As a matter of fact, it is." Ahead of me, something pink fluttered against the windshield of my Cadillac. "Okay, we'll do the meet. But if I hear any more of this self-pitying bullshit, we won't talk for long."

He listed a Los Feliz address, not far from where Nephthys lived. I supposed that he hoped to dodge the news cameras by avoiding his Hollywood Hills home. I glanced up as I pocketed the phone and identified the fluttering pink on my windshield as a parking ticket, my punishment for being taken to Parker Center for questioning and exceeding the two-hour limit. As anyone who lives in Los Angeles knows, parking tickets have been added to death and taxes as the only certainties in life. I stuffed it into the glove box and drove down the hill.

The address Rakaan listed connected to the top floor of a duplex built in Spanish Colonial style, the red tile roof and beige plaster walls shadowed by the gracefully splayed fronds of fifty-foot palm trees, and closer to the ground, the red-and-yellow beaks of birds-of-paradise poked from their green sheaths as though watching me climb the stairs to the front door. Rakaan answered my knock so quickly that I suspected he'd been hovering at the peephole. Lack of sleep bruised his eyes to swollen slits, and he stood with less than the square-shouldered certainty I'd seen on first meeting him. Jail does that to people. He wore the suit he'd been arraigned in, a slick gray model with a creased, slept-in look, top shirt button undone and the tie gone. He stepped back from the door as though aware he carried the stain of murder and that I might want to keep my distance from him. I carried my camera bag slung over my right shoulder, the top conveniently unzipped to allow easy access to the crowbar I'd stashed inside. As a rule, I try not to let my curiosity make me too stupid, and meeting a man accused of murder, alone, was a risk that approached stupidity, if it didn't embrace it.

Rakaan walked toward the couch in the living room. The late-afternoon sun filtered through gauzy white drapes, casting a soft light onto the hardwood floors and beige leather furniture, a spray of yellow roses reflecting from the glass-topped coffee table. I followed him into the room, and when I first spotted the framed candids of Christine on the fireplace mantel I guessed the apartment might have been their love pad, until I noticed that photographs of Tammy held equal pride of place. I realized then that I stood in Christine's apartment. I asked him what he was doing there.

"You didn't recognize the address?" He settled so heavily into the couch it looked like he was falling backward into water. "I thought you'd know it when I gave it to you."

"She's never been here," a voice called from the kitchen.

I backed toward the fireplace, surprised in a not particularly pleasant way. Tamara carried a lacquered tray loaded with pastries into the room and set it on the coffee table.

"At least, Christine never told me you visited, but still, I thought you'd know the address or recognize the number when Jim called you."

It took me a moment to realize she was referring to Rakaan by his first name. She excused herself and slipped back into the kitchen to attend to a whistling tea kettle. I thought back to my brunch with Tammy, earlier that week, and remembered how she'd fled the table when I'd mentioned details of Christine's relationship with Rakaan.

"Now I understand why you claimed you never loved Christine." I moved to a leather chair backed toward the window. "Was Tammy in the room when you called me?"

"I suppose I should expect a tabloid reporter to be cynical." His tar-dark eyes were no less opaque for being sheened in soft, draped light. He watched me carefully as I sat, his glance seeking out mine with a fixed willfulness that soothed as it sought to overpower, like a shot of cognac—or heroin. "Tamara was the one who convinced me to call you. She tells me that you're more interested in the truth than in making sensational headlines, not that I believe it."

"If Tammy is interested in the truth, what is she doing with a huckster like you? She didn't even know about your involvement with Christine. And I think you're far less interested in the truth than in worming your way out of a murder conviction."

He found it difficult to catch and hold my gaze in the shadows the light from the window cast across my face and he sighed, frustrated. "Yes, I acted unethically, but I didn't hurt her, not ever, and I certainly didn't . . ." He shuddered so convincingly I couldn't tell whether it was a trick of theater or came naturally. "I didn't strangle her to death."

"You slept with her," I said, just to get him to admit to facts.

"Yes," he said.

"And you engaged in, what would you call it, acts of sado-masochism?"

"We didn't whip each other, no, but we did explore the, ahh, boundaries of sexuality and cruelty." He wiped at his mouth with the palm of his hand while his gaze sank inward. "Christine and I were too attracted to each other's dark places. You know how, in the early stages of a relationship, two lovers circle each other, looking for advantage? Ours quickly became a spiral and it sucked the both of us down. What started out as therapy became madness, a mutually assured destruction of the self. At first I thought I could help her. But I didn't realize that our dark places were so powerful, not until we'd already fallen in, and by then, I didn't care." He leaned forward and shoved one of the pastries around the tray. "Our roles quickly reversed. She began dominating me as part of her regression therapy, the idea being that she needed to work out her fear and anger at having been murdered in her past life. Some of the things we were doing, she could have killed me, and I wouldn't have objected—in fact, I placed myself completely in her hands. She always seemed to know just how far she could take me out before bringing me back. I'll tell you this, though. Whoever killed her either did it intentionally or knew nothing about erotic strangulation."

Tammy carried another tray from the kitchen, balancing a Chinese teapot and three delicate, bowl-shaped teacups. Herbal tea, she announced, a special blend compounded to promote flows of soothing energy and enhance feelings of harmony.

"And the worst thing is . . ." Rakaan scooted aside and placed his palm on the couch, inviting Tammy to sit next to him. "I hid my relationship with Christine from the one I really do love, the one who is proving to me what love is really about by standing with me now."

Tammy blushed over the teapot as she poured the golden-colored liquid into each cup. It seemed to me she was a girl easily fooled by love, but then, so many of us are. I felt a sudden impulse to dump a pot of scalding tea on Rakaan's private parts. I resisted. "Why do you say the person either meant to murder her or didn't know what he was doing?" I asked.

"My lawyer told me that a ligature was used." He coughed once, uncomfortable, and calmed himself with a sip of tea. "That enough force was applied to damage her larynx and trachea. Ligatures really have no place in erotic strangulation because they can damage cartilage, and they hurt. The idea isn't to cut off someone's air, it's to reduce the flow of blood to the brain." He pressed the fingers of one hand against the side of his throat, just below the jaw line. "You do that by pressing here, against the carotid artery, not full force, not to close it off completely, but to slow the blood, just enough to get high on the lack of oxygen and make the sex more intense."

"Don't try it on me, please," Tammy said.

"If somebody was using a ligature, they weren't trying to make the sex better for her, I can guarantee you that." He dropped his hand gently on Tammy's thigh. "He wanted to enhance his own feelings of domination and control and he didn't care if he had to hurt her to do it. Tell me, what did the video show?"

Never in my young life had I imagined I might one day hold a conversation about erotic strangulation over herbal tea with a past-life regression therapist. As a paparazza working for the tabloids, I suppose I should have been inured or at least accustomed to such things. I wasn't.

"The video showed she was strangled with a strap, from behind," I said, giving him a fraction of the information he wanted. "How did you first meet Stewart Starbal?"

"Who?"

I couldn't tell whether his ignorance was genuine or faked. I repeated the name. He said he'd never met him, never even heard of him.

"Jason Starbal, then," I said.

Rakaan glanced at Tammy and asked, "Isn't he the producer of those intergalactic vampire films, the ones that star Milla Jovavich now?" He received a confirming nod and turned a shrug toward me. "I've heard of him, and certainly I've seen a few of his films, but we've never met."

"Then what were you doing at his house in Trousdale Estates?"

"What house?"

"The one with the statue of Oscar in a fountain in the front yard."

He laughed, relieved, and grabbed Tammy's hand.

"I think I'd remember that," he said. "I was never there."

"Christine's diary says you were."

"You mean the thing she kept on that semipornographic website?"

"She wrote that she accompanied you to Starbal's estate, where you had a session with Jason Starbal while she met his kids."

His face shot through with blood, and he tossed Tammy's hand aside to sweep his palm across his long, black hair. "That bitch was not supposed to use my name on that site. That was our agreement."

"She didn't use your name. She wrote in code."

"She lied," he said.

Maybe blood and sweat rushed to his skin because he was having an allergic reaction to the tea, or maybe he realized how deeply her diary incriminated him, or maybe he just lied badly. I didn't care enough to stay and get the definitive answer, not if it required hearing Christine slandered. I thought I already knew. I had enough problems controlling my temper. If I stayed, I'd be tempted to straighten his teeth with a crowbar brace. I thanked Tammy for the tea and walked out the door, Rakaan's protests chasing me down the steps. I planned to call her later to describe the video's brutal contents, let her know what to expect by trying to show Rakaan what true love was really about.

24

I SPOTTED HIM when the Rott and I left the apartment that evening for a run on the beach, a man reading a newspaper in the passenger seat of a dingy white Toyota Tercel, parked on the side street opposite my apartment building. The way he held the paper to his face, he could have been studying the results of the previous day's running at Santa Anita, looking no more suspicious than any of the other idlers who frequented the neighborhood. I tried to enjoy the run, the Rott racing after seagulls as though he thought he had a real chance of catching one this time. One thing I'd learned from the Rott, the familiar amusements are often the best. He never tired of chasing after seagulls, no matter how often they eluded him, just as I continued to pursue life, liberty, and happiness, no matter how often they eluded me. In the distance, a violet haze shimmered above the curved blue line of the Pacific, the last remnants of a day that had extinguished itself an hour earlier. Then I realized why the man reading the newspaper had bothered me. It was too dark to read a newspaper.

I'm accustomed to watching others, not to being watched myself, and the feeling creeped me out more than frightened me. We ran the back streets home, the Rott leashed at my side, and approached the Tercel from behind. A tattooed hand dangled out the passenger window, smoke wafting from a cigarette clipped between two fingers. Twin lightning bolts arced across the webbing of his thumb. I jogged up the steps and opened the door to the apartment without glancing back.

While I laid out my camera gear on the kitchen table, I considered the probability that the man lingering outside my apartment had chosen a spot next to me on the beach that morning for reasons other than chance. I threaded Tri-X film into the Nikon's spools and sealed the back, then picked up the 500-millimeter lens. The lightning-bolt tattoo was a variation of the Nazi SS symbol, used by white power groups in prison to signify the carrier has done violence to a minority. I'd crossed the color line while serving time, making friends with like-minded women whose skin tones shaded darker than mine, but I didn't think he'd come to exact revenge for betraying my so-called race. I left on the kitchen light and moved the camera and tripod to the draped window in the darkened living room, knowing from experience that the eye is naturally drawn to light. I loosened the telescoping legs on the tripod and raised the camera to window height, then nudged the lens past the corner of the drapes.

The world in extreme telephoto is a disorienting place, and staring through a 500-millimeter lens is like seeing one piece to a jigsaw puzzle. I made out a roofline and part of a wall, then tilted the lens until the sidewalk across the street came into view, close enough to read the number written on the curb. I nudged the camera up and to the side until the Toyota appeared, the ex-con still in the passenger seat, his eyes tracing a line to the kitchen window while smoke drifted from the lit cigarette dangling from the corner of his lips. I ran off a couple of shots to capture the Tercel's license plate, aware that his face, barely discernable through the lens, would be lost in shadow no matter how fast the film. I dragged a stool from the kitchen counter into the living room and sat with my eye near enough to the viewfinder to see when he moved, and then I waited.

Ten minutes after he'd stabbed out his previous smoke the inevitable collision between time and nicotine happened again, the flick of a lighter illuminating his face while he lit another cigarette. I pressed the shutter and held it down. The camera went into overdrive, clicking off three images a second for two seconds. The flick of the lighter probably wouldn't make for a flattering portrait, but it would illuminate the face of the smoker enough to identify him. I made sure the security chain was engaged and braced the stool beneath the door handle as an extra precaution, then stripped down to shower off the run.

The fact that someone watched my apartment made the shower a short one. Even with the stool jammed beneath the handle I felt vulnerable and jumped back into my street clothes before the water dried on my skin. I knew the police could put my apartment under surveillance—Logan's way to convince me to mind my own business—but didn't think the watcher had ever worked for the police except as a jailhouse snitch. Maybe he was the guy who'd dropped the rat in my car. That made sense but didn't reveal what he had against me or why.

The door chime caught me beneath the hair dryer. I wrapped my right hand around the baseball bat I kept in the bedroom closet—the closest thing to a weapon I'm allowed under the terms of my parole agreement—and moved toward the door. When the Rott sat a few feet from the threshold, his expression rapt, I knew I wasn't in immediate danger. I checked the parabolic peephole just to be sure, saw Sean Tyler's face bending away from the lens. I opened the door.

"Getting ready to hit my fastball?" he asked when he saw the bat.

"Somebody's staking out my apartment," I said.

The flicker in his eyes read as fear and guilt.

"I'm pretty sure it's not the department," I added, conscious not to turn my head toward the watcher. "White Toyota Tercel parked across the street. I've got a camera set on telephoto by the window."

He nodded as though thinking it over.

"Aren't you going to ask me in?"

Maybe I'd been wrong about the flicker. I stepped away from the door. Sean paused just long enough to give the Rott a quick scratch and slid over to stick his eye to the viewfinder.

"I don't see anything," he said.

I nudged him aside and bent to look. Shadow and pavement showed through the lens, an empty parking space where the Toyota had been. "I just got out of the shower." I ruffled my hair to demonstrate it hadn't yet fully dried. "He must have moved while I was away."

He nodded as though he almost believed me.

I thought about the coincidence of Sean's knock and the Tercel's disappearance, decided it wasn't a coincidence at all. "What kind of wheels are you driving tonight?"

"Same crappy car last time I saw you."

"Crown Victoria?"

"I drive what the motor pool gives me."

I showed him the webbing between my thumb and forefinger.

"The guy in the car? He has twin lightning bolts tattooed right here."

He took that as an excuse to grab my hand, as though he needed to inspect my skin to tell me what I already knew. "You figure he's a con?"

"He knew the car," I said. "That's why he took off."

"You mean the Crown Vic?" He dropped my hand, leaned over to peek around the edge of the drape. "Sure, if he's a pro, that's possible. You write down the plate?"

The scent of him went to my head like a cocktail, the mix of leather, cologne, and body oils a fragrance as uniquely Sean's as his face. I told him I got the plates on film, and backed toward the open kitchen because I knew what would happen if I remained within kissing distance of him. "I was thinking he was maybe the guy who left the dead rat in my car," I said.

"What dead rat?"

I lifted a bottle of Jack Daniel's and two tumblers from the kitchen cabinet. "Somebody cut a hole in the Caddy's ragtop, dropped a packet of rat poison and a dead rat onto the front seat."

"Why didn't you tell me?"

"I reported it to Logan." I showed him the ice-cube tray, pulled from the freezer. "I didn't think you'd want to get involved."

He raised his forefinger to signal one cube and said, "Somebody threatens you, I want to know about it."

"Really?"

He nodded.

"Somebody threatened me just this afternoon. Right in the middle of Parker Center." I slid the tumbler across the Formica countertop and told him about my interrogation. Sean sipped at his bourbon and shifted away from me while I spoke, a sign, I thought, of personal conflict. He couldn't help me without damaging his career and I didn't think either of us wanted that. It would be simpler just to end it, no matter how I felt about him.

Strong emotions can ruin lives.

I told him that Dougan recommended I go on vacation for a while.

"You might take that suggestion a little more seriously," he said.

"I don't get vacation time, not paid anyway."

"Maybe just a few days, then." He leaned against the kitchen cabinet, staring at me. "Up the coast, somewhere like Morro Bay, or maybe inland, to Death Valley. This time of year, it's just hot enough to drive away the tourists, but not so hot to keep us from hiking the desert."

I took down the bourbon in one pull and poured another, dropping an ice cube into the tumbler to slow my drinking. That he asked shocked me. Whenever I'm surprised my curiosity engages, just before my natural suspicion. I didn't know who Sean was, any more than he knew me. "You worked undercover, how many years?" I asked.

"Seven," he said, continuing to stare at me. "Not straight. I was working organized crime, vice mostly. I'd go under, then come back out, wait for another operation, go under again." He smiled. "I was good at it, but the burn rate for that kind of work, it's astronomical."

"You develop a taste for hiding things while you worked undercover, or were you always that way?"

The question puzzled him at first, but then he considered it, and the implications disturbed him. "A little bit of both, probably." He wandered from the kitchen into the darkness of the main room and spoke with his back to me. "My father is a religious man. A deeply religious man. I'm not. Never was, not even as a child. I grew up pretending I was something I wasn't. Went to choir practice, Bible study, I was even going to study for the ministry until I crapped out for lack of vocation, discovered I couldn't fake faith anymore. I'm not saying I'm a Godless atheist . . ." His laugh was short-lived and bitter. "But I don't have the special relationship my father has. In fact, I probably get along better with the devil." The kitchen light glittered in his eyes when he glanced back at me. "Present company excluded."

"I'm not the devil you think I am," I said. "But I am poison to you. Makes me wonder why you're here."

"The good things in life are always a little poisonous." He sipped at his drink and stared at me so intently I felt myself falling into his eyes. "You like whiskey?"

I nodded.

"So do I." He shook his head at how much he liked it. "Too much will kill you. Alcohol poisoning. You chug a fifth of ninety proof in an hour, you'll die. But just the right amount, your heart beats a little faster, your skin flushes, you feel warm all over."

"The trick is knowing when to stop." I walked toward him, the kitchen light throwing my face into shadow, forcing him to peer to read my expression. "Two drinks, three or four, you feel fine, but then a little time passes and you start to fall faster than you climb, and you don't want to let it go away, that high, that wonderful high, so down go five, six, seven, and then it's not so much fun anymore, it all feels sour no matter how much you drink, and if you drink eight, nine, ten, you'll suffer like you're gunshot."

Then I kissed him, because he'd been truthful, yes, and because if he knew I was poison, it was his responsibility and not mine to know how much would be fatal, and most of all I kissed him because he smelled so incredibly delicious. As good as he smelled, he tasted better. I took him down like that second drink, the good one that's sipped and savored and not bolted like the first, the one that brings the flush of joy to your skin and makes you just the right amount of high so that when it's done you immediately want more, even if more is too much. I backed him into the bedroom. We had time and privacy this time, and savored each other in long, slow kisses and teasing caresses, praising with lips and fingertips the skin we found beneath the leather and cotton we unwrapped from our limbs. We had been barely conscious of making love the first time, too rushed to be fully aware of what we were doing until it was done. We wanted to make up for it the second time, allowing the sexual tension between us to build one kiss, one caress, one dispensed article of clothing at a time, pleasure washing over us in sustained moments of ecstasy as mind-altering as any drug. In the depths of my pleasure I heard the phones ring, first the land line and then the cell, but I was somewhere else by then, floating and darting through a sexual landscape I had always sensed existed but never fully experienced before, a landscape so thrilling but terrifying that I bit him in fear and anger and he bit me, pain fueling passion to streak us into bliss.

The door buzzer jarred me from the postcoital languor of Sean's arms and the excited bark of the Rott yanked me out of bed. When I told Sean I'd check out who rang I was speaking to a moving target, his clothes already bundled against his chest as he slid toward the bathroom door. Maybe that was one of the lessons working undercover taught him, to move fast when uncertainty threatened.

The Rott was stutter dancing by the front door when I emerged from the bedroom, behavior that meant he was excited to see whoever stood on the porch. The bell rang again, the sustained burst of someone leaning on the button in frustration. I tucked a T-shirt into my jeans and put my eye to the peephole. Cassie stood on the opposite end of the parabolic lens, a backpack bigger than her torso towering over her shoulders. I snapped open the door, shocked to see her.

"I was waiting at the bus station for you," she said, her voice so high and stressed that the Rott matched it with a whine of his own. "Why didn't you come pick me up?" She tilted forward to keep from tipping back down the steps under the weight of the backpack.

I pulled her over the threshold and lifted the pack from her shoulders. "I didn't even know you were coming in today."

She wilted once released from the pack, her knees buckling and her shoulders curving into her chest. "I wrote you two postcards!"

I lay the backpack against the wall and winced, not from the weight of the pack but from guilt. I hadn't checked my mailbox. "I'm sorry, but I haven't been around the past couple of days and when I got in tonight I forgot to get my mail."

Cassie glanced at the closed door to the bedroom, her shoulders still huddled toward her chest, and she lifted her chin, sniffing at the air. "I'll bet you forgot." She made an angry but insincere grab at her backpack. "I'll be going now. I don't want to get in your way. I can take care of myself."

I wrapped my arms around her and before she could run or protest I hugged her, hard, telling her that she was staying, and that was final.

"I even called," she said, letting me hug her. "Didn't you hear my voice on the answering machine? Why didn't you pick up?"

"I keep the sound turned down. My parole officer has a habit of dropping in unannounced and I don't want her to monitor my calls."

I released her when the door to the bedroom opened and Sean emerged.

"Thanks for letting me use your bathroom," he said, wiping water from his hands. "The grease from the carburetor was impossible to get off. I hope I didn't leave too much of a mess in there." He grinned at Cassie, the white of his teeth against the black stubble on his jaw making him look like a friendly wolf, and reached out to shake her hand. "You must be Cassie. Great to meet you. Your aunt is incredible, know that?"

"This is Sean, a friend of mine," I said.

"A friend, sure," she said, but she took his hand.

"Don't think too badly of me, but I gotta go. Maybe we'll get a chance to talk later, after you've settled in." He winked at me. "Walk me downstairs?"

I nodded, glanced into the bedroom through the open door, noticed the bed had been freshly made, the bedspread stretched taut to conceal that we'd been twisting the sheets into knots for the past hour. An affair with a cop who once worked undercover had some advantages. I told Cassie she could move her backpack into the bedroom and followed Sean down the stairs. "That was pretty fast thinking," I said at the bottom.

"I didn't want to embarrass you." He turned to give me a lingering kiss goodbye. "I'm going to light a fire under the detectives in Pacific, see if I can get them to assign a patrol to your house, keep an eye on you."

"Sure," I said, not believing that would do any good.

"If this creep shows up again, give me a call, I'll cruise by to check him out. And if you need help with the plates, let me know and I'll see what I can do."

One of the few things I've learned in life about men is that the ones who want more than a midnight fling intrude upon a woman's life in ways that attempt to be helpful, offering to fix things that may or may not be broken, or to buy things that may or may not be needed. It was sweet of him to offer and I thanked him for it as I waved him into his Crown Vic, but I didn't intend to allow that, not yet. I could take good enough care of myself. I didn't want to set him up with false expectations of my dependence or his indispensability, figured that would work better for both of us in the long run.

When his taillights turned the corner I detoured around the staircase to key the box that held my mail, stuffed beyond bursting with neighborhood circulars and other species of junk mail. Cassie's postcards lay at the bottom of the box, one a photograph of Sid Vicious and the other of a saguaro cactus in full bloom, a hurried scrawl announcing the arrival date and time of her Greyhound bus on the backs of both. An oversized envelope stood pressed against the rear of the box, the blank back facing outward. I pulled it free, crumpled the circulars into a ball, and it wasn't until I started to climb the steps that I noticed the Mickey Mouse stamps affixed to the upper right corner of the envelope.

"He's a thief, isn't he?" Cassie asked when I keyed through the door.

"Sean? He's a cop."

I tossed the mail onto the kitchen counter.

Her mouth gaped. "You're kidding. He's too sexy to be a cop."

She followed me into the bedroom, where I opened the door to my closet and pulled a pair of cotton gloves, normally used for handling negatives, from a roll-out bin of photo supplies.

"What are you doing hooking up with a cop?" she asked. "Aren't you afraid he's gonna, like, bust you? Or is it like he's already got something on you, some incriminating evidence, and so he's extorting you for sex?"

I shook my head as I walked back to the mail on the kitchen counter, astonished that she'd asked the question.

"Mom said that kinda stuff happens all the time."

Her mother had worked as a call girl for nearly ten years, before getting into the confidence game. She'd spoken from experience, I was sure, but I didn't want Cassie to think all cops worked like that. "Sean is a friend." I glanced down to slit the lip of the envelope with a kitchen knife. "I hope a good one, but I don't know that yet, and the questions you're asking aren't helping me to figure that out."

"Sorry," she said, as though she didn't mean it.

I turned the envelope upside down and shook out a photograph of a dark-haired man in his thirties, his well-fed face and elegant suit failing to conceal an ice-pick coldness in his eyes and lips sculpted to a permanent sneer.

"My God, it's Andrew Luster," Cassie said.

Heir to the Max Factor fortune, Luster had been arrested the year before on eighty-seven charges of poisoning and date rape. It didn't surprise me that Cassie recognized the man by his photograph; my niece knew criminals like other teenage girls knew boy bands. When the police raided his beachfront home in Mussel Shoals, eighty miles north of Los Angeles, they found scores of videotapes of Luster having sex with unconscious and seemingly drugged women, most of whom had yet to be identified. The search warrant had been issued after a woman accused him of spiking her drink with GHB and raping her. Neither Frank nor I had been assigned to that story but its sleazy blend of spoiled wealth and drug-forced sex had proven irresistible to *Scandal Times,* which gave it extensive coverage. It had been rumored, in the pages of *Scandal Times* and elsewhere, that Luster was part of an international ring of playboy millionaires who traded date-rape tips and video clips over the Internet. I flipped the photo by the edge face down onto the counter. A message of some kind had been scrawled onto the back of the photo in a spidery hand that matched the lettering on the envelope: *J, O, K, E (no S).*

"Who's it from?" Cassie asked, craning her neck to read the message.

"The guy who mailed me the video, the one showing Christine, you know, what happened to her."

"You mean Stewart Starbal?"

I thought about it for a second. We hadn't yet printed Starbal's name in *Scandal Times* and I hadn't mentioned his name to her. I hadn't even met him until she'd already flown back to Phoenix. "How did you know that?" I asked.

"You're not the only one knows about Christine's diary," she said. "I've gone through all her posts a dozen times. I caught the trick with the mirror, 'LA Brats' spelling 'Starbal,' just like Nephthys did."

"You talked to her?"

"Sure, all the time. We're like, girlfriends."

"Suicide Girls, it's an adult website. How did you get in?"

She gave me a scornful look, said, "Please, I've been doing illegal stuff since the day I was born."

"You talked to Nephthys about this?"

"Her roommate Tammy, too," she said, nodding. "I've probably talked with them more than you have. When I heard Stewart Starbal's name on the radio tonight I figured it had to be him that sent you the video, then suicided himself from guilt. You think he helped kill Christine?"

"I don't know, but I think he knew who did." I stared at the letters on the back of the photo, trying to figure out what they meant, then glanced again at the envelope. He'd mailed it two days before.

Maybe if I'd checked my mail, I would have asked the right questions when Stewart called and he'd still be alive.

"'It's a joke, no shit,'" Cassie said, pointing a ragged purple fingernail at the *S* in parentheses. "Maybe it's like a tribute band, you know, Luster is some kind of role model."

I flipped the photo face up and stared into Luster's face.

"If it's a joke, I don't get the humor in it," I said.

25

DETECTIVE ROBERT LOGAN knocked on the door to my apartment at nine o'clock the next morning, responding to a call I'd made to report that I'd received evidence in the mail pertaining to the murder of Christine Myers. I stood in the kitchen, backed against the sink with Cassie beside me, and watched a lawyer in a navy-blue suit that cost more than my entire wardrobe open the door to let him in. The night before, when I'd called Frank about the envelope, he'd insisted I have a *Scandal Times* lawyer present when Logan came calling. He wasn't being sentimental, he said; they'd take away my camera if they arrested me and without my camera I was useless to the paper. The lawyer resembled the jack of spades, hair slicked back over a Botox-smooth face and a cold, knifey look in his eyes. He'd appeared at my door a quarter of a billable hour before Logan, and we'd spent the time discussing the various strategies I might use to keep my mouth shut.

The lawyer introduced himself as legal counsel representing the weekly newspaper, *Scandal Times,* and its work-for-hire employee, meaning me, then backed away from the door to let Logan inside the apartment, gesturing with the manicured nail of his forefinger toward the envelope, lying on the dinette. Logan watched the man's hand until it tired and dropped, a subtle power play to demonstrate he wasn't going to be ordered around by a libel lawyer, then moved toward the envelope, which I'd sealed in a zip-lock bag. "You opened it?" he asked, glancing up at me.

"Ms. Zero opened it as she would any piece of mail addressed to her," the lawyer said, "and when she determined that it contained material that could be evidence in a criminal investigation, she placed the envelope in a secure container and notified the authorities at the earliest possible opportunity."

Logan stared at the lawyer, annoyed, and lifted the baggie by the corner. "What makes you think this is evidence?" he asked, peering at me over the tips of his fingers.

I opened my mouth to speak, remembered I wasn't supposed to say anything until the lawyer approved, and when he nodded, once, an expression of caution focusing his eyes, I said, "The Mickey Mouse stamps on the envelope, for one; those are the same stamps on the video of Christine's killing somebody mailed me."

"If you knew it was evidence by the stamps," he said, letting the plastic bag swing one way and then the other, pinched between his fingertips, "why did you tamper with that evidence by opening the envelope?"

"Ms. Zero didn't notice the stamps until she'd already opened the envelope and looked at the contents," the lawyer explained. "Only after she opened the envelope and noticed it contained a photograph of Andrew Luster did she think to check who may have sent it."

"Who?" Logan asked, as though not hearing right.

"Andrew Luster," I said. "Accused of date rape up in Ventura County."

The baggie swung to a stop and he dropped his hand to his side.

"I'll advise the lab that biological material containing Ms. Zero's DNA may be present in the contents," he said to the lawyer. "The Los Angeles Police Department requests that the publication of any of the material in this envelope be formally cleared with us beforehand."

"That's not the way it works," the lawyer said. "The editors at *Scandal Times* will notify you of what and when they plan to publish, but they're within their rights to publish with or without permission."

Logan made a point of looking at me long and hard, then turned his head to the lawyer. "Remind the editors that cooperation is essential in this case. If they publish this without clearing it with us first, the consequences will be severe."

The lawyer interpreted that to be the threat it clearly was and asked, "Exactly what consequences are you referring to?"

"Consequences to the criminal investigation, of course," Logan said, gracing the lie with an easy smile. "Did the girl come within a foot of the envelope, either before or after it was opened?"

Cassie shook her head, purple-limned eyes enthralled with fascination or fear or a combination of both.

"I suppose if the techs find a purple hair, we can figure it's hers." He laughed as though demonstrating he wasn't such a bad guy after all, then turned and darted away, his shoes clipping down the concrete steps.

Later, when we loaded her backpack and the Rott into the Cadillac, Cassie asked why Logan hated me so much.

"You picked up on that?"

"It's only, like, obvious."

"Obvious how?"

"Just a vibe I had," she said, "that if nobody else was around, he'd beat the shit out of you. I got the same feeling sometimes before, you know, when the cops would come visit my mom and one of the stepdads."

We drove the freeways toward Pop's house with the top down, the radio blasting hip-hop above the roar of wind. Cassie's observation about Logan reminded me that her youth was deceptive when it came to understanding all things criminal. She'd been a passive participant in her mother's cons while still in diapers; when money had been short, Sharon had painted red dots on her daughter's forehead and begged cash from sympathetic men, claiming she needed to take her baby to the hospital. Most of those born into the criminal life continue the family trade well before reaching maturity, often with the self-awareness of a falling brick, and though Cassie might just as easily return to the short cons of her youth, she had an intuitive grasp of the way criminals think that might allow her to build a better life for herself. She was naturally wary of cops too seeming to know how they regarded the people around them, particularly those they suspected of criminal behavior, and unlike her aunt, she understood that it was far healthier to avoid rather than confront the law.

I hoped she might take advantage of her natural gifts by studying law, maybe become a lawyer, and promised myself I'd support and encourage her if she tried, but that may have been more my fantasy than her reality. The night before, she'd stripped down to a boy-beater T-shirt to model her new tattoo, a suggestively winking blonde Betty Boop inked above a banner etched with Christine's name. I hadn't seen too many tattooed, purple-haired lawyers in my travels through the legal system.

I'd hoped to drop off Cassie and her backpack that morning without having to engage Pop in conversation more involved than a wave goodbye, but he stood waiting by the open hood of his Dodge Ram pickup truck and ambled over to meet us before I could take my foot off the brake. He carried a Styrofoam container of hamburger in a grease-stained hand and gave the Rott a good whiff of it before he helped Cassie lift her backpack from the rear seat.

"Brought that toothless dog of yours a little something to eat," he said. "Why don't you come inside, I'll put it in a bowl and he can chow down."

The Rott was all for accepting the invite. I had to grab on to his collar to keep him in the car. "Busy day," I said.

"Sure, I understand, just long enough to feed him the grub."

He gave the meat a little wave to further excite the dog, then he lifted the pack with one hand onto his shoulder and ambled up the walk toward the front door. The thing weighed over fifty pounds, yet he'd picked it up like a sack of groceries. He may have been nearing retirement age but he was still strong, and because he'd figured out a surefire way to get me out of the car, he was craftier than I'd given him credit for. When I let go of his collar, the Rott bounded out of the car and caught up to Pop's heels before whirling around to let out a single bark to encourage me to follow.

Pop had cut the waist-high weeds since my last visit and scattered a seed mix that sprouted small, green blades amid the stubble. The front of the house had been scraped of peeling paint, blotches of white primer soaking into patches where the surface had been stripped down to the wood. Next to the front door he'd painted three strips in varying shades of brown, and he turned to point them out as he crossed the threshold. "You got a good eye for color, let me know if you like one of these," he said, then merged into the interior shadows of the house, the Rott bouncing in behind him.

I stepped into the living room and held my breath as though the air Pop lived and breathed might contaminate me. He continued through to the kitchen, a shadow moving in the open archway, where he clattered a metal bowl to the floor and knelt to feed the dog. Cassie emerged from behind the refrigerator door with a can of off-brand cola, popping the top and swigging away while drifting toward the kitchen table. It shouldn't have felt so sinister to me, that house. My mother had lived there most of her life. I'd loved my mother, even if we didn't talk all that often or well. I let myself breathe in the odors of an aging man living alone, the greasy smell of fried foods mingling with dust, mold, and sweat.

"Hey, what's this?" Cassie asked, hovering over the kitchen table.

"Just an old photo album. I uncovered it the other day while cleaning out some stuff." Pop boosted himself up with a helping hand on the dog's back. "It's got some pictures of your mom in it, back when she was younger than you are now, thought maybe you'd want to see them."

She flipped the album to the first page and squealed, delighted. I edged into the kitchen, watched her bend over a color snapshot of her mother as a baby. My parents owned an early '60s Kodak Instamatic back then, the 126-cartridge film so simple to load that it made photography push-button easy. It wasn't much of a baby shot, angled straight down to Sharon swaddled in her crib, her fat, baby face mottled a sickly blue and purple, the film's chemistry not stable enough to hold the colors true.

"God, she was ugly!" Cassie said.

"All babies are ugly," I said, speaking from the experience of having photographed thousands of them.

"Except your own." Pop leaned his knuckles onto the table and craned his neck to look. "At least, that's what your mom said, that you were all beautiful babies, though to tell the truth I tended to think none of you were much to look at until you got to two or three years old."

I inched toward the kitchen table and looked over Cassie's shoulder while she flipped the page to a montage of baby Sharon photographed in the living room or the front yard, the wheels of Pop's 1959 Chevy Apache pickup truck the most common background. I'd been born ten years later, the image of my sister as an infant as strange to me as it was to Cassie. The beauty of my mother at age twenty-four in a one-piece bathing suit, two years after giving birth for the first time, shocked me. In all my memories she was old, face prematurely lined by worry and abuse, her body settling down and spreading out to a lumpy shape by the time she'd reached forty. She'd been young and beautiful until the years of children and marriage wore her down, my brother, Ray, coming when Sharon graduated to polka-dot dresses, and then, six years later, when she thought she'd finished with pregnancies, I'd come along, unplanned.

Cassie turned the page to a portrait of the family, dressed in our Sunday best circa 1976, though it was more likely our Saturday best because we rarely went to church. "Probably a wedding," Pop said. He'd worn his hair longer then, and the suit he'd donned for the occasion sported the grotesquely wide lapels and bell-bottoms of the times, the fabric a shiny purple that would have served better as someone's bedspread. Mom stood next to him, about a foot to the side and a little behind, her bubble-head hairstyle already ten years out of fashion. Ray huddled on the other side of Mom, shoulders slumping inward, his head raw from the crew cut Pop regularly enforced on him. Sharon stood with her hands on her hips as though annoyed with whoever was taking the photo, about fifteen years old then, her strawberry-blonde hair hanging straight as a plumb line due to the ten minutes she spent every couple of days at the ironing board, ironing it straight. I stood in front of everyone, smiling like a little geek, maybe five years old, my knees scraped red beneath the hem of my lime-green skirt. Something about the photo disturbed me, and it wasn't until I stayed Cassie's hand that I noticed that none of us were even close to touching each other.

That realization saddened me, setting me up for the photo on the flip side of the page. We're all suckers for early photos of ourselves, maybe because they remind us of a time when we still believed in things, when we still had some hope our lives would turn out for the better. In the photograph I'm five years old, sitting on Pop's shoulders, still in the lime-green dress, my legs wrapped around his neck and my hands holding on to his ears like the reins of a horse, my eyes half-closed and face shining with smiling bliss, while he stares at the camera with a look of supreme paternal tolerance, the kind of look men get when their daughters are pulling their hair or ears or trying to see what daddy looks like with his nose pressed flat against his face. The photograph broke my internal ice faster and more irrevocably than any apology, the sorrow for all the trouble that had come between us welling up so suddenly I threw my hand to my mouth to catch the sob spilling out. I turned to latch on to Pop in a fierce, angry hug and I told him that I must have really loved him then. He stood for a moment with his hands to his side, shocked by the sudden gesture of affection, but when I felt his shoulders shift to return the hug I backed sharply away and slapped the side of my leg to command the Rott's attention.

"Sorry, like I said, busy day, gotta run," I said.

I bolted out the front door, leaving Pop stunned speechless, and drove over the pass and down into the San Fernando Valley wondering if I'd unfairly demonized him all these years. Maybe he hadn't been the bad father I'd remembered him to be. We all behave badly at times. We all have our demons.

Maybe I'd allowed his many moments of violent behavior to blot out memories of the times he'd been patient and caring, and as shocking as it sounded to me then, even loving. His violent rages had victimized everyone in the family, but he'd been more than just an angry father. Maybe I'd surrendered to the pity-me ethos of our times, the cult of victimization in which suffering equals personal merit and becomes a source of social status, encouraging us to feel sorry for ourselves rather than to heal and get on with our lives. The photograph implied that within Pop's violent core burned a little family love, and for his young, tomboyish daughter he once possessed genuine paternal caring. This did not excuse his angry sulks and violent behavior. He'd beaten his wife and bullied his children, even if he'd loved us in his own remote and abusive way. I had every right to hate him for that, but any feelings of victimization that lingered from my childhood were my responsibility now far more than his. I couldn't continue to deal with Pop burdened by the pains and resentments of my childhood. Even if he hadn't changed, I was no longer a little girl helpless before him. I was the stronger one now, I thought, and no, he wasn't the same man I'd known as a child. Grief had taught him something about remorse and age had gentled him. I had to learn to deal with who he was now, not what he'd been then.

Under those conditions we might be able to coexist.

26

I RETURNED TO Venice intending to catch a little of the sleep that had slipped from me the previous night but the sight of the white Tercel, parked this time in the grocery store lot down the street from my apartment, made sleep a more distant priority. The slot he'd chosen offered a clear sight line to the apartment steps and the front door to my second-floor unit. I parked in my assigned spot in front of the building, opened the door for the Rott, and led him up the stairs, careful not to tip the guy with a backward glance that I was aware he watched. Sean had asked me to call him if the watcher appeared again, but I didn't intend to play the role of the helpless female. The trip to Pop's left me with a feeling of restlessness. I needed a little action. I called Frank.

"Whoever owns those plates is working some powerful juju," he said, the volume of music blaring in the background signaling I'd caught him in his car, moving from one story to another. Warren Devon, it sounded like. "My guy, he's still searching but the plates don't show in the registry, like somebody's blocked them out. He tells me it's going to take another day at least, and no promises."

"How could somebody block the plates?" I asked.

"A computer hack," he answered. "Or an old-fashioned bribe."

"So we're talking about somebody with a little juice, maybe."

"Or a high school kid with a computer and time on his hands. Give my guy a little more time, he might come up with something."

I'd allowed the ex-con to sit watch on me for days and done nothing about it. I asked Frank if he had time to do me a favor. I didn't even know if the ex-con worked for somebody or was a solitary nut with an inappropriate fixation on me and my dog. A lot of aimless crazy people live in Venice and I couldn't discount that as one of the possibilities. After I hung up the call I pulled open the window in the bedroom and gauged the drop, thinking I might tie a couple of bed sheets together until I realized I only owned two and couldn't anchor them to anything except the doorknob. The two sheets tied together would barely reach the window. The drop measured no more than fifteen feet, but the asphalt below looked hard enough to make my ankles throb just from the thought of landing. Then I remembered the futon in the living room. I stripped away the throw pillows and dragged it through the bedroom door, the Rott watching with the worried excitement dogs sometimes get when humans move things from their familiar places. I propped the futon against the wall and sat on the floor to give the Rott a little quality face time, seeking to reassure him that I was sane no matter how it might look to him.

When Frank's Honda slid into the alley I lowered the futon out the window, held it flat against the side of the building, and let it drop, momentum and gravity tipping the padding flat onto the asphalt no more than a foot from the base of the wall. The Rott barked, once, confused, when I slid my legs out the window. I told him to stay calm and gripped the windowsill with both hands to lower myself. I didn't want to dangle out the window, a coward to let go, and so the moment my body steadied I kicked gently out and released, hoping for the best. I hit the center of the futon with the accuracy of a stuntwoman and tucked into a ball, letting my momentum carry me into a backward somersault, the perfection of my landing marred only by a bump on the head as I rolled back.

Above, the Rott jumped his paws onto the windowsill and barked. I shushed him, pulled the futon behind the trash dumpster, and slid into the Honda's passenger seat, sinking my head below the level of the windowsill as Frank accelerated toward the mouth of the alley. "Is the Rott following?" That was my biggest worry, that the dog would panic and decide to jump down after me.

"Don't worry, he's fine," he said, barely glancing in the rearview. "Nice landing, by the way. You practicing for your next jailbreak?"

I dug into my jacket pocket and handed him a spare set of keys to my apartment and car. "You'll go get him once I'm in place?"

"Somehow, I always imagined it would be a little different when you finally gave me the keys to your apartment." He let a lonely sigh fall from his chest and followed it with a smirk. "Relax, I'll take good care of your dog. You can have him back when we meet Mrs. Starbal the First. You mind coming with me on that? After you take me to lunch, of course."

"What are we meeting her for?"

"She'll talk to us, for one. Not too many people are willing to talk to me about Starbal senior. Certainly nobody who ever wishes to do lunch in this town again."

"What's the angle?"

"Nothing special," he hummed, meaning he wasn't saying yet, and changed the subject. "You know Logan called to twist my arm about the photograph he picked up from your apartment. He does not want to see any mention of Luster published."

"Why's that, you think?"

"I can't figure it out. It's like the connection blindsided him."

"Stewart told me the cops didn't know anything."

"If you look at it from Logan's perspective, he has to treat the whole thing like a gag, right? But what if it's not? He's screwed. If we print it, he'll be forced to deny the connection, and if it turns out Luster is connected in some way? After he's denied it?" Frank grinned and shaped a mushroom cloud with his free hand. "Ka-boom to the old career."

"You mean he thinks somebody mailed the photo as a joke?"

"Isn't that what it said on the back?"

"What it said on the back was *J, O, K, E,* then, in parentheses, *no S.*" Frank turned his face away from traffic to show me a smart-ass smirk. "I know you didn't have the chance to finish college, but that spells joke, singular, as in, *no s.*"

"Why not *J* for James Rakaan? Or even Jason Starbal?"

"Why not *J-O-K-E* for joke? People about to kill themselves, isn't that what they think life is all about, a cruel joke?" He swerved into the driveway of a Budget Rental Car franchise and parked next to a blue Ford Focus. He pointed his chin toward the rental car and dropped open the Honda's glove compartment to show me the keys.

I started the Focus and drove slowly back to Venice, figuring Frank was working on something he didn't want to tell me about, not just yet. We were often competitive, trying to outscoop one another, not with the intention of sucking up to the publisher but to goad each other on. If Frank was interested in talking to Starbal's first wife, then maybe he figured Jason Starbal was involved. That made some sense. Jason Starbal was a filmmaker with ready access to video equipment, and Christine's diary implied that she'd accompanied Rakaan to his house. Maybe Jason Starbal and James Rakaan shared the same sick erotic thrill of strangling drugged young women, video-recording the acts either to enjoy later or to share with other perverts over the Internet. That would certainly freak out Stewart enough to want to kill himself.

Frank veered at Rose and circled the block while I pulled into the grocery-store parking lot across from my apartment, parking two rows behind the white Tercel. I pulled from my jacket pocket a point-and-shoot camera with a 4.5X zoom lens, decent enough for a pocket cam but not nearly as powerful as the telephoto on my Nikon. Seen through the lens, Frank carried something in his left hand as he lumbered up the steps to the second floor of my building. The ex-con lifted a pair of binoculars, the cheap kind that can be bought for under twenty bucks in any drugstore. Frank keyed the door and slipped into the apartment. The ex-con shifted his shoulders and leaned over the passenger seat, the door frame concealing the action of his hands from view. It looked to me like he was writing something down—probably a log of my movements and visitors.

Frank emerged from the apartment less than two minutes after he'd gone in, leading the Rott out the door by his leash and dangling the object he'd carried up the stairs—a donut, the zoom revealed. Frank didn't relate to animals any more gracefully than he did to people, but he and the Rott shared a common passion for junk food, and that formed the surprisingly solid basis of their friendship. He led the Rott down the stairs bite by bite, then tossed the stub onto the floor of the Honda, shutting the passenger door after the dog leapt after it.

The ex-con pulled himself out of the Tercel to watch as Frank sped away, then dropped back into the car to light a cigarette and think about what he'd just seen. A few minutes after he extinguished his smoke, he stepped from the car and approached a raggedy man who pushed a shopping cart crammed with clothing, blankets, old books, and brightly colored plastic toys. He shook his head as the ex-con spoke to him and tried to continue his trek toward the sea but paused when a single bill of money waved in front of him. He snatched the bill as quick as a frog catching a fly and swerved across the street, leaving the cart safely parked just inside the sidewalk while he climbed the steps and rang the buzzer to my apartment. He backed away from the door and hung his head, then rang the buzzer again. Then he just stayed there, swaying from side to side, like somebody had put him into neutral.

The ex-con lit another cigarette, thought about what he was seeing, then lifted a cell phone to his ear. He talked to somebody for a minute or two, finishing the call and the smoke at the same time. He stepped into the car and reached to the right of the steering wheel. The Tercel quaked, exhaust trickling from the pipe. I started the rental and let him jet from the lot before I pulled out of my slot. He drove east on Rose before cutting toward the crown jewels of L.A.'s Westside: Century City and Beverly Hills. Mid-afternoon traffic congealed just enough to slow the Tercel, making it that much easier to follow. I fell a few cars back, speeding forward whenever I sensed a changing signal might separate us. He led me east through Beverly Hills, then north through West Hollywood onto Sunset Boulevard, just east of the Strip. After we hit the 6000 block the glitz of the Westside faded into the grime of east Hollywood. He passed Amoeba Records, signaled left, and swung across traffic into a parking lot beneath a black glass and silver steel midrise, pausing just long enough at a parking arm to insert a card into the code slot. I swept past and pulled a U-turn at the next light, coming at the public entrance to the underground lot from the opposite direction.

A ticket flickered from the box beside the parking control barrier. I grabbed it and sped past the rising arm into the first open slot. The clank of a compact door shutting near the far corner revealed where the ex-con had parked his car. I slipped out of the rental and into the nearest stairwell. I took the stairs two at a time, grabbing the handrail to pull me through the turns with greater speed, then skidded to a stop at the top landing to gather my breath before pushing through into the lobby. Across a granite-tiled floor the ex-con stepped alone into an elevator. I waited for the doors to slide shut and stepped across the lobby, watching the lit buttons above the elevator to mark his progress. The elevator behind me chimed. I rode it up to a corridor of offices with the names of minor-league entertainment companies and professional service corporations—mostly accountants and lawyers. I leaned against the wall and listened. Around the corner, a door hissed and clicked as it shut. I veered to the inside wall and peered around the edge. The moment I read the brass letters on the door at the end of the hall, I knew I'd tracked the watcher to his hole: Ray Spectrum Investigations.

"Oh no, not that guy," Frank said, his mouth stuffed with French fries, when I told him that the ex-con keeping watch on me worked for Spectrum. We met at a Fatburger near my apartment after dropping off the rental and picking up the Caddy, a late lunch at a restaurant of his choosing his price for helping me work the tail. I'd accepted without qualm, knowing he wouldn't choose a boutique Westside restaurant that required a bank loan to pay the bill. Frank preferred hamburger to filet, and pizza to almost anything.

"Why not that guy? What about him?" I asked.

Frank slowly unwrapped the paper from the edge of the hamburger and stared as though he'd lost his appetite, a rare phenomenon. "He's a fixer," he said.

"What's a fixer?"

"Somebody who fixes things."

I didn't suffer from the same loss of appetite. When I bit into the hamburger, the sauce spilled over the paper wrapping and dripped onto the table. "What kind of things?" I asked.

"Embarrassing things." He shook his head, flummoxed. "Let's say you have a celebrity actor who gets his kicks from snorting cocaine suspended by his heels from the ceiling, nude, while a hooker whips him with a wet weasel tail."

"Are you making this up or did it really happen?"

"Stranger things have happened, but I'm making up this one." He looked at his burger as though about to take a bite but held off. "Let's say the guy who deals the coke and the hooker are partners working a blackmail grift. They tell the celeb pay up or the photographs are going to start appearing on the Internet. What can he do about it? If he pays, he'll be on the hook for the rest of his life, and if he doesn't, not only will he be laughed off the screen in his next picture, the ASPCA will sue him for mistreatment of weasels."

"He could always confess to the public and beg for mercy," I said.

"If he made a living playing the kind of guy who might like getting whipped with weasel tails while suspended nude from the ceiling, sure, he could work it into great publicity, but what if he plays priests or tough guys? Not an option. So he hires a fixer, someone who promises to make the problem disappear, one way or another." He lifted the hamburger to his mouth and bit down, then continued to speak while he chewed. "The fixer approaches the blackmailers and offers a deal that won't blow back on the celeb. Unlike the celeb, who only plays tough guys, the fixer is physically imposing, a real tough guy who looks like he wouldn't hesitate anchoring the blackmailers to the bottom of Santa Monica Bay. Of course he doesn't actually kill anybody if he doesn't have to, because the bodies could surface and that might lead to bad publicity. He prefers to give the blackmailers part of what they want—it's only money, after all—with the threat of lethal retaliation if they break the deal."

"And Spectrum, he's a fixer?"

"There are two top-dog fixers in this town," Frank replied, chewing now with great enthusiasm. "Anthony Pellicano and Ray Spectrum. Pellicano got his start as a skip tracer working deadbeat accounts. Spectrum was a cop, originally."

"Local?"

"LAPD. Internal Affairs reprimanded him over an officer-involved shooting—he was working vice at the time—and he quit to join the dark side. The fact that he shot some people while in uniform only adds to his reputation. You know what he likes to tell clients?"

I shook my head, no clue.

"'I only make people disappear as a last resort.'"

"You think he might include troublesome paparazzi in that remark?"

"No doubt." He finished the hamburger with a polishing lick of his fingers. "If Ray Spectrum has been hired to fix you, your problems with Detective Logan are going to feel like a minor case of sniffles before a truck hits you."

"Who do you think hired him?" I asked.

"Starbal, who else?" He suppressed a burp with the back of his hand and fingered out the pack of cigarettes in the front pocket of his T-shirt. "Either direct, or through his lawyer."

"You mean Stewart?"

"I mean his father. Spectrum built his business on guys like Jason Starbal. He wouldn't hesitate to drop a dead rat in your car if he thought it would scare you off the story."

"He'll have to try something worse than a dead rat." I swallowed the last bite of Fatburger and grabbed a sack of takeout for the Rott.

"How about a car bomb?" Frank asked. "You want to have to check the undercarriage of your car with a mirror every morning before starting it up?" He led the way out the door, lighting a cigarette the moment he moved from a violation of the California labor code —smoking in a place of employment—to mere public nuisance. "Let's figure Starbal knows his son is involved," he said, fuming smoke from his nostrils. "He sees we're making a major play on the story and he panics, runs to Spectrum, tells him we have to be stopped. Spectrum hires the ex-con, who drops the dead rat on your seat, figuring it will scare you off."

The Rott jumped his paws to the Cadillac's passenger window when he spotted me, his muzzle pressed against the glass, and tumbled onto the asphalt when I opened the door, too dumb to back away or just too eager to get out to where the food was. I let him sniff the bag before I reached in to tear off a strip of hamburger. "Have you considered the possibility that Jason Starbal is more directly involved?"

Frank peered at me over the smoke curling from his cigarette, his expression as cagey as a card player just asked if he was bluffing. "You mean, have I already considered the possibility that Jason Starbal's oeuvre might include more than vampire flicks? Interesting idea. You think we should ask Mrs. Starbal the First a few pointed questions?"

"There's one thing I don't get about this," I said, feeding the Rott the hamburger patty, bite by bite. "Why is Starbal trying to scare me off? I'm not the one writing the story. Why not drop a rat on the seat of your car?"

"Have you seen the interior? I've got so much junk in there a dead rat would just get lost." He glanced inside his car to remind himself of the mess and smiled. "Besides, why should I be scared of a dead member of my own species?"

27

I IMAGINED SOMETHING a bit grander for the first wife of one of Hollywood's most successful producers than a counter position at Bloomingdale's, even if she worked the more exclusive terrain of men's and women's luxury watches, but Meme Richardson had suffered the great misfortune of divorcing Jason Starbal before he made his Beverly Hills mansion money. According to court records she'd willingly sacrificed her alimony payments from Starbal to marry again less than a year after they divorced, her second marriage lasting a spectacularly brief three months. After that, she seemed to have given up on men—on marrying them, at least. She lived in a modest apartment in Westwood and worked in the solidly upscale Century City Mall, less than a mile from Rodeo Drive, never gravitating far from the center of wealth but continually denied access.

Meme—pronounced *Mimi*—had agreed to talk to Frank off the record about Jason Starbal, ground rules we readily agreed to because so few people seemed willing to talk about Starbal, particularly after the death of his son. She didn't want to be seen talking to tabloid reporters, so to please her taste for the clandestine we waited outside Bloomingdale's for her shift to end and followed her at safe distance to Gelson's, a boutique supermarket where she commonly shopped for groceries. Tall and thin, and stylishly dressed in an embroidered linen skirt and off-the-shoulder stretch silk sweater, she looked like she belonged to the class she sold her products to, a mid-forties woman with taste in quality things as high as her cheekbones. The diet-enforced angularity of her face may have imitated an aristocratic ideal of gracefully aging beauty, but it also gave her a sharp and bitter look. She bought a cup of coffee from the in-store bakery and took it to a table in the informal seating area, browsing through the circular of specials and pretending surprise when we asked if we could join her.

Frank began with a nonthreatening question intended to elicit an easy reply, asking, "How long were you married to Jason Starbal?"

"Five years," she said, then tightened her lips as though remembering how unpleasant those years had been. "I've been waiting for over twenty years to hang Jason by his balls—that's why I've agreed to talk to you—but I have to insist that what I tell you stays off the record. It may not look to you like I have much to lose, but what little I have is mine and I don't want to be sucked dry by frivolous lawsuits."

"Why do you think that might happen?"

"Because that's what rich people do, they throw lawyers at problems to make them go away. If you don't have the money to retaliate—*pffft!*" She flicked her fingers into the air in imitation of a small explosion. "They vaporize you in court."

"Has he done that to you before?"

"What hasn't he done to me?" She brushed her hand over her hair, pulled sharply back into a ponytail. "You'd think he might not be so damned hostile to the mother of his first son, but every time I get within a hundred yards of asking him for a little something he sics his lawyers on me."

"Your son, Jagger, right?"

"My beautiful lost boy." She brought the paper cup of coffee to her lips but pulled it away without taking a sip. "He has his own production company now. He'll take care of his mother when the time is right."

"Do you see much of Jagger?"

"Jason doesn't approve of me so no, I don't." She straightened her back and stared aggressively forward. "As you may have guessed, Jason got custody."

Frank hunched his shoulders and leaned over the table, trying to make himself seem as inoffensive and harmless as possible, a visual cue to the initiated that he was about to open a potentially embarrassing line of questioning. "I thought it was normal, in divorce cases, for the woman to be given custody of the children."

"I was a drunk," she said. "I used a lot of drugs then, too."

"And Jason Starbal didn't?"

A high-pitched chime sounded from her rattan-top purse. She unsnapped the catch and withdrew the offending cell phone, a sleek Nokia with a brushed platinum surface. "He drank and snorted coke almost as much as I did, but he held it a hell of a lot better than I could." Her brow wrinkled as she read the caller's number and she dropped the phone back into her purse, letting voice mail pick up. "It didn't help that over the next three months I was arrested for drunken driving, drunk and disorderly conduct, and then, as the coup de grâce to my hopes of motherhood, felony cocaine possession. It wasn't a lot of cocaine, but possessing any amount of cocaine in those days was a felony."

"Still is," Frank said. "But if everybody who did cocaine in Hollywood was caught, they'd have to hold the Oscars from county jail."

She smiled bitterly, happy to find a cynical shoulder to gnash her teeth on. "I spiraled down after we separated and then Jason's career took off. He could afford a good custody lawyer. All my money was tied up in drug lawyers. So the judge awarded him custody, and since then the more successful he's become, the more difficult he's made it for me to even see Jagger." She hurriedly lifted a tissue from her bag to catch a tear sprung from anger more than sorrow. "But my personal faults and abuses aren't going to help you sell newspapers, are they? I'm sure you're more interested in hearing the dirt about Jason."

"Why did your marriage break up, you think?"

"Whores," she said, stuffing the tissue into her purse. "Jason couldn't stay away from them. And I'm not talking about street whores, the kind that give you the clap if they don't turn out to be a vice cop in drag."

"I heard it rumored that he was in Heidi Fleiss's black book."

"I'm sure he's been in every black book penned in the last twenty years. Before Heidi Fleiss it was Alexis Adams. She ran a call-girl service out of a house on Doheny Drive."

"What drove him to visit whores?" Frank blushed, or at least pretended to, and scribbled a note in his pad. "I'm sorry, that sounds naive, I know, but bear with me."

She flashed her hand across the table to cut him off. "I know exactly what you're getting at. Jason liked rough sex. For a while I was perfect for him because, you know what? I was too drunk or stoned to care. But it wasn't enough for him to dominate his wife. He needed new girls to conquer." Her cell phone chimed again and she sighed, exasperated. "I should just turn the damn thing off."

"Does your definition of rough sex include bondage?"

"Are you kidding? I've still got the strap marks." She held up a single finger to pause the conversation while she lifted the phone from her purse. "Give me a second to get rid of this caller."

She pressed the phone to her ear and answered with her name. Her expression shifted from annoyance to shock, and she glanced the supermarket across as though searching for someone. "What, were you going to chase me all the way to the frozen foods section?" Her voice rang in high indignation. "I just sat down for a cup of coffee and these two characters started asking me questions." She dropped her head and listened. "No, I don't respond to threats. Threats don't work for me. What are you going to do, use your pull to force Bloomie's to transfer me to the luggage section?" She tapped a burgundy, talonlike fingernail onto the countertop and nodded once. "That's better. Okay, we have an understanding. You have all my particulars, right?" She disconnected, dropped the phone into her purse, and then held absolutely still, thinking through the ramifications of what she'd just agreed to.

"Was that Jason?" Frank asked.

"One of his minions. Sorry, but I've got to go." She clutched her purse to her abdomen and glanced at her coffee as though deciding whether to bring it along or abandon it with the conversation.

"Wait a minute, help us out here, we've just gotten started," Frank said, rising to his feet as she backed away from the table and stood. "I'm happy that you've managed to use us to cut yourself a better deal, really I am, but I'm having sudden memory failure here. Our conversation was on the record, right? How would you like me to identify your quotes: as the venomously bitter former Mrs. Jason Starbal or as Meme Richardson, recovering drug addict?"

"You're a bastard," she said, as though she expected nothing less.

"Just doing my job," he answered.

"You want to talk to the woman responsible for ruining my marriage?"

"I think I hear the conversation going off record again," Frank said.

"Talk to Anabelle Lash." She snatched her coffee from the table and prepared to flee. "That bitch has been satisfying Jason Starbal's perversions for twenty years."

28

NORMAL BUSINESS HOURS had long since ended by the time we crossed into the San Fernando Valley, but we drove with some prospect of reaching Anabelle Lash in her office that night. Neither of us was particularly knowledgeable about the phone-sex business—at least, Frank claimed not to be, despite his otherwise encyclopedic range of knowledge—but it seemed reasonable that call frequency would pick up in the evening hours, when the clientele returned from work to pursue their lonely fantasies of subjugation and domination. Frank began dialing Lash's numbers—both office and cell—the moment we left Gelson's. She didn't respond to either.

A dozen cars were parked in the lot of the aging courtyard office complex where Lash worked, encouraging hopes we might find her in. We passed along a concrete walk into a courtyard decorated with dying plants, a standing ashtray overflowing with cigarette butts, and a lost-looking garden gnome standing on the end of a wooden bench. The names of some of the building's other tenants suggested a line of business similar to Lash's, which explained the crowded parking lot and the brightly lit windows circling the interior. Frank rang the bell to Lash's office and waited, then rang again. The blue-white of fluorescent bulbs flickered behind the venetian blinds covering the window above the walk. Frank glued his finger to the bell and peered through the slats, seeing little more than a sliver of carpet at the base. When no one answered after two minutes of insistent ringing, he scribbled a brief message on a sheet of notepaper, asking Lash to contact him as soon as possible, and wedged it under the door. Across the courtyard, a pneumatic blonde and Cleopatra-esque brunette, both dressed in low-slung jeans and halter tops, stepped out of a door marked Wildebeast Productions and lit cigarettes for each other.

"You girls seen Anabelle Lash around tonight?" Frank called.

They shook their heads and turned away to discourage further conversation. I wandered over to ask them if they'd ever heard of Jason Starbal. The one on the left shook her head and looked away, but the one on the right noticed my camera and asked what I was doing. When I told her I was a tabloid photographer she introduced herself as Cherry Laurel, "like the poison," she said. "You're talking about the movie guy, right?"

"Cher," her colleague said, the name spoken as a warning.

"What? Anabelle is a bitch."

"So who isn't?"

Cherry pursed her lips around the filter tip of her cigarette and wrapped her arm around the neck of her colleague. "Take our photo?" she asked.

I pulled the lens cap from the digital camera and directed them toward the courtyard, where I could use a security light instead of a flash to illuminate their faces. I told them to have some fun and ran off a series of stills while they vamped for the camera, then displayed the results on the digital's microscreen. They laughed and squealed at the more outrageous shots, the act of being photographed and then viewing the images animating them in a way mere life did not. Then a bearded head poked out the door and advised them that the cigarette break was over, time to get to work. Doing what, I didn't ask.

"Give me your e-mail address, I'll send you copies," I said.

"My name's my address," she said, and listed a popular e-mail service. "And just so you know, I've never seen the guy you mentioned with Anabelle, I certainly didn't see him at her office last week, no way she set me up on a date with him when I was just breaking into the business, and the rumors that he's a complete fetish freak are completely untrue." She gave me a big, cartoonish wink and slipped through the closing office door.

"What have you got that I don't?" Frank asked, walking up to me.

"A camera," I said.

"The pen may be mightier than the sword, but who uses swords anymore?" He sidled up to the camera to view the images I'd just shot and asked, "Didn't you tell me Christine went to Starbal's mansion with a friend making a *professional* visit?"

"And we thought that referred to Rakaan," I said, advancing from shot to shot. "You think she could have been referring to Anabelle Lash instead?"

"She does practice a variant of the world's oldest profession."

The possibility that Christine accompanied Anabelle Lash to Jason Starbal's estate troubled me for several reasons, primarily because it meant Dr. Rakaan might not have been complicit in her killing. I'd wanted him to be guilty because I considered him a user and abuser and I just didn't like him. As I drove back to the beach that night, I played through my mind scenarios of what might have happened that day. Lash was well aware of Christine's aspirations to be an actress and could easily have invited her along when she visited Jason Starbal. Christine would have gone thinking that she'd visit the mansion of a rich Hollywood producer, might get the chance to meet him, and if he met her, who knows, maybe he'd like her enough to cast her in one of his films. Her diary hadn't mentioned that she'd met Jason Starbal, only his kids, but she might have lied about that, or a meeting might have been arranged later.

It all made a perverted kind of sense to me. Christine was a beautiful young woman educated in the techniques of sadomasochism, a rare combination. Of course Starbal would want her. Lash wouldn't hesitate to make the offer if she could convince Christine to participate. Would Christine agree? Maybe she'd been given ruffies to ensure that it wouldn't matter whether she agreed or not. Or maybe she'd gone willingly and drugged herself to take the edge off the humiliation of having sex with a man for purposes of career advancement. The shadow visible in the lower right corner of the video may have been Anabelle Lash's; given her extensive experience in adult film, she'd know how to set lights and operate a video camera. The only detail that didn't fit was Christine's appointment with the supposed producer of one of Johnny Depp's films; Depp had never appeared in one of Starbal's films, and if Lash arranged the meeting, Starbal had no need of the deception. Like a card that doesn't fit the hand I was playing, I discounted it.

I intended to take a run when I returned to the apartment and got as far as laying out my sweats, exciting the Rott with the prospect of late-night exercise, but instead of running I collapsed on the bed, exhausted in a way that felt new to me, dropping like dead weight through semiconsciousness and down into a deep sleep. When the doorbell rang sometime later I felt jerked from the depths into a gasping kind of consciousness. Cassie and Pop had argued, I thought, and she's hitchhiked back to Venice to seek refuge. I glanced at the clock on my way to vertical—an hour before midnight, not late at all.

The Rott stood before the front door, attentive but not excited. I put my eye to the peephole and was neither greatly surprised nor terribly pleased to see Sean's stubbled face in the parabolic lens. I thought about rushing to the bathroom to splash my face with water, freshen my breath, and spike my hair but decided against it. That he hadn't called before deciding to come over annoyed me. I figured he didn't want to call because phone records can be checked, his extracurricular visits to an ex-con documented by the call lists phone companies keep on their customers. I wanted to inch the door open just wide enough to tell him to go away, but within seconds of seeing him I broke into a pheromone sweat as powerful as any drug and instead I opened the door wide.

"I woke you," he said, and tried to back away.

"I can sleep later." I grabbed the lapel to his leather jacket and pulled him inside. He kicked the door shut with his heel while I kissed him, hesitantly at first but then hard and fast, his stubble scraping against my lips like sagebrush. I yanked off his jacket but pushed him away when he came at me, let him get closer before I pushed him away again, then slipped behind to wrap my arms around his chest and bite his neck. A sound escaped his lips, midway between a moan and a roar, and he spun around, catching me from the back so deftly I couldn't have escaped the move had I wanted to. My hands dropped to his belt while he kissed my neck and when he paused, expecting the jolt of skin-on-skin pleasure, I gave him just the smallest bit of pain instead and turned at the moment of surprise to push him back and lift his shirt above his stomach. He raised his arms to help me strip it off, then pulled me toward him, his hands jerking at my blouse in retaliation. If our first session of lovemaking had been spontaneous and the second smoothly deliberate, our third time together pitted strength against strength and weakness against weakness, the act of making love a physical contest not to cause pain—not much, anyway—but to dominate each other through the force of pleasure. We finished an intertwined jumble of limbs, our skin sweat-slick and flushed with blood, agreeing in our pleased exhaustion to call the contest a tie.

"Are you a mountain person, an ocean person, or a desert person?" he asked, cradling me from behind.

I turned just enough to catch him out the corner of my eye with a look that wondered why he was asking. "That's the great thing about L.A., you got all three within walking distance so you don't have to choose."

"I thought we'd try the desert this weekend," he said.

I considered that for a moment, then rolled on top of him.

"Were you going to ask me if I wanted to go, or just abduct me?"

His teeth glowed in the dark like a Cheshire cat's.

"Which would you prefer?"

"I don't abduct easily, so you'd better ask," I said. "And Stewart Starbal's funeral is coming up, so next weekend is better."

"How'd you learn that? I thought it was private."

"Frank heard about it," I said. "He probably bribed the mortician."

Sean kissed my neck and sat up, saying he wished he could stay but he had to check on some things. I suspect we both appreciated spontaneity more than predictability in a relationship, and mystery far more than certainty. The weekend after next was still far away. I didn't worry about it. "I heard Logan came by to see you this morning," he said, hunting in the darkness for where I'd flung his pants. "Everything okay?" He spotted one leg hanging from the top of the bedroom door and shook his head, amused.

I told him about the envelope I'd found in the mailbox. At the mention of Luster he sat down on the edge of the bed and looked at me in a way I couldn't interpret, the streetlight outside my bedroom window glinting across the surface of his eyes.

"Why didn't you call me last night when you found it?" he asked. "I'd left you, what, fifteen minutes before. I could have doubled back, easy."

"And done what?"

"Helped," he said, exasperated. "You have some guy watching your apartment, you get threatening stuff in the mail, maybe I'd like to hear about it." He jumped to his feet and pulled his jeans over his hips, tracked down his shirt, shoes, and socks in the other room. "I'm not trying to set the tone for a relationship here. I'm not implying that you're weak and I'm strong, or that I'm here to protect you, or any other kind of sexist bullshit. But I have a skill set you should be using. I have contacts and resources that can help you. And no, I'm not going to compromise an ongoing investigation by feeding you information you don't already know, but this looks like a particularly dangerous time for you and I can help keep you safe."

"If I call every time a little trouble comes my way, you'll need a twenty-four-hour hotline," I said.

"You got my numbers, call anytime you want."

I threw myself into a robe and went to the kitchen, thinking I'd pour myself a drink, then decided against it. "Do you think Logan is a good investigator?" I asked.

"You don't make RHD without being a good investigator." Sean hopped into a shoe as he followed me toward the kitchen. "The question is whether he's the right investigator for this case."

"Why?" I asked. "Was he beaten as a child with a rolled-up tabloid?"

Sean gave that the laugh it deserved and eyed the bottle of Jack Daniel's I'd set on the kitchen counter. I poured three fingers into a tumbler for him and he limped over, one shoe on, one off, to get it. "Why are you so interested in attending the Starbal funeral? The poor kid's dead, for Christ's sake, let him rest in peace."

"I don't think he's going to rest in peace, ever."

"He sure as hell won't if you tabloids keep hunting him." He sank half the bourbon in one go and bent his leg to slip on the second shoe, looking like an awkward, one-legged bird while he tied the laces. "You know that cops often moonlight in the movie business, right?"

"Everybody who lives in L.A. knows that," I said. You couldn't drive past a location shoot without seeing a half dozen motorcycle patrolmen working traffic control.

"It's a good source of additional income, and not just for uniforms." He dropped his foot and straightened. "About a dozen years ago Jason Starbal produced a police thriller set in L.A. From a cop's perspective, the film got the details right. Guess who served as the technical advisor?"

I stared at him, thought, no way.

"That's right, Robert Logan, working homicide out of North Hollywood then."

"Your station," I said.

"Before my time." He made a face as he sipped the bourbon. "But his legend lives on. One of the reasons we don't get along."

"You and Logan?"

"The bastard thinks he still owns North Hollywood and I don't encourage his delusions." He closed his eyes, sipped again, shook his head. "It's not so bad as that. We're collegial. I wasn't worried about him until you connected Stewart Starbal to the murdered girl."

"You think he has a conflict of interest?"

"I'd be careful mentioning any links to Starbal, let me put it that way."

"You know the package, the one that came in the mail?" I opened the refrigerator door, suddenly ravenous, and finding it depressingly empty, settled for a carton of milk. "I'm pretty sure it came from Stewart Starbal, and the photograph of Luster, it refers to his father, to Jason Starbal."

He stared at me across the countertop.

I glanced at the carton in my hand, thinking it was that.

"So I feel like drinking milk, anything wrong with that?"

"Help yourself," he said and shrugged. "What makes you think the photo has anything to do with Jason Starbal? I don't get the connection."

"The stamps on the envelope were the same ones used to post the video of Christine's killing." I took another swig of milk, not liking the way he looked at me. "Stewart all but told me he'd sent it. I always figured he felt guilty because he was there when the video was made, a passive spectator maybe, but there. That he'd hooked up with Christine when Rakaan brought her over on a visit to his father. But now, I don't think Rakaan had anything to do with it."

A surprised bark gusted from Sean's chest. "Whatever you do, don't tell Logan that. He'll think you're working for Rakaan's defense team, or worse, inventing stories just to make more sensational headlines. They've got all the evidence they need to convict; believe me, it's just a question of time before Rakaan asks to plea."

"To a lesser charge, like manslaughter," I said.

"From what I've heard, that's what everyone from the district attorney on down agrees is what happened here. They had a history of sadomasochistic practices. He just went too far one night and killed her, then panicked and dumped the body."

"And the shadow moving across the frame? In the video?"

"A dog, a cat, a newspaper blowing in the wind, a figment of your imagination." He shook his head and finished his drink, clattering the glass to the kitchen counter in a gesture of frustration and, I thought, anger. "What makes you think the Luster photograph refers to Jason Starbal?"

"Just a guess," I said, not wanting to go into it.

"Glad to see that degree in criminology is finally paying off."

"I think Stewart feared other girls might be killed and wanted it to stop," I said, goaded into responding. "That was why he mailed me the disk and later, the photo. But why not just step up and turn the killers in, unless he couldn't do that either. That's what made me think his father was involved."

"People do all kinds of things because of guilt, you'd be surprised." He lifted his leather jacket from the kitchen table, where I'd thrown it while undressing him. "If he was part of what happened to Christine—let's say he was in the room with Rakaan when she was assaulted and did nothing about it—he'd do small, pretty much meaningless things to chill his guilt."

"Like mail evidence to a tabloid," I said.

"Rather than turn himself in, yes. And when he still didn't feel any better about himself?" He punched his arms through the jacket, glancing around the room to see if he'd forgotten anything. "You get what you found at the Chateau Marmont, a confused kid dead from an overdose, half suicide, half cry for help. But you know what?" He moved to the door, turned, gave me a smart-ass smile. "You don't have proof for any of this, not even that Stewart Starbal sent you the video or the photo. It's all rumor and innuendo. Perfect for *Scandal Times*."

29

THE SUN STRUGGLED to pierce a June haze hanging over the L.A. basin on the morning Stewart Starbal was scheduled to be buried in Forest Lawn Memorial Park, his body marked for a plot near the crest of a green hillock that offered sweeping views of the foothills of Glendale and north Los Angeles. Frank drove like a lost tourist along labyrinthine cemetery roads named Enduring Faith Lane and Precious Love Drive, searching for one that led to high ground. A gardener had tipped him about the time and location of the memorial service, to be held in Wee Kirk O' the Heather, one of the cemetery's three faithful re-creations of Scottish and English churches, and though we didn't plan to crash the service, we did intend to observe the mourners at a respectful distance.

We weren't the only ones at the cemetery not mourning the death of a loved one; along the way we passed a Japanese tour bus parked near the Last Supper Window Memorial Terrace, which boasted Leonardo da Vinci's immortal work re-created in stained glass. Not even the mortuary business is immune to the fairy-tale kitsch culture of Southern California, turning cemeteries into amusement parks of the dead. Casual visitors were welcomed—no, encouraged—by mortuary management to stroll the sumptuous grounds and admire several exact replicas of Michelangelo's greatest works at no charge whatsoever, with souvenirs of their visit available in the mortuary gift shop. I stepped out of the car and gazed down the slope of grass to the pitched roofs and stone spires of Wee Kirk O' the Heather and nearby Little Church of the Flowers. Below the church two late-model Japanese sedans and a black BMW parked at the edge of the road, where it curved around the hill and widened to allow mourner parking.

"There he is," Frank said, pointing toward a cluster of men huddled near the church entrance. "Ray Spectrum, the guy with the black ponytail."

I aimed the camera and caught in the telephoto frame the suntanned face of a man who could have once played professional football, his black and brilliantined hair swept back above a massive brow and tied in place with a black band, the shoulders of his black matte suit so wide he'd need to turn sideways to fit through the average door. At that distance it was difficult to get a good read on him, an oversized pair of Valentino sunglasses covering his face like an eye mask, but from the way he spoke to the two gray-suited bruisers huddled next to him he was accustomed to command, and when he pressed his hand to his ear and glanced up the hill, directly into my telephoto lens, I knew he was wired and we'd been spotted. The way he looked at the lens, I felt he expected to see me there.

I burned a few images into the digital camera to document his presence and then pointed the lens toward the entrance at the base of the hill, where the first in a convoy of black stretch limousines cruised through the cemetery gates, black ribbons flapping from their aerials like diplomatic flags. I zoomed back for an epic shot, the solemn black vehicles moving amid rolling green and misty sky. At the end of the limousine procession drove mourners in private cars, a steady crawl of sports and luxury metal driven by kids who might have been Stewart's rich friends. The black Corvette in the middle of the pack was not particularly remarkable, neither newer nor more expensive than many of the other cars in the procession, except that I'd seen it before. At the curve beneath the church, the limousines parked bumper to bumper and disgorged their cargo of black-suited men and women in elegant mourning dresses and pantsuits. Spectrum personally opened the passenger door to the lead limousine and whispered into the ear of the balding middle-aged man who emerged.

"Jason Starbal," Frank said. "Can you get him?"

A private bodyguard hustled around the hood with something black in hand that blossomed into an umbrella when he approached Starbal, blocking him from view and shielding the next person to emerge from the passenger compartment. I'd caught a few frames of the back of Starbal's head but nothing more; Spectrum had no doubt warned him that we were watching from above. I'd seen umbrellas deployed before—it was a favorite trick of security teams to shield celebrities from paparazzi cameras. I lowered the camera to locate the position of the black Corvette and noticed two cemetery security guards in a modified golf cart sputtering toward our position on the hill.

"Uh-oh, we're busted," Frank said.

The security guards looked to be nice enough guys, their duties at the cemetery entailing the use of calm authority rather than conflict, a law enforcement posture emphasized by their near-retirement age and dumpling-shaped bodies. The lead officer was a gray-haired black man with crinkled eyes that made him look worried we might cause more trouble than he could handle. "Sorry folks, no photographing the memorial services, I have to escort you off the premises."

"You're telling us you don't allow cameras?" Frank's voice spiked with indignation. "We just passed a busload of Japanese tourists with cameras. Are you going to throw them out, too?"

"Please, sir, we ask you to respect the rights of the mourners to a little privacy." He pressed his palms out in a calm-down gesture while his partner lifted a walkie-talkie to his lips, ready to report a disturbance on Loving Kindness Lane.

I apologized to the officer and walked to the car, glancing over my shoulder when I ducked into the passenger seat. On the road below, a twenty-something with flowing black hair stepped out of the Corvette to exchange fist-taps with two other men in their early twenties, then hugged another young man who approached the group, the last to arrive. I snuck the lens over the doorsill and maxed the zoom to isolate the four of them. The late arrival looked vaguely familiar, but at that distance, I couldn't get a clear enough look at his face to know why.

"You get anything worthwhile?" Frank asked, poking his head through the driver's window, and when I told him about the group of four young men gathered by the black Corvette, he pretended to stretch and checked them out. "The one on the left," he said, referring to the late arrival, "he's Stewart's older brother, Jagger. The Corvette, think it's the same one you saw at Chateau Marmont?"

The feigned casualness didn't fool Spectrum, who hustled to the group the moment he caught the direction of Frank's glance and ushered the boys toward the chapel entrance. I pointed the lens out the side window as we pulled away from the security guards, catching the Corvette driver as he moved toward the chapel. I hadn't seen his face clearly when he'd come down the stairs of the Chateau, but the hairstyle and body type matched closely enough. I suggested we wait outside the cemetery gates, then tail him to see where he went after the funeral.

Frank dropped me off at the Cadillac—like true Angelenos we'd driven out in separate cars—to let the Rott out for a quick patrol while he backed into a parking spot across from the cemetery, using a white panel van in the space ahead of him like a blind to conceal his car. The Rott went about his business efficiently, accustomed to short bursts of activity between hours of waiting, and hopped into the rear seat of the Honda without complaint. To pass the time we talked about Anabelle Lash. Since our visit to her office he'd continued to call and leave messages that Lash had so far ignored. We both speculated that she'd been warned against talking to us; if Starbal watched his first wife so closely that she'd been spotted talking to us, then he'd probably posted armed guards around Lash, who could divulge far more dangerous information than old news about a failed marriage.

"Something else might be interesting," I said. "You ever hear rumors that Logan worked as a technical advisor on one of Starbal's films?"

"Who told you that?"

"A source," I said.

He tapped the rearview mirror to an angle that reflected my face and fingered a lit cigarette outside the window. "How much are you seeing Sean anyway? Like, every night?"

I stared at him in the reflection, stone-faced.

"I never figured he'd move so fast and then stick around."

"He have a reputation for quick moves and moving on?"

"No more than any other guy twice married and divorced by thirty-five."

I waited for the smile that signaled a joke, but Frank didn't tip me that one had been made. He puffed at his cigarette, obliquely watching my reaction as he stared out the windshield. "He didn't tell you," he guessed.

"Any kids?"

"None that he claims formally."

This time he smiled.

I shouldn't have been surprised. Sean and I had been together no more than a few times and though I never felt we couldn't talk to each other, our bodies spoke with far greater urgency—and probable honesty. Neither of us had fully or even partially disclosed the shadows trailing our lives. Not having to talk about the past liberated us from incidents that encumbered us, things we might not have regretted but that required too much explaining to justify to someone else. Animal attraction was one thing and true compatibility something else. I didn't know Sean, not really, no more than he knew me, even though I was already more than a little bit in love with him. We were ciphers to each other, attracted to the mystery of who the other might be as much as the reality of who that person really was. Our moments alone took place in a world of our own making, far from the intrusions of the outside world, and when the time came, inevitably, that the world flooded in, the relationship might not survive it.

The Corvette took good advantage of its speed after the memorial service ended, streaking between the exit gates at the head of a like-minded queue of those who didn't want to waste the entire morning at a funeral. Frank was slow to start the engine and extricate the Honda from its blind, and by the time we were rolling, the Corvette had vanished over the horizon line. My shouts to hurry up didn't improve our speed or Frank's driving skill. Neither of us thought to look behind us. Frank was too enthralled by the hunt to worry about traffic cops, and I was too busy hanging on to the restraint strap with one hand and the Rott's collar with the other. We caught our next sight of the Corvette as it crossed the concrete-lined Los Angeles River and swung left to ramp onto the southbound lanes of the Golden State Freeway. Frank settled back into the seat after we merged into the fast lane, several car lengths behind, confident we could keep up. I put my eye to the viewfinder and waited until shifts in the traffic flow created a gap between the Nikon and the Corvette's titanium exhaust pipes. The license plate that slid through the telephoto frame read *OZZY13*.

"You mean Ozzy like Ozzy Osbourne, the singer?" Frank asked when I read him the plates.

I thought about the kid behind the wheel while Frank called a contact with access to the DMV's database. The kid had met up with

Jagger Starbal and two other boys of similar age at the funeral, the four of them looking like a tight group of friends. What had drawn him to the Chateau Marmont on the day that Stewart had died? Had he been a close friend of Stewart's, his number called either just before or after mine? He might have been responding to a plea for help from a drugged friend. But if he was a friend of Stewart's, why hadn't he phoned the front desk on finding him unconscious? Even if they'd been doing drugs together, he should have summoned help before fleeing—unless he didn't mind seeing Stewart die. I again considered the possibility that Stewart had been given a hot shot, then realized it didn't have to be murder. Ozzy might have gone to the hotel not to talk Stewart out of committing suicide but out of going to the police or confessing to the tabloids. If Ozzy thought Stewart was cracking, about to confess their involvement in Christine's death, then finding him dead or dying of an overdose would be a relief, even if they were so-called friends. He wouldn't call emergency or the front desk. He'd run. He'd let Stewart die.

"All we need now is a Keaton and an Einstein to get the joke," I said.

Frank told his DMV contact to call back with the information as soon as possible and disconnected. "Get what joke?" He asked.

"Jason, Ozzy, Keaton, Einstein."

"*J-O-K-E,* you mean? Like what was written on the back of Luster's photo?"

"Why not *J* for Jason and *O* for Ozzy?" I suggested, voicing the thought out loud to hear how it sounded. It sounded only half right. Ozzy belonged, but not Jason. My head spun from the centrifugal force of reversing suspicions. "No, not Jason. *J* for Jagger."

"Jagger?" Frank shouted the name, incredulous. "First you're so convinced it's Rakaan you almost single-handedly get him arrested, then you decide it's not Rakaan, it's Jason Starbal and Anabelle Lash, and now just to piss everybody off you're saying it's not Jason, it's Jagger?"

"Jason pays women to have sex with him," I said, stroking the Rott's head to help me think. "He's a pervert just like Rakaan but he doesn't need Rohypnol, and even if he decided to try it for kicks, he's too experienced to accidentally strangle someone to death. He's been doing it for years, remember. And where does Charlotte McGregor fit in? She doesn't. And neither does Luster. Stewart sent me the photograph of Luster because he wanted to show what was going on involved more than just Christine. Luster was a serial rapist who used Rohypnol on his victims. That doesn't fit Jason Starbal."

"And Anabelle Lash?" Frank groped the dash for a cigarette, disturbed enough to need a calming hit of nicotine. "Christine connects to Lash and Lash connects to Jason Starbal. Come on, it fits! And it makes a great headline."

"That's how Christine met Stewart," I said. "She went with Lash, not Rakaan. She probably met Jagger there, too. That's how he got in touch with her later. He got her number when she gave it to Stewart and then contacted her, claiming to be Depp's producer."

"And what it said on the photo, *no S?*"

"Not Stewart."

Frank responded with derisive laughter and lit his cigarette.

"He was trying to tell me he was innocent," I said. "That he wasn't part of the group involved in this. It shouldn't be hard to find out who the *K* and *E* refer to. Wait a minute, didn't you tell me that Jagger had a film production company?"

"Right, the one with funny spelling." He swore with the force of sudden realization and fumbled for the notepad in his front T-shirt pocket.

"Illusterious Productions, wasn't it?" I said.

Frank fought the smoke in his eyes while he watched traffic and tried to find the entry he'd made in his notebook. The Corvette headed steadily west, toward the wealthier neighborhoods nestled in the hills or sloping toward the ocean, but instead of turning north toward Beverly Hills it swung south toward Long Beach and Orange County. Frank swore again and tossed the notebook onto my lap, turned to the page of notes he'd made about Jason Starbal's family. "You're right," he said.

I read what he'd written after Jagger's name: Illusterious Productions.

"I don't see any other names here," I said. "Where's his partners?"

"It's a pun on Luster, get it?" Frank stabbed his finger at the page. "Luster is right in the middle of the name of his damn production company. Read it aloud."

"Illusterious," I said, rhyming with *mysterious.*

"No. I'd pronounce it different." Frank grabbed the notebook and peered at the entry. "I'd pronounce it, Ill-Luster-Us."

When the Corvette slid right at the off ramp to Los Angeles International Airport, Ozzy's final destination opened to any number of possibilities. Frank sped around a couple of slow-moving cars in the fast lane, careful to hang close enough to the Corvette to avoid losing the tail at a traffic light. We speculated that he might be leaving the country. It made sense. He needed to show up at the funeral because he would have drawn attention to himself by missing it, but now that he'd deflected suspicion he could take a long, unearned vacation in Mexico, away from worries about the law. We didn't change our minds after the Corvette bypassed the remote lot and entered the terminal itself. Judging by the sticker price on his car, he wouldn't have problems paying the daily rate for short-term parking.

"Time to run and gun," Frank said.

I pulled the film camera from my bag and sped through my preshoot routine, guestimating the shooting conditions, loading extra rolls of film into my jacket pockets, and deciding if the lens on the camera was still the best lens for the job. Run and gun meant guerilla-style journalism, Frank shooting shock questions at the subject while I backpedaled ahead, photographing his alarmed, amused, or violently annoyed reactions. I'd need the greater light sensitivity of film in the low-light conditions we'd encounter in the parking structure and decided to swap telephotos to the faster 28–70–millimeter lens.

The Corvette collected a ticket at the parking control arm and rolled up the ramp to the first parking level, hunting, as almost all Angelenos do, for that one elusive parking space nearest his eventual destination, spending three minutes looking for a spot that might save him a sixty-second walk. Frank hovered one lane over, watching from a distance, and when the Corvette braked by an empty space at last, he sped toward several free slots near the back and squeezed on the brakes. I was already reaching for the door when the Honda lurched and my head snapped back to the sound of crushing metal and splintering glass. Frank cursed and the Rott yelped as the car shot forward, out of control, toward the rear fender of a pickup truck to the right. The moment we struck the fender the world turned white and something smacked me full in the face, knocking me back against the seat. When I opened my eyes, too stunned to move, I realized someone had rear-ended us at speed. The passenger-side air bag had deployed when we hit the pickup truck, the air bag now dribbling from its compartment like a spent condom. The collision knocked the Cubs baseball cap from Frank's head and his hair spiked straight up in protest. I asked if he was okay. He nodded without really being conscious of what had just happened. The Rott barked in the backseat, traumatized, but fine. I felt my neck to make sure the tendons were still attached and elbowed open the door.

Behind the wheel of the blue Toyota Camry that struck us, the driver clutched his hand against his jaw in a way that suggested he might be hurt. I took a step forward, shaking off the effects of the crash easily enough, and saw the cell phone in the driver's hand. Had he been conversing with someone, not watching where he was going, when we collided? Or was he just now calling to report the accident? He spotted me walking toward him. His hand flashed and the cell phone vanished. A moment later the driver's door winged open and he emerged, a large white man in a gray suit. I'd seen him before, one of the two bouncers huddling with Spectrum at the funeral.

"You folks okay?" he called out in mock concern, then glanced back to where I'd last seen the Corvette.

I pretended not to recognize him and pointed toward the Honda, shouting like I was completely freaked out, "My friend! He's not breathing! The air bag! I think he's having a heart attack!"

He hurried forward, reaching into the outside flap pocket of his suit coat for his phone, ready to dial in a medical emergency. He'd been sent to stop, not kill us, and a serious injury could have legal ramifications he'd rather avoid. When he moved toward the Honda I slipped behind the pickup truck we'd hit, then sprinted toward the exit leading to the terminal, the same exit I supposed the driver of the Corvette had taken. I heard a shout behind me but it was too late, I was already gone, out from the shadows of the parking structure and into the bright sunlight, the Tom Bradley International Terminal straight ahead across four lanes of busy airport traffic. The guy in the Corvette was already across the roadway, wheeling a hard-shell suitcase from Louis Vuitton behind him. I shouted, "Hey, Ozzy, wait up!"

He turned when he heard the name. I waved like an old friend and raised my camera. He shook his head, panicked, and bolted toward the terminal entrance. I eyed the flow of traffic. I didn't have time to wait for the light to green. I leapt toward a gap between cars, jerked back, and fell on my butt. The bouncer from the funeral loomed over me, his gray suit blotting out the sun. He'd taken me down so effortlessly I stared up at him in astonished admiration.

"You'll be happy to know your friend is gonna be okay." He extended a hand to help me to my feet. "Sorry if I was a little rough, but he's asking for you."

30

WHEN I RUSHED from bed the next morning to vomit in the bathroom sink, I realized I needed to face a little reality rather than turn my back to it and took the Rott for a walk to the drugstore around the corner, where I bought a package of five test strips. I followed the instructions on the box, the Rott watching from the bathroom doorway, his expression alternating between concern and amusement as I peed into a cup, dipped the test strip into the urine, and laid it onto the comparison chart. I've spent a good part of my adult life waiting, either in a prison cell or in a car, serving time or staking out one celebrity or another. I'm good at waiting. The three-minute gap between application and result was the longest three minutes of my life, and when the second line emerged within the strip's results zone, signaling a positive, I felt awed and overwhelmed, my life consumed by natural forces seemingly beyond my control.

The Rott sensed my emotional change and barked once before nudging against my leg, looking for a reassuring pat. I sat on the floor and gave him a good rub. I'll fight for a woman's right to choose as hard as anyone else, but I was thirty years old and wanted to be both strong and mature enough to take responsibility for the gifts and hardships dealt to me. I hadn't particularly wanted a child and felt more dread at the consequences than joy over the possibilities, but I figured that would change once I came to accept the inevitability of pregnancy and birth. My relationship with Sean was probably finished. I knew that would be just one of the costs of my pregnancy. I wasn't even sure I'd tell him the baby was his. If he wanted to figure out the cause-and-effect relationship of my pregnancy, he could do it without a pointed finger. I'd spent almost a year with the Rott, proving myself capable of caring for another creature. How much more difficult could it be taking care of a baby? I laughed at myself for thinking that. The Rott was easy. A baby wouldn't be. But I knew I could do it alone. The baby might miss out on having a father, but she'd have lots of uncles and a big dog with even fewer teeth than she had.

I needed to clear my head. Walks on the edge of a great wilderness are one of the great benefits of life near the ocean. I leashed the Rott, shouldered my camera bag, and jogged down the steps toward the street, so consumed by my thoughts that I didn't spot the white Tercel parked at the curb just beyond the base of the stairs until the rear passenger door squeaked open. Red flashed too high in the cabin to make visual sense until I realized it was the ex-con's polo shirt, exposed as he leaned over the front seat to open the back door. I jerked on the Rott's leash and pulled up as the ex-con shouted a single command of attack. A streak of brown raced from the rear passenger compartment, too compact to alarm me until I saw the muscular shoulders, blunt snout, and bone-shielded eyes of a pit bull mix.

The Rott turned instantly to meet the attack, the power of his lunge ripping the leash from my hand. The two dogs hit head to head, the pit bull's jaws snapping to the side, deflected by the force of the collision. The Rott whirled to catch the pit bull at the base of the neck, using his superior height and size to advantage. In less than a second Baby became an animal beyond my control, acting from a primitive instinct to attack and survive, completely unconscious of his unsuitability for fighting another dog. Without teeth, his jaw couldn't hold and the pit bull rose up, twisted, and snapped, its teeth digging into the flesh above the Rott's shoulder, near the throat. The Rott bucked, shocked by the pain, but the other dog clenched down, hind legs kicking to raise and straighten its stout body.

I shouted and tried to beat the animal off, my kicks like hitting a concrete block with a stick. The Rott stood his ground, bravely enduring the pain, but the pit bull vised his neck in jaws strong enough to snap wood. I backed away and sprinted up the steps to my apartment, fingers trembling to identify the door key amid the jumble of metal, counting each second in the Rott's blood. I screamed in anguish as the key bounced away from the lock on my first try, the adrenaline so charging my nerves it deflected my aim. I jammed the key into the lock on the second try and opened the door just wide enough to reach for the baseball bat inside the jamb. On the pavement below, the pit bull had taken the Rott down to one foreleg, securing its grip closer to the killing zone of the throat. I charged midway down the stairs and leapt.

As a breed, pit bulls suffer a physical weakness that doesn't hinder their deadly effectiveness as head-to-head fighters, one immediately apparent from a glance at their muscular, sloping profile—all jaws, neck, shoulders, and chest—the narrow join between torso and hips safe from attack by another dog but susceptible to a blow of great force. I landed at the base of the stairs and braked. The pit bull mix didn't bother to glance at me, its teeth sunk deep into the Rott's shoulder and neck. I cocked the bat and swung, the blow crashing down upon the animal's hips. Pit bulls have the highest resistance to pain of all breeds, and though the animal shuddered and yelped, its jaws didn't release their grip until a second blow, a few inches higher, brought wood into contact with bone and shattered its spine.

As I cocked the bat again, I tracked the shouts and charging footsteps of the ex-con as he skirted the hood of his car, and when he curved toward me I whirled and swung. He jerked back and flung his arms to deflect the swing, but the barrel of the bat skipped off his forearm and struck a glancing blow to his forehead. His feet shot out from beneath him and he fell back hard, stunned but still conscious. He rolled once and scrambled to get his feet onto the pavement. I didn't see that as an option. I swung the bat again, toward his ribs this time, and caught him hard enough to flip him onto his back. He screamed more in anger than from pain. Blood streamed down the Rott's neck and pooled at his paws. I didn't have time to negotiate. I golfed the head toward the ex-con's ankle, the crack of bat on bone solid as a struck fastball. The ex-con screamed again, this time not in anger, not at all.

I dashed to open the passenger door to the Cadillac, parked in its slot opposite the stairs. The Rott stumbled toward me, the fur at the wound in his throat flapped open, his eyes sheening like glass. He swayed at the door's threshold, unable to make the jump alone. I stepped over his back and gently wrapped my arms around his chest to boost him onto the passenger seat. It wasn't until I gently nudged the door shut that I looked up and spotted a burly man in a ponytail standing across the street, next to a BMW sedan, a video camera pressed against the right lens of his oversized sunglasses—Ray Spectrum, videotaping the entire incident. I bolted toward my camera bag, left on the pavement near where the Rott had been attacked, and threw myself behind the wheel.

I pushed the Cadillac close to flight speed down Lincoln Boulevard, swerving around traffic without regard for law or safety, pressing a towel against the wound in the Rott's neck to stanch the flow of blood. The anger I felt while striking the ex-con with the bat had flashed through me so quickly it didn't stick, and in thinking about Spectrum my anger directed itself too much at myself. Shortly after the Rott had first trotted to my side, a refugee from a brushfire in Malibu, he'd attacked someone who wanted to kill me and took a bullet as the reward for his heroics. He was a juvenile, less than three years old, but it had taken him months to fully recover, and he still limped a bit when he rose in the morning. How could I possibly allow myself to raise a child if the work I did routinely endangered my dog? What trick would Spectrum have pulled had I carried an infant in my arms rather than led a dog on a leash? I couldn't raise a child in peace and security if I couldn't safeguard my dog.

Maybe I was a fool, too willing to annoy people with the means to hurt me and those I loved, but I could drive, I'd say that for myself. I talked to the Rott while I ran yellows and dodged oncoming traffic, telling him he was a good dog, everything was going to be fine, and slalomed up to the veterinary hospital's emergency entrance in less than five minutes. The vet responding to the bell took a quick glance at the Rott and ran back to grab a gurney. I crouched by his head, noted that his eyes had blanked completely, his breath rapid but shallow, the leather seat beneath him a slick pool of blood. I lowered the seat back and when the vet returned, we lifted him onto the gurney's metal surface. He'd gone into shock, she told me, and pushed him through the entrance at running speed.

After the receptionist directed me to the bathroom to wash the dog's blood from my hands, she gave me a clipboard form and a glass of water with instructions to fill out the first and drink the second. The form gave me something to do, the effort of pushing the tip of a pen across paper focusing my thoughts on something other than the Rott's trauma, one of the calming effects of bureaucracy. What right did I have to think I could have a baby and raise it safe from harm? Aside from the extraordinary events of the past few days, a little rough-and-tumble is part of the paparazza's normal life. Could I risk backpedaling from a star's advancing entourage, seeking the elusive celebrity photograph, when slowed by six months of pregnancy? I doubted it. I'd have to beg for red-carpet jobs, the star-sanctioned photo ops at celebrity events like film premieres and awards shows. I didn't know who would hire me for that. Red-carpet and gotcha photography are not the same trade, as different as a domesticated dog and a wild wolf. I signed my name to the form and wrote a check to cover estimated costs, explaining to the receptionist that I didn't carry credit cards.

Spectrum had set me up like a true pro. He'd staked me out, done his research. He knew I was on parole. He knew how I felt about my dog and knew my reputation for angry outbursts. He'd hired the ex-con first to watch and then to provoke me, sure that he'd found my weakness, certain that I'd respond to an attack on my dog as though it was an attack on my own life. He knew the law made an important distinction that I did not. Assault with a deadly weapon was still assault, provoked or not. Spectrum had video-recorded me assaulting a man with a baseball bat, a felony serious enough to warrant immediate revocation of my parole, even if the State declined to prosecute, or if they did prosecute, failed to convict. Sure, I'd been provoked by a life-threatening attack on my dog, and yes, I had genuine cause to fear for my safety when the other dog's owner charged toward me; these might explain the use of a baseball bat to strike the attacking dog and then the first swing at its owner, but not the second blow to his ribs, and certainly not the third shot that shattered his ankle. Given a good lawyer—and I had a good one—I might win if the case ever went to trial, but even though a sympathetic jury might decide in my favor, the parole system would not. Assault with a deadly weapon was a clear violation of the parole agreement, provoked or justified or not. Arrest and return to prison were inevitable, the only question remaining the amount of time before my parole officer came calling with a pair of handcuffs.

I should have been angry, and I waited for my old friend and confidant, rage, to consume and thrust me toward one irresponsible act or another, but where before I'd burned with a liberating intensity, I now felt hollow and ashen. I burst into tears as I paced the hospital waiting room, just broke down and cried like a normal person whose dog lay near death and who now, pregnant for the first time in her life, faced two more years in prison. Rage always moved me to action. These feelings were different. They paralyzed me. For the first time in a long while I didn't know what to do. I felt helpless.

Then I got a call that put events in a different perspective.

"I got a message for you from Cassie," Pop said, so loudly I thought he'd lost his hearing.

"Things are a little crazy right now," I said. I didn't know where to start. Should I say goodbye to him now, or later? I doubted I'd have time to call again before they arrested me.

"She said it was important," he shouted. "She said if she wasn't back by now, I should call you with this message."

"What message?"

"That she's meeting Mick Jagger's assistant. Said he could get her a role in some new movie, what did she call it? *L.A. Cats? Brats?* Something like that. I told her it damn well better not be a rock band. And she said you shouldn't worry, she wasn't gonna drink anything. You got any idea what she's talking about?"

"Where is she? Did she say?"

"She's somewhere down near your part of town, Hollywood."

"Did she leave any way I could get in touch with her?"

"Well sure, I bought her a new phone yesterday, you know, the kind you kids put in your pocket. Why the little meathead didn't want to call you direct, that's what I want to know. You want the number?"

I grabbed the pen from the receptionist's desk and inked the ten digits he recited into the skin of my forearm. I punched the numbers into the cell and paced, listening to the distant rings with increasing anxiety. "Mick Jagger's assistant" could only be Jagger Starbal. How had she tracked him down? I hated feeling helpless. When voice mail picked up, I grabbed a services brochure from the counter and ran out the door. I knew why she hadn't called me direct. The clever little fool had connived a meeting with someone she knew I'd try to stop her from meeting. I left a message instructing her to call me immediately and started the Cadillac. After I hung up, I called again and left a second message repeating the same information just in case she somehow lost the first.

Ray Spectrum had staked me out and set me up, but maybe he

wasn't aware I knew who he was or where he worked. Midmorning traffic toward Hollywood flowed no worse than usual, the stream of cars trickling through knots near Westwood. I cut north to Sunset Boulevard west of the freeway and tracked a Porsche through the hills, just enough distance between bumpers to spot any traffic cops pulling out to stop him for speeding. The sight of the Rott's blood on the passenger seat and floorboard brought me close to tears again, but I shut them down and mopped at the blood with a towel as I drove. I'd have my time for revenge, and soon. Spectrum had been hired to stop me from looking into the Starbal connection, I felt sure of that. He'd started with threats and harassments, and when I'd refused to back off he decided it would be simpler to get rid of me legally, easy enough to do with someone serving out her sentence on parole.

I parked around the corner from Amoeba Records and took the bloody towel, camera bag, and baseball bat to the trunk. A parking sign near the corner advised no parking one day distant. I'd have to make sure I got the car moved before then. A parking ticket, documenting the presence of my car that close to Spectrum's office, wouldn't improve my legal situation, not considering what I planned to do that morning. I removed the camera and lenses from the camera bag and secured them inside an aluminum-padded case I kept in the trunk, decided to slip the point-and-shoot camera into my jacket pocket just in case. I wrapped the handle of the baseball bat in a sweatshirt from my change-of-clothes suitcase and stuffed the barrel into the emptied camera bag, then shut the trunk.

Nobody paid much attention to me when I walked through the lobby of Spectrum's building, the handle of the baseball bat protruding from the camera bag clenched to my side. I stepped into a parking elevator and rode it to the second subterranean level. The cars to the left were parked by assigned space, all owned by tenants and their employees. I backtracked toward the far-corner spot, where a three-car gap in the line revealed where the ex-con had parked his Tercel on the day I'd tracked him. I didn't see Spectrum's black BMW. Lucky me. He wouldn't have left the ex-con on the sidewalk, writhing in agony. If not worker's comp, then common decency required him to drive an injured employee to the hospital—even if a check of his employee records would find no mention of the ex-con's name. Checking someone into a hospital, that took time. I regretted what I'd been forced to do to the pit bull mix. I wondered what they'd done with him. Put him down, I guessed. I added that to my list of sins and slid under the Ford Taurus parked next to the empty space.

What had Cassie been thinking? On the night she appeared at my door, lugging that towering backpack, she'd shown an interest in the details of Christine's murder that I'd attributed to the morbid curiosity of an adolescent. As I lay under the car and waited for Spectrum to show—I guessed the third space was reserved for the Camry that rear-ended us the day before—I plotted out the days since she'd returned. She could have set up the meeting with Mick Jagger's so-called assistant while still in Phoenix, or at least begun the process. How could she have contacted them? Through the Internet? Pop didn't have an Internet connection. She could have used the library, but not enough time had passed to search, connect, and set up a meeting.

The night she appeared at my door, Cassie already knew about the Starbals through the appearance of the code word, *L.A. Brats,* on the Suicide Girls website. She'd talked to Nephthys and Tammy, and unlike me, she probably navigated the Internet with ease. I now assumed she knew everything I knew, if not more. But why was it so important to her? Did Christine's death fuel such outrage that she was willing to risk her own life to expose the killer? Adolescents make warped calculations of the risk of things, admittedly, and perhaps she didn't understand the dangers of her enterprise. But why had she made such an extreme effort rather than content herself with the usual teenage pleasures of chewing gum, cigarettes, bad music, and hormonally induced mood swings?

But no, she knew the risks. Cassie knew the risks of crime from the perspectives of both victim and perpetrator. I'd underestimated her capabilities a couple of times. She may have just turned fifteen, but she had criminal experience beyond her years and a natural ability that, had it been in a more conventional field, would have been considered prodigious.

When I heard the approaching swish of radials on concrete, I breathed deeply to calm any fluttering of nerves and turned my head to watch for tires swerving into the space next to me. Spectrum didn't seem like the kind of guy who'd be easy to sneak up on, and I knew that if I hesitated or allowed adrenaline to deflect my aim, the consequences could be fatal, if not for me, then for Cassie. If he backed in or carried a passenger, I'd be forced to abandon the plan altogether, but he headed straight into the nearest slot and braked with a scorching screech of rubber, the passenger door on my side of the space. I slid out from beneath the Taurus and pulled my feet under me, crouching in wait between the two cars. The motor fluttered to silence and the moment of inaction that followed stretched to uncomfortable seconds. I gripped the bat one-handed, a few inches above the knob, and focused on controlling my breath. The locks popped and the driver's door on the opposite side clicked open, the car shifting with the weight of someone stepping from behind the wheel. I leapt as Spectrum's head rose above the roof and I jabbed the barrel of the bat forward to spear him in the skull, just above the spine. He never saw me or the bat. He fell like a big bird shot from the sky, arms flapping as he dropped. I glanced around the parking structure. No witnesses, not yet.

Spectrum lay face down beneath the open door, briefcase dropped to one side, sunglasses splayed to the side of his face and keys sprawled a few inches from his fingertips. I snapped the keys from the pavement, and watching the body carefully for signs of movement, I opened the trunk. I'd hit him pretty hard in the back of the head and hoped I hadn't killed him. I grabbed his heels and dragged him to the back of the car. Desperation lent me extra strength. I bent at the knees, dug both hands under his belt, and trying not to cry out with the effort, I hoisted his midsection just over the top lip of the bumper, got my knees under his chest, and rolled his torso into the trunk. A quick frisk yielded cell phone and wallet but no videotape. When I shoved his legs inside he grunted, once, and blinked his eyes. I'd done the job right, hadn't killed him. That made me feel better about things. Technically, they called what I was doing kidnapping.

What the hell, in for a dime, in for twenty years to life.

I slammed the trunk.

31

RAY SPECTRUM DROVE a new BMW 540 sedan with leather seats and power everything, the 4.4-liter, 325-horsepower V-8 engine growling like a beautiful beast when I turned the ignition. I backed the thing cautiously out of the slot, careful not to scrape the car next to me or ding the one across the aisle, far less willing to put a dent in the fender of such a fine car than in the owner's head. He kept his parking card within easy reach, in the padded armrest behind the stick shift. I rolled up to the parking control arm, inserted the card, and accelerated onto Sunset, heading toward the Hollywood Freeway north. The car responded with an awesome surge of speed when I pushed the RPMs and it maneuvered with precision at every twitch of the steering wheel. I could outrun Jeff Gordon's Dupont Chevy in such a car, though I resisted the temptation of demonstrating it. Even a far more talented liar than I might have difficulty explaining to a traffic cop why she was driving a car with the registered owner stuffed in the trunk.

Now that I had Spectrum's attention, I needed to find a quiet and secure place to talk to him. I thought about driving into the parking lot at Dodger Stadium, a vast, empty space at that time of day, or perhaps up into Griffith Park, but neither guaranteed privacy from the awkward intrusion of a witness or cop. I could drive the BMW north, against the base of the desert mountains west of Palmdale, but that would take time. I didn't want to involve anyone else, but in the press of time I couldn't think of another way to work it. I called Pop to tell him Cassie was in trouble and I needed his help to get her out of it. Pop lost his temper, stringing together swear words that brought back less-than-pleasant memories from my girlhood. I waited for him to wind down, told him I needed his pickup truck out of the driveway and the garage door unlocked, enough space cleared in the garage to park a big sedan, and after that I'd need plenty of privacy. He asked me what I planned to do and we disconnected after I told him the less he knew, the better. I didn't want to involve him more than I had to. The scene could play out according to plan, Cassie released unharmed and the Rott recovered with no assault charges filed, or the scene could go bad, with unforeseen consequences. If he didn't know why I wanted his help, he couldn't be charged with a felony. Or so I thought.

I tore the vet's services brochure from my jacket pocket and called the number listed while I merged onto the Golden State Freeway toward the San Fernando Pass. The receptionist transferred the call to the vet. The dog had come through in good shape, she said, considering the loss of blood, but they wouldn't know for sure until a little more time passed. She spoke carefully to give me hope but not false expectations. When an animal goes into shock like that, kidney function is always impaired, sometimes fatally. The risk would decline and the prognosis improve with each passing hour. If the Rott made it through the next twenty-four hours, his chances of surviving the attack were good. I thanked her and promised to call again later that afternoon.

My phone beeped when I disconnected, Frank's name flashing across the display. I took the call, said, "This is not a good time to talk."

He picked up the stress in my voice, asked, "Anything wrong?"

"I won't know the answer to that for another hour."

"Anything I can do to help?"

I thought about it, not too proud to refuse, the freeway asphalt a blur beneath the BMW's long, black hood. "Spectrum have any weaknesses that you know of?"

"Why? Is he bothering you again?"

I glanced back toward the trunk.

"Sort of the other way around at the moment."

I couldn't drag Frank into this, not yet. If I told him what was going on, he'd be an accessory to whatever crime I committed.

"Why'd you call?" I asked.

"Because I get the *J-O-K-E.*"

"What do you mean?"

"I heard back from my guy at the DMV and did some checking at a production database called Filmtracker-dot-com. Ozzy's real name is Oren Flushberg, son of the producer Gary Flushberg, who won an Emmy for *American Firefighter*. Ozzy is one of four founding partners in Illusterious Productions, with Jagger Starbal, Bryan Kane, and Dustin Edwards. Kane and Edwards both have famous dads in the film business."

"Jagger, Ozzy, Kane, and Edwards," I said. "But not Stewart."

"Like I said, I get the joke, but why didn't he just tell you?"

"And rat out his own brother?"

"Isn't that what he sort of did by sending us the video?"

"Just the opposite," I said. "It was his only alternative. He couldn't go to the police without betraying his friends and family . . ."

"So he went to the tabloids?"

"Exactly. Sending us the video, that was meant to warn his brother off, let him know he couldn't keep getting away with it. When I threatened to publish Stewart's name in *Scandal Times,* it flipped him out. No wonder the poor kid killed himself. He didn't have anywhere to go except down that hole he was talking about."

"Suicide is just another word for spineless," Frank said. "If the kid had any character or guts, he wouldn't have killed himself."

"What was he supposed to do? Talk to his father? His father is such a whoremonger and bondage freak he probably inspired Jagger to follow in his footsteps. Was he supposed to go to the police? When the cop heading the investigation once worked on a film for his father?"

"Wait a minute," he objected. "I can't confirm that. Are you sure Sean said it was Logan who worked with Starbal on that film advisory thing?"

I noticed the cars falling rapidly away on my right and glanced down at the speedometer. The BMW was doing one hundred miles per hour like a knife through water. I downshifted to fourth and moved one lane to the right. "Yeah, that's what he said. Why?"

"The Internet Movie Data Base lists somebody else for that film."

"So maybe it's a mistake," I said. The IMDB listed every cast and crew credit for every film known. They couldn't be 100 percent accurate. Why would Sean tell me something like that unless he knew it for fact? I told Frank to double-check his sources and asked him to ring me back in an hour.

The freeway cleared of traffic near the pass and I risked a little extra speed to get over the hump. The briefcase Spectrum had been carrying lay on the passenger seat, next to a bottle of designer water. I pressed the lever and the locks flipped to reveal a Hi8 video camcorder—an older videotape technology. I understood why Spectrum hadn't yet converted to digital. Digital leaves too many records, the possibility for duplication as infinite as the Internet. How many times had I read that police technicians successfully salvaged from confiscated computer data files that supposedly had been deleted? Spectrum was too smart for that, his business too confidential to risk loss of control over the material. It's easier to control tape-to-tape duplication, and, if necessary, destroy all copies completely. Technically savvy young guys with deep pockets, they'd buy the newest and most expensive technology without fully understanding the consequences. They'd buy and shoot digital. Maybe that was how Stewart acquired the video copy of Christine's killing. Brothers have few secrets from each other. He'd hacked his older brother's computer and burned the digital file onto a disk.

I ejected the videocassette from the camera and stuck it into my pocket. The crime recorded on the tape would be minor compared to the crimes I'd be accused of should events spin beyond my control. As I drove, I contemplated an eye-for-an-eye approach: if the Rott died, I'd maim Spectrum in revenge. I tried to fantasize doing it and failed. He may have deserved severe injury for what he'd done to the Rott, but I wasn't going to take that responsibility on myself. I made no such promises if he refused to cooperate and Cassie was harmed as a result.

Pop was standing on the porch when I wheeled onto his street, the garage door propped open and his pickup parked at the curb in front of the house. He tracked the BMW with a slight lean forward. Cars that expensive were a rare sight on his street. He didn't spot me behind the wheel until the tires turned into the drive. I coasted under the garage door into a space cleared of boxes and tools. Pop's image slid into the rearview mirror and he pulled down the garage door. I turned off the ignition and stepped out of the car.

"You want to tell me what's going on?" he asked.

I was surprised to see him inside the garage. On the phone I'd asked for privacy. "Somebody in the trunk," I said.

He looked like he was about to ask the obvious question—why was somebody in the trunk?—but guessed the reason quickly enough. "He know where Cassie is?"

"That's what I'm going to ask him. You mind waiting outside?"

Pop reached into the shadows beside the garage door and pulled a shotgun from the wall. "My house. I'm staying."

"This isn't what I asked you to do," I said. "I need to talk to him alone."

"Sorry, it's either my way or the highway."

He'd used that expression a lot when I was growing up. I'd hated it no less then than now. I glared at him, trying to will him to back off. The fool was going to implicate himself in a crime. He backed toward the trunk, shotgun dangling casually from the crook of his arm. I reached into the passenger cabin to retrieve my baseball bat and contemplated the wisdom of giving him a little tap on the head, just enough to make him go night-night. Hitting someone over the head with a baseball bat isn't a surgical procedure, and I decided I'd be just as likely to do serious damage. "You do not lose your temper, under any circumstances," I said. "If anyone loses her temper here, it's me, particularly considering that shotgun you're holding." I keyed the lock, hoping I'd be able to swing a deal that would get Cassie back unharmed and keep Pop and me out of jail. Pop raised his shotgun and when I popped the trunk, Ray Spectrum's Southern California tan had gone deathly pale.

"Don't shoot, I'm gonna be—" He didn't finish the sentence before he leaned his head out the lip of the trunk and vomited at our feet.

Pop jumped back to avoid the splatter, the barrel of the shotgun dropping less than an inch, the difference between taking Spectrum's head off at the chin or the throat. "What's the matter, boy," he asked, "you didn't like your lunch?"

Spectrum cursed him and looked ready to vomit again.

He wasn't faking it. I backpedaled to the open driver door, leaned into the cabin, and retrieved the bottle of water. The year before, I'd gotten whacked hard enough on the head to make me sick. I knew how he felt. "Drink some water, wash the taste out of your mouth, you'll feel better," I said.

He eyed the water suspiciously and cursed me too but he took the bottle, washed out his mouth, and spat carefully away from our feet. Then he remembered his manners and thanked me. "You got the tape, I suppose?" he asked.

"You'll be happy to hear my dog is probably going to make it," I said.

He grunted. So what.

"What's this about your dog?" Pop asked.

I told him about the pit bull's attack.

"That's just mean," Pop said.

"It's only going to get worse because you're fucking with the wrong people." Spectrum wiped his mouth and looked at the sleeve of his suit as though the stain distressed him. "We tried more polite ways of convincing you to cease and desist but you weren't willing to listen, and one kid's already dead as a result."

"The way I see it, this is a lose-lose situation," I said.

Then I didn't say anything; I just watched and waited for him to engage. He put the bottle to his lips and drank so deeply the plastic sides caved, then dribbled a few drops into the palm of his hand and splashed his face. "Can I get out of the trunk?" he asked.

"No," I said.

He capped the water and lay back on one elbow, the tan seeping back into his face, and calculation trickling into his eyes. "What do you want?"

"Not to lose everything. Just like you and your client."

"Then you're willing to deal?"

"If I didn't want to deal," I said, very carefully, "you'd be under a foot of desert sand right now."

"Tough bitch, eh?" He spat outside the trunk, making a comment as much as clearing the taste from his mouth. "Tell me what you're thinking."

"The son of your client belongs to a group of young men dedicated to meeting gullible young women, slipping them ruffies, then gang-raping and sometimes killing them."

He stared from the depths of the trunk, his eyes as black as his hair but not as lustrous. It was my first good look at him without his sunglasses. He was a good-looking guy, in a block-headed, pugnacious kind of way. "That's just total bullshit," he said.

"Is that what's happening to Cassie?" The shuffle of Pop's feet on the garage floor signaled his agitation, a bad sign.

I shoved the palm of my hand toward his face to shut him up. "It's not bullshit," I told Spectrum. "That's what we're going to print in the next issue unless we come to an understanding."

"*Scandal Times*? Nobody believes anything they read in that rag."

"Guess that's why you're so interested in shutting me up," I said. "But that's only part of the deal."

"Deal? We don't have a deal. What deal are you talking about?"

"The deal that keeps you alive."

"Oh, that deal," he said, nodding. "What do you want?"

"My niece."

He cocked his head and stared at me, clearly thinking I was crazy.

"She got suckered into meeting Jagger Starbal. I don't know, maybe the others are there too Kane and Edwards at least, the ones who help him drug and rape his victims." I got the shakes while I spoke, images of what could be happening to Cassie blowing through my mind. "The thing you gotta understand is, my niece is fifteen years old."

"So what do you want me to do about it?"

I tapped the barrel end of the bat against the concrete, one-two-three, the nerves twitching my arms and brain, telling me to break the guy's leg to encourage better cooperation. I resisted. "Call Starbal, Jason or Jagger, whoever's paying you your fee. Tell him it's a standoff. If he releases my niece, unharmed, I'll stop going after the story and do my best to keep it from publication. I can't guarantee *Scandal Times* won't print anything because it's not my paper, but they won't get the story from me."

"What guarantee can you give that you won't go to print?" A wry smile gapped his lips, as though he found some humor in his situation. "I mean, what you say is good enough for me, particularly that part about staying alive, but to sell this I gotta have something you can't go back on."

The sweat beading on his forehead belied his cool. I didn't know whether or not I could trust him, but I couldn't think of another way to play it. I pulled the Hi8 videocassette from my jacket pocket and tossed it to him. "That's over a year in prison to me," I said. "Assuming I beat the assault rap."

"What's to guarantee you won't just whack me over the head and take it back?" Again, the wry smile, as though he accepted his predicament but didn't fear it.

"Honor among thieves."

When he stretched out his hand, I returned his cell phone and watched him touch two numbers; whoever he called was on autodial. "We've got a problem here," he began, and heard in response an answer that didn't please him. "I don't give a rat's ass whether you're busy or not. You want to extricate yourself from the mess you're in, you unbusy yourself and listen." He rolled his eyes at the reply and cut off the speaker. "That's exactly the problem I'm talking about, a problem that's now part of the solution. Tell me exactly what the situation is, where you are, and what condition everyone's in." He looked up at me, the phone pressed against his ear, and nodded, encouraged by what he heard.

"Somewhere public," I said. "He can name the place."

"The girl's aunt will be there in thirty-five, forty minutes. If she finds the girl unharmed, then the current problem you have with the tabloids will go away. You understand what I'm telling you?" Spectrum listened for a moment, then dropped his voice and whispered, "She's fifteen years old, you asshole." He pressed disconnect, smiled as though everything was going to be fine, and dropped the phone into his side pocket, as though by habit.

"Has she been drugged?" I asked.

"They're in a Starbucks, the one at Sunset and Gower. She was late getting there, something about getting off the bus. He hasn't even talked to her."

That didn't mean she hadn't been drugged. If she'd been drugged, they could deny kidnapping her without fear of contradiction. Anything could have happened and she wouldn't know about it until results from the rape kit came back. "If she's there as promised, you'll be released, no more questions asked," I said. "If she's been harmed in any way, we'll talk again about the deal."

He nodded like that was fair, his eyes tracking my hand as it moved to the trunk lid. "I'll be good," he said. "You don't have to do that."

"Sorry, but I do. Watch your head."

I shut the trunk and backed to the garage door.

"You'll take me with you," Pop said, the shotgun cradled in the crook of his arm. "If something's happening to Cassie, you'll need me."

I told him to hide the gun and then I put my shoulder to the garage door, the afternoon light stabbing at my eyes. I looked at the BMW, then at Pop's pickup truck, thinking about it. "You're right, I need you," I said, words I never thought I'd hear myself say. "I need you here, with the BMW, and I need you to loan me your pickup. Can you hear the phone if I call the house?"

"I can hear just fine," he said, insulted.

"Then listen for it. After I pick up Cassie I'll call to tell you where to drop the BMW. Be sure you wipe down the interior—steering wheel, dash, door handles—anywhere we've possibly touched. The key, too. Don't forget to wipe the key."

He nodded as though I'd told him the obvious.

'The guy in the trunk?" I let the question hang, trying to think if I'd forgotten something while I waited.

"What about him?"

"Don't let him out until you drop the BMW. Don't let him know who you are or where you live. He's a pro. If you give him any advantage, he'll put *you* in the trunk."

"He won't, you can count on that." He tossed me the keys to his truck. "This Starbal you mentioned, he the same guy from the movies?"

I nodded.

"That rich son of a bitch, as if he doesn't have enough already."

"I'm not going after him," I said. "I'm going after his son."

Pop looked at me in a way I remembered from my childhood, when he was teaching me one sport or another and I'd made solid contact with a ball or chin. "Don't know when I'll get another chance to say this so I'd better say it now. You two girls are everything to me. No matter what happens, remember I'll do anything to protect you."

I flushed with unexpected emotion, a mix of pride and regret, and stepped up to kiss him on the cheek, breaking it off quickly to slap at my pockets to make sure I still had my cell phone. Then it struck me, the thing that had been bothering me since I'd walked from the garage, and I rushed back to the trunk, Pop scrambling behind to grab his shotgun.

Spectrum glanced up at me when the trunk popped open, blinking his eyes from the light, pretending to be surprised to see me again. I pointed to the side pocket of his suit coat.

"Your cell phone," I said.

32

POP'S BIG AND ugly Dodge Ram pickup perched me a good four feet off the ground, the better to see the subcompacts crunching beneath its oversized tires. I fiddled with Spectrum's cell phone while I sped the surface streets toward the freeway. He owned a new Nokia, the controls different from my older Ericsson. I'd left him in the trunk with his phone just long enough to make a call. I couldn't immediately figure out how to get to his call list, not while maneuvering the pickup through traffic. Who could he call? He knew his life depended on the safe return of my niece. He could have called the police, but what could he tell them? That he was stuffed in a trunk somewhere? They wouldn't know where to begin to look. He couldn't tell the cops about me. Even if he was willing to risk exposing Jagger to arrest on charges of kidnapping a minor, he didn't know Pop's truck or license plate. He could have called one of his employees—maybe the bruiser who smashed his car into Frank's Honda at the airport. An employee made the most sense. He'd want someone to monitor my meeting with Jagger and intervene if something went wrong. Either that or he'd called his priest to make sure the warranty hadn't expired on his latest confession. I decided not to worry about it. When the cell phone in my pocket chirped with a call, I tossed Spectrum's phone onto the passenger seat.

"I double-checked the production info on Starbal's films and didn't find Logan mentioned anywhere," Frank said, getting straight to the point of his call. "I also ran Logan through both the Internet Movie Data Base and Filmtracker and didn't get a single hit. If he ever worked for Starbal—or on any film for that matter—he kept his name off the credits."

"Can you think of a reason why he'd do that?"

"Not anything that makes sense. I suppose he could have made sure his contribution went uncredited because they paid him under the table. I found out something interesting about Spectrum, though."

I leaned forward in the cab to check the side mirror as I blasted onto the Golden State Freeway south. Spectrum's interrogation had taken too much time, traffic already beginning to thicken as the day spun toward mid-afternoon, the start of rush hour. I flexed my foot against the accelerator and swept a glance toward the rearview mirror, watching for the Highway Patrol. "I don't think Spectrum's going to be much of a problem now," I said.

"Maybe you're wrong there," Frank said, the smugness of a scoop infiltrating his voice. "Guess where he worked when he was with the LAPD."

I immediately thought, *no way.*

"North Hollywood," he said, beating me to it.

"When?" I asked.

"Fifteen years ago. Guess who else worked there at that time?"

"Logan?"

"You got it. Spectrum worked vice and Logan robbery-homicide. They weren't partners but they knew each other, guaranteed."

"Looks like I'm in more trouble than I thought." I ground my teeth and added another foot pound of pressure to the accelerator. The way I looked at it, I was in so much trouble a little more didn't make any real difference. What's another bullet to a corpse?

"You want to tell me what's going on?"

"Not particularly, but if I don't contact you within two hours, call your sources in law enforcement and find out if I've been arrested."

"You want me to call the *Scandal Times* lawyers?"

"It's way past libel lawyers. You know Belinsky, my criminal lawyer?"

Belinsky had represented me on an illegal weapons charge the year before, a Philadelphia-born lawyer in cowboy boots, bolo tie, and fringed leather jacket who pontificated like a cracker-barrel philosopher, an act juries found irresistible. Frank had been at my arraignment and still had Belinsky's number in his address book.

"One other thing," I said. "I need you to get my car. It's parked around the corner from Amoeba Records."

"I'll leave it in front of your apartment," he said. "I know why you don't want to tell me what's going on and I don't know whether I should be grateful or just plain mad."

"A little bit of both," I said.

He wished me luck and disconnected. I veered off the freeway at Gower, a five-block straightaway from Sunset. That Spectrum and Logan worked together at North Hollywood didn't necessarily mean that they'd stayed in touch and exchanged information on cases of mutual interest. It didn't necessarily follow that Spectrum had approached Logan with a request to pressure me. Logan could have been acting independently when he threatened to revoke my parole if I didn't back away from the Starbal family. The connection could have been a coincidence, but it made me feel no less surrounded. I took solace in the fact that I was, at that moment, less hemmed in than Spectrum. The green-and-white Starbucks logo glistened near the corner of Sunset and Gower. I'd never been so happy to see the franchise in my life. I swung into the parking lot and jumped from the cab, leaving the baseball bat and my camera bag behind.

Cassie sat beside a table along the back wall of the franchise, her hands wrapped around a large plastic cup that frothed whipped cream at the top. Next to her, a cockily handsome young man leaned with his back to the wall, the Abercrombie & Fitch distressed denim baseball hat that tilted over his eyes unable to conceal the intense interest he took in my arrival. Cassie noticed the subtle change in the young man's focus and turned her head toward the entrance. When she saw me moving toward the table, her eyes widened and she shook her head as though panicked. "What are you doing here?" She covertly jerked a look toward the guy next to her as though trying to warn me something was up.

"Are you okay?" I asked.

"Of course I'm okay. Why wouldn't I be?"

Four tables away, backed into the corner of the café, two men in their early twenties sat hunched over their creamed coffee drinks, pretending not to observe my entrance. I recognized their faces from Stewart's funeral—they'd greeted Ozzy when he'd stepped from his Corvette—and figured they were the other two charter members of Illusterious Productions, Bryan Kane and Dustin Edwards. None of the few customers that afternoon were large, athletic men in the slick attire of professional bodyguards; if Spectrum had called an employee, he hadn't yet arrived. I pulled out the chair across the table and sat, examining Cassie for any sign of trouble other than the distress she showed at my arrival. Her Goth look was gone for the moment, replaced by a long-sleeved striped cotton shirt and a pair of preppy chinos, her breasts swelling against the shirt as though she'd gained two cup sizes since I'd last seen her. Or three. I flipped open my cell phone, found Pop's number on the call list, and called it.

"She's my aunt," Cassie said, as though my presence embarrassed her. "I don't even know why she's here."

"Please, be quiet for a moment, something's happening you don't know about." While I listened to the signal ring Pop's distant phone, I observed Jagger. He reclined as though utterly relaxed, one arm slung casually over the back of his chair and his opposite hand loosely clenched into a fist on the table, a week-old scab running like a stain across the knuckles. He looked familiar to me, but then, he dressed so much like he'd stepped out of a casual clothing catalog—cargo pants, Timberland hiking boots, and a down vest from North Face worn over a baseball tee—that he looked familiar in the ubiquitous way of all devotees of name-brand clothing. He had Stewart's broad, sloping cheeks and full lips, and though the eyes clearly belonged to a different, more feral kind of human being, I could see how someone might confuse them, particularly if one of the brothers encouraged it. I pointed to his knuckles, said, "You got those from beating Stewart."

His upper lip, plump and ripe, curled into a smirk.

"The time you picked up that girl out in Palmdale you wore your brother's sweatshirt and bucket hat, didn't you?"

He shrugged, maybe yes, maybe no—who cared?

Pop's phone continued to ring like a rock falling through space. He wasn't picking up. His hearing wasn't that great, but it wasn't that bad, either. Had he been so addled with bravado that he'd opened the trunk? Maybe he'd forgotten to open the door from the garage into the utility room and couldn't hear the phone through the closed door. Or Spectrum had called someone on his cell who managed to track down the BMW. But how? It didn't seem possible, unless he'd equipped his wheels with a GPS tracking system, the receiver signaling the car's location to a remote computer. Too much time was passing. I needed to make it look good if nothing else. "About time," I said to the ringing phone. "She's here and okay. You can let him go." I disconnected the cell and stuffed it into the side pocket of my jacket.

"Did you mean to implicate your brother when you raped her?" I shifted in the chair to face Jagger, both feet planted to move quickly. "I'm confused, because I can't figure why else you'd steal his clothes to wear when you abducted her."

"I didn't steal his clothes," he said. "I borrowed them."

"And now, thanks to you, he's dead."

"The little traitor deserved everything he got."

"You don't sound like you're grieving."

"So the weakest bird in the nest fell to his death. More food for us all." He tapped his fist on the table and opened it to reveal a micro-cassette recorder. "Goodness, look what I found."

"You get a kick out of recording things," I said. "I already know that."

"The little bitch was carrying this." He flipped his wrist and the recorder clattered onto the table. "I think she wanted to record something incriminating."

Cassie stared at the drink in front of her, the whipped cream sub-stance melting over the top rim, the flare of her nostrils with each deep breath a sign that she worked to control her temper. Then she looked at me, and from the heat of her glance she seemed angry with me as much as at him. She was working on something, the look said, and I was interfering. If she was working on something, tough. It was my turn.

"You ever meet Andrew Luster?' I asked.

He glanced up, surprised to hear the name, and spun the micro-cassette recorder around the table with his forefinger.

"Your friends at the next table, any of them meet Andrew Lus-ter?"

He smiled and spun the recorder faster and faster, said, "You can't print any of this anyway, so what does it matter?"

"Did you know Stewart had a crush on Christine before you killed her? Or did that make it an even bigger thrill for you?"

He slapped the recorder to stop it from spinning.

"I didn't kill her," he said.

"Who did, then? Ozzy?" I cocked my head toward the table where Kane and Edwards sat. "Bryan, or maybe Dustin?"

Jagger spun the recorder and watched it go with a studied diffidence.

"Stewart didn't betray you," I said. "He knew you were raping and killing girls. He wanted to make you stop. That's why he leaked the video to me. But he never mentioned your name, or the names of the others either."

Jagger lifted a single finger and said, "Just one died."

"Just one? Charlotte McGregor's lucky you didn't kill her, too."

"Charlotte who? Who's that?"

"You don't even remember her name? The woman in Palmdale."

He rolled his eyes, spun the recorder again. "How the fuck am I supposed to know her last name?"

"Maybe because you almost killed her."

He shook his head. I had it wrong.

"I remember that one, just not her name," he said. "She was pretty hot. But this super moral attitude you're copping, it only means you don't understand the scene. These girls are players. They know the score. They get drugged out of their minds all the time. So what if they wake up and can't remember what happened? It's like, what's the big deal? If you ask for it, don't complain when somebody gives it to you."

Cassie said, "Then you admit to drugging her?"

Jagger had the courage to look at my niece that he lacked when speaking to me. "I've got your tape recorder, darling, so go ahead, ask all the incriminating questions you want, or better, just shut the fuck up."

"I first thought your brother had been there, in the room when you raped her." I tapped the table to get his attention. "I figured he felt so guilty about it he sent me the video, but I was wrong about that. He didn't participate, but he knew what was going on. He couldn't go to the police, couldn't tell the cops his own brother was raping girls. The only thing he could do was try to make it stop another way, by involving me."

He spun the tape recorder again.

I lunged forward to stop it with a clenched fist.

"Did your brother beg you to spare Christine? Did you taunt him with an invite to join in the fun of raping and killing her?"

"She wasn't supposed to die." He stared forward, eyes fixed to the table, waiting for me to remove my fist. The physical intrusion on his personal space disturbed him, and he glanced up and away, pretending to be bored with it all. "Ozzy got a little carried away, put too much pressure on the strap, and I didn't notice until it was too late. It was a mistake. Regrettable. But hey, shit happens."

I said, "So it was an accident."

"Totally." He drew out the "o" in that word, sounding like just any another affected Southern California kid. "I mean, half the fun was imagining what happened afterwards, you know, after they came out of their trance." His brows compressed and he leaned forward, animated by the importance of what he wished to say. "You can't take it so fucking seriously. I mean, the girl who died, sure, that was a shame, but the others? It was just a game, a little harmless sport. Most of the girls, they didn't have a clue what happened. They'd wake up the next morning, or whenever, and—I'm imagining this part—they'd go, like, whoa, I'm a little sore, where was I last night?" He laughed, finding that funny. "Only one bitch even got as far as the police. The rest of them? Nothing. Nada. They never knew what happened." He stared at me head on, daring me to understand the logic. "It's a victimless crime, don't you see? Like the tree that falls in the forest. If you don't remember it, did it really happen?"

"If you kill someone, the victim doesn't remember either," I said. "Does that mean you didn't kill her?"

"I didn't think you'd understand," he said.

"She's too old," Cassie said. "She's, like, thirty. She doesn't get the joke."

Jagger slipped his head back to give her a sidelong glance, said, "Well, aren't you the freaky one."

I think he meant it as a compliment.

"Freaky-deaky," she agreed. "How many bitches did you play?"

"Nine. Too bad, you could have been number ten." He shook his head, regretting the loss. "Come back and see me when you make eighteen. I don't want to corrupt the morals of an underage girl."

"I'd cut you up with a knife and stuff the flesh down your throat as you died, starting with your balls," she said. "And then I'd stick your head in a box and mail it to your dad as punishment for bringing your sorry ass into the world."

Jagger inched away from Cassie as though she spooked him.

"You drugged and raped nine girls," I said, stunned by the number.

"And the true shame? You can't do anything about it. Even if you go back on your promise to Ray, I've got other resources you can't even imagine."

"You hired Spectrum?"

He shrugged.

"You've got a rich, powerful daddy."

"The police can be bought. Shocking, isn't it?"

I figured he was referring to Logan.

"Does he know what you're doing" I asked.

"Dad?" The cell phone in one of the multiple pockets of his cargo pants riffed a tune. He ignored it. "Dad taught me everything I know."

"Like father, like son?"

He winked at me, deadpan.

"Look, we're sorry about your friend. We promise not to be bad boys anymore." He glanced at his friends in the corner. "But really, considering the fact that our families practically own this town and your family aspires to the level of white trash, you should be happy that you're not dead or in jail, understand?" The cell phone continued to ring, as though the caller had hung up before the call switched to voice mail and called again. He glanced down to lift the phone from his pocket and gave the calling number a puzzled look. His voice morphed to an agreeable whine when he lifted the phone to his ear. "Hi! What's up?" His smirk straightened and then drooped to open-mouthed surprise. He listened, shoulders slumping as his chest deflated, curling him over the surface of the table. "Yes," he said. "Yes, I will. He can talk to them right now if he wants." He listened again. "Okay. I'm really sorry about this. I'll tell them."

He hung up the phone and dropped it onto the table, still clutching Cassie's microcassette recorder in his opposite hand. "Someone who says he's your father just broke into our house. Can you fucking believe it? He's holding my dad at gunpoint and won't let him go until he knows you're okay."

"Pop?" Cassie backed sharply from the table. "What's he doing there?"

"Give me your house number, I'll call him," I said.

"He won't accept that," Jagger said, calculations of bloodshed flickering in his eyes. "Dad said he demands to see you in person before he'll back off."

"Just give me the listing," I said.

I punched the numbers as he recited them and listened to a distant phone ring unanswered. I wondered then if he'd given me the correct number. I turned to Cassie and told her we had to move—fast.

She stood and thrust her hand palm up toward Jagger.

"Give me my recorder back," she said.

"Fuck off, you skank."

I didn't think about it. My feet shifted and hips rolled with the muscle memory of a right cross, my fist crashing into the smirking point of his full lips. His head snapped over the chair back and he toppled spine first to the floor. I leapt to my feet. He lashed out, his mouth smeared with blood, and tried to stand. I kicked him in the face as he rose, the force and weight of the Doc Marten boot breaking his nose to the side like a branch from a tree.

Kane and Edwards backed from their table in the corner, the sudden violence sucking the testosterone straight from their veins. Across the café, the *barista* bent over the service counter, stunned still while handing a cup of cappuccino to a T-shirted young woman. The recorder clattered to a stop on the floor. Cassie dashed to retrieve it and despite my shouted command to hurry, she stopped to look down at Jagger Starbal writhing on the floor.

"This is just the start," she said and spat on his face.

33

THE RAM'S TIRES played a serenade on asphalt peeling out of the Starbucks parking lot, rubber smoke drifting across my rearview mirror as we sped onto Gower. No one popped from the café to give chase or record our license plate number, and from what I could tell from brief glances in the mirrors as I drove, no one staked us out from a car parked in the lot. I accelerated around a floral delivery van to catch the tail end of a yellow onto Sunset, the pickup truck careening through the turn like a wild beast. We were twenty minutes from Beverly Hills in thickening traffic. I chased the next pack of cars ahead, intent on working to the front and then timing the traffic lights.

"That was awesome!" Cassie shouted, fumbling with the buttons to her blouse. "Will you teach me to hit like that?"

"Ask Pop. He's the one taught me."

"He says my arms are too thin, I got no power."

"If your form is right, you'll have power enough." I sped into the far right lane, cleared of curbed parking at the start of rush hour. "You might not have the strength to lay someone out like that, not unless it's someone your own size, but you can hit hard enough to surprise them, sure."

"We've already been working out together, you know, with the gloves." She plunged her hand into the gap in her shirt and pulled from behind the padding of her bra a microcassette recorder, the twin to the one she still held in her hand.

"You had two recorders? You were recording that?"

"I let him see the first figuring he wouldn't look for the second," she said and pressed the rewind button. "Always give a sucker a little something to let him think he's winning. It's something Mom taught me. And always keep your real stash separate from your giveaway stash—the money or drugs it won't hurt to lose if you're robbed."

"Your mother taught you that?"

"Don't sound so shocked. I did my first cons in diapers." She pressed play long enough to confirm Jagger's voice had been recorded on the tape, muffled, but audible. "Rich daddy or not, I think we got him."

I held out my right hand, palm out, and she slapped it. I'd promised Spectrum that I wouldn't seek to publish photographs or stories about Starbal; I never vowed to keep my niece from taking evidence to the police. Spectrum might expose the videotape in retaliation, a risk I'd be willing to take if it yanked Jagger Starbal and his pals out of the breeding pool. Anger mixed with pride, and I felt compelled to play the role of cautioning auntie. "What you just did was incredibly stupid and dangerous," I said.

"No, what I just did was justice," she replied, her self-certainty unassailable. "You want to see stupid and dangerous, I'll tell you about some stuff I did before I met you."

"They could have seriously hurt or killed you."

"Those punks?" A burst of disdain blew from her lips. "I used to hang with a crew who'd steal the wheels and wallets from punks like that and leave 'em stark naked by the side of the road. Pop get his instructions mixed up?"

"What do you mean?"

"He wasn't supposed to call you for another hour. And then I was late getting here because of the stupid bus. I can't wait until I get my driver's license."

I glanced at her between lane changes. No doubt or remorse troubled her brow. Criticizing her just then wasn't going to help. Later, given time and a quiet place, I might sit her down to explain things. "How'd you set up the meeting?" I asked.

"I called him, said I wanted to hook up, the kinkier the better." She ejected the tape from the recorder and dug into the front pocket of her pants for another cassette. "The first time I called him, it was from Phoenix. I told him I was visiting relatives, I'd contact him when I got back to L.A."

"He didn't think you were a cop?"

She gave me a scornful look, eyebrows furrowed and lips pursed.

"I think I know what cops sound like. Trust me, I didn't sound like a cop. And that shit he was trying to sell you about not knowing my age? He knew. That was part of the turn-on. Besides, how many fifteen-year-old cops do you know?" She stuffed the recorded tape down the front of her pants—another trick her mother probably taught her. "What's going down with Pop? What's he doing at Starbal's, and why are you driving his truck?"

Cassie cursed violently when I told her what happened to the Rott. The swear words she used and the way she strung those words together shocked me. "I know you're mad," I told her, "but you have to learn different language to express it. Those words you're using, they're just plain ugly."

"Okay, Mom," she said. "Next time I lose my temper, I'll hit somebody."

"You're right, I'm an idiot," I said, and we laughed together, laughed a little of the tension off.

"Did he just lose it, or what?" Cassie asked. "Why didn't he stay home?"

"I suspect he thinks he's got something to prove."

"Like what?"

"That he loves you, for one."

"Not just me." She turned away to stuff the recorder back under her bra. "He talks about you all the time, at the house. It's kinda weird, actually, how much he talks about you."

"I'm sure he taught you a few swear words talking about me."

"No, it's like he admires you." She buttoned her blouse over the recorder, then looked down to make sure her falsies lined up. "Says you were the only person with the guts to stand up to him and it taught him something, only he's sorry it took him so long to learn. Says if he ever loses his temper with me, I should stand up to him like my Aunt Nina." She shifted in the seat to face me, asked, "Does it show? The recorder?"

Not to anyone who didn't know she had yet to grow much in the way of breasts, I thought, but just shook my head. "Do you see a cell phone, maybe between the seat and the door?"

Cassie squirmed and reached behind her, the cell phone emerging with her hand. She'd been sitting on it. "Wondered what that was," she said. "Whose is it?"

"Spectrum, the private investigator I was telling you about. Do me a favor and see if you can figure out the last person he called."

She tucked her feet under her and brought the display close to her face, pressing buttons in rapid trial-and-error style. It took her less than five seconds to find it. The ten-digit number she recited sounded familiar. I asked her to repeat it, then said, "Call it."

I grabbed the phone and pressed it against my ear, listening to the signal buzz and then click over to voice mail. One word into the announcement I recognized the voice and flung the phone against the windshield, the cell bouncing off the dash and out the open window on Cassie's side. The tears came to my eyes unasked and brought little solace.

"At least you didn't swear," Cassie said, "Who was it?"

To stay silent was to admit to weakness.

"Sean," I said.

"That cop? Why would the P.I. call him?"

We swung right onto Hillcrest and into Beverly Hills, sweeping past the manicured lawns, sculpted shrubbery, and ornately turned gates of fairy-tale estates that sheltered princes and dragons in equal number. I tried not to think. I needed to get Pop away from Starbal before the cops were called to arrest him on charges of breaking and entering. Holding a shotgun on someone, what kind of crime was that? False imprisonment? Hostage taking? Making criminal threats? If things turned out badly, he could spend the rest of his life in prison.

But we were on a roll, I thought; everything would work out for us. What was I going to figure out by thinking? Spectrum had called Sean. So what? It didn't have to mean anything. It didn't have to mean the realization of the worst fears given to my imagination. My brain spun inside its case of bone, all my assumptions reversing at high speed. Logan wasn't the only cop who worked the same station that Spectrum had—Sean was currently assigned to North Hollywood. I didn't know if the dates lined up—Spectrum might have resigned before Sean made detective—but Sean was well acquainted with Logan and it made sense he'd also know Spectrum by reputa-

tion, if not personally. Given my sudden change in perspective, nothing that happened between us seemed genuine. Little wonder he'd
been so eager to get me away for the weekend. He'd known Stewart
was to be buried then. He wanted me out of the way. And when we
showed up at the funeral Spectrum had spotted us immediately, as if
he'd been tipped that we'd be there. Even his seeming hostility toward Logan could have served a different, insidious purpose. Hadn't
his warning that Logan once worked on a film with Jason Starbal
proved false? He didn't want me talking to Logan. He wasn't trying
to protect me. What I knew endangered Spectrum's clients. He
wanted to distance me from Logan because information we were un-
covering would change the course of the investigation and lead him
directly to the Starbals. Seemingly innocuous things, such as the time
he'd pulled up behind my car when I was staking out the Starbal estate, did not now seem so innocent.

But Sean had been genuinely passionate when we'd made love,
and those times he'd angered me his remorse had seemed sincere. He
didn't have to be a two-faced, lying son of a bitch. I couldn't believe
that night in the darkroom had been staged. And later, when he'd appeared at my door and we'd nearly assaulted each other with sexual
passion, that had been as real as anything I'd ever experienced.
Maybe Spectrum knew that Sean and I were sleeping together and
called him from the trunk to guarantee his safety. Of course. The ex-
con had been staking out my apartment the night that Sean appeared
at the door. He'd made Sean's car as a police vehicle. A man with
Spectrum's resources could track the plates to the vehicle sign-out
sheet or identify him from the ex-con's surveillance photos. He'd call
Sean from the trunk to beg for help, reasoning that a cop boyfriend
would have the power and smarts to restrain me. It hurt to think. I
wanted to run. I imagined the sand beneath my feet as I ran to the
rhythm of high surf, breathing the sea air deep into my blood.

The gilded gates to the Starbal estate hung open at the end of a
sweeping curve. I swerved into the driveway and stood on the
brakes, twisting the steering wheel to the left as the rubber bit into
brick. The pickup fishtailed right, the back end spinning out. We
rocked to a stop just beyond Spectrum's BMW, the grille facing the
gates, ready to throw the car into gear and speed onto the street once
we grabbed Pop. Cassie leapt down from the cab before I jerked the

transmission into park. I shouted at her to stop but she raced away, up the golden brick drive and around the gold-plated monument to Starbal's failed Oscar aspirations. Past the marble colonnades, the double front doors at the top of the steps stood ajar.

I jumped from the pickup truck and sprinted. Cassie took the steps two at a time, her footwork as awkward as a colt's. She paused at the door, looking back to hurry me on, then whirled and dashed into the house. I gauged my speed and distance and hurdled the steps. The door came up fast and I clipped it with my shoulder, bouncing into a foyer tiled with gold, Hollywood Walk of Fame–style stars.

Cassie ran to the end of the hallway, stopped, and turned into a wide, arching doorway to her left, shouting Pop's name. I'd seen the tiles before, on the floor in the room where Christine had been killed. The air split with a sound like snapping metal—once, twice—then a monstrous roar washed through the hall, the unmistakable sound of a shotgun blast. Cassie screamed Pop's name and rushed forward. I yelled at her to stop. She didn't. I caught sight of her heels as I breached the doorway into a room so vast and empty it might have served as a ballroom. She slid into another archway to the right, her scream shredding the air.

I flew across the tiled floor, the biting smell of cordite thickening near the archway, fragments of a room that looked like a study flashing to my eye—a desk, bookcases, and a balding, bespectacled man hugging the far wall next to a floor-to-ceiling window overlooking the swimming pool. The light from the window spilled across a ponytailed man sprawled guts down on a blue Persian carpet stained with a gush of blood, the revolver just beyond his outflung hand pointed toward my niece, who kneeled, keening in her sudden grief, over the fetus-curled body of my father.

The man huddling against the wall watched me as I dropped to my knees, his angular, mid-fifties face frightened as a child's. He risked a few steps away from the wall, toward Spectrum's corpse. I crawled on my hands and knees to Cassie's side, wrapped my arm around her shoulder, and stared down at the dead face of my father, his eyes staring forward like they'd been welded open, his mouth gaped in shock. Two ragged blotches of blood, shaped like deformed flowers, stained his shirt at the back, the fabric blown out at the center of each to reveal the meaty core of his wounds. In the clenched hand that curled toward his chest he still gripped the shotgun by its stock, down near the trigger guard.

"He broke into the house," the bespectacled man said. "He forced Ray to unlock the gates, he held a shotgun on both of us. This is just terrible, a terrible thing." He edged away from the desk, toward Spectrum's heels. "You're his daughter? The tabloid photographer?"

"We were right here," I said. "Why did they have to shoot?"

"He must have panicked when he heard footsteps in the hall," he said. "Ray tried to stop him. He was going to kill us both. This is just terrible."

The presence of death slows time and dulls the mind, and I didn't think clearly about what I'd heard. "We had a deal. Why did he shoot? Pop knew we were coming. Did Jagger lie to you? Did that murderous son of a bitch say something that got Pop killed?"

"No, really, he just went crazy, that's all."

"Do you even know your son is a killer?"

Starbal pulled his chin back, as though my words offended him. "That's pure nonsense. Beneath comment."

"Your son was drugging and raping young women," I said.

"Jag wouldn't do anything like that." He edged around Spectrum's legs. "Why, Ray told me you had some wild ideas, and might try to take advantage of our family in our time of grief. I just lost my son Stewart. A terrible loss. And now, both Ray and your father. This is just terrible."

I'd heard three shots, two sharp cracks from a revolver before the answering roar of the shotgun. A moment of clarity strobed my image of what happened in that room, just before the triggers were pulled. Starbal was lying. I'd frisked Spectrum in the trunk. He'd been clean. Yet he'd pulled the trigger first. "The gun," I said. "Where did he get the gun?"

Starbal glanced back toward the open drawer to his desk and then dived over Spectrum's body toward the pistol on the carpet. I spun and rolled to block the lunge with my curled back and scooped the gun to my chest. He punched at my face, frantic to get the weapon from me, afraid, I suppose, that I wished to kill him. I trapped his arm beneath my shoulder and rolled again, against the grain of his elbow joint. He screamed in pain, gold-rimmed glasses twisting from one reddened ear. I spun free and stood. I didn't bother to point the gun at him. I said, "Stand up and step back."

He held up his hands and backed into the edge of his desk.

"I'm not going to shoot you. I should shoot you, but I won't, not unless you give me more cause than you've already given me." When he cautiously lowered his hands I turned to look again at my father. Cassie had crept around his body to cradle his head, her eyes blood red from crying. I looked back at Starbal, said, "You hired Spectrum, didn't you?"

"I've already lost one son. I can't lose another."

"You knew what Jagger was doing."

"He'll stop," he said. "I promise."

"Bullshit!" Cassie shouted. "He won't stop!"

He held his hands out in a gesture of peace.

"I know this is an emotional moment for you," he said. "I mean, this is just terrible. It never should have come to this. But we can work something out, right? Ray said he'd already struck a deal with you. We can sweeten it." He nodded, impressed by the offer in his imagination. "We can sweeten it a helluva lot. My family is precious to me. What just happened, it's a terrible thing, but we can straighten it all out. There's no reason you two should suffer because of what's happened. The compensation, I promise, will, well, I'll compensate you generously for your loss."

As he spoke, his eyes tracked with the movement of something in the room behind me. I glanced over my shoulder. The light from the window reflected from the tiles onto a black-jacketed man advancing through the archway, the silver barrel of the pistol he pointed at my back glinting as his face breached the shadows. I whispered his name, balanced between disbelief and hope, the name of the man whose baby swam the prenatal ocean of my womb, realizing he didn't know that I was pregnant and knowing that even if he did, it wouldn't deflect his aim if he intended to shoot, even if by killing me he killed a part of himself.

"She's got a gun!" Starbal shouted. "Shoot!"

I glanced down to the pistol in my hand and flung it to the right as I dove to the left, my body spinning with the force of a .38-caliber kick to the back of my ribs, the sound of the shot ricocheting from the marble-plated walls. My body hit the rug and rolled onto the tiles, stunned by the bullet into a blunted, stupefied pain.

Sean shuffled across the room, the barrel of his pistol pointed at my chest. I clutched below my ribs where the bullet had blown out, the blood trickling through my fingers, and raised my head to look at him, uncomprehending up to the moment of my death how it could have come to this. I expected a smile or wink of recognition when he peered at me over the top of his gun sight but instead I saw no more than a detached curiosity as he examined the seriousness of my wound. I tried to speak and couldn't. Recognition sparked his eyes back to life, as though he just then realized that he'd shot someone he pretended to love, and he took the Lord's name not in vain, but in despair. The clack of metal on metal turned his head to the right and his lips compressed with the shock of an expected blow just before the shotgun fired and the pellet spread blasted him off his feet.

Across the floor Cassie knelt on the Persian carpet, the shotgun at her hip. She slid her hand along the walnut forestock, her fingers thin and pale against the darker wood, and pumped another round into the chamber. She shouted at Starbal to call 911, and when he blinked instead, failing to comprehend what he'd just witnessed, she stood and pointed the shotgun at his head.

The pain rushed in with suffocating speed and I tried to take a deep breath to push it away but the air bubbled in my lungs and I gasped, drowning in my own blood. Had the light reflecting off the tiles blinded Sean to the identity of his target? Did he not realize he'd shot me until that last moment before the shotgun blast knocked him down? I pulled the soles of my feet flat on the floor and kicked out, leaving a red smear as I slid across the tile toward the sound of moaning. When my shoulders brushed against a leg I rolled onto my side, grabbed the pocket of Sean's leather jacket, and pulled myself up his body. His pistol lay just beyond his feet. I kicked it away and raised my head. The lead shot had ripped through his right arm just below the shoulder, shattered bone jutting through the red-and-black scramble of shredded muscle and leather. He tried to smile when he saw me looking down at him, recognizing me in a primal way that failed him when he'd pulled the trigger. I wanted to hit and kiss him both. I fought to pull the air deep enough into my lungs to ask, "Why?"

His eyes glassed over for a moment, but he blinked and clarity returned. "Something you said about me, once," he whispered.

I pulled myself higher, asked, "What?"

"My left hand, it doesn't know what the right is doing."

I laid my head on his chest and waited for the ambulance.

34

THE TEMPERATURE ROSE into the mid-80s the morning they held Pop's funeral service, the sky above the San Gabriel Mountains bleaching white with early summer heat as they interred the plain brass urn containing his ashes into a concrete niche, next to the blue porcelain urn that held the ashes of my mother. Not many mourners showed for the ceremony, just my brother and his family and a few coworkers from the machine shop where Pop worked. The publicity surrounding his death might have scared away a few who otherwise might have attended, but Pop hadn't made a lot of friends in his lifetime, and I doubt the crowd would have topped a dozen had he died a normal death. As the oldest remaining member of our dwindling family, Ray bore the responsibility of placing his ashes into the niche. Given the opportunity to say a few words about Pop and what he'd meant to us, he declined.

I don't know more about the ceremony than these few basic facts, because the California penal system doesn't allow funeral leave for prisoners. I'm not sure what I would have said had I been there, whether I would have shown the courage to speak the uncomfortable truth about a man most everybody hated and feared until the last few months of his life, or whether I would have mouthed the usual platitudes. If I'd been granted the privilege to attend the funeral, I would have tried to speak truthfully about his end. He'd tried to subdue the demons that drove him, expressed remorse for how he'd lived his life, and shown genuine love for his daughter and granddaughter. He'd scarred our lives with fits of self-serving rage and violence. He'd wanted to turn that rage at the end to the service of others. That his action did far more harm than good to the ones he'd been learning how to love shouldn't be held against him.

The walls and bars of a prison begin to look alike after just a few days. That's one of the things that makes it a prison. Some days I feel as though I never left, my two brief years on the outside a single night's dream. My current cellmate is a recovering meth addict serving a five-year sentence on burglary charges. She suffers from nightmares. She'd been housed with the general prison population until her screams so unnerved everybody they decided to confine her away with me. I don't mind her so much. She talks a fast and meaningless patter, words like raindrops on a tin roof, then she conks out until two in the morning, when the screams start. The other girls used to beat her when she screamed. I've found it works better to drop down from the top bunk and hold her until the nightmares fade to black. She strikes out at me in her terrified sleep, but I'm stronger than she is and generally avoid much more than a scratch or two. Looks like we'll be together for a while, so I try to make the best of it.

One of my deepest regrets is my lack of contact with Cassie, who remains in the custody of the Los Angeles County Juvenile Justice System. I pass letters to her through my lawyer, Charles Belinsky, who represents us both. He assures me that she's doing as well as can be expected for a teenage girl held in custody at Central Juvenile Hall and facing adjudication on charges of aggravated assault and possibly attempted murder of a police officer. The prosecutor tasked with her case would like to try her as an adult and put her in prison for the next fifteen years, minimum, but Belinsky isn't going to let him get away with that and, oddly enough, neither will Logan.

The deputies charged with Cassie's processing into juvenile detention sealed the tape they fished from her pants with the rest of her belongings, not having a clue to the tape's importance. Belinsky claimed possession of the tape, made copies, and passed one to Logan, who didn't care about Jason and Jagger Starbal any more than the cops in Southern California have cared about O. J. Simpson, Phil Spector, or Robert Blake. Logan interviewed Cassie extensively and matched architectural details from the video recording of Christine's killing to the pool room on Starbal's estate. He didn't gloat at seeing me strapped to a bed in the Los Angeles County–USC

Medical Center Jail Ward, even said it was kind of a shame it worked out that way. He needs my testimony—and more importantly, Cassie's—if any case comes to trial, so I'm not convinced the sympathy he expresses is genuine.

Sean hasn't contacted me, not that I expect or want him to come calling. The department conducted no more than a cursory review of his conduct during the shooting and found his actions fully justified by the situation. He'd entered the house after hearing gunfire and saw the suspect holding a pistol. I hadn't given him time to issue a warning, he reported. He didn't see me drop the weapon when I made a sudden movement. He discharged his weapon in full accordance with his training, fearing not only for his own life, but for the lives of the others in the room.

Belinsky's ability to charm the reason out of prosecutors and juries doesn't extend to parole judges. The videocassette retrieved from Spectrum's pocket unambiguously displayed a fight between two attack dogs that resulted in one owner, a paroled felon, assaulting the other owner, an ex-con, with a baseball bat. My parole officer spoke up for me at the hearing, attesting to my good character and history of exemplary behavior while on parole, both untrue but nonetheless appreciated. The judge said he might sympathize with the mitigating circumstances but they didn't blind him to the clear parole violation he'd just witnessed. "I don't think the State has a dog in this fight," he joked, and then denied continuation on parole.

Sometimes, when I lie in bed at night, waiting for sleep to fall over me and wash away the smells and sounds of incarceration, I try to figure out what was going through Pop's mind that day, why he'd taken heroic measures when more ordinary ones would have served us all better. When the forensics team rifled his pockets, just before tucking him into a body bag, they found a handwritten note in the back pocket of his grease-stained jeans, claiming responsibility for kidnapping Spectrum from his office. He knew the salient details because I'd told him, and he used the information to claim the act as his own. Just before sleep pulls me down, his face in the darkness is the last thing I see.

I didn't expect to escape unscathed, not when events began to spin so wildly from my control. It's not going to hurt me to serve out my sentence. I've put a few photographs on the wall to help me pass the time: my mother standing at the kitchen sink, giving herself a home permanent; a candid I took of Cassie mugging at the beach; one of my dog staring at the camera as though it might be food; and the Instamatic snap I claimed from the family album, the one of me riding Pop's shoulders, my face shining while he stares at the camera with a look of supreme paternal tolerance. It's the look I want to remember him by.

California is a three-strikes state; if the D.A. presses charges and the court convicts me on both the assault and kidnapping counts, that's my three strikes, I'm going down for life. But still, I count my blessings. The Rott recovered from the attack and lives with Frank. It helps me to think of them together, two big, sloppy guys with inexhaustible appetites for junk food. The bullet left some scars, but the baby is all right, and that matters more than my discomfort and scarification. Maybe this is the best place for me, at least for the next nine months or so. The women institutionalized here have been convicted on charges ranging from prostitution to first-degree murder. Since they learned of my pregnancy they have been caring sisters; even those who might normally challenge my right to breathe nod to me in careful recognition. In an institution raging with race warfare, I'm a civilian. We joke that the child will be born with one thousand aunties. If it's a boy, he'll be in heaven. If it's a girl, she'll conquer the world.

ACKNOWLEDGMENTS

The novelist's ability to convincingly render the most arcane subjects is often due to the guidance of persons truly knowledgeable about things novelists only pretend to know. The experts whose advice guided me in the preparation of this manuscript include priests, parole agents, lawyers, filmmakers, and photographers. Special thanks go to Kate Buker, a prosecutor working in Madison, Wisconsin; to Allen Plone, who always seems to know the answer to everything I ask; and to Craig Paulenich, whose collection of poems, *Blood Will Tell,* provided inspiration.

This manuscript was edited by Amanda Murray at Simon & Schuster, who again proved an ideal reader.

I owe a debt of hospitality to the inhabitants of the city of Prague and the Catalan village of Sant Pol de Mar, Spain, where this book was written. *Děkuji Vám, přátelé. Gràcies, amics.*

About the Author

A graduate of the University of California at Santa Cruz and UCLA, ROBERT M. EVERSZ pounded the pavements of Hollywood for a decade before fleeing to Europe to write his five novels about Nina Zero and the American obsession with celebrity culture: *Shooting Elvis, Killing Paparazzi, Burning Garbo, Digging James Dean,* and *Zero to the Bone.* One of the leading literary voices in Prague, the setting for his novel *Gypsy Hearts,* he helped found the Prague Summer Writers' Workshop, now the Prague Summer Program, where he currently serves on the faculty. His novels are widely translated and have appeared on critical best-of-year lists from Oslo's *Aftenposten* to *The Washington Post.*